DATE DUE

√05			

Range of Glaciers

FRED BECKEY

OREGON HISTORICAL SOCIETY PRESS

Range
of Glaciers

THE EXPLORATION AND SURVEY
OF THE NORTHERN CASCADE RANGE

Title page image: Viewing the terminal face of the Stevens Glacier on the southern slopes of Mt. Rainier, 1905 (enlargement). Fred Kiser, photographer, Parsons Collection, Bancroft Library, University of California, Berkeley, 1971.031.1905.04-ALB #324

Support for the research, writing, and preliminary editing of this volume was provided in part by funds from the M.J. Murdock Charitable Trust as part of the Jack Murdock Publication Series on the History of Science and Exploration in the Pacific Northwest. Funds were also provided by the Samuel S. Johnson Foundation. Production was generously supported by funds provided by the Wells Fargo Foundation and the Seattle-based Bullitt Foundation and by personal contributions of Stimson Bullitt. The publisher is grateful to the insitutions and individuals that granted permission to reproduce photographs and images of materials from their collections, as listed in the credit lines that accompany individual images.

© 2003 Oregon Historical Society Press
1200 S.W. Park Ave.
Portland, OR 97205-2483

Printed in the United States of America

Library of Congress Cataloging-in-Publication Data
Beckey, Fred W., 1921–
Range of glaciers: the exploration and survey of the Northern Cascade Range / Fred Beckey
p.   cm.
Includes bibliographical references and index.
ISBN 0-87595-243-7 (cl: alk. paper)
1. Cascade Range—Discovery and exploration. 2. Cascade Range—Surveys. 3. Cascade Range—History. I. Title
F851.7 .B43 1998   917.9504—dc21   98-034488
⊗
The paper used in this publication meets the minimum requirements of American National Standard for Information Sciences—Permanence of Paper for Printed Library Materials, ANSI z39.48–1984.

CONTENTS

MAPS

FOREWORD

Other than Sasquatch, Fred Beckey is the most legendary in the lore of the Northern Cascades. Unlike Sasquatch, he is known to exist. Legend has it that Beckey has climbed every peak, followed every trail, traveled every rivulet to its source. With good reason, Beckey is the guy every mountaineer worries about when the latter thinks he has reached a place no one has been before. Fred Beckey's reputation rests not just on his climbing skills, although they are acknowledged to be formidable, but on the ubiquitousness of his presence. Every peak and valley seems to have a Beckey anecdote attached.

The Fred Beckey of popular legend does not include the fact that besides climbing peaks he is an inveterate burrower into the archives. When I met him a few years ago I was astonished to find that he was the same wiry, middle-aged chap I had often observed going over maps and field reports in the collections of the Oregon Historical Society in Portland (altitude about seventy-seven feet).

Not only has Beckey been everywhere in the northern Cascades, he has familiarized himself with the records and maps (housed in archives across North America) of the explorers and railroad surveyors, the casual climbers among the early settlers and alpinists who came later.

He brings to the thicket of documents an unparalleled awareness of why the terrain looked as it did to the Euro-Americans and the problems they had in understanding what the Native Americans tried to tell them. He can see what the lay of the land they saw seemed to imply about the lay of the land ahead.

Beckey appreciates the wonder of the first comers when they sighted Baker and Rainier and Hood. Understands, too, the bafflement of George McClellan, a cavalry officer assigned to find a route for railroad tracks over the unshrugged shoulders of Mt. Rainier.

He notes with dry amusement Lt. August Kautz's description of marmots as "mountain-sheep" and Hazard Stevens's report that fried marmot, on which he dined one night, "has a strong, disagreeable, doggy odor."

Nobody else could have written this absorbing appreciation of the Northern Cascades, the "Range of Glaciers." Fred Beckey is a master of all he has surveyed and of all the surveyors surveyed.

—MURRAY MORGAN
Auburn, Washington

ACKNOWLEDGMENTS

This book would not have been possible without the vision and the stimulating, cheerful collaboration of Bruce Taylor Hamilton, former director of the Oregon Historical Society Press, who long had an intuitive grasp of my hopes for this book. His extensive critical labors, patience, encouragement, and sense of what this work should attempt have been vital. And he has given the manuscript and my methods his characteristically thorough and perceptive scrutiny and opportunity for discussion with other members of the Press staff.

Special thanks are due Thomas Vaughan, the former director of the Oregon Historical Society, who agreed to the concept of this project in 1986 and helped make a research grant possible. I owe a particular debt of gratitude to the Murdock Foundation, which provided needed funds for study and travel to distant facilities in connection with this project. Stimson Bullitt, the Bullitt Foundation, the Samuel S. Johnson Foundation, and the Wells Fargo Foundation provided funding needed to complete the project.

The staffs of many libraries and historical societies deserve special thanks. The various branches of the National Archives, the Manuscripts and Special Collections divisions of the University of Washington Libraries, and the Oregon Historical Society Research Library, which made resources in their collections regularly available to me, are foremost among these.

It would not have been possible to write a balanced history of early explorations in the northern Cascades without diligent research at the National Archives in Washington, D.C., and the manifold efforts of their competent staff. The chief, Frank G. Burke, pointed me toward various holdings in the branches; a special nod to Stuart L. Butler of the Military Reference Branch and Kathie O. Micastro of the Civil Reference Branch. Early in my search for materials that I could not locate in the Pacific Northwest, I had the benefit of correspondence from Elmer O. Parker and Dale F. Floyd of the Military Reference Branch. Later, I was personally assisted, and again helped through correspondence, by Richard F. Cox, Michael P. Musick, Charlotte Seeley, and Elaine C. Everly, who all searched for documents and made suggestions for further research.

My research visits led me to Richard Crawford, who with enthusiasm led me to documents I would never have otherwise located in the Scientific, Economic, and Natural Resources Branch (now the Civil Reference Branch); James S. Rush, Jr., efficiently located further materials. After my preliminary visit to examine documents of the Northwest Boundary Survey in the 1970s, Milton O. Gustafson, chief of the Civil Reference Branch, located manuscript survey fieldbooks. His staff, which included Larry D. Koger and Sally M. Marks, assisted me several times in identifying and copying documents.

At the Cartographic Archives Branch, Ralph E. Ehrenberg, John Dwyer, and Richard H. Smith more than once located rare manuscript maps and photographs and assisted with copying procedures. The staffs for the U.S. Geological Survey and Department of the Interior records were equally courteous and helpful. All the archives branches not only made information and materials available to me, but also performed services ranging from copying manuscripts and typescripts to making important suggestions concerning collections that I might otherwise have overlooked.

The repository where I did the majority of my manuscript, rare book, and photographic research was the University of Washington Libraries. Karyl Winn, director of the Manuscripts and University Archives Division, along with Janet Ness and others of her competent staff, graciously assisted me in locating specific materials for copying and study. Gary Lundell contributed time for a review of certain papers held in the archives. The experienced personnel of the Pacific Northwest Collection kindly found numerous materials: Carla Rickerson, Gary Menges, and Susan Cunningham spent many hours locating rare books and monographs, and Richard Engeman (now of the Oregon Historical Society) regularly found photographs to fulfill particular needs from a unique collection.

At the Oregon Historical Society, I am indebted to the entire library staff, in particular the late Gordon Manning and Elizabeth Winroth for their gracious and patient assistance and Jack Levin, former OHS documents librarian. Herbert K. Beals is especially remembered for his advice on early navigators in the Pacific Northwest and for his critical reading of an early draft on this subject. Special gratitude is due Lori McEldowney of the Press for her assistance in the preliminary organization of my written material and the illustrations. Betty Fell, Mary Kay Southgate, and especially Anne T. Wilson are to be thanked for typing and retyping my chapter drafts, a massive task. Thanks are also due Roxann Moen, Joan Menefee, Tessa Hinrichs, and Wendy Bolger for their help in ordering photos. Patti Larkin, Allen Willoughby, and Colleen Odell also deserve thanks for their assistance with editing changes.

At the Beinecke Rare Book and Manuscript Library at Yale University, George Miles, the curator of Western Americana, was a great resource in my search of Northwest Boundary Survey manuscripts, and he generously reviewed their contents for my focus. The Minnesota Historical Society Research Library staff was vital in unearthing little-known source material from Northern Pacific and Great Northern railroad explorers. Especially helpful was correspondence with Lucile M. Kane, curator of manuscripts, and Maureen J. Leverty. The efforts of John Wickre, Dallas R. Lindgren, Ruby Shields, and Hampton Smith, both during my visits and afterward, are to be commended.

My research at the U.S. Geological Survey library in Denver, where I studied field photography and journals, was made more efficient by the cheerful guidance of Debbie Rowan and Carol A. Edwards. Before the beginning of this project, Gene Gressley, director of the Western History Research Center at the University of Wyoming, facilitated a study of pertinent collections and proved a most gracious host. Frank Green, librarian of the Washington State Historical Society, courteously gave me insight into the society's resources, and I am also grateful to Elaine Miller for her devoted help with photographic, sketch, and map holdings.

Through the kindness of Constance E. Bignell at the International Boundary Commission in Washington, D.C., I was able to search out and secure rare photographs taken by surveyors of the forty-ninth parallel. Permission to publish this material was given by IBC chief Clyde Moore. Similarly, Dr. Alec C. McEwen, commissioner, and Carl Gustafson of the Canadian section contributed advice on the tracing of valuable field journals.

To Gary F. Reese of Tacoma Public Library's Northwest Room, I owe a debt of thanks for his stimulating counsel and suggestions regarding early army forts and fur-trading posts, for pointing out unique holdings at the library, and for sharing his unparalleled knowledge of regional literature. John Eliot Allen of Portland State University made helpful additions to my geology review and critically read the material on early government topographers. I also benefited greatly from conversations with Professor Paul Hammond, who enhanced my geologic knowledge of the Cascade Range and made suggestions.

Several libraries in Canada rendered invaluable assistance and advice. For bibliographic help at the National Archives of Canada, especially in locating unpublished materials, I am indebted to archivists Sheila Powell, Patricia Kennedy, Candace Loewen, and Doug Whyte and to Timothy Dubé of the government archives. Joy Houston of the Documentary Art and Photography Division kindly located copies of early images from the Northwest Boundary Survey and coordinated reproduction. For his gracious presentation of Hudson's Bay Company post records and other material and for providing a most pleasant environment for study, thanks are due Michael G. Moosberger, archivist of the HBC archives at the Manitoba Provincial Archives, and also to Judith Beattie and David Arthurs.

Various librarians at the Provincial Archives of British Columbia (now British Columbia Archives and Records Service) in Victoria facilitated a rewarding study of early surveyors, prospectors, and fur traders, primarily from the manuscripts and maps of the Royal Engineers and the Hudson's Bay Company. Particularly helpful were Glen Isaacs of the Manuscripts and Maps unit and Robert Davison. In Vancouver, I drew on the Special Collections Library of the University of British Columbia, guided by Ann Yandle, archivist and department head. On several occasions, I was directed to useful material by Frances Woodward, reference librarian.

I am indebted to several persons in England for help and encouragement in the search for maps, manuscripts, and photographs. Particular thanks are due Beverley Williams, assistant curator of the Royal Engineers Museum (Kent) for furnishing rare photographs and copies of letters and for confirming biographical details. I am grateful to William Foot of the Public Record Office (Surrey) and Dr. P.B. Boyden of the National Army Museum (London) for responding to inquiries about holdings and to Tony Campbell of the British Library for guiding me to the original Alexander Ross map and toward pertinent map and manuscript material.

Unexpected assistance came from Switzerland in my pursuit of topographer Henry Custer's background. First, I am most indebted to Dr. Peter Menolfi of Basel, who discovered the location of the Custer family papers for me. Henry L. Custer of St. Gallen was most generous with his time in making accessible unpublished biographical material and in furnishing illustrations. In connection with this long search, Osvaldo Casoni, the consul general of Switzerland, advised me to seek help from Professor Leo Schelbert of the University of Illinois–Chicago, an expert on Swiss emigration. To both I am grateful.

The list of other librarians, associates, friends, and sometimes complete strangers who assisted me with contributions, suggestions, location of materials, and review is considerable. Included are David Wigdor, assistant chief, and Barbara B. Walsh at the Library of Congress; William Moss, archives director, William Cox, Catherine D. Scott, and Nancy J. Seeger of the Smithsonian Institution Libraries; Peter Blodgett, assistant curator–western manuscripts, at the Huntington Library; Gertrude Sinnott and Brenda Graff, reference librarians at the U.S. Geological Survey Library (Reston, Viriginia); Richard J. Sommers, archivist at the U.S. Army Military History Institute (who located the pencil draft of Gen. George Crook's autobiography); Robert M. Frame, assistant curator of the James Jerome Hill Reference Library; Peter R. Christoph of the New York State Library; John D. Stinson of the Manuscripts Division of the New York Public Library; Peter J. Knapp, archivist, of the Trinity College Library; Charles Aston, Jr., of Special Collections, University of Pittsburgh Libraries; James D. Moore, regional archivist of Washington State Archives, and James Scott, director of the Center for Pacific Northwest Studies, at Western Washington University; Christian Frazza, archivist, Washington State University; Connie Manson at the Washington State Department of Natural Resources Library, Division of Geology and Earth Resources; David Van Meer of the Skagit County Historical Museum; Jeanne Engerman at the Washington Room, Washington State Library; Bob Lockerby of the Science Library at Portland State University; Tom Stave and David Barber of government documents, University of Oregon Library; and Mark Takaro of the Bancroft Library at the University of California, for pointing out photographic collections from Sierra Club outings to Mt. Rainier.

Much to my regret, I am not able to name individually all those at various institutions who contributed so much to my search for the raw materials out of which this book was fashioned. In addition to those mentioned above, I am indebted to the staffs of the Washington State Library, Washington State Archives, Lummi Tribal Archives, Whatcom County Museum, California State Library, Yuba County Library, Everett Public Library, Vancouver (British Columbia) Public Library, Coos Bay Historical Society Museum, Lake Chelan Historical Society, Mount Rainier National Park Library, and Federal Records Center at Seattle.

The diligence of Reverend Carl E. Nitz in his translation of the Karl von Zittel account of an early Mt. Rainier exploration is greatly appreciated. Clifford Nelson, historian for the U.S. Geological Survey, kindly searched out and provided background materials on early topographers and geologists, and Rowland W. Tabor in the Branch of Western Regional Geology corrected and commented on some of my interpretations. Both Fred W. Cater and Nellie Carico some years ago recalled details of early geological fieldwork in the Cascade Range and communicated these to me.

Murray Morgan made rewarding suggestions on research and organization at an early stage of the project while hosting me for an afternoon. Both William H. Goetzmann, professor of American Studies at the University of Texas, and Richard A. Bartlett, professor of history at Florida State University, searched their memories and files for documentation on the surveying background of Henry Custer. Correspondence with A.F. Lambert of Ottawa was helpful in the search for Canadian boundary surveyors' fieldbooks. Jerry Olson contributed expert advice on early surveying techniques and provided missing biographical material. Lloyd Berry of the Chelan County Department of Public Works spent time with me on a joint search for Indian-warfare locations of 1858.

Betty Bandel of the English Department at the University of Vermont kindly provided biographical details on railroad surveyor Daniel C. Linsley. Donald Orth of the U.S. Board on Geographic Names joined the search for early topographic fieldbooks, and both Joanne Hohler and James Sweetland of the State Historical Society of Wisconsin located background on the scientist George Gibbs. Tad Pfeffer of the Institute of Arctic and Alpine Research at the University of Colorado generously took time to interpret glacier advances and ice-age dating. Merle W. Wells of the Idaho State Historical Society provided an opinion about the courses and accuracy of Alexander Ross.

Lewis Green of Vancouver, British Columbia, corresponded with me about the location of Canadian boundary-surveyor fieldbooks, while Jon Douglas of North Cascades National Park was helpful in the search for specific materials on several occasions. Mike Ferris, Gail Throop, and Jim Hughes of the U.S. Forest Service's Pacific Northwest Regional Branch; Mike Hiler of the Naches Ranger Station; James A. McDonald of Mount Baker–Snoqualmie National Forest; and Susan Carter of Wenatchee National Forest all provided valuable historical typescripts and photographs. Linda McNeil and Jeff Thomas spent time searching for outing and mountaineering photographs at the Mazamas club. Beverley Bendell of the Alpine Club of Canada, Frederick L. Wernstedt, Harvey Manning, Nile Thompson, and Dwight Watson all gave me the benefit of their correspondence, which included much useful information.

I am most indebted for the hospitality of Anita and Philip Callahan, who turned over for my perusal the Glee Davis collection of pioneer photography in the Skagit River Valley. And special thanks are due Betty Ayer Eichenberger of Ferndale, Washington, for her courtesy in permitting access to the fine Nels Bruseth photographs.

Parts of the manuscript in various stages of completion have been read by experts, and if despite their vigilance errors have gone undetected, the fault is mine. Robert C. Harris of West Vancouver generously reviewed my rough drafts on early exploration in British Columbia and saved me from certain errors. His expertise on early maps of the region led me to conduct further study and use interesting historical cartography. Harley R. Hatfield of Penticton also reviewed material on explorations and fur trading and made useful criticisms.

James W. Aldrich of Falls Church, Virginia, reviewed portions of my draft concerning the Northwest Boundary Survey, collaborated with me on Henry Custer's other surveying activities in the United States, and allowed me to take notes from his study of boundary monumenting, photography, and early maps both drawn and printed by the American and British commissions. Dee Molenaar, an old friend, reviewed questions on the history of mountaineering at Mt. Rainier; Philip Woodhouse added to my knowledge on early Monte Cristo; and Robert Boyd and Robert Miendorf provided expert review and commentary concerning Native peoples in the Cascade Range. Two anonymous readers reviewed the complete manuscript for the Oregon Historical Society Press and offered helpful suggestions.

One of the most delightful aspects of my work was to collate and evaluate the almost unknown journals and letters of the British and American boundary surveyors, manuscript materials that expand on the bare printed documentation. They corroborate each other and together provide a quite complete and voluminous record. Among the records of the Northern Pacific Railroad surveyors and army explorers, the diary of Daniel C. Linsley and the report of Lt. Henry H. Pierce are especially interesting and valuable, as both men were articulate and descriptive writers.

Between the 1960s and the 1980s I was, fortunately, able to visit some Cascade Range pioneers at intervals for the purpose of adding to my research and enhancing my personal explorations in these mountains. It is scarcely possible to exaggerate the importance of dictations taken from the lips of "old-timers," some of them no longer alive, and of the opportunity to peruse their maps, sketches, and photographs. As renowned historian Hubert H. Bancroft noted, "It is early historical knowledge absolutely rescued from oblivion, and which if lost no power on earth could reproduce."

Finally, I would like to thank those people who have given the book its literal and physical shape: the book's thorough and careful editor, Nancy Trotic; designers John Laursen and Veronica Seyd; graphic designer Christine Rains, who prepared the maps; researchers Sarah Gabert and Devon McCurdy; editor Paul Merchant; imaging specialist Richard Jost; and Adair Law, former director of the Oregon Historical Society Press. All have helped me in my ascent of the rich history of the Cascades, and I thank them.

Range of Glaciers

Sturgeon-Spearing on the Frasier, *sketch by Parson, c. 1859 (from John Keast Lord,* The Naturalist in Vancover Island and British Columbia, *vol. 1, R. Bentley, London, 1866; OHS Reference Library)*

INTRODUCTION

Intervening land appeared, beyond which another high round mountain covered with snow was discovered, apparently situated several leagues to the south of mount Rainier . . . This I considered a further extension of the eastern snowy range.

—Capt. George Vancouver, May 19, 1792

The "eastern snowy range" that Capt. George Vancouver and his crew admired from the inland waters of Puget Sound in 1792 remained for the Euro-American world an unknown, mysterious barrier of craggy peaks and high, glacier-clad volcanoes—*sierras nevadas*, as the earlier Spanish discoverers had termed it—until fur traders began to probe the range's secrets from the interior early in the nineteenth century. Vancouver had served with the great naval captain James Cook on his second and third voyages to the Pacific, and he was familiar with the general character of the Northwest coast when he was commissioned in 1791 to command the voyage of exploration that took him back to the region in 1792–1794. Vancouver's tasks were to carry out the terms of the Nootka Treaty and to examine the coast to sixty degrees north latitude in order to find the elusive Northwest Passage from the Atlantic to the Pacific Ocean.[1]

Vancouver's remarkable and extensive surveys have been admired by navigators ever since they were made. He accomplished the first accurate and scientific survey of the Northwest coast, and he assigned nearly four hundred place names—most of which have survived.[2] His maps became the standard for Admiralty charts and were copied by renowned nineteenth-century English cartographer Aaron Arrowsmith. Vancouver drew "A Chart Shewing Part of the Coast of NW America," showing a continuous range of mountains parallel to the coast. The Columbia is the only river shown penetrating the mountain barrier. When Vancouver's lieutenant, William Broughton, sailed up the river to the present-day Sandy River in 1792, he became the first European to reach a glacier-fed river outflow from the Cascade Range.

Broughton's sail along the Northwest coast took place during an age of exploration that would last through much of the nineteenth century. Entrepreneurs and explorers dreamed of new empires, and explorers probed the known mountain ranges of Alaska and Canada, the Himalayas, and the Antarctic. In the Pacific Northwest, explorers found new passages through the mountains from both the east and the west. The Cascades, like almost all other western mountain ranges, were not "discovered" all at once, but were rediscovered through the decades by many navigators and overland explorers, each adding to the accumulated knowledge of the range. Historian William Goetzmann writes: ". . . the explorer is actually one who "*seeks* discoveries." He is not simply and solely the "discoverer." Instead the accent is upon process and activity, with advances in knowledge simply fortunate though expected incidents along the way. It is likewise not casual. It is purposeful."[3]

Like most other early adventurers in the Far West, those who explored the Cascade Range were motivated by curiosity but also by personal ambition, financial reward, economic or political advantage, and greedy boosterism. They were drawn to the Cascades in search of trading routes, railroad passes, or wagon routes; to look for mineral wealth; to mark a boundary; or to map the topography. This book examines the motives and the significant explorations of those pioneers and documents how they added to our knowledge of the northern Cascades.

Although the voyages of exploration between 1774 and 1792 found no Northwest Passage, they revealed to the Euro-American world not only the Pacific Northwest coast and its inlets but the region's mountain ranges as well. The first European to see Mt. Baker may have been Manuel Quimper, an ensign in the Spanish navy. He ventured into the Strait of Juan de Fuca at a time when Spain exerted its greatest strength in the Western Hemisphere, following the establishment of a temporary settlement at Nootka Sound on Vancouver Island in 1789. Quimper was directed by the Spanish viceroy to investigate the newly discovered strait—the one sighted by British trader Charles William Barkley in 1787 and in the following year by John Meares and Boston sea captain Robert Gray. In the sloop *Princesa Real*, Quimper was the first to examine the waterway far inland.[4]

There is no specific reference to Mt. Baker in Quimper's journal, yet he certainly saw the volcano when he was near present-day Victoria. One of the charts by López de Haro, *Plano del Estrecho de Fuca*, depicts Mt. Baker—its first appearance on a map—and the volcano, with the legend "La gran Montaña del Carmelo," is outlined to the northeast of Boca de Fidalgo.[5] On the chart, an artistic rendering of a mountain chain titled "Sierras Nevadas de S. Antonio" matches the location of the Cascade Range.

European and American seafarers also sailed to the Pacific Northwest in the late 1700s for sea otter pelts, which were prized in China, but not until the latter part of the eighteenth century did the British government become sufficiently aroused to seek definite information on a navigable waterway that would facilitate trade with the Orient. The British Admiralty hoped to find a system of waterways by which canoes could carry furs and other trade goods across the North American continent south of the Arctic Ocean, and the 1792–1794 voyage of George Vancouver was the last episode of that dream.

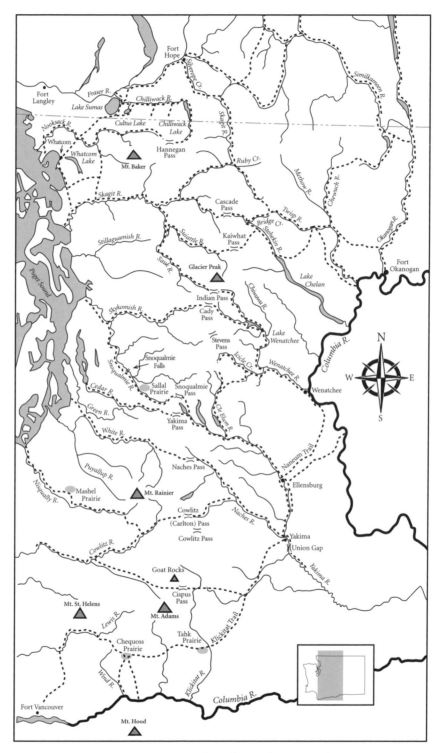

Native American Trails in the Northern Cascades

Vancouver sighted the North American coast at about thirty-nine degrees, twenty-seven minutes north latitude (at northern California), then proceeded to examine it carefully up to the south coast of Alaska.[6] When he passed the latitude "where geographers have placed the pretended Strait of Juan de Fuca," he turned east past Cook's Cape Flattery on April 29, 1792, to begin his assignment "to trace every foot of the continental shore."[7] While Vancouver hoped this was the inland waterway that would fulfill the expectations of the Admiralty, he could not help sighting the Cascade Range and its grand, ice-clad volcanoes. Studying the geography west of Discovery Bay on April 29, 3d Lt. Joseph Baker observed "a very high conspicuous craggy mountain . . . towering above the clouds." Vancouver promptly named it for him.[8]

Vancouver also sighted "a very remarkable high round mountain, covered with snow," bearing S 45 E. Some days later, on May 8, he saw the mountain again near "Marrow-Stone Point" (near present-day Port Townsend) and named it "after my friend Rear Admiral Rainier."[9] Thus, the highest and most majestic volcano of the Pacific Coast, known to the Indians for an eternity as Tachoma or T'koma, acquired another name.

Vancouver and the Spanish navigators missed the mouth of the Columbia River—a failure that later benefited American territorial claims. Capt. Robert Gray, a New England merchant in the sea-otter trade, entered and named the river in May 1792, giving the United States a claim on the vast territory in opposition to the British. Nevertheless, Vancouver pointedly recorded that his lieutenant, William R. Broughton, after exploring the Columbia in October 1792, "formally took possession of the river, and the country in its vicinity" in the name of King George. Broughton was the first European to come close to a Cascade volcano. When he rowed up the river in a cutter to near present-day Washougal, he named the "remarkable mountain" after Lord Samuel Hood. Vancouver estimated it to be over 25,000 feet in height and thought it might be the highest mountain in the world.[10]

The explorations of Vancouver and Broughton, as well as those of earlier adventurers, helped lure others to the Pacific Northwest and the Cascade Range. It would be thirteen years, however, before Lewis and Clark—the most famous American overland explorers—obtained a new vision of the mysterious volcanoes and another forty-nine years before the Americans began a serious effort to map the mountains and their rivers.

When President Thomas Jefferson sent Meriwether Lewis and William Clark in 1804 to trace a route across the Rocky Mountains and then to the western ocean, knowledge about the Far West was so limited that the American public envisioned a vast river system across the Great Basin. The Cascades long remained a *terra incognita* near the western edge of the continent, a barrier of precipitous ridges, dangerous rivers, and thick forests. Lewis and Clark returned with important information about the region's geography and its people, but they added little to what was known about the northern Cascades.

It was the enthusiasm of the Oregon immigrants that stimulated the official exploration of the Cascades. The British had laid broad geographic claims and made their explorative impact largely through waterway probes, the building of a few forts, and the establishment of a fur-trading kingdom, but they had made few mountain-pass explorations. It was left to the Americans to push forward with the surveys and explorations that would finally provide extensive knowledge of the northern Cascade region.

Some of that knowledge came from the surveyors who worked for the Northern Pacific Railroad and the Great Northern Railway. Some came from adventurous settlers who explored the valleys for homesteads, and some came from prospectors in search of mineral wealth on high mountain slopes. Pioneers, mining companies, or government agents turned some of the prospectors' rugged trails into wagon roads. North of the forty-ninth parallel, Hudson's Bay Company brigade trails were widened into wagon roads for settlers, traders, and miners. The few early mountaineers who reached the highest viewpoints in the Cascade Range were succeeded in the 1890s by government topographers and geologists who carried out intense surveying and geologic mapping efforts. Two boundary surveys along the forty-ninth parallel, the first beginning in 1857 and the second in, 1901 furthered knowledge of this especially complex region of British Columbia and Washington state.

The year 1853 was a pivotal one for Cascade Range history. Not only was it the year of the grand Pacific Railroad survey, with its cadre of military explorers and naturalists, but it was also the year that Washington became a territory. In the half century between 1850 and 1900, the population of Oregon, Washington, and British Columbia grew enough to foster those enterprising individuals who saw in the mountains prospects of wealth and, later, physical challenge. Over time, people formed a series of impressions about the mountains that conditioned not only further explorations, both public and private, but also popular knowledge of the Cascades, public land-use policy, and the culture of emerging towns. The exploration of the northern Cascades between the Columbia and Fraser rivers was particularly critical in shaping the destiny of the Pacific Northwest and its people. Before beginning a detailed study of the region's history, however, it will be helpful to review the lay of the land and to consider the region's first residents.

The Landscape of the Northern Cascades

Rising as a wedge between the Puget Sound Basin and the Inland Empire, the northern Cascades stand as one of the grand mountain ranges of the West, spanning over three hundred miles from the Columbia River to the south to the Fraser River in British Columbia. The northern Cascades sprawl over more than nine million acres and include nearly one-fifth of the state of Washington. On the west, the range is bounded by the glacial floodplain of the Puget Sound Basin, on the south by the volcanic rocks of the central Cascades in Oregon, and on the east by the basalts of the Columbia Plateau and the interior highlands beyond the Okanogan River. The northern limits of the range are less clearly defined, but it is bounded geographically on the northeast by the Fraser-Okanogan highlands and on the northwest by the Fraser River, which separates the Cascades from the Coast Mountains.[11]

Nineteenth-century explorers, fur-traders, settlers, and surveyors were awed by the peaks in the Cascade Range. Settlers were struck by Mt. Hood's great height, for example, but they were enchanted by the symmetry of Mt. St. Helens across the Columbia River to the north. On January 11, 1814, fur-trader Alexander Henry the Younger observed: "Mt. St. Helens presented a conspicuous and romantic prospect—an immense cone enveloped in snow, rising from a level country, the base very broad, tapering up to a point without any rugged irregularity."[12] Decades later, in 1853, adventurer Theodore Winthrop wrote: "Dearest charmer of all is St. Helens, queen of the Cascades, queen of Northern America, a fair and graceful volcanic cone. Exquisite mantling snows sweep along her shoulders toward the bristling pines."[13] Winthrop also describedMt. Rainier, which he saw on hiw way from Port Townsend to "Squally" (Nisqually):

> It was a giant mountain dome of snow, swelling and seeming to fill the aerial spheres as its image displaced the blue deeps of tranquil water. . . . Kingly and alone stood this majesty, without any visible comrade or consort, though far to the north and the south its brethren and sisters dominated their realms, each in isolated sovereignty, rising above the pine-darkened sierra of the Cascade Mountains,—above the stern chasm where the Columbia, Achilles of rivers, sweeps . . . Of all the peaks from California to Fraser River, this one before me was royalest.[14]

Although not visible from the Puget Sound Basin, the Wenatchee Mountains—not far from the Columbia River—present a striking view from east of the range. Explorer and geologist George Gibbs called these mountains "the craggy sierra of the Cascades."[15] Early comments on the peaks and subranges to the north came largely from Pacific Railroad surveyors, army explorers, the first navigators, and early settlers. Much more would be learned about these areas during the Northwest Boundary Survey.

Rivers also help define the northern Cascades. With dozens of rivers flowing into Puget Sound and the Columbia and Fraser river systems, the range is a scenic and hydrologic resource. Some five million years ago, the Columbia River, draining a vast territory that now comprises seven states and provinces, eroded its way to sea level, carving the land in the process. Tributaries began to form, and ancient rocks dating to over six hundred million years ago were exposed. The river kept grinding and cutting at the rising mountains, quarrying sediment from them and carrying it to the sea.

While the Columbia River bounds a vast flank of the northern Cascades, the Skagit River finds its entire home in the range and its course reflects the complexity of the landscape. The Skagit's long valley exhibits a beauty and complexity that is remarkable even in a region where drainage relationships are complex. At Newhalem, the Skagit has cut a spectacular canyon into the bedrock gneiss, and its narrowness and steepness suggest that this portion of the range is still rising.[16] The sources of the river are north of the forty-ninth parallel, in Canada. The tributary known as the Skaist River in the Hozameen Range receives the northwest-flowing Skagit, then slices through a gorge to be joined by the southeast-flowing Sumallo tributary. From there the Skagit turns sharply southeast, becoming Ross Lake in the United States. The lake is a dilation of the river, which now trends north-south to the confluence of Ruby Creek and is reinforced by important watercourses on both flanks. In its continuing course, the Skagit is joined by tributaries such as Big Beaver, Thunder, Goodell, Bacon, and Illabot creeks and the Cascade, Sauk, and Baker rivers.

The northern Cascades also experience sharp changes in climate. The mean annual precipitation ranges from more than 78 inches along and west of the drainage divide to less than 20 inches on the east slope. The elevation of the timberline zone rises eastward across the Cascades and the interior ranges. The timberlines are lower on the snowier west slopes where late-melting winter snowpack on the upper forest boundary so shortens the growing season that seedlings cannot survive. A dense, nearly impenetrable forest covers the western valley bottoms, each with a turbulent and often cascading stream. In some localities, narrow rock gorges have cut into the bedrock and valley fill. On the west slopes of the range, Douglas fir, western hemlock, Pacific silver fir, western red cedar, Alaska yellow cedar, mountain hemlock, and subalpine fir are prominent.

Considerable old-growth timber still remains, with certain species living well beyond five hundred years and attaining heights of up to 250 feet. East of the Cascade crest, a changing forest includes ponderosa pine, lodgepole pine, Douglas fir, Engelmann spruce, alpine larch, western larch, subalpine fir, and white-bark pine. The immense and prolific firs and cedars at lower elevations contrast with the smaller and more elegant specimens of the subalpine zone. In that stark landscape, scrub conifers survive by hugging the ground, often behind the protection of rock outcrops. From the subalpine zone to the highest flora, the slopes and ridges of the northern Cascades are endowed with lush floral meadows.

Volcanic activity has helped shape the Cascade Range for at least forty million years, and for the past two million years the range has been among the most volcanically active regions on the Pacific Rim. Geologists believe that the mountains of the northern Cascades—which are high composite volcanos formed by layers of ash, cinders, and lava—are young features built atop a range that had long possessed its present relief and elevation. Between the Columbia River and Snoqualmie Pass, the range is dominated by eruptive rocks of the Cascade volcanic arc. Farther north, the exposed axis of the range consists of metamorphosed, structurally complex pre-Tertiary rocks.

Mt. St. Helens has erupted at least fifty times and over the past few thousand years has been the most active and violent volcano in the contiguous United States.[17] The first published description of the mountain's volcanic activity came in 1836 from Dr. Merideth Gairdner, a physician posted with the Hudson's Bay Company (HBC) at Fort Vancouver.[18] In 1848, Jessy Quinn Thornton remembered an eruption of Mt. St. Helens that he had witnessed in 1831:

> With the exception of a slight red, lurid appearance, the day was dark, and so completely was the light of the sun shut out by the smoke and falling ashes, that candles were necessary. The weather was perfectly calm, and without wind; and during several days after the eruption, the fires, out of doors, burned with a bluish flame, as though the atmosphere was filled with sulphur.[19]

The celebrated 1842 eruption, which deposited ash as far east as The Dalles within three days, was reported by missionaries along the Columbia River and elsewhere. Reverend Josiah L. Parrish, for example, wrote that the mountain had "changed her snowy dress of pure white for a sombre black mantle." Missionary Henry B. Brewer collected an ash specimen, which he presented to explorer John C. Frémont a year later. In February 1844, Peter H. Burnett, an Oregon Trail immigrant, wrote that "the mountain burned most magnificently," and at the end of December he reported that "this mountain is now a burning volcano."[20]

British military officer Henry Warre made the first known sketches of a Mt. St. Helens eruption in 1845. While descending the Columbia River on September 13, he wrote: "Suddenly a long black Column of Smoke & Ashes shot up into the Air, and hung as a Canopy over the Dazzling Cap contrasting strongly with the Clear blue Sky . . . the first Volcano I have ever seen in action." Two years later, artist Paul Kane painted a watercolor of Mt. St. Helens from the mouth of the Lewis River showing a steam cloud hovering above the summit. Kane made another field sketch while at the HBC's Cowlitz Farm. "I had a fine view of Mount St. Helen's throwing up a long column of dark smoke into the clear blue sky," he wrote. When Portland newspaperman Thomas Dryer and his party ascended Mt. St. Helens in 1853, he reported that "the smoke was continually issuing from its mouth, giving unmistakable evidence that the fire was not extinguished."[21] In 1855, George Gibbs reported on the broader volcanic activity:

> The mountains at present active are Baker, St. Helens, and as it has recently been ascertained Mt. Hood and probably Mt. Rainier also, though to a degree hardly perceptible from below. The Indians on Puget Sound state that another smaller peak to the north of Mount Rainier once smoked.[22]

Mt. Rainier, which may have reached its present bulk and height about 75,000 years ago, was aptly described by geologist Bailey Willis in 1883 as "the symbol of an awful power clad in beauty." The last major eruptive period—between 3,000 and 2,300 years ago—saw pumice and lava flows and the formation of numerous lahars, or mudflows. During this period the eastern crater, which marks Columbia Crest, was formed, and the old, hollow summit caldera was filled by the present summit cone.[23]

When settlers first arrived at Puget Sound during the 1840s, Mt. Baker, the most northern of the Cascade Range volcanoes, was intermittently active. Theodore Winthrop mentioned that Mt. Baker was sending up flames and smoke in 1852. George Gibbs wrote that it was "throwing out light clouds of smoke" during 1853 and 1854.[24] A reliable report came from coastal surveyor George Davidson in 1854 while he was making observations in Rosario Strait:

> I had finished the measures for horizontal direction of the summit of Mount Baker, and was commencing a series of measures of the vertical angles for elevation, when I found the whole summit of the mountain suddenly obscured by vast rolling masses of dense smoke, which in a few minutes reached an estimated height of two thousand feet above the mountain, and soon enveloped the higher parts. . . .[25]

Davidson also gave a report of a later eruption: "In 1858 Mr. John S. Hittell of San Francisco was in Victoria, and he informs me that the night clouds over Mount Baker were brilliantly illuminated by the light from an eruption of Mount Baker." Early Bellingham Bay settlers confirmed such eruptions. John Bennett witnessed the mountain spewing fire, and pioneer Henry Roeder watched the volcano erupt periodically for over three decades. From his ship, he saw "the fire of the mountain. It could not have been a forest fire. . . . There is no question in my mind that Mt. Baker is an active volcano."[26] After 1884, the volcano quieted, with only occasional steam emissions.

The higher slopes of the Cascade Range support the largest collection of glaciers in the contiguous United States. With 800 glaciers over 160 square miles, Washington state has an estimated 77 percent of the glacier ice in the forty-eight states.[27] One survey found that half of the 385 square kilometers of glacier ice in the Washington Cascades is on five volcanoes—Mt. St. Helens, Mt. Adams, Mt. Rainier, and Mt. Baker and Glacier Peak. On Mt. Rainier alone, where there are twenty-six glaciers, six important ice streams are nourished from the summit ice cap. Especially numerous on the northern-facing slopes of the range are small ice fields, valley glaciers, and hanging glaciers. The snowfields and glaciers have a vast and complex hydrologic significance, for they act as a reservoir by releasing critical meltwater in dry seasons.

For two million years, glaciation has sharpened and modified the rugged Cascade Range topography. The spectacular landforms owe much of their character to the powerful cutting effect of large, thick glaciers. The repeated advance and retreat of glaciers over the valley floors and in cirques produced deep, U-shaped valleys and glacial basins and wore rock ridges into narrow arêtes. Many of the ice-carved depressions hold lakes, each cirque with its own topographic features, bedrock characteristics, and solar exposure. Glacially ground rock flour gives a vivid green tone to some of these lakes and a milky color to rivers emanating from glaciers.

Geologist Bailey Willis first called attention to the prehistoric existence of immense glaciers in the northern Cascades in 1887. In 1891, Canadian geologist George M. Dawson suggested that a massive glacier (an ice sheet much like that of Greenland), with its center in northern British Columbia, once flowed peripherally in all directions. This Cordilleran Ice Sheet, as it came to be called, formed during the late Wisconsin stage (beginning about 22,000 years ago) as a complex of alpine, piedmont, and intermontane glaciers coalesced in southern Yukon territory, British Columbia, western Alberta, and northern Washington.[28] Many smaller glaciers combined to form this ice mass, which covered all but the highest peaks and ridges and sent long tongues of ice down valleys such as the Skagit, Nooksack, Chilliwack, and Chelan. These alpine glaciers reached their maximum positions 22,000 to 18,000 years ago, cutting deep troughs and advancing far beyond the accumulation centers.[29] The ice sheet advanced into the Cascades from Canada and entered the upper Chelan drainage basin over high passes near the range crest. Thick continental ice that flowed down passes near the Okanogan Valley crossed the Columbia River Valley, forming broad lobes on the Columbia Plateau.[30]

During the peak of glaciation in the Cascades, immense glaciers flowed down principal northern valleys on both flanks of the range far beyond the foothills, greatly modifying river-carved valleys. The Skagit Glacier is estimated to have been over one hundred miles in length and the Chelan Glacier some ninety miles long; alpine glaciers heading on Mt. Rainier gouged valleys, radiating as much as forty miles downvalley.[31] The erosive power of the giant valley glaciers is seen today in the tributary river valleys. There seems to have been a rapid and extensive ice loss in Cascade valleys following an advance between 11,000 and 12,000 years ago. By about 1,000 years later, the ice sheet had nearly disappeared below the forty-ninth parallel.[32]

It was in the northern Cascades that glaciers were first discovered in the contiguous United States. Physician and botanist William F. Tolmie was the first to write about bodies of ice when, on September 3, 1833, from a minor summit to the northwest of Mt. Rainier, he observed that "a few small glaciers were seen on the conical portion."[33] Lt. August V. Kautz, after his attempt on the summit of Mt. Rainier in July 1857, gave this account of the Nisqually Glacier: "The upper end is covered with snow, having immense chasms running across it. The lower end is principally ice, with much débris of rocks, sand, and gravel. It is about fifteen miles to the summit of Mount Rainier, from the foot of the glacier." He described the terminal ice cave of the glacier:

The Nisqually came out from beneath the ice in a stream twenty-five or thirty feet wide, a torrent so muddy and rapid that we would not have dared to ford it. The cavern was not much wider than the stream, and about fifteen feet high. The ice was, in places, clear and blue, but in others mixed with débris.[34]

In 1870, when mountaineer Hazard Stevens ascended Mt. Rainier, little was known about glaciers. Stevens wrote, "The glaciers terminated not gradually, but abruptly with a wall of ice from one to five hundred feet high, from beneath which yeasty torrents burst forth and rushed roaring and rumbling down the valleys."[35] In an 1874 account, George Gibbs mentioned glaciers near the International Boundary at the head of Maselpanik and Glacier creeks.[36] When another early mountaineer, George Bayley, spent the night of August 15, 1883, at high camp below Gibraltar Rock on Mt. Rainier, he singled out what appears to be the Wilson Glacier:

> It was torn and rent with enormous fissures, the blue color of which we could clearly distinguish in the moonlight, even at so great a distance. The surface of the glacier was strewn with detached blocks or masses of ice, that appeared to have been upheaved and thrown out by some mighty power struggling underneath to escape.[37]

Israel Russell, who conducted the first comprehensive glacier studies of Mt. Rainier, realized that the range held glaciers of considerable magnitude.[38] He also observed "that the mountains of the Northwest will win world-wide renown for the beauty and interest of their glaciers, as well as for the magnificence of their scenery, is predicted by all who have scaled their dizzy heights."[39]

Native Peoples in the Cascades

The greater Pacific Northwest was among the first regions in the Western Hemisphere outside of Alaska to be settled by humans. Archaeological evidence indicates that ancestors of the early residents of the interior Pacific Northwest arrived perhaps thirty thousand years ago, before the formation of the Cordilleran Ice Sheet. It is believed that the first inhabitants of the northern Cascades arrived on both flanks of the mountains twelve thousand to ten thousand years ago. Bands from present-day Alaska, after migrating southward behind the coastal and possibly interior ranges, evidently spread northward from the lower Columbia River to both west and east of Puget Sound.[40] They may have crossed Cascade Range passes to the Puget Sound lowland in early postglacial time. Eight thousand years ago, when the climate in the Pacific Northwest was quite similar to today's, prehistoric land-use patterns began to change, possibly because late-glacial large game animals became extinct.[41] People established dwellings and foraged for food, practices that led to food storage and trading. For centuries, Indian tribes and bands interacted through a widespread subsistence network that involved the exchange and trade of food and other items.[42] Native societies were small and inextricably linked to the land. They possessed a remarkable technology, crafting canoes and fishing weirs, and they imposed their own limitations on exploiting the land, collecting food, and using resources.

The Cascade Range and its varied landscapes influenced the Indians' livelihood, their insularity, and their culture. For centuries, perhaps thousands of years, tribes traveled both the Puget Sound and Columbia River basins, using numerous intermountain routes in trade networks established long before Euro-American contact. The largest populations were in the lowlands on both flanks of the Cascades, where salmon and forests provided a remarkable abundance. The western slope was once nearly impenetrable and may have been barely inhabited except for small tribes who used canoes for stream travel. In an environment of almost continuous seasonal rain and dense forests, the mountainous landscape probably held only a periodic interest for hunting, fishing, and berry picking. Some Indian bands, however, appear to have had a detailed knowledge of the mountain areas, kept cross-mountain trading routes in their economic sphere, and even wintered in Cascade valleys.

At least one archaeologist has taken the position that "for most of the thousands of years of the prehistoric period, some Indian bands were mountain dwellers and were well-adapted to the mountainous environment, regardless of what was happening during the few hundred years of the historic period."[43] Historians such as William D. Lyman, however, have concluded that "Indians are much opposed to going anywhere near the mountains."[44] There is some evidence that Indians would not climb mountains because they did not want to anger the powerful spirits there who could cause storms, eruptions, or avalanches. According to one Lummi legend, for example, an angry spirit shot Koma Kulshan (Mt. Baker) with fire from heaven as punishment, causing a large piece of the mountain to slide away.[45] The Indian guides who first led parties to Mt. Baker and Mt. Rainier would not venture beyond the snowline because of such beliefs. Still, Indians made some ascents and demonstrated that they experience climbing mountains. In 1859–1860, Indian guides led the way over dangerous terrain during the Northwest Boundary Survey. Railroad surveyors near Indian Pass in 1870 reported that the Natives accompanying them were experts at glissading, and an obsidian arrow point was found in the early 1900s on the summit of Plummer Peak in the Tatoosh Range. In 1886, seven or eight Yakamas made an attempt on Mt. Rainier. The party, led by Allison Brown, ascended Ingraham Glacier to an unknown height and spent the night near the base of Gibraltar Rock.[46]

A plausible explanation for the apparent contradiction is that the Indians considered certain high snow peaks along the western range front to be guardian spirits. These highly visible peaks—such as Mt. St. Helens, Mt. Rainier, and Mt. Baker—were avoided because of their supernatural associations. Away from those mountains, however, Indian mountain bands and dwellers explored and exploited the inner valleys and even the rocky ridges.

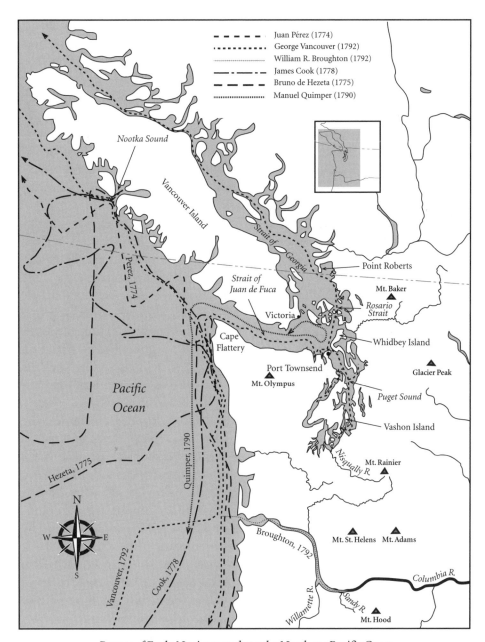

Routes of Early Navigators along the Northern Pacific Coast

Legend:
- Juan Pérez (1774)
- George Vancouver (1792)
- William R. Broughton (1792)
- James Cook (1778)
- Bruno de Hezeta (1775)
- Manuel Quimper (1790)

Tribes of the Western and Northern Flanks

A broad diversity of people lived in the northern Cascade region. The Salish-speaking tribes who lived on the western and northern flanks of the range were the Nisqually, Cowlitz, Puyallup, Snoqualmie, Skykomish, Stillaguamish, Skagit, Nooksack, Stó:lô Halkomelem (including the Chilliwack), and

Thompson. Some tribes chose to reside in more hospitable locations on alluvial river plains or near shorelines. Others took refuge from aggressive neighbors in secluded valleys. Some early census figures for these tribes are available, although they are biased in favor of lowland populations. According to the census for the 1855 Treaty of Point Elliott, the "Sno-qual-moo" (Snoqualmie), "Sno-ho-mish," and allied tribes totaled 1,700 persons; Skagit and allied tribes, 1,300; and Lummi, "Nook-ahk" (Nooksack), and "Sa-mish," 1,050.[47] William Tolmie's 1844 census of west-flank tribes counted 471 "Squalli-a-mish" (Nisqually), 207 "Pu-yal-lup-a-mish" (Puyallup), 373 "Sno-qual-mook" (Snoqualmie), and 322 "Sin-a-ho-mish" (Skykomish).[48] The entire Thompson tribe is estimated to have been 5,000 persons.[49]

To the south, the Nisqually Indians lived primarily in the Puget Sound Basin, although they had houses on the Carbon River, the Mashel River, and the Nisqually River.[50] They traded through the Naches Pass and were the first to use horses on the west slope of the range. The Cowlitz Indians lived mainly along the Cowlitz River Valley, and the Upper Cowlitz were a mountain people who had small villages that extended nearly to Mt. Rainier.[51] In the early historic period, the Snoqualmie had longhouses at various places along the lower Snoqualmie River; their main winter villages were at present-day Carnation and Fall City. In the spring, they fished and collected roots in their gardens and on Sallal Prairie, a historic meeting ground of coastal and interior Indians above Snoqualmie Falls.[52]

Sparse archaeological evidence indicates that Skagit Indians inhabited the upper Skagit River Valley for several thousand years. The Upper Skagits were a Northwest Coast group, although their territory extended eastward to the mountainous crest of the Cascades. Like many other Puget Sound Indians, they relied on salmon and resided in permanent winter villages and in summer camps.[53] The Upper Skagits had thirty-five winter settlements and nine summer villages along the Skagit River and its branches, and they often traveled by "shovel-nosed" canoe or foot trails into the mountains. The largest mid-Skagit village was near present-day Birdsview. Villages were also located on the Sauk branch, and there was a winter house at Baker Lake. The "Mis-kai-whu" band had villages farther upstream, including one at the confluence of the Skagit and Cascade rivers. Some of the Upper Skagit tribe are known to have ascended the Sauk River, where they shared roots with a local band at Sauk Prairie and could make an easy portage to the Stillaguamish River.[54]

In a geographic pocket between Lummi and Fraser Native lands, the Nooksacks had ties with the Skagit, Lummi, Sumas, and Chilliwack tribes. Short portages took the Nooksack Indians to the Chilliwack and Fraser rivers, where they traded with fur traders at Fort Langley and Fort Yale. Their villages extended along the Nooksack River's north fork as far as Canyon Creek, and there was also a village on the south fork.[55]

Along the lower Fraser River (upstream to Spuzzum) lived some twenty-five mainland Stó:lô Halkomelem tribes, all with a common cultural base. The Sumas lived between the Nooksack and the Chilliwack rivers, and Pilalt villages were located between the Chilliwack and Cheam Peak. The Tait covered an area from Cheam Peak to above Yale. Stó:lô villages traded up and down the Fraser River, mainly by canoe.[56] The Chilliwack villages were located along the Chilliwack River between Vedder Crossing and Chilliwack Lake. To reach the Fraser, they followed the Chilliwack and hunted in the Elk and Liumchen mountains.[57] The Chilliwacks apparently moved toward the Fraser after Fort Langley was established in 1827, probably to take advantage of trading opportunities. The fort's journal mentions them often and notes that they were "a tribe that lives on a small river that comes in from Mount Baker."[58]

The Thompson Indians, who spoke an interior Salish language, lived in the southern British Columbia interior and a portion of present-day Washington state to the upper Skagit River. They bartered with the Okanogan tribe, often exchanging dried salmon for tools and animal skins.[59] The Lower Thompson wintered in the upper Skagit Valley, often traveling on snowshoes and sometimes remaining through the summer to hunt and fish. They were regarded as enemies of the Skagits, with whom they had skirmishes (sometimes involving the taking of slaves). East of Mt. Baker was a common hunting territory of the Nooksack, Upper Skagit, Okanogan, Methow, and Chelan Indians; the Lower Thompson also hunted in part of this territory.[60]

Tribes of the Eastern and Southern Flanks

The principal Salish- and Sahaptin-speaking tribes who lived on the eastern and southern flanks of the Cascade Range were the Klickitat, Yakama, Kittitas, Wenatchee, and Okanogan. The Klickitat, Yakama, and Kittitas tribes spoke a Sahaptin language; the Wenatchee and northern interior tribes, including the Okanogan, spoke Salish.[61]

The Klickitat were the most important group of the region north of the lower-middle Columbia River in the early historic period. Headquartered around the Klickitat River, they were strong traders in commodities that ranged from furs to salmon, and they made forays as far north as Mt. Baker.[62] In time, they controlled a good deal of the east-west trade on the Columbia. In addition to various fish camps, the Klickitat maintained summer camps at Trout Lake; Glenwood Meadows; Chequoss, Tahk, and Spilyeh prairies; Huckleberry Mountain; and other locations in the upland north of the Columbia River. There were also renowned racetracks in Klickitat country, points of ethnic gatherings that coincided with the huckleberry harvest.[63]

The Yakama and Columbia Basin Indians possessed a similarly flexible culture, including subsistence techniques for exploiting an environment of hot summers, semidesert vegetation, and harsh, rocky terrain.[64] In the Yakima Valley, explorer and fur trader Alexander Ross—probably the first non-Native to visit the area—came to purchase horses in 1814 and found an encampment of more than 3,000 Indians. The largest Yakama village was one mile north of Union Gap and had an estimated 2,000 inhabitants.[65] The Yakama also had villages on the Tieton and Bumping rivers, southeast of Mt. Rainier. At Rimrock in the upper Tieton River Valley, they kept a permanent village for fishing, hunting, and berry gathering. For generations, the Yakama had frequented the Mt. Rainier region as a summer encampment; and horse pasturing, hunting, berry picking, and racetrack events took place both there and near Mt. Adams.[66] The Yakama and other interior tribes traded Indian hemp, camas root, dried fish, horses, buffalo robes, sheep's wool, bear grass, and tobacco with west-flank tribes, in exchange for dried clams and salmon, dentalium shells, wapato root, and sometimes berries.

In a geographical wedge southeast of Mt. Stuart, between the Wenatchee and Yakama tribes, the Kittitas occupied a large village on Naneum Creek. An important summer camp and salmon trap were at the outlet of Cle Elum Lake, which attracted as many as a thousand Kittitas in summer.[67] A hunting village was located seven miles below present-day Wenatchee at Stemilt Creek.

The Wenatchee were a group of small bands extending from the Wenatchee River to Lake Chelan. They had a large permanent village on the Columbia, below the mouth of the Wenatchee, and other important villages at the mouths of Squilchuck, Mission, and Icicle creeks and at the confluence of the Wenatchee and Chiwawa rivers. The Wenatchees hunted, fished, and picked berries in the nearby mountains, although salmon was their food staple.[68] The Chiwawa River flat near the mouth of Chikamin Creek was apparently a favorite summer camping location for generations. Like the Yakama, the Wenatchee traded with both plateau people and coastal tribes.

The valley of the Wenatchee River was known as the Pisquouse, or "narrow land." The term *Pisquouse* was used by many early explorers to refer to interior tribes from Priest Rapids to the Methow River. HBC Governor George Simpson reported that north of the "Eyakima" (Yakima) River, the tribes were known as the "Piscowes" (Wenatchee), "Intiatook" (Entiat), "Tsillani" (Chelan), "Meatuho" (Methow), "Okinagan" (Okanogan), and "Samilkumeighs" (Similkameen).[69] The Wenatchee Indians were called "Piscahoes" on *Sketch of Thompson's River District*, an 1827 map by HBC trader Archibald McDonald.

The Chelan Indians occupied a quite different environment. With their territory adjacent to Lake Chelan, the largest lake in the Cascade Range, the Chelan used the lake as a waterway. Both Wenatchee and Chelan Indians regularly used mountain passes to hunt and trade with Puget Sound Indians.[70]

Farther north, the Okanogan Indians lived on both sides of the International Boundary. The tribe fished, hunted, and kept trails in the mountainous

Methow River drainage to the west, and sites have been found as far into the drainage as present-day Mazama, the head of the Twisp River, and just south of Barron.[71] The Similkameen Indians, a nomadic interior people whose name means "salmon river," lived between the Okanogan and Thompson peoples at the northeastern fringe of the Cascade Range.[72] At the Tulameen River (north of the forty-ninth parallel), "the place where red earth is sold," the Similkameen dug a red ochre clay that was highly prized as a trade commodity. They also traded wild hemp for salmon and fishnets from coastal tribes.

Subsistence in the Mountains

When ancestors of modern Indians migrated southward from Alaska into the newly deglaciated portions of the Pacific Northwest, they brought with them a heritage of important cultural innovations made in Eurasia during Upper Paleolithic time, a heritage that no doubt facilitated their adaptation to the ecological niches they inhabited along the region's waterways and in mountain valleys.[73] These early peoples continued their long tradition of exploiting the fish resources of rivers and lakes and may have cultivated the land in addition to hunting game and gathering native plants. They also became skilled at making tools and implements of bone, antler, wood, and fiber.

The Upper Skagit Indians—typical of those who inhabited the mountain valleys—fished for salmon with nets, weirs, spears, and hook and line. During a bountiful upstream run of salmon, a family might obtain several months' worth of fish from a river in just a few days.[74] Like other tribes of the region, the Skagit boiled fish and game in woven baskets or in carved wooden troughs heated by hot rocks. Fraser River Indians caught and dried salmon throughout the year. They fished in mountain streams for steelhead, Dolly Varden, cutthroat, and grayling and caught sturgeon in sloughs when the fish moved into the shallow waters of the Fraser to spawn in June and July. They also built smokehouses—shed-roofed cedar structures that housed fish-drying racks.[75]

The Stó:lô Indians constructed weirs of supple brush poles in shallow streams to take salmon, trout, and sturgeon. The Chilliwacks built a brush weir across the Chilliwack River at their main village, and the Sumas had a large sturgeon weir where the river left Lake Sumas.[76] The Stó:lôs also used fine-mesh bag nets of hemp fiber to catch trout and sturgeon and sometimes took fish with a noose at the end of a pole or simply with a prong. The Lower Thompson Indians (below Lytton), fishing from platforms near the riverbank, used a dip net with a hoop frame and a long pole.[77]

The Wenatchee, Yakama, and Klickitat cultures all relied on salmon fishing, drying them on rocks and pulverizing them for basket storage. Both the Yakama and the Klickitat fished with two-pronged spears up to eighteen feet long. They used dipnets made of hemp (from dogbane twine) to fish from platforms constructed with tripod supports and horizontal spars at traditional fishing sites such as Celilo Falls on the Columbia river near present-day The Dalles, Oregon. Fishers also built fencelike weirs to divert fish into traps. Samuel Anderson, while ascending the Columbia in 1862, observed: "The largest & most beautiful rapid is at the Upper Cascades where we found a number of Indians engaged in Salmon fishing & saw them catch a number of splendid fellows from 30 to 40 lb weight."[78] Many families on the lower Columbia shared the rich fishery at Celilo Falls and at other locations along the river. Cascades at the lower end of Tumwater Canyon in the Wenatchee Mountains also produced ideal fishing conditions. In 1870, for example, railroad surveyor Daniel C. Linsley watched two to three hundred Indians spearing fish there. This annual fishing event brought as many as three thousand Indians to fish, gamble, and race horses.[79] Fish weirs were also built across the mouth of the Chiwawa River and below Lake Wenatchee.

The Coast Salish Indians also took advantage of the abundant natural resources of the region, fishing for salmon and using the western red cedar and, to a lesser extent, yellow cedar to make canoes, houses, mats, blankets, clothing, and baskets. They also built temporary houses from cedar or cattail mats. Slender cedar saplings were used to pole canoes, and cedar roots were carefully split to make baskets.[80]

Many tribes depended heavily on roots and berries for food. The Yakama, for example, made use of no fewer than twenty-three kinds of roots—including bitterroot, wild onion, wild carrot, and camas—and eighteen kinds of berries.[81] The Klickitat had a prairie-oriented subsistence economy in a land rich with camas and huckleberry.[82] Tahk Prairie, between the Klickitat River forks, was a favorite place for gathering camas and wapato roots. Indians also obtained roots at many other mountain prairies, including Sauk Prairie on the Sauk River and Sallal Prairie near the Snoqualmie River—both well-known gathering places. At summer camps, Klickitat families gathered berries near timberline around Mt. Adams. Cascade Range tribes made extensive use of other plants as well. Among the Wenatchee, for example, bear-grass leaves were woven into cedar-root baskets; willow was crushed and baked to make tea for colds and flu; arrowleaf balsamroot was dried and ground into powder, then moistened and shaped into cakes that could be eaten or dried.[83]

The Chinook and Klickitat caught deer in pitfall traps covered with brush, sometimes driving game toward the pits with the aid of trained dogs. Using snowshoes, they also pursued deer in winter.[84] The Upper Skagit caught both bear and deer in log deadfalls set in trails leading to water, and deer were sometimes driven over cliffs into ravines. The Similkameen drove elk and deer into narrow canyons, and both the Okanogan and Similkameen Indians used large snares to trap deer, bear, and beaver.

The Lower Thompson Indians—whose weapons included bows and arrows, spears, knives, clubs, and tomahawks—were regarded as especially adept hunters.[85] In winter, they used snowshoes to run down deer and caught animals by using a concealed trap at a fence gate.[86] Little is known about the Indians' use of snowshoes on Cascade trail routes, but it seems clear that hunting on snowshoes was widespread among Pacific Northwest Indians. Railroad explorer Lt. Abiel Tinkham, during his 1853–1854 crossing of Yakima Pass, reported that the Yakamas cached snowshoes eighteen miles west of the range divide for winter travel. George Gibbs reported seeing snowshoes cached at Naches Pass, and sets of snowshoes were later found at Yale on the Fraser River.[87]

Trails

For hunting, fishing, and berry picking, as well as distant trading, Pacific Northwest Indians—both on the flanks of the range and within it—traditionally followed and improved numerous trails, sometimes across passes. A limited number of mountain passes provided good east-west crossings, and it is evident from the location and wide distribution of known trails that the Cascade Range Indians had the navigational skills to negotiate the treacherous mountains. The trails were possibly marked by rock piles (cairns) or broken branches to indicate changes in direction.

The best-documented trade and communication route in the Cascades was the Klickitat Trail, which connected Klickitat and other settlement and subsistence sites; a branch network linked the camas and berry campsites of these Indians. Trails also led to the Columbia River, the Lewis River, and the lower Yakima River Valley.[88] The Nisqually River Indian trail—also well documented—led to Mashel Prairie, then to a river ford near present-day Eatonville (a detour that avoided the Nisqually River canyon) and again to the Nisqually before continuing on to Bear Prairie and across Cowlitz Pass. Another Native trail in the Cowlitz River drainage crossed Cispus Pass, and there were local hunting trails to the Tatoosh Range and from Cowlitz Pass to Goat Rocks.[89]

The Snoqualmie River Valley was an important crossroads of the Native world. Indians came up the river in canoes to the portage around Snoqualmie Falls, then ascended east to Sallal Prairie and into the Cedar River watershed for the ascent to Yakima Pass. (Today's Snoqualmie Pass was primarily a foot-trail route, not favored by the Indians as was Yakima Pass). There was a trail from D'Wamish Lake (Lake Washington) to Snoqualmie Falls.[90] Horses could be taken across Yakima Pass, and trails followed both sides of the Yakima River southeastward from Keechelus Lake. A trail entered the Cle Elum River Valley and extended to Fish Lake, which the Indians called "I-i-yas." Before it was replaced by a wagon road in 1897, Indians told settler Andrew J. Splawn that this trail had long been used to pick berries and to hunt and was a principal Kittitas route to huckleberry sites. Reportedly, there were also trails from the valley headwaters to Icicle Creek.[91]

The Naneum Trail across the Wenatchee Mountains (southeast of Mt. Stuart) was used by Indians and later by the army. It extended from the Kittitas Valley to grassland near Naneum Peak and then on to the Columbia near Colockum Creek.[92] From Lake Wenatchee, a well-known trail followed the White River to Indian Pass, then crossed west to the Sauk River's north fork. Indians told George Gibbs about a short canoe portage from the "Skywhamish" across to the south fork of the "Stoluckwamish" (Stillaguamish) and another from its north fork to the "Sah-kee-me-hu" (Sauk) branch of the Skagit.[93] Gibbs understood that the route continued north by way of Lake Whatcom to the Fraser River.[94]

The Chiwawa River trail, well traveled during the berry season, extended upstream to at least Rock Creek. The Bailey Willis map of 1887 marks a trail leading from Navarre Coulee to Stormy Mountain before crossing the Entiat Mountains.[95] Trails reportedly ascended most canyons from the Entiat River Valley, extended along the Entiat Mountains, and connected to Lake Wenatchee and Chumstick Creek. After HBC posts such as Fort Okanogan were established, trails from the east slope to the Skagit and Stillaguamish rivers appear to have been abandoned because it was simpler for Indians of the area to trade with the new fort.[96] Skagit Indians, who had once carried furs to Fort Okanogan, now traded with Puget Sound and Fraser River posts.

After his 1814 venture into the northern Cascades, Alexander Ross reported that Red Fox of the Okanogan tribe had visited the "Great Salt Lake" (Strait of Georgia) numerous times on trading missions, generally taking fifteen days for the journey. He was probably traveling the route from the Similkameen to the Fraser River, a track of unknown antiquity. The route was later followed in part by a fur-brigade trail and the Whatcom Trail.[97] In the summer of 1853, a Spokane chief, Quiltanee, told George McClellan that Indians occasionally paddled to the head of Lake Chelan, then used a poor, steep foot trail that led to the summit (Cascade Pass) and then descended to the Skagit. There was an eastern variation of this trail from the Methow and Twisp rivers to Bridge Creek.[98] The route was used by army explorers in 1882 and possibly earlier by Alexander Ross.

Many documents from the time of the Fraser gold rush, which began in 1858, refer to Indian trails along the Fraser River canyon.[99] One such trail was rebuilt as the "mule trail" to the Cariboo. The Lower Thompson Indians regularly used a trail from the Fraser River to the upper Skagit for hunting, fur gathering, and occasional raiding. Later, the trail was popular with prospectors and surveyors. A branch, today known as the Skyline Trail (from the Skagit to the Similkameen), was used to hunt marmots and gather berries.

The Northwest Boundary Survey recorded that the "Samona" Indians (apparently a band of the Chilliwack) had numerous goat-hunting trails, one extending from Fort Hope to Chilliwack Lake. Established Native trails also led from the Fraser River via Lake Sumas and portages to the Nooksack River. With the establishment of Fort Langley and Fort Hope, the Chilliwack-Nooksack route became important as a passage to upper Puget Sound.[100]

Because Indians on both flanks of the Cascade Range had already established trails into upper valleys for hunting and gathering food—and sometimes across passes for trading purposes—they assisted early exploring and survey parties as guides and porters. Explorers such as Alexander Ross of the HBC and the field parties of the Pacific Railroad Survey, the Northwest Boundary Survey (both the British and American commissions), and the Northern Pacific Railroad all employed Indians to guide or otherwise assist them. Their knowledge and skills were of immeasurable importance to the Euro-Americans as they penetrated what was for them an unknown land.

Part 1 〜

First Inhabitants

and Early Settlers

Wind Mountain, Near the Cascades of the Columbia River, *sketch by James M. Alden, c. 1859 (E.221, p.i.170, RG 76, National Archives)*

1

MAPPING THE UNKNOWN
AND EARLY EXPLORATION

Country gloomy, forest almost impervious with fallen as well as standing timber. A more difficult route to travel never fell to man's lot.

–Alexander Ross, 1855

Most striking is the wealth of timber. The roads are little more than vast aisles through the forests. Between Mount Baker and Mount Rainier a number of lesser peaks, presenting from the Strait of Fuca the form of a broken sierra, rise to the limits of perpetual snow. They have never been explored, but they appear, from some points of view, like skeletons of formerly more elevated volcanic mountains.

–George Gibbs, 1874

Lack of geographical knowledge of the world did not stop early mapmakers from visualizing the shape of the continents, and maps attempting to present the outline of western North America were published long before Europeans set foot there. One of the earliest cartographers was Ptolemy, whose second-century maps remained the standard until the sixteenth century. He produced sample maps that depicted the North American continent at a time when that landmass was still a projection of the imagination. For over a thousand years, however, Europeans did not build on Ptolemy's monumental achievements. His maps with a rational gridwork of latitude and longitude were replaced by fanciful world maps that combined mythical, geographical, and biblical knowledge—maps that were regarded more as visual summaries of history, learning, and legend than as geographical aids. As Daniel J. Boorstin observes in *The Discoverers*, cartography was "imprisoned in dogmatic geography." Reliance on cartographic knowledge and a belief in a spherical earth—the basis of Greek mapmaking—were not revived in Europe until the Age of Discovery in the fifteenth century. In the centuries to come, a whole new world between Europe and Asia would evolve on maps.[1]

By the eighteenth century, scientific trends and superior instruments, particularly a telescope to determine latitude and a timepiece for longitude, revolutionized mapmaking and made possible an accurate outline of the continents. Despite such advances, the Pacific Northwest remained unknown for over two centuries after Sir Francis Drake's epic voyage in 1577–1580. In the late eighteenth century, however, as more and more geographers were convinced by an increasing number of proponents of the existence of a great stream flowing to the Pacific Ocean, representatives of several nations began to explore and map the Northwest Coast of North America.

Mapping the Northern Cascades

Cartographers and the Maps of Early Explorers

The eighteenth century has been called "a period of groping in the Trans-Mississippi West."[2] Alexander Mackenzie's influential map depicting his 1793 route from Fort Chipewyan to the Pacific Ocean, for example, is impressive for its simplicity and clarity but it contains a geographic error that would not be uncovered for a decade. Based mainly on compass courses and reports from Indians, the map depicts the Fraser ("Tacoutche Tesse") and the Columbia as the same river. Even Baron Alexander von Humboldt's important *Map of the Kingdom of Spain* in 1811 makes errors on waterways in the American West.

By the early nineteenth century, surveys of the territory between the Mississippi River and the Pacific Coast had been made by explorers from England, Spain, and Russia, but most of the maps remained in manuscript form. When the United States purchased the Louisiana Territory from France in 1803, neither buyer nor seller possessed a real understanding of its extent. After the 1804–1806 Lewis and Clark expedition, however, interest in the West grew rapidly. The Lewis and Clark map of 1806, drawn by Nicholas King for the U.S. War Department, gives an impression of the unnamed Cascade Range, which Lewis and Clark called the Western Mountains.[3] The publication of their engraved map of 1814, made from Clark's field drawings, was a monumental achievement and a milestone. The map was the source for a new generation of western maps, and it reflected the complexity of the puzzling system of mountain ranges.[4] It shows a principal chain for the range and includes Mt. St. Helens, Mt. Regniere, and Mt. Baker (the omission of Mt. Adams confirms its confusion with St. Helens). The map continues the error of depicting the Columbia and the Fraser as one river.

Explorers and cartographers slowly pieced together a true picture of the shape of the Cascade Mountains by utilizing all available information (as well as some rumors) to create an image of the range on maps. Most of the information was organized by London cartographer Aaron Arrowsmith, whose patron was the Hudson's Bay Company. This distant compiler drew on the work of the explorers Mackenzie, Lewis and Clark, Peter Skene Ogden, David Thompson, and Vancouver (whose charts were the standard for the British Admiralty). Later, the activities of the HBC provided an impetus for Arrowsmith's mapmaking.

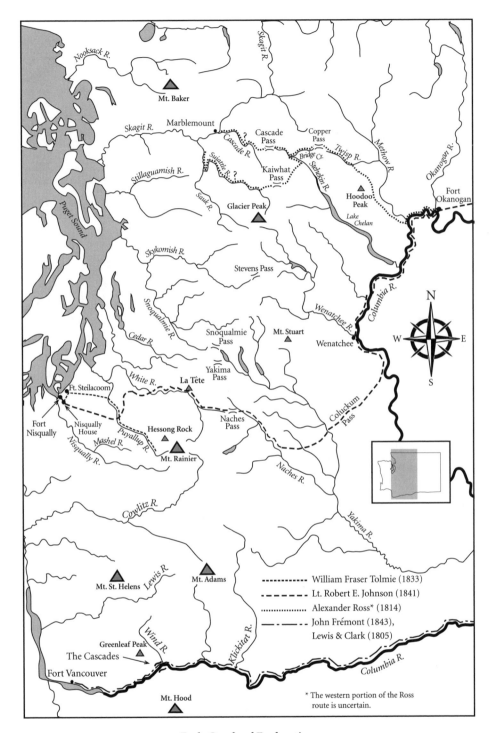

Early Overland Explorations

Within the map:

Nooksack R.

Skagit R.

Mt. Baker

Skagit R.

Marblemount

Cascade R.

Cascade Pass

Copper Pass

Twisp R.

Methow R.

Okanogan R.

Stillaguamish R.

Suiattle R. ?

Kaiwhat Pass

Bridge Cr.

Stehekin R.

Fort Okanogan

Sauk R.

Glacier Peak

Hoodoo Peak

Lake Chelan

Skykomish R.

Stevens Pass

Snoqualmie R.

Wenatchee R.

Columbia R.

N

Cedar R.

Snoqualmie Pass

Mt. Stuart

Wenatchee

W E

White R.

Yakima Pass

La Tête

S

Ft. Steilacoom

Coluckum Pass

Fort Nisqually

Nisqually House

Hessong Rock

Naches Pass

Puyallup R.

Mashel R.

Mt. Rainier

Nisqually R.

Naches R.

Cowlitz R.

Yakima R.

Lewis R.

Mt. Adams

- - - - - - - - - - William Fraser Tolmie (1833)

Mt. St. Helens

- - - - - - Lt. Robert E. Johnson (1841)

· · · · · · · · · · Alexander Ross* (1814)

Wind R.

Klickitat R.

—·—·— John Frémont (1843), Lewis & Clark (1805)

Greenleaf Peak

The Cascades

Fort Vancouver

Columbia R.

Mt. Hood

* The western portion of the Ross route is uncertain.

On Arrowsmith's 1802 map, there is still no hint of the Cascade Range. Despite the river ventures of Simon Fraser in 1808 and David Thompson in 1811, new knowledge about the Pacific Northwest's waterways was absorbed slowly in Europe. London mapmakers in 1813 still showed the Fraser as a prominent Columbia tributary, and Thompson's findings did not appear on an Arrowsmith map until 1814. That map misjudges the course of the upper Columbia, and the Pacific Northwest is still called New Albion. HBC explorers such as James McMillan and Archibald McDonald soon realized there was no large river between the Fraser and the Columbia and that the Arrowsmith maps were in error in drawing a waterway with the name "New Caledonia." The correct drainage of the Fraser did not appear on a map until Daniel Harmon drew his *Map of the Interior of North America* in 1820.[5]

It was Thompson who made the first good map of the region north of the Columbia River. Drawn for the North West Company, his 1818 *Oregon Territory from Actual Survey* was the result of tireless effort. Thompson made frequent stops on his journey to consult with Indians, and he examined the landscape carefully. His map shows Puget Sound and three Cascade Range volcanos in remarkable detail. Although the Wenatchee River (labeled the "Piskowish") is mistakenly elongated to nearly the latitude of Mt. Baker, Thompson's map is surprisingly accurate in its rendition of the Columbia River and the inclusion of Lake Chelan. Historian Carl Wheat calls the map a "magnificent cartographic monument to its maker."[6] The 1821 map of the Columbia Basin by fur trader Alexander Ross corroborates Thompson's map. It shows Columbia River tributaries coming from mountains to the west (the Cascades) but overlooks Lake Chelan. The tracing of Ross's route is evidence of inexact compass bearings and distance; but the general placement of rivers and Indian tribes, as well as the orthography of Native names, is reliable.

Among the Cascade volcanos, Mt. St. Helens and Mt. Rainier appeared on an Arrowsmith map in 1824, and Mt. Baker in 1832. Arrowsmith's early maps followed Vancouver's 1798 chart, showing mountains near the coast and assuming a second chain in the interior, with a great longitudinal valley between the ranges. The cartographer's monumental 1834 map was based in part on Ogden's explorations, and a notable feature of that map was the exaggerated heights of Mt. Brown and Mt. Hooker in the Canadian Rockies. By the 1840s, the barometers of geographical knowledge were the maps of John Arrowsmith, Aaron Arrowsmith's nephew.

Another early map, drawn by William Rector and Isaac Roberdeau in 1818, was first published in 1859 in the second volume of the *Reports of Explorations and Surveys* for the Pacific Railroad. Purported to be a sketch of the West from 35 to 52 degrees latitude, the map shows no streams flowing into Puget Sound, although the "Tapetete" (Yakima) appears as an extensive river. The Pacific Railroad maps of Isaac I. Stevens in 1853 would use this as a base map.

In the eyes of most observers, the mountains of the Northwest coast were a distortion of the landscape that defied artistic expression. These mountains were so far outside the experience of most of those who came to the region that they seemed to violate the natural order of geography. Even HBC traders sometimes failed to comprehend the scope of the Cascade Range. John Work, for example, one of the most well-traveled and knowledgeable company officials, thought he saw Mt. Baker from the Columbia River in 1830:

> From the top of the hill where we are now encamped there is an extensive view and nothing to be seen but mountains and deep valleys as far as the eye can reach, Mt. St. Helen is but a short distance to the northeast, and Mt. Rainier bears north, at still a shorter distance. Mt. Baker, I suppose, is seen at a great distance between the two. We are still but a short way from the Columbia, immediately beyond it is seen Mt. Hood.[7]

Company traders were focused on exploiting the beaver and maintaining their economic domain, not on mapmaking or deciphering the mountain features.

A most peculiar relic is the 1839 manuscript map by a visionary Bostonian and outspoken Oregon enthusiast, Hall J. Kelley. The map, which copied much from Lewis and Clark, is unique in its presidential nomenclature for the major volcanos; for example, Mt. St. Helens is "Mt. Washington" and Mt. Hood is "Mt. Adams." The Yakima River is Kelley's "Tapteal," and it rises near "Mt. Regniere." The "Caledonia" (Skagit) is shown as a small river south of the "Tacooche" (Fraser).

It was American naval commander Charles Wilkes who first used the name *Cascade Range* on a map, and his landmark *Map of the Oregon Territory* in 1844 was a product of diligent and skillful charting. Drawing on the work of Vancouver for the configuration of coastal regions, the map covers the territory north to the fiftieth parallel. The Cascade Range is heavily emphasized as a single chain extending north and south of the Columbia River. The Wilkes map finally charted Mt. Adams correctly. A decade later the Pacific Railroad survey maps made the identification permanent, and "its confusion with the nearby Mount St. Helens . . . was at and [*sic*] end."[8] For the interior—the Rocky Mountains—Wilkes copied largely from British maps. Events that intervened between 1841 (the year of the Wilkes survey) and 1844—such as John C. Frémont's exploration and his 1843 map—also influenced Wilkes's cartography. According to historian William Goetzmann, the Wilkes map was the beginning of accurate western cartography.[9]

Maps in the Age of the Topographical Engineers

The maps left by military engineers are remarkable documents. Beginning with the 1838 *Map of Oregon Territory* by Capt. Washington Hood, for example, the maps of the Corps of Topographical Engineers made many place names permanent. Field leaders in the Corps not only conceived grand new maps and wrote stirring narratives, but they also became geographic detectives. After John Charles Frémont explored the West in 1842–1844 and proposed the true geography of the Great Basin, he created a most important map, the first of a series of scientific mappings of the West. Printed over the face of that 1845 map were excerpts from Frémont's report describing important locations. The explorer's maps, skillfully drawn by Charles Preuss, were the first to be widely carried by travelers.[10]

The view of the Oregon Country was dimly and distantly pieced together during those decades of heightening interest in the West, and the immigration of the 1840s underscored the practical need for improved maps. Frémont's careful survey of Oregon Territory contributed to western mapping but related only to a narrow portion of the lower Columbia River, and maps from individual enterprises were inadequate and unreliable. The entry of the U.S. Army into Pacific Northwest affairs, however, brought a growth of regional knowledge and skilled surveying and mapping personnel.

The military maps show forts and wagon roads quite accurately, Carl Wheat tells us, but they use imagination with respect to the shape of the Cascade Range. Maps prior to the 1850s reflected many misconceptions about the range, with scattered line markings depicting important mountains and rivers drawn erratically. Conjecture focused on two crestlines within the range north of latitude forty-eight degrees. This crestline divergence was popularized by the influential maps of the Pacific Railroad survey, particularly Isaac Stevens's map, drawn by John Lambert and Lt. Johnson K. Duncan in 1853–1854 and published in 1859. Their map synthesized the results of intense fieldwork and compilation of current knowledge.[11] With this map, Duncan (who was with Capt. George McClellan's western-division party during the railroad survey) made one of the first accurate depictions of the Cascades in southern Washington. He described "the main Cascade ranges, which run to the north up to Mount St. Helens and Mount Adams, and centre in Mount Rainier. Thence one main chain connects with Mount Baker, and another runs off to the northeast. These principal chains throw out innumerable spurs."[12]

On the map, the volcanos and Mt. Stuart are the only mountains named. The routes taken by McClellan and his subordinates are indicated—McClellan's route to the "Yahinese or upper Yakima," Duncan's routes in the Methow drainage, and Lt. Henry Clay Hodges's crossing of Naches Pass. The map was the first to show many parts of the fringes of the Cascade Range. The "Pisquouse or Wenatshapam" (Wenatchee) River is marked, but the Cowlitz is so abbreviated that it indicates the survey did not understand its upper drainage. The Skagit, Nooksack, and "Sto-la-qua-mish" (Stillaguamish) rivers are shown breaking through the western chain. Cedar River and Lake are still labeled "Nook-noo," and the Tieton River is the "Atahnam." This map—the result of a hurried survey by McClellan—indicates that Stevens barely understood the location of Snoqualmie Pass. The projected railroad route-line is clearly sketched along the Yakima River and over Yakima Pass to the "Nook-noo" (Cedar) River, but the legend reads "Snoqualmie Pass."[13]

Neither Stevens nor his topographers on the McClellan survey understood the upper Skagit waters. Not until 1908 and the conclusion of the Northwest Boundary Survey, a joint American-British study whose members included highly skilled astronomers and topographers, were the Skagit and other northernmost regions of the range accurately portrayed. The Stevens map leaves the "Cascade Mountains" range east of Mt. Baker a mystery, depicting it as a "region [that] is believed to be a great mountain basin." Glacier Peak is not shown, but Lake Chelan is located with reasonable accuracy and is described as "Mountainous Country covered with pine forest." The map indicates the range dividing near the latitude of Lake Wenatchee.[14]

Early territorial resident George Gibbs—an artist, geologist, and extraordinary explorer and an independent associate of both the Pacific Railroad and Northwest Boundary surveys—was the first person to describe the Cascade Range in writing and to give it a realistic visual form. His drawings and support maps for the Stevens report are good representations of certain parts of the range. Still, the width of the range and the nature of some of the drainages would confound explorers for years to come. Although the east and west fringes of the range had been explored by non-Indians by the time of the McClellan expedition, none of the explorers had penetrated the mountains, so there was little knowledge about the passes and drainages.[15] Before fully understanding the extent of the northern portion of the range, Gibbs wrote that the "Nooksahk" was the headwaters of the Okanogan River. During the time of the Pacific Railroad survey, he believed the eastern branch of the range separated from the main axis at about the latitude of "Winatsha" (Lake Wenatchee). The main axis, he maintained, continued north and crossed the Skagit; the other tended to the east of the Skagit, with the Okanogan River as the eastern limit (this river being the lowest drainage between the Cascades and the Rocky Mountains).[16]

Gibbs, who studied the geography of the Cascade Range more thoroughly than any other person of his day, took the two-divide belief of Duncan and Lambert to heart:

> About the latitude of the Methow River, the range appears to divide, one running parallel with Puget Sound, the other with the Okinakanie [Okanogan] between which lies an interior basin of which nothing is known except that according to Indian account, the Skagit River enters it from the west. Probably it is drained from the north by the Nooksahk and a branch of Fraser's River.

Gibbs was partly correct when he stated in 1854 that the "Skywhamish" (Skykomish) was "probably interlocking" with the sources of "Chelann lake" and the "Winatshapam" (Wenatchee). At the time, he called the Snohomish River the "Sinahomish," and he correctly observed that a southern fork (a

Snoqualmie branch) heads "a short distance north of the main Yakima pass."[17] Gibbs's *Map of the Western Part of Washington Territory* in 1856 shows additional evidence of his regional knowledge.[18] There is a good representation of the range between Mt. Adams and the upper Yakima River, with which Gibbs was familiar. The blank areas to the north of Snoqualmie Pass indicate that Gibbs had not yet visited the drainages of the Skagit and Stillaguamish, though his "Sky-wha-mish" and "Pisquouse" (Wenatchee) appear to be mostly correct and he evidently had examined the lower Skagit. Sauk Mountain is shown as "Mt. Gweht."

The observations of McClellan, Duncan, Gibbs, and others were included in the landmark 1857 general map by Lt. Governor Kemble Warren, the *Map of the Territory of the United States from the Mississippi River to the Pacific Ocean to Accompany the Reports of the Explorations for a Railroad Route.* Secretary of War Jefferson Davis ordered Warren to create the map, which was urgently needed by settlers and for defining the territories of the West. Davis's instructions to Warren were to carefully examine every survey and reconnaissance map, to read every report, and to embody all authentic information in the map. Lauded by historians as a great achievement, the map was the first reasonably accurate cartographic portrayal of the West and "the first map of the western United States which was in any way worthy of the name of map."[19] The style of the illustrations and the text associates the map closely with the tradition of the Corps of Topographical Engineers, but it represented a new degree of accuracy in mapping the Northwest.

Warren must have been perplexed by the discrepancies on the various explorers' maps. The exaggerated distances reported by the first white explorers, who were unable to correct their estimates by precise observations, distort those parts of early maps based on their reports. Considerable sections of Warren's map were, wisely, left blank. In compiling all previous reconnaissances and explorations, Warren was careful to represent only known mountain peaks and to copy as nearly as possible the styles of different topographers from their original maps. Warren's map, like others of the era, shows the range dividing into two distinct chains near the latitude of Lake Wenatchee. It shows the survey routes of McClellan and Duncan, the Cascade volcanos, and Mt. Stuart—all positioned more correctly than on previous maps because of the reference to the Willamette Meridian, which had been established in 1851. Geographic positions were determined mostly from reconnaissances (quick explorations as opposed to the slower, more thorough process of surveying) and could not have a great deal of accuracy. Warren correctly showed the "Sinahomish" (Snohomish) as the Snoqualmie River extending to Snoqualmie Pass; but he erred on the upper Nooksack, which he drew as swinging to the south of Mt. Baker. The upper Skagit became a dashed line, indicating guesswork, to the "Simalla-ow R" (Sumallo River), where the Fort Hope trail is shown.

Other Early Maps and Surveys

Even before the Pacific Railroad explorations, Edwin F. Johnson (who would later become the chief engineer of the Northern Pacific Railroad) was an advocate for a railroad line to connect Chicago and Bellingham Bay. His 1854 map shows that he copied the altitude of Mt. Rainier from Wilkes and that he took from Kelley the name "Cascade or Presidents Range." Johnson's proposed route runs west from the "Barrier" (Methow) River to Puget Sound just south of Mt. Baker; the "Tuxpam R" is apparently the Skagit. In a few years, Johnson would learn from his surveyors how impossible such a route was.

The development of the railroad lines gave birth to some five thousand maps—a testimony to the imagination and ingenuity of the railroad pioneers. Early railroad mapmakers had a difficult task: they often had to try to reconcile information from different and sometimes unreliable sources.[20] The continuation of the Cascade Range into Canada north of the Fraser River, for example, still perplexed geographers in the 1860s. English maps showed a major chain of mountains trending northward from Mt. Baker to the west of Harrison Lake. Gibbs believed that the continuation might be the one that divided the lake from the upper Fraser River. Even at the turn of the nineteenth century, geologist Israel C. Russell was uncertain where the range should terminate: "The Coast Mountains of Canada, although stated by geologists to be distinct from the Cascade Mountains, are in part at least, as determined by the present writer, a direct northward extension of that range."[21]

While Gibbs maintained that there were only two divisions to the northern Cascades, a contemporary from England, Hilary Bauerman—and, later, geologists Reginald A. Daly and George Otis Smith—recognized three divisions. Bauerman recommended the Skagit Mountains, Okanogan Mountains, and Hozomeen Range as divisions of the Cascade Range, but those names did not appear on subsequent maps. Daly, Bauerman's successor on the Northwest Boundary Survey, believed the east and west limits of the three northern Cascade units were clearly defined by the longitudinal valleys of, respectively, the Skagit, Pasayten, and Similkameen rivers.

Knowledge of the upper Skagit region came principally from the exploration of Alexander C. Anderson, an HBC trailblazer, in 1846 and 1847. His map, *Gold Regions on the Fraser River* (1858), shows a small lake near the head of the Sumallo River, but he believed the Skagit River drainage led to Bellingham Bay. The map also shows the Punch Bowl, named for a lake in Athabasca Pass. A line bearing southwest from the "Skhaist-Simallaow" junction has the legend "Supposed to be the Noo-sakh and to discharge near Bellingham Bay."

The complexity of the range that had frustrated Anderson north of the forty-ninth parallel also bewildered Lt. Henry S. Palmer of the British Royal Engineers. On September 18, 1859, he believed he was crossing the mountain backbone, near Coquihalla River: "But so undefined are its general features, and so remarkable is the absence of any prominent and distinguishing snow capped peaks, such as are visible from the 'Dalles', and by which one may determine the general bearing of a range, that it is a matter of extreme difficulty to follow its direction with the eye for more than a few miles."[22]

Palmer and other engineer-explorers from Great Britain, however, had studied and learned the confusing topography, and their pioneering maps are a unique contribution to map lore on the northern fringe of the Cascade mountains. Various maps made during the 1858 Fraser River gold rush, as wagon roads were built along the river and into the interior, provide a litany of early names used north of the forty-ninth parallel. *Fort Hope to Similkameen and Rock Creek* (1861), for example, was drawn by the Royal Engineers for Col. John S. Hawkins.[23] Some well-known features were Lake Sumas (its former size is shown), "Schweltza" (Cultus) Lake, "Tummeahai" (Tamihi) Creek, the trail to Chilliwack Lake, the Punch Bowl, Captain Grant's trail (the Hope trail), the "Sumallow" wagon road, the "Ashnolon" River, and "Mount XLIX."

Meanwhile, misconceptions of the Cascades continued to be portrayed. The 1860 Surveyor General's *Map of Washington Territory* showed an imaginative depiction of spur ranges south of the Skagit River and little indication of a knowledge of important drainages. A large "Unexplored" was placed between the Skagit River and an artistic portrayal of a mountain chain bearing northeast from Lake Chelan, providing continuing buoyancy to the belief in an interior mountain basin. The Northwest Boundary Survey teams from both the United States and Great Britain had explored much of the terrain, but their map (which did not accept this mysterious basin) would not be printed until 1866 and was not circulated in the Pacific Northwest.

Much of the Boundary Survey's knowledge of the upper Skagit River area and the land to the east and west was transmitted to Surveyor General (Public Survey) maps, but not until after 1880. Even on the 1886 map, the Skagit and Chelan drainages are poorly identified, though the legend "Unexplored" no longer appears. In contrast, the Northern Pacific Railroad explorations remained proprietary. An exception was Daniel C. Linsley's exploration west of Lake Chelan in 1870. Within four years, his route would be depicted on the Asher and Adams map.

The 1866 map by the American commission of the Northwest Boundary Survey was made from notes by Lt. John G. Parke of the Topographical Engineers and by civilians George Clinton Gardner, Joseph S. Harris, Henry Custer, George Gibbs, Russell V. Peabody, and Francis Hudson not long after Anderson's exploration of the boundary area. It also took information from the British Boundary Commission, U.S. Coast Survey, British Admiralty, U.S. Engineering Bureau, Pacific Railroad explorations, U.S. Land Office, U.S. Exploring Expedition, and Capt. John Palliser. All the main features of the map are clear, and the rivers are identified by their modern names. The excellence of the 1866 map is due in large part to the keen scrutiny of topographical analysts such as Gibbs.

While government maps prevailed, a few good private maps were being published. The visually attractive maps of historian Hubert H. Bancroft proliferated after 1863 into a family of maps. Prior to the Civil War, there was little need for small, detailed surveys. Then, however, geologist and explorer John Wesley Powell began to advocate making quadrant section maps—maps that would eventually become the standard for accuracy for the U.S. Geological Survey (USGS). In later years, mapmakers in the field often chose local names used by settlers rather than those shown on army maps.

The last of the important army maps was drawn by artist Alfred Downing and shows the route taken by Gen. William T. Sherman in 1883 from Fort Ellis, Montana, west to Fort Hope, British Columbia. In the 1880s, no one was more familiar with the far northern portions of the range than Downing, a civilian associated with army explorations. On Downing's map, Mt. Baker is shown at 11,100 feet and Mt. Shuksan at 9,900 feet. The only other summit shown in that region is "Kakoit Mountain" (Devils Dome). Mt. St. Helens is shown higher than Mt. Adams, Mt. Aix is included, and "Yakima Pass" appears at the location of Snoqualmie Pass. Many names on a similar map of the country Sherman traveled through between old Fort Colville and the Fraser River are taken from the Boundary Survey map. The "Great Rapid" is shown on the Skagit River, the Baker River is "Hukullum," and Granite Creek is "Slukl-te-ko-kai."

Even well after mid-century, the army had considerable gaps in its knowledge of the Cascade Range. An 1881 report by Lt. Thomas W. Symons correctly suggests that the area of Yakima Pass contained sheltered lakes that probably owed their existence to glaciers, but Symons admitted "to the north of this pass very little is known concerning the main chain of the Cascades. . . . It is a region of high and rugged mountains, more jagged and rough than the regions to the south." Another government agency, the U.S. Forest Reserve, created a new kind of map. An 1898 map of the Cascade Range, for example, reflects the influence of settlers and included names such as Eldorado, Mac Millans (McMillans), Orient, Goodell's, and Camp Gilbert. Early Forest Reserve maps depict trails across Cascade, Park Creek, Thunder, Rainy, State, Twisp, Indian, and Crater (Harts) passes. The first peaks noted on Forest Reserve maps were the ones climbed by members of the Geological Survey, and they included Columbia, Pilchuck, White Chuck, Index (Baring), and Pyramid.

More than ninety years had elapsed between the Lewis and Clark expedition and the construction of the first pass roadway by 1898; and the deep, winding river valleys and complex rock structure of the northern Cascade Range was as much a mystery as it had been when Euro-Americans first found its adjacent valleys attractive. The range of glaciers was destined to long remain one of the most poorly mapped regions in the United States.

Early Overland Explorers

For much of the nineteenth century, the northern Cascade Range presented a physical as well as a psychological barrier to fur traders, overland exploring parties, immigrants, curious visitors, prospectors, and missionaries. Because of communication barriers and lack of documentation, few Euro-Americans knew the location or details of Native cross-Cascade routes. Yet, it became increasingly apparent that it was these routes that would be the basis for a further understanding of the range.

In the course of only a few decades, the northern Cascades was infiltrated by American and British explorers, soldiers, fur traders, lone adventurers, and boundary and railroad surveyors. These early to mid-nineteenth-century explorers traveled on foot, on horseback, by boat, and by canoe, often guided by Indians. Some of those men passed along a few of their findings. Others endowed future generations with their literary and artistic representations of a nearly unknown region—a region whose political destiny remained uncertain until 1846.

Sixty years earlier, America's dreams of expanding westward had been frustrated by Spanish and Russian claims on the Pacific Coast, but in 1790 Spain acceded to British territorial demands and relinquished all claims north of Spanish California. A few years later, Napoleon authorized the sale of the vast Louisiana Territory to the United States for $15 million. The treaties were proclaimed and ratified on October 21, 1803, more than doubling the size of the United States.[24]

President Thomas Jefferson had long dreamed about exploring this vast unknown. He became interested in George Vancouver's reports, and he knew about Robert Gray's discovery of the Columbia in 1792 and Broughton's subsequent exploration of the lower river. The limits of the Louisiana Territory had never been definitely established, and it was not clear whether it extended west of the Rocky Mountains. The northern boundaries were also vague (in later disputes with Great Britain over the Northwest Boundary, the United States would claim present-day Oregon, Washington, Idaho, and Montana on the grounds that it was part of the territory), nor did anyone at the time know the location of the Cascade Range or the limits of California and Alaska. Meriwether Lewis and William Clark would change all that.

The Corps of Discovery

Jefferson chose Meriwether Lewis, his reliable private secretary, to head the expedition to the West. Caught up in a vision of new horizons and the opportunity to find the River of the West—in a "country of the mind"—the president instructed Lewis and William Clark to investigate a route across the Rocky Mountains, determine the course of the rumored great waterway to the Pacific, and, if possible, reach the Pacific Ocean.[25] The results of this audacious undertaking would change the focus of international competition for the West.

Lewis and Clark were the first Euro-American explorers to see the Cascade Range from inland. On October 18, 1805, they sighted Mt. Hood—the peaked volcano Broughton had named in 1792. Clark wrote in his journal: "Saw a mountain bearing S.W. Conocal form Covered with Snow." Later, supposing it to be Mt. Hood, Clark wrote, "This mtn. is Covered with Snow and in the range of mountains which we have passed through. . . ."[26]

On October 19, Clark saw Mt. Adams from near present-day Umatilla—its first sighting by a Euro-American—but he thought it was St. Helens: ". . . I descovered a high mountain of emence hight covered with Snow, this must be one of the mountains laid down by Vancouver . . . I take it to be Mt. St. Helens. . . ." Later he wrote, again sighting Mt. Adams, "Mount Hellen bears N. 25° E about 80 miles, this is the mountain we Saw near the foks of this river. It is emensely high and covered with snow, riseing in a kind of cone perhaps the highest pinecal from the common leavel in America." The explorer's first sight of Mt. St. Helens was actually on November 4, 1805, and prompted the entry: "it rises Something in the form of a Sugar lofe." Several times, the men mistook Mt. St. Helens for Mt. Rainier.[27]

On their return trip, on April 2, 1806, Lewis and Clark saw both Mt. Adams and Mt. St. Helens from the "Multnomah" (Willamette) River. Clark described Adams as "a high humped Mountain to the East of Mt. St. Helians." He believed that these mountains lay in the same chain with the conical mountains they had seen in the fall. How much the explorers admired the volcanos' beauty is evident in Lewis's journal entry of March 30, 1806: "we had a view of mount St. Helines and Mount Hood. the 1st is the most noble looking object of it's kind in nature."[28]

Despite their best efforts, Lewis and Clark were unable to unravel the drainage complexities of the Columbia, the Snake, the Clark Fork, and the Fraser rivers. They could reliably map only the course of their own travel. For adjacent areas, they had to depend on maps of uneven validity and on information from Indians. It is apparent that they were familiar with the geography of the West as described by Great Basin explorers Francisco Atanasio Domínguez and Silvestre Vélez de Escalante in 1776. On Clark's map, the Domínguez-Escalante maps are reflected in "Río de San Clemente," a tributary to a river that empties into the "Multnomah" (Willamette). Clark also depicted the Columbia River breaking through the Cascade Range and another river emptying into San Francisco Bay.[29]

Not until 1814 was the Lewis and Clark report published and their map widely distributed. Despite the empty areas and some significant errors, the map solved the first problem of western geography—the width of the continent. Lewis and Clark's explorations captured international attention, cast light on the Northwest, and laid the foundation of the United States' claim to the Oregon Country.[30]

David Thompson

In the early decades of the nineteenth century, the Pacific Northwest mountain ranges and intermontane regions were among the last remaining beaver country. The British Hudson's Bay Company, the Montreal-based North West Company, and American John Jacob Astor's Pacific Fur Company were fervent competitors in the regional fur trade. The North West Company, searching for trade routes and a navigable river that would facilitate trade with Asia, sent Alexander Mackenzie on an exploring expedition in 1793, and he forged a route across the upper Fraser River to reach the Pacific Ocean at Bella Coola. In 1808, Simon Fraser, also with the North West Company, canoed down the river later named for him to near present-day Vancouver (see chapter 6).

It was another explorer with the North West Company who finally journeyed down the Columbia River to its mouth. David Thompson, born in England, was the company's official geographer and explorer from 1799 to 1814. During his twenty-eight years of exploring, he traveled an estimated fifty thousand miles. A skilled geographer and mapmaker, Thompson had no real interest in the commercial fur trade, but he had a passion for science and geography, "a powerful mind and a singular faculty of picture-making."[31]

Thompson worked tirelessly to lay down the principal topographical features of the Columbia River drainage. He mapped with magnetic-compass courses correlated by many astronomical observations by sextant for latitude (Indians called him Koo-Koo-Sint, "the man who looks at stars"). His sextant was a Dollond brass of ten-inch radius, reading to fifteen seconds.[32] To measure distance, he used the rate of travel. His remarkable map of 1814—*Map of the North-West Territory of the Province of Canada. From the Actual Survey during the Years 1792 to 1812*—represents many years of persistent surveying. It was Thompson who named the Fraser River, and the true source of the Columbia River was finally located with Thompson's surveys in 1807 when he crossed the Rocky Mountains to set up the upper Columbia and Kootenay River trade. The practical importance of his efforts was immense. In 1811, he journeyed down the Kootenay and the Clark Fork rivers and then to Kettle Falls, where he built a cedar canoe to take him to Astoria. The voyage made him the first Euro-American to descend the Columbia River to its confluence with the Snake River, and his journals are the first written history of this inland region.

Thompson left Kettle Falls on July 3 with two Iroquois boatmen, five French voyageurs, and two Sanspoil Indians. On July 6, he came to a tribe and village he called "Smeathowe" (Methow), where he went ashore and smoked with the people there. Interestingly, he found that the tribe's knowledge of the Columbia extended only to the next village. He stopped at the large salmon fishery at the Methow River and then portaged around the rapids to the west.[33] Near present-day Wenatchee, on July 7, Thompson came upon a large Wenatchee village at the mouth of the river, which he called the "Piskowish." He was received with dancing by some 120 families. "I invited them to smoke," Thompson reported, "and the 5 most respectable men advanced and smoked a few pipes." He also mentioned the Wenatchee Mountains: "We saw mountains before us whose tops have much snow in places." On July 9, where the river ran west-southwest, Thompson observed a "high Mountain, isolated, of a conical form, a mass of pure Snow without the appearance of rock . . . I took to be Mount Hood." On July 12, Thompson saw both Mt. Hood and Mt. Adams: "a snow mount rather ahead, say 30 miles, another on right, rather behind, say 25 miles."[34] In mid-July, Thompson was welcomed at Astoria by fellow Scots, including three Nor'Westers. Spurred by the Astorians' plans to explore upriver, he started back up the Columbia. At the mouth of the Snake River, Thompson secured Indian horses, then rode overland to Spokane House. Eventually, he returned to Kettle Falls and pushed upstream to complete his survey of the entire length of the Columbia.

Alexander Ross

Alexander Ross was a stalwart twenty-two-year-old Highlander when he emigrated from his native Scotland to Canada in 1805. Lured by the prospect of wealth, he signed up as a clerk for Astor's Pacific Fur Company and sailed from New York in September 1810 on the *Tonquin,* bound for the Columbia. On July 22, 1811, he set out upstream with the David Stuart party to establish Fort Okanogan, arriving there on August 31. In his first year of employ, even though he considered the general aspect of the land "barren and dreary," the enterprising Ross obtained 1,550 beaver pelts valued at 2,250 pounds sterling.[35]

Ross was soon involved in the American and British rivalry for the profitable fur trade. When Astor was forced to sell his small settlement to the rival North West Company in 1813, however, Ross had little choice but to serve as an employee of the outpost's new owners.[36] Much like his contemporaries, Ross was drawn to the frontier. He remained at Fort Okanogan until 1816, during which time the North West Company partners were looking for new post locations and communication routes. In January 1813, Ross visited the Similkameen River en route from Kamloops to his base at Fort Okanogan.

During this early period, Ross contemplated a "project of discovery"—to cross the unknown northern Cascades and locate a feasible, direct trade route to the coast.[37] He allowed two months for this exploration, believing that the distance to saltwater was not over two hundred miles. He had learned that Red Fox—also known as Who-why-laugh, the Okanogan Indian chief—had made crossings of the mountains to trade with coastal Indians and that such trips generally required fifteen days. Ross wrote: "The Red Fox had been many times with his young men at the Great Salt Lake, as they call it, meaning the Pacific, the direct road to which across the mountains is almost due west. . . ."[38]

Ross set out from Fort Okanogan on July 25, 1814, with a guide and two other Natives. Carrying only three days' provisions, they planned to hunt animals for food. He attempted first to follow the trail with his southern Okanogan guides, but the route was so disused by 1814 and so poorly known that its precise travel line was lost soon after the group left the mouth of the Methow River.[39] They had first followed the Columbia's west bank, then crossed the Methow's mouth at a well-known ford.[40] They ascended the south bank of the Methow an unknown distance, and struck off to the left to enter a "pathless desert."

> Here our guide kept telling us that we should follow the same road as the Red Fox chief and his men used to go. Seeing no track, nor the appearance of any road, I asked him where the Red Fox road was. "This is it that we are on," said he, pointing before us. "Where?" said I, "I see no road here, not even so much as a rabbit could walk on." "Oh, there is no road," rejoined he, "but this is the place where they used to pass."

Ross wrote that their course was "due west," but he did not record the distance. Given the directions and compass course he recorded, it is likely that he followed the winding river to near present-day Carlton and then struck west. After a distance, he entered what might have been the forested Libby Creek Valley and traveled about eight miles.[41]

Problems developed almost immediately on the second day. After only a half hour, "we had to steer to every point of the compass, so many impediments crossed our path." The terrain was rocky and uneven. In dense forest, Ross attempted to use his pocket compass.

> On seeing me set the compass, the guide, after staring with amazement for some time, asked me what it was. I told him it was the white man's guide. "Can it speak?" he asked. "No," replied I, "it cannot speak." "Then what is the good of it?" rejoined he. "It will show us the right road to any quarter," answered I. "Then what did you want with me, since you had a guide of your own?" This retort came rather unexpectedly, but taking hold of my double-barreled gun in one hand and a single one in the other, I asked him which of the two was best. "The two-barreled," said he, "because if one barrel misses fire, you have another." "It is the same with guides," said I, "if one fails, we have another."

Ross possibly traveled east of Hoodoo Peak and Buttermilk Butte, and he may have ended the day on Buttermilk Creek. Such a route would shorten the distance to the Twisp River and avoid the bluffs and meanders of the lower Methow.

On July 27, a day hampered by poor weather, the country was "rugged and broken," but Ross experienced fewer problems. He may have descended Buttermilk Creek, then followed the valley of the Twisp—where there was an Indian trail—to near the junction of War Creek.[42] Because Ross does not mention Lake Chelan (although he knew of it), it is probable he kept away from the high crestline of Sawtooth Ridge. The valley of the Twisp River permitted a long trek, "general course W. by N.," on July 28. At the valley head, Ross must have crossed a pass—probably Copper Pass—where he reported snow near the route. That night he may have camped on or near Bridge Creek, which drains westerly into the Stehekin River.[43]

The next morning, Ross "started in a southerly direction, but soon got to the west again." This could have been a route down Bridge Creek.[44] Now that the party was west of the Methow-Chelan divide, the timber was much heavier and the travel difficult. Ross noted the "spruce fir" (Engelmann spruce) on the heights and, in the valleys, poplar and alder (black cottonwood and mountain alder). Of the ascent on July 30 to what may have been Cascade Pass, Ross wrote only that during the evening the party reached a height of land "which on the east side is steep and abrupt."[45]

After being delayed two days by his guide's illness and forced to leave him behind with one of the other Indians, Ross began the arduous descent: "We were still among the rugged cliffs and deep groves of the mountain, where we seldom experienced the cheering sight of the sun. . . . The weather was cold, and snow capped many of the higher peaks." If he had crossed Cascade Pass, Ross logically would have descended the north fork of the Cascade River some distance on August 2. The snow he saw could have been on Johannesburg Mountain or Sahale Peak. In the heavy forest, Ross and the remaining guide blazed some of the larger trees to help them find the way back. Ross estimated they traveled eighteen miles on August 3, the compass courses being predominantly west.[46]

On August 4, the two men began early "and were favored occasionally with open ground."

> We had not gone far when we fell on a small creek running, by compass, W.S.W., but so meandering, that we had to cross and recross it upwards of forty times in the course of the day. The water was clear and cold and soon increased so much that we had to avoid it and steer our course from point to point on the north side. Its bottom was muddy in some places, in others stony, its banks low and lined with poplars, but so overhung with wood, that we could oftener hear than see the stream. On this unpromising stream, flowing, no doubt, to the Pacific, we saw six beaver lodges, and two of the animals themselves, one of which we shot. . . . Courses, W. 8, N.W. 5, W. 7, S.W. 2—distance traveled today, twenty-two miles.

The following day, Ross traveled through a "delightful country of hill and dale, wood and plains."[47] Late that afternoon the pair were disturbed and agitated by a fearful, loud noise:

> Not a breath of wind ruffled the air, but towards the southwest, from whence the noise came, the whole atmosphere was darkened, black, and heavy. Our progress was arrested; we stood and listened in anxious suspense for nearly half an hour, the

noise still increasing, and coming, as it were, nearer and nearer to us. . . . It was the wind, accompanied with a torrent of rain—a perfect hurricane, such as I had never witnessed before. . . . The crash of falling trees, and the dark, heavy cloud, like a volume of condensed smoke, concealed from us at the time the extent of its destructive effects.

The two men perceived the havoc of the rolling cloud "by the avenue it left behind." In his alarm, the guide at first refused to continue. The two camped that night at the edge of some timber felled by the storm. Ross noted that the "little river," which he named the West River, was twenty-two yards wide at that point and so deep that "we could scarcely wade across it." He estimated they had traveled twenty-six miles that day.[48] Ross, estimating it was 151 miles from "Point Turn About" to Fort Okanogan, describes the disappointment of the return: "We shot several red deer, three black bears, a wolf and fisher, and arrived at Okanogan on the twenty-fourth of August, after a fruitless and disagreeable journey of thirty days. And here my guide told me that in four days from Point Turn-about, had we continued, we should have reached the ocean."

Retracing Ross

The routes taken by Lewis and Clark, David Thompson, and Alexander Henry the Younger (the fur-trading partner of the North West Company) may be recovered with almost absolute precision. In contrast, Ross did not make an accurate map, location sketches, or detailed descriptions; and tracing his path is a subjective procedure. Throughout the report of his journey, Ross is inexact about his route. It is unclear whether he was careless and unconcerned with details or simply forgot them over time—his narrative, *The Fur Hunters of the Far West*, was not published until 1855—but his route must be reconstructed by comparing the information he does give with a modern map.[49]

Ross's own map, drawn in September 1821 and titled *Alexander Ross on His Route across Land to Reach the Pacific in 1815* [*sic*], shows a dashed line to "Pt. Turnagain," with no reliable details beyond the lower Methow River.[50] He arrived at the broad alluvial plain of the Skagit, where its meanders would have caused him detours. A plotting of the map's daily courses and distances does not consistently agree with his journal, but many early explorers overestimated their daily travel.[51] Unlike some other explorers in the West, Ross never returned to identify his tracks.

If Ross actually traveled sixty-six miles in three days after crossing the height of land, it would seem questionable that his "West River" was the Skagit, as some writers have proposed. The terrain difficulties along the Cascade River Valley are such that Ross probably could not have kept such a pace nor forded the Skagit.[52] Ross must have been exaggerating considerably. After crossing

Copper Pass, Ross may have gone over the low, forested divide of Rainy Pass, then continued to the upper Skagit River. He could then have crossed to the Fraser River. Rainy Pass is not a "steep and abrupt" divide, however, and the long tangent northwest does not agree with Ross's journal.[53] A stronger possibility is that Ross crossed the range apex between Cascade and Suiattle passes, approximating the 1870 route of railroad explorer Daniel C. Linsley (see chapter 9). It is conceivable that he took a route from Bridge Creek to Agnes Creek and then ascended Spruce Creek to "Kaiwhat" or nearby Ross Pass.[54] There is an abrupt cliff facing east here as Ross describes, and a vista of Dome Peak and its glaciers would account for the snowy peaks he saw. The narrative and compass directions given thereafter could reflect a descent of Sulphur Creek and the Suiattle River; the "small creek" would have been the latter, which Ross could have forded.[55] The "West River" took a northward bend, according to Ross; this would then have been the Sauk. Certainly Ross's descriptions of the landscape fit the Sauk route as well as the Skagit.

Ross covered an immense area by both land and water, but he was no geographer. His pungent descriptions lack geographical clarity, and his eye for terrain generally failed him in the mountains. Still, he was the first Euro-American to penetrate into the Methow River area and likely also the first to explore the Bridge Creek-Stehekin River region.[56]

Because the fur-trading companies found it impractical to cross the northern Cascades to the Puget Sound area (see chapter 5) and because these mountains did not have many beaver, the trappers and traders of the Hudson's Bay and North West companies made only occasional further explorations into the mountains (around the Wenatchee and Yakima rivers and Naches Pass).

William Fraser Tolmie

The successful trek of Dr. William Fraser Tolmie to the slopes of Mt. Rainier in August 1833 was remarkable. Tolmie had taken a position with the Hudson's Bay Company following his undergraduate study in medicine at the University of Glasgow under the patronage of Sir William J. Hooker. At the age of twenty, Tolmie was a wilderness novice, but he nevertheless approached the lower Columbia River with a strong spirit of inquiry. At Fort Vancouver, the enthusiastic youth met veteran trader Archibald McDonald, a fellow Scot who befriended him, oversaw his progress, and led him north to Nisqually (where a new fort was being established) by canoe and horseback. Not long after Tolmie's arrival at Nisqually House, where he took up residence as post surgeon, an employee named Pierre Charles severely cut his foot while swinging his axe at a log. In his first crisis, Tolmie's skillful attendance likely saved the man's life; but his patient's condition remained critical for some weeks, and the physician had to forgo a scheduled venture by boat to Russian Alaska. Still, it gave him time to contemplate an ascent of the greatest mountain he had ever seen—Mt. Rainier.[57]

Contemplation led to a decision: a visit to the great snow and ice mountain. Planning a botanizing expedition to the lofty mountain, Tolmie engaged Puyallup Indians to guide him, although he noted that they were fearful of the mountain's evil spirits. His excuse for taking time away from company duties was a search for herbs to make a medicine that would treat a fever rampant among coastal Indians. The inducement to the Indians was the chance to hunt elk, a staple in their diet. On August 27, Tolmie obtained the permission of Chief Trader Francis Heron to make a ten-day trek. When he left Nisqually House two days later, five Indians went with him. A Nisqually, Lachalet, agreed to supply horses and to take charge. Tolmie wrote in his journal on August 29: "I have engaged Sachalet [Lachalet] for a blanket and his nephew Sashima [Lashima] for ammunition to accompany me and Nuckalkut a Poyaklit . . . with two horses to be guide on the mountains." Quilniash, a relative of Nuckalkut who was described by the adventurer as "a very strong fellow," also accompanied the group.[58]

Starting late on the first day, the party covered some eight miles, camping where Nuckalkut's father lived. On the second day they came upon three Klickitat Indian families who served them a meal of elk. The route was tangled with thickets as they approached the Puyallup River near present-day Orting, and the preferred camp spot was on a gravel bar in the river. Tolmie noted that the had banks were "high and covered with lofty cedars and pines—the water is of a dirty white colour." Prospects seemed gloomy to Tolmie on the morning of September 1, when he recorded that the river was too high to ford and only a day's food remained. The rain would not end.

That evening, Tolmie proposed "to ascend one of the snowy peaks above," but the direction of the route required the group to continue upstream to an "amphitheatre of Mountains"—a description that fits the forks of the Mowich River.

> Our track lay at first through a dense wood of pine but we afterwards emerged into an exuberantly verdant gully closed on each side by lofty precipices. Followed gully to near the summit & found excellent berries in abundance. It contained very few alpine plants—afterwards came to a grassy mound where the sight of several decayed trees induced us to encamp.

For an ascent, Tolmie chose a peak that was near and seemed to hold the most snow. With Lachalet and Nuckalkut, he started

> for the summit which was ankle deep with snow for ¼ mile downwards. The summit terminated in abrupt precipice directed northwards and bearing north east from Mt. Rainier, the adjoining peak. The mists were at times very dense. . . . On the south side of Poyallip is a range of snow dappled mountains.

There, apparently at or near the summit of Hessong Rock, the mist shrouded the view, but Tolmie recorded that Mt. Rainier was a short distance east.[59]

Frustrated by the mists, Tolmie wanted to get his bearings the next morning when the atmosphere would be clear. With Quilniash, he made another ascent. The snow was crisp and the air temperature thirty-three degrees. That evening he wrote that Mt. Rainier bore "SS.E & was separated from it [the peak on which he stood] only by a narrow glen whose sides however were formed by inaccessible precipices."[60] In his journal, Tolmie described

> . . . the eternal snow of Rainier. . . . Its eastern side is steep—on its northern aspect a few small glaciers were seen on the conical portion, below that the mountain is composed of bare rock, apparently volcanic which about 50 yards in breadth reaches from the snow to the valley beneath & is bounded on each side by bold bluff crags scantily covered with stunted pines. Its surface is generally smooth but here & there raised into small points or knobs or arrowed with short & narrow longitudinal lines in which snow lay. . . . Two large pyramids of rocks arose from the gentle acclivity at S.W. extremity of mountain & around each the drifting snow had accumulated in large quantity forming a basin apparently of great depth. Here I also perceived, peeping from their snowy covering, two lines of dyke similar to that already mentioned.

Tolmie grossly underestimated the physical magnitude and height of Mt. Rainier, which has an elevation of 14,410 feet.

Back in Nisqually, Tolmie found himself in charge of the trading post when McDonald was transferred to Fort Vancouver. He mastered the fur trade and developed a deep humanitarian and scientific interest in the Indians, but he never undertook another exploration of Rainier. In 1855, Tolmie was appointed chief factor; but four years later HBC moved its headquarters from Fort Vancouver to Fort Victoria and Tolmie went there to take over its subsidiary farms. Not until 1882 did Tolmie's expedition become generally known, but today he is credited with being the first Euro-American to recognize glaciers in North America (excluding Alaska).

David Douglas

The young English botanist David Douglas is credited with being the first to use the name *Cascade Range* for the grand north-south chain of mountains that dominated western Oregon Territory. Sir William J. Hooker of the Horticultural Society of London recommended Douglas for an appointment with the HBC as a botanical collector. In June 1823, he left London for the eastern United States to collect fruit trees. The mission proved successful, and Douglas was later appointed to explore the present-day states of Washington and Oregon. When he arrived at the company's headquarters at Fort Vancouver in 1825, he was amazed at the immensity of the trees, especially the tall tree that would later be named for him. Douglas was also impressed with the majesty and height of the nearby mountains. Of Mt. Hood and Mt. St. Helens he wrote: "Their height must be very great (at least 10,000 to 12,000 ft.), two-thirds are I am informed continually enwrapped in perpetual snow."[61] The name *Cascade Range* appears for the first time in Douglas's journal for October 13, 1826.[62] The industrious Douglas, whom the Indians called the "Grass Man," introduced some three hundred new names to the botany vocabulary in 1826 and 1827.

On an 1827 visit to the Canadian Rockies, Douglas illustrated the tendency of explorers of this era to make errors in their judgments of height and distance, and the exaggerated heights that Douglas published led to much confusion for later explorers. On May 1, the celebrated botanist set out to make his first alpine climb to ascend what appeared to be the highest summit to the north of Athabasca Pass. Proclaiming that at 17,000 feet it was the highest peak yet known in North America, he named it Mt. Brown in honor of one of his patrons, botanist Robert Brown. The peak to the south he named Mt. Hooker after his other patron. In crossing Athabasca Pass—which he estimated to be 12,000 feet high (it is actually 5,736 feet high)—he passed the Committee's Punchbowl, a small lake with outlets to both the Columbia and Athabasca rivers, before continuing east to the HBC post of Rocky Mountain House.[63]

Charles Wilkes and the Johnson Expedition

Lt. Charles Wilkes, a highly skilled navigator and astronomer, was only the second American naval officer sent by President Van Buren to study the Oregon Country, and he was the first one to enter the waters of Puget Sound.[64] Taking command of the U.S. Exploring Expedition in August 1838, Wilkes sailed from Virginia with severaldistinguished naval and civilian scientists to encircle the globe, a venture he did not complete until 1842. Wilkes was sent west to bolster American claims of the disputed Oregon Country during the nation's joint occupancy with the British. In search of new lands for commercial exploitation, the expedition not only helped solidify American interests, but it also gave policy-makers an impression of life in Oregon.Wilkes wrote glowingly of Puget Sound harbors and urged that they never be surrendered in boundary negotiations.

Sailing near the (Tacoma) Narrows in 1841 and uncertain just what reception his naval vessels would get from the HBC garrison at Fort Nisqually, Wilkes became the first American to describe Mt. Rainier: "We have a splendid view of Mt. Ranier, which is conical and covered about 2/3rd. of its height with snow." The striking mountain rose almost imperceptibly from the Nisqually plain, he wrote, "with a gradual slope, until the snow-line is reached, when the ascent becomes more precipitous."[65] Wilkes, curious by nature, wanted to get a close view of the craters of such volcanos as Mt. Rainier—"The ascent of these mountains has never been effected, but it was my intention to attempt it."— but time did not permit such an attempt. Nevertheless, while visiting Fort Nisqually that summer, Wilkes triangulated Mt. Rainier's elevation from a baseline "on the prairies" (he put the mountain at 12,330 feet). He also observed other Cascade volcanos, noting that Mt. St. Helens was visible from eighty miles at sea, and expressed the hope that he would climb Mt. Hood. On May 6, he saw Mt. Baker with its "conical peak illuminated by the setting sun."[66]

While exploring by land, Wilkes sighted another volcano, later named Mt. Adams: "In my ride I discovered another snowy Peak visible from this plain [the Nisqually area] very much resembling that of Mt. Rainier. It appears to the Eastwd. of the Range. Not being represented on my chart or Map I called it Mt. Hudson after the Comdr of the Peacock." The 1841 expedition filled in many blanks on maps and charts, and Wilkes's water survey became important in the later San Juan Islands boundary dispute.

Wilkes was a navigator, not a land explorer, so he sent Lt. Robert E. Johnson of the *Porpoise* to explore across a pass to the interior. Johnson's mounted inland expedition surveyed the resources of the Pacific Northwest five years before the United States took sole possession of the territory south of the forty-ninth parallel. The party was allocated eighty days to cross the range and return to Nisqually.[67] Johnson had orders to keep a journal, plot daily maps, take observations of the sun each noon and the north star at night, record temperature readings, and take bearings of prominent features. He was to note the size of timber and to designate every unusual object. Heights were to be determined by barometer and distances by taking a horse's pace and timing its movement. A compass was to be used in open country, but in the woods "all your party should be required to keep their own reckoning . . . as at sea." Johnson was instructed to avoid disputes with Indians, to see to the safety and comfort of the party, and to allow the two accompanying scientists every facility for research.[68] The scientists on the trip were Charles Pickering, a thirty-six-year-old naturalist and physician from Pennsylvania, and William Dunlop Brackenridge, a thirty-one-year-old Scottish horticulturist who had been the head gardener at Edinburgh Botanical Gardens. Pierre Charles, the French Canadian trader, guided Johnson and was considered the "main reliance" of the group.[69] Other members of Johnson's party were Pierre Bercier, interpreter; Thomas W. Waldron, captain's clerk; Henry Waltham, cook; and Sgt. Simon Stearns of the marines. They were guided by two Muckleshoot Indians, Lasimeer (or Lashemere) and Pattiewon.

Johnson would have preferred to avoid the mountain travel and camping out, but both Brackenridge and Pickering were excellent walkers and enthusiastic about the outdoors. Brackenridge, in addition to collecting plants, ridiculed the lieutenant and actually led the expedition. His journal for May 17 reports: "Getting provisions & other necessaries ready kept us all busy, & at 4 in the afternoon the party was ordered to leave the Ship, which we all did, leaving a good many of our things on board. Our tents were pitched for the night outside the Fort, & our luggage piled up in a heap . . ."[70]

The expedition left Fort Nisqually on May 19, 1841, following a path around the north flank of Mt. Rainier.[71] Because the trail was seldom used, it was necessary to cut through underbrush, and horses often got their packs wedged between trees and their hoofs entangled in roots. On May 21, the party crossed the Puyallup River (Brackenridge thought this was the Smalocho or White river), and in two days reached the White River. Brackenridge commented:

> Towards eavening we came upon the Smalocho river and encamped at the junction of the Upthascap [Carbon River] with the former. Though deserted of inmates, I here saw a very snug and perfectly water tight house built from plank split out of the Thuja, or Arbor Vitae [cedar], a tree which attains a great size on these mountains. The planks were as smooth as if cut out by a saw & many of them three feet wide. At this place we met several natives awaiting the arrival of the Salmon as their season was now approaching. The snow melting on the mountains we were ascending had swollen the Rivers to an unusual size which made it necessary for us when we had to cross them, to cut down Trees on their banks so as to form a bridge to carry our packs across, making the Horses swim over.

On May 23, Brackenridge described how the horse "carrying our provision Case" fell from a bank into the river, "the lashings giving way the whole pack went down the stream." They could see Mt. Rainier that day and judged to be thirty miles distant. Pickering commented on their route:

> The path we followed had been but once previously traversed by civilized man. It leads over the crest of the Snowy Range, which at a point about twenty miles north of Mount Rainier, seems practicable for horses during four or five months of the year; and indeed the chief obstacle arises from young spruces, that prevent the snow from settling around them in a solid mass.[72]

On May 25, the party crossed the swollen White River. Brackenridge wrote:

> During the early part of this day we had to cross a deep and rapid River—we had for the two past days made a great ascent on the range & were still continuing to do so, and the water from the Snow Mts. rushing down confined valleys acted powerful in sweeping logs and every thing else that came in its way before it, forming bridges, over which we sometimes crossed, & swam our horses.

After a morning of rapid progress, Johnson and the sergeant ascended La Tête—a steep, burnt-over landmark—to obtain bearings.[73] The entire party continued to "Little Prairie" (a half-mile below the confluence of the White and Greenwater rivers), where they found Indians who knew the route.

On May 26, Johnson drew orders for the foot party to cross the mountains. Waldron was entrusted with Pickering, Brackenridge, and Charles as well as ten to twelve Indians who they had hired. On the long ascent, wrote Brackenridge, ". . . the Doctor and Myself had reached the margin of the Snow" long before the remainder of the party. Johnson remained behind with the horses. On the evening of May 26, Brackenridge recorded:

> We now pitched our Tent and there being no water near we melted snow to procure Water for Tea. As the Cooking of the Supper was going on, some one set fire to the moss covered trees, and in one minute all around was one glaring mass of flame. Now was a confusion and bustle—to get all our luggage to windward, & in the midst of the conflagration Dr. P. came near loosing the tails of his Coat by a brand of fire that had accidentally fallen into his pocket.

Brackenridge and Charles crossed the pass on May 27, the distance over snow being some eight miles.[74] The Indians, with their ninety-pound loads, broke through the crust, but fortunately the snow was only ankle deep. That night the advance party camped near the head of the Naches River. The next morning, the Indians brought the horses across while the snow was firm; the scientists walked. Brackenridge described what happened on May 29:

> Towards mid-day several of the Indians from Mr. J's party arrived at the camp. And in the afternoon Mr. J himself came on, having left four of the Horses behind, and came near loosing himself by getting out of the path when the Indians had left him. During the day one of the Indians sent down the river to procure horses, had returned without succeeding. The services of the indians being no more required, the[y] were all discharged with the exception of a smart young fellow named Lashemere, who expressed a desire to accompany us. These indians who had received blankets in advance at the Fort when we started willingly gave them up to us and took an order for the whole amount due them, to be cashed at the same source. All the specimens that were dry, of my collecting, were neatly stitched up in a canvass cover by Mr. J. to be taken back to the Ship. . . .

As Johnson was crossing the stream to camp, he fell and was soaked, causing his chronometer to stop and losing the means for accurate mapmaking. While near Naches Pass on May 29, expedition members discovered the high, rocky peak of Mt. Stuart to the northeast. A day later, Brackenridge noted that the vegetation included *Pentstemon*, lady's slipper, and scarlet gilia. They also found *Polemonium* and antelope brush. On May 31, they met Chief Tobias of the Yakama tribe and smoked a pipe with him, then bargained for dried salmon and horses to replace those left behind. Brackenridge recorded: "These were paid for with a Scotch plaid, some tobacco, a cannister of powder and some balls, and some of their poorer horses." The travelers reached the Yakima River near present-day Ellensburg on June 2. A day later Brackenridge wrote:

> The breadth of the Eyakema may be about 100 yards, and along on both sides of it are large tracks of flat land of apparently good quality though rather of a sandy nature having evidently been overflowed by the river. In the early part of the fore-

noon a sandy prairie with a number of small shrubs on it was passed over. And immediately a group of Mts. set in by degrees upon us. We found these similar to those we had left yesterday.

The crossing to the Columbia was made by Colockum Pass in the Wenatchee Mountains on June 4. "The Ice this morning on water beside our tent was the thickness of a Dollar, & by some accident the Baromiter tube got broke . . ." Brackenridge wrote. "Our road for the first 5 miles was over swampy ground on the brow of a Mt." At the Wenatchee River, which they rafted, Brackenridge commented that the "Piscouas River" rises in "the range of snowy Mts. which lay in a N. West direction from us." On June 6, the Johnson party crossed the Columbia above the Entiat River en route to Fort Okanogan. Brackenridge commented that Johnson had been unfriendly to the Indians and that he was surprised they had helped him cross. The expedition, without a military escort, was vulnerable during such times.

For over two months, the expedition followed a triangular route, proceeding northeast to Fort Okanogan and Fort Colvile, south to Walla Walla, and finally back to Nisqually. Johnson and its party completed the journey on July 15. It was the first organized expedition to cross the Cascade Range.

John C. Frémont

The era of the Topographical Engineers in the Far West began with Lt. John C. Frémont's first expedition to the Rocky Mountains in 1842. The Topographical Engineers were sophisticated, West Point-trained men who worked closely with the foremost scholars of the time. They were concerned not only with the exploration of the West but also with the scientific mapping of its landscape. They revealed the West through maps, photography, and narratives.[75] At the same time, they were influenced by a romanticism that drove them to gather as much data as possible, from the trivial to the exotic, to add to their understanding of what they believed was a great, organic system. They delved into the mystery and grandeur of the cosmos and saw a clear kinship between science and art. Frémont, for example, "saw the West with the eye of an artist, and his narrative reveals the emotional quality of his experience in first penetrating the mountainous wilderness."[76]

With such broad objectives, the Topographical Engineers were linked to the practical development of the nation. Unlike the mountain men who preceded them in the wilderness, they represented the national government's interest fin the West.[77] The engineers promoted wagon roads, located passes, inventoried resources, and helped overcome Indian resistance during two decades of brilliant achievement before the outbreak of the Civil War. In 1863, the Topographical Engineers were merged with the U.S. Army Corps of Engineers.

Even though John Charles Frémont led the most famous official reconnaissance of the American West since Lewis and Clark, he could not always claim primacy of discovery, for others had been in most places before him. His contribution was in the nature of his exploration, his acute observations, his reports, and in his great influence on the public.[78] Frémont's most renowned expedition was his 1843–1844 reconnaissance of the West, during which he surveyed the Oregon Trail. Arriving at Fort Walla Walla on October 25, 1843, he could see the gray shadow of Mt. Hood some 180 miles distant. He followed the Columbia River to present-day The Dalles, where he left his men to rest, and continued alone to Fort Vancouver.[79]

Both Wilkes and Frémont left comprehensive cartographic achievements, yet both confused Mt. Adams with Mt. St. Helens. On October 29, Frémont saw Mt. Adams but referred to it as St. Helens; and he mistook Mt. Adams for Mt. Rainier when returning to The Dalles to rejoin his expedition.[80] Reporting on an eruption on November 23, 1842, Frémont wrote: "St. Helens had scattered its ashes, like a light fall of snow, over the Dalles of the Columbia." Although missionaries and others made the eruption widespread news, Frémont's stature brought special attention to the Cascade Range; and his expedition succeeded in calling the nation's attention to the Oregon Country.[81]

Paul Kane

Irish artist Paul Kane devoted his talents to drawing and painting North American Indians and western landscapes. In 1846, in Toronto, he impressed HBC Governor Sir George Simpson so much that he was given permission to travel freely as a guest in company transport and was commissioned to paint twelve pictures in the Far West.[82] After traveling to the Great Lakes, Lake Winnipeg, and Jasper in the Canadian Rockies, Kane reached the Columbia River and spent the winter of 1846–1847 sketching in the Oregon Country. He made splendid renditions of the people and the scenery. One masterful sketch, which Kane did from near the mouth of the Lewis River, shows Mt. St. Helens emitting a smoking ash pillar on March 26, 1847.

During the time that Kane traveled with the fur brigades, the myths and stories of the Indians fascinated him. He hoped to hire Indian guides for an ascent of Mt. St. Helens, knowing it had not yet been climbed; but he could not get a single companion. On his return, Kane left Fort Vancouver for Victoria in a small wooden canoe with two Indian guides. He continued to work on paintings commissioned by Simpson through 1849 and drew many sketches of Indians, including *Cree Pipestem Bearer* and *Indian Horse Race* and scenic and travel paintings such as *Brigade of Boats, A Prairie on Fire, Boat Encampment,* and *Mt. St. Helen's.* Much of Kane's work is now in the Royal Ontario Museum in Toronto. While Kane was an explorer of secondary importance, his depictions of the Pacific Northwest's geography provide a portrayal of the landscape at a time when the Cascade Range was largely still a mystery.

Theodore Winthrop

In 1853, a spirited, twenty-four-year-old adventurer named Theodore Winthrop shucked his prominent background to follow primitive, dangerous trails in the Cascade Range. Even though Winthrop had graduated from Yale and was a direct descendant of Governor John Winthrop of the Massachusetts Bay Colony, frontiersmen who worked for the HBC—such as William Tolmie, Edward Huggins, and Peter Skene Ogden—gave him friendship and confidence. Traveling from Fort Nisqually to The Dalles with a Yakama guide, Winthrop crossed Naches Pass on horseback on a route that immigrants had recently taken. On August 27, 1853, he obtained his "first grand view of Rainier, the summit of which, seen at this angle, is saddle-like, and perhaps smoking, with a huge cavity below." Enchanted by the highland divide, Winthrop added: "The splendid prairies on top of the pass are like a Swiss Alp after late snows."[83] Once across the pass, he fell in with the railroad-survey party of Capt. George McClellan, and he recorded this scene at the Columbia River:

> At the magnificent Cascades of the Columbia, the second-best water bit on our continent, there is more exciting salmon-fishing in the splendid turmoil of the rapids. Over the shoots, between boulders and rifts of rock, the Indians rig a scaffolding, and sweep down stream with a scoop-net. Salmon, working their way up in high exhilaration, are taken twenty an hour, by every scooper.[84]

Although Winthrop did not pioneer new routes, he turned his astute perceptions of the Cascade Range into a highly popular book, *The Canoe and the Saddle* (1862). Winthrop had a national viewpoint, and he apparently believed it was a shame that few of his fellow Americans had seen the beauties of the Cascade Range:

> The Cascades are known to geography,—their summits to the lists of volcanoes. Several gentlemen in the United States Army, bored in petty posts, or squinting along Indian trails for Pacific railroads, have seen these monuments. A few myriads of Oregonians have not been able to avoid seeing them, have perhaps felt their ennobling influence, and have written, boasting that St. Helens or Hood is as high as Blanc. Enterprising fellows have climbed both. But the millions of Yankees—from codfish to alligators, chewers of spruce-gum or chewers of pig-tail, cooks of chowder or cooks of gumbo—know little of these treasures of theirs.[85]

Many decades later, John Williams wrote that Winthrop "was probably better fitted to study and portray the West than any other Eastern man who attempted to describe it."[86]

Father Pierre-Jean De Smet

In 1821, Jesuit missionary Pierre-Jean De Smet came from his native Belgium to the United States and eventually Oregon Territory, where he preached Christianity and traveled the Columbia River Basin. Through his missionary work, he spread knowledge about the West, immigration opportunities, and the fur trade. His maps were widely used, and William Goetzmann has called him "undoubtedly the best geographer" among the western missionaries.[87] On a typical trip in 1856, De Smet procured an Indian canoe to travel down the Columbia. He found himself in a thunderstorm at "La Chute" in "the great gap of the Cascade Mountains, through which the mighty Columbia winds its way" and recorded a striking description of the Cascades:

> The sublime and the romantic appear to have made a grand effort for a magnificent display in this spot. On both sides of the stream perpendicular walls of rock rise in majestic boldness—small rills and rivulets, innumerable crystalline streams pursue their way; murmuring down on the steep declivities, they rush and leap from cascade to cascade, after a thousand gambols, adding, at last, their foaming tribute to the turbulent and powerful stream. The imposing mass of waters has here forced its way between a chain of volcanic, towering mountains, advancing headlong with an irresistible impetuosity, over rocky reefs, and prostrate ruins, for a distance of about four miles; forming the dangerous, and indeed the last remarkable obstruction—the great cascades of the Columbia.[88]

Father De Smet avoided mountain routes, but he was deeply inspired by the sight of high, glacier-clad peaks. When he ascended the Columbia in 1858, for example, he observed that "the white summits of Mounts St. Helens, Rainier, Jefferson, and Hood, covered with perpetual snow and rising to a great height, offer sublime spectacles which one never wearies of watching."[89] His fascination with the majestic alpine features of the northern Cascade Range was shared by many of the early explorers in these mountains. Those men not only admired the views, but they also added much to the Euro-American knowledge of the range. Some—such as Lewis and Clark, Wilkes, and Frémont—explored to strengthen a national claim. Others sought trade routes, mapped the geography, or in other ways furthered the fortunes of the Hudson's Bay Company—an enterprise that would dominate the greater Pacific Northwest for several decades to come.

Mt. Baker, from below Smess [Sumas] Fraser's R., *sketch probably by Alexander C.*
Anderson, June 1848 (BC Archives, PDP 01236)

2

"ABSOLUTE LORDES AND PROPRIETORS":
THE HUDSON'S BAY COMPANY
AND THE FUR TRADE

Terrible Mountains all over hereabouts.
> —From a map probably drawn by HBC Chief Trader Samuel Black, c. 1833

In 1670, Charles II of Great Britain created Rupert's Land for his favorite cousin, Prince Rupert, who wanted to enter the fur business. Rupert's Land, a huge area east of the Rocky Mountains in what is now central Canada, was a proprietary colony of the HBC. The charter for the colony allowed the company to hold a large part of North America as "absolute lordes and proprietors."[1] The HBC was given all the powers of government according to English law; the right to employ armed force, erect forts, and appoint commanders; and sole trading rights across North America. It was granted

> the sole Trade and Commerce of all those Seas, Streights, Bays, Rivers, Lakes, Creeks, and Sounds, in whatsoever Latitude they shall be, that lie within the entrance of the Streights commonly called Hudson's Streights, together with all the Lands, Countries and Territories, upon the Coasts and Confines of the Seas, Streights, Bays, Lakes, Rivers, Creeks, and Sounds, aforesaid, which are not now actually possessed by any of our Subjects, or by the Subjects of any other Christian Prince or State.[2]

Through this charter, a few noblemen and merchants became the proprietors of some three million square miles of unexplored territory, with further privileges to be added should the territory be found to embrace a land and sea passage to the Far East.[3] Rupert's Land was, in fact, less a colony than a commercial zone.

The HBC had an imperial style. Subjects of the king other than those authorized by the company were forbidden to visit, trade, or travel in its territory. The inhabitants of Rupert's Land were subject to company regulations as well as British criminal and civil law. Its charter required the company to keep its laws as similar as possible to those of England, but informal disciplinary rules that varied from post to post were capriciously applied. In both the HBC and, later, the North West Company, an essentially feudal governing policy persisted. As in England, social classes were rigidly fixed, and society was viewed as a network of interwoven loyalties. Trading and hunting parties were divided by class into Britons, French Canadians, and hired Indians.[4]

As might be expected, there was competition for the vast colony. France disputed the HBC's possession of Rupert's Land. Free traders from Great Britain and what would become Canada defied the company's exclusive privilege there, especially after 1763, when France surrendered Canada to Great Britain by the Treaty of Paris. In 1787, one group of free traders formed the North West Company of Montreal, which was to become a relentless force in the quest for furs. The new company forced the HBC to expand westward for fear of losing its trade with the western Indians that it had gained after the expulsion of France. As a result, both companies expanded their operations and established posts farther from their headquarters, into the country west of the Rocky Mountains in present-day British Columbia.[5]

The North West Company was a daring and energetic vanguard that sent the vigorous and imaginative Alexander Mackenzie across the Rocky Mountains and overland to the Pacific in 1793. Mackenzie "envisioned the Columbia, which he mistook for the Peace-Frazer River system that he had discovered in 1793, as the future western appendage of the main route between the Atlantic and Pacific."[6] In Mackenzie's concept, the "Tacoutche Tesse" (Fraser) was part of the Columbia drainage. He discovered a fork of the Fraser when he found himself "on the bank of a navigable river, on the West side of the first great range of mountains." As he descended the Fraser, he wrote: "The more I heard of the river, the more I was convinced it could not empty itself into the ocean to the North of what is called the River of the West."[7] MacKenzie followed the Fraser to near Alexandria, south of Prince George, before striking westward. He reached the Pacific Ocean at Bella Coola.

The extension of the North West Company's trading area to the Pacific Coast was spearheaded by a tireless trader-geographer, David Thompson, who by 1807 had crossed the Rockies and reached the headwaters of the Columbia River. After continuing his exploration overland and down the Columbia to Astoria in 1811, Thompson claimed the entire area from the Rockies to the Pacific Ocean in the name of Great Britain. Meanwhile, Simon Fraser continued Mackenzie's explorations and proved in 1808 that the Fraser River was separate from the larger Columbia. Not long after Thompson's journey down the Columbia, during which he saw some of the Cascade Range peaks, the first reference to Lake Chelan was recorded by a rival fur trader. On August 27, 1811, David Stuart of John Jacob Astor's Pacific Fur Company, traveling in a party that included Alexander Ross, passed a stream the Indians called "Tsill-ane" (Chelan), which they reported came from a nearby lake.[8]

When the North West Company took over Astor's enterprise in 1813 and established themselves on the Pacific Coast, its bitter rivalry with the HBC increased in venom.[9] Competition led both companies to trap in all seasons

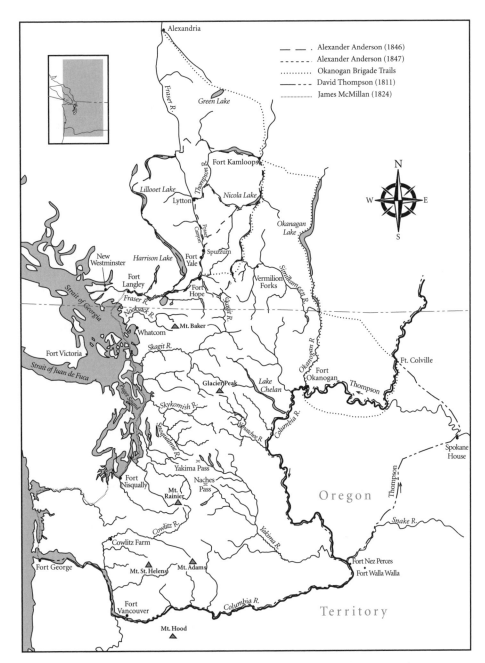

Hudson's Bay Company and Fur-Trade Sites in the Northern Cascades

and raise prices paid to the Indians until there was no longer a profit. The merger of the two companies in 1821, however, led to a policy of energetic expansion. In 1825, Fort Vancouver became the headquarters of the HBC's enterprising Columbia Department.

To ensure against a further outbreak of competition, the British government in 1821 conferred upon the reorganized company exclusive trading rights for twenty-one years in the region lying beyond Rupert's Land, including what was to become Oregon Territory. The HBC found itself with trading posts located in a country of unsuspected wealth, far west of the lands in its original charter. By 1825, the company was in control of a flourishing fur trade that extended from the Rocky Mountains to Fort George (Astoria). Because Indians supplied most of the furs for the trade, however, it was impossible to define the limits of the area exploited by the company.[10] Company partners had taught Indians how to use traps and depended on them to bring in furs. In one season, for example, Ross collected fifteen hundred beaver pelts, most of them bought from Indians.

Until 1846, much of the Columbia River drainage was included under an 1818 convention that allowed people from both the United States and Britain to occupy the region without prejudicing claims, though both nations claimed the area north of the river to the forty-ninth parallel. The Oregon Country was important to the British government not only because of its colonization possibilities, but also because of the rapid decline in the beaver population elsewhere. Because beavers are not highly reproductive and do not migrate, trappers had to move to new sites once an area was trapped out.[11] Furthermore, the British considered the 1,210-mile-long Columbia River a vital route to the sea because the Fraser was too swift and dangerous for navigation.

Sir George Simpson, HBC governor, was eager to win Oregon and turned his attention to rehabilitating the region's fur trade and obstructing the American advance. Beginning in 1822, he directed the economic life of the Pacific Northwest and set out to organize an efficient monopoly, consolidating the trading posts, personnel, and transportation systems of the merged companies. His trip to the Pacific Coast in 1824, when he was thirty-two years of age, was intended to bring profitability and unity to the Columbia Department. During this period, the HBC took to stripping the Snake River country and many other areas of furs, both for its own profit and to discourage American penetration. Fearing competition from American trappers, who undercut the company's trade with Indians on the Columbia, Simpson left Peter Skene Ogden with orders to deplete the beaver as far south and east as possible—a "scorched earth" policy to make the rival American trade unprofitable.

The HBC controlled the fur trade for twenty-five years after the merger before finally yielded to pressure from the Americans. In a sense, that pressure was a result of the American practice of free competition in the fur trade, as opposed to the HBC's monopoly. Under the Americans' rendezvous system, trappers depended less on the Indians to supply furs than the HBC did. Instead of establishing trading posts, independent trappers met once a year to receive pay for the season's work and to purchase new supplies. The Americans' use of the rendezvous system, which opened up vast areas for rapid exploration in a relatively short time, brought the Oregon contest to a head at an earlier date than might otherwise have been the case.[12] The Americans and British brought different visions to the Oregon Country. The Americans saw the fur trade as a transitory stage of progressive settlement, while the British were interested in exploiting the area's resources. The Americans found the HBC a barrier to settlement and believed that some of the Indian hostility was a result of encouragement and aid from supposedly neutral HBC officers.

The Hudson's Bay Company recognized the difficulties of operating south of the forty-ninth parallel, where the costs of trading was exorbitant and the American presence was increasing. The Cascade Range was a significant impediment to fur-trading routes. Passes were high, grass feed limited, and supply lines long from Fort Vancouver and Fort Langley to the Okanogan region. In 1824, Governor Simpson admitted that "our Council know little about that Country."[13] The HBC's also calculated that the territory north of the forty-ninth parallel would remain the basis for a profitable fur trade for many years to come. Apparently expecting an eventual American triumph in the Oregon Country, the company wisely developed the coastal trade by establishing Fort Langley and consolidating on Vancouver Island.

The HBC's interest in settlement, wagon roads, and economic development came too late. By the time the company realized the value of settled diversification and founded the Puget Sound Agricultural Company at Fort Nisqually in 1833, the opportunity was gone. After the Peter Skene Ogden era, British exploration in the Pacific Northwest diminished. John Work, Ogden's successor, disliked the region, calling it "wretched," and resented having to live there. In 1845, the HBC moved to Fort Victoria and effectively withdrew from the lower Columbia. In 1849, a new depot at Victoria became the company headquarters, and James Douglas became the chief factor. The Treaty of 1846, which established forty-nine degrees north latitude as the boundary between American territory and British North America, marked the end of the era.

Settlements, Trade Routes, and Explorations

The activities of the HBC in the Pacific Northwest were motivated by profits from the fur trade. The company established posts in its functional geography and undertook explorations near the northern Cascades only to the extent necessary to serve that commercial interest. Company trading posts were much alike. They were usually built in a square of about one hundred yards; the space was picketed in with logs placed into the ground. Within the bastion were five to six guns (six- or twelve-pounders) mounted as on a ship. Houses were located inside the pickets. Local Indians brought furs to the posts—which the company sold at a great profit—and also bought goods there.[14]

In 1811, David Stuart of the Pacific Fur Company founded Fort Okanogan on a commanding terrace above the confluence of the Columbia and Okanogan rivers—the first American settlement in present-day Washington state. Alexander Ross was the first factor at that lonely outpost, and he remained there during the height of the Far West fur trade. Ross was one of the few men who pushed by boat, on horseback, and on foot up the Columbia and Snake rivers into the Rockies. Fort Okanogan, the pioneer post of the Astorians, was a strategically located base from which explorers and traders could venture. It became an important meeting place for the fur brigades and, after passing into the hands of the British in 1813, was a center of their interests on the middle Columbia. Indians of Oregon Territory and British Columbia also often gathered here for an annual potlatch. HBC maintained the post (which later became a fort) until 1859, when it was sold to the Americans.[15] At such gathering places, one might have heard Chinook Jargon, a trade language developed to facilitate communication between tribes and among the French Canadians, English, Americans, and Indians. This *lingua franca* was based on the Chinook, French, and English languages.[16]

When Sir George Simpson ventured down the Columbia in 1824, he made interesting notes about Cascade Range streams and routes. His journal for November 2 reports: "Four leagues lower down [from Fort Okanogan] a small River [the Methow] falls in from the West." Five leagues farther was a larger stream he called the Piscahouse River (the Wenatchee), "deriving its name from a Tribe who inhabit the banks in the interior, and from the sources of these Rivers there is a communication formed by small lakes narrows and Portages to Puget's Sound the distance not exceeding Six or Eight Days March with small canoes."[17]

Fort Langley, established in the summer of 1827, was the first permanent post on the lower mainland of present-day British Columbia. The party sent to establish Fort Langley, led by James McMillan—an experienced wilderness man—left Fort Vancouver in three light *bateaux* and reached Puget Sound via Grays Harbor. On July 4, they saw Mt. Baker "on a line with the entrance to Possession Bay." From Boundary Bay, they ascended the Nicomekl River and portaged to the Fraser. Chief Factor McMillan, with only twenty-three men, became concerned when what he guessed were five thousand Indians assembled in the area for fishing. On August 8, according to a journal kept by the party, the fort had to be abandoned because the Indians had set a forest fire.[18]

McMillan was succeeded at Fort Langley in 1828 by the resourceful Archibald McDonald, who had been head of the Kamloops post and who would guide the infant fort for four and a half years. In 1839, the original fort was abandoned and Fort Langley was established several miles upriver, where the land was better for agriculture. The colony of British Columbia was proclaimed there in 1858, but the capital was soon moved to New Westminster. Fort Langley then went into a slow decline, the HBC closing its store there in 1896. The fort has been restored and is now a national historic park.

The important post of Fort Vancouver was established on the Columbia River in 1824. Chief Factor John McLoughlin selected the site—Belle Vue Point, where Vancouver's Lt. Broughton had sighted Mt. Hood in 1792. The fort solidified British control of the Oregon Country until 1846, and it remained a major establishment until 1860. Fort Nisqually—the first European settlement in the Puget Sound region—was established close to the Nisqually River tide flats in 1833 as an intermediate station between Fort Vancouver and Fort Langley. In 1838, in an effort to diversify and become self-sustaining, the HBC formed the Puget Sound Agricultural Company at Fort Nisqually, and it became more an agricultural enterprise than a fur-trading post.[19] Dr. William Tolmie came to Fort Nisqually in 1833 and eventually became chief factor there, remaining in charge until 1859. His successor, Edward Huggins, had come to Victoria in 1850 and had then been sent to Fort Nisqually to work under Tolmie's direction.

The "Journal of Occurrences at Nisqually House" offers details of the everyday life and trade of the fort. It mentions, for example, that Indians arrived with furs in August 1833, and "upwards of sixty skins" were traded November 18, "chiefly from the Scadchet & Sannahomish."[20] Indian horses—particularly those belonging to the Cayuse, Nez Perce, and Yakama peoples—became an essential resource for fur traders who worked in the interior. Traders relied on waterways for moving fur bales between posts, yet horses could reach inland depots and provided transport away from difficult rivers. Both methods of transportation had drawbacks: boats had to risk rapids and horses required feeding and posting. In 1855, the company decided that furs from the interior posts should be taken to Fort Nisqually rather than to Fort Vancouver.

Angus McDonald of Fort Colvile was in charge of the brigade of more than two hundred horses and twenty-five men that journeyed to Nisqually over Naches Pass. McDonald, a Scot, was a colorful figure—six feet tall, slim and wiry, with black hair to his shoulders and a thick beard. He wore a dressed deerskin shirt and pants and had a slow manner of speaking, often telling stories to Indians (he could speak several tribal languages as well as his native Gaelic). He was one of the company's last chief traders to conduct a post within the territorial lands of the United States. On June 2, 1855, McDonald arrived at Nisqually with the furs, all nicely packed in bales of about ninety pounds each. Huggins unpacked the furs, aired and beat them, and then repacked them for brigade shipment to Victoria. There were furs from 176 badgers, 576 black bears, 522 brown bears, 270 grizzly bears, 1,531 martens, 588 minks, 2,685 beavers, 345 fishers, 12 silver foxes, 115 crossbreed silver foxes, 322 red foxes, 417 land otters, 7,949 musquashes (muskrats), 572 wolves, 42 wolverines, and 84 lynx.[21]

HBC Routes through the Cascades

Little information has survived on HBC routes in the Cascade Range south of the forty-ninth parallel. An 1868 letter written by Sir James Douglas—an HBC officer who became chief factor in 1839, governor of Vancouver Island in 1851, and governor of British Columbia in 1858—suggests that the company's men did not use any Cascade Range routes: "In fact the only route, north of Columbia River, resorted to, for that purpose by the Hudson's Bay Company, is that which follows Fraser's River."[22] Nevertheless, there is evidence that HBC traders did explore some routes across the Cascades.

Although railroad explorer Abiel Tinkham is credited with the first crossing of Yakima Pass in 1854, HBC trader Alexander C. Anderson may have driven cattle through that pass earlier (or he may have used Naches Pass). Another company fur trader, Pierre C. Pambrun of Walla Walla, and Cornelius Rogers of the Whitman Mission may have explored Naches Pass as early as 1840.[23] In 1840, the two men ascended the Naches River to cross the pass on their way to Fort Nisqually. In December of that year, Pambrun, Pierre Charles, and Pierre Bercier drove horses across Naches Pass. Yakama leaders Kamaiakan and Owhi brought cattle from HBC forts on the west slope through the pass. It was a common practice for Indians of eastern Washington to drive horses through Naches Pass and return along the same route with cattle to be grazed on the Columbia Plateau.[24]

Either HBC trappers or Indians were familiar with the Little Wenatchee River between 1814 and 1840, for there was a blazed trail following an old route over Cady Pass to the Skykomish River drainage.[25] In 1824, Simpson selected James McMillan to lead a forty-man brigade to locate a passage for small boats between the lower Columbia and lower Fraser rivers. Using a tidewater route, the party set out from Fort George (present-day Astoria) on November 18 and made its way to Grays Harbor, then via the Chehalis River overland to Puget Sound, during extremely wintry, wet weather. There they secured a guide, Pierre Charles, and continued to the Fraser with their frail *bateaux*.

Irishman John Work was a clerk in the brigade. He had entered the service of the HBC in 1814 and in 1830 would be appointed as a chief trader. Work's journal for December 8 recorded that "two high mountains were also seen covered with snow to the S. and S.E., another high one was also seen to the S.W."[26] At the time, the group was passing just north of Bainbridge Island in Puget Sound, and the mountains must have been Mt. St. Helens, Mt. Rainier, and a mountain in the Olympics. Near the Skagit River, Work mentioned seeing the "fine looking" "Scaadchet" Indians.

McMillan's arrival at the Fraser marked the first time a non-Native had visited the lower river since Simon Fraser's 1808 exploration. The brigade passed the future site of Fort Langley and on December 17 clearly saw Mt. Baker: "A high mountain covered with snow appeared to the S.W. in the morning and shortly after a ridge also topped with snow was extending from N.W. to N.E. Two peaks in this ridge are very high."

Between 1814 and 1847, goods destined for New Caledonia were transported from Fort Vancouver by canoes and *bateaux* up the Columbia River (after the annual supply ship from England arrived there, generally in June) and then by horse brigade via Fort Okanogan, Fort Kamloops, and Fort Alexandria. The slow route by way of the Columbia, Okanogan, and Thompson rivers was called the Okanogan Brigade Trail and was first explored in 1813 by David Stuart. In the traditional annual brigade, furs from the New Caledonia interior bound for England were first conveyed by boat to Alexandria on the upper Fraser, then by horse portage via Kamloops to Fort Okanogan. From there the furs were taken by boat to Fort Vancouver. After the murders of Marcus and Narcissa Whitman at their mission near present-day Walla Walla in 1847, the brigade route was changed. Rather than risk conflict with Indians, the 1848 interior brigade used the recently probed Cascade Mountains route to the Fraser River. The horses of the Cayuse, Yakama, and Nez Perce became an important intercultural connection between Native and non-Native fur traders, as horses became essential to the success of the north-woods system established by the HBC.[27]

Fur traders were among the first non-Natives to use water transport on the Columbia. Navigation on the river between Fort Vancouver and the interior was hazardous in places and occasionally led to a loss of life. The Columbia River cascades were particularly dangerous, and voyageurs sped bravely through them rather than make the long portage. For travel in shallow waterways and lakes, the men used *bateaux*. Some of the flat-bottomed boats were built at Fort Langley, and there were generally seven men at the oars.[28]

In the fall of 1828, Simpson descended the tumultuous Fraser River to determine its practicality as a trade route. In an 1826 letter, he wrote:

> About 70 Miles from its entrance the navigation is interrupted by Rapids and Falls, so as to render it nearly impassible and according to the best information I have been able to collect, the banks of the River about 150 Miles up, form precipices where the towing line cannot be used. . . .[29]

After hair-raising experiences in the raging waters of the Fraser Canyon between Lytton and Yale, Simpson concluded that the passage would mean "certain Death, in Nine times out of ten." He reached Fort Langley safely but was convinced that another route must be found. He noted a major tributary to the north (Harrison's River) and, on the basis of information from Indians and traders, believed it might be used to bypass the canyon.[30] This observation led Chief Factor Ogden in 1845 to request that the company explore the region to find a superior route.

By 1846, locating a horse-brigade route that was entirely within British territory from the lower Fraser to the interior had become a necessity because of the impending demarcation of the International Boundary. The Americans would soon levy customs duties on imports, and it became imperative to avoid crossing their territory.[31] James Douglas, who was then chief factor of Vancouver Island, ordered Alexander C. Anderson to explore trading routes from the interior to Fort Langley. Anderson was born in India in 1814 and became an authority on North American Indian beliefs and customs. In 1831, he entered the service of the HBC, becoming a chief factor and, in 1858, a collector of customs at Victoria. A scholar as well as an officer, Anderson was the prime initiator of overland exploration east and south of Hope, through the Cascade Range, in search of a route to the Thompson River. Anderson was the first non-Indian man to cross the Cascades between the Fraser River and the forty-ninth parallel, and he drew valuable maps.[32]

The resolute Anderson was a tireless and hardy explorer. He set a fast pace, sometimes setting out at four in the morning and taking a breakfast of dried salmon hours later. Leaving Kamloops on May 15, 1846, Anderson traveled by way of Seton, Anderson, Lillooet, and Harrison lakes to Fort Langley, a route entirely north of the lower Fraser River. He arrived at Langley on May 24. By this time, the valley of the Similkameen was well known to fur traders. The explorer's task now was to locate a route through the mountain barrier to link the Fraser River with the brigade trail that followed the Similkameen and Tulameen rivers and Otter Creek, continuing to Kamloops.

On May 28, 1846, Anderson left Fort Langley for the return trip to Kamloops. After canoeing an estimated sixty-six miles on the Fraser, he reached a river that entered the Fraser from the south, which Indians called the Tlaekullum (Silverhope Creek, west of Hope). There was a defile that the guide from Fort Langley proposed to follow. The route proved to be a narrow pathway with large boulders in the forest. Because the valley trended in the general direction of Mt. Baker, Anderson believed that it could not be the correct route. He retraced his way to the Fraser and then decided to follow a defile farther upstream known as the Que-que-al-la (Coquihalla). On May 31, he left the defile and set out east-southeast through a broad valley. Following the right bank, Anderson reached a small lake at the height of land near the divide between Nicolum Creek and the Sumallo River. There was little underbrush, and the cedars were gigantic. The stream he was following to the east-southeast was called the Simal-a-oueh by the Indians. Although he could not identify the river—"I was at first inclined to set it down as the Skatchett River [it was the Sumallo] and am still in doubt on the point"—he believed it would lead to the vicinity of Bellingham Bay.[33] For guides, he hired a chief of the "Chilwhoe" (Chilliwack) and engaged a Thompson Indian who was hunting beaver in the area and had likely crossed the Tulameen Plateau.[34]

On June 2, Anderson's party set out at 4:00 A.M., following the north bank of the Sumallo. They encountered much fallen timber, sometimes using an axe to cut the way. By six in the evening, they were camped a mile from the Sumallo's junction with the Skagit. Anderson's guides intended to take the east fork of the next junction (the Skagit River), but the new guide wanted to follow the northeast fork (East Snass Creek). Anderson's manuscript describes their progress and what they saw:

> *Wednesday 3rd June.* Set out at 3 1/2 A.M.—A beautiful Rhododendron, with splendid crimson flowers now in bloom abounds in this vicinity. There is some pasture for horses at the spot where we breakfasted and in the neighbourhood. It is scanty but might be improved by burning the fallen wood. With this view partly, and partly to secure a landmark whereon to take a distant bearing I had fire set to the fallen timber. We here leave the little river; strike up east, bending round northward towards the height of land. The name of the little stream we have left is Sk-ha-ist implying, it is said, "a peak standing between the ridges." Set out at 8:20 and at noon reach the summit of the mountain pass. The ascent is very gentle, and perfectly clear of impediment throughout the greater part. Frequent fires have destroyed the timber that heretofore encumbered the ground. Upon nearing the summit of the pass a few occasional snow drifts witness our elevated position, but up to that point there was nothing of the kind to impede the passage for horses. But alas! on reaching the summit a dreary prospect met the view. The whole surface of the valley as well as the confining mountains, was white with accumulated snow. The difference is of course ascribable to the relative position of the opposite sides, that by which we ascended has a southern exposure, lying open consequently to the full influence of the sun's rays, aided by the southern winds and vice versa.
>
> There is a small lake here bearing a marvellous similitude in some respects to the Committee's Punch Bowl in the Rocky Mountains. It is still covered with ice, save in one small spot, where through the limpid water, the bottom is seen shelving off, apparently to an immense depth.[35]

By agreement, the Chilliwack assistants turned back at this point; none of them knew the terrain ahead. Anderson recorded: "The water must guide us."

On June 6, falling in with the tracks of horses, Anderson met the Similkameen Indian chief known as Old Blackeye and his son-in-law a few miles from Otter Creek. The two men were on their way to check on deer snares. Blackeye gave Anderson some provisions as well as information on a shorter route to Red Earth Fork (present-day Princeton), which the group had missed because of the snow cover. The "horse road to the height of land strikes straight across the bend of the river," Blackeye reportedly told them, adding that it was a good road and there was ample pasture. The Indians took this direct road—across the bend of the Tulameen—every summer with horses for hunting. Anderson termed the route Blackeye's Portage and later marked it on a map for Douglas.[36] He continued on, taking the Tulameen's north fork, and Blackeye obligingly sent his son-in-law on horseback to fetch horses for him. The party camped at Blackeye's lodge north of Otter Lake, where he promised to guide Anderson by a better route to Kamloops and provided some fresh fish. "Our provisions are exhausted," Anderson wrote, "but the old man supplies us with a few fresh carp which, though nowise tempting at another time, are very acceptable now." The party reached Kamloops on June 29. The total distance from Langley was 237½ miles.

In 1847, Anderson made another attempt to locate a usable route over the mountains from interior British territory. He followed a Native horse trail from Nicola Lake via Spius and Uztlius creeks, then struck south up the Anderson River and crossed a pass to reach the Fraser below the worst of the canyon.[37] In June 1848, three horse brigades under Chief Trader Donald Manson—the New Caledonia, Kamloops, and Colvile brigades —followed this rough route to Fort Yale with disastrous results. The journey, with Anderson as guide, became a nightmare as fifty men labored to get four hundred horses, many unbroken, with their loads across the surging Fraser current near Spuzzum. Some horses and loads may have been lost. In early August, the inward party also had a difficult time crossing the Fraser and then the mountains.[38] When Douglas later looked at the ferry point near Spuzzum, he ordered a horse trail built to detour west of the river—the rough "Douglas Portage" between Yale and Spuzzum.

After this terrible episode on the Fraser route, Anderson urged Governor Simpson to find alternatives near his 1846 Similkameen route. He recommended a company clerk, Henry Peers (who had been with the return party), to locate a feasible route. Upon his arrival at Kamloops in 1848, Peers began his search.[39] Chief Blackeye's son showed Peers a more direct route than the one Anderson had taken in 1846, one that crossed the notorious and steep Manson Mountain. Peers was evidently under the impression that he had, while east of the Continental Divide, followed the old Anderson route, but he was not quite on it. The Brigade Trail, as Peers's route became known, crossed Anderson's track at Horseguard Camp.[40]

By fall, Peers had reported on a usable route by way of the Coquihalla River, Peers Creek, Manson Mountain, and Sowaqua Creek, and then across the divide to the upper Tulameen River. There the route followed part of Blackeye's Trail, going over Lodestone Mountain and down to the Tulameen River again. Late in 1848, trusting that the Peers route would be practical, the HBC constructed Fort Hope on the delta of the Coquihalla River. In 1849, work proceeded on the Brigade Trail; windfalls were chopped and a path cleared. Contrary to Douglas's hopes, the new trail was not ready to replace the Anderson River-Spuzzum-Fort Yale route for the outward brigade of that year.[41] The Brigade Trail, in fact, would prove to be more difficult and dangerous than the 1846 route; in 1857 or 1858, the company would lose sixty to seventy horses on Manson Ridge in an October snowstorm.

The New Caledonia, Thompsons River, and Colvile brigades traveled the Brigade Trail together, meeting and dispersing at Kamloops. These combined brigades formed a string of as many as four hundred horses, each carrying two ninety-pound loads of furs and goods. In motion, the HBC brigades were an imposing sight, sometimes stretching over a mile in length. They were "a beautiful sight . . . every animal in his full beauty of form and colour."[42] Reporting to London on the new Brigade Trail, Douglas remarked that the trail "may also have an important bearing on the future destinies of the country at large." The trail served as the main route of commerce from Hope to Kamloops until 1860, when traffic followed part of the Dewdney Trail or the Fraser Canyon. At some places on Manson Ridge, the path is still visible today.

The HBC trail up the Chilliwack River to Chilliwack Lake, built in 1855, was intended to provide a way to cross the range to the upper Skagit River (the trail was soon abandoned beyond the lake).[43] Three years later, it became part of the Whatcom Trail, which would be improved by both the U.S. and British Boundary Survey parties. With the decline in the fur trade, the economic forces behind trail-building were the gold rushes and, later, cattle and sheep drives. Still, the trading posts that had served the fur trade became settlements based on other economic pursuits, such as farming.

The HBC had done only what was vital to the fur trade in exploring the northern Cascades. Company men had focused on trade operations, and those who admired the majesty of the range left few written records about it. Angus McDonald, however, with a poetic description of the Cascades' highest mountain as seen from Victoria, indicated that not all traders were indifferent to the mountain aesthetic: "Mount Rainier, the grandest of the Cascade upheavals, and in his perpetual Arctic harness overlooking all the sounds and summits in sight of his, is seen from the skirts of this town. His snow wrapped brother, Mt. St. Helens, I saw burning thirty-six years ago."[44]

The HBC had formed an efficient and profitable trading empire of remarkable dimensions in the Pacific Northwest, but the men were only in the region on assignment, not to settle. The imperial network initially overshadowed the Americans, but by the early 1840s the HBC was losing its means of support as a diminished beaver supply failed to justify the vast and expensive operation. Even without the complexities of American settlers, missionaries, and political agitation, the company would have been forced to shift into other activities. By 1845, the HBC could no longer influence increasing American colonization, and it soon evacuated from the Columbia country.

Mt. Stuart, sketch by George B. McClellan from near Naches Pass, August 26, 1853 (George B. McClellan Papers, Library of Congress)

3

McCLELLAN'S RAILROAD-PASS SURVEY,

1853–1854

There was nothing to be seen but mountain piled on mountain—rugged & impassable.
—Capt. George McClellan, February 25, 1854

The movement for a transcontinental railroad strengthened as the United States approached the middle of the nineteenth century. Asa Whitney, a prominent New York politician and the earliest and most active backer of a route across the northern states, was the first to put the idea of a transcontinental railway into practical shape. He began his public movement in 1845, appearing in Washington, D.C., with a magnificent scheme for a railroad from Lake Michigan to the Pacific Coast—a railroad he would build with money from land grants. Eugene Smalley, in his *History of the Northern Pacific Railroad,* describes Whitney's persistence:

> He got little for his pains, at first, but ridicule; but he was not a man to be put down by sneers and laughter. He believed thoroughly in his project, and soon made others believe in it. A great talker in public and private, eloquent, earnest, and well equipped with convincing statistics and forcible arguments, he returned to the charge in 1846, and in 1847 got a favorable report from the Senate Committee on Public Lands.[1]

Whitney's proposed line and promotional map made the Pacific Railroad one of the great public issues of the day, and his project was a strong factor in the government's eventual interest in surveying routes to the Pacific Ocean.[2]

In the early 1850s, Whitney abandoned the Northern Pacific project in despair of congressional action, but enthusiasm for construction of a northern railroad line was kept alive by Edwin Ferry Johnson, a highly respected civil engineer. Although Johnson had never been west of St. Paul, Minnesota, he gathered and digested all the information he could find on the topography, climate, and production of the United States, including the Pacific Northwest. His knowledge of the Cascades, for example, included the fact that it was "a high range . . . having several lofty conical peaks, one of which, Mt. Baker, is situated near the latitude of 49° No, and another, Mt Ranier, is in latitude 46¾ N." By virtue of his statesmanship, practical experience, and geographic acumen, the forty-nine-year-old Johnson was able to convince the nation's political leaders of the value of the West for settlers and of the merits of railroad expansion to the Pacific Northwest. In 1854, he published a pamphlet, *Railroad to the Pacific,* which included a profile and generalized map of a line across the Midwest to Bellingham Bay.[3]

Johnson discussed the idea of a railroad with Vermont capitalist and railroad builder Thomas H. Canfield, who had pioneered steam propeller navigation on the St. Lawrence River and the Great Lakes. Canfield was a true visionary who would fight a hostile Congress against great odds to promote the Northern Pacific.[4] According to Smalley: "Once launched in Congress the Pacific Railway movement had inherent vitality enough to keep alive." Two factors accelerated the public momentum: peace with Mexico in 1848 had added new territories to the nation, and gold discoveries had enticed adventurers and fortune-seekers across the Great Plains to the Far West. The railroad's location, however, was controversial. By 1852, at least six different routes to the Pacific Coast had been urged on a divided Congress.[5] The decision on where to build the transcontinental railroad would be of paramount importance to the development of the West.

Recognizing that the issue of the railroad's route could not be solved by political means alone, Congress passed the Pacific Railroad amendment on March 2, 1853, authorizing transcontinental surveys under the War Department and ordering the secretary of war to undertake a task that beggared belief. Within ten months, he was to submit a full report to Congress on all practicable routes between the Mississippi River and the Pacific Ocean. The congressional decision to send surveyors and scientists west to examine possible railroad routes gave impetus to western expansion, a movement that would advance Euro-Americans' understanding of the frontier and would force an exploration of the northern Cascades.

The four main surveys, envisioned as an attempt to break the political and economic deadlock over the route the railroad would take, were organized as a series of expeditions that probed the West in isolated reconnaissances some two thousand miles long. Fortunately for the army's Corps of Topographical Engineers, which directed the surveys, the project was limited to reconnaissances rather than the laying of a railroad line.[6] The U.S. Army was in charge and, except for the northern route, the surveys were under the supervision of the Corps.

Closely related to the problem of railroad construction was the need for adequate knowledge of the route transect. To gather the range of geographic and technical information that was required—data on climate, grades of passes, resources of the regions—civilian scientific specialists were needed. Scientists thus had a chance to play a determining role in the choice of route, to compile a great inventory of knowledge, and to serve as an instrument of public policy. The surveys became an unofficial federal patronage of scientists that was linked to the development of the country, even though the pace of the reconnaissances would prove to be too rapid to allow for a full scientific study.[7]

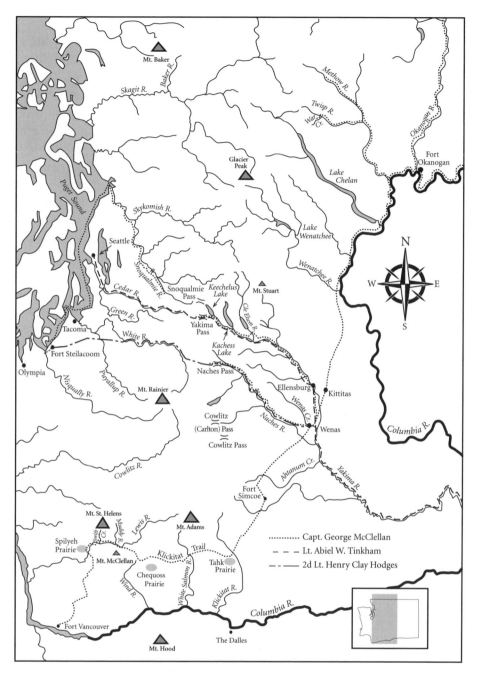

McClellan's Railroad-Pass Survey, 1853–1854

Planning the Survey

The plan was impossibly grandiose—the general instructions to Isaac Ingalls Stevens—the man in charge of the vital northern route—were to "examine carefully the passes of the several mountain ranges, the geography and meteorology of the whole intermediate region."[8] While locating and surveying a practicable railroad route, the Stevens expedition was to determine the winter snow depth at such mountain passes and also the depth of the Columbia River. The forthright and ambitious Stevens, who had just resigned his army commission to become governor of the newly created Washington Territory, had asked Secretary of War Jefferson Davis to place him in charge of the northern route. He was a questionable choice. As governor of a vast territory that would profit greatly from a railroad through it, he was certain to overstate the case for a northern route.[9] Stevens was so enthusiastic about the Pacific Northwest that he maintained that it "far surpasses" the Russian empire for the "cultivation of the great staples of agriculture." At the same time, however, Stevens was credited with being active and intelligent, one who "helps pull on the rope when we get stuck in a mudhole."[10] He had graduated at the head of his 1839 class at West Point and had been wounded and decorated for gallantry in Mexico. He had worked for Franklin Pierce's nomination in 1852 and was a brilliant young lieutenant attached to the Coast Survey in the Engineer Corps.[11] Pierce nominated him as territorial governor, and at the same time the secretary of state made him superintendent of Indian affairs for the territory.

The first, largest, and most elaborate of the survey parties to take the field was Stevens's expedition. In March 1853, Stevens obtained a $90,000 appropriation out of the $150,000 that was allotted for all four surveys. In the next six months, he proposed to traverse and explore a domain 2,000 miles long and 250 miles wide, most of it poorly mapped and inhabited by Indians. The route was long and time was short, so Stevens broke the command in two: an eastern division under his direction and a western division under Capt. George Brinton McClellan of the Corps of Topographical Engineers. Stevens staffed his division with regular army officers and scientists as well as artist John Mix Stanley. McClellan also took competent men from the world of science and managed to secure the services of two naturalists, Dr. George Gibbs and Dr. James Graham Cooper.[12] Because a potential Columbia River route ended far south of Seattle, which was believed to be the best western terminus, Stevens had to locate a direct pass through the Cascade Range if his surveyed route was to prevail.[13] This matter was so urgent that Stevens decided, wisely, that the western division's efforts should commence from west of the Cascades.

McClellan's background bore many similarities to Stevens's. He was born in Pennsylvania and graduated from West Point in 1846, and he was made a brevet captain in 1847 for gallant conduct in the battle of Chapultepec, Mexico.[14] A personable and competent officer, McClellan was commander of the United States armies during the Civil War and later served as president of the Ohio and Mississippi Railroad and governor of New Jersey. While similar in background, Stevens and McClellan were opposites in temperament. Stevens was quick, energetic, and impetuous, while McClellan was more of a thinker and a perfectionist. McClellan had great personal magnetism, and Stevens had great faith in him.[15] His optimism is apparent in an April 7 letter to McClellan requesting him to serve and outlining plans of action. "One word more as to the Railroad Survey. We must not be frightened with long tunnels or enormous snows, but put ourselves to work to overcome them." On May 9, Stevens gave McClellan the quite impossible task of completing an exploration of the northern Cascade Range: "You will thoroughly explore this range from the Columbia river to the forty-ninth parallel of north latitude, making detailed examinations of the passes, and obtaining full information in relation to the range in general." The captain was also asked to construct a "military road from Fort Wallah to Pugets Sound."[16]

McClellan arrived at Fort Vancouver on June 27, 1853, by way of Panama. At the time, the celebrated Capt. Benjamin L.E. Bonneville was in charge of the army post there, and it is likely that he offered McClellan valuable advice on reconnaissance, encounters with Indians, and logistics based on his experience in the Rocky Mountains and Great Basin. McClellan was aware that he would be dependent on the HBC post at Vancouver for saddles and provisions, although he believed it advisable to be as independent of the company as possible. In May, he had written to a member of his expedition, 2d Lt. Johnson K. Duncan: "Still we must keep in their good graces, so that if the worst comes to the worst we can fall back upon them."[17]

At the time, McClellan hoped to mount his entire infantry escort on mules, and he estimated that transporting three months' supplies would require sixty to seventy mules, plus six to eight good horses that would be ridden only when necessary. HBC Chief Factor Peter Skene Ogden had kindly provided a memorandum on the formation of brigades and a strategy for rounding up animals and preparing loads. His "Hints to Travellers" reminded that "the call in the morning for all men to rise should be at the dawn of the day" and that at noon the horses should be permitted "at least 3 hours to eat and rest." The memorandum also suggested that

> the Superintendent of Packers should have his eye over all. No particular place should be assigned him, for men in charge of Brigades are very apt to neglect their Horses, and are too lazy and indolent to stop and manage their loads. . . . Divide your men by Twos. This is commonly called a Brigade, and you can safely give each Brigade 12 Horses. Your Superintendent of Packing should establish it as a rule that one man of each Brigade goes in the morning to collect the Horses, the remaining man of each Brigade should remain in Camp and prepare his loads, so as to be in readiness when the Horses are all brought in.[18]

McClellan's planning was methodical. In his letter to Johnson Duncan in May, he reminded the lieutenant that tent poles must be jointed for packing, although if the expedition could locate abundant timber "we may be able to dispense with poles altogether." Well in advance, McClellan gave thought to how he would feed his ponderous expedition: "If pemmican can be readily provided it will be best to depend primarily upon it—& to take but little pork—of flour we can take but little, must depend principally on good pilot bread [a hardtack]—we must have plenty of coffee, salts & vinegar."[19]

At Vancouver, McClellan hired the scholarly George Gibbs at a salary of $200 per month to take charge of geological observations and to record the vocabulary, history, traditions, and customs of the Indian tribes of Washington Territory, as well as those of Oregon, California, and adjoining British possessions.[20] A descendant of a wealthy colonial shipping family and a Harvard Law School graduate, Gibbs at age thirty-four had been lured by gold, a serious bent for science, and a zest for travel to leave a legal practice in New York and journey from St. Louis to Oregon with a regiment of the Mounted Riflemen in the summer of 1849. During the trip, he had many contacts with interior tribes such as the Sioux, Blackfoot, Flathead, and Nez Perce, which prepared him for his later studies of Pacific Northwest tribes. A versatile man, Gibbs was a geographer and geologist as well as an ethnologist, had twice served on government expeditions, and had acquired a reputation for keeping journals, interpreting, and mapmaking. Gibbs, who would become a founder of scientific geologic studies in the Far West, is among the most enduring individuals associated with the history of the Cascade Range.[21]

Gibbs's most important contributions to the intellectual study of the region were his cataloging of tribal languages, his collection of Native artifacts for the Smithsonian Institution, and his geographical knowledge on both the Pacific Railroad and Northwest Boundary surveys. He collected the vocabularies of twenty-one tribes, publishing them in 1877, and compiled a *Dictionary of the Chinook Jargon* while in Washington Territory. He was a remarkable topographical analyst despite his lack of formal training in surveying, and he made important maps that showed portions of the Cascade Range and locations of Indian tribes. The studious Gibbs read profusely and kept reference lists in copious notebooks. He took compass bearings of prominent mountains, such as Baker, Stuart, and Rainier, and copied Vancouver's latitudes. Collaborating with George Suckley on natural history, Gibbs translated many names of birds and mammals from tribal languages to English. After the expedition was over, Gibbs prepared three important reports on regional geology, Native tribes, and a reconnaissance of "the country lying upon Shoalwater Bay and Puget Sound." McClellan praised Gibbs, his work, and his reports, extolling the benefits of his reconnaissances.[22] Stevens, who first met Gibbs at Fort Colvile in October 1853, later commended him as "a thoroughly educated man" who combined "the habits of a student with the good qualities of a woodsman and mountaineer."[23]

McClellan appointed Lt. Duncan—who was in charge of surveying instruments, mapping, and astronomy—to collaborate with John Lambert, his civilian topographer. McClellan was fortunate to have Duncan, who drew the milestone 1853–1854 map *Preliminary Sketch of the Northern Pacific Rail Road Exploration and Survey from the Rocky Mountains to Puget Sound.* Other members of the expedition included 2d Lt. Sylvester Mowry, a meteorologist; civil engineers J.F. Miller, A.L. Lewis, and Joseph F. Minter; and 2d Lt. Henry Clay Hodges, quartermaster and commissary. Also joining the expedition was James Cooper, a naturalist and physician who spent more than two years in Washington Territory collecting specimens of plants and animals.[24]

McClellan organized a massive expedition, which he later justified by citing "the nature of what little information we possessed at the time in reference to the country we were to traverse, [and] the disposition of the Indians." The pack train's size may be the reason why McClellan saw no deer, elk, or bear during the expedition—nothing larger than a wolf. Although Stevens gave McClellan latitude in organization, he ordered him to make "detailed examinations" of the passes while being "careful to observe the strictest economy compatible with the success of the expedition." Stevens also instructed him to "operate in the mountains until they are thoroughly explored or till driven away by snow."[25] Well past the summer solstice, the expedition was at last ready to depart. McClellan reported to the chief of the Topographical Engineers that he would leave on July 17 "with my command, to explore the Cascade Range of Mountains." He had taken three valuable weeks to get the expedition organized at Fort Vancouver, partly because of problems with supplies and horses.[26]

Setting Out

The party finally left on the July 18 with 61 men, 160 horses and mules, 3 hunters, 15 civilian guides and packers, and 29 soldiers who served as escorts and packers. The men were well armed with United States and Sharps rifles and Colt revolvers. Among the considerable baggage were the surveying and astronomical instruments and gifts for the Indians.[27]

The expedition could not rely on the journals of Lewis and Clark, as Stevens had when crossing the five Rocky Mountain passes. McClellan had to depend instead on Native and other local guides when he struck the Klickitat Indian trail not far into his journey.[28] He had hired A.L. Lewis, who had a stock of practical information and Native legends, as guide for this route. The group adopted some of Ogden's "hints to travelers," and the commanding officer and one or two others scouted ahead, followed by the soldier escort and the civilian brigade. This progression must have produced bottlenecks, for the pace averaged only three miles per day for some time. There were other problems as well. McClellan had not been in the field for three days when the HBC saddles turned out to be completely worthless, and some of the men had to return to

Vancouver to buy fifty Ringgold saddles as replacements.[29] After crossing up-per Salmon Creek on July 25, the expedition camped near the "Yah-kotl," the east fork of the Lewis River. Waiting for the saddles delayed their progress, and it would take them six more days to arrive at Chelatchie Prairie near present-day Amboy. Cooper observed that the two-by-five-mile plain was surrounded by "huge precipitous hills above which towers the snow-capped peak of St. Helens." Following a rough trail on August 1, the expedition made its first crossing of the "Cath-la-poot'l" River (Lewis River) to Spilyeh Prairie.[30]

After leaving Camp Spilyeh, west of present-day Yale Lake, McClellan proceeded northeast to near present-day Cougar. On August 3, they recrossed the Lewis River at a good ford (the group was probably on the south side for only a few hundred yards to bypass a difficult bank where the river turned). After traversing a lava field, the expedition crossed Swift Creek and established camp at the base of Devils Backbone.[31] Below the mouth of the "Noomptnahmie" (Swift Creek), Gibbs studied the flows that he believed were the most recent lava deposits from Mt. St. Helens: "Its surface was everywhere broken into mounds, or gigantic bubbles, produced apparently by the expansion of con-tained gases."[32] The route followed the Lewis River, occasionally crossing it, and then headed southeastward. When passing Mt. St. Helens, McClellan ob-served that the mountains were not as rugged as those near Mt. Rainier, yet no pass appeared (he was still well west of the main Cascade divide). The party's next camp was made below Muddy River.[33]

Ascending to the plateau south of the Lewis River on August 5, the expedi-tion entered the ponderosa pine belt. The distance given for that day to McClellan Mountain—six and one-half miles—is reasonable. Camp Wahamis, where the party spent the night, was probably Paradise Valley.[34] There the hills were covered by huckleberries and the open ground was "carpeted by straw-berry vines with ripe fruit of delicious flavor." By nightfall on August 6, the explorers had reached Wind River at a "boggy" prairie, now known as McClellan Meadows, where they grazed the horses for a day. The "high ridge" they crossed on August 8 was part of Berry Mountain.[35]

From Camp Chequoss, near Big Lava Bed, Gibbs described the lava fields, columns, and "turrets and pinnacles on some of the heights." Later, near the Klickitat River, he wrote that the remarkable vaulted passages in lava were traced at intervals for miles.[36] McClellan mentioned the unusual view that day: "Five large snow mountains were in sight—Rainier, St. Helen, Adams, Hood, and Jefferson. The mountains in this part of the range are generally wooded; they have steep slopes, but seldom present bold or rocky outlines."[37] On the map resulting from Duncan's surveys, Mt. St. Helens and Swift Creek are about seven minutes of longitude east of their true position while Mt. Adams is about twenty minutes too far east.[38] In his topographic report, Duncan mentioned the "several sharp needle-points to the south of Mt.

Rainier" and noted "a curious cathedral-shaped mountain" south of Mt. Adams (Sleeping Beauty Mountain).[39] Like Gibbs, he recorded the large lava field west of Swift Creek. While at Chequoss Prairie, McClellan correctly decided that the trail had been a pocket through the range rather than a pass and that the route would be too expensive for railroad construction. Significantly, he cited an Indian report that the snow was some twelve to fifteen feet deep during the winter.[40]

On August 9 and 10, McClellan recorded what he knew about the Klickitats who lived in the area. They were a proud, nomadic people, he observed, but ravaged by smallpox. At Chequoss Prairie—a popular Indian encampment on the highest plain southwest of Berry Mountain—there were "some 20 lodges of Indians." Gibbs took a census of the Chequoss band and counted 138 persons.[41] On August 11, the expedition passed a "small lake" (Goose Lake), where they encountered several groups of Indians who "were suffering terribly from the small-pox," a disease that expedition members were quite fearful of catching. The "fine creek" where they camped that night, at Camp Hool-hool-se, was southwest of the present-day town of Trout Lake.[42]

The expedition crossed the White Salmon River—the "large stream, the Nikepun"—as the route bore east to a camp on Tahk ("Camash") Prairie. The three-by-ten-mile prairie, 114 miles from Vancouver, abounded with wapato and camas root. Once across the Klickitat River, then in low water, the expedition placed Camp Wa-wak-che on White Creek on August 14. The course then followed the Indian trail across the plateau country to Toppenish ("Pisco") Creek, east of Signal Peak.[43] By August 17 the men had reached Simcoe, where McClellan visited the Indian fortifications. Upon his return to camp, he purchased "4 steers of Skloo at $40 pr. head—had them killed at once—4 days rations issued, & the rest cut and dried."[44] Accompanied by Skloom—a Yakama chief who owned land and cattle—and a Deschutes chief, the men moved northward to the Catholic mission east of Cispus Pass, where they camped.

The following day, McClellan and some members of the expedition visited the mission. "Two priests are there," he reported, "Fathers [Charles] Pandosy and D'Herboux with a french servant. They have some cows & pigs—gave us good fresh milk to drink."[45] McClellan asked Father Pandosy to take a tribal census. At the mission, McClellan met Yakama chief Kamaiakan, who he described as "fine looking." Gibbs wrote that Kamaiakan was "large, gloomy-looking, slovenly in dress, but said to be generous and honest" and that "all of them [the Yakama chiefs] appear to be well disposed and friendly towards the whites." McClellan had what he reported as a long, friendly talk with Kamaiakan and gave him a present. He told the chief that Governor Stevens was approaching and that he would punish whites who committed outrages against the Indians (in his journal McClellan expressed doubts that the whites would discontinue such acts).[46]

Seemingly because of the "beef not being yet dried," the expedition remained encamped on August 9. Although the decisions were his, the slow pace appeared to annoy McClellan and was exhausting the expedition's supplies.[47] The next day, the caravan continued to the Wenas branch of the Yakima, where they made a base camp. Upon hearing that a citizens' party was cutting a wagon road through Naches Pass, McClellan decided to send Lt. Hodges— "an energetic and systematic quartermaster"—over that route to acquire provisions and to return numerous unfit pack horses.[48] McClellan, concerned about being caught in the northern territorial boundary by an early winter, hoped Hodges could obtain fresh mules and supplies at Fort Steilacoom.

The expedition was now characterized by side trips. Hodges left Wenas on August 22 with fifty horses and twenty-six men, returning with provisions on September 16. On August 24, Duncan who "possesses the qualities to conduct any expedition like this," was sent with three men to penetrate the head of the Yakima Valley. McClellan next explored "Nahchess Pass" with a small party of seven men. He followed the uneven Indian trail on the mountain slopes above the Naches River and concluded that the valley was unfit for a railroad; a wagon road would have to follow the stream bottom, with endless crossings.[49] McClellan spent only one day at the pass, which the group determined to be 4,890 feet high. They probably continued westward for a mile, for he saw the "blazes of the party sent out from Olympia to cut a wagon road." McClellan later reported to Secretary of War Jefferson Davis that thick timber near Mt. Rainier made exploration difficult and an extensive view was hard to obtain. A railroad would be very expensive to build, he wrote, citing the black marks on trees as indications that the snow stood five to eight feet deep in winter when "the valley must be choked with snow."[50]

McClellan did get a valuable panorama from the heights near Naches Pass:

> From the summit of the mountains, bordering the pass, there is a fine view of Mt. Rainier. Exceedingly massive, it presents, from near the pass, the appearance of a long ridge with two peaks; the eastern one being rather the higher, and more rounded of the two.

He also described a "belt of jagged cones [Cowlitz Chimneys and Governor's Ridge], extending the whole breadth of the mountain." To the north stood "a vast sea of bare, jagged, snow-crowned ranges extending as far as the eye can reach"—the prominent peaks near Snoqualmie Pass and the Cascade crest peaks of the Cle Elum River drainage. On August 26, probably the day he made these observations, McClellan sketched the dominating peak to the northeast and named it Mt. Stuart after his best and oldest friend, "the late Capt. Jas. Stuart of the Rifles—a gallant soldier & accomplished gentleman. . . ."[51]

During his exploration up the Naches, McClellan must have scanned the divide southward toward Cowlitz and Carlton passes, but apparently he was not impressed with the railroad-route possibilities. Having satisfied himself of the impracticability of Naches Pass for a railway, he returned to the Wenas depot on August 29. Two days later, Duncan returned with his observations on the lakes in the Yakima River headwaters, and a messenger arrived with a note from Hodges reporting that sixteen horses had broken down and that it would not be possible to bring back the provisions ordered from Steilacoom. When the commander realized that he could not supply his cavalcade, he decided to cut its size drastically by sending back the military escort. [52]

On September 3, the reduced party moved northward, close to present-day Ellensburg, and established a base from which to explore what McClellan believed was Snoqualmie Pass. It seems clear that Stevens entertained the geographic notion, current at the time, that Snoqualmie and Yakima passes were one and the same. Taking nine men with him, McClellan traveled about seventeen miles to a prairie along the Yakima River.[53] McClellan must have sighted Mt. Stuart again on September 5 while crossing the Teanaway River. The group made good progress and nearly reached the mouth of the Cle Elum River that day. The Yakima River drainage seemed a logical place to explore for a pass, and McClellan wrote in his journal for that day that it "promises better than the other [Naches]: tho' the Indians say that is worse." Continuing through the valley's light pine woodland, the party passed the outlet of Kachess Lake and, after following the Indian trail, arrived at "two small shallow lakes on a small bench."[54] McClellan later reported to Stevens that the lake at the pass had two source streams: "One is the head of Nooksái Nooksái, which runs to the D'Wamish [Cedar River] and Puget sound; the other into Lake Kitchelus." He continued: "To the northward of the pass the mountains are very lofty, generally bare at the top, often of solid rock, with sharp outlines. . . . As far as the eye can determine, there is no possibility of effecting a passage in that direction; there certainly is none between this and the Nahchess Pass."[55] Strangely, McClellan overlooked Stampede Pass, a route later chosen by the Northern Pacific Railroad.

From the vicinity of the pass, "Mt. Regnier was in full sight—more imposing & majestic than ever." The Indian guide reportedly hinted that the mountains to the north "form the dividing ridge between the Yak-inse [Yakima] & the Linahonis [Snoqualmie]," but McClellan characterized a route through them as "unpracticable."[56] The jagged topography appeared to represent an unbroken mountain landscape that precluded a usable, low pass. By not investigating, however, McClellan missed the chance to locate the true Snoqualmie Pass. Gibbs, accompanying McClellan, described the geology of the higher peaks to the north, which "seemed to be of basalt or conglomerate." He also described the Yakima's source: "a small lake, situated on the very summit of the dividing ridge [Yakima Pass], at an elevation of about 3,600 feet, from which the D'Wamish also, emptying into Puget sound, derives its origin."[57]

The following day, the group crossed into the Cedar River watershed but turned back on the advice of one of the hunters and the guide. McClellan thought that "it would be extremely difficult to carve a road down this stream. It is always narrow & rocky. The guide says that it empties into a lake at the other end of which is a cascade" (present-day Cedar Lake and Cedar Falls). In the afternoon, McClellan and Gibbs crossed to the north branch of the Cedar River, which they followed to a "pretty little lake." In his report, McClellan recorded that at twenty-five miles from the pass the stream emptied into "Lake Nook-noo" (Cedar Lake). Gibbs also ascended to nearby Meadow Pass on the main crest, near the south end of Keechelus Lake. He determined here that "the water also flows in both directions" and that he saw "no serious difficulties in the way of a road."[58]

On September 8, McClellan returned to Yakima Pass. He observed Lost Lake (called Willailootzas by the Indians), which he described as long and narrow: "No outlet is apparent at the E. end, tho' the water clearly runs over there when the lake is high." He then descended to Keechelus Lake, where he took some barometrical observations and superficially observed that the lake was "closed on all sides but the S.E. by lofty mountains." The lakes at the head of the Yakima, he wrote, were "surrounded by rough and lofty mountains, rising directly from the water's edge, and many of them having snow upon them in August." He apparently did not venture north toward Snoqualmie Pass but reported that a foot trail existed from the head of Keechelus Lake to the south fork of the Snoqualmie. McClellan reported that the Indians said it was a very hard foot route and was seldom used: "in fact, there is no trail, properly so called."[59]

The group's examination of the pass was hurried and superficial. McClellan feared being caught by the snow, which piled up twenty to twenty-five feet and was "found in the passes during the most unfavorable months of the year."[60] He may have gotten information about snow depth from Indians and by examining snow marks on trees. In his letterbook, McClellan recorded: "In the Yakima valley, when it opens out, the snow is some 6' in depth. Character of snow, extreme lightness & dryness—too light for the use of snow shoes. About the end of March the snow packs, so that the pass becomes practicable for horses."[61]

When the group passed Cle Elum Lake and descended the Yakima Valley, the air was "perfectly thick with smoke," which reminded an amused McClellan of a West Point barracks room. With apparently little more thought about the pass they had visited, they arrived at "Ketetas," their camp near Ellensburg, on September 12. The exciting news there was that "our people have found gold in the sand all around this place . . . many have the gold fever highly developed." At the camp, McClellan found Chief Ow-hi of the Yakama with a large number of his tribe. The superintendent of the Steilacoom-to-Walla Walla road was also in camp, and he apparently persuaded McClellan to complete contracts to "afford a little assistance to the road cutters," subject to Stevens's approval.[62]

The expedition—reduced to thirty-six men, forty-two riding animals, and fifty-two pack animals—crossed to the Columbia River drainage in two days, probably near Colockum Pass (which became a stagecoach route in 1865). McClellan had expected rolling pine country and was surprised at the view from 5,200 feet. He clearly did not anticipate the scene of "rugged and impassable" mountains to the north: "About west-northwest was a handsome snow-peak, smaller than Mount Baker; as it is not to be found on any previous map that I know of, and had no name, I called it Mount Stuart." Duncan wrote that "Mount Stuart is the most prominent, and is nearest the Columbia" and that the Stuart Range was the "sharp angular range of snow mountains" to the left of the trail.[63] Gibbs also described the Stuart Range: "The craggy sierra of the Cascades reared itself above the lines of forest into the limits of perpetual snow." He described larch trees "as much as three feet in diameter" and, commenting on the change in geologic character, wrote of "sharp peaks, rising singly or in groups, some of which seem to be the skeletons of mountains."[64]

In his search for a railroad pass, McClellan saw only the "rough mountains" toward the head of the Wenatchee drainages. Although he did not ascend the Wenatchee River or its branches, he reported that "it appears certain that there can be no pass at its head for a road." The expedition's map indicates that McClellan's information was limited. Gibbs's own report and map show that he had learned more about the Wenatchee: "The Pisquouse [Wenatchee] is a large and bold stream rising in the main divide of the Cascades, and interlocking with one of those running into the Sound. It passes through a lake, reported by the Indians to be larger than either of those on the Yakima."[65] Beyond the Wenatchee crossing, McClellan noted the watercourse issuing from "Lake Apq" (Chelan): "the lake itself is some thirty miles long, and is shut in by high mountains, which leave no passage along its margin." Gibbs added, quite accurately, that its height was 474 feet above the Columbia.[66]

While the expedition was at the Columbia River near Lake Chelan on September 25, a Spokane chief, Quiltanee, informed McClellan that, after paddling to the head of the lake, the Indians used a steep and poor foot trail "to the summit" and that "½ days travelling more brings them to the Scatchet [Skagit] River."[67] At Fort Okanogan, which the men reached two days later, McClellan characteristically rode to the hill behind the fort to obtain a view. He reported that Joe La Fleur, the HBC factor, "informed me that there was no pass between Mt. Baker and the Hudson's Bay Company's trail from Okinakane to Langley." There was, however, a foot trail that led from the Methow River to Puget Sound, and McClellan spent a week exploring that possibility. Following the Twisp River, a branch of the Methow, the party traveled to War Creek, "the north fork rising a few miles farther on in a high, bare ridge of granitic mountains." The south fork, which the Indians called "Nahai-el-ix-on," came down a narrow ravine, a route soon proven to be impossible for animals. McClellan wrote:

> The trail is said to pass from this ravine, over a very difficult country [War Creek Pass and Purple Pass], to the stream emptying into the head of Lake Chelan, then to cross very steep and lofty mountains at the head of that stream, and finally to reach the Skagitt river on the western slope.

Meanwhile, Duncan examined the upper Methow River. He returned with an unfavorable report, saying that he had continued on foot "until the roughness of the trail and the barometer assured him of its unfitness for a railroad."[68]

From the fort, McClellan continued into British territory, miscalculating his latitude and advancing far beyond Osoyoos Lake at the forty-ninth parallel. He learned about the route to Fort Langley; but after seeing the discouraging canyon of the Similkameen River, he went on to Okanagan Lake, which he called "Great Lake." McClellan finally concluded that the only practical route for a railway between the Columbia and the Thompson was the Yakima River.

Further Attempts

When McClellan met Governor Stevens at Fort Colville on October 18, there was surely an air of disappointment about not finding a satisfactory route through the Cascades. The eastern and western survey divisions, however, did share a night of conviviality and steak with Angus McDonald, the amiable factor at the HBC trading post.[69] Both parties traveled to Walla Walla, where they were chagrined to learn that the James Longmire immigrant party with more than one hundred men, women, and children and some fifty wagons had crossed Naches Pass six weeks earlier. McClellan's failure rankled Stevens. On November 5, he wrote to press the captain to try Naches Pass, reporting that "emigrants got thru 48 wagons in September" and promising "20 fat horses" for the trip. Stevens subsequently talked with A. Dominique Pambrun, who was in charge of the post at Walla Walla, and Peopeomoxmox, a Walla Walla chief. Both men assured the governor that Naches Pass was frequently open until December. Stevens wrote McClellan: "Mr. Pembrum's own father took a band of horses from Walla-Walla to Steilacoom, some years since, in the month of December; and I sent for and closely interrogated one of the voyageurs who was with the party, and who fully confirmed the statement of Mr. Pembrum."[70]

Nevertheless, McClellan firmly objected to another trek to Naches Pass. A frustrated Stevens notified McClellan that he would send Frederick W. Lander, a civilian engineer from Massachusetts who had been with the eastern survey division, to cross the range. Lander was hesitant as well, having heard a story about a wintry blizzard trapping a party in the mountains. On November 8, Lander sent a note to McClellan—who was now the commanding officer at

The Dalles—containing incorrect news about abandoned wagons and lost animals. McClellan replied the same day, declining to order Lander to proceed, and suggesting that he "ought to abandon it."[71] With considerable certainty, McClellan wrote: "I have done my last service [by going to the Snoqualmi Pass from the Sound] under civilians & politicians." Certainly, "I will not consent to serve any longer under Gov. S. unless he promises in no way to interfere—namely to give me general orders, & never to say one word as to the means, manner or time of executing them—even under those circumstances I should hesitate.[72] As McClellan took his party along the trail that followed the Columbia to Fort Vancouver, he met "Billy" McKay, whose account must have delighted him:

> One of the Priests from the Yakama told him [McKay] the other day that the Naches Pilgrims had abandoned all their wagons & lost all their animals—so I was right & Stevens wrong. He says too that there is plenty of snow in the Cascades & that no one ought to think of crossing now except on snow shoes—again the Gov. is wrong & I am right. I hope sincerely that Lander has been guided by my opinion & returned— I think he has.[73]

McClellan spent the next few months in Olympia making reports. His personal report to a discontented Stevens, which assumed that the snow depth in the passes rendered them impracticable for winter use, must have been a hard blow. While at Olympia, however, the governor learned that the story about immigrants having to abandon wagons near Naches Pass was false. Furthermore, no snow had fallen until November 3, and then only four inches. Stevens became even more determined, but who could he find to carry out his orders? In a December 12 letter, Stevens finally directed Lt. Abiel W. Tinkham to carry the line over "Snoqualme" Pass. Tinkham, a hardy assistant engineer with the eastern division, had been sent by Lt. John Mullan to explore Marias Pass in present-day western Montana. Since October 7, when he left the camp in Bitterroot, Tinkham had traveled three hundred miles on foot, so he was obviously in fine hiking condition.[74]

At the Catholic mission in Yakima, Tinkham engaged two Indian guides and the party set out on horses in bitter weather. On January 17, when the snow reached two feet, the horses were sent back and three more Indians were hired for the winter crossing, which was done on foot "and with snow-shoes when necessary."[75] At Keechelus Lake on January 20, the group spent the night in a snowstorm without a tent. Tinkham reported to Stevens on February 1, 1854:

> From Kitch-e-lus lake to the summit [of Yakima Pass], some five miles, and where occurs the deepest snow, the average measurement was about six feet. . . . The whole of the snow was very light and dry, deposited in successive layers of from one to two feet. . . . These snows present little obstruction to removal in comparison with the compact, drifted snows of the Atlantic States, and would cause very little detention to

the passage of trains. Passing on to the western slope of the Cascades, the snow rapidly disappears.[76]

The news of the successful crossing reached an elated Governor Stevens soon after Tinkham arrived in Seattle on January 27. While Stevens was impressed with the lieutenant's energy and judgment, McClellan judged that the winter of 1853–1854 had been a dry one. "I do not think that any important conclusion should be based on the results of Mr. Tinkham's trip," he wrote.[77]

Meanwhile, McClellan was directed to make one last attempt to find a pass, this time from the west. With Minter and a few others, he began without adequate preparations. Unable to secure horses and Indian guides at Steilacoom, the party took canoes on Puget Sound, then up the river system nearly to Snoqualmie Falls, camping there on January 7. Indians told McClellan that there would be about twenty-five feet of snow at the summit and that in about "two moons & a half" the snow would pack down so that horses or snowshoes could be used.[78] McClellan went forward on the trail with two Indian guides. The prairie was soon covered with snow and trail signs were obliterated; the snow was "unfit for snow-shoes, according to the Indians."[79] Although he did not reach the pass, McClellan did learn that it was improperly called "Snoqualme" and that the route went by way of the "Nooksai-Nooksai" (Cedar River).

McClellan's Report

McClellan's general report of his explorations on February 25, 1854, suggested that only two routes were practical for a railroad—the Columbia River and Yakima Pass. He had written Secretary of War Davis on January 31, 1854: "As a simple question of Engineering there can be no doubt that the main Yakima Pass possesses very decided advantages over the other." The survey had gathered sufficient topographic data to veto the Columbia River route because of rocky bluffs and the possibility of flooding. In March 1854, McClellan returned to Washington, D.C., to prepare his reports for Stevens, and Duncan was also there to complete his maps and sketches for the general report.

While McClellan had been eager to leave the range of glaciers—mountains too icy, treacherous, and hostile for his liking—for fame and other regions, Gibbs continued to document the Cascades. At the end of the great railroad survey, the foremost scientist of the region wrote this summary in his fieldbook:

> The Cascade range North of Mt Rainier apparently differs from the portion to the South of it. It is characterised by a back bone of bare & ragged rocks. . . . About the latitude of the Methow river, The range appears to divide[,] one running parallel with Puget's Sound, the other with The Okinakanie between which lies an interior basin of which nothing is known except that according to Indian account. The Skagit river

enters it from the west, probably it is drained from the north by the Nook sahk and a branch of Fraser's River. . . . Several points on the Cascade range nearly approach Mt Baker in Altitude. Mt Baker had been throwing out smoke during the whole winter. One of the men on the Sound told me that he had felt atmospheric vibrations, apparently accompanying jets of smoke.[80]

Gibbs remained in the Pacific Northwest after the railroad survey was completed, accompanying Stevens on a trip along Puget Sound northward to Victoria and also on Stevens's treaty-making expedition in western Washington in 1854. The next year, Gibbs was elected brigadier general of the Washington territorial militia, and he would serve with the American Commission of the Northwest Boundary Survey from 1857 to 1862.[81]

While nothing in Stevens's instructions to McClellan had specified which passes he was to explore, McClellan showed a marked reluctance to examine them. Except on the Lewis River exploration, McClellan failed to examine the west slope of the range carefully and completely bypassed both Stampede and Snoqualmie passes. As historian Philip H. Overmeyer observed, "Compared to the strenuous exertions of the eastern division under the personal command of the energetic Stevens, McClellan's expedition was a mere pleasure jaunt."[82] Yet, it must be remembered that mountain exploration was a new experience and was only a brief interlude in the lives of military officers such as McClellan. Hardships encountered in other terrains do not necessarily prepare a person for a new experience on steep, nearly alpine ground. Men such as Tinkham, Gibbs, Henry Custer of the Northwest Boundary Survey, and railroad explorers Daniel Linsley, Albert Rogers, and John Stevens apparently had exceptional resiliency for such experiences.

McClellan's exploration of the Cascades remains a valuable, pioneering achievement, one that brought geographic knowledge and maps to the public. He was the first to describe for the public much of the east flank of the range, including various watercourses, as far north as the forty-ninth parallel. No one—least of all Stevens—had had a clear notion of how formidable a barrier the Cascades would be, and many of the governor's instructions were impossible to carry out. McClellan had written Stevens that his examination of the passes was limited to a hasty reconnaissance "for the reason that that range was almost wholly unknown."[83] In fact, nothing whatsoever was known of the range between Yakima Pass and the Fraser River. McClellan believed it had been necessary not to delay, to seek the most important facts for each pass, then push on and search for others.

Jefferson Davis must have been aware of the incompleteness and hesitancy of McClellan's explorations, but he nevertheless praised him highly in his 1855 report to Congress on the railroad explorations: "The examination of the approaches and passes of the Cascade mountains, made by Captain McClellan . . . reflects the highest credit on the capacity and resources of that officer."[84]

Deciding on a Route

The Pacific Railroad Surveys, which marked a vital era in the exploration of the West, touched on many aspects of American life, including diplomacy, politics, science, and the process of settlement. The surveys had been on a grand scale—the greatest attempt ever made by the U.S. government to explore the vast, unknown western regions. Philip Overmeyer maintained that for the Pacific Northwest the expedition under Stevens's command was "second in importance only to that of Lewis and Clark." [85]

The massive *Reports of Explorations and Surveys, to Ascertain the Most Practicable and Economical Route for a Railroad from the Mississippi River to the Pacific Ocean*—known as the Pacific Railroad Reports—contained the correspondence and field journals of the various parties that explored the region between 1853 and 1855. The reports constituted a broad encyclopedia of western experience and knowledge, a summary of the information the Topographical Engineers and their scientific partners had gathered before 1857. Partly because prominent natural-history scientists traveled with the field parties, the reports revealed the geographical variety and expansiveness of the West. Nevertheless, the reports proved to be inconclusive regarding the "most practicable and economical route" through the Cascades. Instead, as William Goetzmann points out, "confusion was deepened and rivalry intensified by the most obvious results of the reconnaissance, which indicated . . . that not one but several extremely practicable routes existed." Miscalculations made by the Topographical Engineers, Congress, and the secretary of war in planning and carrying out the surveys doomed any plans for a federally sponsored transcontinental railroad before the Civil War. [86]

Jefferson Davis and Capt. Andrew A. Humphreys of the Topographical Engineers favored a thirty-second parallel route for the railroad. They and some other Corps officers looked unfavorably on the northern route, partly because Stevens had overstated its case and grossly understated its probable costs. They were also influenced by a later report by Frederick Lander about a route from South Pass to Puget Sound. In his report to Congress, Davis stressed the long tunnels that would be needed for a northern route and discussed the severe climate. [87]

Even some members of the Stevens party criticized both the route and the conduct of the expedition. Naturalist George Suckley wrote his relatives that "there was the greatest amount of disaffection in the command throughout amounting almost to open mutiny." He also commented on Stevens's ambition, judging "that his political fortunes are wrapped up in the success of the railroad making its Pacific terminus in his own territory." In regard to the route itself, Suckley pointed out that their railroad-examining engineer had delved into the difficulties that made a northern route both impracticable and expensive: two-mile tunnels, gullies, deep cuts, short curves, and long and heavy bridges. He made a telling comparison: "A road might be built over the tops of the Himaleyah mountains—but no reasonable man *might* undertake. I think the same of the Northern route."[88]

Construction finally began on the Northern Pacific Railway in 1870, and the line was opened to Portland thirteen years later. A line across the northern Cascades—the switchback tracks over Stampede Pass—was not completed until 1887, thirty-four years after the Topographical Engineers conducted their difficult search for the route.

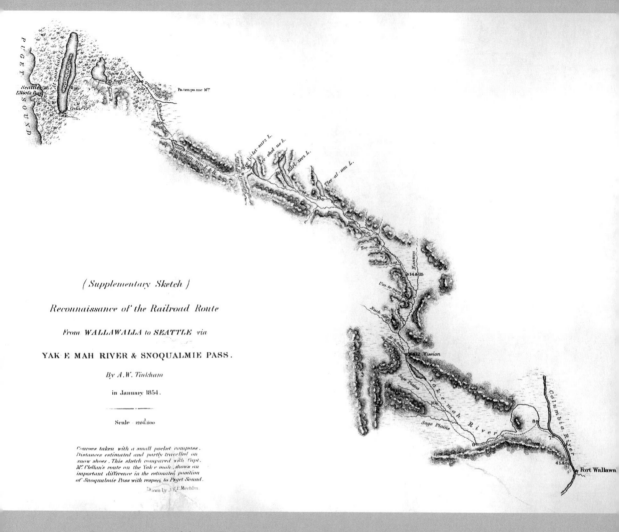

Reconnaissance of the Railroad Route from Wallawalla to Seattle via Yak-E-Mah River & Snoqualmie Pass, *by Abiel W. Tinkham, 1854 (from U.S. War Department,* Reports of Explorations and Surveys, *vol. 11, A.O.P. Nicholson, Washington, D.C., 1855–1860; OHS Research Library, OHS neg., OrHi 86965)*

4

THE FIRST WAGON ROADS

From these alpine pastures [of Naches Pass] the future will draw butter and cheese, pasturing migratory cattle there, when summer dries the scanty grass upon the macadamized prairies of Whulge.

—Theodore Winthrop

When Washington Territory separated from Oregon Territory on May 2, 1853, Olympia was made its new capital, brought into being to secure government aid for the territory's transportation problems. The first settlers of western and eastern Washington were isolated from each other by the scarcity of roads and trails as well as by the formidable Cascade Range, and most early travelers had to follow the river and saltwater networks. In his first message to the Washington territorial legislature, Governor Isaac I. Stevens urged that funds be appropriated for a road through a Cascade Range pass, perhaps up the "Scagitt" to Fort Colville.[1]

The need to connect the eastern and western portions of the territory, which was enlarged in 1859, grew ever more urgent. The army required wagon roads so that it could respond to attacks across the Cascade Range on short notice, and ranchers needed routes for cattle drives. In the end, mining booms contributed most to the building of wagon roads, as prospectors sought dependable routes to their claims. Throughout this period, military wagon roads were the backbone of the road system that connected settlements.

Naches Pass

The most direct link between the Puget Sound Basin and the Columbia Plateau was the Naches Pass route, a strategic pass on the range divide to the northeast of Mt. Rainier.[2] Native peoples had used Naches Pass for centuries as a link for trading, food gathering, and socializing. The Puyallup and Nisqually bands and the people of the White and Green rivers (today's Muckleshoot), who occupied west-slope valleys, communicated across the pass with the Yakama and Klickitat tribes who lived in the broad valleys adjacent to the eastern slope.

Early white travelers through Naches Pass included Pierre Charles and Pierre Bercier, who guided the 1841 Wilkes expedition, and the HBC's Pierre Pambrun and Cornelius Rogers, who explored the pass in 1839 and 1840. The pass was used for travel between HBC fur-trading posts, which were growing in size and importance, and Yakama Indians who drove cattle from the company's western forts across the pass to be grazed on the Columbia Plateau. Once, in 1855—two years after the wagon road opened—the HBC sent a large pack train carrying furs from the interior across Naches Pass to Fort Nisqually, but the company did not repeat this experiment (see chapter 2).[3]

The U.S. Army, under the direction of Capt. George McClellan, had planned to construct a wagon road from Walla Walla to Fort Steilacoom across Naches Pass in the fall of 1853, but that road was never begun. By July 1853, when a promised $20,000 appropriation from Congress had not materialized and McClellan had not appeared, impatient Olympia businessmen, headed by James K. Hurd, raised some $6,600 and organized a volunteer work group. The previous May, twenty-two-year-old Edward J. Allen had been selected to lead a citizens' reconnaissance party that would blaze a route along the forested White and Greenwater rivers. In July, assuming a leadership essential to the venture's success, he set out with the work group to widen the Naches trail into a wagon road.[4]

The route went by way of Connell's Prairie to the White River near present-day Buckley. With R.J. Allen as foreman and Andrew J. Burge as packer, the men spent over three months cutting a trail to the summit. Provisions ran low when they reached La Tête (a peak). At one point, when a bear scattered a cache of beans, rice, sugar, and bacon, the near-famished party had to wait while Burge returned to Fort Steilacoom to fetch more supplies.[5] On August 26, the adventurer Theodore Winthrop, on his trek to Naches Pass, spent a night in Allen's camp, where he met Lt. Henry Clay Hodges of the McClellan expedition who was crossing westward to Fort Steilacoom for supplies.

Allen's party finally crossed Naches Pass on October 15, as immigrant wagons waited close by for the road to be cleared. It was a memorable accomplishment, according to John H. Williams in his introduction to Winthrop's *The Canoe and the Saddle:*

> The "Citizens' Road" is entitled to be remembered less for the service it actually rendered than as an example of pluck and resourcefulness against apparently insuperable difficulties. When the delay and red tape of Captain George B. McClellan held back even the paltry sum of $20,000 which Congress had voted to build a hundred miles of mountain highway, the struggling settlers decided with amazing nerve to undertake it with their own money and labor.[6]

Despite the work party's heroic efforts, the Naches road was never popular. One reason was the need to cross the Naches River sixty-eight times—as James Longmire's immigrant group discovered in a crossing that may be the most celebrated event connected with Naches Pass.[7] In September 1853, the 148-member group from Indiana made the river crossings over four days. For subsistence beyond the Yakima River, the hungry party depended on thirteen bush-

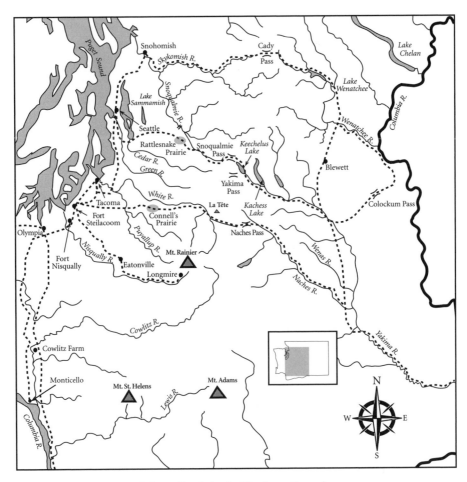

Wagon Roads in the Northern Cascades

els of potatoes they bought from Natives at Wenas Creek. The meadows near the pass provided great relief for two days and feed for the suffering animals.[8]

To the west was "Summit Hill," where the pioneers clambered down a hazardous bluff, lowering thirty-eight wagons, one at a time, for three hundred yards. George H. Himes described the effort:

> It was soon decided that the wagons should be lowered with ropes. . . . Accordingly a long rope was stretched down the hill, but it was not long enough to lower a wagon to a place where it would stand up. Then James Biles said: "Kill one of the poorest of my steers, make a rope of his hide and see if that will be long enough; if not, kill another."[9]

Three animals were killed before the length of rope required was secured. After each wagon was lowered to the end of the rope, a yoke of oxen was hitched to the wagon, and by rough-locking, and attaching small logs with projecting limbs to the rear, it was taken down and across Greenwater River a quarter mile. . . .

Only two wagons were lost. The immigrant party continued westward, making sixteen crossings of the Greenwater and seven crossings of the White River. Their first nutritious food was salmon they obtained from the Puyallup River, where the fish were easy to catch because of low water.[10]

Military Reconnaissance in Naches Pass

In 1854, anticipating problems with the uneasy Yakama Indians who were already conducting sporadic raids, the military again focused on Naches Pass roadwork. A renewed plan was entrusted to Lt. Richard Arnold. In May 1854, McClellan directed him to serve as a liaison for road contracts, with $15,380 remaining at his disposal from the 1853 congressional appropriation.[11] Arnold left Steilacoom with a small inspection party on May 23. He later reported:

> In this examination I travelled the road opened the previous season wherever it was passable, and made a reconnaissance of the entire route to Wallah-Wallah for the purpose of deciding upon the general location, and ascertaining how much of the road cut by the citizens during last season could be adopted.[12]

Arnold's party followed the citizens' route along the Puyallup River:

> Leaving this bottom the road passes alternately through small prairies and timber to White Water or St. Kamish river [the White River]. This stream is a perfect torrent, fordable only three months in the year, and even then the force of the current and exceedingly rocky bed, under the transit with pack-animals and wagons, both difficult and dangerous, particularly for emigrant stock that have crossed the plains. One of the most striking peculiarities of this stream is the milky color of the water, due probably to some earthy substance [glacier flour] found along the northeastern side of Mount Rainier.

Leaving the White River, the road turned to enter the Greenwater River Valley, where the stream often flows in a canyon.

> Near the junction of White Water and Green rivers there is a celebrated peak called La Tête. . . . This is an important point, as it forms the gate of the mountains to the west.
>   Four miles beyond, the only prairie between White Water prairies and the summit is found. This would afford some grass but for the numerous bands of Indians' horses passing to and fro from early spring until late in the fall. . . . With the exception of this prairie and La Tête, the entire valleys of White Water and Green rivers and the surrounding heights are studded with a dense growth of timber. . . . In many instances I noticed thrifty trees three and four feet through, one single shaft from two to three hundred feet high growing upon others much larger, and which, upon inspection, proved perfectly sound. This will give some idea of the amount of labor expended throughout this distance.

During the crossing of Naches Pass (geologically, a broad downwarp in the volcanic rock formation), Arnold reported:

> On my first reconnaissance (about the 28th May) I found four feet of snow for five miles, and in many places from six to ten. . . .
>
> While exploring the mountain I visited Mount Ikes [probably Pyramid Peak], a peak laid down by Captain G. B. McClellan, about 5,100 feet above the level of the sea, and situated near the divide separating the waters of Nahchess and the northern fork of Green river. The view from this peak was grand and extensive. To the west it commanded the valley of Green river and White Water to Mud mountain, and beyond the Olympic range, whose sun-capped peaks were distinctly visible, and the western border of Puget sound, plainly marked by the high clay banks; to the south, Mount Rainier appeared in all its majesty, still towering far above me, and not to exceed fifteen miles distant. . . .

The rest of the survey was not eventful, although the party did meet gold prospectors. Arnold commented that the excitement was unfounded, because the quantities of gold were insufficient to provide a miner's subsistence.

In his 1855 report, Arnold recommended "that the amount expended by the citizens of the Territory in 1853 be refunded. The greater part of the road cut by them from Steilacoom to the mountain has been adopted. But for this, I do not believe the work could have been carried forward as satisfactorily." Secretary of War Jefferson Davis decided not to pay the discontented territorial citizens the $6,000 they had requested for their voluntary work.

After Arnold's reconnaissance, Davis instructed him to adopt the Naches Pass route and immigrant road and to make another reconnaissance. The lieutenant made his second crossing of the pass in July, this time with naturalist George Gibbs as surveyor. Gibbs wrote in his journal that Williamson's Prairie, where a group of Klickitat Indians had a summer encampment on the White River, was a notoriously dangerous ford because the water sucks under the drift.[13] When they reached La Tête on July 6, Gibbs wrote: "It is a high & steep point of hill nearly bare of timber on the left of the trail, & it takes its name from a conglomerate rock resembling the head & neck of man, which stands on its side."

Recrossing the Green River, the party ascended La Tête on July 7, where they had a fine view. "Much to our surprise," Gibbs wrote, "Mt. Rainier bore from here S. showing it to be on the extreme west of the range, the whole pack of mountains lying to the east of it." Gibbs, who with his party was likely the first to traverse the high ridges north of Naches Pass (near Pyramid Peak), was now satisfied that the White River—not the Naches—headed on Mt. Rainier's east flank. He recorded their course:

> *July 8. Up Green River* We have now left white river and the [Naches Pass] road keeps up. Green R. [Greenwater River] crossing 14 times about half way to the foot of the first hills cross a branch comming in from the right half the size of the stream

apparently. Mr. Allen supposed this to be a part of the main river forming an island but it is not. It is probably formed by the union of the streams from the ridge we afterwards ascended. . . . White River comes in from the gap on the right, heading in Mt. Rainier on its eastern side. . . . A short distance beyond we struck the Klikatat [Naches Pass] trail & camped on it at the crossing of a brook. . . . Leaving the Indians here we took a south course up the brook to the top of the ridge on the right and then followed it S.Easterly to a high rock [probably toward Noble Knob] on the edge, for which we obtained a view across the valley.

July 9. We first followed the Klikatat trail [south of the Greenwater River] for some distance until satisfied that it was but a branch of the other, which perhaps avoids some of the crossings of Green River. We then struck S. up the ridge, again reaching a high point overhanging the valley & affording a view to N. & NE. . . . From the N.E. side Lt. Arnold continued along the crest until satisfied that this ridge joined that opposite to or south of us and that no pass existed between. . . .

July 10. We continue to skirt the hills keeping them to our right [south of the Greenwater River] for some distance until descending we struck the wagon road again near the last crossing of Green River.

The party then ascended the notorious hill that the Longmire immigrants had descended (the Cliff) and on July 11 moved up to "Summit Camp" (Government Meadows). Gibbs described crossing the pass and the eastward descent, how the wagon road crossed the Naches River fifty-two times and the balsam fir gave way to pines. On July 13, the men examined a route to Wenas Creek that they had heard would avoid the worst Naches crossings, but they found that "mountains were piled up in every direction—& much broken by rocky precipices." Arnold and his men had undertaken only minor work on the Naches Pass road, mainly adopting the track of the immigrant road. His lasting accomplishment was an odometer survey and map and the record of his traverse.

The last recorded immigrant use of the Naches route was in 1854, although small groups continued to cross the pass in the following decades. In early September 1854, a party under the leadership of Ezra Meeker followed the route taken by the Longmire immigrants, diverging from the Oregon Trail at Walla Walla. On the thickly forested descent from "Natchess" Pass, Meeker later wrote:

[the trees] were so numerous and so large that in many places it was difficult to find a passage way between them, and then only by a tortuous route winding in various directions. . . . In many cases, where not too large, cuts had been taken out, while in other places, the larger timber had been bridged up to by piling smaller logs, rotten chunks, brush, or earth, so the wheels of the wagon could be rolled up over the body of the tree.[14]

Hostilities between whites and Indians curtailed the movement of new settlers through Naches Pass in 1855 and 1856. Army and volunteer troops crossed the pass on at least three occasions, and it was across this pass that Nisqually chief Leschi retreated in March 1856, near the end of the war (see chapter 5). After hostilities ceased, when Native rights to most of the land in eastern Washington were reduced, cattlemen established their herds in the lush rangeland of the Klickitat, Yakima, and Kittitas valleys. Later, Naches Pass became a route for cattle drives to Puget Sound. The stockmen regularly cut out and maintained the road, and it was used for moving cattle and sheep into the 1880s. The Naches Pass road was also the first road across the Cascade Range to be shown on early military maps, such as the 1859 Topographical Engineers' map of Oregon state and Washington Territory.

Yakima and Snoqualmie Passes

Yakima Pass was used in early times by Native peoples and in the early nineteenth century by HBC traders as a pack trail. From the west, the trail ran from Nisqually to Rattlesnake Prairie and then followed the Cedar River and its north fork, crossing the pass to Lost Lake and Keechelus Lake.[15] In the summer of 1855, inspired by a report by Lt. Abiel Tinkham who had made a winter crossing of Yakima Pass in 1854, a large party from Seattle (including Judge Edward Lander) scouted this pass via Rattlesnake Prairie for a wagon road.[16] It was not until the next year, however, that the first documented crossing of Snoqualmie Pass took place. Reports indicate that in June 1856 Maj. J.H. van Bokkelen, a captain in a volunteer company, traveled thirty-five difficult miles from Snoqualmie Falls to the pass through brush, forest, and canyon, surviving for at least part of the time by eating the inner surface of spruce bark.[17] Van Bokkelen described the trail as he came from the west:

> After reaching the summit [Snoqualmie Pass], we lost the old Indian Trail and I took a road with a gradual slope to the south, with the intention of stricking Cichelass [Keechelus] Lake, which I struck after traveling fourteen miles. About four miles before I struck the lake I found an Indian trail which I followed to within one hundred yards of the lake. . . . The trail at this place runs into the lake, and the Indians in using this trail must either cross the lake in canoes or travel round the shores of the lake in the dry season.[18]

In the winter of 1859, the Washington legislature, at the request of people at a mass meeting in Seattle, pleaded with Congress to fund a wagon road across Snoqualmie Pass. In 1860–1861, the House of Representatives appropriated $75,000 to construct a military road over the pass from Seattle to Fort Colville, but Senate approval was blocked by the Civil War. By 1865, Seattle still had no road to the interior, and little help was anticipated from Congress or the state legislature. After a meeting of interested citizens in July, Arthur A. Denny (a leading pioneer and a founder of Seattle), Jeremiah W. Borst, William Perkins, and two unnamed Indians undertook the exploration of Snoqualmie, Yakima, and Naches passes, hoping to find a better way across the mountains than the Cedar River pack trail. Beyond Snoqualmie Pass, the account of their exploration is unclear, but when they returned two weeks later the men announced that they favored Snoqualmie Pass. Surprisingly, they also claimed to have been the first whites to make their way through Yakima Pass, a route virtually trackless and replete with windfalls.[19] Citizens responded by raising $2,500 for wagon-road construction and improvements, and some roadwork was completed. In October, a train of six wagons made it over the pass, although wagons had to be loaded on a log raft and poled across Keechelus Lake. In 1866, King County commissioners selected Snoqualmie Pass as the most practical route to the Yakima Valley. The county surveyed the route, and in January 1867 the legislature authorized $2,000 for the road on condition that the county would match funds. A wagon road of sorts was completed that October.[20]

Edmund T. Coleman, the English mountaineer who scaled Mt. Baker in 1868, accompanied Denny on an early crossing of Snoqualmie Pass. He described Snoqualmie Prairie as "a land flowing with milk and honey" and noted that the peaks at the pass had been named provisionally by Northern Pacific Railroad surveyors. Coleman was well aware of the confusion between Snoqualmie Pass and the higher Yakima Pass and observed that the HBC had been using Yakima Pass for fifty years. He also knew the hardships of crossing the pass. His pack animal sank into a hole up to its girth, and he concluded that "what is called a wagon-road is nothing but a rough uneven trail, full of obstructions, with the trees cut down on either side, very often barely wide enough for a wagon to be urged along."[21]

By the time the HBC's claims to the territory were settled in 1869, cities had grown enough in the Puget Sound region that it was profitable to run cattle drives across both Naches and Snoqualmie passes. Within another ten years, some four thousand head of cattle crossed Snoqualmie Pass from the Columbia Basin and Okanogan ranges. In the winter of 1882–1883, frequent use kept Snoqualmie Pass open, and by 1884 tolls were being taken for animals, men on horseback, and horses with buggies. The wagon toll road was completed to within five miles of Keechelus Lake in 1883.[22]

The transportation route from the Inland Empire to Puget Sound became more important as a rivalry developed between Seattle and Portland businesses in the 1870s. Through its control of the portages at The Dalles and the Cascades, the Oregon Steam Navigation Company enjoyed a monopoly on Columbia River transportation that was lucrative for its stockholders and exasperating for its customers. When the Snoqualmie Pass wagon road was finally opened in winter, there was an alternative to the expensive Columbia River route for getting stock to market. The arrival of the Northern Pacific Railroad ended the brief but vital era of wagon transportation across the mountains. By the end of 1887, the railroad had completed its Cascade Division, providing competition for the Oregon Steam Navigation Company (renamed the Oregon Railway and Navigation Company) for an outlet to tidewater.[23]

Snoqualmie Pass diminished in importance, even though motorized vehicles crossed it as early as 1898, and it was little used until Seattle made plans for the Alaska-Yukon-Pacific Exposition of 1909. The public rediscovered the pass when it was decided to hold a New York-to-Seattle auto race that year as part of the exposition, and county money was raised so that some 150 cars could cross the pass to the exposition. Eventually, new road surveys were made, and the legislature appropriated $350,000 to construct an automobile road over the pass. On July 1, 1915, Governor Ernest Lister dedicated the Sunset Highway, the first automobile highway and truly passable road across the northern Cascades.[24]

Other Passes

The earliest trail route north of Snoqualmie Pass was located north of Stevens Pass, which was not explored until later. In the fall of 1859, pioneer Edward T. Cady and a companion, a man named Parsons, ascended the Skykomish River's north fork to what is known today as Cady Pass. Because it was late in the season and the snow was deep, the two men were forced to return.[25] Subscriptions for roadwork over the pass were nevertheless taken in Snohomish City, although only about two months' work was done before the project was halted. In August 1860, Cady and Emory C. Ferguson of Snohomish crossed the pass with a pack train, bound for the Similkameen mines near the Okanogan River. Travelers to the goldfields in the northeast Cascades and pack trains crossing the range also used the pass.[26] Cady himself promoted the "Cady Pass Road," using a scow to freight supplies on the Snohomish River. Colockum Pass on the eastern slope of the Cascades was opened up in 1880, a year after a wagon trail was pushed from the Kittitas Valley to the mining camp of Blewett.

While early efforts to build military roads were made at Naches Pass and along the eastern shores of Puget Sound to Oregon Territory, it was largely civic enterprise that led to the construction of wagon routes across the northern Cascades. Industrious settlers later improved these roads and built further connections into adjacent west-slope valleys such as the Cowlitz, Nisqually, and Skagit. The military and citizens' roads served as springboards for further exploration of the mountains in the late nineteenth century. Prospecting fever would stimulate the building of the Whatcom Trail to the Fraser River and across the range near the International Boundary in 1858, as well as a much later expansion of wagon roads and trails into the important east- and west-slope valleys. Surveying for those communication routes in the northern Cascades would be financed largely by mining enterprises and the government.

Mt. Rainier from the Grande Prairie, Nisqually, West of Puget Sound, *watercolor by Henry James Warre, September 1845 (National Archives of Canada, C 26341)*

5

INDIAN WARS IN THE CASCADES

At this camp we found a number of snow shoes which it was supposed had been left by the Yakimas, sixty of whom had crossed over to the Sound under Qualston, the son [of] Owhi, and fought at the battle of Connell's Prairie last spring. Distance 12 miles.
—Capt. Walter W. de Lacey, 1856

The Indian wars of the 1850s flared from Puget Sound to areas far east of the Cascade Range. Their roots were in increasing immigration to Oregon, the 1847 killings at the mission run by Marcus and Narcissa Whitman near present-day Walla Walla, and the subsequent Cayuse war, which saw fighting from the Cascade Range to the Rocky Mountains. From 1855 to 1858, both regular army units and territorial volunteers conducted numerous expeditions across the northern Cascades or on the mountain flanks in pursuit of hostile Indians. The interior tribes reacted most against white settlement, fearing relentless immigration and a takeover of traditional lands and hunting grounds. The Puget Sound tribes, who had the closest relationship to early white settlers, felt less threatened and most were friendly (except for the Nisqually, many of whom had intermarried with Yakamas).

The Yakama tribe was initially blessed with its isolation from the main travel routes taken by incoming settlers. When Capt. McClellan's railroad-survey expedition reached the tribe's country in the summer of 1853—the first government expedition to do so—the cordiality with which he was greeted turned to suspicion and indignation when they heard a rumor that the "Great White Father at Washington, D.C. wished to buy their lands and open them up for white settlement." In the following year, Ow-hi, the powerful leader of the Upper Yakama band, warned Washington Territorial Governor Isaac Stevens that they did not wish to sell their lands and that they wanted to be left alone.[1] Despite the brewing tension, however, hostilities did not seem imminent. Lt. August V. Kautz, a regular army officer stationed at Fort Steilacoom who had made an effort to befriend and learn about the Indians, wrote McClellan in 1853 that they were "peaceable."[2]

This early period of non-Indian settlement of the new territory was filled with incidents, struggles, and dangers; and the large number of new arrivals was bound to result in a collision with those who had lived on the land for millennia. Tensions increased when gold discoveries near Fort Colvile attracted miners, who one report described as "not always over-scrupulous in regards to Indian property." When Stevens arrived in the territory in September 1853, he had to deal with a variety of problems among land-hungry immigrants, gold prospectors, and the tribes. Military action against the Indians was the predictable result of settlement pressures and treaties and became a reflex action following attacks on settlers.

The first agreement with the Indians, the Medicine Creek Treaty, was signed late in 1854 after negotiations between Stevens and the southern Puget Sound tribes. While the treaty surrendered lands in return for reservations, guarantees, and annuities, it was a hollow agreement and has been cited as a primary cause of the outbreak of hostilities.[3] The January 1855 Treaty of Point Elliott covered lands north of those ceded by the Medicine Creek Treaty. Stevens negotiated with the tribes north of Point Elliott on Admiralty Inlet to the forty-ninth parallel to relinquish their right to all lands eastward to the summit of the Cascade Range. The 1855 treaties that Stevens negotiated with Kamaiakan, a powerful Yakama chief, and the chiefs of allied tribes at the Walla Walla council were so poorly received by Native people that they merely intensified the hostility that had been kindled by the McClellan expedition. By the papers signed June 9, 1855, the tribes gave up 29,000 square miles of land, for which they received subsidies. When Stevens proclaimed that the ceded lands of the interior were open to settlement, a land rush ensued. Wagon trains passed through Indian territory on their way to Puget Sound and prospectors crossed Yakama lands, a violation of the treaty.

When the conflict erupted, Stevens sought the assistance of Maj. Gen. John Ellis Wool, commander of the Department of the Pacific, which was headquartered near San Francisco. Throughout the years of open conflict between whites and Indians in the Pacific Northwest, there was a bitter policy dispute between Wool and Stevens, who disagreed strongly over the causes and conduct of the wars. To begin with, the seventy-one-year-old Wool, who traveled to Fort Vancouver in November 1855 to direct the campaign against the Indians, appears not to have attached much importance to the problems of Washington Territory. As Pacific Commander, he was already burdened with a host of problems in California, where there were thirty thousand Indians and a small force of only a thousand men for the entire region. Furthermore, Wool placed full blame for the Indian troubles on the governors of Oregon and Washington territories, their militias (whom he thoroughly distrusted), and "the cupidity of whites." Convinced that Stevens was bent on exterminating the Natives and their traditional domain, Wool judged the Indians to be the innocent victims of war, and he blamed increased immigration and white encroachment for making it difficult to preserve the peace.[4]

Believing that the Indians would be peaceful if left alone, Wool preferred a defensive war with secure outposts, conducted by army regulars, and a plan to

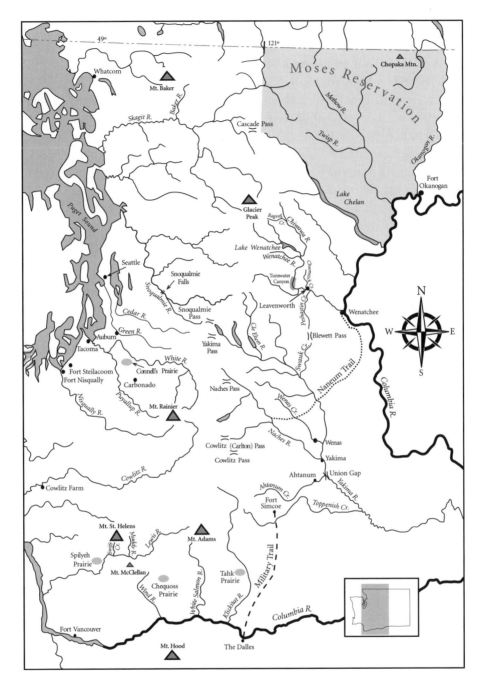

Indian Wars in the Cascades

isolate the "hostiles"—only two hundred of whom were under arms west of the Cascades. In his view, "the Cascade Range formed, if not an impassable barrier, an excellent line of defense, a most valuable wall of separation between two races always at war when in contact." He believed, therefore, that the plateau interior east of the Cascades should be declared off-limits to settlement.[5] Stevens claimed that Wool had joined hands with the Indian enemy. The general's policies revolted the governor, the territorial legislature, and the bulk of the settlers, who had few doubts about the justice of some acts of outrage against the Indians. Congress had offered the new settlers inexpensive donation land claims to make the journey west, and they expected the military to protect them.[6] They expected Wool to combine his troops with the volunteer militias of Washington and Oregon and to make short work of the Indians. Angered by Wool's inaction, Governor Stevens organized volunteer units to conduct his own campaign against the Indians.[7] Without question, Stevens had the welfare of settlers uppermost in his mind, but it is unlikely that he anticipated that less than a year after he took office armed conflict would have broken out on both flanks of the Cascade Range.

Conflict on the West Flank

The initial blow near the Cascade Range fell on settlers' homes in the White River Valley at the close of September 1855, when there were no troops nearby. As Chief Patkamim's Snoqualmie warriors swept through the forests from the Snoqualmie River to Connell's Prairie, then over Naches and Snoqualmie passes, white settlers on the White River and at other localities were killed and non-Indian travelers were endangered.[8] On October 18, Muckleshoot Indians killed nine settlers on the White River south of present-day Auburn. Out of a non-Native population in the territory of no more than four thousand persons, including women and children, over a thousand volunteers took up arms within weeks of the outbreak of what was termed the "hit-and-run" war. Territorial citizens were mustered into U.S. service under Capt. Maurice Maloney, whose unit traveled from Fort Steilacoom across Naches Pass. At the Naches River, Maloney learned by express about the White River attack and heard that the army regulars would not arrive at The Dalles for two weeks. He turned back west to Connell's Prairie (located south of the White River between present-day Sumner and Buckley).

A citizen battalion was immediately sent to the base of the mountains by way of the White, Green, and Cedar rivers. Lt. Pierre Charles, with a force of Chehalis and Cowlitz Indians, scouted the Newaukum and Cowlitz rivers and captured some Indians. Maj. Hamilton J. Mason and his command searched along the Nisqually River, leaving their horses and plunging into the forest. In surprise attacks, they killed a number of Indians hiking in the forest near Mashel Prairie and hanged two of them from an oak tree. On November 25, Lt. William A. Slaughter's small force in the White River Valley was attacked by Klickitat, Nisqually, and Green River Indians. On December 4, Slaughter was shot and killed by an Indian at a cabin near present-day Auburn.[9]

In February 1856, Capt. Maloney moved to the White River Valley with a hundred soldiers, where he was joined by Lt. Col. Silas Casey and two companies from Fort Steilacoom. Capt. Gilmore Hayes and one company of mounted volunteers rode to Naches Pass to assist troops under Major Gabriel J. Rains on the east flank of the range. Because of delays and uncertainty about the best strategic position, however, Hayes and his volunteers returned to the White River. There they learned that Leschi—a Puget Sound Indian who was related to the Yakama and who actively opposed efforts to displace the Indians—had gathered a force. When the troops arrived, Leschi and the other Indians had left, but a fight soon developed when a band from the upper Green and White rivers arrived to bolster Leschi's force. Meanwhile, an attack on Fort Steilacoom brought both regulars and volunteers for battle.[10]

Indians on the east flank of the range sometimes cooperated with Puget Sound Natives to attack settlements and frighten the newcomers into abandoning their locations. Crossing Naches Pass with snowshoes in the winter of 1855–1856, for example, Qual-chan led about a hundred men from the Yakama country to Leschi's camp near Lake Washington, but those bands who crossed to the west flank returned to defend their own land. Without support, the Indians on the west side broke into small groups that could do little more than strike at settlements from hidden retreats.[11]

In early March 1856, a large force of Indians attacked a detachment of regulars who were building roads on the west flank of the range toward the mountains. Fighting on the same ground as Lt. Slaughter had earlier, a command under Lt. Kautz drove off the attackers at White River Hill during an attempt to open the road to Connell's Prairie. A few days later, about 150 Indians attacked two volunteer companies who were at the White River crossing to establish a ferry and build a blockhouse. The Indians were defeated by volunteers under Hayes at the prairie, the final battle west of the Cascades in which Indians appeared in force.[12]

In a report to the secretary of war, Stevens suggested that he cross Naches Pass with two hundred horsemen and drive the Indians across the Columbia River. A volunteer force was located near Snoqualmie Falls, the governor noted, and another group was on the Cedar River to guard against surprise attacks from mountain passes.[13] Early in 1856, Stevens decided to erect a line of blockhouses to serve as supply forts along the Naches "military road" to make the pass route safer. The Pioneer Company made up of sappers (military personnel engaged primarily in construction) and miners was organized. They were a spirited group. According to Urban Hicks, one of their officers, "if we camped at night anywhere within twelve or fifteen miles of a barrel of whiskey or box of tobacco, more than half would be in camp the next morning."[14] Hicks later recalled that after completing the blockhouse on South Prairie (near present-day Carbonado), "about 25 of us" went on a scout toward the foot of Mt.

Rainier, taking along a young, friendly Indian as a guide and carrying guns, cartridge boxes, blankets, and two days' provisions. On the second day out, near the foothills, they found many cedar trees stripped of their bark and a track leading to an enemy settlement. There they had a shoot-out with the Indians, capturing or killing most of them. At the ranch they found items from the residences of families killed on the White River, and Hicks and his party burned the building. It was later reported that most of the depredations were the work of Yakama and Klickitat Indians who had crossed over from the east.[15]

Blockhouses were also built along the Snoqualmie River in early 1856, one at the foot of Snoqualmie Falls and another on Snoqualmie Prairie. In April, Governor Stevens ordered the volunteers' Northern Battalion to make a re-connaissance up "Cedar creek, going over into the Yakima Country."[16] Under a Capt. Smalley, the battalion ascended to Yakima Pass and camped there a few days while scouting ahead to determine where the Indians might be. In June, Maj. J.H. van Bokkelen and three or four men made the difficult crossing through Snoqualmie Pass (see chapter 4). After a fatiguing journey, the major joined the others at their camp and the battalion returned to its headquarters at Snoqualmie Prairie.

The end of the wars on the west flank came soon. Leschi led a retreat through Naches Pass to the Yakama country in March 1856 after the Indians' defeat at Connell's Prairie; he was later captured and executed. On May 19, 1856, Lt. Col. Casey reported that the war west of the Cascades was finished, and Maj. Robert S. Garnett's two companies were ordered to join Col. George Wright (headquartered at The Dalles) east of the range on the Columbia River. By August, the blockhouses were being used to guard portages and the roads that connected settlements. The Cascade Range, as Wool had predicted, had served as a line of defense.[17]

War on the East Flank

The discovery of placer gold near Fort Colville in 1855 sparked warfare east of the Cascade Range, for the route over Naches Pass led directly through land where the Yakama had always held exclusive domain. Kamaiakan, who had been a powerful Yakama chief since 1840, did not want miners in the region, and he sent messengers to both Naches and Yakima passes to tell whites not to come to the interior. Qual-chan, Ow-hi's son, threatened to kill any whites who passed through his tribal domain. The lure of gold was stronger than the fear of attack, however, and the warnings were largely disregarded.[18]

Although the open conflict between whites and Indians on the east flank was hastened when Qual-chan reportedly killed six miners at the Yakima River ford in August 1855, it was the killing of Indian agent Andrew J. Bolon in late

September that precipitated the army's first punitive expedition.[19] Major Rains, the commander at Fort Dalles, ordered Major Granville O. Haller of the Fourth Infantry to lead one hundred men and a howitzer to the Yakama country to make a show of strength and to cooperate with a force of fifty sent from Fort Steilacoom under Lt. Slaughter. When the men crossed the Columbia on October 2, they did not expect the Yakamas to be prepared for war.

The campaign began well for the Indians. An overwhelming force of more than one thousand men, led by Qual-chan, attacked Haller's force at Toppenish Creek. During the battle, which took place on October 6 and 7, the major and his soldiers escaped an ambush under the cover of night as a reported 250 warriors pursued them.[20] When the Yakamas learned that Slaughter's force was coming over Naches Pass to attack them from the rear, Qual-chan was dispatched to meet him with 250 warriors. Trader John Edgar, a guide and scout for Slaughter, met the advance in the Naches River Valley and, using a ruse, raced back to warn Slaughter and tell him of Haller's retreat. The soldiers turned back. Qual-chan hurried after them, but they were already out of range.[20] Rains then ordered all troops into the field, and settlers from both Oregon and Washington territories volunteered to join the force. With 334 regulars and some 500 volunteers, Rains crossed the Columbia on October 30 in a show of strength. The Indians fled, and there were few skirmishes.[21]

In early November, at Union Gap, many important chiefs and some three hundred warriors met the U.S. Army and for the first time confronted bugles, howitzers, and muzzle-loading, long-range percussion rifles. The guns scattered the Indians' stone defenses, and they retreated. Minor fighting resumed in the spring at the Columbia Cascades. About two hundred Klickitats and Yakamas crossed to the Lewis River, but settlers there received warnings of the pending attack from friendly Cowlitz Indians, and they fled.

In March 1856, Lt. Col. Benjamin F. Shaw and 176 mounted volunteers (with 107 pack animals and 25 packers) traveled from Fort Steilacoom across Naches Pass to Walla Walla to cooperate with Col. Wright's regulars. Shaw's offer of cooperation, however, was refused. The volunteers continued to traverse the Yakama country but found no resistance there. Shaw continued to the Grand Ronde Valley, where he knew about a large assembly of Indians; in a battle there, his volunteers killed about thirty Indians.[22]

Capt. Walter W. de Lacy, the expedition's topographer, wrote an account of their crossing of Naches Pass.[23] Although by this time a number of people had explored the pass, Shaw's expedition appears to have been the first large military operation to cross it. The battalion, which spent several weeks preparing for the march to the Yakama country, included a pack train of eighty-two animals, twenty-six packers to carry thirty days' worth of supplies, and twenty-three beef cattle. Six of the pack animals were loaded with ammunition. The volunteers set out on June 12 from Fort Steilacoom, crossing the Puyallup

River and reaching Connell's Prairie after seventeen miles.

On the second day, they crossed the White River and camped after twelve miles at Boise's Creek, where they had the last horse grass until they reached the foot of the pass. De Lacy described the events of June 14:

> Started late as some of the cattle had strayed during the night. Crossed Boise's creek and directed our course towards White River until we reached emigrant road on which we continued most of the day. The road was very rough and hilly, and in passing mud mountain, in horrible condition, a new mass of mud in which the animals sank up to their knees at every step; in fact the whole command led their horse most of the way.

It was necessary to cut trail along the river, for the water was too high for fords. It was fatiguing work.

> *June 16th.* Left Bear Prairie early. Soon after again encountered Green Water. This stream we crossed 17 times before commencing the ascent to the Natchess Pass. It is of course like all mountain streams, rapid and brawling, and in some place difficult to cross. Leaving it, we commenced the ascent, which the road being in excellent order was accomplished in safety; and about 2 P.M. we reached the summit of Natchess Pass, where we encamped on a prairie of tolerable dimensions, and could let our poor animals have, what they much needed, a good feed. At this camp we found a number of snow shoes which it was supposed had been left by the Yakimas, sixty of whom had crossed over to the Sound under Qualston, the son [of] Owhi, and fought at the battle of Connell's Prairie last spring. Distance 12 miles.

At the summit, snow covered the ground for two miles, but it had sufficient firmness to support the animals. De Lacy reported: "Pioneers were sent forward to clear away trees which had fallen across the road and spies two or three miles in advance to see if there were any lurking Indians about." Now that they were in enemy country, Col. Shaw designated a regular marching order.

> *June 18th.* Packed up and started down the Natchess. For a few miles our route passed through a succession of beautiful prairies in the different bends of the stream which we crossed a number of times. We then entered a canyon with high basaltic walls. . . . No Indians were seen and a good camp was found. . . . Distance 20 miles.

The battalion marched down the Yakima and then overland directly southeast to the Columbia River. This was rolling land without water but with "most magnificent grazing for thousands of animals." On June 30, the volunteers moved up the Columbia, nearing Fort Walla Walla. On the riverbank they discovered two Indian canoes, on which they fired. This led to a battle in the Grand Ronde Valley, far from the Cascade Range.

The Wenatchee River Expedition

In June and July 1856, Col. Wright took a force of 450 men to the upper Yakima

River on a reconnaissance and peacekeeping expedition. Wright believed that peace could again reign if the Indians could understand their reservation status and not listen to "radical" chiefs. Following Wool's policy, he made serious attempts to pacify the Indians, maintaining that the Yakama needed all their country.[24] By July 2, Wright had apparently approached Yakima Pass, then traveled eastward, probably via Swauk Creek and over Blewett Pass. He reported:

> On the 3d instant I broke up my camp on the Upper Yakima, near the Snoqualimi pass, forded the river without accident, marched five miles and halted for the night. Marching at sunrise on the 4th, our course lay east of north, following a tributary of the Yakima, until I reached the base of the Mountains.[25]

Route details are vague except for mentions of stream crossings and fallen trees on the trail. On July 6, the force "ascended a high mountain" overlooking the Wenatchee Valley. Wright probably descended Peshastin Creek to the Wenatchee River, where he learned of the fisheries in the vicinity. There were Indian families at a nearby fishing camp (probably near present-day Leavenworth), as well as a priest, Charles Pandosy, and some friendly chiefs. The colonel then descended the Wenatchee to the Columbia.[26]

There was a continuing problem in 1856 with prospectors coming from Puget Sound to the Columbia River region and then traveling on to British Columbia. Because of continued sporadic fighting between whites and Indians, there was still a need for military protection. Fort Simcoe, located on the Yakama reservation and established at Gen. Wool's suggestion, was made the permanent military post for the Yakama region in August 1856.[27] The post was to command Naches Pass, observe troublesome Klickitats, and reduce pressure on the army. To reach Fort Simcoe and the Yakama country, military units had to take a steamer from Fort Vancouver thirty-five miles up the Columbia to the Cascades, make a portage, take a steamer to The Dalles, and then follow a military trail to the fort, thirty-eight miles southwest of Yakima.

Before Gen. Wool left the territory in early 1856, placing his command under Col. Wright, he had issued a fateful proclamation that excluded settlers from all lands east of the Cascades. This edict, which miners generally disregarded, drew Stevens's wrath. Despite the closure, the interior was becoming more and more important to outside interests because of gold discoveries. Brig. Gen. Newman S. Clarke, Wool's replacement, reiterated the settlement and travel policy in Indian country, and the Indians generally halted attacks until 1858. Clarke believed that collisions with Indians would bring on a war if such numbers of men continued crossing Indian land to the goldfields.[28]

The Wenatchee and related northern tribes had not been actively involved in the Yakama war of 1855, but Quil-ten-e-nock (a brother of Quetalican, also known as Chief Moses) swore to avenge wrongs committed by whites. In June 1858, with Qual-chan and twenty-five warriors, he attacked a company of miners who had traversed tribal lands and were camped opposite the mouth of the Wenatchee River. In the attack, which ended in shootings on Squilchuck Creek, Quil-ten-e-nock and one miner were killed.[29]

The remaining miners struggled back to Fort Simcoe and shared their tale with Maj. Robert Selden Garnett, the fort's commander. There was an outcry from territorial residents, who demanded that the army take immediate action against the attackers. Both Stevens, now a territorial delegate to Washington, D.C., and Gen. Clarke believed military intervention was necessary to subdue decisively the interior tribes. Clarke's immediate objectives were to punish the Indians (believed to be among the Yakamas), who had attacked the miners as well as those who had defeated Col. Edward Jenner Steptoe in the Palouse country in May; to impress on the tribes the inviolability of the lives and property of whites; and to force the tribes to deliver the offenders. The views of Garnett, who was originally from Virginia and a Mexican War veteran, illustrate how seriously the army took the situation. The major thought that the Indians were "forever compromised against us" and that hanging was "the only radical remedy for the case."[30] Clarke planned a two-front offensive: Wright would travel toward the Spokane area with seven hundred men, and Garnett would head north near the mountains to catch the enemy in a "pincer." The Indians' ability to disperse and evade, however, made such a hope largely illusory.

In early August, Garnett received his orders at Fort Simcoe: subdue the Yakamas and Wenatchees, going as far north as Okanogan and hunting out those who had attacked the miners.[31] On August 10, setting out with four companies—314 men and 225 pack animals—the major intended to follow Wright's 1856 route to the Wenatchee River. On the fourth day, Garnett's Yakama scouts informed him that several of those who had attacked the miners were camped with a band up the Yakima River near present-day Cle Elum. The first action was to rush the Indian encampment in the dark. During the confusion, Lt. Jesse K. Allen was inadvertently shot and killed by one of his own men. Three Indians suspected of complicity in the killings were tied to trees and shot, and two more were shot in an escape attempt.[32] In all, twenty-one Indians and seventy horses were taken in the raid.

On August 16, the command moved to Cle Elum Lake. There Capt. James J. Archer and a mounted party explored beyond the lake, finding beautiful flowers but no hostile Indians. Garnett then returned to the Kittitas Valley to divide his forces, so that if one command found the enemy it would drive them against the other. Garnett traveled with the main force over the Wenatchee Mountains by the Naneum Trail (which led from present-day Ellensburg past Naneum Peak to a height of 5,786 feet), arriving at the Wenatchee River on August 20. Lt. George Crook, Lt. James K. McCall, and Lt. Thomas T. Turner, with about a hundred men, took another route to the Wenatchee River to a traditional fishing location, where the families of Ow-hi and Moses were camped on the Columbia opposite the Wenatchee River. Qual-chan was recovering from wounds sustained in the scuffle with the miners, while Moses continued to harass miners traveling north.[33]

As Ow-hi and Chief Moses fled eastward, Garnett learned from his scouts that more of the men he sought were camped on the upper Wenatchee River among friendly Indians who were fishing and picking berries.[34] Garnett's August 30 report to Mackall gives the official version of the Wenatchee River expedition:

> We arrived in this camp on the 20th inst. On the following day I despatched a party of sixty men under Lieut. Crook 4th Infantry with Lieuts. McCall and Turner of the same Regt. to follow up the principal branch of this stream into the mountains where it was understood some eight or ten of the hostiles were secreted. On the third day out this party through the instrumentality of the friendly Chief Skimawaw and some of his people, succeeded in entrapping five of these men. They were shot in compliance with my orders. Some incorrect information as to the locality of the remaining hostiles and a shortness of rations compelled this party to return. They got in on the 24. On the next day I put another party of sixty men in motion under Captain Frazier and Lieut. Camp. 9th Infy. to hunt up these remaining men. After clambering over mountain trails the difficulties of which can only be conceived of by one acquainted with this region of country this party came upon the hiding place of these fugitives, but only a few hours after they had been warned and taken flight. They were followed through the mountains with great labor for two days but on the third day their trail was lost and could not be recovered. This party returned yesterday.[35]

Lt. Crook describes his search for the fugitives in his autobiography. With his company of about sixty men and two Indian guides, he set out on August 21 just before dusk, eventually crossing a ridge in the darkness to reach the Wenatchee River torrent. There, perhaps near present-day Plain, some of his men were nearly swept off their pack mules.[36] Turning up the right bank of the river, the expedition entered timber. In the tangle, they had to discharge their guns so that ten men who had gotten lost could find the command.[37] Crook recounted his experiences after starting up the riverine terraces of the lower Wenatchee:

> The trail lay mostly on bottom covered with a dense forest, a species of redwood; much fallen timber. Our trail was circuitous. For instance, we could come to a fallen tree at right angles to our direction, and would have frequently to go a hundred feet to get over the trunk and return again within ten feet of the place we started. When you add to this the soft condition of the ground, with frequent bog holes that our animals would almost go out of sight in, and every few yards a yaller jacket's nest, the inmates of which would cause some grand and lofty tumbling amongst the men, you can form some idea of the fun we had that day.[38]

The "cavorting, snorting, kicking & jumping stiff legged mule" behind Crook's

lead animal created a scene "better than a circus."
After leaving the swamp, the party reached higher and more open ground.

> Just out of this swamp & on the trail were three ponies grazing around with saddles
> & bridles on, we didn't know what to make of it, but the ponies were left undisturbed.
> We had not travelled far on the trail before we came upon a young Indian standing by
> the side of his pony leaning on a gun known as the Queen Bess gun, a long smooth-
> bored rifle sold by the Hudson Bay Company. This Indian was fully six feet high & as
> straight as an arrow, he stood like a statue not even moving a muscle in his face or
> uttering a word, his eyes not fixed on us but past us as tho he wasn't aware of our
> presence. It was some time before we could induce him to talk & even then would
> only answer our questions categorically.[39]

In time, Crook managed to get the man to disclose that he was the son of Chief
Skimawaw and that the horses belonged to some of the men Crook was seeking. His father's camp—where the fugitives were—was a few miles ahead on an
island in a side stream, probably in the lower Chiwawa River area. Aware that
an ambush was planned, Crook, within "a couple of miles of their village,"
dismounted and deployed his men to prevent being taken by surprise. Reasoning that an attack on the village would be futile and dangerous, he explained to
the young chief that a fight would kill men on both sides, including Indian
friends; that it was wrong for his people to harbor the murderers; and that
they could not afford to be his enemies. Crook's account reports that he "suggested that he go to their camp & quiet the fears of the renegades, take his
father to one side & tell him all that I had told him & above all things to keep
the whole business a secret & then bring his father down to my camp." The
suspense was great, but soon the chief arrived. He was followed by numerous
other Indians, including some of those who had attacked the miners. Crook
reported: "The next morning after sun up they would come down with their
people on the pretense of trading salmon with the soldiers & doubtless the
murderers would be of the party."[40]

The soldiers camped that night on the banks of the swollen river, with "overhanging boughs slushing in the angry waters."[41] Each man had one blanket
behind his saddle.

> On the opposite side of the river, rocky crags rose abruptly over 1,000 feet above us,
> with shafts and pinnacles shooting still far above these again, all denuded of vegeta-
> tion from the base of these crags. Some three or four hundred feet above us the
> detached rocks assumed their natural slope to the water's edge. It had rained often
> during the day, and now at dusk it commenced a steady pour. The whole scene made
> an impression not soon to be forgotten.[42]

In the morning, after the Indians entered the company's camp, Crook reportedly proceeded with the charade and "four men were captured." Crook had the
men pinioned, then turned the "execution" over to Turner. Soon after, the
company mounted their animals and headed back to their camp beyond the

dense timber.[43]

After the expedition returned to Garnett's command, Capt. John W. Frazier was dispatched to seek out remaining hostiles. The soldiers negotiated difficult trails and, led by their Yakama guides, continued up the Chiwawa River. On the third day, the retreating Indians in the valley of Raging Creek reached a ravine, where their leader, Quo-lask-en, made a log bridge over which their horses and families could pass. The Indians then destroyed the bridge and escaped.[44] Garnett's information was that there were now only six Indians at large who had been involved in the attack on the miners; ten had already been caught and shot. He was pleased with the results:

> The summary treatment of these men has very badly scared all the Indians in this region and I am of the opinion that even if the expedition should meet with no other success and I fear this will be the case it has already produced a very salutary effect upon these Indians. I think that they will not again be so readily induced by the mere prospect of plunder into an attack upon Whites.[45]

Some skirmishes did occur after Garnett's campaign. Some of the fugitive Indians were still at large in the mountains to the west; the others, who fled east of the Columbia, were with Ow-hi, Qual-chan, Moses, and Skloom. Kamaiakan escaped north of the border and later joined the Palouse tribe. Qual-chan was seized and hanged. Ow-hi surrendered on September 24 and was later shot near the Snake River when attempting to escape.[46]

The Moses Reservation

When Col. Wright announced in late 1858 that his campaign would end, peace was restored in the minds of the new colonists. In March 1859, the U.S. Senate ratified the Stevens treaties. White settlers soon began staking land east of the Cascade Range, even though no territorial survey of public lands had been initiated. To preserve order, the Moses (Columbia) Reservation was created by executive orders in 1879 and 1880, leaving Chief Moses an area from east of Lake Chelan to the Okanogan River, north to the International Boundary, and west to the Skagit River. A supplemental order in 1880 extended the reservation to the south shore of Lake Chelan. The reservation was intended for the permanent use of and occupation by the chief, his people, and other friendly Indians, and settlers were not allowed entry. The Indians were told to settle there and not leave without the consent of the commissioner of Indian affairs and were never to engage in hostilities against the United States or other Indian tribes.

A presidential order opened the Moses Reservation to the public in 1886, settlers and prospectors soon moved in, and considerable prospecting near Palmer Mountain and Chopaka Mountain led to an important tungsten mine discovery in 1904. A few problems persisted between settlers and Indians west of the Cascades. Skagit Indians who had been driven from the lower river, for example, believed the land east of the Baker River was theirs, that they had never ceded it to whites. In October 1880, Dudley S. B. Henry, a U.S. deputy surveyor, was threatened on the Skagit River. Lt. Thomas W. Symons, who took a company of soldiers to the Baker River and met the Indians on October 18, believed that they planned trouble and that the trail they had built that summer across Cascade Pass to Lake Chelan was intended for obtaining aid from Columbia River Indians. Symons negotiated with the Indians, reaching an agreement that would allow surveys to the Sauk River while the troops remained.[47]

As this period of army activity ended in the Cascade Range and on its flanks, the mountains themselves still remained largely a mystery. The military men, including the territorial volunteers, had mostly satisfied themselves with pursuing Indians and occupying posts on both sides of the range. They had learned few of the mountains' secrets and made no detailed maps of pass routes. With the end of the Indian wars, however, settlers and other explorers could now pursue their activities relatively unhindered by fear of violence.

Mount Baker, from the Fraser River, *sketch by Edward P. Bedell, c. 1859. Note the HMS* Plumper *and an American steamer carrying gold prospectors on the river (from Richard Charles Mayne,* Four Years in British Columbia and Vancouver Island: An Account of Their Forests, Rivers, Coasts, Gold Fields, and Resources for Colonisation, Murray, London, 1862; *OHS Research Library, OHS neg., OrHi 84016)*

6

A MOUNTAINOUS CROWN COLONY:

BRITISH COLUMBIA AND THE CASCADES

[The Fraser region] is so wild that I cannot find words.
                                    –Simon Fraser

In the fall of 1807, Simon Fraser received instructions from the North West Company to explore the elusive "Tacoutche Tesse" (the Fraser River) to its mouth and to continue Alexander Mackenzie's courageous westward explorations. For both political and economic reasons, it was vital to find new overland supply routes for the various company posts and to determine whether furs could be shipped to the sea by this river. Fraser, who was thirty-two at the time, set out on a perilous and historic mission to explore the river that Mackenzie had explored in 1793 and had believed was the Columbia.[1] The Columbia River was much in people's minds at the time, especially since Mackenzie had given discouraging reports about the overland route to Bella Coola on the Pacific. By finding a usable water route to the ocean, the British might establish rights to the entire Columbia River region, which had been placed in political jeopardy by the successful American expedition led by Meriwether Lewis and William Clark in 1804–1806.

After building three trading posts in what he called New Caledonia (an area of present-day British Columbia west of the Rocky Mountains) from 1805 to 1807, Fraser began the journey that immortalized his name on May 28, 1808. He set out from Fort George, now the city of Prince George, on what would be only the third recorded journey from the interior to the Pacific. In addition to Fraser, the party included Jules Quesnel, John Stuart, nineteen voyageurs, and two Indian guides traveling in four canoes. Along the deeply incised river, with its flanking cliffs and terraces, Fraser frequently abandoned the canoes for the hazardous and intricate footpaths used by local Indians.[2]

By June 19, Fraser had reached present-day Lytton (then Thlikumcheen, the Great Fork). At the Thompson Indian village there, Fraser reportedly shook hands with over twelve hundred people. From there the group began their adventure down the unknown and dangerous Fraser Canyon. Canoe travel was impossible, and the men inched their way over narrow ledges on precipitous cliffs, crossing some by means of crude ladders made by local Indians. Sometimes poles hung suspended like Jacob's ladders from rock walls, fastened by withes (tough, supple twigs). Near Hells Gate, Fraser commented that he had "never seen any thing to equal this country. . . . We had to pass where no human being should venture."[3]

On June 27, the party passed Spuzzum Creek, where hospitable Indians fed them salmon cooked in wooden vessels on hot stones. Three days later, they passed the Chilliwack River and saw "a round Mountain a head which the natives call Shemotch" (Sumas Mountain). The "Rugged Mountains all around" that Fraser noted on July 1 included the Cheam Range (a northern subrange of the Cascades). Fraser now realized that the river could not be the Columbia, for he knew that river's latitude at its mouth was 46°21', and he was north of 49°. Despite his frustration that the "Tacoutche Tesse" was not the Columbia or a navigable substitute, as he and others had assumed, Fraser did demonstrate that the two rivers were distinct and that the Fraser "emptied into the Strait of Georgia in the vicinity of 49° N—the very area where, sixteen years before, English and Spanish navigators had seen evidence, but could find no river."[4] It was a fitting act of toponymy that the Fraser was later named for him.

Exploring British Columbia

British Columbia was one of the last frontiers in the exploration of North America. Although Spanish and British navigators had landed on Vancouver Island in the late 1700s and Mackenzie and Fraser had voyaged on perilous rivers, further explorations were left to the fur traders. A half century was to pass after Fraser's trip before the British government sent out a serious exploring expedition.

Gold discoveries on the Fraser and Thompson rivers in 1856 drew the attention of the government to that vast, little-known territory, which for decades had remained in the exclusive possession of the Hudson's Bay Company. Although Sir George Simpson, the HBC governor, believed the Fraser River was not a good transportation route, he had long dreamed of the British Empire dominating the Pacific Ocean and the company playing a major role in it. Even before the government decided to take the southern portion of British North America out of company hands, he had thoughts about constructing a road or railway through the territory "to the blooming west."[5]

In May 1857, the British government sent Capt. John Palliser to report on the feasibility of a trade route. Although he did not venture into the Cascade Range, Palliser strongly affected its history. He made adverse statements over several years about the new boundary line along the forty-ninth parallel, which isolated British possessions west of the Rocky Mountains from those to the east and which barred a portion of them from access to the ocean. He thought that the only useful commercial route from the interior of what would become British Columbia was that traditionally used by HBC traders—the Okan-

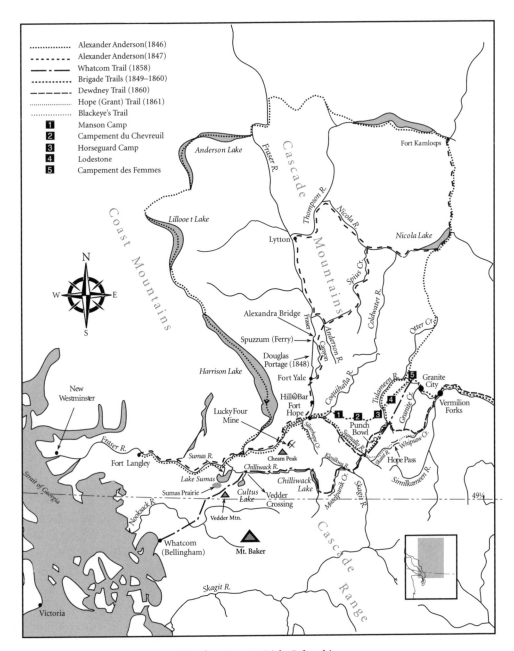

Legend:

- ·············· Alexander Anderson (1846)
- - - - - - Alexander Anderson (1847)
- — · — Whatcom Trail (1858)
- ◂◂◂◂◂ Brigade Trails (1849–1860)
- — — — Dewdney Trail (1860)
- ·············· Hope (Grant) Trail (1861)
- ·········· Blackeye's Trail
- **1** Manson Camp
- **2** Campement du Chevreuil
- **3** Horseguard Camp
- **4** Lodestone
- **5** Campement des Femmes

Southwestern British Columbia

ogan Brigade Trail from the Thompson to the Columbia. The Palliser expedition also examined the Rocky Mountain passes between the International Boundary and the source of the Athabasca River, passes that were known only vaguely to fur traders and even to the Indians in the region.[6]

The Gold Rush of 1858

The Fraser River gold rush began soon after the HBC steamer *Otter* shipped 800 ounces of gold dust from Victoria to the U.S. Mint in San Francisco in February 1858. When the startling news broke, there was a rapid exodus of miners from California—where the frenzied 1849 gold rush had waned—and a stampede to Victoria and Whatcom (present-day Bellingham) on Bellingham Bay. In one day alone, 1,732 persons sailed north from San Francisco.[7]

The first 450 miners arrived in Victoria on April 25, which had begun the year with no more than three hundred inhabitants. Governor James Douglas derisively suggested that the newly arrived were "a specimen of the worst of the population of San Francisco." He later commented: "Crowds of people are coming in from all quarters—The American steamer 'Commodore' arrived on the 13th Instant from San Francisco with 450 passengers and the steamer 'Panama' came in yesterday from the same port, with 750 passengers." Victoria had become a boom town and soon came to have much in common with the American Wild West. If we believe one report (likely far exaggerated), the number of gold seekers exceeded thirty thousand by mid-July.[8] Young Lt. Charles William Wilson, arriving for Northwest Boundary Survey duty, recorded his first impressions on July 13, 1858:

> Vancouver Island itself is most beautiful, but turned quite upside down by the gold discovery, a regular San Francisco in '49. You are hardly safe without arms & even with them, when you have to walk along paths across which gentlemen with a brace of revolvers each are settling their differences; the whiz of revolver bullets round you goes on all day & if anyone gets shot of course it's his own fault. . . .[9]

The miners had arrived by ship, but it was still another 160 difficult miles to the Fraser River sandbars and the goldfields. The *Beaver* and the *Otter*, HBC coastal steamers, were incapable of stemming the river's current, and boats were in such short supply that some miners crossed the Strait of Georgia in Indian dugouts. Enterprising American skippers brought paddle wheelers to the Fraser, but passengers had to be prepared to haul towropes if the current became too fast. The Fraser River—a portal Simpson questioned—had become an important trade route to the rich interior with its gold and furs. Although Douglas was not yet governor of mainland British Columbia, he ordered that all ships entering the Fraser must first call at Victoria, be given a license from the HBC officer there, and be passed by customs.[10]

At one time, some three thousand frustrated men were camped at the new town of Whatcom because there was no trail to the Fraser or the interior. "Some thousands of men were waiting there at that time in the greatest dilemma," one observer wrote, "not knowing which way to proceed to the new mines." The Fraser was running high, but "many would form in companies, buy a canoe, lay in from three to six months provisions, and start, working their way as far as possible, until the river fell."[11] Others waited for a proposed Whatcom Trail to be built across the range. The winding channel and shifting shoals at the Fraser's mouth made it difficult for the larger vessels to enter; but past the bar, the river was navigable as far as Fort Langley, thirty-two miles upstream. Flat-bottomed craft could make it forty more miles to Fort Hope, and some were able to reach Fort Yale, another thirteen miles, and the site of the first rapids. George Gibbs, who was then with the Northwest Boundary Survey, observed that many distracted miners who were camped that spring along Fraser bars found the trails to be very poor and boat passage often insufficient.[12] Discouraged by the obstacles, some returned to California.

The difficulties of traveling on the Indian trail along the Fraser's banks to Fort Yale and the Thompson River are revealed in a letter from prospector John Ledell to a Whatcom newspaper. Ledell, whose weight dropped from 165 to 125 pounds during the journey, described it as "the most awful trail that was ever travelled by a human being. The greater part of the way we climbed over rocks."[13] The gold seekers had other troubles as well. It was reported that the HBC sold some old, worthless pack animals for from $150 to $200 to eager purchasers, and some Indians reportedly stole food and other provisions.

Despite the difficulties, the rush was fanned by the dramatic news that some Californians had discovered a rich bar—Hill's Bar—a mile and a half below Yale. It quickly became the richest site in British Columbia. In a single day in August 1858, miners recovered over eight hundred ounces of gold, and the bar yielded some $2 million in placer gold before the rush ended. The sandbars of the Fraser were alive with tent camps. By summer, there were reportedly over a hundred bars along the Fraser between Hope and Lytton where placer gold had been taken. The names of the bars—names such as Boston Bar, New York Bar, Texas Bar, American Bar, and Union Bar—reflected the predominance of Americans on the scene.

There were many enterprising miners on the river. Volkert Vedder and Jonathan Reece, both from California, took the trail from Whatcom to Sumas and then to Squihala, an Indian village on the Chilliwack River, where they found encamped the American party of the Northwest Boundary Survey. The miners discovered, as had the surveyors, that nearby Sumas Prairie provided good feed for pack mules.[14] Vedder settled in the region, and several geographic features bear his name, including Vedder Mountain and Vedder Canal.

Another early prospector was Urban E. Hicks, who with three others purchased a canoe, loaded it with provisions and mining tools in Olympia, Washington Territory, and headed north on Puget Sound. When they arrived in Whatcom in early June 1858, they found some two thousand miners, most of them from California, camped in tents around the mud flats and wharves. The Hicks party continued by water to the Fraser, where they encountered a British gunboat stationed there to collect a mining tax. Hicks evaded the ship's boat that was sent after them and started up the Fraser. He later remembered:

> On reaching the first rapids in the river (after passing Fort Langley) we came to a large ranch of Indians camped on a low island or sandbar. The whole camp was on a platform erected near the middle of the river, about ten or twelve feet in height, where they lounged and slept, to get above the immense swarms of mosquitoes that rose from the surface of the water in clouds that fairly darkened the sun and stifled the breath. I have seen mosquitoes on the Mississippi bottoms, but nothing to compare with the swarms we encountered on the Fraser River.
>
> We had to carry a brush in each hand, and at every stroke of the paddle brush the face and neck, and yet the blood trickled down each side of the neck from the ears and our faces were swollen from the bites and stings of these desperate insects. At night we generally camped near a large drift, which we set on fire and then got into the thickest of the smoke, covered head and ears with our blankets and managed to sleep a little.
>
> At the first ranch of Indians we hired the son of the chief to pilot our canoe. He assumed command and by his knowledge of the currents and eddies we made much better progress than we could without him. He was followed in a small canoe by his two wives who at night time camped near us. We were lucky in getting the son for a helmsman, as he was well known by all the Indians on the river and his presence saved us from molestation and annoyance. . . .
>
> When we arrived at Port [Fort] Yale we found at least five thousand miners camped just below the mouth of the great canyon, through which it was almost an utter impossibility to push further with canoes or any kind of craft. Still hundreds would try it, only to meet with disaster and death. Large canoes and boats would be caught in the whirl, be upended and disappear, going straight down, only to be seen miles below all in splinters.[15]

Hicks noted that most of the bars and mining camps soon fell into the hands of the Chinese, thousands of whom remained after the gold rush had ended, some later taking railroad-construction employment. Hicks also described the Indians' salmon-drying sheds and how some miners had set fire to them:

> These salmon dryhouses had very much the appearance of old Missouri tobacco dry-houses, tons of salmon being hung up under long sheds, which when set on fire, would create a blaze that could be seen and smelled for miles around. This raid [on the Indians] was gotten up entirely by the American miners, without waiting to consult the British authorities and was over before it was fairly known in Victoria.[16]

The Whatcom Trail

Because of the problems the hopeful miners and prospectors had with floods, robbery, and the Fraser trail, American pressure mounted for a direct route from Whatcom to the gold bars above Fraser Canyon. When Douglas placed a head tax and license fee on all who entered the river, the trail plan was brought into immediate focus.[17] At a Whatcom town meeting in early 1858, it was resolved to open a "road" from Whatcom—Victoria's rival—that would lead to the Fraser River goldfields and also across the Cascades to the interior. That spring, an American engineer, Capt. Walter Washington de Lacy, led an expedition with mules and horses brought from California through the generosity of local citizens.[18] Beginning in July, the Whatcom newspaper *Northern Light,* which fought hard to promote the trail, published de Lacy's reports.

The name *Whatcom Trail* was used for several trails that began in Whatcom and crossed the International Boundary at Monument 43, near Lake Sumas, to connect with the HBC Brigade Trail from Fort Hope to the interior. The Whatcom Trail was first opened to the Nooksack River at present-day Everson, then crossed the forty-ninth parallel northward to Sumas Prairie.[19] It then bore east along Vedder Mountain to avoid Lake Sumas (now drained). One branch went to the Vedder (Chilliwack) River and the other went by way of the Columbia Valley to Cultus Lake, after which the routes joined again. De Lacy proposed to follow an old Indian trail to Chilliwack Lake that the HBC had improved in 1855 and then abandoned. At Sumas Prairie, he apparently met Russell V. Peabody, who was then associated with a Northwest Boundary Survey crew that was cutting trail along the Chilliwack River during the same period. Peabody, who obtained Indian packers and continued with de Lacy to the old HBC trail along the Chilliwack River, had already visited the lake.[20]

While the crew labored hard on the trail, many prospectors waited at Whatcom for its opening. On May 21, the *Puget Sound Herald* reported: "The trail . . . is being pushed through with great rapidity . . . at the rate of five miles per day."[21] Encouraging news from the gold mines was regularly printed in the loudly partisan *Northern Light* to bolster morale among the miners camped at Bellingham Bay. The editor admonished them to have patience: "Wait a little longer! The Trail will go through!" The newspaper printed the names of adventurers who set out, but it usually failed to mention that they only reached "Summit" (Chilliwack) Lake, where a Mr. J. Townsend had built a horse ferry.[22] The *Northern Light* also published letters commenting on the situation that summer. One observer wrote that Fraser boat captains were attempting to get every possible fare, even for poor gold diggings along the lower river. The best route to the Thompson, the writer advised, would be the Whatcom Trail, even though the final portion was uncut. A letter from the trail, printed on July 17, reported that Townsend, who had built a hotel on Chilliwack Lake, "keeps liquors and some provisions."[23]

On June 14, de Lacy wrote Whatcom: "Don't send anybody out on the trail until I report it through. I have made two unsuccessful attempts to get through, but the snow prevents. What I supposed was Summit Lake is not within forty miles of the Summit. I have not been supplied according to agreement."[24] On

July 12, de Lacy—now traveling alone except for Indian guides—sent word that he had ascended "Chuch-che-hum" (Depot) Creek and reached the first pass before being stopped by snow at near 5,000 feet. He had been without food for two days, and one account reports that de Lacy and his Indian assistants had to subsist on the inner bark of pine trees for four days. He returned to Sumas and Cultus lakes for provisions and started again with Townsend for the camp on Depot Creek.[25] De Lacy insisted that the "route was practicable and he was determined to put it through." Indian guides then took him across the narrow mountain pass, following the thickly forested Maselpanik and Klesilkwa branches to the Skagit River, which could be crossed on a logjam.[26]

De Lacy appraised the more open terrain beyond the Skagit as favorable for progress, even though there was "a high range of mountains" and the poor weather limited visibility. Nevertheless, with only a day's provisions remaining, the guides wished to turn back. De Lacy described the return:

> It was raining incessantly, and I had at least fifty miles to go before I could reach Summit [Chilliwack] Lake, and even then with an uncertainty whether I should find the party there. In returning, in order to get as accurate a knowledge of the country as I possibly could, I took a different route; I traveled up the main river and one of its branches in a westerly direction; left the waters of the Skagit and struck the headwaters of a small stream called the Thleh-quennum [*Silverhope*], which flows north into Fraser River, just below Fort Hope [brackets in original].[27]

From Silverhope Creek, de Lacy returned by way of an old Indian route using Hicks and Post creeks to arrive below Chilliwack Lake. This route is circuitous but climbs only to about 3,300 feet.

Fresh men and a pack train with provisions arrived at Chilliwack Lake. Rafts were built to cross the lake to carry the gear to the summit, which de Lacy estimated to be thirteen miles away. Upon his return to camp, the captain found "several strangers; amongst the rest, Mr. Crum, who presented me with a copy of [Alexander C.] Anderson's Map of Fraser River, which was the first time I had ever seen a map of the Hudson Bay Trails—and which was of the greatest service to me afterwards."[28] Spurred by the new arrivals and the map, de Lacy returned to the Skagit River. His route is not given in sources, but he probably retraced his earlier journey. A communication from him dated July 24 indicated he had reached the "Simallow" (Sumallo) River (a branch of the Skagit), he could see campfires in the open country of the Brigade Trail, and he estimated the trail would be open in two to three weeks.[29] Another letter from de Lacy reported that beyond the Sumallo the trail "strikes the Fort Hope trail in what is called on Anderson's Map, 'Blackeye's Portage'" and that the connection with the Thompson River was now made. The Whatcom Trail then passed the Punch Bowl and continued to the Brigade Trail on the Tulameen Plateau.[30]

A special issue of the *Northern Light* on August 19 celebrated the news of the project's completion. Almost immediately, the newspaper printed de Lacy's optimistic evaluation: "The trail is the best, in every respect, of any known route on the whole Cascade range. Bellingham Bay to Thompson River with pack animals, 10–15 days including delays for grazing purposes and recruit of animals."[31] C.C. Vail, an assistant to de Lacy, reported that it was 173 miles from Whatcom to the Brigade Trail and 273 miles to Fort Thompson. There were three ferries on the route: at the Nooksack River, the Chilliwack River, and Chilliwack Lake. "The distance is great" to the interior, George Gibbs observed, and nowhere in California during its mining heyday had provisions been packed over 150 miles.[32]

Nevertheless, Whatcom—which in de Lacy's absence had grown from six hundred to six thousand persons—celebrated the great event in fitting style. One hundred guns "pealing" from the blockhouse on the hilltop announced the trail's completion. At a congratulatory dinner for de Lacy, the first toast celebrated

> Capt. W. W. DeLacy and the Bellingham Bay trail: The fame of the former shall be echoed over the Cascades to the Rocky Mountains, and from the Rocky Mountains to the farthest seas; while the latter shall stand as a monument to his triumph, so long as there are gold regions to explore, or immigrants to be enriched by the success of his labors.[33]

Travelers, however, generally found that the trail builders' stories were exaggerated. Just after the trail's completion, twenty-two men reportedly needed eight weeks to reach the Thompson River, and it is doubtful that any further trail work was done after the fall of 1858.[34] While the *Northern Light* took a patriotic stand against Victoria "and everything British," it soon questioned the trail's usefulness. The trail for the first thirty-five miles was not a "good trail." If it had claimed otherwise, the newspaper assured its readers, "We should subject ourselves to the charge of having uttered a falsehood from every one who has rode or driven a pack mule over it."[35] In fact, hasty construction had left the trail generally muddy and poor, and often laced with roots.

Rains, sickness, shortages of provisions, and the reopening that summer of the Harrison Lake trail that Alexander C. Anderson had pioneered in 1846 all contributed to the eventual failure of the Whatcom Trail, which few prospectors ever actually followed for its entire length. Governor Douglas's proclamation in late 1857 that no person could work in the British Columbia gold mines without first obtaining a license—available only in Victoria—also doomed the Whatcom boom. Riverboats with a $20 fare to Fort Hope now plied the Fraser regularly. The gold rush faded in September and anyway, many American miners were convinced the mines were a failure. R.L. Reid had this analysis:

> In the end, Victoria won, for dominating the situation was Governor Douglas, wise with the experience of years. He had seen Oregon over-run with settlers from the

East, and British authority overwhelmed thereby. Forced to the North, he stood, the protector of the last lands left to England on the Pacific Coast, and without legal authority, but strong in his indomitable will, stepped into the breach and took command. He maintained peace and order along the Fraser River until an authorized Government could be established, and he kept the trade of the mines, so far as was humanly possible for this country.[36]

The New Colony and the Establishment of Order

The mainland of future British Columbia in the 1850s was a vast, unorganized, vaguely defined territory known as the Indian Territory or New Caledonia. It had no government, no roads, and no established transportation. The territory included the land between the forty-ninth parallel and the sources of the Fraser River, and it extended eastward to the Rocky Mountains. The only recognized authority was the HBC, which had exclusive trading rights with the Indians under its 1838 license. Company posts, built to carry on trade with the Indians, were located at strategic points in the region, with Fort Langley as a supply center.

Because James Douglas was both governor of Vancouver Island (since 1851) and head of the HBC on the Pacific Coast, he represented the Crown on the mainland. In that capacity, he issued regulations, to be approved by the British colonial secretary, Sir Edward Bulwer Lytton. There was often a clash of interests among colonists, the governor, and the HBC. Most settlers detested the company and its rule; and as the number of miners increased (most of whom did not respect the company's privilege), the HBC began to lose control of its fur-trading monopoly. Among some Victoria residents, George Gibbs observed on an 1855 visit, "the wish was openly expressed that the American flag was floating over their houses."[37] Miners were unhappy with Douglas's proclamation at the end of 1857 that all persons digging for gold, including British subjects, must have authorization from the colonial government. In 1858, Douglas also forbade everyone except those connected with the HBC to trade with the Indians.

By May 1858, Douglas had appointed a revenue collector, confirmed mining-claim regulations, and made his vigorous and determined personality felt during conflicts. In a dispatch on July 1, Sir Lytton had to remind Douglas that the HBC had no exclusive rights other than its trade with Indians in the Fraser River territory—certainly none to exclude strangers. Miners had to conform to the law, but no restrictions were to be placed on miners entering the gold-fields or on free trade. Douglas thus had to cancel his proclamation requiring a head tax.[38]

As the gold rush swelled the number of miners along the Fraser River, the mainland of New Caledonia superseded Vancouver Island in importance. With the problems created by the gold rush and the fear of that the United States would annex the Fraser River, the British realized that a colony with a properly constituted government would have to be formed immediately. Sir Lytton demonstrated the high value the British government placed on Douglas's services when he proposed that Douglas be appointed governor. Queen Victoria chose the name *British Columbia;* and on August 2, 1858, royal assent was given to the act that created the new colony. Douglas was sworn in at Fort Langley on September 2.[39]

At the end of October, about ten thousand gold miners remained between Fort Langley and Lytton, perhaps two to three thousand between Hope and Yale.[40] Violence and drunkenness were common, and even card games were played for liquor rather than for money. "A reckless man will go to Yale on Sunday, and spend twenty-five to forty dollars in drink and treating others," wrote George Hills, the Church of England's first bishop of British Columbia.[41] The lawless community of miners needed watching.

That summer, the situation on the Fraser had become dangerous as the miners neared the end of their resources. At Hill's Bar, American miners even formed their own rules to regulate claims and keep the peace. There arose the real possibility that the territory might set up its own independent form of rule.[42] Douglas's only recourse to deal with the problems associated with the gold seekers was to call on the HMS *Satellite,* a Royal Navy war vessel that was on boundary-commission duty, and HMS *Plumper,* which was making coastal and island surveys. In August 1858, he made a plea to the Colonial Office for military support. Sir Lytton was already aware of this need, for on July 30 he had written Douglas that he wanted to send an officer of the Royal Engineers and a company of sappers to British Columbia.[43] A few engineers under the command of Col. Richard Moody arrived at Fort Langley in November; the rest arrived in 1859.

In September 1858, Governor Douglas made a speech to the miners at Yale, but it apparently did little to ease the growing tensions. The governor had been unable to prevent a clash in which a group of miners avenged two murders by killing about thirty Indians, but he was able to prevent a war. Carrying out his duty to enforce law and order, Douglas asked for assistance from the Royal Engineers. Although the Royal Engineers had received surveying and military training to complement their mechanical skills, they were called upon to perform few military duties. This was to be the first public service they rendered in the new colony. With Maj. John S. Hawkins and fifteen Royal Engineers from the Northwest Boundary Survey, as well as twenty marines from the *Satellite,* Douglas set out for Yale on August 30. That day, Lt. Wilson wrote his sister:

> In consequence of the very bad reports from the mines up Fraser river, Major Hawkins has gone up with a body of men, to help the Governor to keep the peace. I volun-

teered several times to go up as a little fighting would be much more to my taste than this work; but unfortunately being a Jack-of-all-trades & having most of the work to do, I was left behind much to my sorrow. I am very anxious for news from the party, as there has been a good deal of fighting up there & wise heads in these matters say we are going to have a regular Indian war.[44]

Douglas found that reports of murdered whites were wildly exaggerated and that peace had already been established by the time he arrived. At Fort Hope, he issued a proclamation forbidding the sale or gift of alcohol to the Indians, and he presented the chiefs with presents of clothing "as a token of regard."[45]

Although English law was supposed to prevail in the land, serious crimes might not be tried at all, and it seemed there was no law but the "law of the club and the fang."[46] In 1862, Lt. Richard Charles Mayne of the *Plumper* recorded his impressions on the "rascals" in Victoria:

> The new-found mineral wealth of British Columbia had attracted from California some of the most reckless rascals gold has ever given birth to. Strolling about the canvas streets of Victoria might be seen men whose names were in the black book of the Vigilance Committee of San Francisco, and whose necks would not, if they ventured them in that city, have been worth an hour's purchase.[47]

The arch-renegade was Edward "Ned" McGowan, the king of thugs and gamblers on the Pacific Coast, whom the Vigilance Committee of San Francisco had sentenced to the gallows for a cold-blooded killing. Pursued by various agents, who once managed to put a bullet through his coat lapel, McGowan had fled to Mexico in 1856 and had taken a steamer to Victoria. Now, at Hill's Bar, beneath the rugged peaks of the northern Cascades, the charismatic McGowan had a rich claim and a strong following among the bold and lawless.[48] Governor Douglas had good reason to be concerned.

On Christmas Day 1858, the "Ned McGowan War" began. A saloon shooting and an assault on a local resident were followed by quarrels among local officials and a courtroom fiasco. A rumor reached Fort Langley that McGowan had shot the justice of the peace and the constable at Yale and was conspiring to overthrow British authority. When Col. Moody heard that the Hill's Bar district was in open insurrection, he did not wait for the governor's orders. In January 1859, accompanied by Capt. John Grant and twenty-six Royal Engineers, Moody proceeded in secret from Fort Langley on the *Enterprise*.[49] He also instructed Lt. Mayne on the *Plumper* to order up a hundred marines and bluejackets from the *Satellite* and to proceed at once to Hill's Bar. Advancing along the Fraser, the naval lieutenant was impressed with the beauty of the Cascade Range, even making a sketch of Mt. Baker. Near Fort Hope he wrote: "The Que-que-alla [Coquihalla] is a considerable stream . . . The mountains on either side are from three to four thousand feet high, and are composed almost entirely of plutonic rocks, and at their base is found the 'drift' in which the gold is contained."[50]

The prompt arrival of Grant and his engineers, who Moody ordered to march on Fort Yale, had much to do with the rapid restoration of order. The astonished miners apologized, and Judge Matthew Begbie—who single-handedly brought law and order to Fraser River mining camps—fined McGowan for an assault on a local resident and exonerated him in all other respects. The following day, McGowan escorted Mayne and Begbie to Hill's Bar to show them the mining process. He even invited them to his hut, where they drank champagne with his California chums. The "war" had been trifling, but the display of military force gave the government needed prestige.[51] The stabilization of the Fraser situation was a personal triumph for Douglas. His character and forthright competence impressed the miners, and they learned that the governor and Judge Begbie would not tolerate the same conduct that had been permitted in California.[52]

The Work of the Royal Engineers

The contingent of 165 officers and men of the Royal Engineers under Col. Moody served as a protective force for the new colony, helped in its settlement, and constructed roadways. Sir Lytton believed the Royal Engineers would be more popular than regular soldiers while being useful in surveying and construction, and Governor Douglas was pleased with the choice.[53] On January 5, 1859, Moody was sworn in as chief commissioner of lands and works for the colony. In Moody, Lytton believed he had a man of admirable character and solid colonial experience—a desirable choice for dealing with new settlers and rowdy gold seekers.[54] The Royal Engineers detachment was a select group, with each member chosen by Lytton for the specific service he could render. Capt. John Marshall Grant, a senior officer, was a construction genius, and Capt. Robert M. Parsons was chosen for his surveying knowledge. Many of the early maps of the colony were made from the Royal Engineers' surveys, and they were remarkably well done. One of their major accomplishments was the surveying of New Westminster, the capital of the young colony.

In 1858–1859, the imperative need in the colony was communication with the interior, where the Royal Engineers were in charge of planning routes. An enthusiastic Douglas raised money to finance the operation through loans from England, and three principal routes were initially planned: the Harrison Lake-Lillooet route, favored by Douglas but criticized by government opponents; the Yale-Lytton route (later the famous Cariboo Road), supported by Col. Moody; and the Hope-Similkameen route, well known to HBC traders and envisioned by the governor as part of a transcontinental road.

In the summer of 1858, Douglas put miners to work constructing a mule trail along portages of the Harrison Lake-Lillooet route under the supervision of Alexander C. Anderson. Northeast of Lillooet Lake (upstream from Harrison Lake), the route followed a chain of lakes and a pack trail to the Fra-ser River above the mouth of the Thompson (at present-day Lillooet). By October, the route had been hastily completed.[55] In the spring, in response to a need for a wagon road to the interior, a party of engineers began to improve this route north of the Fraser. After the engineers realized how mountainous the terrain was, Moody explained the project's character:

> By a Waggon Road I do not mean what would be considered as such in England, but a very rude sort of communication 12 Feet wide. . . . It is not the *surface* of the road I am looking to but the Ascents, Descent, and General Direction. The object is to get transport at a moderate cost—and that is only to be accomplished by arranging so that the animals may *dray* much weight compared with what they would *carry* on their backs.[56]

While the Yale-Lytton route along the Fraser Canyon was being considered, an exploration through the mountains progressed from Hope via the Coquihalla River, Boston Bar Creek, and the Anderson River to Boston Bar. This route was examined in 1859 under Lt. Arthur R. Lemprière to avoid the worst part of the canyon. A trail was soon built here via Boston Bar Creek.

With gold mining on the lower Similkameen and Rock Creek (east of the Cascade Range) heralding more traffic and revenue, Moody recommended that the 1849 Brigade Trail be reexamined as a railway line. Lt. Henry Spencer Palmer (then just twenty-one years old) made the official exploration, traveling east as far as Fort Colvile. In September 1859, officers of the new colonial government accompanied Palmer, who wanted an opportunity to find a pass superior to Manson Ridge. Chief Trader Angus McDonald of the Hudson's Bay Company and his Fort Colvile party led the entourage as far as Campement des Femmes on the Tulameen River, where they divided. Some of the men—including Chief Justice Begbie and his staff, who were making their judicial rounds—continued northward to Kamloops.[57] On this traverse, Palmer became the first to fix astronomically the position of points en route, and he made a complete route map. While he covered no new terrain, he named landmarks and made observations about the country, the mountains, and the Indians in the area.

Palmer arrived at Fort Hope on September 11, where he recorded seeing the prominent Ogilvie's Peak and Manson Mountain (Ridge). Following the Brigade Trail on September 17, the large party went up the Coquihalla River Valley, then branched off to the rocky Peers Creek defile, which is walled in by converging spurs from Manson Ridge. In his report, Palmer noted that the streams and waterfalls of magnificent torrents reached the Coquihalla Valley, and he mentioned the geological characteristics of Manson Ridge.[58]

When the party ascended the steep, zigzag Manson Ridge trail, Palmer recalled the disastrous trip of Chief Trader Donald McLean of Kamloops. On this trail, made dangerous by autumn snowstorms, over sixty horses had been lost in 1857 or 1858. Palmer wrote: "Traces of their deaths are still visible, and in riding over the mountain . . . my horse frequently shied at the whitened bones of some of the poor animals, who had broken down in the sharp struggle with fatigue and hunger, and been left to perish where he lay." The day's efforts were captured by young Arthur T. Bushby of the judicial staff: "Up at 5 o'clock. Breakfasted onions Bacon & flour & started at 7 o'clock after a fair spring bath—we had to mount the steep part of Manson's mountain & hard work it was." The climb was made easier by "a cup of brandy some flour cake & some raw salmon an Indian gave us."[59]

Palmer was most impressed with the vista at Manson Ridge, where "an endless sea of mountains rolled away into the blue distance" with a rugged, "naked peak" some thousand feet or more above the summits (probably Mt. Outram). The lieutenant believed he was on the backbone of the main Cascade Range,

> but so undefined are its general features, and so remarkable is the absence of any prominent and distinguishing snow capped peaks, such are visible from the 'Dalles,' and by which one may determine the general bearing of a range, that it is a matter of extreme difficulty to follow its direction with the eye for more than a few miles.

Palmer could not see Mt. Baker, but he believed the divide of the range maintained a general south-southwest direction until "it unites with that peak." Having traveled nineteen miles by trail, the party came to "campement du Chevreuil." The Indians shot some white ptarmigans, which made a good supper. At the camp, Palmer recorded seeing the grave of an HBC trader: "It is here that Mr. Fraser met his death by a tree falling on him when asleep, and within a few yards of the spot where we had pitched our tent, a neat pile of rough hewn logs mark his lonely grave."[60]

Bushby's journal is more chatty, and his September 18 entry is mindful of the ptarmigan dinner: "We all had a fine cold spring bath, then such a dinner. Some Indian had killed 8 or 10 birds so we had a hyyou dinner such a meal—and what with a nip—some hot grog and a pipe we turned in pretty comfortable—eh." Writing some of his thoughts on his shirt, trousers, and moccasins, Bushby described a most pleasant reverie the next morning:

> It was a most beautiful sight the camp last night wild & picturesque in the extreme there was the great log fire blazing away a group of Indians round about it—the opposite tent just glancing in the fire's flame & some dozen tall cedar trees brought out in bold relief from the fire & utter & mysterious darkness behind oh it was a grand sight—I dreamed a good deal last night—I thought I was married to Agnes—& she kissed me at the altar.

That day, Palmer observed that to the east the mountains were "more soft and rounded in appearance," and he expressed disappointment in not seeing Mt. Baker. What he described as a remarkable conical peak, an exceptional landmark, appeared at S 64° E.

At McDonald's suggestion, Palmer gave the mountain we stood on the Gaelic name "Stuchd-a choiré," from a beautiful "choire" or recess situated about halfway down its eastern slope.

On the summit, and invisible except from the rocks immediately surrounding it, lies a pretty sequestered little lake, guarded by one solitary stunted oak, and lower down on the eastern slope is a larger one, on whose banks, there being plenty of firewood, travellers from the eastward frequently camp.[61]

The "little lake" became known as Palmer Pond. He later learned this peak (Mt. Chopaka) was near the forty-ninth parallel, so he named it "Mt. XLIX," or "Mount Forty-nine."[62]

Descending from the divide through a more open forest, the men followed Podunk Creek, which meets the Tulameen River at Anderson's Horseguard Camp. They then ascended 1,800 feet, taking Blackeye's Portage to avoid detouring by the horseshoe sweep of the Tulameen. Keeping to a general northeasterly direction, the party camped at Lodestone Lake. "Mount Forty-nine" was still visible. The next evening, they pitched their tents at Campement des Femmes (downstream from present-day Tulameen), which had been named after the Indians' custom of leaving their women and children there while en route to Fort Hope. The party then followed the Tulameen, where the good trail had excellent bunchgrass for horses. The route led to the junction of the Tulameen and Similkameen, known as Vermilion Forks because of the presence of red clay (ochre), which the Indians used to make face paint. The Similkameen country featured broad valleys, open forests, good camps, and stock feed. Palmer then continued to "Keereemaous" (Keremeos). Along the way, he noted the "Na-is-new-low" (Ashnola) River and again "Mount Forty-nine." Observing Polaris at night, he gave a latitude of 49°03'20" on the night of September 26.[62]

A report in September 1860 from the *Daily British Colonist*'s "special correspondent at the Similkameen" corroborates the trials of this tiring route:

I arrived here yesterday from Fort Hope, in five and a half days, by the Brigade Trail to Camp des Femmes. . . . We had to carry our blankets and provisions, etc., amounting in my case to 40 pounds, as packing at 20¢ a pound to Rock Creek is rather too expensive a luxury for prospectors. The first day out we camped at the foot of Manson's Mountain, having had to wade across the Co-que-alla River, which feat was accomplished without any accident beyond two loaves of bread coming to grief in the stream. The trail at the foot of Manson's Mountain commences to be very swampy and difficult to traverse, and the descent on the other side is just like rushing down an almost perpendicular gulch or mountain stream. This, for a man with a load on his back, is a rather fatiguing operation. . . . The next day (Sunday) we spent in the profitable occupation of climbing Deer Mountain, one of the highest of the Cascade range, and I can truly say that I have never worked so hard on the day of rest before. For eight miles between Deer and Manson's Mountains the road is nothing but one vast swamp, in which we often sunk up to our knees. It reminded me strongly (being well read up on Pilgrim's Progress) of the slough of Despond; whilst a Cockney whom we met returning from the Similkameen was of the opinion that it was like going to "'ell by a short route." Although not in a state of mind to admire nature, the view from the top of Deer Mountain struck me as being magnificently grand. A large portion of the Cascade range, with the usual pine tree accompaniment, stretches forth on all sides, forming an almost impenetrable barrier to the fertile plains beyond.

Signed, Argus.
Forks of the Similkameen
13 Sept. 1860[63]

Along the route Lemprière examined in 1859, a mule trail was built in 1859–1860 by merchants at Hope with the assistance of the Royal Engineers. It led east of the Fraser River via Boston Bar Creek and the Anderson River to reach Boston Bar and established trail routes. The route failed, however, because of its length and the inconvenience of long closures because of snow. Later, in 1876, the first portion was used for the government cattle trail from the Coquihalla River to Nicola Lake.[64] James Turnbull, a sapper, explored the Coquihalla River in the spring of 1862, but he recommended against trail- or wagon-road building because of the prevalence of avalanche tracks. Nevertheless, trail construction began in 1875 in response to cattle ranchers' demands for access to the coastal market.[65]

Governor Douglas was aware of the need for good communication and transportation that was wholly on British soil and would link the two capitals, Victoria and New Westminster, to interior mining camps. In 1860, as Similkameen trade prospects increased, Douglas instigated a review of the old Alexander C. Anderson exploration from Fort Hope to the Punch Bowl summit and the Tulameen River. He envisioned a "British Canadian Colonization Waggon Road" to firm up the colony's relationship to the British Empire and to counteract the Americans' Columbia River trade benefit. The route would begin at Fort Hope and cross British Columbia to the Rockies.

In the summer of 1860, a detachment of engineers under Sgt. William McColl and Cpl. Charles Sinnett located the old Anderson trail. They generally followed Anderson's route but bypassed the Punch Bowl by following the main Snass Creek (not the east fork) to Paradise Valley. It was an unfortunate choice because the canyon held snow late into the spring. The route crossed the Tulameen headwaters eastward to Granite Creek, then ran northward to Vermilion Forks.[66]

When the magistrate's office in Fort Hope examined the public tenders for the contract of "a good mule road from Hope to Semilkameen," Edgar Dewdney's was lowest bid. Taking Toronto engineer Walter Moberly (the second-lowest bidder) as a working partner, Dewdney forged the "road" to the Similkameen River by the fall of 1860. Pack trains used it immediately, even during construction. The trail was extended in sections during 1861 and 1865 to reach

Fort Steele on the Kootenay River, thus becoming the principal route to the interior. Governor Douglas called it a "great boon to the country."[67]

Almost before Dewdney's extended trail was completed to present-day Princeton, Capt. John Grant opened a bypass south and east of Dewdney's. The twenty-two-mile diversion bypassed the Snass Canyon section and crossed the Cascade divide at what is now Hope Pass to become the principal packing route to the Kootenay region. The Grant diversion (the Hope Trail) was open for a longer season than the Snass canyon.[68] During this 1861–1862 project, which involved eighty sappers and ninety civilians, James Turnbull discovered that beyond Skagit Bluffs, the broad valley of the Skaist River led easily to Hope Pass—a good location for crossing the range.

The Dewdney Trail initiated the pattern of settlement in the Similkameen and Okanagan valleys. It also led to the development of the Kootenays, whose chain of rich mining camps later produced vast mineral wealth. The trail was paid for by taxes on gold, not fur. Its cost of $74,000 was financed partly by excise taxes on gold exported by American prospectors. Concurrently with mineral development, thousands of cattle and some sheep were brought to market over this trail; cattle were driven west to Hope, then loaded onto Fraser River boats. The extended Dewdney route served as a vital communication link to the coast, where pack trains could transport goods without crossing into the United States and paying customs duties.[69]

The Cariboo Road

By 1859, the center of gold-rush activity had begun to shift north to the district above Lytton.[70] Rich gold strikes in 1860 brought thousands of miners to the Cariboo, the Fraser River region north of its juncture with the Thompson. Packing in this hinterland, however, was both tedious and treacherous, and in places "one slipping foot would open the gates of eternity."[71] Jackass Mountain, for example, was so named because a mule had plunged over a cliff to its death. The Cariboo Trail, also known as the Mule Road, was nevertheless an alternative to crossing the northern Cascades for pack trains heading to the goldfields, even though travel on the trail was difficult or impossible for much of the year because of high water or snow. Costs were high because the four thousand miners in the region depended on pack animals.

Governor Douglas wanted a wagon road to the Cariboo region in order to better exploit its gold resources. In 1861, when he launched his plan to build the road, the colony had two good wagon roads: the Douglas Road west of the Fraser and the Dewdney Trail. After cutting a twenty-five-mile mule trail from Yale to Boston Bar (then on the west bank of the Fraser River), the Royal Engineers began in 1861 to survey the entire route from Yale to Cook's Ferry (now Spences Bridge) on the Thompson River. Col. Moody wisely ordered

Capt. Grant and his fifty-three sappers to begin construction in May 1862 with the hardest stretch of the road, the critical first six miles (to Pike's Riffle). Private contractors would build the remainder under military supervision.

The Cariboo Road was among the last works done by the Royal Engineers in British Columbia. Eventually, stagecoaches and freight wagons were put into service to haul passengers and supplies to the goldfields.[72] The gold rush peaked during the construction of the road. In November 1861, the *Otter* docked in Victoria with a single load from the Fraser River worth $300,000. By year's end, gold shipped from Victoria to San Francisco amounted to $1.6 million.[73]

The Railroad Arrives

When John A. MacDonald swept back into power as prime minister in 1878, he set out to fulfill an election promise to link Canada from the Atlantic to the Pacific Ocean with a railroad and to settle the Northwest. In 1872, Sir Sanford Fleming's party was sent westward to study routes to bypass or cross the Selkirk Range. After the discovery of Rogers Pass (see chapter 11), the line's completion was imminent.

Construction of a railway line through Fraser Canyon began in spring 1880 when Andrew Onderdonk, an American, secured his first contract with the Canadian government (British Columbia joined Canada in 1871). Onderdonk was a seasoned contractor with a reputation for promptness, efficiency, and organization. To alleviate his problems with labor costs and supply, in 1882 he brought ten vessels from China with six thousand laborers. At the peak construction, he had an estimated seven thousand Chinese in his employ, all of them prepared to work for lower wages than white laborers were.[74]

The hardships of the canyon—the most difficult in North America—were so extreme that it required eighteen months to build a line two miles out of Yale. An explosives factory serving the construction turned out four thousand pounds of nitroglycerine each day.[75] In only seventeen miles above Yale, thirteen tunnels were blasted out. The dangerous work was plagued with a high accident rate, as hundreds of men drowned, were maimed, or were killed by blasting mishaps and avalanches of rock or snow. On July 29, 1884, Onderdonk completed the lines between Port Moody and Savona's Ferry, a section nicknamed "Onderdonk's Railway." The Canadian Pacific Railway, finally completed in 1885, ran from one coast to the other.[76]

Further Mineral Discoveries

In the Similkameen region, placer gold and platinum were found from 1860 to 1900 near the Tulameen River and along Granite and Whipsaw creeks. The rapid growth of Granite City in 1885 was the result of John Chance's placer discoveries on Granite Creek.[77] In that locality, which geologist George Dawson had investigated in 1877, silver-lead ores were discovered in 1895 at Summit Camp near the Tulameen-upper Coquihalla divide (the Cascade divide). Successful lode mining later augmented the exhausted placers and led to the development of rich mining camps.

Summit Camp (on Treasure Mountain) had important mining properties. The original discoveries by Fred Sutter led to much excitement and staking, but no real work was done until 1910. Claims were also staked near the head of Whipsaw Creek in 1908–1909. To the northwest, the entire Coquihalla Valley contained a variety of mineral wealth, but it was difficult to access. Some silver-lead deposits were located and some gold was mined in this drainage (the chief properties being situated near the mouth of Dewdney Creek).

Gold discoveries at Hedley in 1897 by George Allison and James Riordan led to the growth of Penticton. In 1888, copper was found ten miles south of Princeton, inspiring the name Copper Mountain for the nearly flat-topped spur between the main Similkameen River Valley and the more shallow valley of Wolfe Creek to the east. High-grade copper ore was discovered there, but the site was not staked until 1892. Copper mining became an important industry in the early 1900s. After several stops and starts, Copper Mountain Mine is still operating.[78]

Near the Fraser River, only seven miles from Fort Hope, an Indian discovered mineral ore in 1868 while hunting goats. This location, high on Silver Peak, became known as the Eureka-Victoria Mine. After a company was formed the next year, Indians packed the ore out over the rough mountain slopes until it could be transferred to horses for transport to Hope. The mine, which became an important Crown-patented claim, was successfully operated as a high-grade silver property until 1874; it reopened in 1920.[79]

A 1915 report indicates that pioneer miner C.O. Lindeman (after whom Mt. Lindeman was named) located ore at Chilliwack Lake.[80] The report also mentions that six prospects showing iron ore were found at 5,300 feet on Custer Ridge, near the head of Paleface Creek. The Pierce Mountain group of claims, a gold property exploited by G.O. Pierce, was located west of Chilliwack Lake near Pierce Lake and high above the Thurston ranch. Another group of claims was developed a half mile from the head of Chilliwack Lake. Owned by the Silver Chief Mining Company, the eight locations could be reached in 1924 by fifteen miles of wagon road from Chilliwack, then thirty miles of good horse trail to the lake.[81]

In 1915, some prospectors traveled the rough northern frontage of the Cascades from Hope to prospects located between Silver Peak and Cheam Peak. Near the foot of a glacier on the northeastern flank of Foley Peak, the miners staked the Lucky Four group of claims (the entire range informally took the same name). High-grade samples attracted mining engineers, and the owners packed in a diamond drilling outfit with a gasoline engine and installed it on the glacier's surface in order to bore through the ice and evaluate the ore. The difficulties of drilling and excavating, however, were virtually insurmountable.[82] In the spring of 1917, a pack trail to these alpine claims was developed from Laidlaw, near the mouth of Wahleach (Jones) Creek on the Fraser River. In 1950, a small camp was built on the ridge crest by Rice Copper Mines.

Pack trails also proved helpful to reach the divide between Lightning and Nepopekum creeks—a route taken by the first boundary surveyors—and the country now traversed by the Skyline (Centennial) Trail. Both Hilary Bauerman and Reginald A. Daly made detailed geologic explorations in this region.[83] Mineralization was discovered in 1911 at the nearby Skagit-Sumallo claims (the prospects were called Twenty-three Mile Camp). Drilling began later at Mammoth Mine, underlain by rocks of the Hozameen Group.

A small group of claims —the Silver Bell—was also developed near the head of Silverdaisy Creek, not far from the Skagit-Sumallo junction.[84] An aerial tram was built in 1935 from the Skagit River to the Norwegian group, near the head of this creek; but, as often happened in this rugged country, it was destroyed by a snowslide three years later. West of the Skagit River, near the boundary and in the alpine, close to the head of Galene Creek, were the International and Grandview claims.

Today, those driving the Trans-Canada Highway along the lower Fraser River can recall Governor Douglas in statues and in the name of a principal street in Victoria. The Cariboo and Dewdney wagon roads are identified only by historic signs, and the work of England's stalwart Royal Engineers in British Columbia is all but forgotten. Nevertheless, these are the varied influences that helped weld the colony into a strong political and economic force.

Illustrations ~

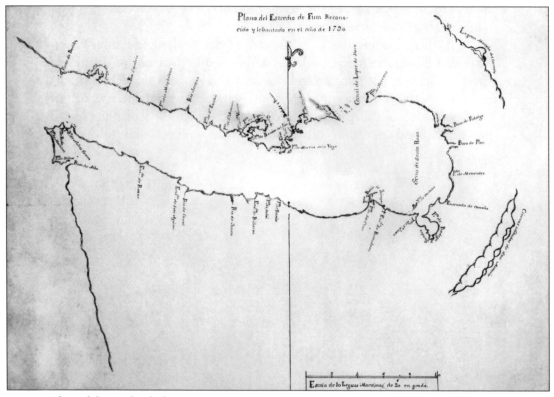

Plano del estrecho de fuca reconocido y lebantado en el ano de 1790, *by López de Haro of Manuel Quimper's expedition. The plan shows the Strait of Juan de Fuca, the Cascade Range, and, in the upper right, Mt. Baker, identified as "La gran Montaña del Carmelo." British Columbia Archives and Records Service, CM/A447.*

Surveyor's pack train along Keechelus Lake, about 1900. Walter C. Mendenhall, photographer, U.S. Geological Survey Photographic Library, Denver.

(Above) Mt. Baker from West of Protection Island, Puget Sound, *lithograph from a sketch by Henry James Warre, September 27, 1845. This is the first drawing of Mt. Baker after López de Haro's in 1790. From Warre,* Sketches in North America and the Oregon Territory *(London: Dickinson & Co., 1848); OHS Research Library, OHS neg., OrHi 793. (Below)* Mt. St. Helens, *painting by Paul Kane, spring 1847. Courtesy of the Royal Ontario Museum, Toronto, Canada, #912.1.78.*

(Right) Capt. George B. McClellan, sketched by Joseph F. Minter. From Theodore Winthrop, The Canoe and the Saddle, or, Klalam and Klickatat *(Tacoma, Wash.: J.H. Williams, 1913); OHS Research Library, OHS neg., OrHi 85672.*

(Above) Mount Rainier, from the South Part of Admiralty Inlet, *sketch by John Sykes, 1792. From George Vancouver,* A Voyage of Discovery to the North Pacific Ocean and Round the World, *vol. 1 (London: Printed for G.G. and J. Robinson, 1798); OHS Research Library, OHS neg., OrHi 87185.*

(Left) Lithograph portrait of Alexander Ross, many years after he crossed the Cascade Range at age twenty-nine. *From* The Fur Hunters of the Far West: A Narrative of Adventures in the Oregon and Rocky Mountains *(London: Smith, Elder and Co., 1855), Beinecke Library, Yale University.*

(Below) Map prepared by George Gibbs during the Northwest Boundary Survey, c. 1859, probably based on one drawn by the guide Thiusolac. Its geographic features include the Nooksack and Chilliwack rivers. Map 26, cartographic series 69, RG 76, National Archives.

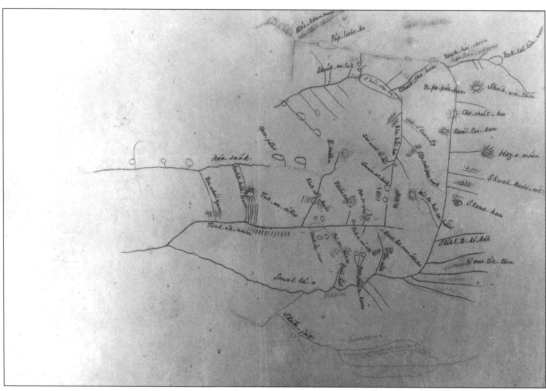

Map of the Gold Regions of the Frazer River and the Washington Territory on the Western Coast of America, *by James Wyld, 1859. British Columbia Archives and Records Service, CM/W103.*

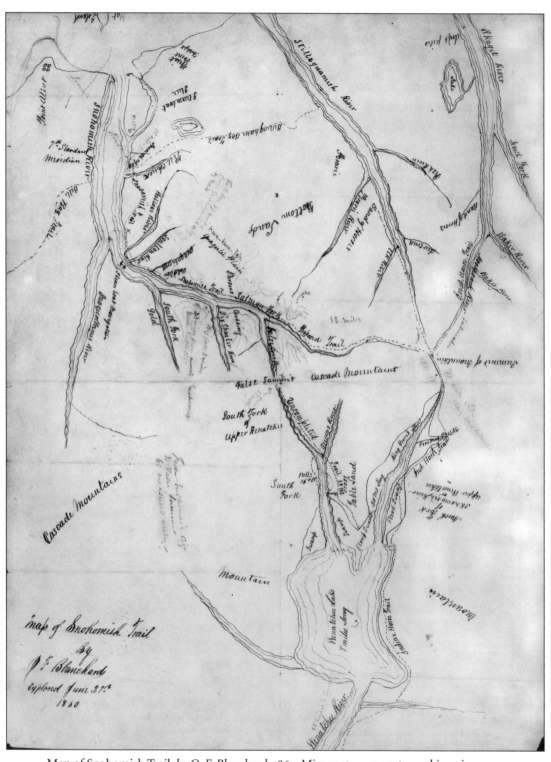

Map of Snohomish Trail, *by O. F. Blanchard, 1860. Misc. map no. 5, cartographic series 69, RG 76, National Archives.*

Ow-hi (above left) and Kamaiakin (above right), as sketched by Gustav Sohon at the 1855 Stevens Treaty Councils. Kamaiakin was Palouse on his father's side and descended from a prominent Yakama family on his mother's side. Of the various Yakama leaders, he was perceived to be the most powerful. Ow-hi, a head chief of the upper Yakamas in the Kittitas district, was related to Kamaiakin by marriage and was the father of Qual-chan. Kamaiakin: OHS neg., OrHi 4349; Ow-hi: from Hazard Stevens, The Life of Isaac Stevens (Boston: Houghton, Mifflin, 1900), OHS Research Library, OHS neg., OrHi 4341.

(Left) George Simpson's career with the Hudson's Bay Company spanned the years 1820 to 1858, and for most of that time he was director of field operations. Engraving, 1857, by James Scott from a portrait by Stephen Pearce, Hudson's Bay Company Archives Documentary Art, P-206 (N5394), Provincial Archives of Manitoba.

Part 2 ～

Surveyors and

Railroad Engineers

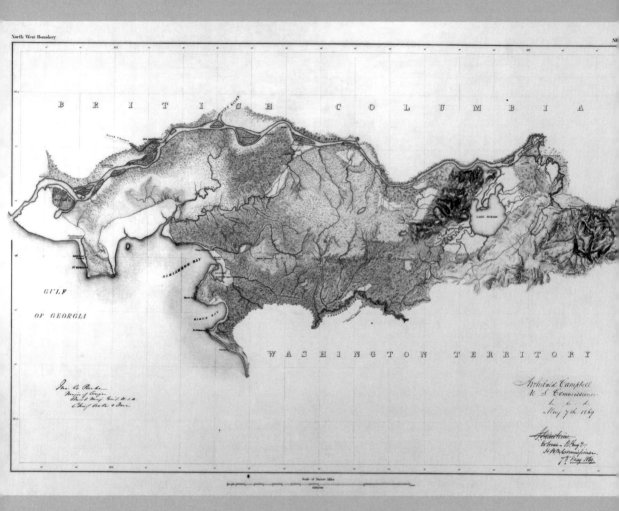

Map of the Northwest Boundary, signed by the American and British commissioners on May 7, 1869, showing (scale 1:120,000) Semiahmoo Bay, trails to the Fraser River and Lake Sumass, and Camp Chiloweyuck (map 7, cartographic series 66, RG 76, National Archives)

7

ALONG THE FORTY-NINTH PARALLEL:

THE NORTHWEST BOUNDARY SURVEY, 1857–1858

Nowhere do the Mountain masses & Peaks, present such strange, fantastic, dauntless, & startling outlines as here. Whoever wishes to see Nature in all its primitive glory & grandeur, in its almost ferocius wildness, must go & visit these Mountain regions.
–Henry Custer

The boundary line that divided the territories formerly belonging to the English and French crowns in North America seems never to have been precisely defined. After both nations made nearly contemporaneous voyages of discovery to the East Coast and formed settlements on the new continent, each laid proprietary claims to an extensive domain that it had no power actually to possess.[1] These excessive claims would inevitably become incompatible. The belief that the forty-ninth parallel was fixed by British and French commissioners who had agreed to the provisions of the Treaty of Utrecht in 1713 as the northern boundary of Louisiana formed the basis of later agreements. In a 1763 treaty, Canada and Louisiana east of the Mississippi River were ceded to Great Britain; the remainder of Louisiana continued as before, bounded on the north by the forty-ninth parallel.[2]

The definition of the boundary between the United States and Canada began with the 1783 Treaty of Paris, which described the dividing line from the Atlantic Ocean to the Great Plains between British North America and the American states. The treaty was basic to discussions concerning the boundary for sixty years after it was signed, but it was an unrealistic agreement because international frontiers on the continent had been drawn by men barely acquainted with the geography and history of the land and none of the vast territory west of the Mississippi River was covered.[3]

British claims in the Pacific Northwest were originally based on the discoveries of Sir Francis Drake and then on Capt. Cook's 1778 explorations, Capt. Vancouver's circumnavigation of Vancouver Island and his exploration of Puget Sound, and Alexander Mackenzie's 1793 journey from northern Alberta to the Fraser and Bella Coola rivers. The American claims were based on the voyage of Robert Gray, who entered the Columbia River in 1792, the 1804–1806 expedition of Meriwether Lewis and William Clark from St. Louis to the

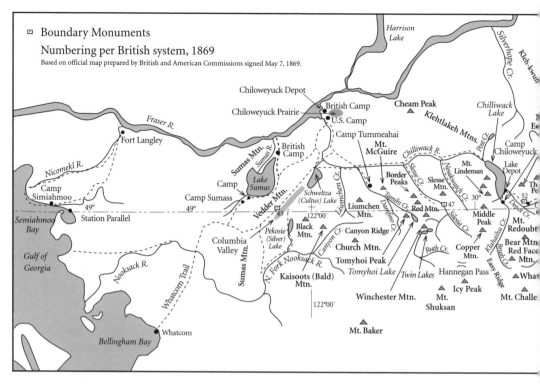

The Northwest Boundary Survey, 1857–1862

mouth of the Columbia, and the 1811 settlement of Astoria near the river's mouth. During the controversy of 1818, neither Great Britain nor the United States had sovereignty in the region. No government ruled the large span of territory between forty-two and fifty-five degrees of latitude.

In the Convention of 1818, the two nations agreed that the northern limits of Louisiana should be the forty-ninth parallel from Lake of the Woods to the "Stony Mountains" and that they would jointly occupy "any country that may be claimed by either party on the northwest coast of America, westward of the Stony Mountains."[4] Nationals of both countries had the right to hunt and settle at any unoccupied point, and each nation had the right to establish posts and protect its subjects. Although the Louisiana Purchase had not specified the ownership of the land west of the Rocky Mountains, it is certain that most of the Oregon Country fell into the United States' hands as a consequence.

Other negotiations and treaties also affected the final location of the Northwest Boundary. The United States and Spain reached agreements in 1819 in which Spain, for a consideration, ceded all territorial rights north of forty-two degrees as far west as the Pacific Ocean, thereby giving up the Oregon territory. In 1824, Russia and the United States agreed on a boundary line of 54°40', and Great Britain and Russia signed a similar treaty in 1825. After Spain and Russia withdrew from the imperial contest, the United States and Great Britain were left to vie for the vast "Old Oregon," located between the

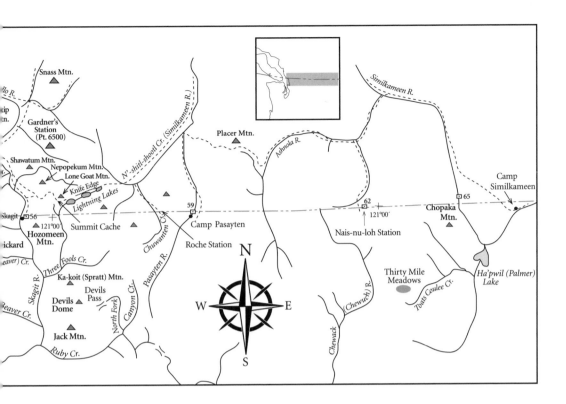

Columbia River and Alaska. At the time, the American government was almost totally ignorant about most of the vast Oregon Country.

During joint occupancy, the sprawling Hudson's Bay Company dominated the region with its posts at Vancouver, Nisqually, and Okanogan. Britain, however, sensing the increasing power of the Americans, pulled north of the Columbia River and built a fort at Victoria on Vancouver Island in 1843 to keep sea lanes open for its fur trade. Before the Oregon question seemed important, the only American settlers in the region lived south of the Columbia River, while most of the British fur traders were to the north. Eventually, however, conflicting interests made it urgent to settle the boundary and determine jurisdiction. Although settlement by the Hudson's Bay Company along the Columbia River gave Britain the better claim, it was largely offset by American immigration. When in the late 1840s a significant number of immigrants settled north of the Columbia in the region administered as a private holding of the HBC, there was enormous potential for conflict. By 1844, the increasing number of immigrants caused company employees so much uneasiness that they requested protection from their own government. When American immigration reached three thousand in 1845, the settlement of the Oregon question became imperative. On February 3, 1845, the U.S. House of Representatives passed a "Bill to organize a Territorial Government in Oregon Territory. It appeared to Great Britain that the United States was assuming sovereignty of the entire region west of the Rockies and north of the forty-second parallel.[5]

Relations between the two nations were increasingly strained in 1844–1845. The Oregon boundary question became part of the presidential campaign, and Democrats adopted the slogan "Fifty-four forty or fight." The Americans did have an advantage: the United States was physically close to Oregon, Great Britain was far away, and settlement was continuing. Although the Americans' legal arguments were weak, their threats were meaningful: in 1843, a Senate committee had already hinted at war. While the British wanted to see the boundary follow the Columbia River and the Americans hoped to gain territory to the fifty-fourth parallel, both sides were willing to settle for less.

The contest for the Oregon Country spurred Britain to seek more information on the region from the HBC. Sir George Simpson, HBC's governor, proposed that British officers should make a military survey of the Oregon Country, including an examination of and report on all British posts. In 1845, Prime Minister Robert Peel, who by 1844 had become concerned about American intentions, dispatched two agents to conduct a secret reconnaissance mission. Lt. Henry James Warre, a distinguished army officer and a skillful artist, and Lt. Mervin Vavasour of the Royal Engineers were to pose as gentlemen tourists on a hunting and fishing expedition. For this disguise, they wore expensive beaver hats and clothing and carried the accessories of high-class travelers. The two officers were to report on American settlements and military strength as well as on potential military action should the Americans declare war.[6]

Warre and Vavasour left Quebec in May 1845. Their mission is now remembered not for its effect on political events—the boundary dispute was settled during their journey—but for the officers' descriptions of the Rocky Mountains and Oregon Country. Warre's illustrations are a rare visual record from that period of what was then a little-known region. His lithograph depicting Mt. Baker from near Protection Island, published in London in 1848, was the first widely available depiction of the mountain. Vavasour drew a number of maps that contributed to knowledge of the region.

When Polk won the U.S. presidential election, the British found that he had become even more adamant about establishing the boundary. In his inaugural address, he claimed that "our title to the country of Oregon is clear and unquestionable." The president understood Manifest Destiny, and he was quick to realize that the quest for the Oregon Country was no longer based on naval power.[7] In December 1845, Polk took a fateful diplomatic step: he asked Congress to serve notice on Britain of the termination of the joint-occupation agreement. Had the United States not been occupied in war with Mexico, Polk's slogans might have led to a serious confrontation in the Pacific Northwest. Britain was also in a difficult period. With war in India and famine in Ireland, there was little sentiment for a conflict in distant North America. Complicating the issue was the decline of the fur trade south of the parallel and Britain's troubles with both Indians and the growing numbers of American settlers.[8] In the end, the wisest strategy seemed to be peaceful negotiation. When in 1846 the British proposed that the boundary be a continuation of the forty-ninth parallel west from the Rocky Mountains, the Americans quickly accepted. Both sides received some advantageous territory: Puget Sound and half of the Strait of Juan de Fuca went to the United States and the mouth of the Fraser River and all of Vancouver Island went to the British.

The Treaty of Washington, signed on June 15 and proclaimed on August 5, 1846, stipulated that the boundary "shall be continued westward along the said forty-ninth parallel of north latitude to the middle of the channel which separates the continent from Vancouver's Island." The treaty failed to designate which of the three principal channels the boundary should follow through the San Juan Islands to the Strait of Juan de Fuca. In the following years, the U.S. and British boundary commissioners would disagree as to the location of this water boundary. With the San Juan archipelago at stake, it was important to determine whether Haro Strait, which Wilkes had examined in 1841, was to be the boundary channel. James Douglas, who became governor of Vancouver Island in 1851, was convinced that the treaty meant the boundary was to follow Rosario Strait. The American occupation of San Juan Island and the confrontation between U.S. troops under Capt. George Pickett and four British men-of-war in July 1859 would affect the cordial relations between the American and British boundary surveyors in the Cascade Range.[9] The dispute continued until 1871, when the two governments agreed to submit the matter to Emperor William I of Germany for arbitration. He decided that in the true interpretation of the treaty, the boundary should pass through Haro Strait.

"An Unnatural Boundary"

The settlement of the land-boundary question ended a colorful chapter in American history and set the stage for a new era of systematic exploration in the northern Cascade Range. The HBC and British presence retreated northward, leaving as their legacy a few buildings and many geographical names. By 1849, the company had completed shifting its operations from Oregon Territory to Victoria, and U.S. troops took over its Columbia River properties.

The 409-mile boundary between the United States and the Dominion of Canada from the summit of the Rocky Mountains to the Pacific Ocean is usually referred to as the Northwest Boundary. It is not at all realistic in the topographic sense, for it follows no natural features. The line, which was easy to define on paper but very difficult to locate on the ground, was decided upon by men who had only the vaguest notion of its geographic aspects. According to one evaluation,

> the drawing of an astronomical line upon a map, without reference to the territory through which it passed, seems to have been an unimaginative way of proceeding.

The 49th parallel, which cut across heights of land, sliced through valleys, segmented rivers, and isolated small areas, was an unnatural boundary.[10]

The factors that prompted both nations to compromise on the boundary "were based on traditions and predilections held by Americans in the East, rather than by the practical implications the boundary might have had for those who would ultimately be required to cope with it."[11] At the time, few people were living along its course. By the early 1900s, however, it had become clear that some parts of Canada were, as a result of geography, commercially related to the United States. Both mining and agriculture, for example, were affected by a boundary that isolated some enterprises.

Ten years after the treaty, Great Britain and the United States created commissions to demarcate the land boundary. Congress provided for the American commission, and the British staff was appointed by the Queen.[12] Authorities from both nations agreed that a survey and marking of the forty-ninth parallel was vital because of legal and title problems.

The American Surveyors Organize

On February 14, 1856, President Franklin Pierce appointed Archibald Campbell to head the American commission, and Lt. John Grubb Parke of the U.S. Army Corps of Topographical Engineers was named chief astronomer-surveyor.[13] The two officers were charged with representing the United States on all land- and water-boundary questions. Campbell, born in 1813 in Albany, New York, graduated from West Point in 1835, briefly served with the infantry, and then worked as a civil engineer on various topographic, railroad, and canal surveys. In 1845, he was appointed private secretary to the secretary of war and was then promoted to chief clerk of the War Department. Because of this background, he organized the American survey party in quasi-military fashion: subordinates reported to Parke, and Parke reported to Campbell. The taciturn Campbell remained in the post of commissioner until the end of the survey in 1869.

Parke, born in 1827, entered the Corps of Topographical Engineers directly from the U.S. Military Academy in 1849. After surveying in the Midwest and the territory of New Mexico, he was involved in studying California passes for the Pacific Railroad in 1853, then took command of the important railroad survey of the thirty-second parallel in the Southwest.[14] He remained with the Northwest Boundary Survey until spring 1861, then left to serve in the Civil War, where he was promoted to brevet major general. Parke was reported to be "not only talented, but industrious, & systematic, and an ornament to his particular Corps."[15] Because of the rigid organization of the survey party, Campbell was generally not accessible to the field personnel, but he was fairly well received by his men. Among the party, however—which, in the opinion of one of its members, Joseph Harris, "promises to be a very decent one"—Parke was singled out as "a very fine upright fellow as far as I have seen."[16] The British government appointed separate parties to undertake the land and water surveys, with the experienced Capt. John Summerfield Hawkins in charge of the former. Robert Walsely Haig, a captain in the Royal Artillery, was the chief astronomer.

Campbell assembled an elite, diversified, and experienced field party. His most important recruit was George Clinton Gardner, who was to have complete charge of the American field party. Gardner, who came from a prominent Washington, D.C., family, was only seventeen when in 1849 he began a five-year stint as an assistant on the United States-Mexico Boundary Survey. From 1854 to 1857, he had been occupied in public and private surveys on the Pacific Coast, and he gained considerable field experience surveying in Oregon Territory. He joined the Northwest Boundary Survey when he was twenty-six years old.[17] On Gardner's recommendation, Campbell secured the services of forty-two-year-old George Gibbs. By 1857, Gibbs's reputation as a linguist (he was also a geologist and ethnologist) had grown to the extent that Campbell was keen to have him join the expedition; his accumulated knowledge of Native languages would help the survey's progress in the wilderness. Gibbs prepared numerous maps and sketches of both the volcanos and the rugged peaks near the International Boundary. He remained with the survey until the end of May 1862.[18] Another key assignment was Joseph Smith Harris as assistant surgeon and naturalist. His official title was misleading, for Harris, born in Pennsylvania in 1836, was a surveyor and civil engineer with experience as an astronomer on government surveys.

On the recommendation of Lt. Parke, one of the two topographers chosen for the survey was Swiss-born Henry (Heinrich) Custer, a technical engineer who had remarkable field-sketching and cartographic talent.[19] Born into an aristocratic family in the canton of St. Gall in March 1825, Custer was an enthusiastic, many-sided person with a speculative bent. He had accompanied his physician father on the first botanical exploration of the Alpstein Range in eastern Switzerland, where he had become familiar with mountain hiking, scrambling, and topography. As a teenager, Custer had attended a technical school in Nuremberg, where the headmaster was noted physicist Georg S. Ohm. He then spent three years studying mechanics, mathematics, chemistry, drawing, and architecture at a polytechnical school in Vienna. After graduating with high honors, he was employed as an engineer with the company that built the Zurich-to-Baden railway line, the first such line in Switzerland.[20]

In 1849, Custer immigrated to the United States, perhaps measuring the uncertainty in Swiss railway construction against the allure of California gold and surveying opportunities on a new continent. He searched for gold in the Sierra Nevada foothills and was employed by Capt. John A. Sutter to survey townsites and to map the Feather River.[21] He worked for the U.S. Coast Survey and was an assistant to Parke during the railroad exploration along the thirty-second parallel in 1854–1855.[22] After he worked on the Northwest Boundary Survey in 1864, Custer became second topographic assistant to Clarence King on the historic Fortieth Parallel Survey from 1867 to 1870. [23] It is regrettable that the meritorious record of George Gibbs and Henry Custer never achieved significant recognition.

West to San Francisco and Victoria

The field party sailed from New York on the steamship *George Law* on April 20, 1857, hailed by a cannon-fire salute. In addition to Campbell, Parke, Harris, and Custer, the party of fourteen included William J. Warren, secretary; John J. Major, clerk to the commissioner and clerk and computer to the astronomer; Francis Herbst, the second topographer; Dr. Caleb B.R. Kennerly, an ebullient young surgeon and naturalist; J. Nevin King, quartermaster and commissary; and J.V. Wurdemann, Francis Hudson, and James Nooney, all assigned as computers. Gardner, the assistant astronomer and surveyor, was to join the party upon its arrival in San Francisco, and Gibbs was to meet it in Victoria.[24]

On the ship, even before the assembled party had the opportunity to become acquainted, Harris wrote, there arose "the most furious rain storm that I have ever seen through the whole day."[25] During heavy seas outside Sandy Hook, some of the men became seasick and "toppled over pretty fast." Though the skies were showery and the conditions stormy, the group often went out on deck together.[26] Harris observed that the men "all seem sensible and pleasant and I think the party bids to be a pleasant one. The Commissioner seems very affable and Parke is very free & easy though not at all loweringly so." Custer and Herbst "are married men I believe and the first quiet & decent."[27] Harris, like most of the others, had never been to the Pacific Coast. An expedition to the scenic Northwest—with its glacier-clad mountains, cascading streams, and wilderness—had all the trappings of a romantic adventure, offering the chance to escape from a settled life in the East. As the days at sea progressed, Harris learned more about the country in which they would be operating: "Bear, deer, elk, moose & sheep are said to be abundant and salmon cod haddock duck & snipe." The survey staff, he judged, was a special group: "We dont cultivate the society of others as much as we might."[28]

The party arrived in San Francisco on May 15. On June 17, they sailed on the Coast Survey's steamer *Active* to Victoria, arriving on June 22. There, Campbell and Parke learned with frustration that James Charles Prevost, the British commissioner for the water boundary and captain of the man-of-war *Satellite*, had no authority to determine the land boundary and that the British government had not yet provided a commissioner for that survey. Furthermore, Prevost had only been in Victoria for fifteen days and was not yet prepared to enter an agreement on the water boundary.[29] After two meetings during which the problem was inconclusively discussed, Campbell and his entourage proceeded to the contiguous western terminus of the forty-ninth parallel to establish a depot and locate an observatory. Campbell returned to Victoria on the *Active* and on August 2, 1858, met Capt. Hawkins.

It was already well into summer, and the American commission understood the urgency of getting underway. In mountains such as the northern Cascades, whose serrated and snow-clad forms were already visible to the southeast, the field season was short. The Americans worked alone during the remainder of 1857 and into 1858 before the British survey party arrived on the mainland. By July 15, the Americans had landed all their equipment at Semiahmoo Bay, and a military escort was camped near Bellingham Bay.[30]

Beginning the Survey

When Campbell and Parke arrived on Vancouver Island, they certainly glimpsed the Cascade Range from a distance. At first, neither realized just how alpine, baffling, and difficult the mountains were or that the forty-ninth parallel, easy to plot on a map, would be impossible to trace precisely on the terrain. In a letter to the secretary of state twelve years later, however, Campbell demonstrated his acquired wisdom:

> The 49th parallel extends over rugged and precipitous mountains that attain great elevation, and in the Cascade range on and near the boundary, perpetual snow covers many of the peaks, whose northern gorges are filled with immense glaciers.[31]

Soon after beginning the survey, Campbell became fully aware that the greatest problem would be the section of the land boundary through the Cascade Range, whose "rugged and snow capped ridges, independent of the forest, present serious and formidable obstacles to the prosecution of Astronomical and Geodetic work." In December 1857, Parke added that "the primeval forest extends from the very shores of the Gulf of Georgia to the crest of the Cascade Mountains, and is so dense that it is impossible to take a pack animal in any direction from the trail without constant use of the axe."[32] The use of wagons was "out of the question." It was difficult to know where to begin.

By November 1857, Harris had identified a few important mountains: "To our right towers the eminence of Mt. Baker while farther away lie like white clouds along the horizon the snow capped peaks of Mounts Rainier and Olympus." (He actually saw Mt. Angeles in the Olympic Mountains, not Mt. Olympus.) While on the Fraser River, Gardner and his men could admire Mt. Baker, which, Gibbs later noted, appeared roof-shaped compared to the perspective from Puget Sound. The commission's surveyors, particularly Gardner and Harris, were at first naively optimistic about traversing the range. That month, Harris wrote: "We can go up the Nooksahk River which I have marked just south of the line and crossing the mountains near its head can probably take a nearly straight course across the country intervening between the two ranges of the Cascades."[33] Russell V. Peabody—who worked with the commission from August 1, 1857, to January 15, 1861—guided the party, procured mules for inland transportation and acted as interpreter with the Indians. During California gold-rush days, Peabody had been an associate of an important Whatcom pioneer, Capt. Henry Roeder, and was also one of Whatcom's founders. Usually attached to Gardner, he had a talent for correctly estimating distances and directions.

Semiahmoo Bay, seventy miles from Victoria, proved to be a fortunate site for the American base. Camp Simiahmoo was in a protected location on the saltwater fringe of present-day White Rock, B.C. (named for light-colored Quaternary glacial deposits exposed on bluffs), closely northwest of the forty-ninth parallel on the bay's inland shore. The stream channel near the camp afforded a useful boat exit when tides fell. The American party used the steamer *Constitution* out of Olympia as a liaison and for mails, and they kept whaleboats that could move under sail (these boats were later towed up the Fraser by steamers in order to take supplies to a depot). Quartermaster Nevin King was in charge of the camp, its horses, mules, stores, and boats. The camp had an unobstructed view for triangulation and for determining latitude with the zenith telescope from a semipermanent observatory the men built. Gardner made all the latitude observations, with additional transit sightings by Harris and Parke.[34] As a work base, they used a wall tent pitched over a truss.

A military escort under Capt. D. Woodruff also built quarters at Camp Simiahmoo, including two blockhouses, to protect the site from the northern and Vancouver Island Indians. Harris recorded that the Indians living near the camp, whom he considered to be quite uncivilized and "not fastidious about their dress," had such an abundance of fish, clams, mussels, ducks, and deer available that they stored little for winter. He also remarked that they traveled in families—men, women, children, and dogs—and estimated that there were a hundred Semiahmoo Indians at one village. There is little record of what interaction occurred between the commission members and their escort on the one hand and the nearby tribe on the other. We do know, however, that the quartermaster, King, shot a soldier because after a warning, "he spoke to a young squaw again" in a neighboring hut.[35]

At first, the American party employed local Natives to pack supplies on foot. Indians were also hired for numerous other tasks, including cutting hay, herding horses, transporting canoes, and carrying messages.[36] Both the American and British commissions appear to have possessed some sense of objectivity in their dealings with the Indians. Custer's narratives provide valuable information about Indian activities in the northern Cascades. He saw the Indians as aboriginal peoples, not the mock heroes or villains of romance, and he admired the Native employees and their survival skills. He held the people of the Sumas, Nooksack, and Chilliwack valleys in high esteem and reportedly treated them with some respect, recognizing their good judgment, reliability, and competence in wilderness travel. In one of his reports, he wrote that the American party, by employing the tribes, had secured the goodwill "so necessary to our success."

Custer also credited the Indians with giving the surveyors "most of our first knowledge of the country, as also many of the names of its mountains, smaller streams & lakes." An untitled map of Mt. Baker and the Nooksack-Chilliwack area, probably drawn by Custer in 1857, shows Native nomenclature (including Mt. Baker as "Te-kó-meh"), probably provided by a Nooksack Indian. A "Samona" chief named Thiusoloc was most helpful to the surveyors, and a map he drew provided valuable guidance. Custer noted, however, that the Indians had a limited geographic range. The mountain country was "a perfect terra incognita to them, which they neither need nor care, or have the curiosity to explore."[37]

The American commission's permanent and temporary personnel included guides, hunters, packers, expressmen, chainmen, laborers, carpenters, stonemasons, axemen, sappers, boatmen, boat builders, blacksmiths, herders, cooks, and stewards. The party's number eventually reached thirty or forty (not including the military escort), and the quartermaster depot at Camp Simiahmoo resembled that of an army command. The annual subsistence budget provided for 96 persons for 365 days and 75 persons for 240 days.[38] The surveyors' supplies ranged in cost from $585 for a zenith telescope to two dollars for logarithmic tables.[39] The largest camping purchases were twelve conical tents at $1,046 and twelve reconnaissance tents at $402. Medical items included bullet forceps, an amputator, a tooth extractor, catheters, and a penis syringe. There was also a wide variety of notebooks, pocketbooks, tools, and drafting supplies.

It appears that the commission members ate well. Food purchased included clear pork in barrels, venison, duck, geese, salmon, hams, flour, sugar, potatoes, water crackers, cornmeal, molasses, pilot bread, beans, rice, dried apples and peaches, cranberries, preserved vegetables and fruit, vinegar, black tea, and Batavia coffee (an ample number of mousetraps were necessarily kept on hand). Beef "on the hoof" was also procured. The HBC's Puget Sound Agricultural Company stocked some four hundred head of cattle on a 1,000-acre prairie near Fort Langley (the "Low-el-loh-wuch" prairie), seventeen miles distant. Game was inexpensive: ducks cost twelve and a half cents each and salmon eighty-five cents apiece until the Fraser River gold rush inflated prices.

Survey Party Interactions with Indians

In August and September 1857, Sumas Indians took Gardner's party by canoe to Fort Langley on the Fraser River. It was not possible to make an inland reconnaissance southward because of hostilities among the Stó:lô tribes, and none of the Indians available to accompany the party would venture beyond Sumas Prairie. Parke realized that the Indians, who subsisted on salmon, had little occasion to leave the watercourses known to them, so "No old, well-marked trails were met, and little definite information" was acquired.[40] The surveyors decided to attempt a more southerly approach along the Nooksack River. Peabody, Custer, Herbst, one other man, and an Indian boy as cook left Camp Simiahmoo on August 24 in a whaleboat for Bellingham Bay. Nooksack Indians—who had not been on friendly terms with white settlers, fearing occupation of their land—initially were uncooperative, but the surveyors managed to hire them to transport the party up the Nooksack in canoes.[41] The group ascended the river to near present-day Lynden, then followed small creeks and prairies northeast (the route of the Whatcom Trail) to the "To-tah-la-o" (Sumas) River.

The next undertaking was to establish a camp near the range front at Lake Sumas, about twenty-five miles from Semiahmoo Bay. Parke and Gardner apparently believed that the escort and the larger number of Natives accompanying them would overcome possible reticence by the Sumas Indians, who lived in a large stockade at the mouth of the Sumas River. Gardner, Peabody, Major, Herbst, and six other men—with an escort of seventeen soldiers under a Lt. Douglas—left Camp Simiahmoo on September 25, taking a whaleboat around Point Roberts into the Fraser River. With them were sixteen Indians in five canoes. Gardner was a little concerned about Indians living near the base of Mt. Baker. They had never had any contact with whites and were "but little known by the other Indians that we have seen." He believed their number so small, however, that they would not "give us much trouble."[42] Gardner's party made camp on a prairie near Fort Langley. They discharged the large canoes because only small craft could ply the prairie streams. A group of Sumas Indians took the surveyors to the shallow lake, which was on a large prairie covered with luxuriant grass. Camp Sumass was established north of the forty-ninth parallel and about three miles southwest of the lake.[43]

Francis Herbst made the first reconnaissance of the Sumas Valley. He located for mapping many of the spectacular peaks to the east, and he undoubtedly could see the Cheam Range, Mt. McGuire, and Liumchen Mountain. Herbst also prepared a sketch map of the area from Camp Sumass to the Nooksack River. For five nights, beginning on October 13, Gardner used a zenith telescope to take latitude observations from Camp Sumass. For the survey's initial exploration into the Chilliwack River Valley, Gardner, Peabody, Kennerly and five Indians left the camp on October 28. A mile and a half before reaching the mouth of the "Tummeahai" (Tamihi Creek), the men crossed the river and struck the HBC trail, "said to lead to a large lake at the head of the Chiloweyuck."[44] It was the closest the boundary surveyors had come to Chilliwack Lake. They then returned to Camp Sumass, traveling mainly in canoes hired from Indian villages. During this reconnaissance, Gardner commented, the Indians seemed well-disposed toward them. At one Chilliwack village, the chief offered the survey party protection and asked the same in return. Because the Indians seemed quite explicit in explaining their territorial limits, Gardner suggested to Parke that it might be best to tell them that the survey's purpose was to make a regional map. He sensed that it would be difficult to explain they were running a boundary line between nations.[45]

Probably reasoning that it would be wise to explore more than one route eastward near the boundary, Gardner wanted to probe for a route southward and to try to get around "Lai-yone-san" (Liumchen) Mountain to the east of his camp, on the Chilliwack-Nooksack divide.[46] On November 3, Gardner and Peabody followed the Samona Indian trail by a gap southeast of Camp Sumass (between Vedder and Sumas mountains) to the Columbia Valley, then south to the Nooksack. Because it was late in the season, they decided not to press on. After speaking to the local Indians, Gardner believed that it would not take more than four days to ascend the Nooksack to where the forty-ninth parallel crosses near its headwaters.[47]

Near the end of the 1857 season, because of the intimidating array of mountains visible to the east, Campbell and his subordinates wisely decided that they should not survey directly along the parallel but intersect it via valley and ridge approaches from both the north and south. Concerning a potential route from the Nooksack's north fork to the Chilliwack, Gardner wrote Parke in November:

> This branch of the Nook-sahk heads to the north of Mt. Baker and runs in a south west direction, while the west branch of the Okin a kane runs in a north east direction and the ridge separating them is said to be lower than the head waters of the Nook-sahk—The mountain spur which forms the divide between the Nook-sahk and the Chilosayuck is much the highest and was the barrier to the Hudson's Bay Company's trail; so by following the valley of the Nook-sahk we will avoid them.[48]

At the time, Gardner did not know the position of the Skagit River. He would soon obtain this information from both Indians and HBC factors.

The Water Boundary

In a December joint meeting on the water boundary, both the British and American commissioners remained firm in their interpretations. Prevost wrote Campbell from the *Satellite* contending that Rosario Strait was "a continuation of the Gulf of Georgia." Campbell claimed that the division should be along the middle of Haro Strait, in strict adherence to the treaty's terms, and he refused to compromise.[49] A stronger man than Prevost might have secured American acceptance of Rosario Strait, but Prevost was able to win nothing from the highly political Campbell, who unyieldingly insisted on his interpretation in order to deprive the British of the San Juan Islands. Capt. George H. Richards, the British maritime surveyor and second commissioner for the water boundary, later read the Campbell-Prevost correspondence and was contemptuous of Campbell's case, finding that "he has not one single argument whereon to rest his claim."[50]

Winter Break

In the late fall of 1857, the Americans had time for reading, wood carving, and canoeing. The men also wrote letters to family and friends, although mail sometimes took two months to reach the East Coast. There was occasional social drinking, and, as Harris observed, "if you dont drink at all you are considered a queer fellow." When the weather broke, the view of the mountains from the shoreline reminded them of the coming season's work. "Tonight you can [see] range after range growing higher and higher until you reach the dazzling snow capped peaks of the Cascades," Harris wrote one evening in October.[51] In February, Gibbs sketched Mt. Baker from the camp.

The British survey vessels appeared regularly near the Americans' winter camp and engaged in considerable shooting practice (regulations obligated them to fire a certain number of rounds each year). The American party met the crews of both the *Satellite* and the *Plumper*. They reported dissension on the *Satellite* and labeled its skipper "Dismal Jimmy" (an apparent reference to Prevost), but the *Plumper*'s crew was considered a splendid set of fellows. To Harris, the English officers seemed "rather reserved on first acquaintance and it takes some time to get to know them well."[52]

By late fall, the isolation and rainy weather apparently began to affect the American survey team. They were unused to heavy underbrush in a cold, wet wilderness and "mountains everywhere." Harris wrote to his mother in late November: "To go up the face of some of these mountains would [be] impossible as well as useless." The surveyors were cheered by a grand Christmas dinner at their base camp, however, with beef, mutton, turkey, duck, venison, pastry, figs, raisins, olives, and almonds. The Indians received a gift of "a barrel and a half of flour, several fathoms of molasses and several fathoms of tobacco for tobacco here is put up in strings and measured by fathoms instead of pounds."[53] To avoid boredom, the American surveyors spent some of the winter in the San Juan Islands. In December, Kennerly cruised to Orcas Island in a sloop and explored the archipelago, which, he observed, originally belonged to the Lummi and "Cowitchin" tribes. He noted that the absence of predators made the islands excellent for the HBC's sheep-raising enterprise, and it was reported that the mutton there was "remarkable for its delicacy of flavor."[54]

The British Surveyors Arrive

The British land survey began with the 1858 season. Col. John Hawkins, born in 1812, spent much of his life in the Royal Engineers. He obtained the army rank of major in June 1858 and became a lieutenant colonel that December. He retired in 1881 with the honorary rank of major general and was knighted. The British commission also included Lt. Charles John Darrah, an astronomer who would receive the Crimea Medal before his premature death in 1871. Dr. David Lyall of the Royal Navy was the medical officer. Appointed to the *Plumper,* the forty-one-year-old surgeon had accompanied both Sir John Franklin and Sir Edward Belcher in the Arctic. His collection of plant specimens, which he dried and sent to the Herbarium at the Royal Gardens at Kew, contained 1,375 species, some newly discovered that he named after himself or other members of the commission. John Keast Lord, the naturalist and veterinary surgeon, had served with Turkish forces in the Crimea, and his collection of plant specimens is in the Natural History Museum in London. Hilary Bauerman, a geologist had been born in London in 1835 and had studied in England and Germany before his appointment to the commission. With George Gibbs, he was the first to study the complex geology of the northern Cascade Range. Bauerman subsequently undertook assignments as a mining geologist and wrote textbooks on mineralogy.[55]

Lt. Charles William Wilson of the Royal Engineers, was the secretary and transport officer. As secretary, Wilson was responsible for all accounts and records. He was also in command of the Royal Engineers detachment that was to accompany the commission for surveying and other work and acted as commissariat, store, and transport officer—duties that were to prove exceedingly arduous. He was only twenty-two years old when he left England for the boundary survey. Wilson was one of those nineteenth-century British officers whose contributions to science were of greater significance than their battle service. He was educated in Germany and England and, after receiving his commission in the elite Royal Engineers in 1855, spent most of his life surveying and mapping various parts of the globe. Among his diplomatic duties was his service as British commissioner for demarcation of the Serbian boundary after the 1878 Treaty of Berlin. Wilson was eventually knighted and made a major general. With his observant eye on history, he kept a detailed record of his impressions and activities and also created watercolor illustrations. Wilson's diary, originally intended for the amusement of his sister, combines the serious and accurate with the trivial.[56] In it, he commented on the social life of frontier towns and on HBC employees, American settlers, and Indians. Given the vastness of the terrain surveyed, Wilson's writing was bound to be impressionistic rather than comprehensive. Lt. Samuel Anderson, the second secretary to the commission, arrived the next year.

Because the boundary country to be surveyed was wild and mountainous—much of it barely explored and some of it completely unknown—the commission made careful preparations before leaving England, expecting the survey to last three to four years. The month of March 1858 was spent obtaining a large array of field equipment (ranging from rifles to a portable boat) and testing the astronomical and terrain-survey instruments, including one seven-inch and three five-inch theodolites, two sextants, chronometers, prismatic compasses, and measuring chains (the Americans loaned them a zenith telescope). In addition to the instruments, the most expensive field items out of a £2,471 estimate were tents, tools, camp equipment, clothing, and blankets.[57]

The voyage of the British commission from Southampton, England, to Colón, Panama, took the entire month of April. The surveyors then rode the recently completed railway across the isthmus to Panama City. Wilson described the stretch of land between the two great oceans, a taste of the untracked wilderness they would soon encounter in the northern Cascades:

> The railway from Colon to Panama is certainly one of the most wonderful and curious works in the world. Directly after leaving Colon the train rushes into a dismal swamp, which comes right up to the rails on either side. It is no wonder that the labourers died like rotten sheep, working, as they must have done, up to their waists in water, and in the rank vegetation.[58]

At Panama City, the British frigate HMS *Havannah* was in port, ready to convey the commission to Esquimalt Harbor (near Victoria) on Vancouver Island. After taking men and stores on board, it sailed on May 1. The ship crossed the equator four times before favorable winds permitted it to head north, and it did not cast anchor until July 12.[59] The ship was sheltered by timbered hills, and the picturesque harbor lay across from the snow-capped Olympic Mountains and with an open strait to the ocean. When the detachment of Royal Engineers landed, they were proud to be the first British troops quartered on Vancouver Island—5,068 miles due west of London—in the same year that the mainland became a colony. On arrival, Wilson's biographer Charles Watson writes, the staff was concerned that "the summer months were slipping away" while the American team was already in the field.

In preparation for the survey, the Foreign Office had purchased land and buildings in Esquimalt Harbor. The *Plumper,* a man-of-war under Capt. Richards, was available for surveys and latitude observations. Previously engaged in New Zealand and Arctic waters, the vessel was slow but suited to its purpose. The energetic Richards, then thirty-eight years of age, served as the chief astronomer-surveyor.

When Hawkins arrived at Esquimalt, he learned that the American party had already made a reconnaissance along the International Boundary to the western mountain uplift. After consulting with Parke, Hawkins decided to send an astronomical and reconnaissance party to the American station near Lake Sumas. His July 26 dispatch to the Foreign Office read in part: "I think it right to state . . . that the American reconnaissance, at least as much of it as I saw, seemed to be almost entirely confined to the British Territories; but this might in a great measure be explained by the fact that a great portion of the Sea and the Cascade Mountains must be approached from the Frazer River."[60]

A Measure of Latitude

Gardner—then only twenty-seven years old—was in charge of the American field party for 1858 while Parke took general control of the commission's working force. When Gardner was absent, Harris directed the field party. Warren, the secretary, kept all records and accounts, paying the men quarterly and acting as postmaster. Gardner's field party was a youthful group—most of the men were not beyond their thirties—that was accustomed to hardship and for whom the pursuit of knowledge was almost an obsession. They began the fieldwork—delineating, marking, and defining the western section of the boundary—in early 1858. The first project, from March to May, was the survey across the Point Roberts peninsula and the establishment of "Station Parallel" on latitude forty-nine degrees, closely southeast of Camp Simiahmoo at land's edge.[61]

Delineating a boundary line depends on accurate triangulation, and in a mountainous region this requires that survey stations be placed in prominent locations. Still, surveying and marking the forty-ninth parallel involved a great deal of compromise. Both the American and British surveyors approached the parallel via stream valleys because they could not sight along the boundary line, and the astronomical surveyors established observation points on peaks and ridges so they could determine the latitude and longitude of each station. They could then use triangulation to determine the exact location of the line.

From 1858 to 1862, twelve latitude stations (not including the observatory at Camp Simiahmoo) were set down at prominent stream crossings along the parallel from Camp Sumass to Camp Osoyoos. As the terrain permitted, specific stations were connected by survey lines, according to which intermediate monuments were placed by computed offsets upon the forty-ninth parallel. After triangulation determined the location of the parallel, it was marked by stones piled around a five-foot post. During the survey, forty-three monuments were placed from the west shore of Point Roberts to the Columbia Valley, and a continuous line was run and marked to latitude stations. The line from monuments 35 to 43 was projected eastward on the observed parallel.[62] By 1861, cast-iron monuments five feet high replaced the stone pyramids, and 161 markers were eventually placed on the entire span from Point Roberts to the Rocky Mountains. Because the geodetic, or true, parallel could not be determined, both commissions agreed to adopt the mean astronomic parallel as the boundary.

The American commission's immediate tasks included surveying triangulation nets along the boundary area from Camp Simiahmoo to the foothills south of Lake Sumas, the identification of boundary points, and the projection (where practical) of straight lines between them. The boundary points had to be connected with the triangulation to compute their geographic positions. The extremely mountainous nature of the terrain precluded the extension of a continuous net of triangulation. During the 1858 season, astronomical observations to determine three points on the parallel in the Chilliwack Valley drainage were completed.

The astronomical parties had to make nighttime observations at the latitude stations, and the usual procedure was first to send a reconnaissance party ahead to blaze a rough trail. Teams of surveyors and astronomers followed, setting up stations for making exact astronomical observations and tracing the line with a compass survey. Laborers cut vistas that were twenty feet wide on each side at astronomical stations, near settlements, and at important stream crossings.[63]

The two topographers, Custer and Herbst, worked closely with the surveyors and astronomers and were as much artists as surveyors. Their duties were to measure a few control points, then to sketch topographic features from good vantages and determine the barometric altitude of hundreds of locations. The preliminary field sketches, along with the connection of triangulation points, resulted in correct maps covering the boundary region.

In the earliest phase of the survey, the Americans used waterways whenever possible; pack animals were not generally used until operations were well inland. In March, using a canoe and with an Indian guide, Custer made a reconnaissance of the terrain between Camp Simiahmoo and the Nooksack and Sumas prairies. While ascending a hill in this area, Custer could see the Nooksack and Fraser rivers, which "wound their way like silvery threads."[64] He drew a map to depict the terrain best suited for a trail. He also probed the route to Lake Whatcom (Gibbs had made a map of the lake in 1854). With Indians and a canoe, he made a shoreline survey that summer from the American base to Whatcom and then to the Nooksack thinking that the drainage could provide a supply route to the parallel. By the end of the 1858 season, using his Schmalcalden compass and a watch to measure distances traveled, Custer had "tramped over and mapped a good deal of ground and has been in the field more than any other member of the Survey."[65]

Distant Terrain Observations

In March, Parke sent a party to ascend the Fraser River to make distant terrain observations and study possible access routes to the parallel from the north. Gardner, Peabody, Gibbs, and Kennerly left Camp Simiahmoo in a large canoe and proceeded around Point Roberts into the Fraser, reaching Fort Langley on March 10. After exploring nearby prairies, the group continued to the mouth of the Chilliwack River. Venturing north, they entered "Harrison River" to reach the outlet of a large lake, "Pook-pah-kohre" (Harrison Lake). They canoed onward about twelve miles to a remarkable hot sulfur spring, whose bubbly water threw out a vapor cloud "so strongly impregnated with sulphur as to make it unpleasant to remain."[66]

Continuing the reconnaissance, Gardner's party arrived at Fort Hope on March 23, where a Mr. Walker, who was in charge of the post, gave them a report on the HBC trail to Fort Colville. He had little reliable information on the nature of the boundary-line terrain. The company's trade west of the mountains, Gardner wrote, "is mostly with canoe Indians, who seldom leave the margin of the streams and consequently have no well worn trails."[67] A few Natives, however, provided vital knowledge. The "Saa-me-ma" chief "Pa-haa-luk" told them that the trail from the fort along the "Kleh-kwun-num" (Silverhope Creek) crossed to the "Kleht-la-killa" (Post Creek), following it to the Chilliwack River, then the "En-saaw-kwach" (Nesakwatch) and around to the south of Mt. Baker. The Indians used the trail in hunting, Gardner wrote, but they "know of no such stream as the Nooksahk." He inferred that the trail bore east of the Nooksack's headwaters, a conclusion that Gibbs agreed with. Gardner learned about Chilliwack Lake from the chief's son, "Hwee-tah-lich-kun," whom he regarded as a most intelligent Indian and the person best acquainted with the country. Hwee-tah-lich-kun told Gardner that a mountain trail used for goat hunting led from Silverhope Creek to a stream that fed Chilliwack Lake. On learning that deep snow would impede crossing the divide to the lake, Gardner decided to retrace his route for a western approach.

While descending the Fraser on March 31, the Gardner party saw miners working river placers for gold. The group stopped at Wahleach (Jones) Creek, which the Indians had told them came from a lake. Passing beneath Cheam Peak, they continued downstream to the mouth of the Sumas River to get supplies for the new exploration.[68] After obtaining ten days' food at Fort Langley as well as fish and meat from local Indians, Gardner's party along with eleven Indians to carry loads followed the old HBC trail cut along broad, timbered benches from the Fraser's alluvial flats to mountain-bound Chilliwack Lake. Gardner observed that the "Chilowchuk" River's "banks are abrupt in many places, but a good trail can be made up the valley."[69]

During the four-and-a-half-day venture along the rushing river, Gardner sighted potential routes to reach the forty-ninth parallel, which crossed rocky, precipitous mountain ridges and untracked, forested river valleys. Obtaining the names of feeder streams from the Indians (there were villages five miles up the Chilliwack River and two miles above Slesse Creek), he correctly concluded that the line could be reached by the "Tum-mea-hai" (Tamihi), "Sen-eh-sai" (Slesse), and "En-saaw-kwach" (Nesakwatch) valleys, where branch trails could be built to supply work parties.[70]

Gardner and Peabody were the first members of the survey party to reach Chilliwack Lake on April 7.[71] They could see a magnificent panorama of forest-clad ridges rising steeply above the lake, the ridges capped by snowy peaks gleaming in the springtime brilliance. The men built a raft resembling a flat-iron, using two dry logs with wooden pins through poles that were laid across the logs and tied with willow withes. The next day, Gardner, Peabody, and four Indians crossed to the far shore, where they found a low beach at the sandy mouth of the "Klahihu" (upper Chilliwack River), the lake's principal feeder.

After the reconnaissance party returned to camp at the mouth of the Sumas on April 11, they learned more about the upper Skagit River from an Indian who had crossed the divide eastward from Chilliwack Lake. The country east of the Skagit was reputedly open timber terrain, and Gardner learned that the HBC traders had not availed themselves of the shortest route beyond Chilliwack Lake. Gardner also entertained plans to explore the Nooksack River drainage above the point he had reached in 1857. He had learned that small streams led to a pass through the mountains northeast of Mt. Baker (probably Hannegan Pass), and he thought he could make an alpine crossing to the upper Chilliwack River. Though the Stó:lô Indians were willing to pack loads to the Nooksack River, they did not like to travel during this season, because their winter food was depleted and they were about to begin potato planting.

Summer Season Activities

The midsummer field party—which included Kennerly, Harris, King, Herbst, an additional twelve to fifteen men, packers, and an escort of twenty-five soldiers from the 9th U.S. Infantry—left Camp Simiahmoo on July 21 to establish a depot at a slough by the mouth of the Chilliwack River. Because of the gold rush, Gardner was unable to charter a steamer to take the large group to the depot and had to settle for a slow schooner scow. When the boat entered the Fraser, the steamer *Surprise*, its decks laden with prospectors, towed the clumsy craft to Fort Langley. On entering the river at low tide, however, the scow was swamped when the steamer backed off, and the men had to climb up the steamer's side to save themselves. Because the scow was virtually destroyed, the men remained on the steamer to reach the fort and then returned to Simiahmoo on foot to get supplies and charter another schooner from Whatcom for the trip back.

Chiloweyuck Depot, on the east bank of the Chilliwack River at Chiloweyuck Prairie, was about a mile and a half from the Fraser, where river vessels could enter with supplies. There the American commission built log storehouses. Salmon and sturgeon were plentiful, but the depot proved to be an insect haven. Dr. Kennerly reported: "We thought ourselves comparatively safe here from musquitoes, but we were able to sleep but very little last night. I was forced to get out of bed twice in order to make a smoke around the bed; we have yet to learn how they got through the fine meshes of our bar." Fleas were also a problem.[72] Despite the insects, however, Kennerly—along with Gibbs, Bauerman, and Lyall—was interested in studying the natural environment and its wildlife. Much like the scientists did on the Pacific Railroad Survey, they gathered data on natural history and geography.

Kennerly, a collaborator with the Smithsonian Institution, was keen to bring back specimens from the Pacific Northwest. His 1858 diary included observations of the magpie, fish crow, teal, mallard, grebe, Carolina dove, hooded merganser, ruffed grouse, gull, osprey, and swallow.[73] In September, he caught a thirty-inch trout at Chilliwack Lake. An Indian arrived at the lake with six hoary marmots, a real prize to the naturalist, since he believed there were no specimens at the Smithsonian. Kennerly stuffed birds with cotton and skinned animals, sprinkling the skins with arsenic to preserve them.

On August 2, Peabody arrived at the depot with a pack train from Whatcom. Two days later, Gardner, King, Peabody, and ten members of the escort left on a four-day trip to Chilliwack Lake, with Indians carrying the surveying instruments on their backs. At the lake, the party found that a ferry had been established by "Mssrs. Townsend and Stott" and that the two entrepreneurs had built a ferry house "and were keeping tavern for the entertainment of man and beast, giving the place quite a civilized appearance, compared with April last."[74] The members of the survey admired the picturesque mountain lake, hemmed in by rocky shores, with waters "very deep, clear, and transparent." The "views it presents," Gibbs wrote, "are almost unequalled, even in this region of wild and solitary grandeur."[75]

Meanwhile, the men at the depot found the pests and the rain impossible. On August 5, Kennerly deplored the "Rain, Rain, incessant rain! All Day long nearly it has been pouring down." Kennerly had been left in charge of the depot for part of the season. On August 21, a large group of Chilliwack Indians in ten canoes landed at the village north of the depot.[76] Rumors abounded that forty-two white men had been killed by Indians above Fort Yale, and the local Chilliwacks, innocent of those deeds, wanted advice about how to avoid violence. Kennerly suggested they go to Fort Hope and determine the truth of the rumors that miners of the Fraser were going to kill some of them. By September 21, he had learned that only fourteen whites had been killed, and he wrote that he was glad the Indians could distinguish between the surveyors, who hired them, and the miners, who were the "cultus tillicum" (worthless people).

Custer reported to Chiloweyuck Depot on August 9. With Harris, he made a triangulation of the prairie and located the prominent mountain peaks in view. They began measuring the angles of a triangulation system laid out from a four thousand-yard east-west base, from the prairie to the depot's flagstaff.[77] From this station they would determine the position of such peaks as Slesse, McGuire, Tomyhoi, Liumchen, Church, and Amadis.

At Chilliwack Lake, Gardner deemed it necessary for the commission to build its own boats rather than rely on the ferry company for transportation on the lake. First they constructed a flatboat with gunwales. It was made of fir or cedar, large enough to carry twelve mules, and sufficiently broad to be propelled by oars.[78] Spikes, oakum, and pitch were used in construction; and the lumber for the scow's two-inch boards was obtained near the lake camp. For Herbst's survey of the lake and the valley beyond, Gardner ordered the construction of a canoe. Peabody had brought along a canoe-maker from a Chilliwack village who began work on August 20. He hollowed out a log with an adze, used a fire to shape the bow and stern, and then tied thwarts to brace the gunwales and preserve the form. Everyone was surprised to find that the craftsman finished the canoe in five days rather than the expected two months. Because the pack animals were exhausted, Harris and Herbst did not join Gardner at the lake until the third trip. They left Chiloweyuck Depot on August 21 and arrived at the lake in four days. Herbst's fieldbook shows profiles and directions of peaks from Camp Chiloweyuck and the lake.[79] While based at this camp, Harris completed a full set of magnetic observations.

With their own boats, Peabody and Gardner could now locate Camp Chiloweyuck on the west bank of "Kla-hai-hu" Creek (upper Chilliwack River) near the parallel (at latitude 49°00'22"), about three-fourths of a mile south of the lake. By August 26, Gardner was able to mount the zenith telescope and transit for astronomical observations. He began work at the camp on August 31, obtaining 106 results on 42 pairs of stars. While waiting for the weather to clear, he found the valley to the south, beyond the parallel, "walled in by immense mountains."[80] While the main survey crew established the new camp, Gibbs explored the middle Skagit River—whose course through the range was still a mystery—to determine whether a portion of the parallel could be reached from downstream. He learned, however, that the Indians had not been above the canyon "on account of a tremendous rapid or cascade."[81]

Preparing Plans on How to Mark the Boundary

On August 2, three weeks after the British commission arrived in Victoria, Col. Hawkins, Capt. Haig, and Lt. Wilson boarded the *Active* to visit Archibald Campbell and set a plan to meet on the mainland.[82] Social events for the British officers were also soon on the schedule. That evening the three men went to a ball given by the *Plumper*'s officers, where they met the young women of Victoria. Wilson recorded his impressions: "They only number about 30 & are not very great beauties; however I enjoyed myself very much, not having had a dance for such a time." After a picnic dinner two days later,

> . . . we sat down & smoked until the fair sex or 'les belles sauvages' had taken their siesta. One horrid event which happened I must not forget to relate. A shower of rain came on & we had to take refuge in an Indian hut & on coming out I found myself literally covered with fleas, actually swept them off my clothes & have been in agonies ever since. The most rigid shaking of blankets & clothes & sweeping out cannot get rid of them though I manage to polish off a few every evening.[83]

On August 9, Hawkins, Haig, and Wilson left Victoria on the *Satellite* on their way to meet formally with the American commission. The sail through the islands in the Strait of Georgia was delightful, the open glades in the forest and scattered clumps of trees looking "exactly like an English park scene."[84] Three days later, exactly one month after arriving at Victoria, the British saluted the American commissioner when he came aboard their ship in Semiahmoo Bay. The following day, the British went to the American camp on shore to prepare a protocol on how to mark the land boundary.[85] Wilson wrote of the Americans:

> We found them all very pleasant people & will, I am sure, prove capital companions on our journey to the mountains; indeed Mr. Campbell and Parke are very clever, well informed men & have much more of the Englishman than the American in their manners. In the evening Capt. Prevost of the *Satellite* gave us a grand dinner party, at which all the officials on both sides attended. It was enlivened by the presence of two ladies, Mrs. Prevost & Mrs. Alder the wife of a Capt. in the American navy.[86]

As Hawkins and Campbell met face to face, the hope was expressed that the coordinated efforts of the survey would prevail over differences and national interests. Hawkins was determined that there be no friction, and he later reported that on several occasions he had yielded on a point against his better judgment in order to ensure harmony. Considering the discord between the two governments, it is remarkable that the two commissioners worked together as well as they did, and at times their relations relaxed almost to the point of friendship.[87]

The commissioners determined that it was inexpedient to mark the entire boundary by cutting a forest vista. They decided instead to make convenient astronomic points on or near the boundary by cutting a track one-half mile or more on each side. They would similarly mark and cut at important streams, settlements, permanent trails, "or any striking natural feature." Of the entire line, 190 miles were eventually cleared and marked, leaving 220 miles untraced, unmarked, and unsurveyed.

The agreement between the two men obscures the fact that Hawkins argued in favor of more forest cutting than Campbell did and in favor of erecting frequent iron markers, as on the Maine-Quebec boundary. The British favored monuments at one-mile intervals, although Hawkins did not feel he could recommend such an expense to his government. They finally agreed to erect iron monuments between Point Roberts and Camp Sumass and to use stone cairns to mark the remainder of the line. They later learned that many of the cairns fell apart, so Hawkins's misgivings appeared to have been justified.[88]

"At Last We Have Begun to Work"

In late August—nearly five months after leaving home and with summer fast nearing its end—Haig, Darrah, and Lyall started for "Sumass," the first point on the parallel to be fixed astronomically. The three officers, along with non-commissioned officers and sappers of the Royal Engineers, left Esquimalt and proceeded via the Fraser River by steamer, *bateaux*, and canoes. They made camp at the south end of Lake Sumas on August 30. Wilson recorded a word of relief in his diary: "I am very glad that at last we have begun work."[89]

Wilson's responsibilities included keeping the party supplied with provisions and equipment, organizing mule trains, arranging for Indian packers, and hiring labor to cut the vistas. Fortunately, the HBC in Victoria was well stocked with provisions, and soon after his arrival Wilson had begun making purchases and arrangements to supply the survey crews on the mainland. The commission's progress was slowed, however, by its dependence on the transport of supplies from Victoria and Fort Langley by steamer. The gold rush had caused a considerable increase in the price of labor and supplies, as well as frustration and delay for the British. Furthermore, Hawkins traveled up the Fraser with Governor James Douglas and troops to monitor disturbances between gold miners and Indians, and he did not return to the Sumas camp until September 23. He then went to Victoria to coordinate logistics. It was not until October 13 that mules were sent by steamer to Fort Langley.[90]

Supplies were first conveyed to the principal depots by river steamboats and then by canoes, *bateaux*, scows, pack trains, and Indian packers. While the canoes had been made and manned by local Indians, the *bateaux* were of the HBC pattern. Some of these large, flat-bottomed boats had been built at Fort Langley (where there is a replica), and they were used to cross Lake Sumas and ply the Fraser. Seven or more men rowed the boats, which could carry a considerable amount of stores.

Parke visited the British camp on September 28 and pointed out the position of the station mark on the parallel. At the time, Hawkins was not aware of the amount of work the American commission had done during the past season, but he had reason to think that it did not exceed the fixation of three points on the parallel by the party detached from Simiahmoo on the 21st July mentioned to your Lordship in my previous Report; one point being at the Chilukweyuk Lake about 70 miles east of Simiahmoo, one between Chilukweyuk and Schweltza [Cultus Lake], and one about 10 miles east of Chilukweyuk towards the Cascade Mountains.[91]

The British sappers made a reconnaissance survey of the mainly lowland district between Sumas, Cultus Lake, and the Chilliwack and Fraser rivers in early fall. There was no displeasure to learn that "the whole of the valuable Prairie land in this neighbourhood proved to be within British Territories."[92]

In the late fall, Wilson took a reinforcement of seven sappers and four axemen from Fort Langley to Sumas Prairie (near the American Camp Sumass). When the steamer that was supposed to take the party upriver did not arrive, Wilson and Lord hired a large *bateau* from the HBC at Fort Langley (the mules were to follow under a corporal when the steamer arrived from Victoria). On October 21, amid torrents of rain, they blithely launched themselves onto the Fraser, fighting wet, cold conditions and a strong current. Wilson related the ordeal: "My first night's experience of camping out in the bush was anything but cheerful. The rain continued heavily all night, and the only wood we had being sodden drift wood, made a very poor fire. So we stowed ourselves between the blankets, and, under the influence of a hot tot of grog, composed ourselves to sleep."[93] He also described the Indian village on the spit, whose inhabitants came to visit the landing party:

> They were a much superior race to the Victoria or Tsaumas Indians, and, most of them being able to talk the jargon, we got on pretty well. The village is protected by a strong stockade which surrounds the houses. These are built of enormous pieces of timber, roughly hewn, which must have cost an immensity of time and labour to place in position. The interior of the houses were very dirty, and had a dreadfully fishy smell.[94]

On October 23, Wilson and Lord and their party started at daylight in seven canoes engaged from Indians. The Sumas River was crowded with wild duck, but it was so rainy that Wilson could not keep the nipples of his gun dry. Upon entering Lake Sumas, "we called a halt and served out some grog, which was of great benefit to all, as we were quite wet through."[95] Serious problems soon arose when about a mile and a half from shore the water became so shallow that the *bateaux* got stuck. The canoes continued another mile, with difficulty:

> This was a climax to our misfortunes. Lord & I could not help laughing at each others black faces, however there was not time to idle, as the camp was a 4 mile march after landing, so out I jumped into the water, & we all set to work to land the stores, for 4 hours we were all hands in water, in many places up to our knees, working like slaves, & got everything landed even to the heavy barrels of beef which I slung on the shoulders of 3 or 4 Indians; the Indians are dreadfully lazy but by dint of swearing at them in every language I could think of, & liberal promises of tobacco I managed to

get on. The camp being now only 4 miles off I determined to push on leaving a guard with the heavy baggage, but soon had reason to repent it, as we found the trail led through a marshy prairie, the grass of which reached the shoulders of the men. Several of the men gave out, but I cheered them on till it began to get dark, when head over heels I went into a dike, out of which I managed to scramble.[96]

When the men arrived at the camp, Wilson was barely able to speak because of exhaustion, not having "tasted a crumb since breakfast," but a first-rate supper "soon set me to rights again."[97]

By that time, Haig had completed observations for fixing the position of the Sumas station. The British surveyors opened a second camp to the east on November 13 at the north end of "Schweltza" (Cultus) Lake. They used a rubber boat to reach the astronomical station at the opposite end, where they took systematic astronomical readings until the rains forced them to stop.[98] The first axemen had to cut the boundary line through gigantic firs near Sumas Prairie, some of them 30 feet in circumference and 250 feet high. In his survey of natural history, *The Naturalist in Vancouver Island and British Columbia*, Lord referred to them as "Douglas spruce." He was also studying other flora and fauna. It did not take him long to discover devil's club, "that most prickly and unpleasant plant named the 'Devil's Walking-stick' (*Panax horridus*)." In his first natural-history study, however, he concentrated on the sedges and grasses of shallow Lake Sumas. In nature's inevitable progression, insect swarms accumulated as the prairie dried, to be followed by birds who built their nests and reared their young. Lord observed the swallow, flycatcher, yellow finch, northern swift, and raven. Roundfish on Sumas Prairie were so profuse that "it was only requisite to stand in the stream and bale out the fish."[99]

Lord, a tall, "big-shouldered" Englishman who sported a great black beard, was a spirited and opinionated personality. Taking the pen name "the Wanderer," he had quietly and unexpectedly forsaken a veterinary practice for a new life as a naturalist and sportsman in the "North-western Wilds." His book offers not only taxonomy but also personal reminiscences and reflections. He delighted piously in the natural world, admiring, for example, the squirrel's useful pouch as "striking evidence of Divine wisdom and forethought." Unlike other members of the British commission, who rarely expressed wonder at the wilderness or the allure of the mountain peaks, Lord was an observer in the spirit of the poet-romanticists. His years in and near the Cascade Range seem to have been the most important in his life. Although by all accounts always a British gentleman, Lord possessed a knack for adapting to changing circumstances and environments. He recorded practical advice on how to catch fish, build a log house, swim a horse across a raging stream, and cook trout in the most artistic fashion.

As assistant naturalist, Lord was subordinate to Lyall but he seems to have worked quite independently (Lyall, for example, fails to mention him in his botanical report). The collection that Lord deposited at the British Museum apparently contained several new species, and he was the first to describe the Rocky Mountain pika. He was more professionally accomplished as a veterinarian than as a naturalist, however, and testimony from the commission's members indicate his concern for the pack animals' well-being and diet during the winter of 1859–1860 on Sumas Prairie. Lord commented in his book on the acute problem of feed amid the forest and bush of the western Cascade slope: "A great proportion of the loads carried by horses and mules travelling this way necessarily consist of grain for themselves." The expense was enormous, with the commission's pack animals consuming a thousand pounds of grain per day.

The field experience of 1858 was an apprenticeship in a wilderness environment that required exhausting foot travel and sometimes awkward stream crossings. Autumn rains often made trails a morass, with slippery footing for the horses, but there was also the exhilaration of riding through a sea of uncut grass and the occasional evening rest around a campfire. By December 7, snow two feet deep and a temperature of eleven degrees Fahrenheit brought an end to British field operations and a return to winter quarters in Victoria. The steamer trip back had some excitement. Mutinous miners drew revolvers and attempted to take possession of the ship, Wilson wrote, but fortunately the captain prevailed.[100] Victoria was quite a contrast to Sumas. The sociable Wilson could enjoy "a round of balls, private theatricals, and duck shooting." Good barracks had been built at Esquimalt, where the commission carried out the indoor labor of calculating the observations and plotting the surveys.

Col. Hawkins acknowledged in his report to the British secretary of state for foreign affairs that the season's results had been "not very satisfactory." He accounted for the limited progress by citing the commission's late arrival, unavoidable delays in getting to the survey work, widespread disorganization in supplies, the great difficulty of moving about and getting transport, and much unfavorable weather. He was optimistic, however, that their experiences would help prepare them for the 1859 season, and he was "happy to inform your Lordship that the general health of the expedition has been very good throughout."[101]

The Americans East of Chilliwack Lake

The primary task confronting the American field party late in the 1858 season was to begin a reconnaissance east of Chilliwack Lake, an area for which Gardner still had little information except that "the country along the boundary must be rough indeed." A chance encounter with Whatcom Trail builder Walter W. de Lacy yielded the valuable information that the next main drainage was the Skagit, not the Nooksack.[102] Leaving Kennerly in charge of Camp

Chiloweyuck, Gardner and Peabody with one other man and two soldier escorts followed the Whatcom Trail along glacier-fed "Chuch chehum" (Depot) Creek on September 25. They established Camp Chuchchehum on the parallel in heavy timber at a calculated elevation of 3,405 feet, north of Mt. Redoubt and near the north branch of Depot Creek.[103]

Gardner and Peabody sent their men, with mules, to follow the Whatcom Trail down Maselpanik Creek, while they crossed the mountains by a more direct route, traveling as nearly due east as possible. Fortunately, they had fine weather on the trek. "We soon found ourselves at the base of the Chuch chehum glaciers," Gardner wrote, "where we had to take a north east course down a ravine to the Skagit River."[104] The high mountains to the south of camp took the informal name "Chuch-che-hum Mountains"; the pass to Maselpanik Creek (at 4,533 feet) and the Skagit was called "Chuch chehum Pass." During the crossing to the Skagit, Gardner and Peabody were immersed in wilderness grandeur. On the ridge they crossed, estimated at 5,000 to 6,000 feet in altitude, they found one or two small lakes formed by melting snow. The dazzling sight of glacier ice (apparently the Maselpanik Glacier) prompted Gardner to write: "The glacier before which we stood made a grand picture." Gardner also noted the stunted firs with their branches drooping from the pressure of winter snows. Down the ravine, the underbrush was so dense it tore their clothing, so that on their return to the lake they were clad "somewhat in Highland costume, shorts, considerably above the knee, beautifully fringed, but not in a very appropriate dress for the weather as the snow continued to fall all day."[105]

Because Gardner and Peabody reached the Skagit River just north of the forty-ninth parallel, it is likely that they crossed from the Maselpanik drainage to St. Alice Creek before descending to the Skagit. Gardner was surprised to find a well-worn Indian trail along the Skagit's banks. They found their party at the mouth of the Maselpanik and returned to Chilliwack Lake via the Whatcom Trail. They had been gone a total of eight days. This extraordinary trek ranks with the adventurous high ridge and pass crossings that Custer and his party would make in 1859.

During October, helpers were busy building a trail to the Skagit River. It was a difficult project, and much corduroying was needed because of swampy slopes. When early snows appeared on the mountains, it was apparent that crossing the range again would be unwise—in fact, three Indians who arrived on October 19 had come from near Fort Hope on snowshoes.[106] Parke, Gardner, and Peabody attempted observations of stars at Camp Chuchchehum late in the month but had little success because of cloudy skies. Custer, who joined Gardner at the camp on October 30, had completed his triangulation of Chilliwack Lake and located all mountains in view. To find his way around the upper end of Chilliwack Lake when returning from Depot Creek one night, Gardner had to resort to lighting cedar torches, "passing many places that day light would have made frightful, for at times we had but a foot hold on a perpendicular wall of rock, with the deep lake only a few feet below."[107] He had also measured the parallel and extended his chain-and-compass survey to the summit beyond Camp Chuchchehum (this would have been the Maselpanik divide).

On October 10, there was an accident to the British detachment at Chilliwack Lake. Upon leaving the ferry-house tavern after dark, the canoe under the command of Lt. David B. McKibben capsized with three men in the frigid water. Michael Brown drowned, and the others nearly froze as they followed the rough, rocky flanks of the lake through the night to their base. At an inquest, affidavits concerning the death were made by Dr. Kennerly, Gibbs, McKibben, Townsend, and Custer.[108] A work party found Brown's body the next summer—perfectly preserved by the cold lake water—and he was buried near the trail to Camp Chuchchehum.

To Gardner's surprise, Campbell paid a field visit, arriving with a mounted party to meet him and Parke at Camp Chiloweyuck. There had been some problem with Indians at the depot, so it was decided to send Peabody back to induce them to return to the survey's employ. On November 7, Peabody, having successfully negotiated with the Indians, arrived at Camp Chiloweyuck with a number of Indians and a pack train to transport the remaining supplies to the depot for the winter. The men placed the boats in safe positions at the sandy beach on the lake's north shore, then started outward. Townsend and Stott were leaving the lake because of insufficient business, so Parke authorized the purchase of the ferry company's effects.

Parke hoped to set up another astronomical station between Camp Sumass and Chilliwack Lake before winter storms ended the season. The plan was to establish an astronomical point on the parallel at "Tummeahai Gap." On September 18, Harris left the depot with a corporal and seven privates as escorts for a reconnaissance into the untracked Tamihi Creek Valley. He began by building a bridge across the "Chiloweyuck" River. "It proved a difficult undertaking," Harris reported, "owing to the breadth of the river and its rapidity: one bridge was carried away by a freshet, and it was not until the Seventh of October when another was completed, and the trail carried over the first mountain in the Gap." After delays and another survey priority near Camp Sumass, Harris was able to continue the survey. Herbst joined him on October 4, and Parke arrived two days later. They established Camp Tummeahai on October 12, about three miles above the mouth of Tamihi Creek, barely north of the parallel (at 1,146 feet). Harris reported: "The valley just above for quarter of a mile became a rocky gorge and the stream a mountain torrent."[109]

Unfavorable weather prevented the completion of latitude observations until November 4. This painstaking task extended over five cold nights and consisted of 166 observations on 48 pairs of stars. Harris made a theodolite survey from Camp Tummeahai on November 8, and Herbst carried out chaining. Meanwhile, axemen cleared a line southward along the valley.[110]

On his return from Chilliwack Lake to the depot, Gardner took the transit and chronometers and left the packtrain to visit Harris on November 14 (meeting Parke, who was returning to Chilliwack Lake). Ascending the Tamihi, whose waters were swollen from autumn rains, proved to be a difficult undertaking for Gardner. At one crossing, the water, rushing over a bed of boulders, was so high he feared losing the instruments. He gave up all ideas of making observations for longitude:

> The approach here to the 49th parallel is rough beyond description. . . . At Camp Tummeahai the mountains rise on all sides, and through the dense timber, which it would seem the sun could never penetrate, added to the rumbling noise from the rushing waters of the creek, it was to me indeed a gloomy spot.[111]

When Gibbs later described the convoluted wilderness terrain near the boundary line, he had Tamihi Creek in mind when he wrote: "The affluents of the Chilowynck are themselves torrents." He added: "On the south fork of the Tummeakai, just at the line, a fall of forty or fifty feet in height marks the boundary, and others above it make in all some two hundred feet."[112] The torrents and waterfalls were a prelude to what the surveyors would see at the head of the valley the next season, where the higher peaks "rise in almost acicular points of naked rock, accessible only to the foot of the mountain goat." Some of the precipices here seemingly overhung the stream heads, "among which are inclosed small but deep lakes."[113]

As the 1858 season ended, Gardner left most of the camp equipment at Chiloweyuck Depot with an escort, and the animals were taken to the coast where forage was inexpensive. Harris and his men returned to the depot on November 27. The American party could look back on its first full season's work with a certain satisfaction. The line had been covered by reconnaissance from an initial point on the Strait of Georgia eastward to the Skagit River near the 121° meridian, an estimated ninety miles. The late-starting British commission had conducted no original reconnaissance at all and had just barely reached the American Camp Sumass. By January 8, 1859, Harris was moved to remark that the British "seem doomed to be a millstone about our necks." In later recalling their delay, Gardner wrote: "We laid in a beautiful state of almost perfect inactivity for one year . . . waiting for the English Commission."[114]

A season's wilderness and mountain experience meant that the Americans were also ahead of the British in physical conditioning, hardiness, and confidence for 1859. Lt. Parke's direction and planning were important factors in the survey's good progress, but there had been indirect complaints concerning Campbell's protocol, delays, and selfishness. There were complaints, for example, about his taking as many animals to the field "to pack him and his attendant" as it took "to move an astronomical party." Campbell, some believed, worked for his own comfort and credit.[115]

Because the oil lanterns that illuminated their instruments were unreliable in cold temperatures, Gardner took a steamer to San Francisco in December, hoping to improvise a more dependable lighting system. He also had some tents made in San Francisco, one being of a conical design; open-end "A" tents were made for reconnaissance work and to cover stores. Both Gardner and Parke (who had left in January) returned at the end of March.[116]

That winter, the Americans were quite isolated in their camp at tidewater, with almost no settlers nearby and only Indian villages between them and the wilderness. Canoeing, sailing, and taking whaleboat trips were the only diversions. In the absence of Parke and Gardner, Harris was in charge of the camp, while Gibbs, Kennerly, and Custer made a reconnaissance of the San Juan Islands beginning February 21. Herbst, meanwhile, tendered his resignation from the commission.

The winter was less monotonous for the British commission. The Victoria settlers were hospitable, and there were parties and dinners to attend. The Royal Engineers, joined by the men from the *Satellite* and *Plumper,* gave a grand ball for the women of Vancouver Island on March 15. The ball committee, which included Lt. Wilson, decorated a "dismal looking" marketplace with ship's flags so that "not a particle of the building was visible." A blaze of light helped the revelers—about two hundred of them, including the governor— forget the dreary winter and some "kept the dancing up with great spirit till ½ past 3 in the morning."[117] Wilson approved of the women's dress and dance, but commented that it would be an improvement "if they would only learn to wear their crinoline properly." He described what happened after the ball:

> I conveyed some ladies home who lived about a mile out of the town. You would have laughed to have seen us at that time of night floundering away through the mud, the ladies with their ball dresses tied up round their waists & long boots on, your distant brother smoking a very long cigar & "standing by" as the sailors say to help any unfortunate petticoat who should become irretrievably stuck in the mud . . . [118]

In January, Hawkins, Haig, and Lord traveled to Nisqually to purchase animals to augment those left to winter at Sumas.[119] Lord went to Nisqually again in April to make a final selection of horses, then conveyed them to Whatcom by sea and to Sumas by trail. Some bullocks were brought for fresh beef. At the same time, in both the British and American camps, plans were underway for the next season.

View on Cascade Range—from Chiloweynck River, near 49th Parallel, *sketch by George Gibbs, c. 1859, with Sleese Mountain (center) dominating (from* Journal of the American Geographical Society of New York 4 [1874]; *OHS Research Library, OHS neg., OrHi 87187)*

8

ALONG THE FORTY-NINTH PARALLEL:

THE NORTHWEST BOUNDARY SURVEY, 1859–1862

... we could see the bare peaks of the Cascades all round us, many of them clothed in snow, whilst towards the west we recognized our old friend Mount Baker raising his hoary head high above the others ... There is something indescribably pleasant rambling about a mountain at such an altitude; the air sharp & clear, the magnificent panorama before the eye & a buoyant & elastic feeling both of mind & body, which is never felt elsewhere.

—Lt. Charles Wilson, 1859

As the Americans formed plans for the 1859 season, they decided to have two astronomic parties, headed by George Gardner and Joseph Harris, and one surveying party. James Nooney became Gardner's assistant, and Francis Hudson was to assist Harris. Gardner's brother, "Charlie," was assigned to survey the Chilliwack Valley. The Americans would coordinate their efforts with the British but would work independently. Fifty laborers and boatmen, thirteen axemen and cooks, and sixteen recorders and chainmen were hired.

When the British and American commissioners met at Camp Simiahmoo in April to arrange the season's work, it was once again apparent that they were not in accord over the manner of marking and cutting the boundary. Capt. John Hawkins, who was in charge of the land survey for the British, and Capt. Robert Haig, the chief astronomer, believed it was their duty to mark the line by a continuous vista to prevent future disputes among settlers, in accordance with instructions from the Foreign Office and the precedent set in marking the New Brunswick-Maine boundary.[1] Archibald Campbell, the head of the American commission, agreed to undertake the cutting of vistas only in forested valley bottoms, not on open ground and prairies. He was content to confine operations to ascertaining points on the line and cutting a track twenty feet wide and at trails and settlements on each side of important stream crossings. In fact, the ruggedness of the terrain generally kept vista cutting to a minimum. John Parke, chief astronomer-surveyor for the U.S., deemed it impractical to transport and erect cast-iron monuments in the mountains, and both commissioners ordered that stone monuments, or cairns, be built.[2]

Despite a reduction in the congressional appropriation for the American party, Hawkins believed the boundary definition would be largely completed before year's end. Campbell had told Hawkins he hoped the appropriation would not be less than $115,000, an amount the British commissioner thought "may tend to cripple his proceedings." Hawkins added: "Meanwhile I am arranging to carry out those operations which appear to me indispensable and undoubtably necessary for the performance of our joint duties."[3] Because the American commission was one season ahead of the British in its work and their most recent camps were therefore quite distant, the two men rarely met. Each acted independently of the other and, according to British surveyor Samuel Anderson, were "extremely tenacious of each others rights." Anderson also reported that the British men believed it very probable that both commissioners would be replaced in hopes of "getting two others who would agree better."[4]

Despite the differences and distance between the commissioners and the two field parties, Lt. Parke courteously escorted Col. Hawkins to the boundary line in June 1859 to determine the site of astronomic stations. Hawkins found nothing to complain about and even thought the Americans were well trained.[5] Anderson described another friendly encounter the following winter when the British visited the American party at their base quarters:

> Mr. Campbell seemed tremendously afraid of us and there was no sign of cordiality about him so we soon put an end to that visit. We then went and saw some of the American officers of the escort, all of whom I must say are exceedingly nice fellows and display a[n] openness and goodhearted sort of manner which it is a treat to see in a Yankee.[6]

"Where the Foot of Man Has Never Yet Trod"

Although they were following routes marked and sometimes pioneered by the Americans, the British found the logistics trying and progress difficult. In thickly forested country, survey lines could seldom be over 150 links and the rate of progress about three miles a day.[7] Lt. Charles Wilson's diary gives some idea of the difficulties encountered in the survey work:

> From Semiahmoo to Sumass the country is low, in many places very swampy, and covered with perhaps the densest forest that can be seen anywhere, for not only are many of the trees of enormous girth, from 25 to 35 feet in circumference, but the spaces between them are filled with an almost impenetrable mass of underbrush and fallen timber. . . . This part of the country is so infested with mosquitoes, from the middle of June to the middle of September, that even the Indians cannot stand it, and move to some other part of the country for these three months. Between Sumass and Schweltza the Cascade mountains commence, and from this point to the Shimilkameen, 110 miles on, the country is of the most rugged description, and it was only by taking advantage of the valleys and mountain glens running in a north and south direction that the parallel could be reached.[8]

The British built log storehouses at the mouth of the Sumas, but they could not depend on local resources for provisioning. The mainstays of pork and bacon were sporadically augmented by the plentiful grouse, ducks, and geese and an occasional deer. In summer, there were various berries, and salmon ran upstream in great quantities from August to October. Like the American commission, the British had to depend on the pack train once they were away from rivers and lakes. During 1859, the British had fifty-five mules and forty-four horses available—twenty of which would die in accidents—hardly sufficient for the seven parties scattered from the Chilliwack to the Similkameen River.[9] Because grass was scarce west of the Cascade divide, forage for the animals had to be carried along with provisions. Each pack mule ate from ten to twelve pounds of corn daily, or about 150 pounds during a two-week journey, and the riding animals had to be fed as well. The group had to import grain, the high cost of which dismayed Hawkins, and considerable management was required to keep all parties properly supplied.

All the British commission's horse packers and muleteers were Mexican and were paid about eight shillings a day. These invaluable men never took a tent and slept on the ground with one blanket. The Mexican saddles were called *aparajos*, and even the American party preferred them to those issued by the army.[10] The mules generally gave little trouble on the trail, according to most accounts. "They all follow one another," Anderson wrote, "the front one being ridden by one of the packers and having a bell round its neck, . . . at night they will never stir from the one with the bell."[11] When the loads were packed, however, there was much shouting and swearing in Spanish. Once saddled, the mules were girthed up tight by two men with their feet against the animal's sides to prevent it from kicking the saddle and pack off. Wilson wrote that he had seen "a refractory mule leap clean off the ground & come down on his back, so that crockery would not be a safe article to carry about."[12]

By May, some of the British had penetrated the mountain stronghold. Wilson recognized the adventure of surveying "in places where the foot of man has never yet trod." At one location, the mountain gorge was so deep that the sun was visible for only three hours of the day, "the huge precipices literally hanging over you & the mountain torrent rushing along at your feet."[13] In preparing for these mountain surveys, the British set up "Chilukweyuk Depot" near where the Chilliwack River joined the Fraser. The depot was close to the river for easy access to supplies, while the headquarters camp was two miles away. On June 16, Wilson had his "office marquee" set up at the camp, and by then Hawkins, Lyall, and Lord were also there. Wilson, who was in charge of payments, sometimes had as much as £1,000 on hand, and later in the season he lamented that he did not have a dog for security.

On the prairie, as one might expect in early summer, the insects were fearful. While Wilson was erecting a store, clearing brush, and building a shanty on

June 10, the vicious mosquitoes drove their stings through his corduroy trousers. He wrote in his diary: "The scenery is most lovely but as far as I have seen the place abounds in snakes, mosquitoes, sand flies. . . ."[14] The sand flies were a particular bother:

> There is a small kind of gnat here called the sand fly which is even worse than the mosquito, as it is so small it gets through the mosquito curtains & its sting is very venomous. At present my skin is something like a leopard's, all spotted; . . . Lord & I turn out before 6 every morning & rush across the prairie to take a bathe in a beautifully clear stream, but *awfull!* cold; we then jump into our clothes scarcely stopping to dry ourselves & rush away from the "squitoes."[15]

Except for the irrepressible insects, the British lieutenant was enamored with the locale. The prairie was

> . . . covered with flowers & strawberries & even in this early period of the year the grass is nearly up to the waist. The Chilukweyuk stream is a tributary of the Fraser & rises in the far recesses of the Cascade mountains & by its valley we penetrate the mountain range later on in the season. The Indians give a wonderful account of a lake near the summit, where bears, marten, marmot & salmon abound; a reconnoitring party sent forward give glowing accounts of the fishing. . . . the view from the camp is superb . . . with snow capped mountains on either side; on the right, the Chilukweyuk valley, at the head of which stands a very prominent & peculiar peak of the Cascades with its snowy summit. . . .[16]

There were not only mountains to admire, but wild animals as well: "[Lt. Charles] Darrah spied a bear through his theodolite the other day, trotting across the parallel & Lyall met one face to face two days ago . . . our mule trains coming home in the evening have come across them several times but none of our party has yet bagged one. . . ."[17]

Lt. Richard Roche of the Royal Navy was called into land-survey duty in the summer of 1859, and he proved to be the explorative forefront of the British. When he was later recalled to the *Satellite*, his place was taken by two civilians. Roche made a reconnaissance of the Slesse and Nesakwatch Creek valleys to set up astronomic stations. When he reached Chilliwack Lake, the American party was already there. A party led by Roche set out from the depot in mid-June but found the water at Tamihi Creek so high that the pack train had to turn back. Then, on June 18, Roche left for the Skagit River with a mule train. The next day, a team coming back from the gorge of Tamihi Creek brought bad news: an entire load had been lost when a mule toppled off a cliff and broke its neck; one man had broken his leg.[18] Another man was swept off his horse by high water twice on June 21 and nearly drowned while fording a stream.

On July 2, Wilson and Lyall rode to Cultus Lake, located between the lower Chilliwack and the boundary.

> . . . here we exchanged our horses for a boat, constructed by our men and a very good one it was . . . We found Haig encamped on the edge of the lake & went in for a heavy

breakfast & luncheon combined after our morning ride; our journey home however was by no means so agreeable. It began to rain before we got half way across the lake and such a ride we had through the woods, dripping wet and every step we went bringing down showers from the trees down our backs; the trail on the hills too, had got dreadfully slippery and we had to get off & lead our horses down the hills. The mosquitoes have now regularly set in; it is perfect agony performing even the regular actions of life. Washing is a perfect torture, they settle *en masse* upon you perfectly covering every portion of the body exposed. We sit wrapped up in leather with gloves on and bags round our heads & even that cannot keep them off; none of us have had any sleep for the last two nights & we can scarcely eat. . . .[19]

The mosquito plague was so bad that on July 11 all work had to be stopped. "After having killed every one" in his tent, Wilson went to sleep, "but in less than two hours awoke in great pain, literally covered by mosquitoes, which had even got under the blankets."[20]

Difficult, Untracked Valleys: Custer's Nooksack Reconnaissance

The American commission's goal for the 1859 season was to survey and study the forty-ninth parallel eastward with a view to making the next winter quarters on the Columbia River. To cope with the possible hostility of the Okanogan and related Indians, a larger escort was planned. The first event of the season occurred on April 18, when George Gardner, J. Nevin King, and Henry Custer, with an escort, left their shoreline camp in whaleboats for Chiloweyuck Depot. At the Fraser River rapids above the Sumas, a snag nearly capsized one boat. On arrival at the depot, this advance party found the stored supplies in good condition after the winter.[21]

Custer began the first overland survey on April 25. It extended from Camp Sumass to Sweltcha Station on the south end of Cultus Lake, along the mountain foothills east of where he had conducted his 1858 reconnaissance; he continued his survey to Camp Tummeahai. Custer's sketches along Lake Sumas and the Chilliwack River are detailed, showing river bars, channels, and tree groupings. When Harris arrived at the depot on May 4, bringing with him eleven chronometers, Gardner began a series of latitude observations along the parallel with the new zenith telescope.

Because of the springtime surge and consequent flooding—by May 8, the river at the depot had risen over five feet, much of it from the Fraser's backwater—the men feared that supplies being brought over the Whatcom Trail might become mired at Sumas Prairie.[22] Fortunately, the *Maria* arrived with stores from San Francisco on May 14, and more supplies arrived four days later. Provisions had previously been brought by whaleboat from Camp Simiahmoo, but in 1859 the Americans used the steamers *Constitution*, *Maria*, *Governor Douglas*, *Wilson G. Hunt*, and *Colonel Moody* to transport freight and food supplies from Victoria to the Fraser River and Chiloweyuck Depot.

The commission's first priority was to make the trail to Chilliwack Lake practical for pack mules. The trail required considerable bridging, grading, and corduroying. Because of the snowpack and fallen timber from winter storms, building the trail was much like beginning anew along the glacial till of the valley bottom. On May 17, under Custer's direction, a party of men began work to open the trail to the mouth of Tamihi Creek. The next day, Charles Gardner and another group of men began clearing farther in the Chilliwack River Valley. The nine-mile section to Tamihi Creek occupied fifteen to twenty men and took two weeks of hard labor. In some places, windfall so blocked the route that the men found it simpler to bridge the trees than to cut through them.[23] Fortunately, Peabody's pack train from Whatcom managed to cross the prairie by May 24 before high water closed the trail. Because of the full streams and rivers and the difficulty of preparing a mule trail, Indians were hired to pack into the Tamihi Creek Valley.

Harris left Chiloweyuck Depot on May 26 to define the parallel at Tamihi Creek. By June 3, he had reached the parallel south of Camp Tummeahai, having been forced to replace footlogs that high water had swept away. Although his principal duties were to make triangulations and geodetic observations for latitude, Harris also built stone monuments and had vista timber cut for about one mile. His project was finished on June 9. On June 23, he again left the depot, this time for Chilliwack Lake.[24]

Custer was charged with making his own topographic reconnaissance of the mountains between the Chilliwack and Nooksack rivers.[25] It was difficult to obtain the help he needed from Indians, partly because of the shortage of adequate footwear but also because snow remained at even moderate elevations. By June 4, however, Custer had assembled a reconnaissance party and arrived at the camp. The party consisted of eleven Indians (including a Samona guide named Thiusoloc) along with "Mitchly" (John Midgely) and the "Kentuckian" (probably Michael Kavanaugh). The Samona Indians, a band of the Stó:lô Chilliwack tribe, had a village near Slesse Creek ("the Samony village"). Custer called the tribe "true Mountain Indians" and obtained the Native names for regional geographic features from Thiusoloc.[26] Some of the Indians had been associated with Custer in the 1858 season. By all reports, he dealt honestly with them and judged them to be hardworking.

On June 5, taking provisions for twelve days, Custer's party left Harris at a cache on Tamihi Creek. That night they camped on the American commission's new trail from Cultus Lake, near the crossing of Liumchen Creek (west of Tamihi Creek) at about five hundred feet.[27] The party ascended the difficult, brushy east flank of the creek, then a thickly forested slope of Douglas fir and western hemlock. Camp 2 was located about three and a half miles from the first camp, below the west fork near one thousand feet.[28] Their course now bore southeast up the timbered spur dividing the eastern and middle (main) fork of Liumchen Creek. From the "inclined ridge which we had been ascending," the view at five thousand feet included the "Sowack Mountains" (Church Mountain) south of the forty-ninth parallel. As the day progressed, the men passed above the mountain hemlocks near timberline and moved rapidly across extensive snowfields. The air was "bracing & singularly exhilarating."[29] Custer's party continued to a high point on the ridge, triangulated at 5,576 feet.[30] Camp 3, sheltered by subalpine fir, was situated between this point and Liumchen Mountain ("Layomesun"), just north of forty-nine degrees. A welcome addition for dinner that night were two blue grouse brought in by Thiusoloc. There was no water on the ridge, so the men melted snow for cooking.

On June 8, looking eastward under a flawless mountain sky, Custer admired the high peaks of Slesse, Larrabee, and Tomyhoi, "their summits, exceedingly brocken & rugged & utterly inascendable." To the west, he could plainly see Point Roberts and the line marking the terminus of the land parallel, which appeared "like a white thread."[31] To reduce the effort with their heavy loads, the men traversed the flank of Liumchen Mountain rather than scramble over it, remaining on snow above the last trees. From a point on the divide between Liumchen and Canyon ("Cowap") creeks, Custer admired "Mount Baker [which] showne forth in all its serene beauty & majesty the king among the mountains here." He observed: "It apears very near & to judge from the gentle outline of its massive cone easy to ascend."[32]

That morning, while descending a point on Canyon Ridge on steep and frozen snow, Custer took a fall:

> While stepping into the footsteps of those before me . . . I glided out, and fell, and was imediatley rolling, at a fearful rate over the steep & slippery descend, lower down I fell over a rocky wall, some 10 feet or 12 feet high, against the stump of a decayed tree which fortunatley obstructed my further downward course.[33]

Miraculously, Custer was unhurt. Several Indians lost their loads, the contents rolling into the timber. At mid-afternoon, they reached the foot of "Kaisoots peak" (Bald Mountain), then traversed around its north flank to a snow-free campsite. For sport, the Indians ascended the steep cliffs of the main summit, and the guide-hunter returned with two whistling marmots.[34]

Early on the morning of June 9, Custer made a quick ascent of Bald Mountain. He ascended snowfields on the southwest flank, probably alone. From this vantage, the whole country spread out like an "immense map, and all I had to do, was to make a reduced copy." Custer could identify distant Vancouver Island, and he drew a useful map. Mt. Baker and Mt. Shuksan in particular stood out, towering "over the rest of the peaks." Custer returned to camp in time to push onward with the party, and by ten o'clock the entire party had traveled west-northwest to "Signal peak" (Black Mountain).[35] From the forested summit ridge, Custer could see Silver, Cultus, Sumas, and Stave lakes.

A steep descent from the slope below Black Mountain's middle summit took the party toward "Pekosie" (Silver) Lake, where they placed their fifth camp. The descent was comparable to going down a staircase, with the men "using stick, arms & legs freely. . . . Several Indians lost their loads, which came thumbling down, scattering Pots, Kettles, hard tak & pork." The young Kentuckian refused to descend, pleading "that his state was old Kentuck, that it was a level state, & that he had never done such climbing there." Two of Custer's "best Indian climbers finally brought the recreant Kentuckian down almost literally carrying him in their arms."[36]

That evening, Thiusoloc came into camp reporting the capture of a large black bear. To allow time to bring in the game, Custer decided to remain at the lake the following day, and some of the men built a raft so they could sail on the lake. The bear proved to be enormous, over seven feet from the tip of the nose to the beginning of the tail and weighing four to five hundred pounds. On the night of June 10, "an enormous feast began," and, according to Custer,

> the Indians formed a ring, cooking carving & devouring bear meat. A more determined set of fellows could not be seen, extending their feast, through the small hours of the night—the fun often breacking out in downright riot . . . to finish up the whole carcass of the animal.[37]

Custer sent two Indians back to Chiloweyuck Depot with the skin.

The men pressed on the next day, striking a Samona Indian trail that led from the Nooksack River to Silver Lake, Columbia Valley, and Cultus Lake.[38] At the Nooksack, Custer noted the "much discolored" water, which originated from glaciers on Mount Shuksan and Mount Baker. At about four o'clock, they reached a campsite on the north fork of the Nooksack River, several miles east of present-day Maple Falls. The men continued upstream on June 12, taking to the gravel alluvium of river bars when the river was constrained by the canyon bedrock. That night, they made Camp 7 opposite present-day Glacier.[39] Before reaching Canyon Creek, Custer noted the variety of minerals in a river bank. He also found fossil flora, a "beautiful impression of willow & other leaves, imprinted in soft slate rock."[40]

In the morning, progress was slowed by the bordering canyon incline, where "one false step would precipitate the unlucky traveller into the surging waters of the stream."[41] Before noon the valley widened to permit faster progress, but by the time they camped everyone was "duly tired and worn out." Near midday on June 14, the party reached a boggy section just above Swamp Creek, which Custer termed "Nuquoichum." From a marsh where the river branched out into three smaller streams, the Indians told Custer, it was eight miles to the head of the river at a mountain called "Spech" (probably Ruth Mountain or Icy Peak).

Camp that night was made near the western foot of Mt. Sefrit, below where Ruth and Razor Hone creeks enter the main stream. Custer recognized that the valley was "a perfect cul-de-sac, and its Easterly end is closed up, by impassable Mountains." Late that day, he took a short hike above camp, crossing Ruth Creek. He saw no point in continuing eastward because of the forthcoming rendezvous with other survey members at the Tamihi forks, and he already knew where the Chilliwack River tributaries were located.[42]

On June 15, Thiusoloc led the men northwest through the forest to the area of Welcome Pass. The guide, selecting a direct route to the rendezvous point, clearly knew the region from previous visits, and Custer was acutely aware of his dependence on him: "It is a peculiar skill which these Indians have, to select the best route in a given direction, a quality which to the white man, unused to travel in these woods, completely fails, and who is sure to select always the most awkward places of the route."[43]

Camp 10 was pitched near the pass on a small bare spot beneath a subalpine fir clump and surrounded by a solid wall of snow. A dense fog driven by a furious wind chilled the men, and "a cold drizzly rain set in." Gusts of wind made the campfire a source of annoyance. In this "wretched place," the choice was to shiver in the cold "or to be stiffled with smoke." In the morning, while the men were on the Damfino Creek divide, the fog held on "with a stubborn tenacity," the wind chasing it in all directions. For a time, the fog shrouded Custer, Mitchly, and Thiusoloc so completely that they could barely see each other. Custer reported: "The guide was bewildered, by not seeing the country, & hesitated, which way to proceed, for fear our onward course might bring to some impassable precipice." When the fog finally lifted, they could peer down into the deep valley ahead.[44] Custer termed Damfino Creek the southwest, or middle, fork of "Tumehay" Creek.

In the difficult, untracked valley, the men made a steep, slippery descent, first on snow, then through subalpine brush. Travel became easier along the streambanks, but thickets of Sitka alder (*Alnus sinuata*) were frustrating. Camp 11 was made at an estimated 2,100 feet at the forks of Tamihi Creek, only a few miles above the cache where the reconnaissance had begun eleven days earlier. Custer must have been relieved to find a helper and an Indian awaiting their arrival, and he decided to wait for provisioning from the cache below.

On June 19, the party—now reduced to Custer and ten men, eight of them Indians—moved on. Because of an open understory in the heavy timber, it was a relatively easy half-day journey to Tomyhoi Lake. Along the way, the waterfalls cascading off Tomyhoi Peak were spectacular, some over five hundred feet high. The environment—which had been "spring like," with flowers and bushes blooming—changed "abruptly to a perfect Winter landscape. The vicinity of the lake is covered with a deep crust only slowly yielding to the influence of the sun." The lake itself was still partly frozen.

The men made camp below the lake's outlet under a group of firs. That evening, the hunter-guide killed a small grizzly bear amid "steep & almost perpendicular Cliffs oposite" the camp. The bear tumbled over brush and rock, Custer reported: "The Indians brought it to camp in Triumph, 4 men carried it on 2 poles.—This was of course the signal of another enormous feast . . . it continued vigorously through the whole night, until the last vestige of the carcass had disapeared." Custer found the bear's meat coarse and not very palatable, "except the tongue, which is really an excellant morsal."[45]

On June 20, Custer decided to ascend "Putlushgohap mountain" (Tomyhoi Peak). It seems clear that his experience in the Alps and memories of his father's excursions kindled his longing for adventure in isolated places. The rough terrain beyond the lake, particularly the steep slopes of frozen snow, challenged the men. On that extraordinary day, Custer saw the tracks of a mountain goat and some hair on bushes for the first time. On a plateau at about 5,500 feet, Custer collected specimens of scrub evergreens (*krummholz*) and blooming red and white heather. At that point the party was southeast of the summit of Tomyhoi Peak on a plateau separating upper Damfino Creek and the deep cirque of Tomyhoi Lake.

Farther along, Custer noted the last specimens of "balsam [subalpine] fir," "reduced here to a mere shrub, about 3–4 feet high." Beyond, the bedrock was covered with a deep layer of snow and a glacier. At about noon, Custer and the Kentuckian reached the "highest ascendable point, the real sumit being still about 500–1000 feet heigher, but the ascend to it so steep & rocky that I did not deem it advisable."[46] From this vantage, non-Natives saw for the first time the grand extent of the northern Cascades, including Mt. Rainier and the sharp peaks of the Picket Range.

In the evening, Thiusoloc came to camp with the skin of a goat and some of its meat. With no little apprehension, the party saw as many as four grizzlies "prowling about in the bushes of the steep cliffs oposite to our camp. They seemed to watch us closely," Custer wrote. The night stillness was interrupted by the "loud, thundering & grating noise of an avalanche [from some cliffs on Tomyhoi Peak], pouring its vast volumes of snow, over the precipices." The next day, Custer sent two Indians to the Tamihi Creek depot with animal skins. He remained at Tomyhoi Lake to explore the area. On June 22, he ascended some of the peaks near the camp and visited the nearby Twin Lakes—still frozen—at the head of Swamp Creek.[47] His route was via Low Pass, then a snow traverse on the flank of Winchester Mountain. Taking a different route back to camp, Custer made the first climb of Winchester Mountain.[48]

By June 24, the Indians had not yet returned from the cache, so Custer decided to leave for Silesia Creek without them. From Low Pass, he studied the steep descent at Winchester Creek with apprehension, but the men made their way down the dangerous slopes by scrambling and sliding.[49] Soon Custer could relax a bit, and he took some time to examine and collect blooming flowers that were new to him.

After struggling through thickets of alder and willow along the valley bottom of the "middle fork" of Silesia Creek (Slesse creek south of the boundary), the men arrived at the main stream, where they camped. Following the united watercourse the next day, they moved along rapidly during the rainy morning and soon struck an old Samona trail. Progress came to a virtual halt, however, when the valley narrowed into a rocky canyon, where "waters sped with torrentlike rapidity." Thiusoloc pointed out the only feasible passage—a contrivance left by an earlier Indian party consisting of "a small log, leaning in a slanting direction, from the water's edge, to the nearest protruding point of rock"—and with some trepidation each person climbed the slippery log. Shortly after noon, the men passed a turbulent, milky stream descending from the glaciers of the Border Peaks.[50] Their camp that night was not far from the mouth of Slesse Creek.

When the river took a more gentle fall and was divided into channels that permitted travel on gravel bars, requiring "occasional wading up to our knees," the party made rapid progress. When they reached the final campsite on the left bank of the Chilliwack River in midmorning on June 26, they found the two Indians who had come from the cache to meet them. Because there was no known nearby crossing of the swollen Chilliwack River, they crossed Slesse Creek and then continued upstream about three miles (probably about opposite Chipmunk Creek). To Custer, the river—now at its seasonal peak—"looked anything but practicable. One half of the river was bridged over by a good substancial log, the other half on our side was unbridged."[51]

Custer allowed the Indians to make a trial crossing, but not without considering the risk of failure. First the Indians split a small cedar lengthwise, and "by dint of great exertions, & by going freely into the cold waters of the stream, up to their armpits, they finally succeeded to lay the 2 pieces of the cedar tree, on 2 rocks." This made the transit possible, although the supple timbers—Custer estimated they were not more than six inches wide—"had a strong oscilating motion, that underneath was a roring turbulent stream."[52]

While the crossing was improved by stationing two Indians on the underparts of the bridge, "holding tight rope between them," Custer later reported to Parke that "we can not but confess, that the crossing over such a frail contrivance, was altogether one of the most hazardous, dangerous, undertakings, which I have ever attempted."[53] It took the men the entire morning of June 27 to complete the bridge and then the crossing. Relieved that all were still alive, they continued that day to the main depot, eighteen miles away—a long, and remarkable day. Gardner, recognizing the difficulty of Custer's explorations, later wrote that this reconnaissance completed the commission's topographical work "as far as the Senehsay Creek through a country that will never again be visited except by some energetic hunter who may perhaps penetrate its rocky wilds."[54]

Custer's Exploration South of Forty-Nine Degrees

When the *Governor Douglas* brought Lt. John G. Parke to Chiloweyuck Depot on June 3, Gardner could start for Chilliwack Lake to begin field operations. He left the depot on June 4 and arrived at the mountain lake four days later. There, boats were repaired and Lake Depot was established at the mouth of Depot Creek. The men also built a log storehouse with a canvas roof and worked on the trail to Camp Chuchchehum. Surveying commenced at Camp Chiloweyuck, and they began to cut a vista across the "Klahaihu" (upper Chilliwack River) Valley to mark the boundary. The vista, which was completed on July 11, was 850 yards long, and the boundary was marked by two cairns, six to eight feet high.

Dr. Kennerly continued studying the natural history of the region. He observed the salmon and their migrations in the Chilliwack River and the lake and made careful lists of the fauna and birds he saw, including loons and grebes along the lower river.[55] In July, Custer gave Kennerly a goat skin, and he noted in his journal that the explorer had seen a grizzly bear southeast of Chilliwack Lake. The doctor also wrote about the hoary marmot, whose squeaks often surprised surveyors from both the American and British teams:

> The heads of the gulches running towards the Skagit were inhabited by colonies of the hoary marmot whose whistle was heard constantly among the rocks. We saw numbers of them sitting erect at the mouths of their burrows or running from one to another. Their whistle is shrill and one of their calls so nearly resembles that of a man that when I first heard it, I answered, supposing it to be the signal of one of our men who was hunting.[56]

With orders from Parke to explore the mountains near the forty-ninth parallel between Ensawkwatch Creek (called Nesakwatch Creek north of the parallel) and the upper Chilliwack River, Custer left Chiloweyuck Depot on July 14 with Mitchly and probably Kavanaugh and eleven Indians. Each Indian began the journey with a pack of fifty to sixty pounds, and Thiusoloc again served as Custer's guide. The Indians' help in packing supplies was critical, and the start was delayed because one of the men "would not proceed without his better half." Custer was impatient with what he saw as "the disturbance which these Indian damsels produce in a party by their willfulness & extent of influence."[57]

The well-established valley trail near the Chilliwack's north bank brought the cumbersome party to a place opposite Nesakwatch Creek, where they planned to enter the mountains by a route unknown to any white explorer. On the night of July 15, the party camped at a river bar by a Samona village. Crossing the river—which rushed along "with almost furious speed," Custer later observed—would be impossible without a suitable footlog. They decided to camp in order to fell a tree for the dangerous crossing in the morning.

Custer then sent Setwahm, a Sumas chief, with a message to Gardner at Chilliwack Lake.[58]

On July 17, Custer followed an Indian trail to a narrow valley that was "bounded by high & very precipitous Mountains, which increase in height as we ascend." Unlike the lower gradient of the upper Chilliwack River Valley, here there was a pronounced narrow profile with heavy underbrush and timber fallen downslope—one of the most rock-bound valleys of the northern Cascades. The east valley wall culminated in the slabby, granitic Illusion Peaks and Mt. Rexford (Custer's "Ensawkwatch Mt"), while on the opposite flank were the even more precipitous walls and buttresses of Slesse Mountain, carved by Pleistocene ice from Chilliwack batholith (a Tertiary granitic body).

Custer had anticipated "Silesie Mt" (Slesse), which he had already seen several times, but his notebook sketches indicate that he first misidentified it during the difficult hike. Later in the day, however, its position became evident, and he described the peaks as "exceedingly broken & steep near their summits, which seem to be inascendable."[59] The hike had been a difficult one:

> Our march was a most tedious one, winding our way along the steep slopes of the Mountains bordering the Stream, or breaking our way through dense tissues of bush vegetation, always found in the bottoms of these streams. They are the vine maple & another bush whose name I do not know [Sitka alder]. They extend along generally the margins of the Creek clear up to the Mountain sumits, & their is no alternative, but to break your way through it, to do so you have to work with hand & foot, to break, or hold away the very elastic twigs of the bush, which if not careful, will give you such a lesson, you will not soon forget. Add to this a most disageable thorny plant [devil's club], with large leaves & red berries, which obstructs itself continually in your way.

While they were constantly pushing boughs and twigs aside, an "intolerable swarm of musquitoes" plagued them. Perhaps the only inspiration that hot day was the view of the bordering mountains, "composed of whitish granite." At times, the party's traverse was obstructed by avalanche debris, where "large masses of snow" had slid down and "left a broad track of destruction."

All the trials and frustrations must have made this one of Custer's most arduous days. Shouts and rifle shots were eventually necessary to bring straggling members of the party together in camp, where they luxuriated in "a pleasant, cool camp, a good fire, & a simple hearty meal." Suddenly, "in the midst of our peaceful camp," a large dead tree crashed without warning, "some of its branches playing havoc, with our cooking arrangements, & the main trunk smashing one of our most valuable tin kettles." No one was injured, but this was a sobering narrow escape. The camp was about a mile and a quarter north of the forty-ninth parallel, just below 3,000 feet.[60]

A cool, clear morning prompted an early start on July 18, and in little over an hour the men reached several marshy prairies near the creek's headwaters.

They were now near the terminal forks of Ensawkwatch Creek and would soon be able to sight Pocket Lake in a hidden rocky cirque to the west. When ascending eastward along a ridge spur proved to be difficult, the party was forced into a lateral ravine. That afternoon, they made camp along a small feeder stream, "a fine alpine pasturage," replete with flowers and luxurious grass.

To gain an overview of the mountains to the south and west, which he still but dimly understood, Custer ascended the "prominent peak on our left" with Thiusoloc and Mitchly. From its summit, which Custer's barometric reading indicated to be about 7,000 feet, he could for the first time look into the valley of the upper Chilliwack River. Custer and his companions had reached the southwest summit of Middle Peak (7,160 feet plus), about six-tenths of a mile from the true summit, from which they would have also seen Chilliwack and Hanging lakes. The men were now well south of the forty-ninth parallel on the upper Ensawkwatch–Little Chilliwack divide.

Custer was spellbound by the jagged and glacierized peaks he had only glimpsed earlier from a distance: "The view from here was fine & extensive to all directions of the compass. I leave it to a better pen to describe the sublimity of true Mountain scenery in the Cascade Mts. . . . It must be seen it cannot be described." Dominating the eastward view were the grand peaks of what is now known as Custer Ridge, the highest being Mt. Redoubt and Mt. Spickard. Custer recorded that the glaciers "cover the Mountain sides to a considerable extent, [dazzling] in the reflected light of the sinking sun." Most apparent would have been the Challenger Glacier and various segments of ice on Whatcom Peak. The Redoubt Glacier is the largest in the mountains to the east, but from this vantage only a small edge of it could be seen.

Near the parallel, a fire in the Skagit Valley sent up "vast columns of smoke." To the west, Custer saw Mt. Shuksan and Mt. Baker; and the "Tumeahay" (Border Peaks) and "Sanisseh & Ensawquatch Mts" (Slesse and Rexford) presented "vast masses of whitish Rock, steep perpendicular & inascendible." Custer had good reason to be pleased with his reconnaissance and what he had learned of the complex topography, which had never been documented.

The next day, the entire party packed camp across the dividing ridge to the Little Chilliwack drainage, where the snow cover on a long, open slope provided an opportunity to practice "sitting a straddle of our Mountain sticks." After locating a campsite, Custer took Mitchly for an ascent "of a Mountain on the south side of the Southwest fork of the Klaheih." This was a minor summit of Copper Mountain (at about 6,760 feet) between the Little Chilliwack and the upper Chilliwack River, much of it in the forest. From the summit, they saw Mt. Shuksan, or "Thuskan," "as an imense rocky perpendicular wall." Custer was the first explorer to obtain this view of the broad Nooksack Cirque of the mountain, and from there he could define the main crest of the Cascades, located eastward. From that vantage, he considered that Baker and Shuksan did not belong to the main body of the range. A sketch he made from the ridge of Copper Mountain shows the peaks of the "Chuch-cheh Mountains": Mt. Redoubt is labeled "I Klahoih," Nodoubt is "Lower Klahaih Mt.," and Bear Mountain is "II Klahoih." Custer also noted that between 6,000 and 7,000 feet, only a few plant specimens existed, predominantly heather with red and white blooms.

By early afternoon on the final day, the party reached "the main Klahaih stream," also known as Klah-neh and Dolly Varden, and a valley floor that features a gigantic western red cedar forest.[61] Custer passed the vista cut of the parallel and the now-abandoned Chiloweyuck astronomical station before reaching Chilliwack Lake. At the shore of the lake, the group hailed the main survey party, which dispatched a canoe to bring them to Lake Depot on the east shore.

On July 23, Kennerly wrote in his journal that Custer and Gibbs made a significant one-day ascent of the principal peaks above the west shore of Chilliwack Lake, a subrange that appears as "Sem-i-tic Mts" on the 1866 map. No details about the route have been located, but the two may have ascended the northwest ridge of Mt. Webb and then traversed Mt. MacDonald. Kennerly wrote only that they climbed to 7,000 feet opposite Lake Depot to get views. They were certainly the first to visit this subrange.[62]

The British at Chilliwack Lake

In early July, when British Lt. Darrah had a camp on Sumas Prairie near the boundary, Chilliwack Lake was so high that Wilson reported it was feasible to paddle across the flooded prairie. From their camp on Cultus Lake, Wilson and Haig walked to the parallel on July 14:

> . . . we laid down a bottle at the exact point & erected a cairn of stones over it. . . . The walk down to the parallel along the stream was excessively beautiful & reminded me very much of the Dargle near Dublin. There were some pretty cascades & great numbers of the Anna's humming bird, a nest of which with 3 eggs was found by one of the men, hanging to the leaf of a prickly shrub which grows in great quantities in the woods. There are a great number of marmots & rabbits about here, one of the former one of Haig's Indians killed with a stone. I spent some time watching the little humming birds; they have a peculiar note & fly very rapidly, making a noise something like a humming top with their wings.[63]

On the way to Chilliwack Lake on July 29, Wilson found "a first rate fruit garden, black currents & raspberries in profusion." One species (probably the yellow salmonberry) "was unequalled in flavour even by the best in the garden at home." He also commented on the "lofty snowy peaks, glaciers close above our heads."[64] In trekking the last six miles on that day, the British party passed through an area where there was a large fire:

. . . the fire extended right across the valley & up the mountains & was very grand, the flames rushing right up the immense trees with a hissing crackling noise, whilst every now & then the crash of a burnt tree falling on the mountains rolled along like distant thunder. . . . every now & then I had to leap my horse over a burning log. When I got to the lake I found that this fire had been lighted by some of the American party for amusement, they had been too careless to put it out & now it will probably burn till rain falls.[65]

At the end of July, the large Skagit Valley fire also interfered considerably with the work of the surveyors of both nations. Wilson commented:

One of Roche's men came in from the Skagit valley beyond the Cascades & told us that a fearful fire was raging there. He had great difficulty in passing it. This also originated from an American camp fire, which they had been too lazy to put out properly; I am rejoiced to think that nothing of this sort has occurred amongst our men.[66]

The British party crossed Chilliwack Lake to Haig's camp in a boat they had constructed. Dirty from the survey work and riding, Wilson wrote: "You can have no idea of the luxury of undressing after having had your clothes on for nearly three weeks."[67] The beautiful lake could turn into a demon when a sudden wind arose, and Wilson described the difficulty of such conditions:

I was steering and precious hard work it was; to let the canoe get broadside on in the least would have been an instantaneous upset & the water was so cold there would have been no chance of swimming; besides, we had to work away with the paddles to keep up with the wind or we should have been swamped by the water coming over the stern. The canoe literally flew through the water with the rain and spray flying past us.[68]

On August 5, the British party at Chilliwack Lake learned that the American commander, Gen. William S. Harney, had landed troops on San Juan Island in connection with the ongoing boundary dispute. The British commission hoped the controversy would not blow up into a war and interrupt the work of both parties. At the time, however, a major conflict seemed imminent. The shooting of a pig that belonged to the HBC and a dispute over payment for it brought American troops to the island under Capt. George E. Pickett, and Governor James Douglas sent British warships (in an incident later known as the Pig War). A clash was avoided, however, and both nations agreed on a joint occupation until a settlement could be reached.

The bears were thick in the Chilliwack River Valley during the summer of 1859, and Wilson hoped he could take time off for hunting.[69] On August 16, a day after he had canoed across Chilliwack Lake to reach Darrah's camp at the mouth of Slesse Creek, Wilson was walking his horse across "Grizzly Flat" when he was suddenly jerked upright by the rearing animal as it was confronted by a black bear no more than seven feet distant:

We stood looking at each other for about a minute during which my feelings were anything but pleasant as I had not even a revolver. If the bear had advanced another step my horse would have backed out of the path & gone rolling down the hill & been killed & my only chance would have been to trust to my heels down the trail; however, Bruin seemed quite as frightened as I could have been & made off along the side of the hill at a pace which astonished me. . . .[70]

On August 28, Wilson and Dr. Lyall rode up Slesse Creek to visit Darrah, who had left for his station on upper Silesia Creek (as Slesse Creek is called north of the boundary). After about nine miles, they came to the end of the mule trail. Continuing on foot, they were rewarded by what Wilson considered the finest view yet:

We were right under the peaks of the Chekoimuck mountains [Border Peaks], which formed a kind of semi-circular basin in which lay four glaciers high above us whilst another was close beside us, not more than 200 yds off. From the four glaciers somewhere about 30 cascades fell down from 150 to 200 feet in height & uniting close above us formed the Chekoyoun stream, whilst the Slessé ran away to the left; the mountain peaks shutting out all the cold winds formed a kind of hot bed in which we found strawberries, black currants and raspberries in great profusion to which you may be sure we did ample justice. After gratifying our eyes & our insides we pushed on to Darrah's camp. . . .[71]

On August 31, Wilson bid "good-bye to the jolly old mountains for this year."[72] Lt. Roche, meanwhile, continued explorations beyond the Skagit, selecting a site for an astronomical station on Chuwanten Creek, a tributary of the Similkameen that Haig had named Roche River.[73] Snow began to fall in late September, forcing a return. In October, Haig crossed the pass east of Chilliwack Lake through two feet of new snow, much to Wilson's concern. With Lyall and Bauerman, he returned to the Chilukweyuk camp.

Custer's Reconnaissance to the Upper Skagit

After their reconnaissance to the Skagit River in 1858, Gardner and Peabody concluded that the Whatcom Trail could be shortened by using a lower pass between the north fork of Depot Creek and Maselpanik Creek. Leaving Lake Depot on June 29, 1859, Harris joined Peabody to study the situation. By the next day, they had located a gap that saved about eight hundred feet in elevation and about one and a half miles in distance. The new trail, which required only some three miles of new construction, Gardner wrote, passed "lakes of a deep cobalt blue that form a very picturesque feature in the scenery of these wild mountains."[74]

Gardner, who had been at Camp Chiloweyuck, arrived at Camp Chuchchehum with his party on July 13. (At this time Parke was based at Chiloweyuck Depot; on July 21, he moved to Lake Depot to join Gardner.) An express soon arrived from Capt. James J. Archer, notifying the surveyors that his command had arrived at the Okanogan River to ensure the safety of small parties traveling east of the divide. At Lake Depot, Gardner had prepared large wooden boxes for packing the delicate astronomical instruments, which were made to be used in pairs. Each instrument needed to be transported in a horizontal position, with the lens facing upward.[75] To open the trail from Lake Depot to the Skagit River at the parallel—an estimated thirty-five miles—required a force of ten to eighteen men for nearly a month. During that period, an axe flew off its helve when two men were cutting a tree, requiring Dr. Kennerly to be called from Chiloweyuck Depot to treat the injuries. Further, a great fire, caused by an unextinguished campfire, broke out on the side of the mountain, endangering the tents at Camp Chuchchehum. "The atmosphere was filled with smoke and cinders," Gardner wrote, and the already hot weather became almost unbearable.[76] This was the same fire that raged in the Skagit Valley at the end of July and hindered the British.

Various ridges and minor summits near Chilliwack Lake were occupied by surveyors for sighting and topographic sketching, such as Lake Hill station (which appears to have been Point 6044) and nearby Mt. Edgar (Hill Station). The distinctive Williams Peak was known as Custer's Peak, although Custer did not ascend it; apparently, it was sighted for triangulation but not climbed.

On July 25, Custer received orders from Parke to explore the region north and east of Chilliwack Lake in order to reach "Klequannum" (Silverhope) Creek (a Fraser tributary) and then the Skagit River. Custer's party of two whites and ten Indians was assembled the next day. Instead of Thiusoloc, he took a young Samona Indian who reportedly knew the country to be explored but whose knowledge, Custer later reported, "proved to be very slight." The entire party crossed Chilliwack Lake in flatboats, then ascended the "Koechehlum" (Post) Creek Valley, where there were faint traces of an Indian trail. Following the northeast-trending defile called "Noo-kwch-kwa-lum valley," the party reached Lindeman Lake in a few hours. Finding good travel along a wider valley floor, they came to the larger Greendrop Lake, which was surrounded by "high & perpendicular cliffs." To avoid climbing over a spur, Custer built a raft out of the abundant dry logs, using flexible fir branches and pack ropes to bind the parts together.

On July 28, the men descended "Pip-kwai-kwit" (Hicks) Creek, which led to the Silverhope Creek Valley. The ravine had a uniform course, "in which a good trail would be easily located, in fact it is, as we subsequently ascertained, the usual route, which these Mt Indians take to reach Fort Hope, from the Chiloweyuck lake, which they make sometimes their habitation during the winter." The route then bore southeast, and the men camped that evening at about the altitude of Chilliwack Lake. Continuing in the morning, they pushed through the dense forest of the Silverhope Valley, which widened as they continued. At first there was little underbrush, but it thickened gradually in the bottomland. Where the main creek turned sharply west, the party came to a series of marshy lakes, above which there were mountains on the left that "have lofty sumits and are still partly covered with snow." This parallel subrange to the northeast was called "Kleh-kwun-num," the same term used on sketches and maps for the Silverhope-Klesilkwa Valley. At about noon, the explorers came to a deserted Indian hut among giant cedars.

Custer, accompanied by his regular mountain companion Mitchly and an Indian, made a "very steep & tedious" ascent of a ridge point (Point 6827, about one mile west of Mt. Payne) high above the valley. The ground was still hot from the recent fire, and the dry ascent proved to be nearly suffocating until they found snow to quench their thirst.[77] There was little time to contemplate the mountain landscape, but Custer's report indicates that he could identify the lateral valley of the upper Skagit River. That afternoon, the Indians in the party killed three beavers, preserving the skins but eating the meat.

Travel on the morning of July 30 was tiring because of underbrush and a boggy surface. But after a walk of about five miles, the party "crossed unknowingly the here almost imperceptible divide between the Fraser and Skagit rivers." In late afternoon, "a general hurrah of the Indians" meant the party had struck "a broad & well travelled trail" (the Whatcom Trail). That night the party camped near the junction of Maselpanik Creek and the Klesilkwa River. The next day, they continued downstream by the trail to the Skagit, which flowed "with beautiful clear water" fit for canoe travel. Crossing the river on a large footlog, they found the forest to the east still smoking from a large burn that had been started by recent campers. The Indians were delighted to have reached the river, of which they apparently had no previous knowledge.[78]

Because they were at the eastern limit of the reconnaissance, Custer decided to camp at the river. He ascended a nearby hill, but the smoky atmosphere prevented him from seeing very far. Custer estimated that it was fourteen miles to the parallel by the new trail cut by the American party (it is actually about nine miles). He noted that the Skagit intersects the main range lengthwise, the mountains to the west (the "Chuch-chech Mts") being "the main backbone of the Cascade Mts." He proposed that "every ravine, almost every indentation in these Mt regions contains a living stream or a stationary reservoir of water." Where two streams drain the land in a directly opposite direction, Custer observed, they often do so at a comparatively low altitude, the course lying "in a continual gap or pass through the Mts, with only a comparatively low and thin saddle" between them. He also commented on potential and existing trails:

A good trail could be located, through this pass from the Skagit to Fort Hope, connecting this with the upper and lower Skagit, and would have been, from a topographical point of view, far preferable to the now existing Whatcom trail, but would have certainly gone entirely through brittish Territory. As a general thing the information received from officers of the Hudson bay company was very meagre and scanty, and is almost incredible, how little information of the Country they possessed even of the nearest vicinity of their Forts, aside from their usual lines of comunications. We found an Indian trail leading through the Klesilkwa valley, faint though as all these trails are, & observed subsequently its continuance through the entire length of the Skagit valley explored by us. My plan was now to return to the Chiloweyuck lake.

The next morning, following the trail near Maselpanik Creek, the men found the fire still raging, and they were barely able to get through. Taking the ravine that shortened the Whatcom Trail, they camped near a small lake "of singular blue color, the intensity of which is remarkable." Custer noted that the stream entering the lake came from a nearby glacier, which nearly reached the bottom of the ravine. This glacier, the western Maselpanik, is on the north flank of Peak 8630 ("Mt. Custer"). The topographer remarked on the greenish color of the glacier stream flow, although he did not know the tint was due to reflection from suspended glacier flour. He found mosquitoes—"this pestiferous insect"— everywhere below 6,000 feet but not higher.

On August 2, Custer ascended a nearby peak to obtain a better understanding of the area. The mountain slopes to the north were "covered with meadows of excellent pasturage," with two small, clear lakes nearby (northwest of the old Whatcom Pass trail summit). After a few hours of rather easy climbing, Custer, accompanied by Mitchly, arrived at the highest point to the northwest, Thompson Peak (of which this was the first recorded ascent), where he could absorb "a complete Panorama of the Mt regions in all directions of the Compass." He also visited Peak 6600 and perhaps Paleface Mountain and Point 6405. Spellbound by the contrasting colors, the multiplicity of stark, rocky peaks, and the succession of glaciers and snowfields, Custer made this report:

> To the East, deep down in the valley, the Skagit winds its peaceful course, through the dark masses of the woods adjacent, its clear & limpid waters, glittering & glistening, in the reflected light of the sun rays. The Mts to the East of the Skagit rise to considerable height. In the first Ridge we observe 2 Peaks especially prominent, the Shawatan, and the Hozomeen, the latter is a huge masse of grayish blak rock, ending in 2 sharp points, of considerable altitude, the height of the Mts, toward the South & Southeast, increases greatly, at some distance from Hozomeen peak, the Nokomokeen [Jack Mountain] rises its broad & bulky sumit far up in the air, covered with eternal snow & ice. . . . Imediately to the South of us, the rocky, whitish, masses of the Chuch-chech Mts, elevate themselves far above the surrounding Mts, covered with ice, & broken up in a thousand peculiar forms, castles, columns & walls; they are broad & massive, & seem properly to constitute the main matrix of these Mts. Toward the West we observe a vast sea of Mts, Peak on Peak, valley on valley. Mt Thuscan, & Mt. Baiker (Tako-meeh) loom up gloriously grand as ever, the latter with his usual companion, a little cloud, covering its sumit, maybe due to the vapors, which arise, or seem so, out of its craterlike sumit.

He spent hours sketching on the summit, "the eye luxuriously feasting in the matchless diversity of forms & colors." No fewer than nine lakes were in view.

On August 3, the final day of the journey, the party followed the trail through virgin forest to Chilliwack Lake. A glimpse southward showed that Depot Creek's main branch rose in a lake "fed by numerous glaciers & snowfields" (the Redoubt Glacier is the largest of these). A few hours later, Custer could describe his successful reconnaissance to the large party at the lake.

The topographer's next expedition was his most important, although it contributed little to the reconnaissance and marking of the forty-ninth parallel. As on his three previous ventures, Custer was unafraid, ambitious, and self-reliant. His exploration of the mountain rim of the upper Chilliwack and his crossing to the Skagit River rank as one of the outstanding episodes of Cascade Range pioneering. Custer left Chilliwack Lake on August 8 with Mitchly, a helper named Williams, and nine Indians. A flatboat carried the men to the south end of the lake. Traveling up the "Klah-neh" through the forest was relatively untiring through light underbrush and some cedar deadfalls.[79] In the soft alluvial valley bottom, the immense trunks of the giant cedars often leaned, "probably due to a want of firmness in the roots." Sometimes using gravel bars for faster progress, the party passed Bear Creek.[80] They made camp about ten miles from the lake near an Indian hut of cedar bark, not far above the mouth of Brush Creek.

To obtain an overall view and plan their route, Custer and Mitchly set out at daybreak to ascend the slope to the west. It soon became apparent that the deeply incised Bear, Indian, and Brush creeks form the three Chilliwack tributaries on the east valley flank; in the opposite direction was Ruth Mountain, with "a peculiar, sharply defined . . . sumit." To determine their course to the Skagit River, they decided to ascend what is now known as Easy Ridge. The entire party pushed onward about one mile, then bore upslope, all of them "animated by a spirit of curiosity." None of them had been on the ridge or to the pass they would soon cross.

The upper crest was broad and spacious, with white granite outcrops "covered with fine pasturage, a regular alp, such as one sees in the Mts of Switzerland or Tirol." There were many small, clear ponds and clumps of subalpine fir, and the explorers were surrounded by peaks that few people had ever been so close to. From the ridge, Custer recognized the distant Skagit Valley. He also jotted down other geographic features, including the "Zakeno" (upper Baker River), the precipitous anchor of Easy Ridge (Whatcom Peak), the high "Chuch-che-hum Mts," and the reddish rock of what is now Red Face Mountain (the granodiorite has a zone stained with iron oxide that caps the peak). Custer named the ridge "Mt Goat Mt" because of the many mountain goat tracks they found there.[81] When he returned to the campsite, the Indians were rejoicing because a goat had been killed. There ensued the usual feast with song, "mirth, and frolik," together with music made by striking a stick on a tin kettle.

In the morning, the party made a steep descent of about 2,000 feet to "Red Mtn [Brush] Creek." A crust of snow over the creek bed made for quick travel to a beautiful meadow slope carpeted with heather—"the 2 minute shrubs bearing white & red flowers," Custer noted. Proceeding over the alpine meadow, the men reached the brink of a sheer precipice, and they looked down to see a wide, rugged gorge with a stream winding through it—the Skagit tributary (Little Beaver Creek, called "Sko-mel-pua-nook" by the Indians). They had arrived at present-day Whatcom Pass.[82]

Custer was bedazzled by the "imense glacier which covered the Mt side on our left" (Challenger Glacier). The glacier formed "a solid wall of pure ice, to a height of over 5000 ft to near the Sumit of a very high Mt." Custer learned from the Indians that the peak's name was "Wilakin-ghaist" and estimated its altitude at between 9,000 and 10,000 feet.[83] The glacier's "matchless grandeur" prompted a comparison: "Imagine the Niagara Fall, tens of times, magnified in height & sise, of this vast sheet of falling water, instantly cristalised, & rendered permanently solid." From the glacier's uneven surface, Custer concluded that the process of ice formation must be continuous and correctly conjectured that the heavy winter snowfall would secure "the perpetuity of this splendid creation of nature." He thought that this section of the Cascades was "worthy to stand beside the most famous Mountain parties [parts] in the Alps of Europe."

Late in the day, Custer decided to risk the descent into the gorge, "the steepest and most dangerous I have ever made." He later reported: "It could only be overcome by the utmost caution on our part, by using our hands, arms legs & stiks, freely in a multitude of novel positions. Once to have lost foot hold here, nothing would have been left to the unlucky climber" but the fate of being "dashed to pieces on the sharp & frighttful rocks below." They located a good campsite in the forest opposite the glacier, whose waterfalls and cascades sent "their dustlike waters" over the cliffs. At times the next day, Custer found that wading knee-deep in the silt-colored "Glacier Creek" was preferable to clambering through the "dense tissues of wine maple & other bushes, with which the whole Hillside was overgrown." By the evening of August 13, the difficult portion of the valley had been overcome. At camp, however, the cook gave Custer the disconcerting news that there was enough food for four more meals.

To best determine their position, Custer and Mitchly left at daybreak the next day to ascend some distance northward onto the ridge, where they could see the tortuous course of the Skagit River and the valley's dark forest cover. The route to the survey's camp on the parallel was obvious, and it would be easy compared to what they had endured. Custer termed the ridge they had ascended (which appears in some sketches) "Disapointment Mt" because clouds and rain kept him from getting a good view of the Picket Range. The party soon continued to the river, and by afternoon they camped well toward Camp Skagit, a recently established astronomical station. The adventure concluded after a few hours' march.

Parke had left orders for Custer to explore the Skagit River for ten miles north and south of the boundary.[84] While a skilled Nooksack Indian built a canoe, Custer and Mitchly prepared to ascend the river. Opposite their camp was Shawatum Mountain, whose isolation and height made it logical for a topographic observation point. Custer followed his basic travel rule:

> If . . . your intentions are simply to ascend a peak, on the foot of which you stand, always select the longest leading spur, following the direction of its sumit. . . . Never select a ravine or watercourse, coming from the peak to be ascended [because here are] sudden drops, dense bushy vegetation, and an increasing steepness.

As Custer, Mitchly, and an unnamed Indian ascended Shawatum's lengthy slopes on August 24, they feasted on the tempting berries. Custer counted "at least 4 or 5 different varieties" of huckleberry, including the red ones in the forest zone and blueberries on the subalpine slopes and open meadows. The summit, which Custer estimated to be at 6,500 feet, provided a fine view in all directions, particularly of the "steep & rocky cliffs" of Hozomeen to the south and the "Chuch-che-hum Mts" to the west. Eastward, toward the Similkameen and Pasayten terrain, "straight lines are exchanged for curves, pointlike sumits, for table, or plainlike ones." Custer compared the somewhat desolate landscape "to that observed in the territory of Arizona."

Custer's downstream exploration of the Skagit began on August 27. While some of the party walked, Custer and three Indians took the canoe, although large logjams sometimes required them to haul it. The next day, there was pleasant canoeing on an unobstructed river. "The motion is so gently," Custer wrote, "the air on the water, cool & pleasant & the scenery, which is continually shifting, occupies mind & eye pleasantly." Below Three Fools Creek, they passed to the west of "Nokomokeen Mt" (Jack Mountain), which, "with its snow & ice covered sumit" rising to over 9,000 feet, dominates the upper Skagit River Valley. Custer noted the deep, narrow stream canyons entering the valley from the much-dissected Hozomeen Range.

As the valley narrowed, the canoe passed the "Tseh-neeh" (Big Beaver Creek), a large western tributary. Custer speculated that the stream's headwaters interlocked with the Baker and upper Chilliwack rivers. They encountered rapids when the party was still some miles above the east fork (Ruby Creek, which Gardner called "Sluklkokai"), and the Indians were "shouting and singing at the same time, as our canoe sped on with the rapidity of an arrow." Custer judged that "nothing equals the pleasant excitement" of dashing through the stream's swift waves "with a good canoe & skillful crew." The river's increasing flow rate between rocky banks, however, caused concern even to the experts.

Just in time, a little eddy enabled them to find a secure nook in the bank, and the crew gave a yell of satisfaction. To continue would have meant disaster. A hundred yards downstream the river formed a small waterfall, which "would have engulfed the whole party." Farther down the canyon, to where Gibbs had ascended in 1858, Gardner reported that the Skagit passed through a canyon with innumerable falls and rapids.[85] Nearby, the high, rocky bank of Ruby Creek was "bridged over by a small fir tree . . . one of the Indians, was rapidly crossing & recrossing, looking with perfect coolness in the dizzy chasm below, where the waters were dashing & roaring in their onward course." The Indian invited others to join him, but without success.

The next day, August 31, after making a latitude observation, the party abandoned the canoe in order to return by the Indian trail. For some time, Custer had wanted to climb the "Kakoit Mts" to study the topography of the Skagit-Similkameen divide. Ascending a spur to the south of Lightning Creek, the men endured a hot, dry day before reaching a snowpatch in a meadow where they could quench their thirst. That afternoon, from the first "Kakoit" peak (Spratt Mountain's south peak), Custer looked through the smoky air at the intricate ridges, spurs, and valleys east of the Skagit. The deep ravine of Three Fools ("Skweh-kway-et") Creek was to the north. Custer wanted to climb Hozomeen—a gigantic, double-fanged rock peak located just south of the International Boundary—but the "whole country is covered with clouds & smoke." The undertaking would be useless if he could not get a good view. They camped that afternoon on the ridge northwest of Spratt Mountain. Custer estimated that he had traveled over three hundred miles so far on his series of reconnaissances.

The next day, after Custer climbed the second "Kakoit" peak (Spratt's north peak), they moved camp about four miles to the east, on Devils Dome.[86] The view from the summit disclosed a low saddle (Devils Pass) to the east and a prominent summit that appeared to lie on the semicircular dividing ridge between Jack and Hozomeen mountains. During a cold night at the camp—their highest yet—a violent wind blew down the tent.

On September 3, Custer, Mitchly, and an Indian boy named Tom crossed the ridge slope to Devils Pass and then made an uneventful ascent. Custer thought they were on the Cascade Range watershed divide—he could scan the Pasayten River drainage and make out the Methow terrain, still some distance to the southeast—but the stream flowing southeast (Canyon Creek's north fork) did not lead to the Methow drainage, as he believed. The slopes beyond Devils Pass had the "finest alpine pasturage, room & food for extensive herds of cattle." The party resumed their march up the Skagit on September 5, but bush and fallen timber slowed them down. They reached Camp Skagit the next day. At Custer's request, Parke had sent a new barometer to replace the one Mitchly had broken when he stumbled and fell in the forest.

Custer deserves much credit for his courageous reconnaissances between the Chilliwack and Nooksack rivers and the upper Skagit River drainages. Of his explorations, those in the Tomyhoi-Silesia Creek high country, from Nesakwatch Creek to Chilliwack Lake and from the upper Chilliwack River valley to the Skagit River, are outstanding pioneering journeys over terrain new not only to surveyors but often to the Indian guides as well.

The Gardner Party Continues East

Joseph Harris, who by now had moved forward to make new latitude and magnetic observations and to mark the parallel, had established Camp Skagit on July 26 at a river bend on the east bank. Latitude observations from camps were made using the zenith telescope on as many as 150 pairs of stars, using an oil lantern to read instruments. Chronometers were used to determine the longitude differences between camps. When Gardner arrived at the new camp on July 30, he arranged for a reconnaissance eastward to locate other astronomical stations. He was joined by some Similkameen Indians who had accompanied Capt. Archer's expressmen. The expressmen gave a favorable account of the route to the east via the gap of Nepopekum Creek.[87]

Campbell decided that the American party should be pioneering and cutting trail, not cutting the vista, and that the Similkameen Valley was to be the site of the next astronomical station. On August 1, Parke, Gardner, and Peabody left with an Indian guide and a fifteen-man escort under Lt. McKibben. Following the guide onto Skyline Ridge, the party apparently descended into the Nepopekum Creek Valley before reaching the route's highlight—the memorable "knife-edge" crest, whose southern slope dropped steeply to the Lightning Lakes chain.[88]

Gardner observed that, with the exception of "Showatrum" and "Hozameen," the mountains east of the Skagit lose some of their abrupt character: "There seems to be a monotonous rounding of the mountains, making them look so much alike that it is impossible to distinguish one from another." The sighting and identification of distinctive peaks had always been important for mapping and positioning the parallel. "Our reconnaissances theretofore through the Cascade Mountains and to the west of them," Gardner wrote, "have been mostly made by the aid of the sharp, well defined peaks, whose positions were determined from the prairies on Frazer River, as well as from the Astronomical Stations along the Boundary."[89]

On August 5, Peabody returned to Lake Depot, while Parke and Gardner continued eastward. The two men descended from the "knife edge" to near Gibson Pass, then continued to the valley of the "N'shitlshootl" (upper Similkameen River) and on to Nicomen Ridge. That night they camped on a divide, where they found ripe strawberries to eat. There were also western larch, which had "straight burnt sienna colored trunks" that gave the Similkameen country the "appearance of a private park in civilization."[90] Gardner wrote that the Indians were not well acquainted with the country but that "we frequently struck upon old Indian trails used in hunting and followed them." Now that they were east of the main Cascade Range divide, the survey party came upon some birds they had not previously seen on their trips, including barking crows, magpies, Franklin's grouse, white-bellied swallows, and American ravens. Kennerly wrote that ptarmigan had been seen near the Pasayten River.

By August 9, with the help of four axemen, the party made its way through thick pines to the main Similkameen Valley with its lengthy terracing and narrow bottomland. The soldiers were exhausted by the long march, and trail dust hardened the perspiration in their cotton socks, causing blisters. After striking the HBC Brigade Trail, the reconnaissance party followed the route to the Okanogan River.[91]

Returning from the Similkameen, Gardner wanted to avoid the long northern detour, so he ascended the "Naisnuloh" (Ashnola) and its east fork (today's Ewart Creek). An Indian hunting trail eased the trek through the lower valley and its steep scarp. After reaching the boundary and setting up the Nais-nu-loh astronomical station, Gardner traveled from the main fork of the Ashnola across high country and past Placer Mountain to the lower Pasayten River, an estimated twenty-five miles. At the time, the Pasayten, not the upper Similkameen, was considered the main stream, with the name *Similkameen* used for the river below the junction.

When Gardner reached Camp Skagit on August 23, the great fire had spread into the upper Skagit and was enveloping the entire region in smoke. The blaze interfered with surveying activities, and at one place "a mule transporting ammunition of the escort had the hair of its tail almost burnt off, but fortunately for us its load was not reached by the fire."[92]

Meanwhile, Gibbs had been placed in charge of a "road" party to improve the trail between the Skagit and the Similkameen. Parke sent an express requesting Peabody and the work party to construct a trail by the Nepopekum gap, but the dispatch did not arrive in time and the trail was built via Skyline Ridge instead. The route approximately coincides with today's trail to the open ridge, where Summit Cache was established near Lone Goat Mountain.[93] Gibbs sketched and made topographic observations from several small peaks, including Lone Goat, near this divide. On August 8, he was at Point 6500, four miles northeast of Shawatum Mountain, a point also known as "Gardner's station" (Gardner apparently used it for observations) and "2nd summit." Gibbs also used Nepopekum Mountain as a triangulation station.

Harris left Camp Skagit on August 29 with a small party to set up an astronomic station in the Pasayten River Valley. Camp Pasayten, located closely south of the boundary, was established by September 5. Harris made triangulations and geodetic observations for latitude, assisted by Hudson, a mathematician just arrived from Washington, D.C. Together, they made 150 pairs of observations on 50 pairs of stars before leaving the camp on September 18. The two men also located three boundary points and built monuments.

Gardner—along with Parke, Charles Gardner, and Peabody—broke Camp Skagit on August 31 and proceeded eastward to establish an astronomical station on the Similkameen River. On night of September 1, they camped at Summit Cache, east of the Skagit River on Skyline Ridge, where they witnessed the most brilliant aurora Gardner had ever seen:

> The camp had been at rest for an hour or more with the exception of a few packers, who were repairing some of their gear and when the aurora was most brilliant it had the appearance of a clear bright sunrise giving the packers the idea of perpetrating a joke upon the rest of camp. They awoke the cooks, scolding them for being so late as the sun was up and no breakfast ready—all of them turned out and started their fires and might have gone further if not for our timely interference.[94]

After leaving the picturesque "knife edge," which now had a trail, Gardner and the escort took the old trail down the upper Similkameen and crossed the Pasayten where the two streams meet. There they were joined by Harris, who had just explored south to the boundary line. Roche, a member of the British commission, had already crossed to the valley of the upper Similkameen— and, in fact, had located the route over the "knife edge" ahead of the American party. The British lieutenant continued to the mouth of the Chuwanten and ascended it to the boundary. Haig then accompanied Gardner up this drainage, where they established Roche Station barely south of the parallel.[95]

The Gardner party descended eastward and on September 9 arrived at Camp Similkameen on the valley bottom. The camp was located on the Similkameen River about one mile south of the forty-ninth parallel, northeast of Palmer Lake and west of Osoyoos Lake. The pack trains, which had been on the move throughout the 1859 season, finally reached the Naisnuloh Cache (Gibbs had apparently gone ahead of the main party and established this cache). Capt. Archer's escort greatly helped Gardner's party in completing the mountainous portion of the survey before the late-autumn snows fell.[96]

On September 10, Custer, along with Mitchly and a small party, left Skagit Cache on a trek eastward to the Similkameen River. Following the Whatcom Trail, the men traveled north of the forty-ninth parallel on the head branches of the Skagit, a region Custer thought had "an indescribable charm." The route crossed the "T's-kai-ist Mts" (where he wanted to obtain topographic notes) to reach the 1849 HBC Brigade Trail.[97] As Gardner noted, the area had never been accurately mapped even though the fur brigades had traveled it for years.

On September 13, Custer ascended a lesser peak of Snass Mountain, above the junction of the two principal head branches of the Skagit. His route took him past the Skagit-Sumallo forks and then across the divide to the Similkameen, passing the Punch Bowl. After intersecting the Brigade Trail near Campement des Femmes on September 20, Custer visited Otter Lake. Others were on the trail as well. He met two men heading for Fort Hope who were with Capt. John Palliser's employees. Beyond a place the Indians called "Yake-to-lo-meen" (present-day Princeton), he met two friendly travelers on horse-back—Angus McDonald of the HBC and Lt. Henry S. Palmer of the Royal Engineers. Meanwhile, Peabody's pack train cleared Lake Depot on September 20. After an eighteen-day journey, that group arrived at Camp Similkameen on October 7.

During the encampment of the main party at Camp Similkameen, many of the men washed for gold in the river with remarkable success. On October 6, Gardner saw "ten or twelve dollars in gold flakes & dust that had been washed out in a very short time. I found it necessary to allay this gold fever in order to progress with the work."[98] Survey members and prospectors reportedly found less than $2,000 in gold along the sandbars, yet the news caused a minor rush.

On October 3, Custer and Mitchly began a reconnaissance southward from the camp into the valley of "Help wil" (Palmer) Lake to Toats Coulee. Their route probably followed the south fork of the Toats westward to the divide with the Chewuch (Chewack) River near Thirtymile Meadows. Continuing on to the Chewuch, the men traveled through the balsam fir forest and Custer made accurate observations about the Methow drainage. The explorers re-traced the route to the "Help wil" Valley, where on October 11 Custer men-tioned the high "Tcho-Pah'k [Chopaka] Mts" opposite them. They then fol-lowed a coulee east of present-day Loomis (via Spectacle Lake) to the Okanogan River. On the way back to Camp Similkameen, which they reached on October 19, Custer saw a remarkable creature, a bighorn sheep, with fur of a "bluish gray color, and large horns, a species of mountain goat, or chamois, it bounded from my presence with the swiftness of an arrow."

Camp Similkameen was broken on October 23, and Harris and Parke trav-eled eastward to establish the next station—beyond the Cascades. In his sum-mary report to Campbell, Parke reviewed the 1859 season's reconnaissances, which had covered some 6,000 square miles. The survey, taking the nearest practical line to the parallel and connecting the astronomical stations, had covered an estimated chained distance of about 370 miles.[99] Parke was pleased that the party had come through the season's work without any damage to the astronomical instruments—although they were less fortunate with the mag-netic instruments, as a mule carrying them had "missed his footing and rolled down a precipitous bank." The report discussed the difficult terrain, the rug-ged mountains, the peaks covered "with perpetual snow," the discovery of gla-ciers, and the labor of building trails and bridging for pack-mule transporta-tion. Parke also mentioned the dangerous watercourses his men had faced. He believed "the entire region is eminently unfit for occupation or settlement."

Joint Demarcation

Although the Americans had earlier rejected the British proposal for joint demarcation of the western portion of the boundary, when the commissioners met officially at Fort Colville in November 1859, their discussions were virtually frictionless. The iron markers provided at the expense of the British government were to be erected from saltwater to the base of the mountains. Each commissioner agreed to recognize the work of the other, subject to examination and revision on completion of the fieldwork. This proved a relief to Hawkins, for he wanted to be certain his work would be acknowledged. During the 1859 season, the British had established astronomical stations at five miles east of Semiahmoo Bay and also at Cultus Lake, Slesse Creek, Nesakwatch Creek, and Chuwanten Creek.

Haig assumed charge of the British commission during the winter while Hawkins traveled to England to report to the Foreign Office on the survey's progress and to discuss the San Juan Islands crisis. Operations shifted to the western frontal terrain and to winter quarters on Vancouver Island.[100]

November proved to be so cold and snowy, even in the lowlands, that the men remaining on the mainland had to fight for survival at times. On December 12, when ice blocked their canoe while they were traveling on the Fraser, Wilson and his two Indian companions decided to trek overland the final miles to reach Fort Langley. A harrowing and frigid "crawl" through four miles of brush along the river took seven and a half hours, the snow sometimes coming up to their knees. At times they "crawled along the ice at the edge of the river which would ever & again break through & let the luckless leader up to his armpits in the river, then wading up to the waist in an open piece of water or creeping along the trunk of a fallen tree. . . ." Finally, they saw the light glimmering in the HBC fort at Langley.[101] Darrah had a camp on Langley Prairie at the time.

Hawkins was quite displeased with the instruments the British were using at the end of the 1859 season. Both the twelve- and fifteen-inch altazimuths were too cumbersome and heavy for the rough terrain, and they were also inaccurate and antiquated. The instruments were packed up and "not again brought into use." Haig asked Hawkins for two seven-inch transit theodolites with perforated axes for laying out azimuths.[102]

Samuel Anderson's Commentaries, Winter 1859–1860

Samuel Anderson, "a clever young Engineer officer," arrived to join the British staff in the winter of 1859–1860. He had received the finest technical and military schooling—at St. Andrews University, the Military Academy in Edinburgh, the Royal Military Academy at Woolwich, and the School of Military Engineering at Chatham —and had been commissioned as a lieutenant in the Royal

Engineers the year before. Eventually, he would replace Wilson as secretary to the boundary commission. His letters to his relatives paint a picture of what life was like for the members of the British commission during that winter at Victoria and Fort Langley.[103]

Anderson was relieved to arrive at Victoria on December 2 after a two-month voyage on an American steamer, where, he wrote his brother Jack, "comfort is wanting, cheapness being the only thing thought of." As for the Yankees themselves, "their conceit is beyond all bearing," and they "have a peculiar way of pronouncing ordinary words," such as "criks" for "creeks."[104] The surveyor found a sparse social culture in Victoria, although there were enough men around from four warships and some twenty women "to get up a little dance" and some theatricals.

When Anderson first went to the mainland, shortly after arriving in Victoria, he stayed at Col. Moody's camp at New Westminster because the frozen river had stopped all traffic to Fort Langley (where Darrah and Wilson were at the time). When he did reach Langley on December 15, the inconveniences included a "very hard bed" with five blankets, and the newcomer complained there were no luxuries such as sheets, pillows, or mattresses.[105] The British officers had servants, however, which lessened the discomfort. At the temporary British headquarters camp at the Sumas River, the men were allowed a pint bottle of wine and a bottle of beer per day, and they generally contrived to keep a good supply. Anderson found the brandy keg rewarding, it being "very acceptable sometimes on a cold winter's night when we have to sit up till sunrise observing the stars."[106]

The December survey work was difficult because of the bitter cold snap. The first morning chore—often performed by Indians—was to get a good fire going. The effect was to be "toasted on one side and frozen on the other," so that the men had to "keep up a continual rotation to make our blood circulate everywhere." If they wished to warm up, it was usual to get an axe and fell a tree, although Anderson was unhappy at the way the men "cut down young and old trees."[107] Tree bark was a better fuel than coal, Anderson wrote, and in his bag he carried what the Indians called "gumstick" (obtained from tree trunks), which "flames up as soon as a match is put to it."

The lieutenant does not seem to have focused on the terrain. Not only did he seldom comment on the Cascade Range, but he also held the misconception that "the Boundary passes over nothing but Mountains all the way from the Pacific to the Rocky Mountains, and it is impossible to tell where one range of mountains ceases and the next begins."[108] Still, Anderson found the Fraser River Valley country quite different from his native England and seemed to prefer the outdoor life to that of his contemporaries who were "doing nothing in Victoria but spending money and going to balls and parties." There was ample wild duck and sometimes grouse for variety. An HBC farm near Fort Langley provided beef, butter, and milk. Fresh beef was on the table for Christmas Day, augmented with venison, plum pudding, and plenty of sherry and beer.[109]

Of all the British officers, Anderson appears to have been the most interested in the Indians. He admired their way with horses and wrote to his brother that one could expect good bargains in trading, "as they will often give a fine horse for an old red jacket, and also some valuable furs."[110] He found their appearance striking:

> The Natives of this country are the most extraordinary looking individuals I ever saw. They all have long black hair hanging over their shoulders, have thick lips, flattened noses, and foreheads flattened, by their parents in their childhood. There are a great number of different tribes scattered all over the place, and a few years ago, there used to be constant fights between one another. Most of them are armed with the old flint muskets and they are very good shots with them.[111]

Concerning the Indians' culture, Anderson observed that they were very superstitious; that the Chinook Jargon was easy to communicate in; and that the local Indians occupied themselves during the day with fishing in their canoes for salmon, which they dried and saved for the winter months. He also admired their capacity for work:

> We keep a certain number of them in employment . . . to act as messengers, to cut fire wood and for the various odds and ends in a camp, and what they can do, they do well. They can carry tremendous loads, strapped either to their forehead or across their breast. . . . Those we employ we make cut their hair to a rational length, and send them down to the river every morning with some soap to have a good wash, which they would not think of doing otherwise.[112]

The British also employed Indians to gather cranberries; for the equivalent of a dollar, they gathered enough to last three weeks. The British also paid one shilling for each grouse brought in.

The men generally did not see bears during the winter, as the animals hibernated, but there was one exception near Fort Langley:

> One of our working parties a few days ago came across two [bears] inside a tree which they were beginning to fell. One of them escaped the other one tried to escape, but a Canadian axeman of the party jumped and seized hold of him by his neck and by his tail and rammed his head in the snow. The bear tried to bite but the man held on to the back of his neck like grim death till another man secured a rope round his neck (the bear's) when the animal followed them quite quietly into the camp. We are going to try and buy him and if possible take him home as a trophy.[113]

Mister Tom, as the bear became known, was soon sufficiently tame to "eat out of our hands."[114]

During the cold January and February weather, the men often sat around the campfire with waterproof clothing and made themselves "as jolly as possible with a halfglass of grog." The tents were too small to be comfortable, except during sleep. When it rained, the party was "obliged to remain under canvas most of the day, and read, and write letters, or amuse ourselves."[115] Any newspapers that arrived were usually three months old. Camp provisions usually arrived every seven days by mule. Field rations included one and a half pounds of fresh meat and flour for each man and three-quarters of a pound of potatoes per day, although in fact there was no restriction in quantity for the officers' mess. Occasionally there was the luxury of Worcester sauce or pickles.

Winter at Victoria

The remainder of the British party, including Wilson and Haig, enjoyed the relative comforts of Victoria. As during the previous winter, there was a ball, held this time at the HBC fort in November and given by explorer John Palliser, Capt. Haig, and Lt. Wilson. "We had the dancing room rigged out with flags & I had the floor well waxed to make it slippery," Wilson wrote, "the effect of which was two tremendous tumbles during the course of the evening."[116]

After his duty on the mainland, Anderson returned to Esquimalt on March 6 to find the other members of the commission awaiting the return of Col. Hawkins from England. The lieutenant had much to say about social life on the barely settled island and about the slow-paced daily routine. Anderson usually arose at about nine o'clock, when he would read the newspapers, take a few solar observations with a Sextant until noon, have luncheon, and ride up to town about two o'clock, lounge about the town paying visits and shopping until three, then go for a ride until half past four, get home about five-thirty, have dinner at six, cup of tea at half past seven, rubber of whist (for love) until eleven, and then turn in.[117]

In his spare time, the young officer amused himself by playing the flute. The officers all had horses for luxury rides, and there was occasional racing. The men received good quantities of food on the table, with champagne for special occasions, and Anderson once wrote that he had gained fourteen pounds since leaving England. As an officer, he expected the obligatory invitation from the governor and the admiral, when

> there will be the bother and formality of dining with them which is objectionable tho' not the less necessary. There are 2 Miss Douglas's daughters of the Governour and of course the greatest flirts on the island and I certainly have very little desire to make their acquaintance in consequence.[118]

When Anderson—who was obviously a popular officer—attended one luncheon with the governor with "12 or 14 gentlemen and only one other lady besides his two daughters. . . . The Governour gave us a capital luncheon, and there was plenty of champagne going."[119] He wrote his brother that

> there is a very good show of ladies here [in Victoria], but the most of them have been spoiled by the host of naval officers and others running after them. Of course they

are very different to our ladies at home, as the most of them have been in this country all their lives, and have consequently had few advantages in the way of education and accomplishments. They are all very fond of dancing.[120]

He wrote his sister that the bishop, "who taught all his clergymen to go about for subscriptions in a most barefaced way," had been giving "some very severe lecturing sermons to the ladies about gossiping, which I am afraid will do little or no good, as they have no other way (as they think) of passing their time."[121]

In his letters, Anderson also described the commission's photographers, who took some of the first photographs of the region, including some of the survey activities, HBC forts, and members of the commission. Anderson wrote that the photographers had not been busy lately "on account of sickness or bad conduct," although he hoped to send some pictures to England soon.[122] That spring, Anderson received orders from Col. Hawkins, who had returned to Victoria unexpectedly on March 15 to resurvey a portion of the boundary line between Chilliwack Lake and the Skagit River. The colonel also had to plan a more extensive boundary demarcation because of the recent gold discoveries on the Similkameen River.[123]

The Last Mountain Surveys, 1860

The general plan formulated by the British commission for the coming season's work was to outflank the Cascade Range in spring and early summer by traveling south to the Columbia, then from The Dalles to the Similkameen. The commission wanted to avoid further encounters with the mountains by establishing a supply and winter base at Fort Colville. Hawkins planned that Haig, Anderson, and the Royal Engineers would begin at Roche River, the farthest point reached in 1859. In late April, Darrah commanded a party of engineers, muleteers, and packers—along with a pack train of seventy-seven horses and mules—by steamer from the Fraser River to Nisqually, and on to Fort Vancouver.[124] The remaining members of the commission took the *Otter* directly to Fort Vancouver, leaving on April 28. The men left their friends at Esquimalt with mixed feelings. There were particular farewells to the navy personnel, the church, and the barracks, which they relinquished to the Admiralty. Anderson described the *Otter* as

a little bit of a screw steamer, about as big as a ½ boat on the Thames, only with the sides a little higher. The Yankees however never speak of a screw steamer, but always call it a propeller. It was with great difficulty that we stored ourselves away on this boat, as we had so much baggage. . . .

At Fort Vancouver, which the HBC would abandon the next year and which was being used by the U.S. War Department as a military post, the American garrison officers welcomed the British with hospitality. Taking the steamer for the Cascades of the Columbia on May 16, the commission walked from the

Lower to the Upper Cascades, admiring the wildflower pageant. At The Dalles—now a temporary base for the commission—the group met Capt. Haig, "who hurried us off to drink sherry cobblers at the Mount Hood."[125] Wilson described The Dalles and the Indians he saw there:

> The river runs through a wide channel of basaltic rocks & is only 150 yds wide, the current is so strong that it quite stops the navigation of the river. There are a great number of Indians here fishing, quite different fellows from any we have met before; they have large bands of horses & are all mounted & some of them look very well on horseback with their feathers & streamers flying in the wind.[126]

The British found The Dalles rather lawless; and although there had been an average of one murder or attempted murder a month, the locals boasted that no one had been hanged for murder during the past three years.

On May 25, the resourceful Lord, who had been sent to California in late winter to obtain more animals, arrived safely at The Dalles with seventy-seven mules and one horse. He and his party had had a long and adventurous journey. Lord had decided not to take the regular mail route through Oregon, but a shorter way farther inland through Klamath Indian territory. The party had been threatened by Indians at Klamath Lake, and two horses had been stolen.

Haig moved from The Dalles to the north bank of the Columbia River to prepare for his trek to the boundary line, where he would connect with the previous season's surveying. He began his journey on June 4, traveling by way of Fort Simcoe and up the west bank of the Columbia and arriving at Osoyoos Lake on June 28. Haig's party included Anderson, Lyall, and Bauerman, along with four other officers, twenty noncommissioned officers and sappers, the packmaster, twenty packers, and twelve axemen. They took along provisions for 125 men for fifteen months, as well as a forage supply. The grand cavalcade included ninety pack mules, thirty horses for officers and packers, and twelve head of cattle for fresh meat.[127] Wilson, meanwhile, began an overland journey from Walla Walla to Fort Colville to establish a new depot. Taking with him only a sergeant and his servant, with no baggage but blankets, some bacon, and flour, Wilson reached the fort on July 1. There he set about arranging the stores brought by wagon and mule train. Hawkins arrived soon afterward, and they began the season's work with vigor.[128]

Haig's advance to the boundary on the east flank was so hindered by the swollen Ashnola River and fallen timber on the valley slopes that it took his group twenty-one days to ascend to the chosen astronomical station—twenty-two miles from the river mouth on the east fork, closely south of the parallel. The party arrived at the boundary on July 26 and completed observations by August 5.[129] Anderson, meanwhile, began the resurvey between Chilliwack Lake and the Skagit River on July 26, returning to Roche River (Chuwanten Creek) on August 13.

The men feared rattlesnakes in the low and hot Similkameen country. On August 12, Wilson wrote that one of his men was carrying a large snake over a stick, one he had just killed in Wilson's blankets. The lieutenant had a frightening experience the next day:

> I went out to sketch the dark gorge of the great bend of the river and had nearly completed . . . when, to my horror, a large rattlesnake dropped off the lappets of my coat, where he had probably found a pleasant resting-place. The brute seemed quite as frightened as I was, and made off at a good pace.

Wilson was pleased, though, that the HBC kept a farm with some cows and oxen in the valley, "so that we had a good drink of milk, a thing not to be despised in this part of the world."[130] Wilson proceeded on foot with his gun to Haig's camp, at over 6,000 feet, arriving on August 16. It was the first time he had met Haig and the rest of his party since leaving The Dalles.

Leaving the Ashnola, Haig's party crossed a mountain ridge at the tree limit and then descended to the Pasayten River. Near the ridge summit, on August 20, Wilson experienced a conflict between Old World standards and New World wilderness:

> . . . I fell in with a fine lot of grouse, the mother & 5 well grown young ones, they seemed quite unsophisticated, not the least idea of danger & did not care at all for the report of firearms; I fired four shots at the old one with my pistol . . . After this I dismounted & got the whole brood, killing one with my gun, two with stones & two with sticks; what would some of the English sportsmen say to this wholesale kind of butchery! I was almost ashamed of myself, but the inward man crying out that fresh grouse was better than stale bacon overcame any conscientious scruples I might have had as to this unorthodox manner of procuring game.[131]

The next day, they reached the junction of the Pasayten and the Similkameen:

> Near where we camped the Pesayton joins the south fork of the Similkameen, which makes a tremendous bend to the north from this point . . . Some distance up we found an old Indian vapour bath, which shows that Indians must have lived at some time near this, which we had before thought a *terra incognita*; we had great fun fording the rivers, the stones being very slippery & the water very cold, it was a difficult matter to keep in the perpendicular without shoes & stockings.[132]

While Haig returned to his camp on the Ashnola in order to move it to Osoyoos Lake, Wilson ascended the Pasayten to Anderson's camp, over the "worst road I ever travelled." Anderson rejoiced in the letters and English newspapers Wilson had brought. The surveyor was in good spirits but had, as Wilson observed on August 22, only "the remnants of his last pair of boots, through which his toes protruded to a considerable distance, his evening occupation being generally to sew the soles on to last over the next day. . . ."[133]

On August 24, Wilson and Dr. Lyall returned eastward. Marmots abounded in the meadows along the route, their shrill whistles echoing among the cliffs.

From the summit, at about 7,500 feet (they were apparently on the Pasayten-Ashnola divide, perhaps between the boundary and Flat Top Mountain or near Park Pass), there was a magnificent view:

> . . . we could see the bare peaks of the Cascades all round us, many of them clothed in snow, whilst towards the west we recognized our old friend Mount Baker raising his hoary head high above the others . . . There is something indescribably pleasant rambling about a mountain at such an altitude; the air sharp & clear, the magnificent panorama before the eye & a buoyant & elastic feeling both of mind & body, which is never felt elsewhere.[134]

From August 14 to September 5, Anderson surveyed eastward to the Ashnola River headwaters. Between July 9 and September 7, he covered the entire region from Chilliwack Lake to the Similkameen River.

At the beginning of September, some eight inches of new snow fell in the high country. Camping near timberline on September 1, about fourteen miles from the Similkameen, Anderson heard his servant shoveling about the tent:

> it instantly occurred to me that my tent must have been covered with snow and I found out that in one night, a foot of snow had fallen and we ran a very good chance of losing all our camp necessaries as they had been left about the night before, and in the morning nothing was to be seen but one mass of snow.[135]

When descending the Similkameen, Anderson saw some thirty to forty men working along the river for gold, sometimes damming portions of the river to find the precious metal in the streambed. He noted that the miners made thirty-two to forty shillings per day (twenty shillings equaled one pound), barely sufficient to tide them over in the winter when they could not work. By late 1861 he was astounded by the discoveries in the Cariboo, where £6,000 to £10,000 could be earned in four to six weeks.

Fieldwork Completed

By the end of the 1860 season, the American commission had essentially completed surveying and marking of the entire land boundary from Point Roberts to the Rocky Mountains. The American and British commissioners held a joint meeting at Harney Depot at the beginning of November. Relations, it seems, were barely tolerable. Hawkins wrote to the British Foreign Office: "Mr. Campbell addressed himself to me with much arrogance, and even not refraining from insult; to which I replied with I hope firmness and forbearance."[136] Campbell—together with Warren, the artist Alden, and Gibbs—left the region on November 25, 1860, and reached Washington, D.C., forty-six days later. In spring 1861, the two Gardners, Custer, Hudson, and Nooney left for the East Coast. In the last quarter of the year, Parke, Harris, Major, and Wurdemann also returned, bringing records, instruments, natural-history specimens, and the remaining baggage.[137]

By December 1860, the British were settled into winter quarters at Fort Colville. Wilson wrote of the lack of communication with the outside world and of reminiscing about seasons past:

> You can picture the Commission on a winter's evening sitting in a circle round a huge fire of logs, a kettle singing merrily by its side with sundry suspicious looking tumblers standing on a table close by & then the yarns that are told, where everyone has his little troubles & adventures to talk over, of weary nights with mosquitoes, of rattlesnake bed fellows, of onslaughts on grouse, toiling over mountains & fording rapid streams, what one's feelings were when he saw the mule with all his household property go rolling over a precipice, or another's when he broke the stock of his pet double barrel, all is talked & laughed over & often looked back to with a sort of pleasure.[138]

The winter cold was so excruciating that ink froze in one's pen, despite attempts to keep it warm by a fire. According to Lord, "the steam rising from the teacups would freeze into a kind of sleet," then fall onto the table.[139] Surprisingly, however, the men could shoot grouse, even with the deep snow. There were various entertainments throughout the winter. In February, the British invited the Americans to a grand ball hosted by the HBC at the fort. (Anderson later commented that the only two things required to "get up a Ball" in that part of the world were "a Gallon of Whiskey and a Fiddler.") The British played four-handed cribbage, and the Americans' card games—played by all classes, the caste-conscious British noted—interested them considerably.

In February 1861, Wilson left for San Francisco to repair some scientific instruments. He and his servant, each on a horse and driving two packhorses with instruments, journeyed through a country deep in snowdrifts, with temperatures that dropped to thirty degrees below zero. It took them eleven days to travel from Fort Colville to Walla Walla, and from there they took boats down the Columbia and then a steamer to San Francisco. Wilson returned to Colville, then went with the commission to the Rocky Mountains as surveying continued east of the Cascades during the 1861 season. He left for England later that year.

The second winter for the British commission at Fort Colville was especially severe, as the thermometer dropped to twenty-eight below zero night after night. "It is impossible to keep anything thawed," Anderson wrote on February 2, 1862. "Today is almost the first day I have been able to write without the ink freezing in my pen."[140] The British seem to have been continually amused by the Americans' oddities. In January, Anderson and Wilson paid a visit to the American garrison (seventeen miles from the fort), where there were two companies of California volunteers. The American officers, Anderson thought, "were more or less rough as you may imagine, and had not paid much attention to the rules of English grammar, but they were exceedingly hospitable."[141] Later he wrote his sister:

I dined at their mess and had a tolerable dinner, and one of the many things that amused me was being pressed to take some cheese with my mince pie. It is amusing to see how many things they pile on their plates at the same time, and one and all make a practise of putting their knives in their mouths a barbarous custom which I believe exists even in the more civilized parts of America.[142]

Making their way across the Columbia Plateau in the spring of 1862—on their way to The Dalles, headed back to Victoria and then to England—the British were detained an entire week "at that dreary sandy place called Walla Walla waiting for the steamer." Anderson called it "a miserable place, no wood to make a house with, not enough to make a fire." He also told of a tragedy:

> It was along this road that 11 men had started, loaded with gold dust, 2 months previously, but only 3 reached their destination unharmed. Three were frozen to death, and 5 had their feet or toes frozen so badly as to have to undergo amputation. One man that perished was found afterwards with 30 pounds weight of gold dust on his person.

After their arrival at The Dalles late at night, the British succeeded in getting an oyster supper. Anderson reminded his sister of the torture of having to

> sit at the same table with a lot of Yankees. They all put their knives into their mouths, then thrust them into the salt, then into the Potato dish, pile up all sorts of things on their plates and gobble up everything with barbarous rapidity. . . . We went to the Theatre in the evening, saw a Tragedy and a screaming farce played, and everything was very creditably done. They acted also a portion of "Othello" tolerably well.[143]

On their arrival at Victoria on May 14, there were final farewells and a "snug dinner" with Col. Moody and his officers.

During their work in the Cascade Range, the British surveyors apparently did not climb any significant summits, although in 1861 Wilson hiked to the top of a minor point in the Rockies, the higher peaks being "seemingly inaccessible." During the same period, the British became skilled mountaineering pioneers in the Alps. Anderson's letter describing his final descent of the Columbia River in April 1862 is perhaps indicative of the attitude the British had toward the northern Cascades: "We soon got rid of the Mountains again, and then the country as far as I could see from the river seemed level."[144] The one member of the British commission who paid close attention to the Cascade Range was the geologist, Bauerman; but without mules, assistants, tents, and supplies, he was limited in where he could go and what he could do.

Compilations, Reports, and Maps

After completing its fieldwork in the spring of 1861, the American commission returned to Washington, D.C., to compile reports and prepare maps. When Hawkins returned to England nearly one year later, he urged Campbell to collaborate with him on the final report, but his suggestion fell on deaf ears. He therefore drew up his own report for the Foreign Office.

At its Washington office, the American commission proceeded with the computations, plottings, map drawings, and preparation for the final report. Gibbs, Custer, Alden, Hudson, Nooney, and Charles Gardner were instrumental in this effort. Custer and Gardner assembled and replotted all of the commission's notes. They used computed field positions from reconnaissance notes, and Custer made the preliminary field maps. During this work, word came of Dr. Kennerly's death at sea, which caused much sadness.[145] The computations and drafting continued until 1866, and it would not be until October 1869 that the commission declared its assignment completed. For the United States, surveying and marking the boundary to the Rocky Mountains between 1857 and 1860 had cost about $600,000, or $1,463 per mile.[146]

When the British and Americans met to prepare the official survey maps, they discovered many discrepancies in their findings with respect to the location of the boundary line, but this was to be expected because of varying astronomical observations and calculations. Magnetic forces that could not be offset with available instruments caused most of the discrepancies, and they thought some were due to differences in the season of the year in which observations were made and differences in which stars were observed.[147] These complexities and incongruities were apparent in the final document. Still, the two commissions were, according to Hawkins, quite in accord on the problems of producing a joint map—an agreement he had not anticipated only months earlier.[148] In fact, considering the crisis in British-American relations because of the dispute over the San Juan Islands and the water boundary, both sides cooperated unexpectedly well.

The minor disagreements were reconciled at conferences and over the drafting tables by drawing a mean between the original American and British lines, but this solution failed to deal with the problems created when the parallel was marked. As historian George F. G. Stanley observed,

> Easy and convenient as this was, it only compounded the pressing problems of titles and jurisdictions when squatters and other settlers moved into the boundary areas and found not one but two and sometimes three lines cut through the woods and several sets of boundary markers.[149]

Because of the difficult topography and limited field season, the line could not be marked continuously. In 1869, summarizing the field observations, Campbell noted the necessity of carrying the line over the nearest practicable route for a pack trail in order to connect the astronomic stations. These stations "were established by parties of the joint commission at almost every accessible point from which the boundary line is ascertained, and marked by a vista across all valleys and trails, where rough stone monuments were erected over posts buried in the ground. . . ."[150]

The British produced seven final maps at 1:120,000 (and additional, detailed maps of the immediate boundary area at 1:60,000), corresponding to the Americans' seven land-boundary maps at the same scale.[151] The two countries' maps are nearly identical, differing mostly in the technique of hachuring the terrain features. It would seem that the "joint effort" consisted mainly of checking each other's maps for consistency. The manuscript field maps drawn by the surveyors during the course of the four-year project illustrated in detail their journeys, with some maps showing the locations of campsites, astronomical stations, and Indian villages. There were nineteen manuscript-map compilations signed by the American and British commissions, with a ten-sheet map covering the boundary in detail. Included in the final joint report was the lithographed set of seven numbered maps covering the summit of the Rocky Mountains to the Strait of Georgia. Elevations along the parallel shown on the 1866 map—"Map of Western Section"—were chiefly measured barometrically, but a few were determined by triangulation. The final cartography shows the boundary zone quite accurately but falls into some error and vagueness north of the head of Lake Chelan, probably because of a reliance on Washington territorial and Pacific Railroad Survey maps, which at the time were considered authoritative.

A last meeting of the joint commission was held in Washington in 1869, during which Campbell and Hawkins signed the final joint report.[152] This report was never published because the American secretary of state deemed its publication too expensive in light of Civil War debts.[153] It was loaned to Campbell in 1872 when he prepared to survey the northern boundary, but it was never returned and was lost.[154] Not until 1900 was a partial American report made available through the efforts of Marcus Baker of the U.S. Geological Survey.

In the absence of proper archives, the American papers became scattered among several government agencies. The survey's correspondence and its topographical, astronomical, and meteorological data remain the only original sources on its operations; and the reports of field parties, the reports of subordinate officers and personnel to the commissioners, field journals, letters, maps, and sketches are all now preserved in the National Archives. The beautiful series of watercolor paintings made by James Madison Alden to accompany the final report and the topographic sketches of both George Gibbs and Henry Custer also survived.

By a strange coincidence, the British commission's records were also lost for many years. In 1898, Dr. Otto Klotz, a government astronomer, accidentally discovered the missing records at the Royal Observatory in Greenwich. Years later, he described how he found them:

> The writer was sent by the Dominion Government to London and Petrograd on a
> special mission, in which was included the obtaining of information regarding the

records and final report of the survey. All of the Government offices in London were visited in which there was the faintest likelihood that the records might be stored, but all to no avail, and no one seemed to be able to give any assistance. Before leaving England, however, the writer, as Astronomer for the Dominion Government, naturally paid a visit to the Royal Observatory at Greenwich. By chance his eye caught the initials B.N.A. on some boxes on the top of the library shelves—letters at once interpreted as possibly standing for British North America. The boxes were taken down, the dust of years removed, and in them lay the long-lost records of the international survey of the forty-ninth parallel.[155]

Lt. John G. Parke's expedition was a pivotal one in Cascade Range history. The Northwest Boundary Survey was instrumental in transforming the public view of the most poorly mapped region of the United States. Mountains formerly drawn in artistic hachures, with errant river drainages, now began to take their correct shape. The survey also marked the end of the era of the Topographical Engineers in the West—an era in which these architects of national development blazed and explored trails, mapped the frontier, and collected natural-history data, bringing important new knowledge to mid-nineteenth-century America.

As the American field-party commander, Parke could look back with considerable pride on the survey's achievements. He had led a survey of two-fifths of the boundary country west of the one hundredth meridian, and he and his men could claim to be the first to have explored it. The astronomical labors of both the Americans and the British, which involved thousands of precise observations, ranked with the best such work yet done. Important contributions to natural history, through observations and the collection of samples of species, were made by members of both commissions—Gibbs, Kennerly, Lord, Lyall, and Bauerman. Much as with the boundary survey between Alaska and British Columbia/Yukon—in the St. Elias Mountains in 1912–13 and in the Coast Mountains even earlier—the monumental frontier placed high premiums on field operations, logistics, and endurance. It is likely that the individuals from both commissions of the Northwest Boundary Survey were unaware that their achievements would eventually become the material of an alpine mystique.

Virgil Bogue and his Northern Pacific Railroad Survey party with a camp outfit (Washington State Historical Society, Tacoma)

9

LEGACY OF THE LAND GRANTS:

THE NORTHERN PACIFIC RAILROAD SURVEYS

Oh! What timber.
   –Samuel Wilkeson

Forests in which you cannot ride a horse . . . forests into which you cannot see, and which are almost dark under a bright mid-day sun.
   –Samuel Wilkeson

As historian William Goetzmann observed, "The acquisition of a Pacific empire in California and Oregon forced Americans to think primarily in terms of transcontinental transportation when they addressed themselves to the problem of populating, developing, and defending their new Western domain."[1] Though railroad-building came somewhat later in the Pacific Northwest than in California, similar concerns arose for the territory near the Columbia River, especially when scouts and pioneers laid out the wagon road through the Rockies' South Pass. The construction of a railroad to the Pacific Northwest was inevitable. The questions were only how and where.

The northern route explored by Isaac Stevens and George McClellan in 1853 was without a champion after Stevens's death in the Civil War—that is, until Josiah Perham, an eastern railroad promoter, stepped in to use his political influence in Congress. Perham saw in national defense an argument for the need of a northern route. A congressional act in 1864 empowered the Northern Pacific Railroad Company to build a line from Lake Superior north of the forty-fifth degree of latitude to Puget Sound and granted the railroad sections of public land adjacent to the line, thus giving the company a federal charter with an immense subsidy. The act required the company to begin work within two years and complete the entire road by 1876 (construction, in fact, began at the Duluth terminus in 1870).[2] To grant a new railroad line was one thing, but to realize its potential was quite another. Stevens's surveying parties had probed the passes and river valleys for the most suitable route across the Rocky Mountains and then nominated the military wagon road through the Coeur d'Alene Valley—a trading route where Lt. John Mullen had begun road construction in 1859. The best crossing of the Cascade Range, however, was still a mystery.

In May 1866, Edwin Ferry Johnson was appointed chief engineer of the Northern Pacific Railroad Company. Although Cascade Range surveys began the following summer under J. Gregory Smith, who was president of the company until 1872, it was not until April 1869 that the reports of engineers at both ends of the line were ready for presentation. The optimistic Johnson portrayed his speculations about the geography of the Cascade Range on an 1867 map that depicted the Skagit River entering Washington Territory from a "Garden of Eden" in Canada.[3] In 1867, Johnson was ordered to make a reconnaissance of the country between the Columbia River and the Strait of Juan de Fuca. Systematic field surveys began that summer when Gen. James Tilton, the former surveyor general of Washington Territory whom Johnson had appointed to take charge of the surveys, sent parties into the field.

Exploring the Options

On August 1, 1867, Tilton initiated the surveys by dispatching civil engineer William H. Carlton and surveyor Jared S. Hurd to explore, respectively, Cowlitz and Snoqualmie passes. Probably because Cowlitz Pass was almost opposite Olympia, the new state capital, it was one of the first cross-Cascade routes to be considered for a railroad. When Carlton, guided by settler William Packwood, left for "Packwood's Pass"—it was later called Cowlitz Pass in reports—he followed a route that pioneers had established from the Nisqually to the Cowlitz River. The surveyed route on the west slope crossed the Muddy Fork of the Cowlitz, then projected sidehill cuts to distribute the ascent to the pass. At the pass, which Tilton estimated was 125 miles from Olympia, was a small lake from which the water flowed in both directions.

The survey established Cowlitz Pass—now named Carlton Pass, north of what is today's Cowlitz Pass—on the summit of the range at 4,210 feet. Carlton ascended the creek named after him to the divide summit and then descended the Bumping River. Across the pass, the party was the first to see "Lake Tanim" (Bumping Lake).[4] Tilton, who was highly impressed with the mountain scenery, visited the pass himself, commenting that this lake, filled with salmon, was "the most beautiful lake known in the Cascade Mountains." Surveyor R.M. Walker, who reviewed the entire route, described the "Tanum" as a "bold, rapid, and beautiful stream without a single perpendicular fall of even a foot."[5]

Walker, who plucked a few alpine flowers on the summit to press into his fieldbook, praised the "extraordinary" work of the survey party, reporting that they even worked on Sundays:

> Every man was a *Pacific Coast* man. No going into the work on horseback, but every one took the field on foot, marching through the swampy bottoms of the innumerable streams of the lower country, wading the rivers, and climbing the mountains, has been the daily routine, and when night came on and bacon, beans, & coffee were

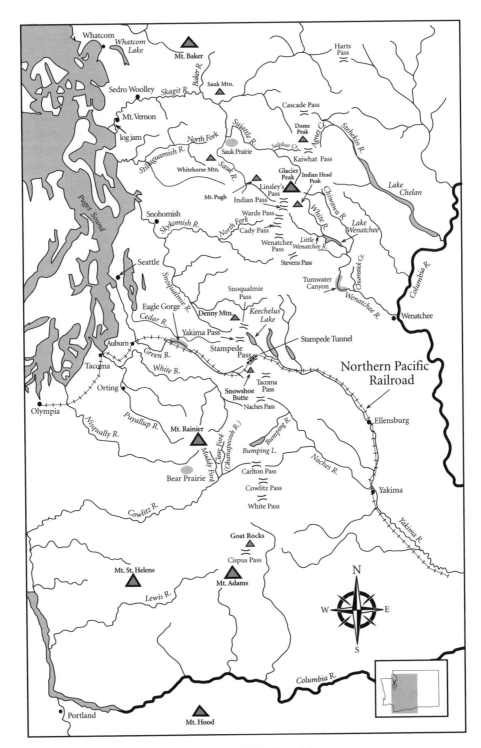

The Northern Pacific Railroad Surveys

disposed of each man would seek a friendly tree, wrap himself up in his blanket and sleep like a top until the cook at the peep of day would sing out "come to grub" when every cuss would spring up with a yell of an Indian.[6]

Upon completion of the Cowlitz Pass survey, Walker wrote that the surveyors

cut their way through the nearly impenetrable forests of the mountains, have climbed the loftiest peaks of the range for observations, have run a spirit level and compass line of about 70 miles . . . and have carried the whole caboodle from foot hill to foot hill with a maximum grade of 60 feet to the mile.

Walker affirmed his faith in the Cowlitz Pass route after a 140-mile foot march over "Nah-chess" Pass, the route of the 1853 immigrant wagon train. He judged that Cady Pass would also be favorable, but that "Sno-qual-a-mie has been found to be impracticable without a heavy tunnel."[7]

Tilton had proposed that Carlton cross to the east slope of the Cascades, obtain supplies at the Yakama mission, proceed north to Wenatchee, and then cross the range again over Cady Pass. Logistics and distances doomed this plan, however, and Carlton returned to Olympia. The magnitude of the range of glaciers was thwarting the Northern Pacific's zeal for completing the line. "The country is so difficult to traverse and the means of supply in the mountains so difficult," Tilton wrote in mid-September, "that I fear I cannot explore as much as I would wish during this season."[8]

Initially, both Tilton and Walker believed that a Cowlitz Pass route would be superior to one over Snoqualmie Pass, which was steep with a narrow canyon to its west.[9] Walker particularly disagreed with an army report by Gen. Oliver O. Howard to the president of the Northern Pacific that favored Snoqualmie. The report's reference to a "broad and open pass," Walker wrote, "ain't worth a d—n." Hurd, meanwhile, left Olympia on August 3 with nine men and three horses to survey Snoqualmie Pass. His exploration included the "Cedar River" (Yakima) Pass, Keechelus Lake, and the Yakima Valley. The party scrambled to the top of "Mount Gregory Smith" (Denny Mountain), "quite 7000 feet high."[10] Both Hurd and Tilton (who accompanied the survey party for a time and also visited Yakima Pass) eventually came to regard Snoqualmie as more favorable than Cowlitz Pass, although Tilton was surprised at the deep snow in sheltered locations despite the late season. Hurd's party returned to Olympia on October 12.

Almost immediately after Carlton returned from Cowlitz Pass, Tilton sent him to the Skykomish River Valley to investigate "Cady's Pass," which ambitious pioneers had already crossed (see Chap. 1). There was such urgency that Carlton and his party did not wait for a steamer from Olympia but instead traveled by Indian canoe on Puget Sound.[11] Reaching the Skykomish's north fork, Carlton followed the Indian trail, which to his chagrin crossed a sharp backbone far above the true pass summit "without regard to [the backbone's] elevation, showing that the trails are unreliable as guides to the best Passes for the purposes of a railroad."[12] This was not the pioneers' Cady Pass; the survey-ors likely crossed by the higher ridge to the south, Saddle Gap. Johnson re-ported that the backbone would need to be tunneled three miles at a cost of $151,000 per mile because of the high grade.[13]

Carlton descended to the southeast, where he located a "summit" between the main, or south, fork of the Skykomish and the Wenatchee at 5,117 feet. He dismissed the route as barely practical. Poor weather prevented the party from examining the south branch (in fact, they had brought no tent). According to Carlton's report, the stream branch rose in a summit lake. This exploratory crossing may have been by Rapid River, Pear Lake, and Lake Creek.

Tilton, satisfied that there was no "eligible or practicable Pass leading from the Skagit to the tributaries of the Columbia or the Okinakane south of the 49° of north latitude," still held out hope for a pass to the Wenatchee River despite Carlton's evidence that a Skykomish route would be unduly expensive. Ac-cordingly, on September 30 he sent engineer Albert J. Treadway to examine the "Sawk" branch of the Skagit. Treadway, who was the U.S. deputy surveyor in Washington Territory from 1860 to 1870, had F.M. Brown as a guide.[14] After hiring on Indians and canoes on the lower Skagit, Treadway changed to smaller craft at the Baker River. Now with five Indians, all serving as canoemen and packers, he arrived at Sauk Prairie, the camp of Chief Whowetkan (Wawetkin). This, the farthest permanent Indian camp, was about three miles beyond the Suiattle River fork.

On October 8, when the party was seven miles beyond present-day Dar-rington, heavy fall rains made it impossible to continue along the Sauk River with canoes. On the final day, they managed an estimated ten more miles, which placed them near Pugh Mountain.[15] The river rose dangerously—three feet in twelve hours—and the Indians informed Treadway that they were still twenty to thirty miles from the summit. They "declared winter had set in, and all would perish in the snows unless they retreated."[16] The surveyor agreed, for conditions were intolerable and low clouds prevented him from seeing any-thing of the rugged landscape. Treadway estimated he had ventured twenty-two miles up the Sauk River beyond the Suiattle.

Before the year's end, Tilton concluded that the Skykomish Pass route stud-ied by Carlton had a high grade and would be expensive "and not as favourable as the Cowlitz or Sno-qual-mie." Yet, Johnson took a tenacious view, suggest-ing that the question was still open. He reported to the railroad's board of directors in November that "north of [Cady Pass] is a pass leading from the We-nach-ee to the Saak branch of the Skagit, and another from the Skagit to Lake Chelan, both of which are supposed to be more elevated than Cady's."[17] The chief engineer had widely disseminated the notion that a northern Cas-cade route to Bellingham Bay might be feasible, an idea that engineer-explor-ers in the field continued to dwell upon.

The Northern Pacific Railroad took no immediate action after the 1867 surveys. The company did not have enough resources to start construction, and it was not until April 1869 that Johnson placed the reports of Gen. James Tilton and Gen. Ira Spaulding (a senior engineer) before the board of directors. Tilton had concluded that Snoqualmie Pass could not be overcome from Snoqualmie Falls directly but by a loop from the Cedar River. After crossing the pass, reported to be only 3,145 feet, the line would continue on the west side of Lake "Kitch-e-lus." The cost would not exceed $70,000 per mile, "and there is abundant coal, timber and stone, especially on the western side of the mountains." By the end of 1869, Johnson had indicated a preference for Snoqualmie Pass over Cowlitz. He pointed out that Snoqualmie was not only 1,100 feet lower than the Cedar River Pass, but it could be tunneled at the level of Keechelus Lake. Yet, in 1870, Tilton made a survey over Cowlitz Pass to develop a line from Olympia to the Yakima Valley.[18]

The Northern Pacific Meets the Cascades

By 1870 St. Paul had become the primary railroad center northwest of Chicago, and track construction of the Minnesota Division had begun. During that year, surveys were conducted across the Great Plains, and a committee visited Puget Sound to locate the mainline and to select future townsites.[19] The Northern Pacific was interested in settlement to generate traffic, and there was the added spur of profits to be gained from land sales. The picture emerged of a vast grazing domain, interspersed with suitable agricultural valleys.

Engineer Thomas B. Morris disagreed with Johnson's 1869 report that stated that "the [1867] surveys so far as made, show the passage of the Cascade Range by the Snoqualmie Pass can be accomplished without encountering any formidable obstacles."[20] By this time, the surveys showed conclusively that the line approach on the eastern slope must be made via the Yakima Valley. Morris concluded that what remained was to select the best terrain between the Yakima and Puyallup rivers and "to adapt the character of the road to the nature of the topography." It was the rugged, precipitous topography that continued to perplex the mountain-wise engineer.

To determine the snow depth at Snoqualmie Pass, the Northern Pacific in 1870 employed two men to keep accounts of the weather. William Milnor Roberts, who later replaced Johnson as chief engineer of the Northern Pacific, believed it was his duty to remind people of the formidable nature of any route over the pass and to stimulate more critical examination.

> The observers stationed at the Snoqualmie summit, frequently heard terrific noises, caused by avalanches of snow; and on the Skagit Pass route, the survey showed twenty immense slides . . . where it would be exceedingly difficult to build a Railroad, and which it might be still more difficult to maintain.[21]

The investigations of Morris and others in 1871–1872 indicated it would be necessary to build twenty-five to thirty miles of "very strong snow sheds." In comparing the avalanche potential of the Cedar River route with that of the Sierra Nevada, Morris wrote:

> I have seen no country, where evidences of snow slides are so abundant as along this grade line. The route of the Central Pacific is not to be compared with it. There are no such snow slides common on the Sierra Nevadas, they are trifling slips of a mass of snow with one or two trees, and not like these, which take everything along with them, and stop only at the bottom of the valley. To these remarks I would add that the slides are immense in extent and show evidences of power only equalled by the earthquake, often they extend to the very tops of high mountains.[22]

The Roberts Exploration

To market the construction bonds, the banking firm of Jay Cooke & Company was proffered the financial agency of the Northern Pacific Railroad in 1869. It delayed a definite decision on the offer, however, until its own agents could examine the route and determine the value of the land. For that purpose, the firm sent out two field parties that summer. Their reports eventually convinced Jay Cooke that the railroad land grant was of immense value and afforded a legitimate basis for credit.

One of the parties, under William Milnor Roberts, was directed to examine Puget Sound and the Columbia River, and then to cross the Cascade Range eastward either through Snoqualmie Pass or along the Columbia.[23] Roberts's party was made up of Thomas Canfield, the general agent of the company; Samuel Wilkeson, the company secretary; Reverend Claxton; William G. Moorehead, Jr.; and Edwin F. Johnson's son. They traveled three months by horseback, railroad, steamer, wagon, and canoe. Altogether, Roberts studied fifteen passes in the Rockies during Jay Cooke's regime.

While some favored Portland as a terminus because it precluded the problem of the mountain barrier, Canfield insisted that the railroad should construct its line over the Cascade Range to Puget Sound. He believed that a great commercial city of the Pacific Coast would be built on the Sound, receiving vessels that traded with the world through the Strait of Juan de Fuca. After securing large land tracts on Puget Sound and studying which would be the ideal railroad terminus and approach, Canfield concluded that Tacoma was the logical connection and purchased a large tract of land there.[24]

After this latest reconnaissance, Roberts estimated that the total cost for building a railroad from Lake Superior to Puget Sound was $85,277,000. Extolling the Puget Sound landscape, he wrote: "Mount Baker, Mount Adams, and Mount St. Helens, with their elevated snow-clad peaks, are the pride of Washington Territory." Samuel Wilkeson wrote Jay Cooke in 1870 that the region was still a vast, undiscovered wilderness. The girdling mountain slopes were imprinted with the marks of the glacial era, and timber monarchs stood over 250 feet high. "Of all the marvels, and all the beauties, and all the majesties of this region, these forests of giant trees are chief," he wrote. "On the Atlantic slope, where it was my misfortune to be born, and where for fifty-two years I have been cheated by circumstances out of a sight of the real America, there are no woods."[25]

Wilkeson described an enchanting land "with a rim of glaciers"—a land, he prophesied, that someday would become the world's summer playground. "The waters of Puget Sound evoke wonder and reverence," he wrote. "Its waters in summer mirror the loveliness of the most augustly lovely things on earth—snow-clad mountains skirted and girdled with green." Moved by the beauty of both the Cascade Range and the Olympic Mountains, he added: "From every part of the sound the snow-covered peaks of both ranges can be seen at once. The distance between these crests of frosted silver . . . is one hundred miles."[26]

Roberts concluded in 1870 that the Northern Pacific route was a most favorable one and in a few years would pay fair dividends. He believed the route would be minimally obstructed by winter snows because of its relatively low altitude and because of the climatic effect of the warm ocean current. At about the same time, Johnson predicted that the population of the United States, then over forty million, would greatly increase near the Pacific Coast because of the abundant timber supply and the good, arable land.[27]

Daniel Linsley's Explorations

After Tilton's efforts in 1867, the Northern Pacific needed both field leadership and a new impetus to study further the northern Cascades for the projected railroad line. On April 13, 1870, Johnson appointed Daniel Chipman Linsley, a forty-three-year-old newcomer to the region, to explore in Washington Territory near the forty-eighth parallel to "determine the practicability of carrying the main line" after it left the Clark Fork Valley.[28]

Monumental though the achievements of other railroad explorers may have been, Linsley was the most diligent of all. The innovative engineer was an outstanding representative of the adventurous professionals who came west in the late nineteenth century. His journal is an invaluable record of discovery, containing descriptions of Indians and their canoeing skills as well as observations on the natural history of the land. Linsley seems to have been less aware of the alpine splendors than some of his contemporaries were, but he displayed a sensitivity to the forests and an appreciation of his Indian helpers:

> I found them invariably disposed to assist me. I trusted them many times and in various ways, and in no case did they abuse my confidence. They are good campers and packers and the most superb boatmen I have ever seen. If kindly and judiciously

treated I think they can be made of great service in the construction of your road, especially in its earlier stages.[29]

A man of broad ideas and brilliant engineering conceptions, Linsley had political acumen and a talent for organization. He was born in 1827 in Middlebury, Vermont, into a prominent family of jurists and clergy. He studied civil engineering, then entered the transportation field with a three-year survey for the Rutland and Burlington Railroad.[30]

Before Linsley left New York, the chief engineer had given him instructions and offered some advice. Johnson, although concerned about the shortage of time, wanted Linsley to visit Snoqualmie and Cedar River passes and to "act as your good judgement shall suggest for the best interest of the company . . . within the time at your command." Johnson had yet to learn about the roughness of the terrain, for he advised: "If you can reach the Suiatle pass with horses or mules from Whatcom you will probably be able to use them all the way around to Seattle." Stressing the importance of obtaining complete information about the region, he asked Linsley to explore "not only . . . the Suiatl Pass but all other passes and their approaches which you may consider to be eligible" east of the Skagit. Considering the option of terminating the railroad at Bellingham Bay, Johnson also emphasized the need for secrecy: "The facts of importance which you may obtain in your explorations you will communicate only to the Company and you will observe . . . discretion in your intercourse with others."[31]

On May 2, Linsley left New York by rail for San Francisco, then continued to Whatcom and set about organizing men and supplies in the frontier town. At the suggestion of settlers and with the help of local Indians, he contacted John Tennant, who lived near present-day Ferndale. Tennant, a southerner who had arrived at Bellingham Bay in 1858, had taken part in the first ascent of Mt. Baker in 1868 (see chapter 13). Linsley also engaged H.C. Hale, an Indian agent who had previously been stationed at the Tulalip Reservation, and Frank Wilkinson. Provisions for the three-week expedition were limited to rations of flour, tea, and bacon. Aside from blankets and their instruments, the party carried nothing else, apparently judging that tents would be an extravagance.

When the four men left Whatcom on May 25, they were accompanied by six Indians paddling two large canoes. In two days the party entered the Skagit River, where they hired two more Indians. To lighten the canoes in the four-mile-per-hour current, the explorers walked the riverbank to reach the well-known "raft," or Skagit logjam, downstream of present-day Mt. Vernon, an obstacle that stopped navigation and hindered early settlement. Above the jam, they traveled on the river to the village of the Skagit chief Sosumkin, with whose help Linsley procured canoes and Indians to continue upriver.

On the riverbank near present-day Mt. Vernon, Linsley measured an immense cedar and found its circumference to be twenty-four feet, eight inches at six feet above the ground. Accustomed to the smaller forests of fir and birch in his native Vermont, Linsley must have been astounded at the size of the trees. Soon they "passed the last settler's cabin" and were "fairly in the Indian country." On the following day, May 28, the party proceeded eastward in three canoes manned by eight skilled Indians. Despite a rain shower and a strong current, which required poling, spirits were high. Above present-day Sedro Woolley, the current was estimated to be from five to seven miles per hour. The final three hours of the day's journey were a strain because the waters were rapidly rising. Linsley kept careful records of hourly barometer and thermometer readings.

On May 30, the party camped at the mouth of a turbid tributary, whose source, Linsley noted, "is among the glaciers of Mt. Baker." He learned that "the Indian name is Novcultum," meaning "white water." The next morning, they saw some impressive scenery, including the glacier-clad Snowking Mountain. Linsley wrote in his journal: "The morning was very fine & the snow peaks on every side of us reflecting the first rays of the morning sun presents a most magnificent spectacle." The first summit in the range that Linsley referred to, on May 31, was "To-Wuge," today's Sauk Mountain (less than three miles north of present-day Rockport). Despite its moderate height, the massif's nearness to the river makes it quite noticeable.

That day, the Indians informed Linsley that there was "no prospect of finding any pass through the mountains to Lake Chelan." Linsley, mindful of Johnson's directive, decided at least to make a hurried venture in that direction, leaving the bulk of the party on the Sauk River. Turning into the Sauk with their canoes, by evening the smaller group had come several miles from present-day Rockport. Linsley stopped early to allow the hunter to bring in an old bear and two cubs. Linsley consulted further with the Indians and wrote: "The only Pass the Indians think at all possible from the Skagit to the Columbia is at the upper end of the Sawk valley & of this they speak in the highest terms." The Suiattle River route was "the only possible route to Lake Chelan."[32]

On June 1, Linsley's party remained in camp preparing rations for the Suiattle River explorations, the Indians still objecting to continuing. During a meeting on the morning of June 2, it was decided to pay the Indians an advance of thirty cents a day for canoeing. Traveling up the Sauk and Suiattle rivers, Linsley expressed surprise at the progress the frail canoes made in the fast water. Sometime that day, the explorers saw Whitehorse Mountain, which stands at an elevation of nearly 7,000 feet, very close to the low passage between the Sauk and the north fork of the Stillaguamish. Because of its low footings and valley vista, the glacier-hung mountain is remarkably conspicuous. Linsley recorded it as "Sumallealle, . . . a high bare peak."

The next day, in the densely forested Suiattle Valley, the explorers walked in order to lighten the canoes. They saw several specimens of the rare and beautiful water ouzel. Linsley noted the more abrupt and rocky nature of the terrain, as well as mountains "capped with snow." There was also "evidence of a heavy fall of snow last winter," and freshly broken timber on the steep and rocky valley slope indicated recent avalanches. Spotting various mountain peaks, Linsley wrote in his journal, "Mt. Hihai . . . bears S 15 W." This was 6,989-foot White Chuck Mountain. The journal also refers to "Sahtsaht," possibly Glacier Peak as seen beyond the valley of Lime Creek.

On June 5, the men left their canoe and baggage to follow a faint trail. Chief Sosumkin had told Linsley that in his father's youth this trail was broad and much traveled (see chapter 1). It seems that the Indians traded to the east but changed when posts west of the mountains, such as Fort Langley and Fort Nisqually, became more accessible than Fort Okanogan. At noon the party reached a side stream that the Indians called "Kaiwhat" (Sulphur Creek).

> From the north bank of the creek the snow peaks rise almost perpendicularly. Any number of little rivulets creep out from under the enormous snowbanks & tumble down the rocky sides of the mountains. I noticed one which I estimated fell a thousand feet in a nearly perpendicular descent. The timber on the Kaiwhat is the best I have seen. The cedar particularly is most remarkable. I think on some acres twenty trees might be cut that would square fifteen inches for fifty feet & be perfectly straight.

The peaks he noted included Downey and Sulphur mountains. That day they probably traveled about eight miles—although they estimated it to be fifteen miles—and they may have gone over halfway up Sulphur Creek.

The next day, the men faced a long and difficult ascent of the "Kaiwhat Creek" Valley "through open woods of magnificent fir & cedar timber with occasionally an alder thicket." Linsley mentioned windfall obstacles four to six feet in diameter, and the "exceedingly bold and precipitous" sidehills were a solid mass of granite. At three o'clock, Linsley saw

> two Cinnamon or Brown bears quietly feeding in plain view & not more than three hundred feet distant. One was a very large animal & the other apparently but one or two years old. Mr. Tennant had the only rifle in the party. He fired at & wounded the large one but it escaped.

The Indians informed Linsley that the ridge ahead led to the desired pass. They reached the snowline before the valley head and found two to three feet of snow in the "abundant & good" forest.

Eager to avoid the valley's warm daytime temperatures and to examine the expected pass, Linsley, Tennant, and the Indians left "at 4¼ this morning over which is the Pass to Lake Chelan. The sky was clear & every thing indicates a hot day." The ascent, only about one and a half miles, was on a hogback between two stream forks. Linsley must have seen Dome Peak in the "very fine" view, which also included "two bodies of snow more than one year old" and a high peak supposed to be "Sahtsaht."[33]

The snow at the pass was estimated at six feet deep, "very soft in the bright sun & thermometer at 61° in the shade. The elevation of the Pass is 6135 ft above tide. The old Indian trail passed through it at its lowest point." The dividing ridge, Linsley noted, "is a solid mass of granite."[34] As for railroad engineering, Linsley concluded that the "Kaiwhat Pass" route could be practicable only with a tunnel. In bare spots, the explorer saw "Scottish Heather," ptarmigan, and granite with "possibly some veins of quartz." The party also saw some reddish snow, whose tint is due to the presence of a one-celled alga containing a reddish pigment (alpine hikers frequently see red snow in the Cascades and inland ranges).

The men made a quick descent on the soft snow, aware of the danger "from the liability of the snow to slide in large masses." On June 7, Linsley wrote:

> One such slide occurred on the opposite side of the ridge we were travelling. Of course we could not see it, but it was evidently no slight affair as it sounded like heavy thunder & continued for some two minutes. In coming down I practised the plan pursued by the Indians, to wit, sitting down upon the snow & allowing the force of gravity to take me down using a stout stick as a break to regulate the speed. It may not have been, & indeed I am convinced it is not the most dignified mode of travelling known. . . . We reached our camp of last night at 11½ o clock A.M. & . . . we were thoroughly soaked with the melted snow.

With a typically early start on June 8, the party proceeded down the valley. Linsley wrote that "the hot weather of the past two days has had the effect of raising all the streams in this region & every little brook is brimming full. As we walk along by the creek we can constantly hear the noise of the granite boulders grating & pounding on the rocky channel."

The descent of the Suiattle the next day proved almost too exciting. The Indians in the canoe used their poles, clearing rocks with powerful thrusts.

> [A pole] is broken in a twinkling but before your eye has assured you of the fact the holder has grasped a paddle & is working it with desperate energy. . . . A mass of spray flies over you & a barrel of water pours into the canoe. You work your bailing dish with all the strength you can muster. Your eye catches a glimpse of the rocks as you fly by. The canoe tosses & whirls in every direction apparently ungovernable but really controlled with amazing dexterity. The water now dashes over the side of the canoe incessantly & you literally bail for life. A moment more & the triumphant shout of the Indians rises above the roar of the waters & announces that you are for the moment safe. After several miles of this kind of navigation the Indians pulled up & announced their conviction that it was unsafe to proceed further until the water falls. In this opinion I heartily concurred & was glad to step on shore drenched through & through every shred of clothing with the ice cold water. The sun was shining bright & clear with the thermometer at 85° in the shade so that with the aid of a good fire we rapidly dried our soaked garments. A rather important matter as none of us have a change.

On their return to Sauk Prairie, Linsley and Tennant received a warm welcome from the four men, six women, ten children, and sixteen dogs at the village. Most of the Indians were with the chief on a fishing expedition. The explorers took an inventory of their supplies and found they had insufficient food to reach the opposite slope of the range. On June 12, Tennant and Hale started up the Sauk to cut a trail toward Indian Pass while supplies were obtained. On June 16, the Sauk had become clear enough for the party to kill four salmon using a seventeen-foot spear forked at the end, "with a barbed point of iron or horn stuck loosely on each prong." Linsley's journal gives a graphic description of how fish were caught from a canoe:

> When the canoe has been brought up the stream abreast of where the salmon is lying & about a full spears length off, say about fifteen feet, (this being about as near as the game can be approached without disturbing it) the striker casts his spear which enters & generally passes through the fish. The spear is instantly withdrawn. The barbed points pull off the end of the spear but the fish is held & pulled on board by the thongs which attach the barbed points to the spear. If the barbs were fixed rigidly on the end of the spear the floundering of the fish would break the slender spear which is of cedar & not more than an inch in diameter at the thickest part. It seems a long distance to strike at a fish some two or three feet under water & yet the Indians rarely miss them. I have seen many taken & I do not recollect seeing but two misses.

On June 19, while the party was traveling up the river above present-day Darrington, everything in the canoe was soaked in a rapid. Fortunately, Wilkinson was carrying the instruments on the shore. In his journal, Linsley described the "wide opening in the mountains toward the Southwest where the ground appears nearly level; the Indians here traditionally dragged their canoes to the 'Steilaquamish.' " They sighted Glacier Peak, which is clearly visible through the wide opening of White Chuck Valley: "Mt. Quoku a conical pointed snow peak bears S 84 E."

Linsley and Wilkinson continued up the Sauk Valley on foot, carrying the instruments to avoid a river soaking. At the mouth of the White Chuck River (a side stream), Linsley found "large quantities of Pumice stone." By evening the entire party was drenched by the rain and wet brush they had been traveling through. Just before reaching camp, they met Tennant, who had dispatched Wawetkin's brother, Jim, to the Columbia River to procure horses.

On June 22, Linsley sent Tennant with eight Indian helpers to finish blazing the trail to Indian Pass, while he remained at the Sauk River forks. Days of cold rain without tents for protection—a poor situation in the mountains—caused much delay, and Linsley also needed to wait for money to pay the Indians. Wilkinson was sent to examine the trail from the Skagit River via the Nooksack's south fork to Whatcom, and Hale went to cross the Stillaguamish portage. Both took Indians and a canoe.

On June 29, Linsley and his men took a difficult trail from the Sauk forks camp at dawn, soon entering the north-fork canyon. The long day ended with a cold, rainy, uncomfortable night. The precipitous valley slope, Linsley wrote, "terminat[ed] in bold peaks of granite" (Bedal and Sloan peaks), and he saw Mt. Pugh immediately northward. They found Tennant camped at "Sauk Pass," where Linsley estimated was at 5,042 feet and 50 miles from the mouth of the Suiattle River. To judge by marks on the stunted firs, Linsley estimated that the snowpack, now seven feet, could total twenty. The men remained at Indian Pass for over a week.

In their explorations both north and south of the pass, Linsley and Tennant climbed Indian Head Peak, estimated at 8,000 feet high and a good position from which to study the defile to the north ("North Pass") as a possible railroad crossing.[35] The snow was soft that day and progress was "dangerous as we climbed over some of the immense drifts whose crests seemed just ready to plunge to the bottoms of the gorges thousands of feet below."[36] Because no messenger had arrived at Indian Pass yet with the money, Tennant was dispatched down to the Sauk. The Fourth of July was a festive occasion, as Tennant and Hale returned with six hundred dollars and, instead of fireworks, eight quarts of wild strawberries from Sauk Prairie.

The explorers' course now followed the White River to Lake Wenatchee—a route previously unknown to whites. The Indians who had been sent east returned to the White River with horses, and by July 7 the party was not far above Lake Wenatchee. Although the lake—a "sheet of water" that Linsley estimated at eight miles long—had been passed by earlier explorers, he named it Lake Pattief. Below the lake, Linsley made careful observations of the direction of the stream drainages and added details to his field map. The map was the first to depict streams originating in the rugged mountains to the west and north of the lake, including Nason Creek and the Little Wenatchee, White, and Chiwawa rivers. The explorer noted the changing character of the land, as ponderosa pine replaced lodgepole, white pine, and fir. By evening the party had reached the head of Tumwater Canyon, which Linsley examined and described the next day:

> The Canyon of the Wenachee proves a hard spot and I spent the day in exploring it. It is some 12 to 15 miles long—rather crooked and walled in by mountains of rock from one to five thousand feet high. In this Canyon the river makes a long detour to the South West and the trail to the Columbia leaves it at the head of the Canyon and meets it again [at present-day Leavenworth] just below the foot.

Tennant, meanwhile, examined the trail along "Happy Brook" (Chumstick Creek).[37]

During his two-day exploration of Tumwater Canyon, Linsley studied craggy Icicle Ridge: "The Hills or more properly the mountains, on each side rise to a height of several thousand feet. . . . The Upper positions of these Mountains are precipitous masses of Rock." When he ventured into the lower end of the canyon on July 10, he observed the traditional Native fish harvest:

> The stream flowed over & around huge boulders of granite & seems one mass of snowy foam. Here the salmon collect in great quantities & hither every year come swarms of Indians to lay in their years stock of food. Some two or three hundred are now camped along here all busy as a swarm of bees. The fish are taken by means of a barbed hook attached to the end of a slender pole from fifteen to thirty feet long.
> . . . The Salmon is caught on the hook taken & thrown on shore. The women then take them cut them up & hang them on poles to be dried & smoked.

Linsley's route continued along the Wenatchee River, a valley of "fine grazing land" where the only timber observed was the "Yellow Pine" (ponderosa pine). "There is no underbrush," he wrote, "& one might drive a ladys carriage with comfort in almost any direction." At this point he estimated it would cost $13 million to build a railroad by way of the Sauk and Wenatchee rivers; the shortcut using the Stillaguamish portage would shorten the route by ten miles.

On July 12, Linsley, Tennant, and Wawetkin, with his brother Jim, ascended the Columbia River. Reaching the gorge at the outlet of Lake Chelan on the morning of July 14, Linsley wrote: "The water is bashed into a perfect mass of feathery and milk white foam." He and Tennant continued on foot along the lakeshore, and Linsley concluded: "A road can be cheaply constructed along the North shore thus far and for some distance beyond." The next day, they started for the lake head "in order to take advantage of the still water, our canoe being a wretched affair and entirely incapable of living in the least sea." Fortunately, after Linsley and Tennant went on shore, they came upon some Indians from whom they were able to procure another canoe and two guides.

Severe weather delayed the group for two days. They reached the lake head on July 19 and continued another seven miles on the "Chelan" (Stehekin) River by poling. On entering the river, the two explorers and one Indian again traveled on foot to lighten the canoe. In his journal entry for July 20, Linsley indicated that the Chelan Indians knew about the pass route (Cascade Pass) to the Skagit River, although they did not know of the War Creek and Bridge Creek routes to the Methow River.

> I have little hopes of finding any favorable route by the North Fork [Stehekin River] but as it is desirable every *possible* route should be explored I divided our little party here and despatched Mr. Tennant with two Indians up the North Fork while I started myself with the other two Indians to examine the middle fork [Agnes Creek] and connect our survey with the one made up the Kaiwhat.

The following day Linsley traversed above the canyon of Agnes Creek, with its perpendicular rock walls. Travel was rough over the rocky hillsides, fallen timber, and tangled thickets. Looking into the steep valley of the west fork of Agnes Creek, heading in glaciers, Linsley must have known that there was no hope for a route there. By noon the party had reached another stream fork, and "Kaiwhat Pass" was "in sight bearing S 55 W." After ascending a small canyon (Spruce Creek), the explorers reached the "foot of the Divide drenched to the skin with the cold rain" (they were actually still some distance from the divide). As the rain "continued through" unabated, Linsley sent the Indians to the pass to mark the barometer reading while he explored the valley below. The best route lay along the mountain slope, a course that avoided the dense alder thickets. Other features combined to reinforce a dismal impression. Linsley remarked: "Some four or five small brooks tumble down the precipitous mountain sides from the immense snowfields and glaciers that cover the peaks." Under these conditions, it is improbable that the Indians reached the pass. Visibility was only about a hundred yards, and Linsley "found it utterly impossible to keep the instruments dry" among the thick understory and endless windfalls. That evening, completely soaked, the party reached the west fork of Agnes Creek.

In the morning, after finishing their last ration of flour and pork, the men headed back toward the canoe depot below the mouth of Agnes Creek. When Linsley again met Tennant, waiting a few miles below, he learned that the upper Stehekin was "utterly impracticable" for a railroad. Tennant had explored the valley for a few miles but had halted far short of Cascade Pass. Linsley, probably discouraged by the incessant rain and formidable mountain precipices blocking the routes, made no comments on what is today considered a spellbinding alpine wilderness. His description of the upper lake and Stehekin Valley was abrupt: "The timber is short and scrubby and the land of little or no value."[38] By late evening on July 25, the party had canoed down the Columbia to the mouth of the Wenatchee River.

In the most detailed descriptive report given on the region by any of the explorers, Linsley summarized that railroad construction from the Skagit to the Columbia via Lake Chelan would require heavy grades and the cost per mile would be "much greater than by a more Southerly route."

Alternate Routes

Despite Tilton's reluctant conclusion in 1867 that a Skykomish River route was unduly expensive and too high in altitude, the Northern Pacific in 1872 continued explorations north of Stevens Pass. The railroad's search for a pass through the Cascades, now under the supervision of William Milnor Roberts, aimed to find a route that could be suitably tunneled and safe from avalanches. Beginning on June 1, James Tilton Sheets—on instructions from Thomas B. Morris, engineer of the Cascade Division—ran a rapid, preliminary line survey from the mouth of the Skagit to the Sauk River and Linsley's Pass, following Linsley's 1870 trail.[39]

That summer, Morris retraced Sheets's route. His party kept up a hardy pace in the field: "We were up at 3:30 and after a breakfast of bread and bacon—with a small piece of salmon caught the day before were off." From Indian Pass, which they reached on July 18, the party ascended a peak and then descended to Linsley's Pass by sitting glissade. "I found [the] best way of getting down to be to sit down and shut your eyes," wrote Morris. The engineer judged this was the best pass in the area. The return trip was difficult. On July 23, they "travelled in canoes walking round the worst rapids—our canoe was ⅓ full of water for the 1st four hours and our blankets, grub and selves well soaked in *ice water*."[40] Sheets also explored the Skagit-Methow headwaters in July, calling present-day Harts Pass "Skagit Pass." At the same time, Northern Pacific surveyor Hubert C. Ward examined the Methow River drainage.

Later in 1872, Ward began a survey running along the crestline south of Indian Pass. On September 18, he reached "Ward's Pass," whose altitude he gave as 4,295 feet and which he estimated was five and one-half miles from Indian Pass. It was historic Cady Pass, on the trail along the north fork of the Skykomish. Ward then surveyed eastward down "Bald Eagle" Creek. He also surveyed down Cady's Fork of the Little Wenatchee and determined the height of "Chusallie Pass" (likely Wenatchee Pass), before returning from Cady's Fork to the junction of "Bald Eagle" and "Chusallie" creeks. Together, these valleys merged with the Little Wenatchee River. There, he heard from the Indians about a low pass at the head of the "Nahum" (Nason) fork of the Wenatchee. The mountains at the head of the Skykomish have "no high snow peaks" and were less rugged than those in the south; and if the reports were reliable, Ward believed it would be the lowest pass in the area.[41] Had he continued southward to probe the pass, he would have been the first to reach Stevens Pass.

After Morris's exploration, Linsley's (Little White) Pass was preferred for a Skagit–Sauk route. Morris's report stressed that a "Skagit Pass route," from the Skagit River's mouth to Pend Oreille Lake, would be shorter than a route over Snoqualmie Pass. Still, he expressed concern over the "Snow Slides" on the Skagit: "I hardly know what importance to give those as yet."[42] Surveyor Ward Sheets outlined a tunnel route from the Sauk continuing to Lake Wenatchee; another tunnel would be bored through the ridge to Chumstick Creek, a proposal that wisely avoided Tumwater Canyon. Morris also warned of slides in the canyon and of the expenses for immense trestles and numerous snowsheds on the east slope, but the Great Northern later did not heed his advice.[43]

From Olympia to Whatcom, towns competing for the Puget Sound terminus anxiously awaited the railroad's decision. Northern Pacific President George W. Cass and a committee examined the Sound for the best location:

> The committee cruised about the Sound for a week on the steamer North Pacific, accompanied by the company's chief engineer, W. Milnor Roberts, looking for a good location for the big city which it was expected would spring up wherever the

company elected to fix its tide-water terminus. There were no towns on the Sound at the time worthy of the name; the only settlements, beside the village of Olympia, the capital of Washington Territory, being a few saw-mill hamlets. . . . Seattle, then a petty lumbering place of, perhaps, two score of houses, was objectionable because of its steep hill and lack of level ground for depot, yards and sidings.[44]

Tacoma, on Commencement Bay, appeared to best fulfill the requirements, with an ample harbor, good shore wharfing, and a "background of primitive forest, facing upon a beautiful bay, on which the gleaming summit of magnificent Mount Rainier looked down like a pyramid of ivory from the blue heavens." The board of directors in New York narrowed the choice to Mukilteo, Seattle, and Tacoma and finally adopted Tacoma on September 10, 1872.[45]

Refining the Information

The financial panic of 1873 destroyed Jay Cooke & Company and severely crippled the Northern Pacific Railroad. Although the panic lasted only a month, its effects continued for years, causing a reduction in both railroad building and immigration from Europe and stalling surveys in the Cascade Range. A high rate of interest on company bonds caused a great floating debt to grow at a rate of over $2 million annually. When Charles Barstow Wright was elected president of the railroad in 1874, bankruptcy proceedings began. The Northern Pacific's affairs were at their lowest ebb.[46]

To keep the existing 575 miles of track in place and to resist the clamor for forfeiture of domain not yet traversed by the railroad, financier Frederick Billings devised an ingenious reorganization plan that erased the company's debt. When Billings was chosen as Northern Pacific president in May 1879, the company's finances finally stabilized, and the future looked bright for a transcontinental line.[47] Coal, which had been discovered in the Mt. Rainier foothills in 1868, enticed the railroad to broaden its interests; and in 1876, it built a thirty-mile Puyallup branch line to the coal-mining town of Wilkeson.

As economic conditions improved, it was not only possible to sell railroad bonds but it was also clear that the solution to finding a pass over the Cascades was imminent. In July 1880, Northern Pacific tracks were approaching the junction of the Snake and Columbia rivers, opening up the entire Yakima and Kittitas valleys to settlement.

The Northern Pacific had mounted new pass surveys in 1878, when three expeditions were sent to review the earlier explorations. In March, a twenty-three-day barometrical reconnaissance was carried out to Cowlitz (now Carlton) Pass. Col. Samuel A. Black, general superintendent of the railroad's Pacific Division, organized the eight-man expedition from Tacoma, with surveyor David Dexter Clarke in charge and settler James Longmire as his guide.[48] Clarke's route from Yelm Prairie essentially followed the old Indian trail to

Bear Prairie and then to the upper Cowlitz River. The route crossed the Muddy Fork and continued to the Ohanapecosh branch, then fourteen more miles to Carlton Pass. The party's hunters killed deer and caught salmon in the Cowlitz, but in the end provisions ran low. Arriving at the pass on March 28, Clarke found some seven feet of winter snow, and the men spent one night camped on the snow. Clarke left the inscription "N P RR March 28 1878" on a pine tree.

With plans for an instrumental survey that summer, Chief Engineer Roberts arrived in Tacoma on July 18. Clarke, who was optimistic about the Cowlitz Pass crossing, was in charge of the field survey, which began at Orting. His seventeen-man party had the experienced Longmire as its guide. Clarke ran the survey southward to Bear Prairie, where on September 20 he met Charles A. White, a U.S. deputy surveyor and engineer, coming from the Cascade divide to conclude the 102-mile route between Orting and the pass. White had devoted several days to examining the crest both north and south of Carlton Pass before beginning the survey westward down Summit Creek to the Clear Fork of the Cowlitz. He ascended to 6,000 feet south of Carlton Pass and also crossed "Tieton Creek," noting that it ran into a large lake (Clear Lake). Today's White Pass, crossed by a major state highway, is named for him.[49]

In 1880, Clarke took a thirteen-man party to complete a portion of the instrumental survey to Cowlitz Pass. This time, the party traveled directly up the valley bottom, taking two weeks to open a trail to the Muddy Fork. They began the survey on June 25 at the mouth of the Muddy Fork and returned there July 31. On the divide summit, Clarke proved that present-day Carlton Pass was considerably lower than Cowlitz Pass, some five miles to the south. From high points on the watershed divide, Clarke also concluded that the rugged slopes and canyons west of the passes made any approach difficult and expensive.[50]

While Col. Isaac W. Smith, the supervising engineer, camped below White Pass awaiting the completion of the pack trail, Clarke and two companions spent three days conducting a barometrical reconnaissance north of Carlton Pass, continuing immediately east of Mt. Rainier (placing them near present-day Chinook Pass). They then descended the "Clearwater" (Ohanapecosh) fork of the Cowlitz to their Muddy Fork camp. That fall, Smith learned of the existence of the Green River Pass from Natives who had used it during the Indian wars. The six parties he sent in search of the pass examined it from both the upper Yakima and the Green and followed the divide north from Naches Pass. James Sheets discovered Tacoma Pass at about this time and studied the range to the north (nearby Sheets Pass now honors him).[51] The field parties labored until December 5, when snows suspended their work.

Smith, who joined the upper Yakima group one week after their arrival, believed that a 5,500-foot-long tunnel in this area would reduce the summit height to 3,150 feet and that the costs for crossing Green River Pass would be less than for any other pass. A route there would be eleven miles longer than one through Naches Pass but twenty-three miles shorter than one through Snoqualmie Pass. Smith was "disposed to think that the Green River route will be the best." For Charles Wright, who expected Tacoma to be the terminus, a Green River route had a logical advantage over one using Yakima or Snoqualmie pass.

In the 1880 season, Northern Pacific survey parties traversed the extensive range crest from Mt. Adams to Naches Pass, finding tolerable snow depths with little wind drift. Virgil B. Bogue studied the Cispus River and pass route, and an examination west of Snoqualmie Pass by James R. Maxwell showed only two slides crossing the surveyed line. No slides had been observed on the Green River Pass survey. Smith believed "that the track could be kept clear of snow without the use of snow-sheds, on embankments, and in places where room could be made for the deposit of the snow displaced by the snow-ploughs."[52] He commented on the avalanche potential:

> On the timbered slopes of the Cascade Range no slide is possible in standing timber; but on steep slopes, where soil has but little depth and is saturated with water from the melting snow, slides, which may be designated as land slides, are of frequent occurence, and in their course carrying away the timber and soils.[53]

Smith concluded that no railroad to Tacoma could be built south of Naches Pass at a practical cost except through Cispus Pass—which opened to the Klickitat, not to the fertile Yakima Valley, as he projected. His verdict was that the route choice was limited to Naches, Green River, or Snoqualmie.[54]

Surveying Tacoma and Stampede Passes

The railroad's Tacoma faction was impatient to get the line completed, partly because of the threat that Seattle promoters would construct a Snoqualmie or Cedar River line to the Yakima Valley. Thus, after the fall 1880 explorations to the Green-Yakima divide, Col. Smith instructed engineer Virgil Bogue, who had been given charge of the Cascade surveys, to make an instrumental survey of Tacoma Pass and to explore the neighboring crestline on snowshoes. Tacoma politics were pressuring the railroad to speed the survey along, but wintertime work meant traveling in heavy rainfall with fresh snow in the foothills. Bogue did have the advantage, however, of a reconnaissance made in the fall and a resident winter party camped far up the Green River Valley.

Bogue's party, complete with ponies for a pack train, assembled in January 1881 at McClintock's, a ranch on the slight divide between the White and Green rivers. Experienced woodsmen and packers had been equipped with saws, axes, tools, snowshoes, sleds, blankets, small fly tents, and rubber blankets. Provisions consisted of coffee, bacon, beans, flour, and baking powder, and they carried a coffee pot, tin kettle, and frying pan.

The men headed toward the Green River, struggling to cut trail through the heavy forest and over fallen logs. In some places, the snow's weight had bent the tangled underbrush nearly horizontal, sometimes forcing the men to choose between scrambling over supple willow and alder limbs and crawling on the boggy ground. Bogue wrote:

> At night, worn out by a day of such toil, bruised, scratched and sore, soaked to the skin, our reflections were such as would hardly bear publication. As usual in winter, the rain fell in torrents much of the time, forming morasses. After having cut trail through masses of forest debris, our party was frequently obliged to return and lay corduroy or build rough bridges of cedar puncheons to afford footing for the ponies.[55]

It took ten days to travel sixteen miles, and the forty men reached the Green River on January 26, apparently near present-day Palmer. At an advance base camp, which they reached on February 8, they spent a wet week, during which they attempted to build a canoe. Worse yet, deep snows stalled the pack train when it climbed out of the river bottom to heavy timber.

When the party could advance again, the men floundered in the snow. They used snowshoes to haul sleds when they could, but at times it was easier simply to backpack loads. A rainstorm caused the river to rise dangerously, marooning the party for four days on a rock ledge. On February 24, the men, on the move again, caught sight of "a large eagle flying in widening circles"—which they considered a good omen. On March 2, camp was made near Smay Creek, eight miles above present-day Eagle Gorge Reservoir.

On March 3, Bogue took a few provisions and pushed ahead with two Indians, known as Peter and Charley, and a Canadian, Joseph Wilson, in hopes of locating cabins and the winter party at Thorpe's Prairie (east of present-day Lester and an estimated five miles from Tacoma Pass). Fearful of bears and wolves whose tracks had been seen in the snow, Bogue waited alone a few days while Wilson went back for food (the Indians had already been sent for provisions). The isolation affected Bogue's self-reliance. Sleepless and tired, he was frightened by a noise that proved to be the indomitable Wilson arriving with supplies and food.

Bogue's camp 15 was located on a gravel bar at Sunday Creek. After finding the first cabin, Bogue followed the winter party's trail, then continued to Tacoma Pass in a snowstorm, arriving on March 9. His party crossed the Yakima divide to camp on Cabin Creek, explored nearby passes, and then returned to Thorpe's Prairie where they found the winter party. Fortified with food and improved spirits, the group—which included Andy Drury, James Gregg, and Matthew Champion—accelerated its exploration as it followed the range northward on March 16:

> We travelled on snow shoes, the men packing such provisions as we had. . . . In the morning we climbed to the summit and followed the ridge to a high butte, which is south of, and overlooks Camp Creek and the head-waters of Sunday Creek. Here

one of the men stumbled and fell down quite a steep slope, plunging in the snow. As the snow-shoe was the cause of the fall, we named the mountain Snow-Shoe Butte. That night we camped lower down on the ridge between the Butte and Stampede Pass.

The next evening, the men camped on snow at a 4,400-foot spur. Dismal weather delayed the search for a pass the men had seen from Snowshoe Butte. A cold gale was blowing from the southwest, a thick fog "added to the gloom of the balsam forest, made our movements groping and uncertain" and the frozen snow crystals made it difficult to face the wind. The party crept along a ridge, frustrated by their concern that they had circled to "near our previous night's camping place." Improved visibility when the weather broke the next morning, however, confirmed that they had been going in the right direction. Bogue reported on March 19: "A little after nine o'clock appeared a sharp bend in the ridge to the north, as anticipated. We descended along a well-defined crest so rapidly that in less than an hour the barometer marked only 3,495 feet elevation at a point where for a little distance about us there were no trees. It was evidently one of the lowest points of the divide."

The men continued north to discover three more passes and apparently reached Meadow Pass. Reaching what would later be called Stampede Pass—eventually judged the best route—the men could scan Sunday Creek and the forested valley of the Green River to the west. To the south rose the wintry, sharply defined "snowy mass" of Mt. Rainier. Bogue called the low point Pass No. 1, but railroad officials named it Garfield Pass.[56] Years later, Bogue reminisced about the order that led to the name Stampede Pass:

> I had a trail-cutting party camped near Stampede Lake. This party was controlled by a foreman who I thought did not accomplish much work. When the other party which had been cutting the trail from Canoe Creek up Green River to my camp near the mouth of Sunday Creek, finished its work, I sent its foreman to the camp . . . with a letter authorizing him to take charge. A large number of the former mentioned party then stampeded.[57]

The stampede was apparently caused by the foreman's "no work, no meals" edict. The remaining men used campfire charcoal to print "Stampede Camp" on a large fir-tree blaze, and the name came into use.

The Railroad Reaches Portland

Despite the optimism of Wright and others, Tacoma's future as a terminus and the completion of a route across the Cascades remained uncertain. The economic outlook had brightened, but the Northern Pacific still had cash-flow problems and trackage gaps on the mainline—a legacy of Jay Cooke's failure. The railroad was in sufficiently thin financial shape that the shrewd German-born financier and journalist Henry Villard was able to gain control of the company.[58] Villard, whose interests centered in Portland, wanted a controlling influence over the Pacific Northwest through a syndicate he had formed with American and European business associates.

In 1881, Villard approached Northern Pacific President Frederick Billings with an irresistible offer: the railroad would lease Villard's existing tracks along the south bank of the Columbia River and in return Billings would waive any claim to damage from Villard's Oregon Railway and Navigation Company's operations. The Northern Pacific would retain its chartered right to build a competing north-bank line. This leasing arrangement meant the transcontinental line would funnel traffic to Portland instead of Tacoma.[59] To obtain money to complete the mainline, Billings arranged a $40-million sale in first-mortgage bonds to a J.P. Morgan syndicate. When the Northern Pacific's operating profits proved insufficient to service the debt, Villard raised millions to purchase enough stock to win control. Billings soon resigned, and Villard became president of the railroad in September 1881.

Both Villard and, later, James J. Hill of the Great Northern Railway sought to bring thousands of immigrants to the Pacific Northwest. In 1883, Villard recruited farmers in Germany, Sweden, and England for railroad labor. His agents distributed circulars about the rich agricultural opportunities in the Midwest and the Pacific Northwest and gave out some two and a half million pieces of illustrated literature in seven languages.[60] One bulletin announced:

> 200 Scandinavians can find employment on the Construction of the Cascade branch of the Northern Pacific Railroad in Washington Territory at $2. per day and numbers can secure contracts on Station Work.
>
> Half fare to Washington Territory for Scandinavian Families. None but married men with families will be taken on these rates. . . .
>
> There will be work for the next 12 months or more. These workmen can become settlers on Government or Railroad lands and take up farms and secure good homes.[61]

Villard favored a railroad route that would avoid the Cascade Range and run directly to Portland and a Columbia River port. Although he was able to delay the more expensive route over the Cascades, the pressures of population eventually prevailed, as Washington Territory grew from 75,000 inhabitants to over 357,000 in the 1880s. He had financial problems as well. In the spring of 1883, with hundreds of miles of track still to lay, costs were far beyond original estimates. As the value of Northern Pacific shares plummeted, Villard was forced to resign. His tenure as president had been brief—from 1881 to January 1884—but his influence was tremendous. By fall 1883, he had completed the line to Portland, although tracks had not yet crossed a Cascade pass.

A Railroad through the Cascades

In August 1882, Bogue returned to Stampede Pass with engineer J.L. Kingsbury to locate the route for a tunnel, a proposal that was approved at a board of directors' meeting late in the year. In July 1884, Chief Engineer Adna Anderson wrote Vice-President Thomas F. Oakes with his recommendation, and the Stampede Pass route was accepted.[62] The route was projected at sixteen miles longer than the Naches Pass route but was considered the most favorable for construction and operation because the slopes allowed a lesser grade and there were no indications of past slides. The rumors of coal discoveries in the upper Yakima Valley also may have influenced the decision. There were other advantages as well. Bogue, who favored the Stampede Pass route and had examined its entire course except for a part of the Yakima River, pointed out that "about the Upper Green River is a region of the finest timber in the Cascade Mountains, which will be accessible by the line as located." He also called attention to the "abundant timber about the Kachass and Kleallum Lakes."[63]

In 1885, with Portland still in control of inland commerce, Thomas Burke and others organized the Seattle, Lake Shore, & Eastern Railway Company to build a line across the mountains. Concerned Northern Pacific officials decided they must move quickly with their own crossing of the Cascades. The final Stampede Pass grade was too steep for a railroad, so a 1.8-mile-long tunnel was planned at 2,880 feet. The Northern Pacific awarded the construction along the Yakima and Green rivers, as well as the building of the tunnel, to the fearless and sometimes "slave-driving" Bennett brothers of Tacoma and gave them a twenty-eight months to finish the work, with a penalty and bond that would surely break them if they were late.[64]

With the use of telescopic sights, a true line was cut in the timber over the divide to connect the portals of the tunnel. Near Stampede Pass, crews rushed under dangerous conditions to shovel snow, clear the right-of-way (usually fifty feet on each side of the centerline), build track, dig the tunnel, and construct timber trestles over Green River side canyons. At any given time between 1886 and 1888, an average of 350 men, many of them Chinese, were laboring on the tunnel.[65] Spurred by a financial reward and the dinners and alcohol promised the first crew to poke through to daylight, this army of workers saved the Bennett brothers from bankruptcy and gave Tacoma the competitive edge. The line opened in 1887 with a tortuous, hastily constructed seven-mile switchback bypass system, with grades reaching 5.6 percent, that would serve until the tunnel was finished in the spring of 1888.[66]

The Northern Pacific was the last of the three great transcontinental railroad lines to be completed. The historic event was widely heralded, with praise for the foresight of Asa Whitney and the engineering skill of Edwin F. Johnson.[67] As railroad lines stretched from the Atlantic to the Pacific, the mapping that preceded the lines and the work of the railroad-pass explorers became part of the romance and reality of the West. Successful railroad magnates, grasping the economic potential of the West, persuaded individuals and communities to relocate there. The completion of the Northern Pacific played a dominant role in westward settlement and sparked population and economic growth in the Pacific Northwest, which was now linked with the rest of the nation.

Public Lands

During this period of expansion and railroad construction, a public-lands giveaway was seen as a logical way to develop the West. The Pacific Railroad Act of 1862 granted twenty alternate sections of public land per mile of road on each side of the railroad line in the territories (only ten sections were granted in states) and gave a four-hundred-foot right-of-way through the public domain plus the right to remove stone and timber from adjacent land. The Northern Pacific selected every odd section on the 2,100-mile strip from Lake Superior to Puget Sound for every mile of railroad completed before 1890. The railroad chose the best timber and mineral land in those lots. The national forests were converted to checkerboards, and great timber assets passed from public to railroad ownership. During the four decades following the Civil War, the railroads received 183 million acres from the public domain. By 1924, the Northern Pacific had realized from granted lands more than the entire original cost of the railroad. Of the forty million acres transferred to the company, it sold all but about five million.[68]

Vast frauds were committed in disposing of the land and in the expenditure of revenues from granted lands. Moreover, some fifteen hundred miles of road were not constructed within the time limits, yet grants were still patented.[69] Land grants and their abuses, as well as the demand for forfeiture of unearned lands when grant conditions were unfulfilled or breached, became campaign issues in 1884. The transcontinental railroads had taken on a "robber baron" image and were the target of growing public hostility.

Thomas Griffith described what happened to part of this immense acreage. James J. Hill, the empire builder who fathered the Great Northern and eventually took control of the Northern Pacific,

> approached his neighbor . . . a rich, reclusive German immigrant named Frederick Weyerhaeuser. Hill offered him vast territories: the land around Mount Rainier, the land around Mount St. Helens, a swatch of land west of the Cascades extending from Snoqualmie Pass in the mountains to Puget Sound, dense forests near the mouth of the Columbia, great scenic stands in central Oregon. Hill asked $7 an acre; Weyerhaeuser offered $5, and they settled for $6.[70]

Weyerhaeuser is still Washington state's largest private timber holder. The timber assets of James J. Hill's Burlington Northern were acquired by Plum Creek Timber Company, which now owns 228,000 acres in the state.

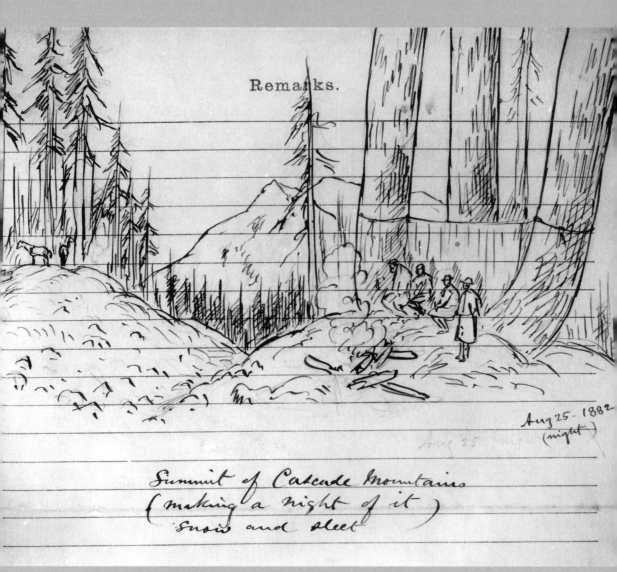

Sketch by Alfred Downing of the Pierce expedition, August 25, 1882 (Alfred Downing notebook, p. 53, Washington State Historical Society, Tacoma)

10

ARMY EXPLORATIONS NORTH OF LAKE CHELAN

Clear-cut, white and blue, against the azure sky, a hundred miles away, a chain of snowy
peaks, bold and serrated even in the far distance. These peaks are the cradle of the lake.
–William D. Lyman

By the end of the 1870s, the exploration of the western United States had moved beyond the Age of Discovery. The exploits of John Wesley Powell in the canyons of the Green and Colorado rivers and the explorations of Yellowstone by Ferdinand V. Hayden had revealed the last unknown regions outside the Cascade Range. With the reconnaissances of both Capt. George McClellan and the members of the Northwest Boundary and Northern Pacific Railroad surveys, the range had been mapped and described sufficiently to become a familiar part of the geography of the West.

The leaders of the U.S. Army explorations, both before and after the Civil War, had created elaborate teams. The assignments of officers in the Department of the Columbia, as in other frontier army units, included surveying, mapping, gathering topographic and route information, and constructing and repairing public and military roads. In the 1850s, as the army was strengthening and adding to its posts during the Indian wars east of the Cascades, concern grew that the military should have a route across the northern part of the range. While the army did not penetrate the rugged and complex region north of Glacier Peak and Lake Chelan at the time, a few troops escorted the members of the Northwest Boundary Survey.

Several army undertakings had an impact on the exploration of the area. Beginning with McClellan's expedition to search for a railroad pass in the summer of 1853, the military possessed only fragmentary knowledge obtained from Native people. McClellan found that Lake Chelan was "shut in by high mountains" and left "no passage along its margins." With a small party, he cautiously attempted the Indian trail up the Twisp River and War Creek (the south fork of War Creek, or "Nahai-el-ix-on," was the locale of a trail crossing to the head of Lake Chelan), but the route was too steep for his horses. Farther north, he reported, the prospects for a railroad route showed little promise.

As concern over Indian unrest east of the mountain divide revived in the 1870s, the army was reminded of the incomplete task of finding a northern route across the Cascade Range. As a precautionary measure to protect white settlers, the military established several temporary or permanent forts in the area. With the formation of the Moses (Columbia) Reservation in April 1879—in an area extending from the lower Methow River to the forty-ninth parallel and from the range crest to the Okanogan River—the army set up the temporary post of Camp Chelan on the Columbia River near the site of present-day Bridgeport. In March 1880, the reservation boundaries were extended to the south shore of Lake Chelan.

Under orders from Gen. Oliver O. Howard, commander of the Department of the Columbia, Lt. Thomas W. Symons (recently appointed chief engineer of the department) and Lt. Col. Henry Clay Merriam began a search for a more suitable location for the post. Symons, a native of New York state who had graduated from West Point at the head of his class in 1874, had just served under Lt. George M. Wheeler's U.S. Geographical and Geological Surveys west of the 100th Meridian. In spring 1880, Symons and Merriam decided on an attractive site near the outlet of Lake Chelan, where there was "unlimited timber" and where the post could serve as a buffer between the reservation and white settlers.[1] In the spring of the following year, the army erected a small camp near present-day Chelan, where troops built shelters, a sawmill, and a steep road up from the Columbia River. Howard soon ordered the men to abandon the post because of its strategic disadvantages, however, and they moved to the newly founded Fort Spokane.[2] In 1883, a presidential order eliminated a fifteen-mile swath of the Moses Reservation immediately south of the forty-ninth parallel, and the entire reservation was opened to settlement and mining in 1886.

In September 1879, Symons and Merriam had engaged In-na-ma-setch-a, a chief of the Chelan Indians, and his two sons to take them up Lake Chelan in a dugout canoe. Paddling some twenty-four miles—perhaps to Safety Harbor Creek—they found that the mountain terrain increased in rugged grandeur "at every paddle stroke." Although Symons was not the first white person to see the lake, he was the first to record its beauty:

> Lake Chelan is a wonderfully beautiful sheet of water. . . . It seems to be and is in fact a dammed-up mountain cañon of the most rugged and pronounced description. The water is of diamond-like clearness and yet in places no sight can penetrate to the bottom of its liquid depths. It is supplied from mountain-springs and from the melting snows of the mass of snow-capped mountains lying about Mount Baker.

He concluded: "It is the most grandly beautiful lake that I have ever seen."[3] Later he admired "the granite walls rising smooth and shiny, without a tree or blade of grass, for a thousand feet or more from the water's edge."

Other explorers were also enthralled by the lake's pristine beauty. Geologist Israel C. Russell, comparing Lake Chelan to the famed lakes of northern Italy, wrote: "The mountains inclosing the hidden gem of the Cascades rise abruptly from the water's edge to great heights. . . . The lower slopes are dark with forests of pine and fir, and the bare serrate spires above are white with snow

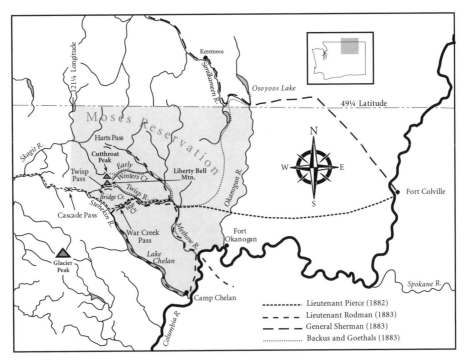

Army Explorations North of Lake Chelan

long after the spring flowers have faded." Twenty years later, William D. Lyman, on the first Mazamas Club outing to the lake's headwaters, described how the "cathedrals, organ-pipes . . . stand out in bold relief against the blue-black sky of those lofty altitudes." The "vast pinnacles of rock," he wrote, "deceive the eye by their sheer immensity."[4]

The steep slopes of the lake were also notable for the presence of mountain goats. Fur-trader Alexander Ross had seen "the ibex, the white musk goat" below the Chelan River in 1811, and both Symons and Merriam noted the abundance of game trails along the lake slopes in 1879.[5] When Lt. Samuel Rodman canoed up Lake Chelan in August 1883, he reported that "the mountain goat, unsuspicious of danger, browses on the slopes. We landed several times and stole upon them, bringing down several fine specimens."[6] In 1893, Lyman described numerous goats on "a stupendous line of cliffs, four or five thousand feet high." He continued: "On the ragged crags of Goat Mountain, secure in their inaccessible Fortresses, these beautiful creatures can be seen leaping about like lambs at play."[7]

In July 1870, Daniel C. Linsley, who was exploring for the Northern Pacific Railroad, became the first non-Native to reach the lake's head.[8] Ten years later, Merriam explored the full length of Lake Chelan by canoe, and he and Symons made a notable discovery near the lake head: "At the extreme upper end he found solid vertical walls of rock and on these . . . were a large number of hieroglyphics written in a horizontal line, evidently by people in boats when the waters were at this higher level."[9] Symons, who lamented the brevity of his visit, hoped to make sketches and learn the history of the markings, but he never did.

The Pierce Expedition

Military exploration continued eastward and northward from Lake Chelan in 1881 and afterward, even though the lake bordered the Moses Reservation. Both Symons and Alfred Downing, who had probably become acquainted on the Wheeler survey, were members of the U.S. Army expedition that investigated extending steamboat navigation on the upper Columbia in 1880.[10] Downing worked as a topographer and artist after emigrating from England in 1872, and he accompanied exploring parties for the Department of the Columbia in 1880–1883. He distinguished himself in the exploration of the Fort Hope trail under Lt. George Goethals in 1883 and in the north-central Washington tour under Gen. William T. Sherman the same year. He remained with the Department of the Columbia until 1888, when he left to work for the railroad.

Downing was a gifted landscape artist, and he took good advantage of the horizontal lines of skylines, valleys, and massive escarpments juxtaposed across a scene to indicate relative spacing and distance. Like the earlier artists of the Pacific Railroad Survey, the HBC, the Royal Engineers, and the Northwest Boundary Survey, Downing had to illustrate the terrain realistically while also expressing its beauty. He arrived in October 1880 from the Wheeler survey to join Symons's Columbia River expedition as topographic assistant. The expedition went ashore at the confluence of the Columbia and the Okanogan River, the site of Fort Okanogan, which the HBC had abandoned in 1860. They found three Indian tepees near the water where men were making spears and women were making moccasins. Downing wrote: "Snowcapped mountains are visible to the N.W. and by noon we find ourselves at the Methow Rapids; they are not bad at this stage of water and we go spinning through easily."[11]

In 1882, Gen. Nelson A. Miles, commander of the Department of the Columbia, selected Lt. Henry Hubbard Pierce to lead the first military exploring party across the northern Cascades. The forty-eight-year-old Pierce was a graduate of Trinity College in Connecticut, a classical scholar who became a professor of mathematics and military tactics. After serving in the Civil War, he was appointed first lieutenant in the U.S. Army. Pierce is remembered at least in part for his articulate and perceptive narrative, which fortunately was published as a separate report, not as a congressional document.

The expedition's route would cross from the Okanogan River to Lake Chelan, Miles wrote Pierce in July, and "thence if practicable . . . cross the mountains to Skagit River." The objective was to reconnoiter and obtain information about the country between the northern interior and the northern Puget Sound. The establishment of the temporary Camp Chelan in August 1879, unrest among the Indians in the Columbia Basin and on the Skagit River, and Symons's subsequent reconnaissance of the Columbia River in 1881 were all factors in planning this overland exploration for a possible military and settlement route.

Pierce's plan for the westward journey was based on Symons's and Merriam's exploration of Lake Chelan and on previous surveying and military expeditions into the Skagit River region. Information obtained from Indians over the years indicated that they used a route from the head of Lake Chelan to the Skagit, and Pierce assumed that this route could be followed with a guide. He may also have obtained a copy of the printed Northwest Boundary Survey map of 1866 to gain an understanding of the area's drainages. The geographic conception of the exploration is indicated on Symons's *Map of the Department of the Columbia*, drawn by Downing in 1881, and Pierce relied on this and other existing maps for the overall route plan.

The expedition assembled at Fort Colville, where men were recruited and animals and provisions gathered in preparation for their departure on August 1, 1882. Pierce was accompanied by a small but capable party: his chief assistant, Lt. George Benjamin Backus (1st Cavalry), a West Point graduate and Pennsylvania native who was a skilled woodsman, marksman, and fisherman; topographic assistant Alfred Downing; assistant surgeon Dr. George F. Wilson; sergeants Doyle and Worrell; principal musician and soldier Alford; a packer (probably F. S. Sherwood); four privates; and the mixed-blood guide and interpreter Joseph La Fleur (then stationed at Fort Okanogan). The expedition included a train of fifteen Cayuse horses and fourteen mules.[12]

On the first leg of the journey, the party crossed the rolling Kettle Range to the Okanogan River. After crossing the Okanogan Valley—which was "devoid of protection from the burning sun except along the river banks"—the expedition was guided by the Chelan Indian Swa-u-lum. On August 15, Pierce was nearing the Cascade Range.

> As one looks down from the commanding table-lands upon the Methow Valley, a scene of peculiar loveliness is presented. Westward, the mountains, thinly grown with yellow pine and fir, rise abruptly, towering peak on peak, until, in the distance, their summits are clad in perpetual snow. To the north and south are pictures of rival beauty. Far from our standpoint a jutting spur divides the prospect. Through the midst of each the Methow, fringed with poplars, balms, and evergreens, winds its tortuous course as if reluctant to quit so fair a landscape. . . . The streams, where beaver dams are frequent, throng with splendid trout (no less than two hundred having been caught during our stay), and their banks with tufted grouse, while thousands of deer are said to roam the fruitful uplands.

Two days later, on August 18, while traveling up the Twisp River Valley, Pierce had his first view of striking mountain scenery:

> While riding leisurely with my guide over a fine, grassy plateau, a glance to the left revealed through one of these openings a picture of such startling effect as to call

forth an exclamation of surprise: two friendly peaks, apparently thirty miles away—the one shaped like the point of an egg, the other like a pyramid—lifted their snow-clad summits to the clouds. So grand and sudden was the vision, that I named them Wonder Mountains [Hoodoo Peak and Spirit Mountain] on the spot. The blue of the distance framed in the green and gold of the foreground completed a landscape worthy of the highest efforts of the painter.

Westward in the direction of our trail another majestic prominence of the Cascade Range appeared. Its vast proportions, sharply outlined against the sky, assumed to our eyes the form of some quaint temple of worship, with its painted gables, grained, dark-ribbed central dome, and snow-covered roof. So close was the resemblance, that all united upon the name of Cathedral Mountain [Reynolds Peak].

The difficult Indian trail "ran between lofty mountains: those to the south [Black Ridge], sloping to a stupendous height, those to the north . . . crowned by forbidding crags of granite." Pierce continued: "The last mile of our march was by a badly defined zigzag path up a steep, grassy declevity, where the animals found great trouble in securing a foothold."

On upper War Creek, the expedition met two prospectors, the older one claiming to have explored the mountains for the past seven summers "in search of a rather legendary mountain of golden quartz."[13] They

begged for a little flour, of which they were nearly destitute, in exchange for a shoulder of mountain-goat. The request was granted, much to their relief, and thenceforth they clung to us for companionship to the very top of the main cascades, where bewilderment and the loss of their strongest pack-horse down the mountain turned them homewards a discouraged and disappointed pair.

The prospector told the lieutenant about a pass to the north "where creeks nearly sever the mountain," a low-profile route that Indians used and that he had explored earlier. He also told Pierce that Lake Chelan had two heads, which led the army to mount further expeditions and later caused Pierce some embarrassment, as he had reported that this "intimation . . . of two heads . . . was afterwards from undeniable proofs and the testimony of our guide found to be the truth."

Even though the prospector's guide, "Captain Jim," knew the route and apparently had talked with Pierce's guide, Swa-u-lum, that evening, the expedition took an unnecessary route the next day to a higher pass on the flanks of the valley.[14] The "loose, yielding rocks" caused a pony and a mule to roll "headlong down the steep, landing among jagged granite fragments below. The sight of their helpless, struggling bodies bounding in the air was pitiful." Downing sketched the scene of the animals tumbling hundreds of feet downslope, one of the forty-nine pen-and-ink drawings he made on the expedition. His map of the expedition (included in Pierce's report) indicates the error of the intricate route, and the guide later set a course for the correct pass. On August 19, the prospectors apparently dismissed their own guide, who arranged with

Lt. Pierce to attempt to retrieve the injured horse and mule. It is probable that Captain Jim became the guide for the expedition at that time.[15]

On August 20, the Pierce party reached Purple Pass, where the lieutenant could see Lake Chelan and such distant, high Cascade peaks as Fernow, Bonanza, Dome, and Tupshin.

> As I gazed westward from a height of 6,850 feet above the sea, and 5,800 feet above the lake, a scene of remarkable grandeur was presented. To the south and west were the rugged peaks of the Cascade Mountains covered with everlasting snow. At our feet reposed Chelan, in color like an artificial lake of thick plate glass, while Pierce River [the Stehekin] brought its clay-tinted waters with many a winding down the narrow canyon that opened to the north. No painter could place the view on canvas and be believed.

Leaving three privates at the "snow lake" to tend the pack animals, the party began its wearisome descent to Lake Chelan.

> Reaching the canyon bottom, camp was made for the lack of a better place, on a sand bar one mile from the mouth of Pierce River. . . . This head of Chelan, evidently unknown except to Indians, and possibly a few old miners, bears no likeness in any feature to that described by Colonel Merriam and others. The head visited by them is believed to be 20 miles to the south, beyond an impassable range, and into it the Sta-he-kin River flows [Railroad Creek]. A reconnoissance in that direction will establish the correctness of this conclusion, and thenceforth give the lake an entirely different form from that upon the maps. The peculiar conformation of the mountain spurs has doubtless so concealed the divergence of the newly discovered arm, that those passing in boats here deemed it but a simple indentation of the shore.

From his high vantage, Pierce may have been believed that an arm of the lake existed at Railroad Creek. Assuming that Merriam had reached another head of the lake in 1880, he named the Stehekin River the "Pierce."[16] He also called present-day Bridge Creek "Backus Creek" and the upper Stehekin River "Symons Fork." These names did not survive, although his "Agnes Creek" did.

The route along the Stehekin was exasperating, as rocky banks, cottonwood and willow thickets, and rocky bluffs impeded progress. On August 24, the men forded Bridge Creek. Pierce recorded that "just above the ford was a rude bridge of drift-logs, joined with strips of cedar-bark, and ballasted with stones, built by the Indians, and doubtless often used by them instead of risking the formidable current." The crude bridge may have been built by Skagit River Indians in the summer of 1880 to improve communication with interior Indians at a time when trouble was brewing on the Skagit.[17] The men followed "a wretched foot-path" for an estimated eight miles. The pack train "toiled and floundered" through "almost impenetrable underbrush and swampy areas," and fallen logs and steep slopes sometimes forced them into the streambed.

Pierce and Downing made an early start the next day for "the passage of the main Cascades."

Midway, on glancing upward, I saw the old miner hastening down the steep with a look of utter discouragement upon his face. Upon inquiry, he advised me with great earnestness to return; saying that the ascent was impossible for packs, that his best horse had tumbled from the cliffs ahead, its body lying in the brush close by, with two others probably lost by Indians, giving ample proof, and that altogether the summit was a strange, inhospitable place. It forcibly recalled the passage in Bunyan's inimitable allegory, where the timorous pilgrim meets Christian on his way up the hill.

Shaking hands with the old man, who bade me a sorrowful farewell, and sending back word for the train to come on, we gained the height without mishap, the last few hundred feet becoming exceedingly treacherous by reason of a sleety shower.

La Fleur and the packer could not get the train up the boggy, slippery trail, and several mules with their packs rolled off the path.

The Downing map suggests that the wilderness the party was traversing: "Snow Peaks" appears northwest of Backus Fork, where Mt. Buckner and Goode Mountain are located, and to the south, in the area of Tolo Mountain and the Seven Sisters. The map correctly identifies the "summit of Cascade Mountains" and gives an altitude of 5,050 feet for Cascade Pass (which is over 5,360 feet). In the fading afternoon, Pierce selected a sheltered spot beneath "somber firs" and with difficulty kindled a fire using wet wood.

Meanwhile, Backus, with habitual energy and unselfishness, had examined the region ahead. Returning late in the evening, drenched from head to foot, he reported a small grassy prairie some distance beyond, but expressed fears of a precarious, if not wholly impracticable, path down the mountain to the west.

In a sketch of this miserable bivouac at Pelton Basin, closely east of Cascade Pass, Downing depicted himself, Pierce, Backus, and Wilson. The camp was screened from the elements by a "shelter-tent stretched between two trees." The sleet continued into the night, saturating cargo bundles and blankets.

During the night the sleet became snow, and what with the weirdlike darkness, the thunder of falling masses of ice [off Johannesburg Mountain] into the neighboring canyons, the ceaseless roar of the torrents, and the howling of the wind, the situation was dismal beyond description.

After breakfast that morning, August 26, the men discussed whether to continue or retreat. Apparently all but one man wanted to continue. The dissenter likely was Dr. Wilson, who was a tenderfoot compared to Pierce, Backus, and Downing. Pierce, deciding to push on, wisely sent Doyle and the packer with all but three of the Cayuse horses back to Fort Colville. There were now eight men to complete the journey to the Skagit River and, eventually, Vancouver Barracks.[18] They moved their wet camp a half mile closer to the pass at a more sheltered location. Close by were the abandoned shovel and frying pan of the discouraged prospectors, who had apparently crossed Cascade Pass ahead of Pierce before their packhorse fell to its death on the west flank.[19]

After the expedition crossed the pass, they found specimens of quartz rich in gold at what was later to become the Soldier Boy claim. Pierce noted that "extensive croppings were seen high up the mountain to our right. Surely the Eldorado of the old man's dreams." The difficult route crossed "a tangled growth of trailing alders" (Sitka, or slide, alder) that reached far above their heads. The explorers passed a waterfall and traversed a three-hundred-yard-wide avalanche track coming from Boston Basin. Pierce commented: "No sturdy lumberman could have cleared the densely wooded slope more completely, for not a tree or shrub was left standing."[20] There was "grave uncertainty" about the stream they had been following—the north fork of the Cascade River—because "the maps from Lake Chelan have been declared erroneous."

On August 28, the party forded the Cascade River and its north fork four times. Travel was difficult, "exceedingly serpentine," yet they marched an estimated fifteen miles. Downing's failure to portray on his map the large south fork of the Cascade River indicates that the party was traveling on the forested north side at that point. They found two canoes at the riverbank at the end of the next day's travel, indicating that they had reached navigable waters with prospects of a village downstream (the Indians took canoes as far as Marble Creek). Their march of over eleven miles "was through a thick forest of splendid cedars, pines, and cottonwoods."

The expedition crossed Monogram Creek on August 30. After continuing an estimated eight miles, the trail suddenly ended at a river ford, where a "swift, turbulent stream, that went whirling and foaming over the granite bowlders, brought us to a standstill." Pierce sent La Fleur across on the strongest horse to search for "an Indian ranch, located, according to Major Babbitt, on the north bank of Cascade River, near its mouth." Late in the afternoon the guide returned, reporting no sign of a trail or ranch. Camp was ordered, "and after a scanty supper of bread and coffee we spread our blankets for the night." Downing's sketch of camp 27 depicts the hungry party with a small bacon allowance.

Pierce was, understandably, worried about the river crossing:

To form a foot-bridge whereby to avoid the dangers of the stream, and at the same time lessen the burdens of the animals, I sent La Fleur at daylight to fell a tall pine that stood near the opposite bank, and had been selected for the purpose the evening before. With but one dull axe this was soon found to be a forenoon's labor. Time being too precious, I at once decided to attempt the fording, which was happily accomplished by ten o'clock, the two strongest ponies making no less than twelve trips each. During the passage Lieutenant Backus and the guide narrowly escaped drowning; the latter with his horse being carried down the stream to the deeper and more furious waters, where both were for a moment overwhelmed. Compelled to abandon the pony to its own salvation, with perfect presence of mind, the courageous man at last gained the shore, drenched and chilled by the icy flood. . . . We pursued a rather bewildering trail for four miles along the south bank of the river, when one of its loops was passed by swimming the animals and carrying the baggage over by a bridge of logs.

The final crossing took the party to the north bank of the river, not far from the summer fishing camp of Miskaiwhu (near present Marblemount).

> Judging that, if on the Cascade River, we must be near its mouth, and urged by an almost providential anxiety, I sent Backus with the guide . . . to search for Indians, and, if found, to make arrangements for our journey down the Skagit. The result of their mission was awaited with more than doubtful hearts. At the end of two hours, however, success was announced, and for a time the welkin rang with cheers.

Hearing the men calling, an Indian and his wife crossed from a summer lodge beyond the Skagit. La Fleur could speak their language, and an agreement was soon made for the Indians to bring two canoes to the explorers' camp at daybreak. Still,

> they refused to believe that we had arrived from the summit, the old man, apparently 70 years of age, claiming that he had never seen a white man go or come that way, and that it was impossible for anyone but an Indian to keep the trail. They also said that, a winter's supply of salmon laid in, they had intended to quit their temporary lodge and go down the river early the next morning. Had we therefore failed to s[p]end that night, or been delayed 24 hours on our journey, an insecure raft, on an unknown rapid river filled with snags, would have been our only recourse.

Having traveled an estimated 295 miles, Pierce added to the understanding of the geography of a country previously unknown to army cartographers— one that still appeared as large blank areas on maps. The map of a part of Washington Territory to accompany the 1860–1861 Surveyor General's report has the legend "Unexplored" between the head of Lake Chelan and the Skagit River. Downing's 1881 *Map of the Department of the Columbia*, Lt. Johnson K. Duncan's Pacific Railroad Survey map of 1853–1854, and the Northwest Boundary Survey map of 1866 were the best to show drainages, yet they were all incomplete. Although Pierce did not examine Lake Chelan as planned, he and Downing gathered sufficient information to provide the first accurate depiction of the upper Lake Chelan drainages, a major cartographic contribution.

In forwarding Pierce's detailed, readable account of the grueling expedition, Gen. Miles praised the officer's efforts: "Lieutenant Pierce is entitled to much credit for the efficient manner in which he performed this duty and in obtaining valuable information regarding sections of the country little known." In December 1882, Gen. Sherman submitted the report to the secretary of war, advising that it be published along with Downing's map. Sherman explained:

> Further Explorations will be made, and publication of the information gained should be made, as it is to the national interest that the timber and minerals of that Region should be brought within the reach of the Emigrants who will throng to Oregon and Washington Territory as soon as the Northern Pacific Railroad is completed.[21]

The route that Pierce explored was far too difficult for a military and settlement road. The width of the northern Cascade Range misled the lieutenant, causing him to believe that the mountains were a sufficient barrier to keep interior and coastal Indians from forming an alliance and that a small army force in the Methow or Okanogan area would be enough to maintain peace.

Lt. Symons lauded Pierce's report, but after conversations with Col. Merriam—who later thoroughly explored Lake Chelan in boats and examined the shores for timber—Symons had "no hesitation in recording my belief that Lieutenant Pierce has been entirely misled concerning the second head of Lake Chelan, and that the river called by him Pierce's River is in fact the Ste-he-kin."[22] The report from the prospector Pierce had encountered about a pass located north of his route, where creeks heading close together nearly "sever the mountain, to form a natural road with a low gradient"—a pass presumed to lead to one of Puget Sound's finest harbors—encouraged the army to explore the Methow Valley region further in 1883. Pierce was apparently assigned to command another expedition, but he succumbed to an illness near present-day Bridgeport on July 17, 1883.

Rodman's Route

The U.S. Army wanted to examine Lake Chelan again because of the geographical differences reported by Pierce and Merriam. In June 1883, a small party under 2d Lt. Samuel Churchill Robertson went by boat to the lake's head, verifying that there was but one head and that it was the same one Pierce had visited.[23] Other than Pierce's route, however, little was known about the passes of the Methow River drainage through the center of the Moses Reservation. Lt. Samuel Rodman, with a small party that included Alexander Smitkin, an Indian guide, made an exploration in this region in July and August 1883.[24]

Crossing the extremely hot sagebrush country of eastern Washington, the party found little to break the monotony except taking easy shots at sage hens. They followed an Indian trail to the Methow River, then explored canyons near its headwaters where there were no signs of previous visits by explorers. There were two distinct trails up the main valley, one for use during high water and one for use during low water. "Steep, rocky mountains enclose the river in a narrow gorge," Rodman wrote, "where travel is impossible except in the river bed." He also went several miles up the Ne-quam-tum before deciding to follow the Twisp River. Rodman was clearly awed by the "snow capped peaks of the Cascade mountains." "Nature had selected this spot," he wrote, "far away from the abodes of civilized man, for her own children; for surely these rugged peaks, with saw-tooth forms, seemed to bid defiance to any but the wild beasts."

Returning to the Twisp and frustrated by the search for a pass near the Methow, the Rodman party basically retraced a portion of Pierce's 1882 route—without the unnecessary detours near the head of War Creek. At camp one evening, the cook was careless about the fire, which after dinner spread through the ground layer of dry pine needles. Rodman told what happened next:

> The doctor . . . was awakened by the smell of smoke. . . . In attempting to find some receptacle for water in the dark, he fell over our tinware . . . which awakened the cook, who promptly seized his rifle and shouted out: "Who's there?" The doctor, not hearing him, made no reply, and our cook . . . raised his rifle with the intention of shooting. Fortunately, he called out once more, this time receiving the answer, "It's me." . . . he again shouted, "Who's me?" whereupon, the Doctor answered again, and established his identity. The story as related the following morning created a great deal of laughter, and the cook confessed that he was so sure a grizzly bear was around the eatables, that he could not be convinced to the contrary, at first, even though a human voice had replied.

One morning, after the smoky air had been cleared by a brief precipitation, Rodman "obtained a fine view" of Lake Chelan, "nestling away down below me, its waters were a perfect emerald green, and as smooth as glass." The task now was to determine the form of the lake's head. Smitkin and another Indian were to descend to the lake and plant a long pole with a white rag to mark the lake head; then the whole party would return to the Methow, descend to the Columbia, and continue to the foot of the lake for an exploration by water. At the lake, Rodman was as ecstatic over its beauty as Symons had been:

> Nature has given this place all the delights of beauty and grandeur. The waters, clear as crystal, are very deep. Natural wharves of rock exist at intervals, and in some of the sheltered harbors level plateaux stretch back to the base of the mountains, and are so fascinating to the eye that it seems strange that there are not handsome villas to occupy the sites. Farther up the lake the steep banks barely permit a good foot-hold.

Their boat was a large, flat-bottomed scow that was fitted with a square sail made of two tents. With a favorable wind, the party made good progress without using the oars. On the third day, they found the pole the Indians had placed at the head of the lake, which settled the question of whether the lake had but one head. Rodman observed the snow-capped peaks that hemmed in the Stehekin River Valley beyond the head of the lake, and he examined the figures Col. Merriam had seen drawn by unknown Indians on the cliff.

The Backus and Goethals Route

After Pierce died, Sherman appointed Backus to take charge of the army's scouting for a pass across the northern Cascades. On an 1883 expedition, the thirty-two-year-old Backus was accompanied by twenty-five-year-old Lt. George Washington Goethals, who was to report on the expedition and make route maps. Both men traveled with Sherman's expedition from Fort Colville to Osoyoos Lake.[25] Backus's party included four men in addition to Goethals: interpreter Arthur Chapman, a packer, a private, and a Cpl. Rheinhardt.

Each man had a saddle horse, and there were four pack mules. The expedition left Osoyoos Lake on August 15.

The route led through the Moses Reservation by way of Toats Coulee and the Conconully area, then approximately followed Pierce's route to reach the Twisp River. The expedition map, drawn by Downing from Goethals's notes, shows "Looch-oo-pan Mt." (now McClure Mountain) on the west side of the Methow. The name of the mountain—also noted by Rodman—means "broken stone." The party veered from Pierce's route on August 25 and kept to the main, or north, fork. The next day they covered only about six miles on "a very dim " trail where there was much chaparral and many gnats and hornets. During an attempt to jump animals over fallen timber, "Corpl. Rheinhardt's horse snagged himself in the crown of the hoof, and became so lame that the corporal could not ride him. The yellow jackets were numerous."

Backus was certain from his interpretation of the story of the two miners, as well as from recent reports from Indians at Foster Creek, that the pass they sought was at the head of this branch. Smoke interfered with interpreting the valley and ridge topography, however, and travel was made difficult by tree branches that tended to knock men off their animals. It was hard to see through the "thick growth of chapparal."

On August 28, Backus and Goethals hiked to the pass at the valley head:

> To our west, appeared the zigzag peaks, covered with snow, and their outline resembled sawteeth. . . . A short distance to the west of our camp . . . arose a high conical peak with sides very steep. Though towering many feet above the snowline, still none could be seen on it. This we called Silver Peak.

The "zigzag peaks" would have been Lincoln Butte, Twisp Mountain, Hock Mountain, and a ridge of Stiletto Mountain. "Silver Peak" (Lincoln Butte) was so named "on account of the number of small silver ledges we found on its sides." The explorers picked their way along the flank of a snow basin on the south slopes of Silver Peak "over loose rock slides, chiefly trap, and along precipices where in places scarcely a foothold could be obtained, and the sensation was anything but a pleasant one, when a stone we had just stepped on, was heard the next moment tumbling hundreds of feet below." Goethals received such painful yellow-jacket stings on his hand that day that he could barely take notes, which may have affected the accuracy of his map.

The men apparently reached Twisp Pass, where they recorded the altitude as 6,500 feet (over 400 feet too high). They believed that they were on the true range divide and, judging from their maps, that "the stream beyond was one of the branches of the Skagit River." It was in fact Bridge Creek, which drains to Lake Chelan. Goethals reported that "deer, bears, mountain sheep and goats can be found along the route, and in our walk to the summit, the 'whistler' was heard. This is a species of ground hog, whose whistle resembles that of a man calling his dog, and puzzled the hound we had with us not a little." He added that a good mountain wagon road could be constructed over this route to the summit, but nothing could be seen clearly beyond it because "the smoke was too dense." Exploring farther along the Methow, the party continued to the Papoose Methow (Early Winters Creek). On September 5, they made their camp 18 near the stream junction. Travel was difficult along the valley of Early Winters because of the thick cottonwood, brush, and fallen timber.

On September 8, when the two officers and Chapman were cutting trail, they came to an opening about three miles from camp 21. This location—apparently on the west bank below Cutthroat Creek, where there were good grazing meadows for the animals—became their final camp, and the party remained there from September 9 through 11. During a storm, they had to huddle under a tent fly, but the weather cleared in the evening so they could see the snow-covered, zigzag peaks resembling those at the head of the north fork of the Twisp (probably the Liberty Bell massif with a dusting of fresh snow).

On September 11, Goethals was taken ill. Backus and Chapman were gone all day, hiking upstream about five miles before coming to a branch. "Each basin [Cutthroat and upper Early Winters creeks] was carefully examined," Goethals wrote, "but the mountains rose up so abruptly, that they did not attempt to reach the summit." Thick brush in avalanche paths was an impediment, with one swath two hundred yards wide. Backus judged that to get to the top would have meant "a hard day's tramp for a foot passenger, and . . . he doubts if a horse could get up at all." By afternoon, Goethals felt better and walked near the creek for about a mile, where he saw an enormous slide. "The side of the mountain from its summit has been swept clean of all its timber," he reported, "which lay at the bottom broken in all sizes, by the stones." He concluded that the Indians apparently did not reach the Skagit by this route.

On their return to the upper Methow, the explorers noted a horse track, which had been made by a member of Lt. Rodman's party. The Backus party did not ascend the Methow, where "the country looked rough and uninviting," because their rations were low and they knew Rodman had been there. Goethals, differing with Rodman, noted that there was a good trail along the Methow and suggested that Indians traveled from there to the Skagit. On September 14, near the Chewuch (Chewack) River, Goethals wrote there was a trail into that valley where Similkameen Indians went on annual hunts and to fish for salmon.

The Backus expedition is of particular interest because it was the first group known to have visited Early Winters Creek and to have seen the Liberty Bell group of peaks. Otherwise, it accomplished nothing new. Backus and Rodman both failed to locate Harts Pass because they concentrated on the Twisp River. Apparently, Backus and Goethals were inclined toward a certain pragmatism in which caution prevailed over the heroics of climbing to a summit (or even a high ridgetop) to search the terrain for a suitable pass. They certainly missed the Washington-Rainy Pass route now used by the North Cascades Highway.

General Sherman in the Cascades

Another expedition in the region, notable not only for having explored new terrain but also for the importance of its leader, was the western portion of Gen. William Tecumseh Sherman's 1883 continental inspection tour, which began at Fort Ellis, Montana. On August 7, eighty-one men, sixty-six horses, and seventy-nine mules organized at Fort Colville for the mountainous march to the Fraser River. The route went along the Similkameen River and followed the trail built by British troops during the boundary survey in the 1850s. On August 14, the expedition arrived at the site of an old HBC trading post (at present-day Keremeos). In his account of the journey, Sherman's aide, John C. Tidball, wrote that the "valley is inclosed by high mountains. . . . The mountains are exceedingly precipitous, in fact, in places are quite perpendicular."[26] A thundershower two nights later provided relief from the smoky atmosphere.

The route passed Allison's cattle ranch, made a bouldery ford, and then followed the old trail along canyons and ragged slopes. On August 17, the expedition ascended Hope Mountain (now Hope Pass on Skaist Mountain), where the trail became a wagon road. Tidball's account notes "the gloomy gulches of the headwaters of the Skagit River" and later the high and precipitous mountains along the canyon of the Skaist River. "All along are evidences of the terrible work of avalanches and torrents," Tidball wrote. "The snow of some of these avalanches, mingled with rocks and trees, was still unmelted. In some cases the débris of the avalanches filled the entire bed of the cañon." The road of the Royal Engineer troops proved to be remarkably well built, though some bridges had rotted away. After the party passed the source of "Lake River" (Nicolum Creek), Tidball wrote, "the mountains again close in, forming a cañon." He observed that the Fraser River was about the same size as the Missouri and was of a grayish-brown color, caused by mining and the "washing of clayey bluffs along its course." Sherman's expedition continued to Yale, then took a steamer to Victoria.

Defeated in its search for a useful route across the northern Cascades, the army satisfied itself with occupying posts on the periphery. Pierce's 1882 expedition and those that took place the following year were the last of the regional scouting parties, for the official, large-scale army explorations—such as the Wheeler survey—ended, except in Alaska. By 1877, President Ulysses S. Grant was gone and the military had lost its dominance in Washington, D.C. Like the railroad explorers, Pierce, Rodman, Backus, and Goethals had found their hopes of an easy mountain crossing frustrated by precipitous slopes and a complex landscape. Prospectors, surveyors of the Great Northern Railway, and—beginning in 1895—the professional topographers and geologists would be the ones to give new, firsthand accounts of the rugged high peaks and ridges and the narrow canyons that blocked continuous routes from east to west.

Tracklaying on switchback bridge no. 1 on the west slope of Stevens Pass, December 15, 1892 (Washington State Historical Society, Tacoma)

11

THE GREAT NORTHERN RAILWAY'S
SEARCH FOR A PASS

You can lay track through the Garden of Eden but why bother if the only inhabitants are
Adam and Eve.

–James J. Hill

In an age of commercial giants, James J. Hill was among the most power
ful. With an almost euphoric vision, he saw the opportunities of that
vast region more clearly than most men, and his Great Northern Railway became the backbone of settlement and prosperity in the northern Midwest and, later, the Pacific Northwest. Known as the "Empire Builder," Hill was
a ruthless and decisive entrepreneur whose basic philosophy was simple: "A
railroad through virgin territory creates its own business." In other words, the
railroad would attract new settlers, who would in turn provide business for
the railroad.[1] The Great Northern was not a land-grant railroad, however,
and Hill was sometimes required to purchase land.

Like the U.S. Army engineers, Hill and his circle were explorers, although
with private profit in mind, not a broad sense of national purpose. As his
railroad was being constructed across the Great Plains in the 1880s and he
committed the Great Northern to multimillion-dollar expenditures, Hill was
concerned about the uncertainties of crossing the Rocky Mountains, bridging
river canyons, and, finally, building through the avalanche-swept Cascade
Range.[2] He took heart, however, from Isaac I. Stevens's Pacific Railroad survey
report about the possibilities of a northern route. The explorations of such
men as Albert B. Rogers and John F. Stevens would make it possible to locate a
railroad line through the forbidding mountain barrier.

Rogers's Survey in the Cascade Range

The Great Northern's first field party in the Cascades went out in the summer
of 1887, when Hill hoped to pursue a northern crossing to the Skagit River. He
selected for the exploration Albert Bowman Rogers, a gruff veteran of mountain surveys for the Canadian Pacific Railway (of which Hill was a director).
The fifty-eight-year-old Rogers had received his engineering degree from Yale,
had been a prairie railroad surveyor and had acquired his title of "Major"

while helping to fight the Sioux in 1861. Rogers had a reputation as a miser who regularly underestimated field rations—largely beans, bacon, and alcohol—needed for his men. He was generally disliked because of his insulting profanity and his practice of mercilessly driving his employees. Rogers's expeditions had many desertions, and few men worked for him more than one season. Hill was aware of this, and his decision to employ him to locate a practicable railway route through some of Canada's most perplexing mountains, and later the Cascade Range must have seemed unlikely. Hill's faith in Rogers, however, rested on Rogers's success in locating the best pass through the difficult Selkirk Range in 1881–1882.[3]

In February 1881, Hill had made a shrewd offer that the ambitious Rogers could not resist. If the explorer could find a pass through the Selkirks that would save the railroad a possible 150 miles, Hill would name the pass for him and give him $5,000.[4] Although nearly every pass had already been explored by Sir Sanford Fleming's engineers, this did not deter Rogers, who J.H.E. Secretan characterized as "a short, sharp, snappy little chap with long Dundreary whiskers" who was "a master of picturesque profanity, . . . continually chewed tobacco and was an artist of expectoration. He wore overalls with pockets behind, and had a plug of tobacco in one pocket and a sea biscuit in the other."[5] In the fall of 1882, the explorer proved out the route through the Selkirks from the Beaver River Valley, much to the delight of his sponsor. True to his boast that fame, not money, motivated him, Rogers framed his bonus check and hung it in his brother's home in Minnesota for all to see.

For Rogers and Hill, it was now time to probe the Cascade Range for a pass north of the Northern Pacific line. Although advised by both Indians and settlers that it was too early in the season, Rogers and his party (including his nephew Al and his cousin John G. "Jack" Rogers, both of whom had come with him from the Midwest) started up Lake Chelan on July 6, 1887. At Chelan, homesteader and government surveyor Ignatius A. Navarre—who had arrived early in 1886—discouraged Rogers in his plan to explore between the Methow and Skagit rivers, especially since Capt. George McClellan had condemned the route. Navarre's wife told Rogers that Indians knew of a pass from the head of the lake but that they would not divulge its location. She added that the west-slope Indians who crossed the range hid canoes at the lake head by sinking them in marshes. Despite the uncertainties, an Indian known as Wapato John told Rogers about the Methow-Twisp River route to the lake head and its continuation to the Skagit. Through Navarre, Rogers met William L. Sanders, whose boat the party used.

On July 9, the explorers arrived at Railroad Creek, which was then called the Stehekin (a legacy of Lt. Henry Pierce's 1882 army expedition). There Rogers learned that civil engineers had explored the creek valley for a short distance the previous year.[6] Three days later, the group reached Hart Lake, estimating

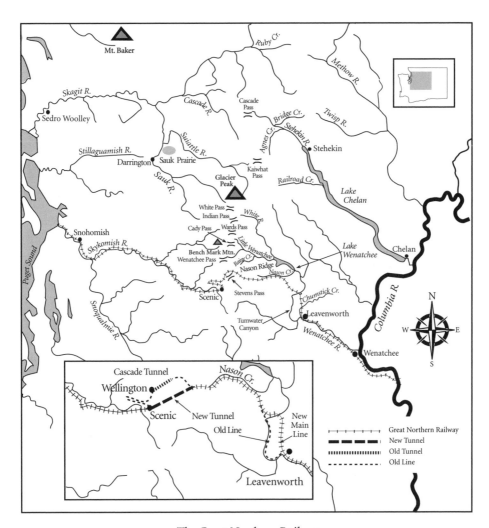

The Great Northern Railway

it at twenty miles up the valley (it is actually about fourteen). At the mountain lake, Rogers wrote in his diary that there were "splendid glaciers north of camp and a magnificent cascade in view about 4 miles farther up the creek." The glacier was the Isella on Bonanza Peak; the cascade was Crown Point Falls. Avalanches had swept away acres of large timber in this steep-walled, U-profiled valley.

The following day, Rogers started for a high viewpoint to study the terrain between the Wenatchee, Entiat, and Skagit River drainages. After several miles he cached his supplies, then continued about two more miles. He gave the height of the viewpoint—probably a position short of Cloudy Pass—as 5,850 feet. The weather was poor, with snow squalls. The exploration continued after the party canoed to the "Pierce" (Stehekin) River at the head of Lake Chelan on July 15. Sanders informed Rogers that the Indians used Bridge Creek to cross to the Skagit River. Jack Rogers wrote in his diary that the party saw a grizzly that day.[7]

On July 18, from a hill on the route to Bridge Creek, Rogers saw what was undoubtedly Dome Peak—"a 3 peaked snow capped mountain" above the forks of the southwest branch (Agnes Creek). He correctly noted that the north river branch (the Stehekin) appeared to be in alignment with the "Skagit branch" (the Cascade River). Now low on supplies—a problem that had burdened him in the Canadian mountains as well—Rogers had insufficient time to follow any of the Stehekin River sources.

Dismissing this exploration, Rogers decided that an approach farther south by the Wenatchee River offered a solution for crossing the main divide.[8] Collectively, the tributaries of the Wenatchee form a peak flow through the confines of Tumwater Canyon. Near present-day Leavenworth, just below the canyon, Rogers hoped to find an Indian known as "Salt Chuck," who was familiar with the upper river, but Salt Chuck was too busy fishing at the mouth of Icicle Creek to be gone the required time.

On July 30, the party ascended Chumstick Creek, a quick route that took them to near the mouth of the Chiwawa River. From a hill (Natapoc Ridge) north of camp the next day, Rogers sighted the Nason Creek Valley, leading to what would become known as Stevens Pass: "It looks as if a gap in the divide lies about West of us—and a low one." By August 1, Rogers had moved his party to Lake Wenatchee. The next day, he climbed Dirtyface Peak to about 5,000 feet, where he gained a perspective on the Little Wenatchee and White River drainages. Rogers learned that the Indian names for these rivers were "Te-te-ak-um" and "Tehko," respectively.

The expedition traced a trail to the White River, where trees were felled for a crossing. On August 4, Al Rogers and Sanders attempted to cut a horse trail into the valley of the Little Wenatchee River, where it was brushy and "terrible." The next day, the party built a bridge of drift logs across the White River and then cut a trail to the Little Wenatchee, which Rogers named "Sanders Creek" for his assistant. On August 6, he noted a blazed trail along the stream, estimating that the markings—the work of "Hudson's Bay men"—were some fifty years old. He also mentioned the good stands of Douglas fir and western white pine in this valley. In two more days, the party reached the second large creek from the southwest (Lake Creek), where Rogers again located old blazes. They camped close to Cady Creek, about seventeen miles from Lake Wenatchee.[9]

On August 10, while Sanders remained at camp with the horses, Rogers and his nephew hiked to the range "summit," which they estimated at 5,300 feet. This location was probably present-day Wards Pass, although it could have been Dishpan Gap. Then continued northward one mile through a northern basin of the Little Wenatchee and to a "ridge sag" that led to a valley fitting the description of the north fork of the Sauk River. The pair encountered a grizzly "with 2 big cubs" that day, an alarming event, since they had no firearms.

The following day, the two men inscribed "Aug-10-5300" on three trees on the "summit" before following the divide "southeast" (actually south-south-west) to a lower gap (Cady Pass). There they again blazed a tree, marking it "Aug-11-4350." Rogers's diary for August 11 describes a short and steep divide heading directly against a stream trending west and southwest (Pass Creek and the north fork of the Skykomish River). He wrote:

> Climbing along the divide very difficult & often dangerous. Part of the way abruptly piled rocks & again were forced to cut foot holds in the snow. Found a blazed trail in the lowest gap . . . (at least 15 years old). This may be the mythical "Ward's Pass."

This sharp divide was the crest or steep incline of Skykomish Peak, which could still hold snowpatches with a crusty surface in August. Rogers believed the pass had been visited by Hubert C. Ward of the Northern Pacific survey. In a letter to Hill on August 19, he recalled the fearful effort, the men "sometimes creeping along on a narrow ridge of promiscuously piled rocks, and again cutting footsteps in the snow, to prevent falling over the bluffs."[10]

Hiking west a mile and a half, Rogers and his nephew climbed to 5,600 feet for a view. This would have been on Bench Mark Mountain (now triangulated at 5,816 feet). On August 12, they followed a grade line five miles noting cuttings and an old survey stick, which they attributed to one of Ward's old lines. It appears that they descended Cady Creek's valley slope to where Fish Creek enters the main valley. The next day, the two men returned to their seventeen-mile camp on the Little Wenatchee River. They spent a day a short distance down valley where there was feed, mending shoes and recuperating. Rogers observed that a good trail and tote road could be built along the stream terraces of "Sanders Creek."

On August 15, Rogers wrote that the party camped upstream on the "Cady Trail," where they met three men arriving from Snohomish with one horse. The next day took them up the brushy north fork of this creek, the divide summit here being 4,130 feet. This description best fits Wenatchee Pass (4,200 feet plus), with an approach from Lake Creek. Rogers correctly noted that the hills to the west (Fortune Mountain) were higher than the true divide. On August 17, the party traveled up the southwest branch of the creek to an altitude of 4,000 feet, within a mile of the summit (this appears to have been the basin east of Grizzly Peak). There they found traces left by previous surveyors. The party did not cross the divide but returned to the Little Wenatchee. They then traveled to the White River, where on August 18 they met a group of Indians picking berries.

In his letter to Hill on August 19, Rogers stated that examining "Sanders Creek" had been helpful but that it was impossible to take a pack train on the route because of brush and windfalls. Present-day Cady Pass, he concluded, was the wisest choice. Another pass six or seven miles to the southeast (Wenatchee Pass) was two hundred feet lower than Cady but would need a longer tunnel. Rogers admitted he was unable to determine whether the route northwest from the divide to the Sauk River would prove to be a good one. His comment on the topography was not favorable: "North face of mountains on both sides divide are almost as continuous as sloping roof of a house."

On August 21, Rogers, his nephew, and Sanders took a pack train seven miles up the White River. Two days later, they were twenty and one-half miles from Lake Wenatchee, north of Mt. Saul. They made camp at 4,400 feet, estimating that the summit was 6,000 feet (White Pass is in fact 5,904 feet). On August 24, Rogers followed Ward's line into the extreme northern fork of the White River to within two and a half miles of the divide. There was much brush and windfall, and the route did not appear practicable for a railroad line.

The following day, Rogers climbed to Little White Pass, estimating it to be at 5,330 feet. The explorers found a blazed tree marked "N P R R SURVEY," and Rogers himself blazed a tree, marking it "Aug 25 Sag 5330." The route then followed the divide southeast and at two miles passed a gap (Indian Pass) at 4,920 feet. Rogers correctly believed that this pass was within two and a half miles of the northern pass he had explored earlier. Returning to near Lake Wenatchee on August 27, Rogers again wrote his employer that he was certain he had noted all the northern passes and he had found the marks of two Northern Pacific surveys.[11] Nothing there impressed him as favorable for a railroad line. He pointed out that the Indians did not take their horses farther than his party did on the "Tehko" (White River). He believed that the "Skywamish" route was the shortest and, with the exceptions he noted, the lowest summit. It had the best general direction and route for construction, with fewer snowslides than the others. All the maps he had seen were "fearfully incorrect—and mislead one in almost every instance." He planned to cross the divide to the Skykomish on foot the following day.

Rogers, his nephew, and Sanders set out for the north fork of the Skykomish River on August 30. They may have traveled up Fish Creek and its north branch, then to a sag south of Saddle Gap before traversing to Cady Pass. In two days, they struck the Cady Trail, about twelve miles west of the summit at the confluence of West Cady Creek and the north fork of the Skykomish River. Fallen logs and brush made it difficult to follow the trail, and they ended up twenty-three miles from the summit (which would place them above Index). On September 3, the party came to an empty logging camp and dried their blankets. The following day, they struck Haggerty's logging camp en route to Snohomish and then continued to the Skagit River. Rogers planned to follow the Sauk River's north fork to its source and intersect his survey line from the west. On September 11, near present-day Birdsview on the Skagit River, he found it difficult to hire Indians to pack for the planned ten- to fourteen-day trip, for they were working in the hop fields. On September 14, Rogers and his companion Alex Arguet traveled fourteen miles by canoe from Birdsview, continuing to about present-day Van Horn. The next day, they stopped at Jackman's camp for help in reaching Albert Bacon's, eight more miles up the river (below the confluence of the Sauk and Skagit rivers). Bacon agreed to go with them to "Prairie" (Sauk Prairie, about two miles above the Suiattle River) or continue until they met an Indian guide, Sauk Charley, who was then berry picking. According to Bacon, Johnny Qualken (a chief, Sauk John) and Sauk Charley were the only Indians who were familiar with the route.

On September 16, the men traveled from Bacon's to Arguet's, near Sauk Prairie (sixteen miles from the mouth of the Sauk), poling the canoe because of swift water. They continued to Stillaguamish Portage (present-day Darrington), where, Rogers noted, the Indians portaged canoes from the Sauk to the Stillaguamish. The party crossed the portage on September 18, and Rogers observed that the divide was only fifty feet higher than the Sauk. Continuing the next day in poor weather, they progressed only some four and a half miles.

By September 20, the explorers had canoed upstream to about two miles past the east fork (White Chuck River); they made about six and a half miles that day. Since passing the forks, they had seen ten black bears catching salmon in the riffles. That night, Rogers wrote that he was "in full sight of the high mountains near the summit." He may have caught a glimpse of Glacier Peak from the valley, but he does not mention the spectacular nearer summits, Pugh Mountain and Sloan Peak. Moving upstream six miles on September 21, the party reached the Sauk's north fork, then followed its canyon. Now on foot and being forced to ford the stream more than ten times, they experienced difficult travel in the forest, encountering brush and beaver marshes, progressing only five miles. Fortunately, at the stream forks they found a blazed line and trail. By September 23, the men were within sight of Indian Pass, and the effects of snowslides in the valley were apparent. They had come thirty and one-half miles from the Suiattle River. On September 24, Rogers arrived at Little White Pass, the same location he had reached on August 25. The barometer read 5,130 feet at the summit, against the earlier reading of 5,330 feet. By September 27, the explorers were able to return to the canoe, and the next day they reached present Mt. Vernon.

In early October, Rogers wrote Hill that "the only route connecting the Skagit with the Wenatchee" was the one he had explored. He warned that avalanches on the western slope of the Cascades were fearful—"much worse than any in the Selkirks"—and again asserted that Indian and Wards passes were not as favorable as the Skykomish route.[12] By October 14, Rogers had returned to the Little Wenatchee River. From the top of a hill south of his camp, he saw the valley of the "Co-co-mil-le" (likely Rainy Creek) coming through a gap some twelve miles distant (the west end of Nason Ridge). Indians told him that the "Nat-a-poo" (Nason Creek), the Co-co-mil-le, and the Skykomish all headed near one another. The Indians did not travel the Nat-a-poo and said that it was not visited by whites. The year 1887 would be the last one in which Rogers worked as a trailblazer. While in Idaho, he pitched off a stumbling horse and within two years was dead from the effects of the injuries.

Plotting a Route for the Great Northern

J.J. Hill and his associates did not make the decision to extend their railway line to Puget Sound until 1889. At that time, the main line of the Great Northern had been pushed westward from Minnesota to the small settlement of Havre in north-central Montana. To complete the Pacific Extension and open up new territory, Hill now had to solve the considerable engineering problems of crossing Washington. Fortunately, he was able to arrange the financing and to progress rapidly before the United States fell into the grip of a major depression a few years later.[13]

The task of selecting the route was given to the New Englander Elbridge H. Beckler, who was appointed chief engineer of the Pacific Extension in 1889. Beckler sent his two most skilled locating engineers, John F. Stevens and Charles F.B. Haskell, to examine passes in the Rockies. The industrious Stevens had an aptitude for both topographic observation and decision. When he discovered Marias Pass late in 1889, the stage was set for the railroad's extension to the Kootenai River and then to the Cascade Range.

In 1890, when Hill sent Stevens to the Cascades to determine the route the Great Northern would take across the mountain, there was little information available about passes aside from what Rogers had provided (a few reports of the Northern Pacific surveys had been published, but the railroad did not have access to the reconnaissance information). The slopes were known to be heavily timbered, the winter snows abundant, and the grades steep. Still, Beckler wrote his employer that "the work is in good hands & I know of no one more competent than Mr. Stevens."[14] Stevens, born in Maine in 1853, had earned a reputation in the West as a location and construction engineer and had supervised and helped locate the Canadian Pacific line from Winnipeg to Shuswap Lake.

In early 1890, when Stevens was in Montana, an army unit apparently made explorations along the Methow River for Beckler. A party under Lt. James A. Leyden ascended the Twisp River to near its head. Leyden, who may have previously crossed Cascade Pass, wrote: "As an engineering problem, I considered the gradual rise and approach to the summit offered by the Twisp and Methow rivers much more desirable than the abrupt and very rocky slopes of the Cascade pass." The chief packer for Leyden's party reported the route northwest as practicable for a trail. Yet, the lieutenant was skeptical about prospectors' reports indicating an easier pass than Cascade up either the Methow or the Twisp to the headwaters of the Skagit, judging that "the great American frontiersman is, generally speaking, the greatest liar in existence."[15]

By mid-June 1890, Beckler, who was headquartered at Fairhaven (later Bellingham), was conducting surveys on the west side of the range, and there was pressure from commercial interests to make a crossing from the Skagit. By June 22, after reviewing discouraging Northern Pacific reports, Beckler concluded that Lake Chelan would "force us into some hard work." From those reports, which he only "lately became the possessor of," he also learned that the Sauk River approach was not hopeful.[16]

While Stevens was exploring Lake Chelan, four engineers with parties were exploring up the Methow, Entiat, and Wenatchee rivers as well as around Lake Chelan. One group at Indian Pass was studying the crest from the Suiattle River to Cady Pass, coming in from the west. C.W. Root explored Indian, Cascade, and Ruby passes and also the valley of the north fork of the Nooksack River. Beckler had a large party under John Joseph Donovan examining the Skagit River headwaters and "everything from the Snattle [sic] northward."[17] Another engineer under Beckler, a man named Sterritt, was on the Methow with pack trains. He planned to attempt a crossing from "Nakeetan" Creek to "Backus" (Bridge) Creek on June 12 and then report on the Stehekin and Cascade rivers route. Stevens was of the opinion that "there is a low pass from the Methow . . . but whether into Backus or into North Fork of Skagit, time only will tell. I have been in the saddle from 10 to 12 hours daily for the past ten days and am pretty well tired out."[18]

The letters of Stevens's assistant engineer, Charles Haskell, provide a glimpse into the frontier surveyor's life. Typically, he rode a horse when possible, and obtaining fresh meat was seldom a problem. In early 1890, Haskell had written to his mother from Demersville, Montana: "I wore the same suit that I wore last Summer, and took no overcoat. I used a flannel shirt, the only change. Wore heavy dutch socks and overshoes. We took one blanket apiece. . . . Our cooking utensils consisted of a frying pan, a coffee pot & three half pint cups."[19] Typical provisions consisted of flour, sugar, tea, coffee, bacon, salt, and baking powder. The cooking operation was basic: "Open the flour sack and sprinkle in baking powder and salt. Pour in cold water, then stir. Knead by hand to form dough; flatten and place in frying pan. Bake by the fire." An axe was used to pound coffee in the corner of a deerskin, and the men ate using their fingers and jackknives.[20]

Finding Stevens Pass

Before midsummer of 1890, Beckler had concluded that the Skagit, Chelan, and Methow routes should no longer be considered. In a letter to Hill on July

2, he called the reports of Ward's Pass also "unworthy of consideration," citing Hubert C. Ward's report to Thomas B. Morris of October 31, 1872, on the terrain for ten miles north of Little White Pass: "Here the main ridge is from six to ten thousand feet in height with numerous snow peaks [Glacier Peak] among which the north forks of the Wenatchee and Sauk head in glaciers." On August 30, he wrote Hill that "the Cascade pass is next to impracticable even with 12,000 foot tunnel and can only be used with Lake Chelan route which is also exceedingly difficult." Ward's, Chusalle, and Indian passes would require tunnels. The best pass found to date was another route near the head of the Methow, "near the junction of the Chelan range and the Cascade range."[21] After learning of the discovery of Stevens Pass, however, Beckler believed it was the best choice.

John F. Stevens now became the prime catalyst in establishing the line across the Cascade Range.[22] In May 1890, he had been optimistic about locating a route westward from the Wenatchee to the Sauk River. Meanwhile, he continued to entertain the idea of running the railroad line along Lake Chelan's shoreline and through a Skagit pass.[23] Sterritt had made a steamer trip up Lake Chelan, giving a more favorable report on the practicability of a line along the lake than expected. After rowing up the lake and making an exploration across Cascade Pass, however, Stevens concluded that "a direct line to Bellingham Bay was not feasible." As for Indian Pass, he later wrote that he "didn't like it at all." In his words: "There then was left the Wenatchee. From my studies I had found that the narrowest part of the Cascades must lie somewhere at the heads of the Wenatchee and Skykomish; in other words the Cascades were in a way like an hour glass with its waist at the heads of those rivers."[24]

Although his itinerary is difficult to follow, Stevens stated that he explored from Indian Pass along the crest to Snoqualmie Pass.[25] Years later, he summarized his rambling Cascade Range explorations:

In the early spring of 1890 I was placed in charge of reconnaissance and surveys of the country from Spokane to Puget Sound and from the Northern Pacific Railway to the British Columbia line, an area of some 45,000 square miles, with orders to find and locate the best line for the Great Northern Railway to the Sound. The only suggestion made to me was that only as a last resort would a parallelling of the Northern Pacific be considered. My instructions were very broad—"Get the best line." There had been some exploring done before my time, but I had no reports of its results then, and never have had. . . .

The process of reconnaissance for a railway line is largely one of elimination—to find out where not to go. Starting down the Spokane River I examined the Columbia River clear to Pasco. I studied the Northern Pacific from there to west of Stampede Pass. I also went through Snoqualmie Pass and down several miles into Cedar River. I went from the Columbia River west across the Rattlesnake Mountains, I think they were called, to Ellensburg and on again up to Snoqualmie. The stretch of country as far as Ellensburg is very forbidding, apparently being made of the remnants of rock and greasewood left over when the world was made. . . .

I examined every stream coming into the Columbia River from the north—Okanogan, San Poil, and Methow. There was naturally a strong desire on the part of the people there that the line should reach Bellingham Bay directly, and I could not afford to make any mistakes. I had an idea that I could get across from the Methow to the head of Chelan Lake and so on up and over Cascade Pass, but found it impracticable.[26]

During his traverse along the Cascade divide, Stevens noticed a particularly low gap. After making a hand-level elevation observation, he made up his mind "that the small creek which led east from this gap must of necessity be the head of Nason Creek."[27] In a 1928 memorandum, he remembered his reconnaissance and his intuition:

On one of the trips up Wenatchee Lake, I marked a creek coming into the foot of the Lake from the south, I followed this creek up but a short distance and found it turning sharply to the west, that is, coming directly from the high range. I had already noted a favorable looking gap through the top of the range, which apparently lay directly west of the turn in the creek above noted. I became convinced that this creek could head nowhere but in the gap I had crossed some time before on one of my trips along the crest of the range, and if so, the problem was solved.[28]

Upon returning to his Waterville headquarters, Stevens asked Haskell to travel to Lake Wenatchee and follow Nason Creek, examining the head of every fork.[29] He told Haskell of "the gap I had noted and that it must be a head of Nason Creek."

The result of this trip was exactly what I had hoped, and expected. The creek—afterwards named Nason Creek, headed directly in the gap, where Mr. Haskell blazed a large tree and marked it "Stevens Pass" which is the name it bears and which is carried on maps of that country. The Great Northern Ry. goes through this pass, as does also a motor car highway built and maintained by Chelan and King Counties, and which connects the Puget Sound region with Eastern Washington, this highway being officially known as "The Stevens Pass Highway."

There was no evidence whatever that the pass in question was known to anyone, although it may have been. There were no signs of any trails leading to or from it, within ten miles or more in either direction. No blazes on trees and no signs of any wanderers' camp or camp fires. Heavily timbered—covered with almost impenetrable brush, and not offering any hope that the mountains contained minerals, the region promised nothing to the prospector, while the Indians and Whites crossing the mountains used either the Snoqualmie on the south or the Indian Pass on the north for route of transit.[30]

Stevens recalled in a 1929 speech how he investigated the pass:

Immediately on Mr. Haskell's return I went to Stevens Pass and confirmed in every particular his report. Then I put two parties at work, one from the pass east, and one on the west side, as winter was coming and I had to know what was what. The east side party got along all right, but when I got the results of the preliminary survey from the party west, I was rather discouraged. The line as hastily run was impracticable, but deep snow prevented any further work that season. I thought of but little else that winter. I felt that I had not failed and that a line was there, and waking or sleeping it was on my mind.

Now you all may think that I was crazy and that only Conan Doyle could see it as I saw it, but I woke up one morning early in March with an idea. I have always thought that I dreamed it subconscious mentality probably. I started at once (I was living in Snohomish) and, picking up my faithful co-packer, John Maloney, at Sultan, went up into the mountains. We had no snowshoes, but by starting early the crust on the snow would hold us up for a few hours. We went on up the valley, and standing on a point above it I sketched out what was afterwards known as the Marten Creek loop. As soon as the snow melted enough, I sent the field party back there, and it laid the line as I had sketched it, and as it was built. This solved the problem.

I will add that when I had the preliminary lines of the switchback laid, I laid the line of the old tunnel, alignment, and gradient, 7 years before it was completed, and not a rod of new line had to be built nor a rod thrown away to make connection with the permanent line.[31]

The actual locating of the railroad line that would cross Stevens Pass began in late spring 1891.[32]

Avalanche and a New Tunnel

Hill eventually became impatient with the progress on the line. Uncharacteristically, he ordered speedy construction that took precedence over safety and route quality. The result was that his engineers designed a twelve-mile switchback complex over Stevens Pass that had four percent grades.[33] The last spike in the transcontinental railroad was hammered on January 6, 1893, near Scenic, almost three years after the first horse trail was built across Stevens Pass. Beckler's engineering and track-laying accomplishment was unequaled. He had built over eight hundred miles from Havre, Montana, to Everett in two and a half years.

The unwieldy switchback route served traffic from January 1893 to December 1900, when the Cascade Tunnel was completed. Tunnel work began in 1897, with six to eight hundred men working continuously. The Wellington and Cascade tunnel camps sprang up on opposite sides of the pass, typical construction sites with rowdy saloons and gambling. When the 2.63-mile tunnel was completed—at a cost of $25 million—the track elevation was reduced from 4,059 feet to 3,383 feet, and all grades over 2.2 percent were eliminated.[34]

Even though the Cascade Tunnel was a widely heralded engineering achievement, snowslides both east and west of the tunnel posed a constant danger in winter and spring. There were also sections of track exposed to snowslides in narrow Tumwater Canyon. At first, there had been little evidence of avalanche problems on the heavily timbered western slopes along the line located by Stevens, but the slope was avalanche-prone because timber above the line had been destroyed by fire. "Snowslides of increasing extent developed and the need of protection became apparent as early as 1903," one engineer wrote.[35] Snow depths to twenty feet were recorded in the winter of 1897–1898, and at least fifteen hundred men struggled to clear the road. There were also heavy snowfalls in the winters of 1909–1910, 1912–1913, and 1915–1916, and trackage covered by sheds increased rapidly between 1911 and 1917.[36]

A disregard for the avalanche danger west of Stevens Pass resulted in one of the world's great train disasters. In one of the worst storms in Pacific Northwest memory, heavy snowfall in late February 1910—sometimes as much as a foot per hour—had brought accumulations of eleven feet in six days. On all steep Cascade Range slopes, especially those denuded of timber by previous slides or fire, there was an extreme potential for wet-snow avalanches.[37] "Huge drifts block all trains," screamed an *Everett Herald* headline on February 23, and the paper reported that three trains were stalled on each side of the tunnel.

Despite the continuing heavy snowstorms, local train Number 25 persevered, pulling through the Cascade Tunnel on February 25. About four hundred yards west of Wellington station, the train was stalled by the heavy snow accumulation and could not back through the tunnel because of slides at the eastern portal.[38] A snowplow stalled at Horseshoe Tunnel to the west could not reach the Wellington siding. Backing the train into the tunnel to avoid a potential slide was considered, but the heavy coal smoke would have been too dangerous in the insufficiently ventilated tunnel.

For six days, the Great Northern's passengers were marooned as record drifts piled up from the unabated snowfall. Extra trains and workmen sent from Everett were powerless before the winter onslaught, but a few passengers escaped by trudging through the storm to Scenic. Helped by the train crew, five men dressed in business suits, coats, and shoes walked down the track to Windy Point, then slid some eight hundred feet to safety. The "escape party" made it to the bottom unhurt by "pulling their overcoats over their buttocks and their coat tails up between their legs."[39]

On March 1, at 1:20 A.M., an immense, thousand-foot-wide avalanche on the barren and burnt mountain slope struck the train, hurling the cars chaotically into Tye Canyon, leaving most of the bodies of the 101 victims under twenty feet of snow. Only seventeen persons survived; engineer Charles Andrews, who was not in the train, was the only witness.[40] Not long after the accident, the railroad changed the name of Wellington station to Tye. Even with the tunnel, crossing Stevens Pass was still tedious, and a seven-car passenger train required three locomotives. Despite the availability of rotary snowplows, clearing off after a winter storm took valuable time.

By 1925, the company had concluded that a 7.79-mile lower tunnel should be built to permit the railroad to abandon the portion of the west-slope line that was subject to avalanches. The Chumstick Line was projected to eliminate the high grades and snowslide menace in Tumwater Canyon, and a seventy-five-mile electrification was planned from Wenatchee to Skykomish. Electrification and the new line changes would allow the operation of five-thousand-ton freight trains, which could reduce running time by three and a half hours. Construction began in late November 1925, with field camps at Berne and Scenic. The main tunnel, eighteen feet wide and twenty-five feet high, was begun on March 6, 1926.[41]

Stevens, now serving as project engineer, was as indefatigable and compulsive as ever. Ralph and Muriel Hidy remind us of his importance:

> There were times when he was simultaneously checking and pushing almost two dozen significant projects. He directed construction of about a thousand miles of new railway. To admit that he attracted able assistants and worked under vigorous top management does not detract from Stevens' indisputably outstanding service to the railroad. The tasks called for a driver with technical skills and imagination; the railroad benefited by having such a man.[42]

With improved technology and engineering methods, the new Cascade Tunnel beneath Stevens Pass—the longest railroad bore in America—was completed on December 24, 1928, in a remarkably short time. The cost for the tunnel, line relocation, and electrification was over $25 million. About thirty-four miles of high-speed track replaced forty-three miles of steep and winding line; track elevation was reduced to 2,881 feet; and high grades, curvature, and miles of snowsheds were eliminated.[43]

At the dedication of the new tunnel on January 12, 1929, when the first train ran through, a coast-to-coast radio broadcast with President Herbert Hoover as principal speaker was made from a banquet at the Scenic construction camp. Stevens made a speech, recalling the discovery of the pass named for him. For the immense celebratory feast, attended by some six hundred prominent citizens, one of the cooks made a five-foot-long relief-model cake of the Cascade Range.[44] L.C. Gilman, vice-president of the railway, proclaimed: "The eastern and western sections of the state have been separated by the barrier of the Cascade Mountains, and to-night for transportation purposes that barrier has been removed." The Wenatchee River watershed lay distant from the primary routes of trade by overland explorers, fur trappers, and immigrants in the nineteenth century. Ultimately, however, its corridor, like that of the Yakima, became a route of travel and communication.

Encouraging Tourism

Lake Chelan had not been a satisfactory railroad route for Beckler and his engineer-surveyors, but early in the twentieth century the Great Northern began to encourage tourism there, as it already had in Montana's Glacier

National Park. In August 1916, well-known author Mary Roberts Rinehart and her entourage arrived at Stehekin at the railroad's invitation, and the story of her trip was later featured in *Tenting To-Night*. Accompanied by local photographer and naturalist Lawrence D. Lindsley and horsepacker Dan Devore, the Rinehart party went on a hunting expedition, riding over Cloudy Pass to Agnes Creek and from the Stehekin River across Cascade Pass to the Skagit. The party was well equipped for hunting, with shotguns, a Savage repeater, and two Winchester rifles. "Silent Lawrie" Lindsley, who knew all the ferns and flowers, carried a Colt revolver, and the accompanying forest supervisor had a .38 revolver. "We were entirely prepared to meet the whole German army," Rinehart wrote, but "it is rather sad to relate that, with all this preparation, we killed nothing."[45] One consolation was that the northern lights were visible from Lyman Lakes. Rinehart, who was not as accustomed to the mountains as the railroad surveyors, was concerned about the "horrors" of the trail across Cascade Pass. Inevitably, she commented about the mosquitoes: "There was no getting away from them. Open our mouths and we inhaled them. They hung in dense clouds about us and fought over the best locations."[46]

The railway continued to promote the scenic lake as a place for saddle and camping trips. A 1921 brochure praised "a Summer Playground for the People of the Pacific Northwest," touting the many vacation destinations such as Glacier Peak, Cloudy Pass, Cascade Pass, Trapper Lake, Doubtful Lake, Agnes Canyon, Bridge Creek, Boston Peak, and the great glaciers of Sahale and "Arrowhead."[47]

It would still be some time before most of the alpine spectacles in the northern Cascades were known to the public as they are today. The persistent Great Northern surveyors added much to the knowledge of the Cascades between Stevens Pass and the Skagit River, and they successfully located a difficult cross-mountain transportation link. By the 1890s, when the frontier era in America was drawing to a close, the new railroad—spurred by James Hill's philosophy—stimulated logging, agriculture, and commerce in a once-remote part of the nation.

Illustrations ∼

Semiahmoo Bay, from Bluff near Entrance of "Mud Bay," with Camp Semiahmoo, Drayton's Harbor, and Distant View of Mt. Baker to E, 1857–1862, *by James M. Alden. Mt. Baker is the dominant pe1ak, with Mt. Shuksan to its left. The Twin Sisters are to the far right. The American camp is on the shoreline directly beneath Mt. Shuksan. The ships in the bay are the* Active *(left) and the* Satellite. *Alden sketch 5, cartographic series 70, RG 76, National Archives.*

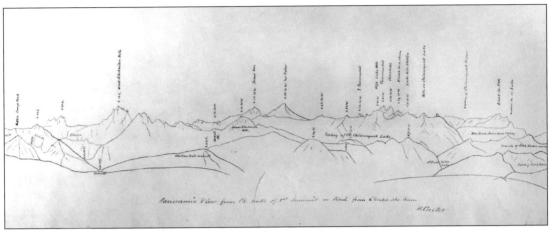

Panoramic View from Pk. north of 1st Summit on Trail from Chuch-che-hum, *sketch by Henry Custer, August 1859, from the top of Peak 6600 feet (plus) east of Chilliwack Lake, redrawn as an office sketch. In the left foreground are Camp Peak and Mt. Custer (behind), then the Depot-Maselpanik Creek pass, the higher Whatcom Trail summit. To the right is Paleface Creek ("1st Creek below Lake"), the Post-Hicks Creek valleys ("Noo-kweh-kwa-lum"), and upper Silverhope Creek ("branch of Kleh-kwun-num"). On the skyline are Twin Spires (Mox Peaks) on the left, with Mt. Spickard missing; Mt. Redoubt ("West Klahaihu Mtn"), Mad Eagle Peak, Nodoubt Peak ("Lower Kla-hai-hu Mtn."), Mt. Shuksan, Mt. Baker, Mt. Larrabee ("? Tummeahái"), Mt. Lindeman ("High Lake Mtn"), American Border Peak (ATummeahái), Slesse Mountain ("Senehsái"), Mt. Rexford ("Ensahkwachum"), Mt. Webb ("Mtn. on Chiloweyuck Lake"), Welch Peak ("Kleht-la-keh"), and Williams Peak ("Custer's Pk. on Lake"). Custer marked summits on this view with magnetic north bearings. Map 39, cartographic series 69, RG 76, National Archives.*

Henry Custer, from a funeral card, 1862. Custer participated in the Pacific Railroad Surveys and was a topographer with the Northwest Boundary Survey. OHS neg., OrHi 91223.

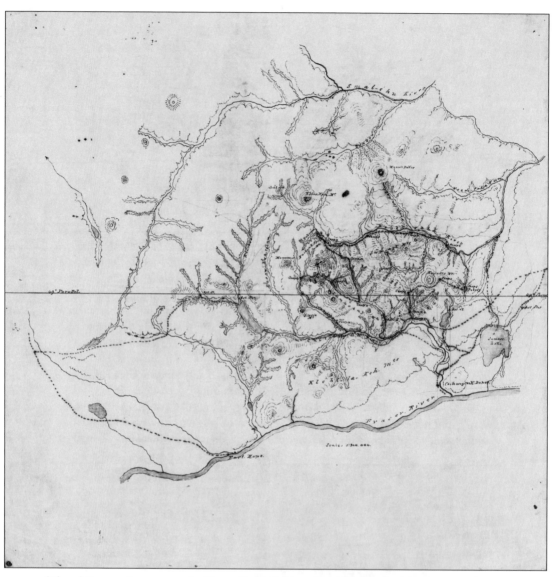

(Above) Reconnaissance map by Henry Custer (although not his handwriting), 1859, scale 1:300,000. Note that south is at the top of the map. Map 19-2, cartographic series 69, RG 76, National Archives.

(Above right) Map of the Country from Lake Superior to the Pacific Ocean from the Latest Explorations and Surveys, *to accompany the report of Edwin F. Johnson, Northern Pacific Railroad, 1867. Library of Congress, Geography and Map Division.*

(Below right) Officers of the British North American Boundary Commission, 1859. Standing (left to right): Lt. Samuel Anderson, astronomer; Capt. John Summerfield Hawkins, head of the commission; Lt. Charles W. Wilson, secretary and supply officer. Sitting (left to right): Capt. Charles John Darrah, astronomer; John Keast Lord, assistant naturalist and veterinarian; Capt. Robert Walsely Haig, senior astronomer. BC Archives, HP 13970 (A-05429).

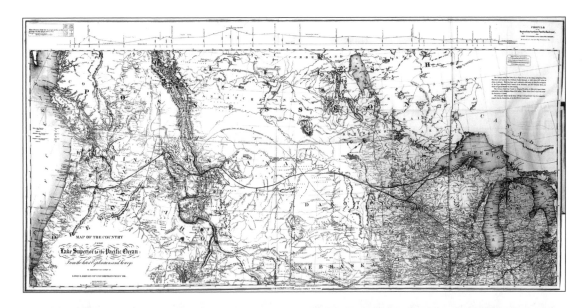

Lt. Henry H. Pierce, leader of the expedition that crossed Cascade Pass in August 1882. Trinity College Archives, Hartford, Connecticut.

John G. Parke of the Topographical Engineers as brevet major-general. Special Collections Division, U.S. Military Academy Library.

(Above) Fording the Cascade River near the mouth of Boulder Creek, August 31, 1882, sketch by Alfred Downing . Pierce is on the left, with officer's stripes on his pants. Guide Joseph La Fleur is in the river on the left, after being swept from his pony; Lt. Backus, in the center, is in the same predicament. MSCUA, University of Washington Libraries, UW22020.

(Left) Mountain on Klahaihu Creek (Bear Mountain) from the upper Chilliwack River, lithograph from a sketch by George Gibbs in 1859. From Journal of the American Geographical Society of New York 4 (1874); OHS Research Library, OHS neg., OrHi. 87188.

Pencil drawing of tents at Camp Sumass in 1859, by Francis Herbst. E 208, RG 76, National Archives

Sappers clearing the International Boundary vista in the forest near the Moyie River, between the Cascade Range and the Rocky Mountains, 1860–1861. Joseph Smith Harris Papers, MSS S 1293, Beinecke Library, Yale University.

Part 3 〜

Miners, Mountaineers, and Tourists

Davis Ranch Mile 21½

The Davis Ranch on the Skagit River trail, c. 1898. Darius Kinsey, photographer (Glee Davis Collection, courtesy Mrs. Jeanita Davis Callahan; OHS neg., OrHi 85678)

12

FROM WAGON ROADS TO HIGHWAYS

It is doubtful if the snow ever leaves these so-called passes, and any further expenditures would be a waste of money.
                                        —Washington State Road Commission, 1895

Wagon roads in the northern Cascades were at first piecemeal enterprises, funded and built by cattlemen, miners, and citizens of towns that stood to profit by their construction. The Kittitas Valley wagon road to the Blewett mines, for example, was built in 1883 along a wagon-trail route to serve both livestock and mining interests. No road project, however, captured as much public attention as the one through Snoqualmie Pass, which was vital if commerce other than that served by the railroad was ever to link the western and eastern parts of the state. After the Pacific Railroad Survey failed to find a suitable pass through the range in 1853 and in view of the continued uncertainties of the Naches Pass route, the U.S. Army made a study of Snoqualmie Pass. In 1859, it was estimated that a good wagon road of 250 miles over "Snoqualmoo Pass" would cost $100,000.[1] After Arthur A. Denny and his party explored the pass in 1865 and Seattle residents raised money for construction, a rough trail was completed in 1869 and cattle were driven to market across the pass. The trail was trampled thoroughly in 1879, when it was reported that four thousand head of cattle had been driven across. Improvements were made slowly, and a toll road, sponsored by cattlemen, was opened in 1884 (see chapter 4). Many immigrants also passed over the road on their way to Puget Sound.

Boosters continued to support other passes as well. Both Snohomish and Chelan counties proposed the old Cady Pass trail as a highway route. In 1913, county officials went with a party that included photographer J.A. Juleen to scout the route and found its scenery better than that of Stevens Pass.[2] Nevertheless, state and county highway officials came to favor Stevens Pass because it was more direct. The road across this important defile north of Snoqualmie, named the Cascade Scenic Highway, was completed on July 11, 1925.

To the south of Snoqualmie, a road over Chinook Pass was constructed in 1930, with an elaborate series of switchbacks across the fragile subalpine terrain. The poorly conceived route was open only seasonally, however, while both the Snoqualmie and Stevens crossings became year-round roads. There were also those who promoted the old Carlton Pass railroad-survey route, but they had been unable to get the state and the U.S. Forest Service to adopt their plans. Eventually, nearby White Pass was chosen as a more suitable route.

Many special-destination roads were built on the slopes of Mt. Rainier, Mt. Adams, and Mt. Baker. One of the most unusual proposals, put forward in 1943 by the American Legion, was a plan for a toll road to the summit of Mt. Pilchuck. Various political and civic groups endorsed the road, which would wind its way through the forests and rocky cliffs to a vista house at the craggy summit. In seeking funds for the scheme, the sponsors even tried to persuade the military to use the mountain as an observation point.[3] Across the International Boundary, the Hope-Princeton Highway was completed in 1949, approximately following the route surveyed by the Royal Engineers. Part of the highway crosses the E.C. Manning Provincial Park.

While the Stevens Pass route proved to be a success, business groups in Wenatchee kept probing for a road elsewhere, to the north. One of their schemes was a route through Buck Creek Pass (near Glacier Peak). As late as 1937, the Forest Service was petitioned to approve a road through this pristine mountain wilderness. The hopes of the boosters were eventually fulfilled—though not until 1972—with the construction of the North Cascades Highway across Rainy and Washington passes.

One of the first attempts to find a suitable cross-Cascade route north of Stevens Pass came in April 1886 when the Banning Austin party made an effort to explore the north fork of the Nooksack River and locate a route to the gold prospects of Ruby Creek. Apparently, the party—which included Hamilton C. Wells, E.P. and C.E. Chase, William Garrett, and William Thompson— followed the Nooksack and then Bagley Creek to reach the watershed divide east of Mt. Baker that would later be known as Austin Pass. In 1891, in another attempt to find a northern wagon road, Austin, Wells, and Charles Bagley followed prospecting trails to their end and then apparently continued into the headwaters of the Nooksack's north fork.[4]

In 1893, miners and cattlemen petitioned Whatcom County commissioners to build a trail from the Nooksack road end (Maple Falls) to Little Beaver Creek on the Skagit in order to avoid the treacherous Skagit Canyon. An appeal to the state legislature resulted in a $20,000 appropriation for a two-hundred-mile-long road from Whatcom to Ruby Creek and on to the Columbia River.[5] Also in 1893, the Board of State Road Commissioners engaged Austin and R.M. Lyle to survey for a Ruby Creek toll road. Both men were from the Whatcom area and had considerable mountain wilderness experience. Taking enough supplies for a month, they left Thompson's ranch on September 7 for Austin Pass (which they named at that time).[6] Austin blithely reported that the pass was practicable for either a wagon road or a railroad.

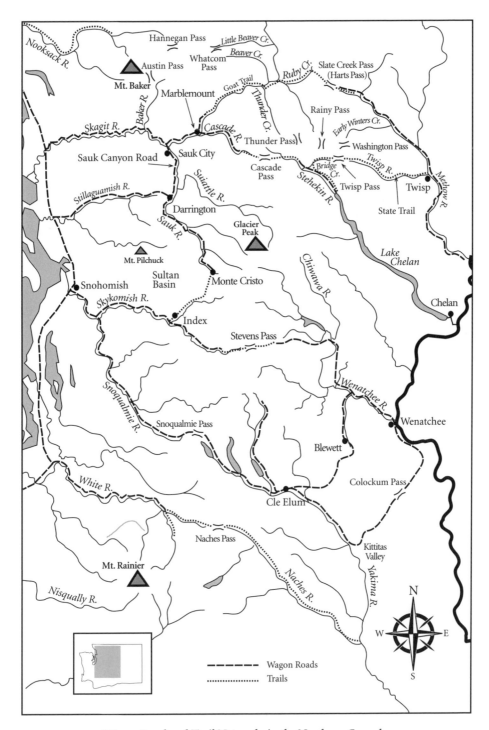

Wagon Road and Trail Networks in the Northern Cascades

The two men hiked the trackless Ruth Creek Valley (naming Ruth Mountain for the daughter of President Grover Cleveland; the creek later took the same name) to the pass at its head (which they named for road commissioner Thomas P. Hannegan). The two men noted blazes in the valley and saw signs of an Indian camp. "From a mountain near 'Hannegan Pass' [probably Hannegan Peak]," they reported, "we could see the range as far as the boundary line." They were correct in concluding "there is no other pass between Shuksan and the boundary line."[7] According to their report, the men retraced their route to follow the main branch of the Nooksack River (the north fork), then explored to within three miles of its head (the Nooksack Cirque). "The mountains on each side began growing steeper until ending in a perpendicular wall, on the north east side of Mount Shuksan and formed an impassable barrier." They were blocked by "cliffs . . . rising sheer and abrupt above us to a height of 4000 feet shutting out the sunshine like a black cloud."[8]

Sources disagree on what happened next. According to the account published by Percival Jeffcott, the men followed a faint Indian trail for the opening they saw in the Chilliwack-Skagit River watershed, then crossed Whatcom Pass and later Beaver Pass to reach Ruby Creek. Halted by the canyons downstream, they hiked north to Fort Hope. Other sources deny the account, and Austin was soon contradicted because he described Hannegan Pass as leading into the Baker River even though the mouth of Ruby Creek was their objective. The minutes of the October 13, 1893, State Road Commission meeting indicate that the men returned from Hannegan Pass (or Whatcom Pass) and then ended the exploration by examining the Nooksack Cirque.[9] One newspaper story discounted most of Austin's reconnaissances, complaining that his "excursion"— which cost an estimated $600—was a "wild goose trail." C.W. Root, who accompanied William Garrett of the 1886 Austin party and reportedly crossed four times between Hannegan Pass and the upper Skagit in the summer of 1894, claimed that Austin simply sat on mountain crests and let his imagination roam.[10]

The State Road Commission ruled that Austin Pass was too difficult and, further, that the route did not lead to Ruby Creek. In his report, Austin had proposed that a wagon road be built over Hannegan and Whatcom passes to the Skagit. But the commission, wisely, vetoed the route, concluding: "Several glaciers are close to the line and mountains 8000 to 9000 feet high are all around. It is doubtful if the snow ever leaves these so-called passes, and any further expenditures would be a waste of money." Because Whatcom County failed to appropriate its share of the road money, the state withheld its road-construction funds. Despite certain geographical inaccuracies in Austin's report, he did reach and traverse important new alpine terrain. A trail was later built over the route he and Lyle explored, and in 1896 pack trains were taken over Hannegan Pass to the drainage of the Chilliwack.

In 1894, the State Road Commission hired Bert Huntoon and H.M. Wellman to search for a route near Mt. Baker. They followed the south fork of the Nooksack River, reaching a "Baker Pass" south of the mountain. For the adventure and to gain a grand viewpoint, they also visited Austin Pass. They concluded that no good location for a wagon road existed near Mt. Baker.

In 1895, Whatcom and Skagit County legislators cooperated to pass a bill for a state-supported Cascade route. The legislature approved funds that year for a road from Bellingham Bay to the Skagit and also up the Skagit Valley to Marblemount. Beginning on July 22, road examiners E.M. Wilson, R.O. Welts, and J.H. Watson studied four potential cross-Cascade wagon-road routes. In all, some five hundred miles were examined and evaluated before the survey ended on September 11. With pack animals, the three men began to explore the Slate Creek route, where they hoped to make use of mining trails, but they proved useless because of steep grades and the rocky Skagit Canyon. The examiners hiked the famed Goat Trail and later reported: "It is a picturesque place and rugged enough for the most ardent mountain climber." The route was rejected because of the heavy rock work, excavation, and bridging that would have been necessary.[11]

Building a four-foot-wide wagon road from Marblemount to Twisp via Slate Creek (Harts) Pass, a distance of ninety-seven miles, would cost $20,739. The more expensive Thunder Creek Pass route would require a ninety-foot bridge to cross the deep Skagit gorge, and it had a ten-mile alpine section where even a trail had never been built. The terrain "in places is so steep it is almost impossible to get a foot hold." The Board of State Road Commissioners eventually favored the Cascade (Skagit) Pass route, which also crossed Twisp Pass; the distance was 78½ miles, and the estimated cost was $31,362. "Cascade Pass has an icy appearance in summer as the Glaciers hug it close," the report cautioned, while Twisp Pass "was green and inviting . . . ornamented with a profusion of wild flowers." The route via Granite Creek, Rainy Pass, and Early Winters Creek was calculated at 105½ miles with a cost estimate of $24,962. The examiners noted that "a trail had never been even blazed" for eighteen miles on Granite Creek. A blueprint map of the route shows "The Towers" positioned near Washington Pass (the Liberty Bell massif).[12]

Some work was contracted in 1896 as a result of the previous year's surveys, and Merritt E. Field of Stehekin obtained a contract to build boardinghouses and camps.[13] At the time, there was a four-foot-wide wagon road from Marblemount to Gilbert's cabin and from Pershall's to Bridge Creek on the Stehekin River. Work continued fitfully on the "Cascade Wagon Road," but the result of the project was nothing more than a pack trail across Cascade and Twisp passes, although state road maps soon marked it as a wagon road. Three years later, in 1899, the legislature appropriated $20,000 to build an actual wagon road along the route, but apparently little construction took place.

One of the last attempts to locate a way through this part of the northern Cascades was actually a railroad survey conducted in 1900. A locating party for the Bellingham Bay and British Columbia Railroad completed a reconnaissance over Hannegan and Whatcom passes, essentially retracing the route followed by the Austin-Lyle party seven years earlier. Between August 23 and September 7, engineer J.J. Cryderman led six men in mapping, photographing, and recording observations of both natural and cultural features in the region. Traveling by rail and then wagon road, the men reached the end of the road at Shuksan, where a few mining cabins stood near the north fork of the Nooksack River. Continuing with horses, the party traveled eastward, heading up and over Hannegan Pass. Cryderman noted:

> On the east side of Hannegan Pass there is considerable timber. . . . Indications of minerals are good mostly as on the west side of the Pass, gold and copper. However owing to the present inaccessible location of the country, few [mineral] locations have been made and practically no work has been done. . . . Horses have been taken from here to Whatcom Pass and to the mouth of Indian Creek, but it was when the River was low and the bed of the Chilliwack was used for much of the distance. From Whatcom Pass there is no trail until within two miles of the mouth of Big Beaver creek, where there is one from McMillan's ranch on the Skagit River.[14]

When the reconnaissance was completed, Cryderman wrote a report for John Joseph Donovan, the railroad's general superintendent. He stressed the scenic views, the game (bear and goat), and the "abundant peaks for the mountain climber to struggle with," but no construction was ever undertaken.[15]

In 1906, the State Highway Commission estimated that three-quarters of the $85,200 in state road funds appropriated had been spent—along with $14,000 in county funds—with "no passable roads to show for it."[16] The net results of this expenditure are a horse trail from Marblemount to the summit of the Methow range, a distance of about 30 miles; about 12 miles of wagon trail between the head of Twisp River; the town of Twisp; and a road and trail about 14 miles in length of the Stehekin river.[17] In 1909, the legislature appropriated $30,000 for the cross-Cascade road, but the road commissioners refused to spend it. The legislature appropriated even more money in the years following, yet little construction was done.

On June 9, 1921, Charles I. Signer, locating engineer for the Department of Public Works, left Marblemount with packhorses for a survey of the Skagit Canyon and then Cascade Pass. He was impressed with the difficulty the canyon presented for a roadway and the steep slope to the pass. For example, he described Boston Creek as "a glacier stream that is almost on end with a wide boulder bar cut by many channels and is the path of a perpetual snow slide." After studying Slate Creek and Cascade passes, Signer concluded: "I do not consider either route practical for a highway at the present time, or in the near future, but I recommend that a good pack or horse trail be constructed."[18] Yet, by 1933, the Bureau of Public Roads naively believed that the Cascade-Twisp Pass route was a logical one, principally because of pressure on the legislature and state officials by county commissioners, chambers of commerce, and the Cascade Highway Association of Skagit Valley.[19] In 1932, a U.S. Forest Service survey recommended a route over Washington Pass and Cascade Pass, but nothing came of it. The Forest Service also surveyed Twisp Pass, favoring it as the best crossing from the Methow Valley, and funds were appropriated to clear a roadway west of Twisp.

A Cascade Tunnel survey bill was introduced in the Washington state legislature in 1933. Chambers of commerce throughout the region had urged construction of a tunnel as part of a "Cascade Highway." Urgent requests had been made for a "master highway" across the northern counties to develop agriculture, logging, and mining in the region. This appeal from the Colville Grange was typical: "Automobile facilities, together with the development of the country and products have increased to such an extent that Trans-Pacific Highway in the northern part of the State has become a necessity."[20]

In 1933, the Cascade River road was built twelve and a half miles beyond Marblemount, and Mine to Market Roads funds were used to extend the road to the junction of the north and south forks (at Mineral Park) in the 1940s.[21] Soon afterward, a mining road on the opposite drainage was extended into Horseshoe Basin from the Stehekin River Road, and the cross-range wagon road continued to appear on many maps as if it actually existed. After World War II, the concept of a mine-to-market road persisted, and ultimately a roadway was built from the west to within three miles of Cascade Pass.

In 1945, the Washington state legislature authorized yet another study, one that unfolded into years of survey effort, mapping, plans, and road proposals. Conservationists preferred the Slate Creek (Harts) Pass route, but planning engineers disliked the route's high cut and the tunnel and bridging costs required and preferred the Rainy Pass–Washington Pass route.[22] By 1959, the final agreements were concluded, and thirty-five building contracts were awarded for the work. On September 2, 1972, the North Cross–State Highway Association held an opening-day "victory ceremony" to celebrate the completion of an automobile road near the route Alexander Ross had scouted more than 150 years earlier. Although the Washington State Department of Highways claimed that it had built the North Cascades Highway without destroying natural beauty (an impossibility because of the scars remaining from road cuts), conservationists did not wholeheartedly agree. While the highway encouraged tourism and provided new access to recreational areas, its value as a transportation corridor is debatable. Given the buffers of legislated wilderness areas and the establishment of North Cascades National Park, this highway seems destined to be the final traffic corridor built across this mountain heartland.

Adventurous Settlers

All of the hundreds and then thousands of pioneer settlers who encroached on the Cascade Range valleys were explorers in a sense, as they learned about new places and added to the regional lore. Although the settlements around Puget Sound grew rapidly after 1850, both exploration and the development of resources were affected by the available methods of transportation and communication. Inland travel to the foothills of the Cascades was largely limited to the use of canoes and horses. Almost impenetrable coniferous forests impeded not only exploration but also prospecting, hunting, and trapping. There were few wagon roads, and the early trails were rough and difficult to maintain.

Most of the new arrivals on either flank of the northern Cascades were occupied clearing land for agriculture and livestock and erecting buildings. They used existing wagon roads for travel and to carry their goods to market and found they were too busy to explore in the mountains or appreciate the scenery. Some settlers turned to prospecting and ventured beyond existing trails, but few left a record of their movements. Fortunately, details of some trailblazing journeys have been preserved, and they have contributed significantly to the recorded knowledge of the region.

One of the earliest settler-explorers who struggled through the forest wilderness was James Longmire. After his party of immigrants came over the Naches Pass trail in 1853, Longmire settled south of the Nisqually River near the base of Mt. Rainier. His prairie homestead—beyond the lands grazed by stock of the HBC's Puget Sound Agricultural Company—was the first permanent settlement within the present-day boundaries of Mount Rainier National Park. Longmire built trails and, as an expert on the area, guided surveying and exploring parties through the Nisqually and Cowlitz wilderness. Together with William Packwood, who had settled in the fertile Nisqually River Valley bottom in 1847, he explored an old Indian trail up the Nisqually in July 1858 and considered building a wagon road across the range. The following summer, with the hope of finding a route to the Naches River, Packwood, Longmire, and W. Kirtley again went up the Nisqually. They reached the Cowlitz River Valley but thought they had arrived at the opening of the Naches, an error due to their misconception that Mt. Rainier was on the Cascade summit. This pioneering party, which left a blazed trail, believed it had found an easy route across the range, but no road was built here.[23] In 1867, when the Northern Pacific Railroad sent surveyors across Bear Prairie to the Cowlitz, there was still no horse trail.

In 1883, when returning from an ascent of Mt. Rainier (see chapter 13), Longmire followed his stray horse into a meadow and discovered mineral springs there. He immediately filed a mineral claim for about twenty acres and built a trail from Bear Prairie to Longmire Springs. In 1884, he erected buildings amid the tall evergreens in an area that is now within the national park.[24]

After the toll road to Mt. Rainier was completed to Longmire in 1891, following the old Cowlitz trail, both Indian Henry's farm on the Mashel River (near present-day Eatonville) and Longmire Springs became popular stopovers for recreational travelers. The success of the resort also helped accelerate the movement for a national park.[25]

Some of the settlers in the Cowlitz River Valley were part of a migration that began in the 1890s of southern Appalachian highlanders to the mountain communities of the Pacific Northwest. The highlanders brought their backwoods style, idioms, woodcraft skills, and traditional subsistence methods of hunting and farming to the upper Cowlitz, the Lewis River Valley, and locations in Snohomish and Skagit counties. They found fertile land for farms in the alluvial river bottoms, where they cleared land, hunted, and developed dairies. The creation of the Rainier Forest Preserve in 1897 halted new settlement in the upper Cowlitz Valley until 1906. Then, until 1914, settlement was restricted to those who received permission from the Forest Service. The forest boundaries were later changed to exclude valley bottoms.[26]

Other newcomers included Snohomish pioneer Emory C. Ferguson, who built a trail up the north fork of the Skykomish and over Cady Pass in 1860 with a view to transporting goods directly to the British Columbia goldfields, avoiding the Fraser River. The Cady Trail was soon abandoned, although forest supervisor Albert H. Sylvester found evidence of it sixty years later.[27] West of Stevens Pass, almost beneath the steep flanks of the spectacular Index Peaks, Amos Gunn settled in 1889 at what became the town of Index. There he built a home that also served as a hotel for prospectors and surveyors. Originally from Illinois, Gunn had served in the Civil War before coming to the Cascades. He also became an active trail builder.

The low divide between the Sauk River and the north fork of the Stillaguamish, long used by Skagit Indians as a portage and tribal meeting place, became the site of Darrington. When the Wilmans road to Monte Cristo was completed in 1891 (see chapter 14), settlers began to arrive at the scenic watershed. By 1895, at least twenty homesteads had been established between Darrington and the foot of Mt. Forgotten.[28] Among those who came to the area were the Neste brothers—Knute, Ole, and Ted—who staked claims on Jumbo Mountain. Charles Wellman discovered gold on the north flank of Whitehorse Mountain. In about 1891, miners Matt and Charles Niederprum came to Whitehorse, leaving a cabin that many hikers and climbers would later come across. Homesteader Walter H. Higgins had a mountain named for him in 1887, and five years later John Higgins and his companions climbed to the summit.

Darrington received its name from a committee of settlers charged with finding a name for the post office (even though the town and area had not yet been surveyed). Someone suggested "Norma," while a Mr. Christopher proposed "Darrington," his mother's maiden name. The vote was tied four to four, so papers with the two names were thrown into the air, and "Darrington" fell face up. Some soon called the place "Daring-town," an appropriate nickname for the rough-and-ready backwoods locale.[29] Timber harvesting was the mainstay of economic life in Darrington, with special value placed on western red cedar because of its durability and versatility. The focus returned to mining in 1903, however, when a promising copper ore was discovered on nearby Canyon Creek. A trail and tramway were built for hauling machinery, but the boom project was never completed.

Other pioneers who located along the Sauk River Valley included William Pugh from Missouri, who homesteaded below the mountain that took his name. Sam Strom, a Norwegian, settled just upriver from Darrington in 1893, where he studied the English dictionary during the winter. Strom was the regional constable for fourteen years, and he and his neighbor A.H. Dubor assisted with the first government mapping surveys in the Sauk, Suiattle, and White Chuck River drainages.[30]

There was no more versatile pioneer family in the northern Cascades than that of James Bedal, who moved from Illinois and married the daughter of Wawetkin, a Sauk Indian chief. In 1892, the family moved from Sauk Prairie to the Sauk forks (which would become Bedal), where they made a living cutting cedar and driving the logs downriver for shingle bolts. Son Harry worked for the U.S. Forest Service, trapped on Bedal Creek (where he had a claim and cabin), mined at Goat Lake, and helped construct the lookout building on Three Fingers. In 1925, he packed supplies for The Mountaineers on an outing from Barlow Pass to Glacier Peak. Sisters Edith and Jeane, meanwhile, picked berries and ran a packing service for miners. Nels Bruseth, a forest ranger, later told a story about a Mrs. Moorehouse who had stopped at Bedal. She exclaimed, "This must be China, I can't go any farther," and Sauk forks became known as Orient. The Moorehouses established a trading post that would compete with Bedal's, but the Bedals absorbed their homestead in 1896.[31]

Settlers on the Skagit River

A few pioneer settler-prospectors braved the Skagit River Valley. One of them was John McMillan. Lured by Fraser River gold, he came from Ontario and in 1884 homesteaded about two miles above the mouth of Big Beaver Creek.[32] In running trap lines for marten and beaver along the upper Skagit, he must have been one of the first non-Indians to enter the remote Big and Little Beaver Creek branch valleys, whose glacier-water sources are in the jagged Picket Range. McMillan panned for gold along Ruby Creek and ran a packing business for miners with his string of horses and mules. During his homesteading years, he opened the old Fort Hope trail to Ruby Creek. He wintered his animals at Big Beaver Meadows and got grass at the Whitworth ranch, about four miles north of the International Boundary on the Skagit.

A close friend of McMillan's was George Holmes, the first African-American in the locality. A former slave from Virginia, Holmes came to the Skagit in 1895 and built a cabin near Ruby Creek, where he became a successful prospector (reportedly clearing $7,000 in a single year on a lease of the Original Discovery Mine). Possibly because of the location's value to the Forest Service, the agency did not try to remove Holmes, as it had other squatters on its land. After he died in 1922, the Forest Service used his buildings as a guard station and as a camp for packers and trail crews.[33]

Tommy Rowland, another settler on the upper Skagit, arrived from Canada in the early 1880s. He built a large log cabin and barn, cultivated vegetables, and grew hay on a terrace of the Skagit's east bank across from the Big Beaver; he also mined along Ruby Creek. Periodically, he and McMillan lived on each other's property. Rowland's lower location was eventually taken over by the Forest Service, and by 1917 it was listed as the Rowland guard station. In the late 1930s, the dammed waters of the Skagit flooded the area.[34]

On the Cascade River, French Canadian prospector Gilbert Landre, who arrived in 1888, built a small log cabin closely beneath the north face of Johannesburg Mountain. Avalanches often threatened the location, and a slide leveled the cabin in 1893. His second cabin, which measured eighteen by twenty-five feet, was expertly cut from large logs. With its bunk beds, "Gilbert's" became a hostelry for passing prospectors and wagon-road surveyors. Landre prospected and mined at this location until 1905.

Remi Durrand, a French Canadian trapper and prospector who came to the Skagit area in 1893, built Middle Cabin on remote Thunder Creek. He died in 1915 from mistakenly drinking wood alcohol.[35] Another trapper, John Dayo, arrived in the upper Skagit Valley in 1920. Based at Marblemount, he ran trap lines along Thunder, Fisher, and Bacon creeks and in the Cascade River Valley. In the late 1920s, he built Rock Cabin near Fisher Creek, where he spent two winters.[36] Two other Skagit homesteaders of interest were William Thornton and Burton Babcock. Thornton kept a ranch east of present-day Marblemount on the Skagit's north bank, where he patented 166 acres, and Babcock had a 138-acre claim nearby. The junction of the Skagit and Cascade rivers—land once occupied by an Indian village—was ideal for homesteading. Seeing an opportunity, William Barrett operated a ferry across both rivers for some years.[37]

Even before the Ruby Creek prospecting boom (see chapter 14) and the arrival of such upper Skagit pioneers as McMillan and Rowland, settlers moved into the lower Skagit Valley. Their livelihood came mostly from logging the virgin coniferous forests. Once the two great logjams that hindered upstream development were finally cleared in the late 1870s, boats could ply the Skagit beyond present-day Marblemount and supply gold seekers.[38] When prospectors began to work on the upper Skagit, outfitters quickly followed, and the confluence of the Skagit and Cascade rivers became a portal to the mining region.

N.E. Goodell of Portland set up a small miner's store at what is now Newhalem, where the river was sufficiently slow for canoe navigation. Goodell's Landing, as the flat became known, was sixteen miles above Marblemount. Harrison Clothier and Ed English, two mining promoters, established a new trading post at the landing, probably in 1880. It was soon a hub where miners exchanged gold for food and supplies. August Dohne purchased this roadhouse in 1897.[39]

Perhaps the most notable pioneer family on the Skagit was that of Lucinda J. Davis, who came to the Cascade River in 1890. Davis moved to Cedar Bar with her family when the Cascade flooded out her homestead in 1897. To reach Cedar Bar (present-day Diablo), they had to hike the Goat Trail on the north bank of the river canyon, beginning fewer than four miles from Goodell's. The first Davis residence, a log cabin, was built in 1898.[40] The soil of the bar, on which grew gigantic western red cedars, was excellent, and the family operated a roadhouse to serve the second Ruby Creek boom. Such delicacies as vegetables from the garden, apples, fresh milk, chickens, and homemade pies were available to weary travelers. Meals and a bed cost fifty cents, and hay for horses went for one hundred dollars per ton. The Davis family became so successful that they built a third house in 1907, this one with a veranda supported by log posts.

Because the land settled by the Davises had never been surveyed—a prerequisite for filing a claim—the Forest Service, which wanted the flat for a ranger station, withdrew much of the land from homestead entry in 1908. In a controversy that continued for years, the family was finally able to patent forty-three acres in 1910. Power proved to be the greater public need, however, and the Davis land—even though it was within the Mt. Baker National Forest—was condemned in 1929 to make way for the Diablo Dam, a part of the Seattle City Light hydroelectric scheme. The utility obtained the homestead for $15,000.[41] The project's hydroelectric plants, power lines, and dams are visible today from the North Cascades Highway. The Skagit, which pioneer settlers saw as a torrent rushing through a deep rock canyon, is no longer a fearsome place; and the dangerous foot trails, bridges, and wagon roads have disappeared.

Among the few Skagit settlers who became trappers, the most persistent was Gaspar Petta, who came from Greece to Marblemount and trapped in the winters from 1912 to 1956.[42] Such men were unquestionably the first non-Native people to enter certain deep and remote mountain valleys. Petta, who built a cabin at the foot of Jasper Pass and purchased another one about twelve miles lower in the valley of Goodell Creek, explored the flanks of the Picket Range. He ventured alone into the trackless valleys of the Baker River, Bacon Creek, Big Beaver Creek, and the south fork of the Cascade River. In the winter of 1930, for example, he traveled to the Baker River Valley for weasel and marten (at the time, marten furs brought thirty to sixty dollars apiece). In 1929, he earned $606 from marten, and in 1933 he trapped over fifty of the animals. According to Petta, the last fisher was trapped in 1912. Petta used small snowshoes for winter travel on the steep valley slopes and to buck the brush, and he usually packed an axe, frying pan, and cooking pot. Avalanches were a frequent hazard, and he was occasionally so close to them that he felt their frightening wind blast. He was once struck by a winter slide near Jasper Pass but luckily rode it out and was stopped by a rock. His last season of trapping was in 1956.

Ernest Kobelt, a settler from Sultan, must have been one of the first non-Indians to explore the rugged mountain region southeast of Mt. Baker. In July 1922, with his companion Jim Jaeger, he hiked into the wilderness of the Baker River Valley to investigate the story that Indians from British Columbia had once killed local Skagit Indians near Baker Lake. The brush in the valley was so thick that it took the men, with their heavy packs, three and a half days to cover seven miles. The adventurers then crossed the divide to Bacon Creek (perhaps by Bald Eagle Creek), discovering Berdeen Lake along the way. Continuing on their difficult route, they followed the valley of Bacon Creek to the Skagit.[43]

Settlers at Lake Chelan

Across the range, on the east flank, miner Henry Dumpke and his partner William Sanders packed across the high Sawtooth Ridge to Lake Chelan in the summer of 1886 (their horse Prince was killed in a fall at what is now known as Prince Creek). The two men built a canoe at Canoe Creek and paddled to the foot of the lake, where with Ignatius A. Navarre they became the first white settlers in that location.[44] The head of the magnificent lake attracted homesteaders, packers, trappers, and prospectors. Merritt E. Field, who arrived at Stehekin in 1892, purchased a small hotel and in 1900 constructed an elegant architectural landmark.[45] By 1910, the Field Hotel could accommodate one hundred guests. Another notable hotel was the Moore, built in 1889 by James R. Moore from New York state.

The Pershall and Kingman brothers, prospectors and mining pioneers, also settled at Stehekin. Henry F. Buckner, who worked Horseshoe Basin mines from 1898 to 1910 and was also a packer to prospectors, is remembered in the name of one of the area's highest summits. Dan Devore, who arrived in 1889, ran a packing business to mining camps from Stehekin and guided tourists through the region. He probably constructed trapping cabins along the north fork of Bridge Creek in 1906. Throughout the Stehekin River drainage, trappers caught goat, bear, and lynx at the turn of the century. The Weaver brothers, for example, trapped and also prepared skins for visiting hunters, and Hugh and Ray Courtney trapped along Company Creek and in other valleys near the head of Lake Chelan.[46]

Sightseers were attracted by the striking scenery around the lake, and tourism provided employment for nearby settlers. One magazine story reported: "The head of Lake Chelan is in the midst of mountains upon whose sides the everlasting snows of ages lie."[47] An 1899 tourist advertisement in the *Chelan Leader* included this encouragement: "Animals gentle and accustomed to trails. Guides and packers furnished if desired." Settlers, prospectors, and tourists could use boat transportation on Lake Chelan as early as 1888, when the *Belle of Chelan* began to work the lake. By the next year, it was taking passengers to Stehekin. In the fall of 1889, the *City of Omaha*, brought by wagon from Ellensburg, was also operating on the lake waters. The first boats burned cordwood, furnished by a settler at Stehekin.[48]

Guy Waring, who arrived in 1891 and opened a general store at what became Winthrop, may have made the largest contribution to the lore of the Methow River. In 1892, Owen Wister—an intimate of Theodore Roosevelt, Rudyard Kipling, and Oliver Wendell Holmes and the author of the classic western novel *The Virginian*—came to the Methow River valley to visit Waring, a former classmate from Harvard. Wister was also on the prowl for story material, which was certainly in abundance among the adventurous settlers of the northern Cascades.

The Cornice, *sketch by Edmund T. Coleman (from* Harper's New Monthly Magazine, *November 1869; MSCUA, University of Washington Libraries, 8682)*

13

EARLY MOUNTAINEERING ON THE VOLCANOS

For anyone who has the courage, the hardihood, and the physical strength to endure the
exercise, there is no form of recreation or amusement known to mankind that can yield such
grand results as mountain climbing.

–George O. Shields, 1889

The early ascents of the ice-clad volcanos of the northern Cascades—
much like early mountaineering in the world's other mountain ranges,
including the Alps, the Himalaya, the Andes, and the mountains of
Canada and Alaska—were true exploratory endeavors that rank with the surveys of the Northwest Boundary, the search for railroad routes, and the explorations by the U.S. Army. After about 1900, the approaches and early ascent
routes in the Cascade Range were largely proven.

Mt. Baker

Various early navigators, from Manuel Quimper and George Vancouver to
Cmdr. Charles Wilkes, were impressed by Mt. Baker's snowy volcanic cone.
From near Port Townsend in 1841, Wilkes, who was conducting the American
naval survey of Puget Sound and adjacent waters, sighted the high summit:
"From this point, Mount Baker is distinctly seen to the northeast, and forms a
fine sight when its conical peak is illuminated by the setting sun." Dr. William F.
Tolmie, who was a physician for the Hudson's Bay Company, also mentioned
the "lofty snow clad mountain" as well as a "lower range of snow tipped summits" rising over the "woody bank of sound" to the south. In 1859, from the
rugged terrain north of Mt. Baker, topographer Henry Custer of the Northwest Boundary Survey wrote that the peak "shows forth in all its serene beauty
and majesty, the King among mountains here." It was, "to judge from the
gentle outline of its massive cone, easy to ascend," he added.[1]

The view of the white mountain from Vancouver Island could be compelling, especially if a person was charmed by alpine landscapes. Edmund Thomas Coleman, who had left England in September 1862 and moved to Victoria,
soon became enamored with the vista of the glacier-clad volcano, which he
believed rose to 12,000 or 13,000 feet. He wrote admiringly: "It is remarkable
for its beauty of outline bears a considerable resemblance in this respect to the
Jungfrau, the queen of the Bernese range of the Alps." He also noted its isola-

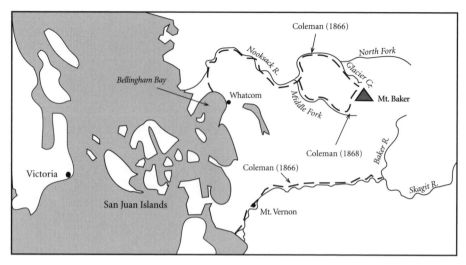

Coleman's Ascents of Mt. Baker

tion and that its height was "rendered the more apparent" because there were no neighboring peaks to compete with it. "Tukullum," the Skagit Indians' name for Mt. Baker, brought wistful memories of his beloved Alps.[2]

Coleman was tall, slender, and fair and was judged to be polite and urbane. An early Bellingham resident described him as having polished manners and "what you would call esthetic tastes." He was an unusual figure in Victoria—a librarian, amateur botanist, and accomplished artist—and he was certainly the only one there at the time with a serious interest in mountaineering. A charter member of the prestigious Alpine Club, Coleman had spent the 1855 to 1858 seasons making expeditions in the Mont Blanc region while sketching its splendors. He had ascended Mont Blanc twice and had made a first ascent of the Dôme de Miage. He had left the traditional paths of the Alps for the "unexplored heights of the West," as he put it, and he brought along some of his alpine equipment, including hemp rope, crampons, and ice axe.[3]

To ascend a mountain such as Baker in the middle of a tangled, unknown wilderness, however, Coleman needed comrades and support. The only countrymen of his who had been near Mt. Baker were the Royal Engineers of the British Northwest Boundary Commission, but they had already returned to Britain. The logical place to find companions was Washington Territory, a land of pioneers, farmers, and timber cutters. He could not hope to locate mountaineers, but perhaps he could find hardy pioneers with a yen for adventure. He himself would plan and finance the expedition, as well as provide the mountaineering equipment and knowledge.

In mid-July 1866, the forty-two-year-old Coleman crossed the Strait of Juan de Fuca to Port Townsend, where he was joined by Dr. Robert Brown, a Scot, and Charles B. Darwin, a U.S. magistrate. Taking passage in a cedar canoe, the

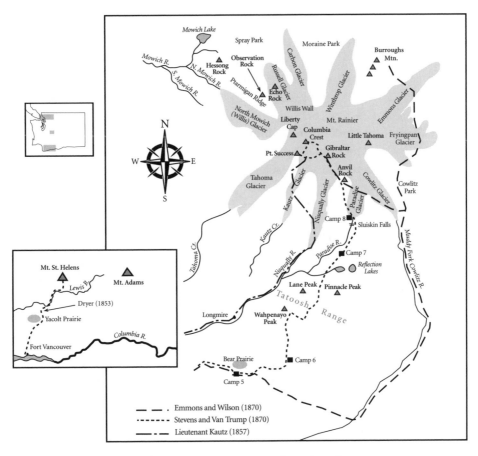

Early Ascents of Mt. Rainier and Mt. St. Helens

trio arrived at the Skagit River, which Coleman had chosen because prospectors had used the river as an approach to the mountain. About six miles upriver, they encountered the famous logjam, which required three exhausting portages. They also met an elderly Indian on the lower river, who told them that Mt. Baker had once erupted with great violence and all the fish in the Skagit had been killed. When a band of some sixty Koma Indians blocked the three men from continuing, the expedition was aborted at the mouth of the Baker River (at the site of present-day Concrete). Nevertheless, Coleman persisted, making a second attempt that summer. At Bellingham Bay, he met Edward Eldridge, a settler who suggested that the best way to reach the mountain was by way of the Nooksack River, partly because the Lummi and Nooksack tribes along that drainage were friendly. With Eldridge and another settler, John Bennett, Coleman hired Indian guides and canoes at the mouth of the Nooksack. Bennett, who was born in Scotland in 1818, had some training in botany and had sought gold along the Fraser River.

While the Indians were taking the canoes around a logjam, the rest of the party visited John Tennant, hoping to enlist the strong and enterprising settler who had extensive backwoods experience. Tennant, who was born in Arkansas Territory in 1829, had some education in law and civil engineering and had served as Whatcom's representative in the territorial legislature in 1859.[4] He agreed to join Coleman on the climb, and his knowledge of the region and influence with the Indians made him invaluable to the expedition.

With two Nooksack Indian guides, the men ascended the Nooksack and its north fork, then turned up Glacier Creek ("Noochsakatsu"). By August 17, they had reached the northwestern base of Mt. Baker, where they pitched camp.[5] The following day, Coleman and Bennett began the ascent by what is now called the Coleman Glacier, while Tennant remained below (Eldridge did not continue on the adventure). The day was beautiful, but they were stopped well above the final western saddle by "an overhanging cornice of ice." The two climbers retreated to the saddle and endured a frigid night without blankets at about 9,000 feet. Spending the endless hours moving about was a most wretched experience, Coleman recalled long afterward. Although fatigued, the two men attempted the ascent again the next morning but were stopped by the same ice barrier. The situation was "very dangerous on account of avalanches and sliding ice."[6] They were probably near the top of the Roman Wall on the upper Deming Glacier, only a few hundred feet from success. After they descended, Coleman spent some two weeks at Eldridge's cabin, sketching, before he could hire Indians with a canoe. He then returned to Victoria.

Coleman made another expedition to Mt. Baker in 1868. He traveled from Victoria to Bellingham Bay by canoe, this time accompanied by David Ogilvy, who supposedly had some mountaineering experience. Thomas Stratton, a customs inspector, met the men at Eldridge's cabin, and Tennant joined the group as well. On August 7, the men set out up the Nooksack River with four Indians. After a few miles, the large canoe was exchanged for "two small shovel-nosed canoes."[7] Stratton reported that "at times we were obliged to lie flat down in the canoe to pass under logs and trees that obstructed the river."[8] At camp the first night, Coleman discovered a utensil shortage—there was only one plate and spoon for the entire party—and rations were limited, strangely, to bacon, bread, and tea. On August 9, Stratton wrote, the party was

. . . camped for the night at the village of "Hump Clallam," the chief of the Upper Nootsac tribe, a venerable looking old fellow, with hair as white as snow. He is apparently 80 or 90 years old. He sent us potatoes and salmon, for which we presented him some tobacco. He made us a short speech, saying he was glad to have the "Bostons" come to his country, that we should be treated well, and telling the Indians that they were responsible for our safe return to the village.[9]

The Indian guides, Squock and Talum, recommended a route along the middle fork of the Nooksack. Because of the many shoals, bars, and rapids, the mountaineers had to walk most of the way while the Indians poled the canoes. After two days, the party cached the canoes and set out with sixty-pound packs loaded with blankets and ten days' supply of food.

On August 13, Squock and Talum went on a scout, Coleman sketched, and the others searched (in vain) for gold. The guides returned with marmots for dinner and the good news of a prospective route. During the following two days, the party climbed well out of the forest, camping on Marmot Ridge near 6,000 feet (Camp Hope). There was a low cloud and visibility was poor, yet Coleman must have had a good view of the jagged Black Buttes (part of an extinct volcano's crater rim). He was sufficiently impressed by their prominence to name them Lincoln and Colfax peaks, and he compared the features "of the Red Ridge with its glaciers" to the " 'Aiguilles Rouges,' as seen on the north side of the Valley of Chamounix" in the Alps.[10]

On the night of August 15, avalanches shook the ground. Stratton wrote: "The Indians were much frightened, and devoutly made the sign of the cross, like good Catholics."[11] After breakfast the next day, Tennant and Stratton undertook a route reconnaissance, taking along alpenstocks and "creepers" (iron spikes with chains and straps, a primitive crampon worn on boots for gripping on hard snow or ice). The two ascended about 1,000 feet to the base of the Black Buttes, where they could look across at crevasses on a large glacier.[12]

Early on August 17, each mountaineer took a blanket and provisions for twenty-four hours in case they needed to camp on snow. Each also took a small brandy flask, a practice Coleman had become fond of in the Alps. Coleman brought his twenty-five-fathom hemp rope and an "apparatus for making tea by alcoholic fire." By eight o'clock that morning, the group had reached the ridgetop and donned their creepers. The first procedure was a 300-foot descent to reach a site suitable for crossing the glacier. Probably because he wanted to avoid the extensive field of crevasses and "great blocks of ice and snow that had fallen from the peaks above," Coleman suggested that the party follow the jagged ridge to Colfax Peak.[13] They never would have succeeded in completing this traverse and fortunately followed Stratton's lead instead:

> At 9 o'clock we reached the first chasm [crevasse] across our route. We had to make an abrupt descent of about three hundred yards to reach a point where we could cross it. Here our rope was brought into service—we tied ourselves at equal distances apart, the person ahead cutting steps to afford foothold for those who followed. Our course after crossing the first chasm was up steep benches of snow and ice, around chasms, some of which I looked into, seeing no bottom—all looked dark blue, like the ocean depths. At times we had one on each side, not over six yards apart—we were literally walking on a wall of ice.[14]

Stratton pulled ahead and found the route through the crevassed glacier.

A crevasse with an upper lip higher than their stance posed a technical problem. "The difficulty was formidable," Coleman later explained, but I made a leap, ice-axe in hand, with the pick pointed downward, so that I might easily anchor in the snow. As I made the spring Mr. Bennett pushed me with his pole, and I managed to alight and catch on to the slope. Fixing myself firmly in the snow with the aid of my pole, Mr. Bennett made a leap, and at the same time I gave him a good tug with the rope, and he managed it also in safety. . . .

We were in considerable anxiety concerning Stratton. Divested of rope and without a pack, he had made rapid progress. At one time we saw him crossing a spot exposed to avalanches of ice, and shortly afterward were greatly alarmed to see him take a jump, and then suddenly disappear, being lost to view by projecting masses of seracs. It appears that he had fortunately fallen in with the tracks of a grizzly bear, and wisely concluding that what would bear its weight would sustain his also, he had followed it without hesitation across snow-bridges over the chasms.[15]

At about two o'clock that afternoon, the others reached Stratton, who was waiting at the high saddle between Mt. Baker's summit cone and Colfax Peak, the point Coleman and Bennett had passed on the 1866 attempt. While the crater's nauseating, sulfurous fumes occasionally drifted by, Ogilvy made a brandy cocktail with ice, a drink later called the "Mt. Baker cocktail." Above them was the final, steep slope that had frustrated Coleman and Bennett earlier. Blankets and provisions were left behind, but Coleman was careful to take the barometer, thermometer, and sketching items. The men, all wearing creepers and carrying "staves" (alpenstocks), put on the rope again.

As the leader, Stratton found the route on both the ascent and descent. On the steepest portion of the upper Deming Glacier, he used Coleman's ice axe, cutting some 350 steps.[16] The ascent was made late in the day, and the exposure to the sun must have been great. While cutting steps, Stratton had a frightful experience: a snow block about twelve feet wide suddenly slid from the ice directly above. "Paralyzed with terror, he was about to warn us, when it fortunately stopped," Coleman wrote.[17] Stratton remembered what happened next:

We soon gained the rock, where we rested for a time. Our ascent from this point was not very difficult, and at 4 p.m. we stood on the summit of Mount Baker! What an indescribable feeling passed over us! No word was spoken, as we stood with clasped hands, contemplating the majestic grandeur of the scene. At such a time and such a place one feels the spirit of inspiration that led the Psalmist to exclaim, "Great are Thy works, O Lord!"

After singing a doxology, we looked around the summit and saw another peak due east from where we stood, apparently higher than the one we were on, and about a quarter of a mile distant, with a depression of about two hundred feet between the two. We went to it, and found it to be, by the barometer, of the same hight as the one we were first on.

I approached the edge of the crater and looked into it. It was an awful sight. Down, down—all dark and sulphury, with green, black, red and yellow sides.[18]

The men left two flagpoles on the summit, and Coleman named the peak (the high point of the summit-dome ice mass) after Gen. Ulysses S. Grant. He produced a flask of brandy, while everyone sang a patriotic song and shook hands.[19] Coleman called the other small point on the summit plateau Sherman Peak (after the general), a name cartographers later applied to the highest point on the south crater rim. He also noted

> a peculiarity in the snow [at the summit] which covered this plateau that I have not observed in the Alps. In form it resembled small tongues of flame, all leaning in the same direction, and was evidently caused by the violent eddies of wind. It seemed as if there was some mysterious sympathy between the volcanic fires within and the snowy surface without.[20]

Those thin, leaning "tongues" of snow, known as *nieve penitente*, are caused by the effects of the sun's radiation.

While the Englishman was sketching the summit dome, his partners ventured toward the crater and found an excellent vantage. Their accounts indicate that the crater was ice-free at the time, probably as a result of higher internal temperatures than at the present time. To the east, Stratton saw Mt. Shuksan and the remote Picket Range. The men also heard avalanches in the direction of the steep east flank of the volcano and near the crater. When Coleman was finished with his hurried sketches, the party re-roped and began the dreaded descent, which concerned even the experienced Englishman:

> The sun was already sinking, so that we had no time to lose. Urged by the fear of having to pass the night on the mountain, we plunged after Stratton down slopes, across snow-bridges, by walls of ice, as if pursued by a fiend. Vain were my remonstrances, fearful of an accident, but my companions hurried on in a manner that would have sent a Swiss guide into fits. Such a helter-skelter mad-brained party was never seen on either Mont Blanc or Mont Rosa.[21]

Twilight turned to darkness, and Stratton described the return to camp: "At 11 P.M., worn out with fatigue, we arrived where we left the Indians, who joyfully welcomed our return. After taking some tea, . . . we wrapped ourselves in our blankets to dream of glaciers, chasms and craters."[22]

It was probably on the following day that Coleman made his sketch of the Twin Sisters Range. After comparing barometric readings, he concluded that the summit height of Mt. Baker was 10,613 feet (not far from the present figure of 10,781). The Coast Survey during this period gave a long-distance triangulation measurement of 10,814 feet. They arrived back at their canoes on August 21 and descended the Nooksack with a sense of fulfillment. The ascent of Mt. Baker was the greatest mountain conquest in the northern Cascades up to that time. The only principal Cascade Range volcanos that had not yet been ascended (north of the lower Columbia River) were Mt. Rainier and the unknown Glacier Peak.

Coleman worked his field sketches into finished illustrations (which were made into wood engravings) and prepared a narrative from his diary, which was published in *Harper's New Monthly Magazine* in 1869. The account of the ascent in a leading publication brought national attention to a Pacific Northwest mountain for the first time. When Coleman returned to London in 1873, he wrote a series of articles that appeared in *Illustrated Travels* describing his trips to Mt. Baker, his visit to Mt. Rainier and various Cascade passes, and his railroad journey across the continent.

Mt. Rainier

To some early Washington Territory residents, the ascent of a 14,000-foot mountain only fifty miles from the shores of Puget Sound was a coveted accomplishment. Mt. Rainier has always been a compelling sight for ambitious adventurers. Adding to its aloofness and mystery is its tendency to remain hidden in a cloud canopy for so much of the time. Theodore Winthrop, in 1862, had judged that "of all the peaks from California to Fraser River, this one before me was royalest." In 1873, Coleman described how Rainier dominated the landscape: "As it can be seen from . . . Victoria . . . a distance of upwards of 140 miles on an air line, its height must be great. The general form of the mountain is that of a great pyramid."[23] Coleman's ascent of Mt. Baker had spurred additional interest in climbing Mt. Rainier, but settlers tended to criticize anyone contemplated an ascent. It would be a young army officer who would take the risk.

Lt. August Valentine Kautz arrived at Fort Steilacoom in March 1853 as a newly-minted West Point graduate. Slim and nearly six feet tall, the young officer with black hair and a full beard was restless at the fort, where "there was plenty to eat and little to do. . . ." Mt. Rainier was often in full view, and Kautz envisioned an alpine adventure to interrupt a summer of monotonous garrison duty. "On a clear day," he wrote, "it does not look more than ten miles off." The mountain appeared to him mysterious and compelling, especially after he came to believe that no white man had ever attempted its ascent.[24] Although Kautz had an active field career, he was a complete novice as a climber of mountains. Yet, he had read accounts of the ascent of Mont Blanc and had a keen curiosity about mountains. Born in the Grand Duchy of Baden in 1828, he had immigrated to Ohio with his parents. While still a teenager, he enlisted in a volunteer infantry under Gen. Zachary Taylor in the Mexican War. After graduating from West Point in 1852, he was assigned to Columbia Barracks before his transfer to Fort Steilacoom.[25] During his first years at the fort, Kautz guarded Nisqually chief Leschi, who had been charged with murder during the Yakama war. The lieutenant, who came to believe in Leschi's innocence, hoped that he could accompany him to Mt. Rainier as a guide, and he acquired information from the chief on the route to the mountain. Leschi recommended another Nisqually as a guide, Wapowety, who knew the region best among his people.

Others at the fort did not take Kautz's climbing plans seriously: "I had expressed so often my determination to make the ascent, without doing it, that my fellow officers finally became incredulous and gave to all improbable and doubtful events a date of occurrence when I should ascend Mount Rainier."[26] His resolve strengthened in 1857, however, when he found that others would accompany him. One of them was assistant surgeon Robert Orr Craig, who soon enlisted two privates, Nicholas Dogue from Germany and William Carroll from Ireland.[27]

Kautz studied the mountain from afar and judged that the "southern slope seemed the least abrupt." He recounted the planning stage in his 1875 article about the expedition in *Overland Monthly*:

> I made preparations after the best authorities I could find. . . . We made for each member of the party an *alpenstock* of dry ash with an iron point. We sewed upon our shoes an extra sole, through which were driven four-penny nails with the points broken off and the heads inside. We took with us a rope about fifty feet long, a hatchet, a thermometer, plenty of hard biscuit, and dried beef such as the Indians prepare.[28]

Their equipment also included a field glass, prismatic compass, spirit lamp, and revolver.

The historic adventure began on July 8, 1857. The party, with pack animals and four soldiers from the regiment, left for a homestead near present-day Roy—beyond which was unmapped wilderness. Kautz and Craig went by way of the Nisqually Reservation to engage Wapowety as a guide. The Indian took along his rifle so he could provide the men with fresh meat. Following an old Nisqually Indian trail into the old-growth forest, the party reached "Mishawl Prairie" (southwest of present-day Eatonville) on the second day. This was as far as the horses could be taken, so two soldiers were left to tend them. Each person who continued carried a blanket, a tin canteen, and a haversack with two pounds of dried beef and two dozen crackers. Kautz found that

> there was no path and no open country—only a dense forest, obstructed with undergrowth and fallen timber. The sun was very hot when it could reach us through the foliage; not a breath of air stirred, and after we crossed the Mishawl, not a drop of water was to be had until we got down to low ground again. We toiled from early morning until three o'clock in the afternoon before we reached the summit. As the doctor had taken whisky instead of water in his canteen, he found it necessary to apply to the other members of the party to quench his thirst, and our canteens were speedily empty.[29]

When the doctor developed painful leg cramps, he paid Wapowety ten dollars to carry his pack the rest of the trip. Kautz observed:

> Here was an illustration of the advantage of training. The doctor was large, raw-boned, and at least six feet high, looking as if he could have crushed with a single blow

the insignificant old Indian, who was not much over five feet, and did not weigh more than half as much as the doctor; but, inured to this kind of toil, he carried double the load that any of the party did, while the doctor, who was habituated to a sedentary life, had all he could do, carrying no load whatever, to keep up with the Indian.[30]

On July 10, the party camped in the forest without water. The next day, however, having passed the river canyon, they turned south and reached the Nisqually River. There they were wet much of the time, wading between gravel bars, but at least there was drinking water. Early on July 13, Wapowety killed a deer, the first animal they had seen since a "large red wolf" two days before. By nightfall, they reached the west bank of the "milky" stream now known as Tahoma Creek. Although the weather seemed to be changing, the mountain appeared to be very close.[31] The next day, Kautz made the fortunate decision to continue along the Nisqually rather than its Tahoma Creek tributary, but it was weary progress through the forest with thickets to struggle through, cold stream torrents to wade, and avalanche paths to cross. Finally, the party reached the "foot of an immense glacier, from which the River emanates."[32] They camped near the glacier terminus, and Kautz explored the ice toe and sketched. He estimated that it was four or five miles long and "probably half a mile deep." He also discovered that the river

> emerged from an icy cavern . . . The ice itself was of a dark-blue tinge. The water was white, and whenever I waded the torrent my shoes filled with gravel and sand. The walls of this immense mountain gorge were white granite . . . The water seems to derive its color from the disintegration of this granite.[33]

Although drizzle and then fog had turned into rain and sleet by the morning of July 15, the party crossed the lower portion of the glacier, which Kautz described as "very large" and having "immense furrows and a ridge of boulders on each side. The whole thing seems to move at times."[34] Kautz and his companions were the first non-Natives in North America to set foot on a glacier; they were also the first to use metal-spiked alpenstocks. Noisy boulder falls from the steep flanking moraines made the party apprehensive. Bringing out the rope, they crossed to a moraine on the west flank, where they located a camp amid the stunted evergreens.

At camp, the men saw whistling marmots feeding near their burrows, and Kautz mistakenly described them as

> mountain-sheep, a small animal with long shaggy black and whitish hair, with the appearance and attitude of a small dog, and the motion and feet of a sheep. They are exceedingly wild—burrow in the earth, and at the least alarm, make for their holes.

While the whistles were amusing, the sound produced by the nearby Nisqually Glacier "was startling and strange. One might suppose the mountain was breaking loose, particularly at night." Without alpine experience and familiarity with the foreshortening effect of large mountains, Kautz erred in assessing the volcano's size. "I estimated that I should not require more than three hours to go to the summit," he later wrote. The next morning it snowed until eight o'clock, and when the weather cleared, Kautz, Carroll, Dogue, Craig, and Wapowety plodded upward, hardly concerned with the late start. As they gained height on the gradual southern slopes of the mountain, Kautz saw, above a sea of clouds, the "snowy peaks of St. Helens, Mt. Adams, and Mt. Hood, looking like pyramidal icebergs."[35]

The men's beards protected their faces from the sun reflecting from the glacier's surface, but not their lips and eyes. The rarefied air dehydrated the climbers, causing them to gasp for breath and slow their pace. They were further weakened by their inadequate diet, and the difficulties of the approach had taken their toll. The wind numbed the men and froze their fingers and faces, and ice crystals formed in their canteens. With a commendable effort, the sedulous Kautz managed to ascend high on the mountain, perhaps to the saddle area between Point Success and Columbia Crest at about 14,000 feet.[36] He later remembered: ". . . although there were points higher yet, the mountain spread out comparatively flat."[37] He climbed on alone for more than a half hour with the others out of sight. When a wind gust carried away his hat, he realized that there would be no overnight survival without blankets and that a dangerous, dark descent was imminent. Noting the shadows rapidly forming behind lower ridges and on the Tatoosh Range, he decided that he dared not linger after six o'clock. The climbers' long day ended well after dark. According to Aubrey Haines,

> Kautz wished to make another try for the summit, in the hope of determining its elevation by an observation of the boiling point, but in the morning the Indian's [Wapowety's] eyes were so inflamed he was blind. Also, a check of their provisions showed that they had but four crackers and a pound of dried meat each for the return journey to Mashel Prairie. Since Wapowety would no longer hunt, they dared not linger at the mountain.[38]

When the party returned to the fort, nobody was readily recognizable. They were sunburned, haggard, and tattered. Kautz was wearing a cap made from his shirtsleeve, and the doctor had replaced a trouser leg with a flour sack. During the two weeks they were gone, everyone had lost weight. Wapowety nearly died from gastritis, and both soldiers had to undergo medical care. Carroll even applied to Kautz for a discharge pension, claiming permanent disability. The doctor "was taken with violent pains in his stomach, and returned to his post quite sick. He did not recover his health again for three months."[39]

Thirty-six years later, forester Frederick G. Plummer—who had incorrectly marked Kautz's route on his recently made map of Mt. Rainier—was embroiled with mountaineer Philemon B. Van Trump and Kautz in a trivial dispute when he argued that Kautz should be credited with the first ascent of the mountain. In an embarrassment to the lieutenant, Plummer wrote the *Tacoma Ledger*, that Kautz, Craig, and Dogue "reached the crest of Mount Tacoma . . . and were the first white men to reach [the] summit." His claim involved the definition of "summit." When the climber turns the crest, he argued, "he is on top, and is entitled to that honor, whether he splits hairs by standing on Crater Peak or not."[40] Certainly, Kautz and his party must be credited with exploring a route to the mountain and disproving the prevalent belief that the ascent of Mt. Rainier was impossible.

After the expedition, Kautz traveled extensively on both flanks of the Cascades and visited other mountain regions of North America and Europe. He predicted:

> When the locomotive is heard in that region some day, when American enterprise has established an ice-cream saloon at the foot of the glacier, and sherry-cobblers [*sic*] may be had at twenty-five cents half-way up to the top of the mountain, attempts to ascend that magnificent snow-peak will be quite frequent. But many a long year will pass away before roads are sufficiently good to induce anyone to do what we did in the summer of 1857.[41]

Unknown to Lt. Kautz, a scouting party of three or four men—apparently the earliest one on the mountain—had in fact traveled up the Nisqually River Valley in 1852 and later pioneered a route on the west flank of the great volcano. An Olympia newspaper carried this report in September of that year:

> About four weeks ago, a party of young men, consisting of Messrs. R.S. Bailey, Sidney S. Ford, Jr., and John Edgar undertook an expedition to Mt. Rainier, for the purpose of ascending that mountain as far as circumstances might warrant. . . . On arriving at the foot of the mountain the party secured their animals, and pursued their way upward by the backbone ridge to the main body of the mountain, and to the height of as near as they could judge, of nine or ten miles—the last half mile over snow of a depth probably of fifty feet, but perfectly crusted and solid. . . . The party remained at their last camp, upward, two days and two nights, where they fared sumptuously on the game afforded by the mountains. . . .[42]

Benjamin F. Shaw, who may or may not have been in the party, said in an interview a half century later that "no other point seemed higher whereon his party stood."[43] This could mean that they seemed to be above other visible peaks—which in itself would have been an amazing accomplishment—but there is no evidence to support the story.

At some time in the mid-1850s, two Englishmen are believed to have gone onto Mt. Rainier from its east or north flank, possibly for surveying. Their Yakama guide, Sluskin, told the story about sixty years later to a settler in Yakima.[44] He reported that he had guided the two "King George men" to the foot of the mountain and that they climbed to what he indicated was the summit. The account has been given some credence because Sluskin said that the men had put on special boots with nails and he described a crater lake on the summit with smoke or steam coming out, as in a sweathouse. It is doubtful, however, that surveyors of the time could have made an ascent and descent of 8,000 feet in one day by way of the heavily crevassed Emmons Glacier, as Sluskin's narrative suggests.

Among those Puget Sound-area residents who took an interest in climbing Mt. Rainier in the late 1860s was the peripatetic Philemon Beecher Van Trump, a recent arrival in Olympia. Born in Ohio in 1838, Van Trump was a casually educated, self-made adventurer who went west to prospect. Although reputed to be somewhat impractical, he was the private secretary to his brother-in-law, Marshall F. Moore, who was territorial governor from 1867 to 1870. Van Trump first saw Mt. Rainier in 1867. As it happened, he had "a long cherished desire to scale such an ice-crowned and unconquered peak."[45] In the small community of Olympia, where an ascent of the mountain was generally thought to be impossible, it was not difficult to ferret out what like-minded adventurers there were. Hazard Stevens was one of them.

Stevens, born in Rhode Island in 1842, had come to Washington Territory in 1854 when his father, Isaac I. Stevens, was appointed its first governor. He gained valuable experience among Indian tribes and in the outdoors and crossed the Rockies twice. Although he was at times judged to be undisciplined and arrogant, he was nonetheless a serious, able man who pursued success zealously. As a captain in his father's regiment during the Civil War, he was wounded in the same battle in which the elder Stevens was killed, on September 1, 1862, and he was later given the Medal of Honor for gallantry and promoted to brigadier general.[46]

Sometime in 1868, Van Trump and Stevens agreed to climb Mt. Rainier, but circumstances were not favorable until 1870. Coincidentally, Coleman hoped to visit the mountain that summer and ascend it if he could locate partners. He proposed an ascent to Stevens, but none was made that year.[47] It is uncertain how firm Van Trump's and Stevens's plans were before Coleman arrived; but they were certainly aware of Coleman's alpine experience, and he undoubtedly deserves credit as a source of motivation.[48]

An unlikely but tangible alliance began to emerge: "official" Olympia and the "upstart" Englishman, who must have been delighted at finding companions. Coleman took on an important role in planning, organizing, equipping, and possibly financing the 1870 expedition. Although Van Trump and Stevens examined his equipment with some skepticism, Coleman's preparations increased the likelihood of success. He had brought along a one-hundred-foot-long hemp rope, creepers, an ice axe, a spirit lamp for making tea, green goggles, deer fat for their faces, and three alpenstocks. As for provisions, there were references to one flour sack, bacon, coffee, beans, dried beef, tea, and yeast. They also took along a kettle, a frying pan, two coffee pots, and tin plates and cups.[49]

The attention to detail has tended to obscure an important fact about this expedition: it was a generally unplanned and haphazard effort. Although Coleman had made preparations and brought specialized equipment, the two Americans took the adventure rather lightly. They drove to Yelm Prairie on the Nisqually River to meet James Longmire for route advice and to seek his services as a guide. Longmire told them that the trail up the Nisqually had not been traversed since the Northern Pacific Railroad survey of 1867 and was entirely illegible to anyone not versed in woodcraft. Because of his harvest and a pending cattle drive, however, he was reluctant to leave; and Longmire's wife further discouraged his going, mindful of his thin and haggard appearance after his last wilderness journey. "The bountiful country breakfast heaped before us, the rich cream, fresh butter and eggs, snowy, melting biscuits, and broiled chicken, with rich, white gravy," Stevens conceded, "heightened the effect of her words." He continued: "But at length when it appeared that no one else who knew the trail could be found, Mr. Longmire yielded to our persuasions, and consented to conduct us as far as the trail led, and to procure an Indian guide before leaving us to our own resources.[50]

It was likely that Longmire's sense of adventure as well as his concern for the men led him to decide that he would take them to Bear Prairie and then locate an Indian guide. Later, Coleman readily admitted that had it not been for Longmire's knowledge of the land, "we should never have been able to make the journey." Coleman later summarized the beginning of the adventure:

> We left Olympia on the 8th of August, 1870, and were accompanied for the first thirty miles by a large party of friends and relatives, who desired to see us off and enjoy a picnic at the same time. A good road extends from Olympia in a south-easterly direction, through a succession of large prairies, divided by belts of timber.... Late in the afternoon we drove up to the last farmhouse on the borders of civilisation.[51]

With such a complement of guests, the night naturally became boisterous, with drinking, horseplay, and practical jokes played on Coleman, the outsider. It is a tribute to the Englishman's ambition that he decided to carry on.

The hot, oppressive weather affected everyone, slowing their pace. In the mossy gloom of the old forest, with its thick understory and huge fallen trees, the men and horses made slow progress, with frequent halts to adjust packs knocked loose by the thick growth. Historian Aubrey Haines described an incident that nearly ended the expedition just above the Ohop Creek ford:

> At that point the stream was a waist-deep, icy flood of milky colored water one hundred yards wide; so the animals were used to get over. Van Trump led on the saddle mule, with Coleman mounted behind him holding the neck-rope of the pack mule, which carried Longmire as an additional load. He, in turn, held the neck-rope of the packhorse on which Stevens was mounted. Soon after entering the water, Coleman let go of his rope and the two pack animals turned down stream, requiring strenuous effort on Longmire's part to keep them from the rapids below the ford.[52]

Another mishap occurred east of the Mashel River when a packhorse fell under its unbalanced load and rolled down the slope.

Beyond the Nisqually canyon, west of Elbe, the men passed an interesting structure on August 10. Coleman described an

old Indian vapour-bath house on the banks, which formerly belonged to a Tomanawos or "medicine-man," who also lived on the spot. These erections are very small, and are constructed of wood, about eighteen inches above the ground, sometimes square, sometimes of a rounded form. The earth is scooped out about six inches below the surface. When used, a fire is made inside, good-sized stones being placed on and round it. A small hole is left, just big enough for the invalid to creep into; the stones being then heated, cold water is poured on, which induces a profuse perspiration. The hole is then closed up and covered with mud, sometimes buckskins, or both together.[53]

Gradually, the differences between the Americans and the Englishman became apparent. After a hard day's travel, Coleman enjoyed his pipe and undertook sketching, while others did the camp chores. Probably from the outset, Stevens and Van Trump ostracized the methodical and fastidious Coleman, and he was subjected to some humiliation in their published accounts. Van Trump complained:

To all our representations in favor of an energetic campaign against the mountain his one knock-down argument was, "We didn't travel so in the Alps." He was a profound crank on the subject of bathing. If it be literally true that cleanliness is next to godliness, then our companion was phenomenally near to exemplary piety. Twice a day, with all the regularity and certainty with which that division of time begins and ends, did our devotee to personal comfort or cleanliness perform his ablutions. If our tent happened to be pitched too far from the Nesqually to permit of a plunge into its turbulent and icy flood or into the less cool and bracing waters of some other stream, then the less satisfactory sponge bath was resorted to. . . .[54]

Coleman's indulgence in brandy mixed with water threw him behind the train, according to Van Trump, and he frequently became lost, forcing the rest of the party to search for him. "Unfortunately," Van Trump remembered, ". . . our new acquaintance proved a clog on the expedition rather than an aid to it. Mr. C. did not get as far as the base of the mountain. . . ."[55] The Americans' accusation that Coleman slowed them down, however, was largely specious. The real difficulties in reaching Bear Prairie were the poorly blazed trail, huge fallen timbers, and problems with pack animals; and Stevens may have treated Coleman with disdain because of their different backgrounds.[56] Stevens's experience in combat spurred him to gamble on the unknown, and he may have had a general dislike of the British, who had sided with the Confederate during the Civil War. His account of the expedition, published in *Atlantic Monthly* in 1876, contained some rancor and some untruths—particularly suggestions that Coleman was inexperienced, "an Alpine tourist."

Because Longmire had planned to escort the mountaineers only to Bear Prairie, he and Stevens made the arduous hike down Skate Creek on August 13 to a small Cowlitz Indian camp to find a Native guide. Most of the band was away picking berries, so only one man was available.

> He was a friendly fellow, this Sluiskin, welcoming Longmire and Stevens with dignified hospitality. With much hand shaking, they were seated beneath the little shelter of hides to be served cakes of dried huckleberries by his squaw; then there was talk through the medium of Chinook jargon. Longmire soon explained the purpose of the visit, obtaining Sluiskin's services as a guide, with the understanding that he would present himself at their camp the following day.[57]

As promised, Sluiskin rode into camp the next day with his family and was treated to a substantial dinner. Sluiskin proposed to start by ascending the steep, forested scarp behind camp—the 5,475-foot Lookout Mountain, a spur of the Tatoosh Range. Van Trump reported:

> When our plans and the object of our expedition were made known to him he evidently looked upon it all as a colossal joke. The idea of these three white men, two "Bostons" and a "King George" man, coming such a long distance under the hallucination and with the vain idea that they would be able to climb the mighty "Tahoma" . . . was to him, evidently, the very acme or crown of ridiculousness.[58]

Van Trump later explained that Sluiskin had made some shrewd financial calculations:

> We understood in the end why he was so partial to the Tatoosh route to the mountain. Although he had never heard the oft-quoted Franklinian maxim, he acted in this instance on the theory that "time is money." The bargain with him called for a dollar a day, and of course the more days the more dollars, and therefore the Tatoosh route had a financial value in Sluiskin's eyes that the Nesqually route failed to present; and we, not really knowing the facts in the case, fell easily into the trap. And then I am confident that Sluiskin had, in selecting the Tatoosh route, another object in view . . . he expected to "take the starch" out of us, so to speak, and to show us . . . that mountain climbing was not by any means the boy's play that perchance our fond fancy had painted it.[59]

The remainder of the party favored the Nisqually approach, which Kautz had taken. Being unfamiliar with the region, however, they decided to follow Sluiskin's advice.

That afternoon, the men selected their indispensable articles and packed them into forty-pound loads, and Sluiskin led the way upward, carrying a pack and, on his head, a Hudson's Bay Company rifle. On the laborious ascent across the Tatoosh Range, the older and somewhat ill Coleman fell behind and the others were barely able to keep the pace. While scrambling on a rock cliff, Coleman dropped his pack, expecting it to catch on a bush; instead, it bounded out of sight, and he started back down the mountain. The Americans did not return for him—even though he carried all the bacon in his pack—because they judged him "too infirm to endure the toil before us."[60] Van Trump later remembered:

> After debating the situation for some moments we decided that Mr. C. must have given up, for the time being, his design on Rainier, and that the best thing for us to do was to push on without him. Sluiskin all the time had been watching us with one of his peculiarly amused expressions of countenance, which said, . . . "One has already fallen by the wayside; you, too, though fleeter of foot, in the end will also have to give up this wild goose chase."[61]

Crossing the west spur of the Tatoosh Range, Stevens thought it "seemed incredible that any human foot could have followed out the course we came." They looked down thousands of feet into terrible defiles, and on Mt. Rainier "the glaciers terminated not gradually, but abruptly, with a wall of ice from one to five hundred feet high."[62] At the campfire that night, Sluiskin again attempted to dissuade the two adventurers from continuing, but to no avail. The party went on to a grove of alpine fir near the Paradise River for a high camp at just over 6,000 feet, where the mountaineers named the cascade immediately below the camp Sluiskin Falls.

Stevens and Van Trump then ascended for four hours to the foot of Cowlitz Cleaver (near present-day Camp Muir) to view the contemplated route along the face of Gibraltar—the great rock cliff of Mt. Rainier's south flank standing between 11,800 and 12,800 feet. It appeared possible to cross the cliff to the upper Nisqually Glacier, and the pair were in a cheerful mood on their return to camp. Speaking in Chinook Jargon and "eloquent pantomime," Sluiskin urgently portrayed the perils of the ascent, still hoping the men would renounce their plan. He reportedly told Stevens and Van Trump that "Takhoma" was an "enchanted mountain, inhabited by an evil spirit, who dwelt in a fiery lake at its summit. No human being could ascend it or even attempt its ascent, and survive."[63] The guide assured them he would wait for them in camp for three days, and if they did not return he would proceed to Olympia with their belongings and relate their tragic fate to their friends.

Lacking experience with perspective foreshortening and higher altitudes, the two mountaineers were convinced the ascent would not take long. Consequently, they took no coats or blankets the next morning, fully expecting to be back in camp by evening. Part of their optimism was a result of the rapid time they had made on the reconnaissance, and the effects of altitude were not noticeable at that elevation. For the final ascent, they took the hundred-foot-long rope, two flags, Coleman's ice axe, two alpenstocks, a tin canteen, a brass plate inscribed with their names, and a lunch. Stevens had a thick-soled, well-calked pair of boots, while Van Trump had the homemade creepers for the ice.

On the morning of August 17, the two left Sluiskin Falls at six o'clock, far too late, but they did reach the crumbling lower Cowlitz Cleaver in about three hours. Ascending the "very narrow, steep, irregular backbone," they came to the base of Gibraltar. Stevens described it as "a vast square rock, whose huge and distinct outline can be clearly perceived from a distance of twenty-five miles." Van Trump later recalled: "Greatly to our satisfaction, we discovered a shelf or narrow ledge that seemed to extend along the entire west face of the cliff."[64] Striking their toes against the "cement-like debris," Van Trump continued, "was a somewhat thrilling experience, for had any of these footrests crumbled under our weight, or had we lost our balance, we would have been hurled to death on the Nisqually glacier." Stevens later remembered that the cliff was "rapidly disintegrating and continually falling in showers and even masses of rocks and rubbish, under the action of frost by night and melting snow by day."[65]

At noon, as the two mountaineers reached the ice chute beyond the Gibraltar ledge, stones whizzed down from above. One struck Van Trump's alpenstock and wrenched it from his grasp. Taking turns cutting steps with Coleman's axe, the men climbed the icy chute and the steep glacier slopes. When they reached the corrugated suncups, which looked "like a violent chop sea," it was no longer necessary to cut steps.[66] With the altitude came fatigue, however, and the hours were passing. As they bore westward toward Point Success, a crevasse barred the route. Stevens threw the looped rope end over an ice pinnacle on the upper edge of the crevasse. Each man held the rope to swing into the crevasse, then climb hand over hand to gain the upper edge. They were now obliged to travel more slowly:

> In that rare atmosphere, after taking seventy or eighty steps, our breath would be gone, our muscles grew tired and strained, and we experienced all the sensations of extreme fatigue. An instant's pause, however, was sufficient to recover strength and breath, and we would start again.[67]

The men continued westward toward Point Success, and in a cold, fierce wind crawled and staggered to its summit, "unfurling there our flags." They probably believed they were on the true summit and had decided to climb Point Success once they were above Gibraltar, where the southwestern summit would have appeared higher and closer. Seen from the vicinity of Olympia, the central summit cone is unmistakably the highest point, and we can only assume that Stevens and Van Trump had not carefully studied Mt. Rainier from a distance.

Surveying the remainder of the summit mass, the two climbers realized there was yet a higher summit, and they decided that there was still sufficient daylight to climb it. By the time they reached the west crater of the summit cone, however, the effort and altitude had thoroughly weakened them and they were chilled to the bone by the cold and biting wind. It was now probably near six o'clock, only about two hours before dark, and both realized that it was too late to descend before nightfall.

On the northern rim of what they called Crater Peak, the two men found an ice cave, which emitted unpleasant hydrogen sulfide fumes. Despite their fatigue, they piled blocks of ice in front of the cave to break the wind and built a circular rock wall around the steam jet. Their backs were frosted and their clothes saturated as a driving mist clouded the summit. Van Trump later wrote: "The night was, to us, a succession of dozes and rude awakenings, the latter occasioned first by a freezing blast from above." It was "more like stupor than sleep."[68] Unquestionably, the steam cave saved their lives in the strong, icy wind. Stevens and Van Trump had overextended themselves foolishly in taking a grand detour to Point Success and had failed to perceive the mountain's true size, but this is not surprising given their lack of alpine experience.

In the morning, the frigid blast kept the men hovering in the cave rather than exploring "Crater Peak." They were worried that they might be trapped, even as Stevens deposited the brass plate "in a cleft in a large bowlder on the highest summit,—a huge mound of rocks on the east side of our crater of refuge. . . ."[69] The mountaineers left their cave at about nine o'clock, and then apparently circled around the Columbia Crest snow dome to avoid the wind and crossed the east crater (which they discovered that morning and whose ice caves they did not find).[70] They descended the steep Gibraltar chute by tying the rope over a rock to serve as a hand line. Below Anvil Rock (near McClure Rock), Van Trump slipped on steep snow and gashed his leg badly on the rocks. In camp that night, Van Trump and Stevens dined on four fried marmots, which, according to Stevens, "has a strong, disagreeable, doggy odor."[71] When Sluiskin returned to camp, Van Trump reported, "he thought it was our ghosts, for he could not believe it possible for men to spend a night on the summit and get back again in the flesh."[72]

This historic conquest of Mt. Rainier set the stage for more exploration on and near "the mountain that was God." After the ascent, Stevens pursued ambitions other than mountaineering, eventually moving to the East Coast. Van Trump continued to be fascinated with Mt. Rainier and made several ascents.

The Emmons and Wilson Ascent of Rainier

Several notable pioneers in the sciences made their mark in mountaineering by ascending Mt. Rainier. Among them was a well-known geologist, Samuel Franklin Emmons, who arrived in Washington Territory in the fall of 1870 with his companion, topographer Allen Drew Wilson. Emmons had a reputation as a serious explorer and a competent mountaineer (see chapter 15), and Wilson had served from 1867 to 1870 with Clarence King's U.S. Geological Survey of the fortieth parallel. A natural leader who had mastered alpine surveying, Wilson would later see extensive service with the Hayden survey in Colorado, where he would climb many high peaks.[73] He later became chief topographer of the U.S Geological Survey. Both men had been engaged with King's survey and had spent five days with him on Mt. Shasta to survey its glaciers, and they were now to visit Mt. Rainier to continue a study of Cascade Range volcanos. They were in excellent condition from their surveys in the Great Basin and their recent acclimatization on the California volcano, and it is doubtful that they were much concerned about the climb until they arrived in Olympia, where they learned of the Stevens-Van Trump ascent.

In late September, Stevens gave Emmons and Wilson useful information about the mountain and then sent them to Longmire at Yelm Prairie. Fortunately, Longmire decided to undertake the trip—although his wife was again opposed—and Emmons later wrote that it was probably only a feeling of duty to the advancement of science and a fear that the scientists might meet misfortune that prompted Longmire's decision.[74] Because King was expected to join the expedition, some mules and provisions were left at Yelm (King's survey work in California, however, apparently took priority, and he never joined his colleagues). Led by Longmire, the party, with five animals, followed the trail through "stately pines, cedars, and firs," a forest of giant trees that "became ere long gloomy and oppressive."[75] Persistent rain hardly improved the spirits of men who had spent three years in a sunny climate.

On September 30, they made their way up the Nisqually River and followed "Longmire's trail" to the Cowlitz River Valley, where the scientists hired two guides. The route took them up the Muddy Fork of the Cowlitz to north of the Cowlitz Glacier. Ascending to Cowlitz Park through the wet forest on October 4, they located a campsite near timberline, where they could peer far down to the glacier.[76] Postponing the ascent of Mt. Rainier because King was still expected and two barometers had been damaged, Emmons and Wilson measured a baseline for map triangulation and explored the mountain's lower slopes. They crossed the glacier divide between the Ohanapecosh and White rivers at near 7,000 feet.

While crossing slopes below yet-unnamed Little Tahoma, Emmons recognized (by its stratification of andesitic lava) that the satellite peak had become separated from Rainier by glacial erosion: "An outlying mass of lava, forming a jagged peak with overhanging cliffs on every side which rises some 2000 or 3000 feet out of these névé fields . . . shows by its bedding lines that it originally formed part of the main mass."[77] They made a pioneering exploration around the mountain's east flank, carrying provisions, blankets, and surveying instruments, and crossed the Ohanapecosh and Fryingpan glaciers. In crossing Emmons glaciers, a total of three miles, they had to cut steps because it was so bare and then camped to the north. On October 8, they climbed what was probably Burroughs Mountain, observing eight glaciers on Mt. Rainier. From the summit, they could look thousands of feet down the north flank to the Winthrop Glacier.[78] Back at Cowlitz Park, alone after Longmire and the Indians left, the scientists spent four days waiting out a gale on a daily ration of one cup of flour, four spoons of coffee, and the remains of the goat the Indians had sold them. They first descended and crossed the Cowlitz Glacier, then reached a high camp at the tree limit, where a gnarled pine provided firewood. Concerned about the limited daylight and the risk of freezing to death on the summit, Wilson and Emmons headed across the Paradise Glacier before dawn on October 17, aided by moonlight.[79] Higher up, the long ridge of andesite outcroppings of Cowlitz Cleaver, with loose blocks and scree, slowed their pace. Nevertheless, they reached the great cliff of Gibraltar in only five hours.

The two men readily located the narrow ledge used by their predecessors. They kept beneath the headwall to avoid the dangerous rock showers from above—rocks hit the ledge beyond them, then bounded noisily to the Nisqually Glacier in the void below. In the narrow gully adjacent to Gibraltar, they saw the rope that Stevens and Van Trump had left hanging.[80] When they gave a pull on the rope, it dropped. As Emmons cut steps in the ice with his geologist's hammer, his rucksack came loose and slid away. He now had less weight to carry, but he had lost his overcoat and ice creepers as well as the brandy, coffee, and firewood. From a higher ledge, Emmons hauled up the theodolite, then kept a tight rope on Wilson with his big pack.

As the men completed their remarkably rapid ascent, the remainder of Mt. Rainier's ice dome was less of a problem, for the experienced pair found a route where crevasses were bridged or could be jumped. At one o'clock that afternoon, they stood on the highest crater rim. Emmons, without his overcoat, soon suffered from the violent wind, "which seemed almost sufficient to blow away the very rocks." Fortunately, the ice cave was open, so he could regain body heat and thaw his icy fingers at a steam jet. Wilson's attempt to set up the theodolite during their two hours on the summit failed because of the gale.

The descent of the summit ice dome was perilous for Emmons, who was now without his creepers. He tried to use the spiked theodolite tripod for balance and to nick holds. Wilson kept in front, hoping he would not need to catch his partner. At the ice chute, the two were able to anchor the rope left by Stevens and Van Trump and grip it for sliding.[81] As the sun sank, the mountaineers observed the shadow of the mountain mass travel slowly eastward until it reached the horizon, then rise up against the sky like a second, gigantic mountain. By the time they reached the foot of Cowlitz Cleaver, it was pitch-black.

On the day after the ascent, both men were footsore from walking on volcanic rocks. Although their provisions were low, they did not return to Olympia through the arduous forest and underbrush but hiked eastward along an Indian trail, crossing the range divide to the Indian agency at Fort Simcoe.[82] Rain and the first snow of the season fell on Mt. Rainier on their third outbound day. They arrived at the fort hungry and gaunt, with torn clothing. When they reached The Dalles, they found they had been given up for lost.

Emmons did not write a description of the ascent, but he did report to King on the mountain, its geology, and its glaciers; and King published Emmons's letter in 1871 as part of a larger account. Stevens did not publish his ascent story until five years later. In that account, he claimed that he and Van Trump were "the only ones up to the present time, who have ever achieved the summit of Takhoma," thus attempting to discredit the Emmons-Wilson ascent and setting off a dispute.[83] In 1877, Emmons presented a paper before the American Geographical Society that gave more than adequate proof of the October 1870 ascent as well as the first scientific information about the great volcanic peak.[84]

The 1883 George Bayley Ascent of Rainier

Forty-three-year-old George B. Bayley came to Mt. Rainier in the summer of 1883 to test his alpine skills. He had begun climbing by the age of twenty-two and had settled in California a decade after the gold rush. "As a mountain climber of some experience," he wrote,

> I had long felt the ambition to try the difficulties of Tacoma. . . . [I had] achieved the summits of a number of western peaks, among them Mounts Whitney, Shasta, Lyell, Dana, Hood, Pike's Peak, Lassen's Butte, and, last though not least, a mountain in the Sierra Nevada named by John Muir and myself the "California Matterhorn." . . . Mount Tacoma could afford the only parallel on this continent to Mount Blanc, the Jungfrau, or the Matterhorn; and to it I turned with that eagerness which can best be appreciated by those who have been infected with the same sort of ambition.[85]

In early August 1883, Bayley joined Van Trump, Longmire (who had now lived in the shadow of the mountain for thirty years but had not yet climbed it), and William C. Ewing, the son of an Ohio congressman, for an ascent of Mt. Rainier via Gibraltar Rock. By this time, the wagon road from Olympia had been extended to Mashel Prairie, where the party was hosted by an Indian known as Henry (Sotolick or Soo-too-lick), a Klickitat who had settled there. After negotiations in Chinook Jargon, it was agreed that Henry would serve as guide and be paid two dollars per day.

Beyond the prairie, the men and horses struggled through the forest, arriving at the foot of the Nisqually Glacier on the fifth day. Bayley described the unforgettable torture from insects at a grassy bank on the Nisqually:

> We all needed rest and refreshing sleep, but were denied either, for no sooner had we unpacked our animals than we were assailed by myriads of small black gnats and ravenous mosquitoes. . . . We anointed ourselves with mud, buried our heads in our blankets, and tried to snatch a little sleep, but all to no purpose. The gnats crawled down our backs.

They rode across the rich, grassy meadows of what is now Paradise Park to the last stunted firs, where their barometer incorrectly indicated an altitude of

8,200 feet (about 2,000 feet too high). Ascending on snow with the pack animals, they finally had to halt. "Henry, who had not spoken a word the entire day," Bayley reported, "and had looked as blue as possible, here made a last persuasive appeal to Longmire not to persist in his foolish attempt to scale the mountain. . . . He said we should never get back alive."

Despite the warning, the foot climb began. With twenty-five-pound packs, the party (without Henry) ascended the narrow ridge of "burnt and blackened rock" to an estimated 11,300 feet. They made beds in the lava scree, as others after them would do, and then lit a fire with the wood they had brought. From their high camp, Bayley was awed by the tumbling Wilson and Nisqually glaciers:

> Lying due west of us, some three miles away in an air line, was the largest glacier any of us had seen, with a length which we estimated at five miles, and a perpendicular depth of probably fifteen hundred feet. It was torn and rent with enormous fissures, the blue color of which we could clearly distinguish in the moonlight, even at so great a distance. The surface of the glacier was strewn with detached blocks or masses of ice, that appeared to have been upheaved and thrown out by some mighty power struggling underneath to escape.

The "grinding of the glaciers" kept them awake. Bayley continued: "Avalanches of snow and ice from the sides of the gorges fell with a sullen crash, and every puff of wind brought showers of stones from the tops of the crumbling cliffs to the glacier. . . . The mountain seemed to be creaking and groaning."

The ascent to the summit, on August 16, was relatively uneventful—aside from the stonefall on the dangerous Gibraltar rock cliff and in the ice gully, where they needed to cut every step. The Gibraltar face traverse was difficult and was later described by Ernest C. Smith who made an ascent of the mountain in 1898:

> Besides being narrow, it shelves away from the rock, and does not always afford a firm footing. . . . I set my alpenstock, then firmly plant my foot, then set the alpenstock again. There is little chance to take hold with one's hands, for nine out of ten projections which offer themselves are rotten, and give way at a vigorous strain. We walk, we crawl, we go singly, we use the rope.

On an ascent in 1894, which was led by guide Henry Sarvent, journalist Olin Wheeler wrote of the danger of falling: "nothing short of a miracle would prevent being carried down to the glacier and into the crevaces, even if not dashed to pieces on the sharp rocks first encountered." Wheeler also described their method of ascent:

> Sarvent would climb up for the full length of our rope—200 feet—then sitting down, plant himself firmly, with one end of the rope fastened to his waist. Then grasping the trailing rope, at intervals of twenty-five feet apart, we would "follow the leader." We soon found that simply holding the rope line in the left hand without bringing any

strain to bear, was all that was necessary. It gave us the confidence required to get along by ourselves.[86]

On the 1883 ascent, Bayley reported: "The snow was frozen into ice-waves, running across the face of the mountain, and resembled a heavy chop sea, solidified and set up at a considerable angle—the hollows being three feet deep, hard and slippery." Near the summit, the mountaineers spent an uncomfortable night close to a steam jet. "The long night at last wore away," Bayley wrote, "and by morning we were fairly cooked by the steam. We could face it but a few moments at a time, and when we turned around, our clothing was instantly frozen to sheets of ice." A wind estimated at one hundred miles per hour hurled the men about on the descent and numbed them with cold. At times, they were literally blown over and had to crawl a few feet at a time. With frozen clothing, they barely survived until getting under the lee of the summit dome. To Bayley, all other climbing in which he had indulged now seemed like "boy's play." Aubrey Haines described the party's euphoria upon returning to the low country: " Van Trump felt it vindicated him in the eyes of some neighbors who did not believe he reached the top in 1870; Bayley felt he had at last climbed a mountain worthy of the effort; and Longmire found he was still a good man despite his sixty-three years of hardships.[87]

The Ascent by Fobes, James, and Wells

The earliest success on the northeast flank of Mt. Rainier was a result of uninformed, youthful zeal that persevered after two false starts up the mountain. Apparently not even aware that the volcano had been ascended, three young, naive climbers from Snohomish were astonished to find a pole on the summit in August 1884. That J. Warner Fobes, George James, and Richard O. Wells reached the summit at all is surprising, considering their lack of planning and their complete lack of mountaineering experience.[88] Their ignorance and inexperience easily could have led to tragedy, for they were completely unaware of the danger of hidden crevasses. In his account of the journey, Fobes, the pastor of a Snohomish church, admitted their lack of knowledge:

> As we pursued the route which will doubtless be the one used by climbers in the future, our experience may be of some value. . . . We knew nothing of the trails or about the locality; and we went in a very plebeian manner, without guides or packers, and carrying our tent, blankets, food, etc., for ourselves.[89]

The three had calculated that two weeks would be needed for the ascent. On the evening of August 15, however, "as we threw on the biggest logs for our night fire and sat around waiting for them to light up, we were happily confident that before our next night fire was lighted we would have explored the summit." With an alpenstock and creepers for each man and one hundred feet of light rope, they headed for Ptarmigan Ridge, a technically difficult north-face route that was not conquered until fifty-two years later. When crevasses began to appear, Fobes reported,

> we did not quite understand them at first; we would walk up near them, try the snow all about with our staves, then creep up gently and, holding our breath, peep over and gaze down their depths with greatest awe. But how familiarity breeds contempt; within three days we would with the utmost nonchalance walk up to their very edge, pole down pieces of snow, [and] contemptuously spit into the abyss.

At about 11,000 feet, they clambered up the highest rock spur and found themselves "on the verge of an immense abyss" (the sharp rock spur on Ptarmigan Ridge that crests at 10,100 feet, separating the North Mowich and Carbon glaciers). The sight of forbidding walls of sheer rock satisfied them that it was "next to impossible to make the ascent." The next day in camp, Fobes saw

> . . . a great gray fellow, twice as large as a Newfoundland dog. . . . I called to the boys, who were still in bed, to hand out the rifle quick. As they came crouching up the wolf ran off about eighty yards and turned, when I fired quickly at his shoulder, feeling perfectly certain that his skin was ours. But the ball must have struck too far back, for he doubled up and started with his tail between his legs on the keen jump down the snow drift. There were no more cartridges in the rifle so I could not shoot again. We expected at every jump to see him roll over, but he went down the drift at an angle of forty degrees, leaving a crimson trail as he ran. Over the rocks and across the valley he went at full speed till we lost sight of him a mile away.

The three men separated to make solitary explorations. Fobes hiked eastward and found the Carbon Glacier, which presented "an odd appearance, much resembling a dried worm with its skin all cracked open, only on a somewhat larger scale." The upper surface was full of crevasses, "its profile being much like a saw." Fobes astutely observed that where the glacier was convex, the crevasses were more open, "but where it is concave they are closed." He headed for a depressed area, where there was not much difficulty in crossing. From the opposite side, a view from the flanking ridge convinced him that a suitable route lay beyond—on the northeast flank of Mt. Rainier.

When the men hiked east of the Carbon Glacier the next morning, they surprised a large goat, which they killed and ate:

> We judged that he weighed considerably over three hundred pounds. . . . though we took his tenderest porterhouse steaks, and tried them boiled, fried and roasted, and all three together, still the billy taste and the seventeen-year toughness were there. But his skin is a beauty, pure white, with long soft hair.

Skirting the foot of the mountain, they ascended to the last wood that could be found and pitched their tent near the glacier's edge. "Several times during the night," Fobes wrote, "we were awakened by great masses of falling ice [from Willis Wall], thundering and shaking the ground like discharges of artillery."

In the morning light, as the party crossed an ice bridge above a deep crevasse in the Winthrop Glacier, an incident occurred that Fobes later considered to be "the base of a most thrilling tale." As the leader was cutting steps with the axe, one of the others became impatient and started ahead.

> He slipped a little, and then began sliding toward the big crevasse at a fearful rate of speed. The only hope of safety was in his alpine-stock. Grasping this close to its sharp point, and turning over upon his face, he stuck it into the ice with all the force he could command and clung to it for dear life. It had the desired effect. The point cut a deep ridge in the ice, making the frosty chips fly into the air, and taking a liberal quantity of skin from off his hand, but it checked the speed. . . . It was the most exciting three seconds of his life.

Although fatigued, the three men persisted and reached the summit "arm in arm" on the next day, August 20. After shouting "Cheers!"—believing they were the first on the summit—they spotted a "walking stick protruding from the snow." Fobes studied the great panorama spread out before them, which he found

> . . . confusing in its vastness. To the north Mount Baker, one hundred and fifty miles distant, seemed near at hand, and we could plainly see the mountains of British Columbia, more than twice the distance. We traced the shores of the Straits past Victoria far up the side of Vancouver Island. Below us the Cascade Range, with its peaks six and eight thousand feet high, seemed scarcely more than a potato patch. . . . through a semi-transparent sea of haze, were seen the tortuous outlines of Puget Sound. The cities were marked by their smoke, and even the steamboats announced their position in the same manner. . . . Oregon was shrouded in smoke, Mount Hood and a few other points alone lifting themselves above the gloom.

With eyes painful from the brilliant reflection of the snow and faces peeling from sunburn, the trio staggered back to Wilkeson. It had been a pleasant and innocent, though careless, adventure. The 1896 Israel Russell party (see chapter 15) must not have been aware of this ascent, for they supposed that they pioneered Mt. Rainier's northern flank.

John Muir on Rainier

John Muir ascended Mt. Rainier by the Gibraltar Rock route in August 1888 with several other distinguished individuals, among them Van Trump and photographer Arthur Warner, who carried fifty pounds of camera equipment to the summit. The naturalist later wrote: "The mountain is very high, 14,400 feet, and laden with glaciers that are terribly roughened and interrupted by crevasses and ice-cliffs. Only good climbers should attempt to gain the summit, led by a guide of proved nerve and endurance."[90]

In his reverent and sometimes humorous style, Muir described the expedition's start:

With a cumbersome abundance of campstools and blankets, we set out from Seattle, traveling by rail as far as Yelm prairie, on the Tacoma and Oregon road. Here we made our first camp, and arranged with Mr. Longmire, a farmer in the neighborhood, for pack and saddle animals. The noble King mountain was in full view from here, glorifying the bright, sunny day with his presence, rising in god-like majesty over the road, with the magnificent prairie as a foreground. The distance to the mountain from Yelm in a straight line is perhaps fifty miles; but by the mule and yellow-jacket trail we had to follow it is a hundred miles. For, notwithstanding a portion of this trail runs in the air where the wasps work hardest, it is far from being an air-line, as commonly understood.

Warner described the bivouac at what is now Camp Muir (previously called Cloud Camp but renamed by Edward S. Ingraham, another member of the party): "The night was like a night in Minnesota in December; there was a strong north east wind and our camp was not well sheltered. Dan [Bass] and I dug a hole in the sand, then got some large flat stones . . . as to make a house."[91]

Muir painted a vivid picture of the discomforts: "After eating a little hard tack each of us leveled a spot to lie on among lava-blocks and cinders. The night was cold, and the wind, coming down upon us in stormy surges, drove gritty ashes and fragments of pumice about our ears, while chilling to the bone. Very short and shallow was our sleep that night. . . ." Warner added: "I was the only one who was not sea sick." He had two chunks of hard bread and some cheese, but the others would not eat.[92] It was likely that none of them drank enough liquid.

Muir remarked on the "desperately steep" ice and the fortunate appearance of "innumerable spikes and pillars which afforded good footholds." The upper curve of the summit dome was dangerous:

> The surface everywhere was bare, hard, snowless ice, extremely slippery, and, though smooth in general, it was interrupted by a network of yawning crevasses, outspread like lions of defence against any attempt to win the summit. Here every one of the party took off his shoes and drove steel caulks about half an inch long into them, having brought tools along for the purpose, and not having made use of them until now, so that the points might not get dulled on the rocks ere the smooth, dangerous ice was reached. Besides being well shod, each carried an alpenstock, and for special difficulties we had a hundred feet of rope and an axe. . . . by noon all stood together on the utmost summit, save one, who, his strength failing for a time, came up later.
>
> We remained on the summit nearly two hours, looking about us at the vast map-like views, comprehending hundreds of miles of the Cascade Range, with their black, interminable forests and white volcanic cones in glorious array reaching far into Oregon; the Sound region, also, and the great plains of Eastern Washington, hazy and vague in the distance.

On the descent, one man "shot past" Muir toward "certain death," but he managed to keep his presence of mind. He "threw himself upon his face and, digging his alpenstock into the ice, gradually retarded his motion until he came to rest." From this expedition, American readers received the first detailed description of Mt. Rainier and its beautiful alpine parks.[93]

Other Early Climbers on Rainier

One of the most persistent of the early Cascade Range mountaineers was schoolteacher Edward Sturgis Ingraham. He had attempted an ascent of Mt. Rainier in both 1886 and 1887 before joining Muir's party in 1888. In late December 1895, Ingraham led an attempt that was sponsored by the *Seattle Post-Intelligencer* to both experience a winter ascent and to determine whether an eruption had occurred. The well-outfitted party took snowshoes and a toboggan, rifles, and a double-barreled shotgun to shoot blue grouse and ptarmigan in the event their 225 pounds of food ran out. The provisions included bologna sausage, hardtack, flour, coffee, rolled oats, condensed milk, cheese, raisins, fresh beef, beans, salt pork, butter, and sugar. Each man had two woolen suits of underclothing, a canvas suit coated with linseed oil, and a sleeping bag—possibly the first use of one in the Cascades.[94] Homing pigeons were taken to carry out messages.

At Wilkeson, the starting point of the winter journey, coal miners "shook their heads solemnly when the nature of the expedition was explained."[95] Ingraham and his companions spent a "no sleep," frigid Christmas Eve at St. Elmo Pass, and there were icy crossings of the Carbon River and a heavy toboggan to pull.[96] The men attempted to ascend via the Winthrop and Emmons glaciers, but the elements proved too violent and they never reached the summit. Still, the exploit proved that the mountain might be assaulted in the winter.

The early climbing events on Mt. Rainier were sporadic, often involving men from outside of the region (such as Emmons, Russell, Bayley, and Muir) who had the time and means or were on a scientific project. Before the turn of the twentieth century, there was no indication of how popular the mountain would become. Historian William D. Lyman had predicted in 1883 that the ascent of Mt. Rainier would not be a frequent occurrence: "The Cascade branch of the U.P.R.R. will doubtless pass not very far from Tacoma. It will then be more easy of access, though it will probably never be a common subject for mountain climbers."[97] He could not have foreseen that, a century later, the ascent would be made by over five thousand climbers a year.

With their summer outing to Mt. Rainier in 1897, the Mazamas ushered in the modern era of mountaineering clubs, when an individual could undertake mountaineering by participating in a club outing. Returning to the mountain in 1905, the Mazamas invited members of the Sierra Club and Appalachian Mountain Club to join them (Gen. Hazard Stevens was also a guest). Thirty-seven Mazamas and fifty-six members of the other clubs reached the summit.

Mt. St. Helens

Mt. St. Helens was the first high, isolated mountain to be climbed near the Pacific Coast. With its symmetrical, glacier-clad cone rearing high above dark evergreen forests, "Loowit" was a majestic beacon to early overland travelers and settlers both north and south of the Columbia River, and it must have stirred considerable curiosity. While Mt. St. Helens was close to the Columbia, however, the tangled wilderness between the river and the mountain discouraged close investigation.

In the summer of 1853, George Gibbs, who had ascended the Lewis River with Capt. George McClellan's railroad-survey party, contemplated an ascent of either Mt. St. Helens or Mt. Adams, but the more urgent business of the survey had taken precedence. That same summer, a group organized by Portland newspaperman Thomas Jefferson Dryer made the first serious attempt to ascend Mt. St. Helens. The group included John Wilson, a Mr. Drew, and a Mr. Smith. Dryer, forty-five years old at the time, was a native of New York state and had come west during the California gold rush in 1849 before setting up a printing house in Portland. Wilson, Dryer's employee at *The Oregonian*, was twenty-seven years old. "Mr. Drew" may have been Oregon Indian agent Edwin P. Drew.[98] The expedition's first stop was on August 16 at Fort Vancouver. There the HBC chief factor, Peter Skene Ogden, loaned them a pack animal and bade them farewell with "a substantial dinner."

During the first night on the trail, one horse ran off, possibly because of a "serenade" by wolves or coyotes, and a messenger had to chase back to the fort to fetch it. The trail was so rough that "some portions of it baffles description. We have gone up chasms several hundred feet in height that would puzzle a goat." They were in burnt land, where game tracks abounded (this area would be the site of the 1902 Yacolt burn). At Yacolt Prairie, the horses munched good grass while Dryer's three companions hunted birds, which the men later "devoured with a relish."

Following a trail "which we care not to travel again" (the one cut by McClellan's survey party), the men saw Mt. St. Helens looming majestically, "apparently only a few miles off—but probably some twenty-five or thirty. It looks much more formidable and difficult of ascent than when seen at a longer distance." Indians who passed by carrying dispatches for the survey party reportedly told Dryer that the mountain was "four sleeps" distant. Eventually, the party reached a volcanic field (the Swift Creek lava flow) that extended some three miles. Not knowing the topography, they followed the survey trail too far east and saw Mt. Adams, which they thought was Mt. Rainier. They discovered their error on August 22 and retraced the route.

On August 25, the men took three days' rations and left the horses in camp. They followed upper Swift Creek to the lava field at the edge of vegetation. Dryer wrote that the "appearance of the mountain upon a near approach is sublimely grand, and impossible to describe." The "blackened piles of lava" were thrown into ridges "hundreds of feet high." The route took them to a small cluster of evergreens at a campsite on the south slope of the volcano, where the party kindled a fire. A long but easy lava ridge led to the summit, a route that required no glacier travel. Dryer's account, which may have been embellished for his readers, stated that

> we were enabled to reach the highest pinnacle of the mountain soon after meridian (August 26). The atmosphere produced a singular effect upon all the party, each face looked pale and sallow, and all complained of a strange ringing in the ears. . . . Blood started from our nose, and all of us found respiration difficult.

These effects, however, were more likely from fatigue than altitude.

Dryer reported that they could plainly see the ocean and that the snow-covered peaks of Mt. Hood and Mt. Adams seemed close by (he again mistook Mt. Adams for Mt. Rainier). Bearings told him that the crater was on the northeast portion of the summit, and he made the first description from close range of an active volcanic crater in the Pacific Northwest: "Smoke was continually issuing from its mouth, giving unmistakable evidence that the fire was not extinguished." After examining crevasses "several rods across," the party built a pyramid of loose stones on the highest spot.

An ascent in 1860 was made by some prospectors, whose largely unknown story appeared in an obscure pamphlet. Five of the party reached the summit on September 28.[99] Believing theirs was the first climb, they left a flagstaff and banner there.

Mt. Adams

A missionary made the first attempt on Mt. Adams in September 1845. The Reverend Henry Bridgman Brewer of the Fort Dalles Methodist mission and Penassar and Howat, two Indian assistants on the mission farm, likely would have succeeded had they not become exhausted because of poor decisions during their approach. The party swam their horses across the Columbia River as they ferried themselves by canoe and followed the trails to summer berry grounds near the mountain that Penassar and Howat knew about. At dawn on September 16, the men were still twelve miles from the foot of the mountain. After taking horses to the snowline, Brewer and the younger Indian picked their way over rock ledges, but the missionary gave out within a thousand feet of the summit. They had made thirty hours of almost continuous effort on only a few berries.[100]

What was probably the first complete climb was made in August or early September 1854 by Andrew G. Aiken, Edward J. Allen, and Andrew J. Burge. Pioneer George Himes, a founding member of the Oregon Historical Society, reported the ascent, which he learned about in a conversation with Aiken.

Aiken, seventeen at the time of the ascent, had crossed the Great Plains in 1853 in the same wagon train as Himes. Himes wrote: "As I have a personal acquaintance with all three men, I have no doubt as to the fact of their making a successful ascent."[101]

The three men (there may have been a fourth) belonged to a party working on the military road being constructed through Naches Pass. It was while the party was camped a few miles northeast of the base of Mt. Adams that the three made the ascent, apparently without difficulty. In a newspaper account, Aiken described the adventure, reporting that they took one day to reach the foot of the mountain and that they had made a rock pile and left an American flag on the summit.[102]

What appears to be the first complete climb of Mt. Adams from the south took place on August 2, 1864, nineteen years after Brewer's attempt. A.C. Phelps, Henry C. Coe, and Josie Fisher were led by "Johnson," a favorite Indian guide who had remained on good terms with whites during the Indian wars. It was reported that Coe, in the course of the descent, made a six-mile slide on a tin pie plate in twenty minutes.[103]

The true pioneer of Mt. Adams was prominent mountaineer Claude Ewing Rusk, who first climbed the mountain in 1889 and then made its first circuit near timberline.[104] Rusk (who in 1910 would lead a small expedition to Mt. McKinley to investigate the first-ascent claims of Dr. Frederick A. Cook) conquered Mt. Adams's east face. This successful exploit encouraged other mountaineers to attempt more difficult routes on the Cascade volcanos after the turn of the century.

With an elevation of 12,276 feet and its easy route from the south, Mt. Adams became popular for outings and mass ascents by early outdoor groups who followed in Rusk's footsteps. The early explorer-mountaineers probably had no inkling that their example would encourage thousands of climbers in the following decades. As roads and trails were built and improved and the population grew, the lure of the glittering peaks became irresistible.

The Deer Fly Mine in the Agnes Creek Valley, August 1909, L.D. Lindsley, photographer (author's collection)

14

PROSPECTORS AND THE MINING BOOM

Only in Washington are there such terrible forests and gulches intermingled and distorted, as if especially to retard the progress of mankind. Giant trees fallen and broken across each other and grown over with an impenetrable thicket of underbrush; gulches that seemed like gigantic wounds in the bosom of nature. . . . It was too much! I gave a man $20 to pilot me back the three miles to the trail.

–E.W. Saportas, 1897

There is nothing that appeals to the mind of man so strongly as the chance of finding gold and silver ore.

–*The Everett Herald*, April 7, 1892

Although mining never dominated the economy of the Cascade Range region as it did in the Rocky Mountains for over half a century, it was important to the life of the settlers and fostered an intense exploration of the mountain areas. The first gold discoveries in the northern Cascades were reported on the Yakima River during the Pacific Railroad survey, and there was a large influx of prospectors to Washington Territory in the last two decades of the nineteenth century. Most of the significant mineral prospects in the Cascades were discovered before 1900.

Prospectors—the most persistent and the least documented explorers of the northern Cascade Range—thoroughly investigated the principal mountain valleys and many of their slopes. They ranged along stream courses, literally foot by foot; and sometimes, when prompted by their intuition or a promising mineral sighting, they climbed the most precipitous of mountain slopes in the hope of locating a rich strike. Miners developed a particular intimacy with the Cascade wilderness. Many prospectors led a solitary existence in the mountains, relying totally on their own resources for survival and on their own skills, luck, and enterprise to discover ore deposits. They were generally tough, fearless, and highly motivated, often performing prodigious feats in their search for treasure.

Prospectors typically sampled stream placers—or deposits—by panning, and they recovered gold from sluice boxes. Where placers were exhausted, they searched out lode deposits (ore veins in bedrock). They depended on assays—a costly and often inaccurate procedure in those days—to determine the richness of a vein.[1] In most districts, silver was found to be a widespread accessory to gold (although at Index, the Carbon River, and Railroad Creek, most of the value in veins came from copper minerals). In the Cascades, most veins were very irregular and hard to follow, intercept, and mine. They also tended to be shallow and narrow, and prospectors and mining-company share-holders were often disappointed when high-grade ore pinched out not far below the surface. Mines often failed because stamp mills to treat the ore were built before enough ore had been found to justify their cost.

The moderately successful prospectors in Washington produced several million dollars' worth of gold and lesser amounts of copper, silver, and other metals by the early 1900s. Most mining promoters made more money from investors and speculators than from actual mining, often selling their claims for profit or obtaining funds for development. In addition to the rich Monte Cristo area (see page 347), there were six major mining districts in Washington's northern Cascades: the area stretching from Mt. St. Helens to Darrington, the Chiwawa River to the Okanogan River, the Skagit River to Ruby Creek, Stehekin to Horseshoe Basin, Thunder Creek, and Mt. Baker.

The Mining Boom

Mt. St. Helens to Darrington

In 1855, Edward Eldridge and two companions who had prospecting experi-ence in California crossed Naches Pass to search for gold on one of the earliest prospecting expeditions in the region.[2] At Fort Steilacoom, Dr. William F. Tolmie tried to persuade the adventurers to abandon their enterprise, but he also gave them route information and told them they would need horses to cross the rivers and carry provisions. Warning the men against admitting they were "Boston men" (that is, Americans), Tolmie advised them to tell any Indians they met that they were "King George men" (British). Each of the three men had a load of over eighty pounds, which included two sacks of flour, fifty pounds of pork, and some tea and sugar along with a rifle, shotgun, axe, pick, pan, and shovel. Each had two blankets, an overcoat, and a change of clothes.

At the first crossing of the White River, the muddy water occluded its depth. "With our axe we cut a stout walking stick for each," Eldridge later remem-bered, "then taking off our clothes we had to secure them with our packs in such a way that we could carry them on our backs." They crossed the White River seven times in this manner. The men were concerned about running out of provisions:

> At first we had been prodigal with our provisions, as the more we ate the lighter our packs became; but we soon saw that that could not be kept up indefinitely or we might find ourselves in the middle of the wilderness with nothing to eat, and no knowledge of where anything could be got. Before we crossed the summit of the

Mines in the Northern Cascades

mountains we had used up what few luxuries we had with us, and were living on flour bread and fat pork, which we ate raw, and found a good substitute for butter.

We had three pairs of blankets and by putting them together we could have one pair under us and two pairs over us, and in this manner after traveling twelve or fourteen hours through the day we could have as refreshing a sleep at night as ever we had in our lives.

Eldridge was also concerned about becoming lost, but he had the confidence of having studied maps and knowing the star positions at different hours of the night.

Near the Columbia River, the three men encountered an Indian camp of perhaps two hundred people. Remembering what Tolmie had told them, they exchanged flour and pork for salmon and potatoes. Someone suggested that they hire an Indian guide on the opposite side of the Columbia, and they were warned of "a long distance to be crossed where there was no water." That night, they

> . . . spread our blankets down and went to sleep wondering whether we would wake up all right in the morning or not. But whatever our thoughts may have been, we were very soon unconscious of all trouble and the next thing we knew the sun was shining on us, and the Indians were shouting, in their canoes, catching fish.

Other prospectors began to search the upper Lewis River for gold, silver, and copper as early as the 1850s. Between 1892 and 1911 alone, over four hundred claims were filed for the area north and east of Spirit Lake as miners sought high-grade vein deposits. The Sweden Mine of the Mt. St. Helens Consolidated Mining Company was the most active operation at the turn of the century. To meet prospectors' demands, the county built a wagon road from Castle Rock to Spirit Lake in 1901 so the mine could be reached by boat, and some fourteen tons of copper ore was hauled to a Tacoma smelter from the mine in 1905.[3] Sulfur was mined as high as the glacerized summit of Mt. Adams. In 1932, workers dug test pits over much of the mountain's crater, spending nights in the abandoned summit lookout. The next year, a camp for packhorses was established at 9,000 feet, and some twelve hundred loads of sulfur ore were carried down from the summit over several years.

East of Mt. Rainier, along Silver, Morse, and Union creeks, placer mining was energetically pursued after 1880. At the head of Union Creek, the Fife brothers staked the Blue Bell group of claims. One colorfully named location was Pick-handle Point, a spur near Crystal Mountain with valuable discoveries. Bullion Basin, adjacent to the present-day ski area, is another of the many features whose names are a legacy of prospecting times.

In the Yakima River drainage, placer gold mining on Swauk Creek dates to 1860, the same year Benjamin Ingalls discovered rich gravels on nearby Peshastin Creek. Edward Blewett's mining company erected a twenty-stamp mill, and arrastras were built nearby for treating ore.[4] Countless miners heading for the Similkameen region took the trail over Blewett Pass and later used the wagon-road route built in 1879 from Cle Elum. There were several thousand mineral locations in the region, both placer and lode quartz, most of them along Ingalls, Negro, and upper Icicle creeks. Allen Van Epps was an active miner in the Icicle Creek Valley and must have been one of the first to traverse the high timberline ridges near Jack Creek and the upper Cle Elum River.

By 1881, there was reportedly a good belt of copper and gold ledges all the way from the Teanaway River west to Kachess Lake. S.S. Hawkins and others made valuable claims on Camp Creek, Fortune Creek, and the cliffs of Hawkins Mountain in the Cle Elum drainage, and soon a wagon road was built from the Yakima River north to Salmon la Sac. According to mining reporter Lawrence K. Hodges, who accumulated information on mine locations and made extensive reports on the region, "the big Salmony Sac" was

> a gorge with precipitous, craggy walls rising a sheer 500 feet from the water, through which the river pours in thunderous rapids to a series of deep pools. These rapids prevent the salmon from ascending further up the river, hence the name, which is a corruption by the Indians of the French words "Salmon le sac." The baffled fish gather in the pools below the rapids and fall an easy prey to the Indians. About this point, too, are the first placer mines, which were worked years ago by Chinamen.[5]

In about 1882, an Indian discovered the King Solomon ledge of galena ore on the Icicle-Cle Elum divide. Hodges described the picturesque area: "In the foreground is the sharp-pointed King Solomon peak, with a pile of rock on each side like an ass's ears." Mt. Stuart dominated the landscape, "a triangular pile of rock shooting one point into the sky . . . so perpendicular as to be bare of snow."[6] Discoveries in the district were sufficiently productive that by 1896 a stamp mill had been erected at the mouth of Fortune Creek (a tributary of the Cle Elum River) to smelt the ores found nearby, and John Lynch built a mill on the mountain slopes above Fish Lake.

Not far to the west, miners took a boat up Kachess Lake, then walked a few miles to copper deposits on Mineral Creek. Numerous claims were staked and several cabins built in the little valley. Prospectors must have crossed the Mineral Creek divide to the head of Gold Creek, where claims were centered in Ptarmigan Park. Prospecting began in about 1890, and soon trails led from Keechelus Lake to Joe's Lake and to the head of the Gold Creek Valley. In 1896, Arthur A. Denny built a cabin near timberline at 4,489 feet, near the Esther Mines and south of the rock formation known as Four Brothers. Denny, a prominent pioneer, had seen Indians bring back pieces of mineral ore from the mountain and discovered ore deposits on August 2, 1869, when he saw iron-rust streaks on what is now known as Denny Mountain (flanking Snoqualmie Pass).[7] Another early discovery was made by F.M. and John W. Guye, who developed a small iron mine near Snoqualmie Pass. Guye Peak retained its name, but adjacent Kate's Peak became Snoqualmie Mountain. After the toll road was built across the pass in August 1884, countless miners probed the Snoqualmie Pass backcountry, and features soon had colorful names such as The Tooth, Red Mountain, Silver Peak, and Chair Peak (which appears to be a huge armchair).

A logical route from the Snoqualmie River Valley into the heart of the range was the rock-rimmed and brush-choked middle fork. Beginning in the 1880s, prospectors staked many claims in the rough mountain terrain above Burnt Boot Creek. The Dutch Miller lode at 5,700 feet near La Bohn Gap—named for Andrew Jackson Miller, who found copper deposits in 1896—was the most intensively developed in that era.[8] Before the turn of the twentieth century, prospectors thoroughly explored the Snoqualmie River drainages, crossing alpine divides to the Cle Elum and Skykomish River watersheds. At times, they ascended dangerous stream canyons, and certainly some of those adventurers scrambled up cliffs and rocky ridges that would challenge modern technical climbers.

The Skykomish River drainage eventually became a much more successful mining hub. The Cady Trail, which bore toward the main crestline of the range, permitted reasonably easy access early on, which led Amos Gunn to settle at what is now the town of Index in 1889 and establish a roadhouse there. Prospectors made important discoveries near the river's north fork and entered the rock gorge of Silver Creek, which led to the surprising discoveries at the head of the Sauk River in the area that would become known as Monte Cristo. Combing the mountainous terrain of the Skykomish River drainage, prospectors discovered the Apex ledge of galena and copper in 1889, near the head of the tributary Money Creek. This was the first property to develop and ship ore in the district; and by 1901, the ledge reportedly produced $80,000 worth of ore. A wagon road and, later, a tramway were built to the property.[9]

On another Skykomish tributary, the west fork of the Miller River, the Cleopatra Mine was established at 3,400 feet, and ore production began in 1897. In 1940, a tram was built to the property, which produced $250,000 worth of ore during one year. At the same time, energetic prospectors searched the Skykomish north-fork tributaries for ore veins. Near upper Trout Creek (on the "back side" of Gunn's Peak, some six miles northeast of Index), Col. Benjamin Townsend and Andrew Merchant located the Copper group of twenty-six claims in 1892.[10] Claims named Troy and Utica were indicative of prospectors' nostalgia for their homes back East.

A rich copper deposit found at Trout Creek in 1897 by A.C. Egbert eventually became the Sunset Mine, the greatest copper producer in western Washington.[11] The success of the Sunset started a boom at Index, which had been a wintering place for miners who could not reach high-altitude lodes during the season. A surface tram was eventually built from Index to Trout Creek, and two tramways ran up the mountain slope to the mine. Another important mine, the Non-Pareil, was located on the mountainside above the Sunset, and nearby Howard Creek had producing properties by 1891.

The region around Darrington, midway along the Sauk River drainage, became an important prospecting area in the 1890s. Wealth-seekers explored the valley of Clear Creek known for Devils Thumb, a towering rock that overlooked their efforts, and searched the flanks of Whitehorse Mountain, high above the townsite. Charles Burns, originally from Ohio, gave his state's nickname to Buckeye Basin, where he built a trail and staked claims. Buckeye Creek became the scene of arduous claim-staking in the 1890s, and its silver ledge was only 2,500 feet beneath the precipitous summit ridge of metamorphosed volcanic sediments.

Another Whitehorse pioneer was Charles Wellman, who probed for ore in the 1890s. On adjacent Jumbo Mountain, the country rock (phyllite and schist) carried gold in veins up to a hundred feet wide between slate and porphyry walls. Across the Sauk, on Gold Mountain—a lesser summit that consists largely of slate with porphyry dikes—some one hundred claims were located between 1895 and 1900.

Chiwawa River to Okanogan River

By 1897, a trail had been built from north of Leavenworth to the upper Chiwawa River, where mineral discoveries had been made in the Chiwawa and Phelps basins and on Red Mountain. Lawrence Hodges reported that in 1893, a trapper told prospector George N. Watson that he had reached the head of the "Chewah" River twenty-five years earlier and "saw a great copper mountain." The trapper may have been Moses Splawn, who in about 1868 ventured to Phelps Creek and brought back ore samples. On Phelps Ridge, where intrusive breccias have been altered and mineralized with sulfides, prospectors found minerals carrying gold and silver. After visiting this mining district, Hodges wrote: "A single glance suffices to satisfy a man that Red hill, which stretches away to the left from the upper rim, contains mineral . . . [there were] red stains of oxidized iron all along the line of cliffs . . . shining red in the sunlight."[12] Hodges found Spider Meadow, three miles above the Red Hill Company's cabin, to be an enchanting mountain garden: "Flowers of every tint . . . of every form and texture, grow in profusion. . . . The horses gorge themselves on [the meadow grass] and never care to wander."[13]

Prospectors soon arrived in number, hiking along the rivers and the nearby Entiat divide, where they found free gold and made claims in Rock Creek, in Maple Creek, west of the Mad River, and south of Whistling Pig Mountain. By the fall of 1901, they had crossed Buck Creek Pass to find the rich copper deposits on Miners Ridge. As prospectors, railroad surveyors, and, later, highway builders learned, avalanches in the high Cascade Range valleys could be devastating. In 1896, Hodges vividly described the "evidence of one of those terrible exhibitions of nature's forces" in Phelps Basin:

> On December 26, 1895, a snowslide started from far up the mountain on the other side of the creek and swept down with a force increasing every second, snapping off every tree in its course, stripping them of limbs and bark and carrying their naked trunks into the creek and far up the other side. The log cabin with a shake roof, in which were Charles Allen, William Nack, and John McKenzie, was buried under snow to a depth of twenty-five feet, the roof being swept off and the interior filled. Allen was by the fire, which softened the snow, and he trod snow until he reached the surface. Nack crawled up the chimney. . . . McKenzie was completely buried and only got what air came in along a beam which fell quartering over him. The other two men set to work to dig him out and in two hours reached him and dragged him to the open air. He was so nearly suffocated that his reason had begun to fail and he was insanely biting his flesh when released, but fresh air soon brought him to himself. The snow still lies deep around the cabin and the logs lie far up both sides of the creek and half choke its bed.[14]

In 1887, across the divide north of Phelps Basin, Great Northern Railway surveyor Albert B. Rogers noted some heavily mineralized outcrops. James H. Holden explored them five years later and in July 1896 discovered a large deposit of gold- and copper-bearing ore near Railroad Creek. He immediately staked claims in the copper sulfide ore, which was chalcopyrite with important amounts of gold. The ore extended through Copper and Irene mountains, and the claims became the site of the famed Holden Mine. Between 1938 and 1957, the mine yielded over $66 million worth of copper, gold, silver, and zinc.[15]

Developing his claims with hard work but little money, Holden built a cabin and dug a tunnel to bring out ore samples. He staked claims near Bonanza Peak (then known as North Star) before the winter forced him out, then shouldered a heavy pack filled with samples and began the twelve-mile walk through the snow to Lake Chelan.

> It was a perilous all-day trip. On the way down, he slipped and sprained his foot. Then while crossing Railroad Creek on a log that was slick from the rain and snow, he lost his balance, fell in the water and was soaked completely. He eventually arrived in Chelan by steamboat, tired and broke, and took a room at the Lakeview Hotel.[16]

Holden also owned the Mary Green Mine in the forest east of the Isella Glacier on Bonanza Peak. In 1900, he leased his claims to Chelan Transportation and Smelting Company, whose development plans included a smelter and a twelve-mile railroad between the lake and the mining property.[17] The company cleared and graded a 3 percent right-of-way for a railroad, but tracks were never laid and the grade was used as a pack trail (the name Railroad Creek survived). In 1902, the company built a road up the valley to the Holden Mine.

In 1907, machinery for a power plant was taken by wagon from Lake Chelan to the Holden claims. In the following years, there were plans for powerhouse and railroad construction, and it was expected that Lyman and Hart lakes would supply water power. Granby Mining Company, the new owners of the Holden claims, spent some $25 million on drilling during 1916 and 1917. Then a subsidiary of the company paid Holden $28,750 for his titles. The year-round operation was now attracting attention.[18]

Early in the century, the Crown Point Mining Company built a cabin at Crown Point near lower Lyman Lake, which company president O.R. Dahl called Aurelia Lake after his mine. In a scheme to defraud investors, the company printed false assertions in 1920 that it had staked valuable mineral claims in the upper Railroad Creek Valley and that it had built a wagon road and a railroad to the locality. The Forest Service alleged that Crown Point's claims were nonmineral and that they were located purely to obtain investment.[19] A judgment by default in 1922 canceled the claims, and the land was then administered as public domain.

By late in the nineteenth century, prospectors had scoured the rocky parapets of Sawtooth Ridge (east of Lake Chelan) and the nearby Methow Valley. During their explorations in these areas for the army in 1882 and 1883, Lt. Henry Pierce and Lt. George Backus encountered men who had spent years combing the uplands, and Backus discovered silver ore on the upper Twisp River. The first claims were staked on the slope of rugged Gilbert Mountain in 1884 and at North (Glacier) Lake in 1892. John Gillihan reportedly penetrated North Creek and traced ore ledges in 1884, but the most important discoveries came as a result of P. Gilbert's claims the next year. By 1896, the busy Gilbert camp was served by the State Trail constructed up the Twisp Valley.

The valley-slope terrain was difficult and rocky, as indicated by a claim called the Mountain Goat; and the claim-staked locale near the Twisp River and South Creek was appropriately dubbed Goat Park Mountain. Farther north and east, an American boundary-survey party found placer gold near the "Big Bend" of the Similkameen River in 1859. Soon a busy prospecting camp developed there, and within ten years the locale was known as Chopaca City. Later, when this area was included in the Moses Indian Reservation, soldiers were called to drive out miners who had entered illegally. Claims were also staked on nearby Chopaka Mountain, some on the high, prominent summit.

After Hiram "Okanogan" Smith made a claim along the Okanogan River in 1867, reports of gold brought claim-stakers to the fringe of the range near the International Boundary. When the reservation was opened to prospecting in 1886, mineral discoveries were made along Salmon Creek (northwest of Okanogan); Ruby City sprang up here. In 1888, Ruby City reached its heyday with a population of over a thousand. According to Guy Waring, who called the lawless camp "the Babylon of the West," killings were common, and "nothing ever happened to the guilty parties. Either they bribed the Justice or escaped from the territory."[20]

In 1904, a party from the second boundary survey discovered tungsten veins carrying wolframite in granitic rocks near timberline at the northern headwaters of the Chewuch (Chewack) River.[21] The veins were developed in 1915, and tungsten from the Tungsten Mine was carried out by mules for many years along a wagon trail through Horseshoe Basin and eastward to the Okanogan River Valley.

Skagit River to Ruby Creek

In the 1850s, the Skagit River was so poorly known that the territorial maps only conjectured its upper reaches, and no non-Natives were known to have traveled its entire course. Alexander C. Anderson and other Hudson's Bay Company explorers who were aware of the river's headwaters were uncertain where it flowed through the Cascades and where it entered Puget Sound. In July 1858, George Gibbs ventured to the Skagit Canyon and drew a sketch, noting the branch from Mt. Baker ("Hukullum") and the Sauk ("Sakumihu") with its Indian trail. The same year, a civilian prospecting group that included Maj. J.H. van Bokkelen found gold on river bars and then continued north to Baker Lake, where they met friendly Indians. Jack Rowley, George Sanger, and John Sutter may have hiked as far upstream as Ruby Creek in 1872 and found gold nuggets. If so, their expedition was the first through the steep-walled, dangerous mountain canyon. In 1875, Rowley took up a claim near the junction of the Skagit and Baker rivers and prospected near present-day Marblemount.[22]

Otto Klement, who in 1873 had left his native Wisconsin for the Puget Sound region, became involved in the great task of clearing the Skagit logjam (near present-day Mt. Vernon) two years later. The Seaam brothers circulated a story in 1877 that Indians had discovered placer gold at a Methow River tributary, which induced Klement to organize an exploring party to investigate. In mid-July, Klement, Charles von Pressentin, Jack Rowley, John Duncan, John Sutter, and Frank Scott left the lower Skagit in a shovel-nosed canoe. At the mouth of the Cascade River, they left the canoe with a subchief (Cascade Charlie) for safekeeping and, guided by Joe Seaam and carrying sixty-pound packs, began walking the thickly forested valley of the Cascade River.[23] On the third day, Klement's party met a group of thirty Indians with ponies who, presumably, had crossed from the Methow Valley. While crossing "Cascade River Pass" on August 1, Klement was enthralled by the sight of "Mountains piled upon mountains, stretching away in every direction, presenting the most startling scene imaginable." An avalanche "of thousands of tons of ice, snow, and rocks" (probably from Johannesburg Mountain) fascinated the party. At night, the thundering roar was such as "to awaken us from a sound sleep and lead us to almost believe that the world was coming to an end."

Following the Indian trail, they came to an overlook of a small lake, which Klement named Spirit Lake. At the lake's head, the guide found canoes hidden by the Skagit Indians. Seaam and Klement paddled down the lake, then hiked to the Columbia River, where the guide knew an Indian (known as Wapato John) who had a stack of provisions. After the two explorers returned to their companions, the group proceeded eastward—without the guide, who "suddenly took violently ill"—to the summit of a high mountain bordering the lake. The party prospected in creeks of the Methow drainage, but found no gold. "It commenced to dawn on us that we had been gulled," Klement wrote.

Undaunted, the party returned to the Skagit and turned up the main river on August 17, with another Indian taking Seaam's place. At the rapids, about ten miles above the Cascade River, misunderstood signals resulted in the canoe tipping. Duncan and Sutter "sprang into the canoe, and with sticks in lieu of paddles, pushed down the stream in pursuit of such articles as might be expected to float. In this they were successful, recovering a half dozen rolls of blankets, four sacks of flour, a number of sides of bacon."

Near present-day Newhalem, the men searched for gold and built sluice boxes. The guide reportedly refused to continue any farther, saying that the region was inhabited by demonical spirits (known as the Stetattle) that did not tolerate the intrusion of Skagit Indians. Klement remained to guard the camp while the rest of the party continued its explorations. Returning in two weeks, the prospectors reported they had found some gold. Their adventures led to new names: Sourdough Mountain was so called because Rowley slipped and spilled a pail of sourdough; and Ruby Creek because of nuggets found in the creekbed. The men also named Canyon Creek, Granite Creek, and Jack Mountain—the last for Rowley, who had the most prospecting experience among the group. Enough gold had been found on the expedition to warrant another trip in 1878.[24]

It was during the third season, in the spring of 1879, that the big strike was made. Albert Bacon and his partners made a claim called Nip and Tuck eight miles above the mouth of Ruby Creek and quickly washed out $1,500 in gold, while Bacon reportedly picked up a twenty-three-ounce gold nugget. Meanwhile, Rowley and his partners went up Ruby Creek to Canyon Creek and took $1,000 in gold dust.[25] When Rowley, Bacon, and Klement returned to the lower Skagit River, the news spread quickly.

On April 12, the steamer *Josephine* left Seattle full of excited prospectors. The great logjam had been cleared in 1878, and steamboats could travel eighty miles to Portage City in high water. By August 1879, over sixty men were working the placers of Ruby and Canyon creeks. Some miners, disenchanted by the earlier Fraser River rush, came to try their luck at Ruby Creek; and during the winter, several hundred men rushed through Hope and the upper Skagit to reach the placer diggings.[26] The stream gravels of Ruby Creek yielded some $100,000 in placer gold, but the rush was short-lived because of limited placer ground and the difficulty of direct access up the Skagit Valley. The only feasible approach route was a circuitous one, from Fort Hope in Canada via the Sumallo River to the upper Skagit, then by Indian trail to Ruby Creek.

A Skagit Canyon trail to reach the gold properties had its beginnings in 1879, when N.E. Goodell (who built a roadhouse at present-day Newhalem and was a pioneer trader in the Skagit mining district) tried to raise construction funds. A December meeting at Yesler Hall in Seattle resulted in contributions of $1,517.[27] The difficult trail was called the Goat Trail, and its most notorious portion was the Devil's Corner, or "elbow," with its overhanging rock and vertical drop to the river.[28] Catwalks and handrails were added, but the place was always dangerous, and above the "elbow" people had to use a forty-foot Jacob's ladder to traverse the exposed corner. At Gorge Canyon, a man known as Capt. Randolf built a shed across the trail and for a time charged miners fifty cents' toll to pass through.[29] At Hanging Rock camp, a hollow under a rock that afforded shelter, the cliff was so low that people had to walk, not ride. From Cedar Bar, a small river flat, the precipitous trail continued eastward by the "long bridge"—a catwalk that followed the canyon face of Stetattle Mountain (now Davis Peak). After ascending a portion of Sourdough Mountain, the Goat Trail traversed Box Canyon, then descended into the "Punch Bowl," where Thunder Creek joined the Skagit before Diablo Lake was formed. At one time, a bridge crossed the Skagit near Cedar Bar, but it burned when a miner tried to rid the area of hornets and accidentally set fire to the structure.

The first horse bridge to span the Skagit was built by miners in 1891–1892, about two miles above Goodell's. By crossing the river there, packers could avoid bringing loaded animals through Devil's Corner. The bridge used large boulders in the river for support, and someone built a cabin on a central boulder and charged a toll for crossing. Miners sporadically used the bridge to reach Thunder Creek, but it suffered washouts (a rebuilt structure in 1902 was partly financed by Thunder Creek Mining Company). In about 1896, a bridge was built across the Skagit Canyon at Ruby Creek, which eliminated the need for a canoe crossing a mile above the canyon.

The names of features on the Goat Trail testify to its frightening nature: Jacob's Ladder, Abraham's Slide, Frightful Chasm, Perpendicular Rock, Wilson's Creep Hole, and Break Neck Peak.[30] Winter experiences on the icy trail could be especially harrowing; and press reports were replete with accounts of avalanches, broken limbs, and narrow escapes. A letter from an H.C. Pierce described an encounter with a snowslide:

One man so narrowly escaped an avalanche that he was actually thrown into the river by the force of the wind caused by the slide which alone saved him from being crushed by the mighty mass of rocks, snow, and debris which composed the avalanche. It was some two hours before he could be rescued by ropes, let down to him by his fellow adventurers.[31]

Early settler Lucinda Davis wrote her daughter about an avalanche of snow falling from a big fir tree in January 1907. "It nearly suffocated me but I just stood still and let it come."[32] Unable to reach their home on Cedar Bar that day, Davis and her son, Glee, built a fire on the trail. After little sleep, the pair had a difficult and perilous trip the next day:

We hurried all we could for fear of the slides and were glad to find that Twomile Creek had not slid at all. We got to the midway point where the trail was blasted into the rock, afraid every second that the ice would break and fall, then here the trail seems to have broken off, but we are not sure. We clung to the bluff till we reached the last section of the bridge and I could not see how we could get over the snow and ice was much higher than the bridge railings and up to a sharp point, but by bracing himself against the bluff Glee got over the worst. Had he slipped, he would have gone between the bluff and the bridge and it was all ice to the river about sixty feet.[33]

In 1880, G.M. Johnson of Ship Harbor described what was involved in a journey to the mines:

We left Mount Vernon on the 22nd of March and arrived at Goodell's (head of navigation) on the 29th in about 44 travelling hours, having laid over two days on account of storm. The cost of transportation from Mt. Vernon to Goodell's is $40 for two Indians and one canoe with carrying capacity for 4 men and 1000 to 1200 pounds of freight, or $10 each to the man; besides this the boatman must be fed by the passengers on the trip, and the principal part of the propelling power is with pole and paddle which must come from the passengers. Every man should furnish himself a pair of long gum boots; then there is no occasion for wet feet. On the morning of the 30th we started with 50 pound packs; passed over Skedadle Mountain and camped for the night at Tunnel Bar, foot of Sour-Dough Mountain. On the 31st we passed over Sour Dough arriving about noon at Ruby. We came to this point in company with men who have travelled over the worse trails in the world, and the unanimous verdict of all is that this trail or track from Goodell's to the mouth of Ruby Creek is the worst ever known.[34]

Devil's Corner was a nightmare for packers, and U.S. Forest Service ranger C.C. McGuire wrote about the danger when he took a horse across it in the fall of 1909:

We had a pack horse with us and when we got to Devil's Elbow the drip from over head had completely blocked the half tunnel with ice. We chopped our way through but it was very dangerous for the horse to get through for one slip would send him over the cliff into the river 50 feet below. So we tight-lined him across. . . . A rope was fastened to the horse's neck and I carried one end across. Another rope was tied around the horse's tail and the loose end with a couple turns around a tree. I took a turn around a tree with the lead rope and as my partner let out a few inches I would take up the slack, so at all times the horse was in the center of the tight line. Though the horse fell several times we inched him across.[35]

The year 1880 began with excitement, with six hundred new claims reported along Ruby Creek. Three steamers were carrying passengers on the Skagit—the *Chehalis*, the *Josephine*, and the *Fanny Lake*—and everyone was demanding an improved trail. At the height of the boom, a mining district was formed and surveyors platted the land near Ruby Creek, even though snow from a heavy winter still covered the ground. The newspapers exaggerated the number of men going to the goldfields, but it is estimated that at least a thousand made their way to Ruby Creek.[36] A visitor to the area in April "found every foot of the way taken up along Ruby and Canyon Creeks."[37] Despite the stampede of 1880, placer-gold yields in the upper Skagit region did not fulfill expectations. As the boom ended, there were abandoned sluices, wing dams, and prospecting equipment littering the banks of Ruby Creek. In October, the *Puget Sound Mail* curtly pronounced the rush "a failure."[38]

The pioneer mining location in the upper north fork of the Cascade River was the Soldier Boy. A soldier from Lt. Pierce's 1882 expedition found a piece of rich float (a gold nugget in the stream) and later returned to locate the claim. In September 1889, George Rouse, John Rouse, and Gilbert Landre traced a ledge high in Boston Basin (west of what was then called Boston Glacier, now the Quien Sabe), perhaps the first people to explore the now-popular alpine basin west of Cascade Pass. The Rouses located the Boston claim and Landre claimed the Chicago. The rich ledge, at an altitude of more than 6,000 feet, was found to contain twenty-four to forty-eight inches of solid galena ore. Higher, at about 7,000 feet, was the San Francisco claim. The Midas claim was located on the east side of Boston Creek, and the Diamond was nearby.[39]

Mining journalist Hodges visited the Boston Mine in the summer of 1896, guided by Landre. He wrote about the beauty of Boston Basin: ". . . Gilbert's basin, named after its lone inhabitant . . . has all the rugged grandeur of tall cliffs and pinnacles towering above broad glaciers, gulches of awful gloom, precipices which no man can scale, beneath which the forest forms its silent aisles of dark columns." Hodges also heard the Indian story that the glacier once covered the basin to the tops of the bars (moraines). "Above it is a line of sawteeth," Hodges wrote, "through which the great Boston ledge cuts. . . . The trail crosses the moraine below the glacier foot." He added:

> The view of the mountain [Boston Peak] further north is cut off by a line of cliffs, split into high, narrow caves. A roar and rattle draws your attention to the mountain opposite [Johannesburg Mountain], where every gulch between the unscalable sawteeth is filled with a narrow, tumbling stream of ice, broken into huge waves. The

roar is caused by the falling of blocks of ice from the tail of one of these glaciers, to be shattered on the rocks beneath and pour in a white cascade, with an accompanying shower of snow, over the precipice beneath.[40]

Because of their inaccessibility, these discoveries did not lead to a rush. Trails built in the 1890s finally opened the Cascade River Valley to horses. By 1897, there was an eight-mile wagon road from Marblemount, with twenty-one miles of trail continuing to Cascade Pass. When Hodges visited the site of Mineral Park (once the Eldorado post office) in 1896, however, he noted:

> This is a town without any people. During the lively times immediately following the discovery of mineral on the Cascade it boasted a population of about 90 persons and had a hotel, store and saloon, but now all is left to the chipmunks, mice and woodrats. The first building passed after crossing the bridge is the store. . . . The door stands open and gives a view of two bunks on each of which is a spring mattress. . . . An old whisky barrel, a flour barrel and grocery boxes litter the floor, the scales hang on the wall.[41]

At Landre's cabin—"the last human abode west of the pass"—Hodges heard the "roar of the cascades, creeks and the wind rushing down from the pass." Huge ice blocks tumbling from the glaciers with a crash "accompanied by clouds of snow."[42]

Hodges also visited the nearly inaccessible Johnsburg claims on the precipitous lower north face of Johannesburg Mountain (the name is an incorrect rendering of "Johnsburg") west of Cascade Pass. The claims were at 3,700 and 5,000 feet, both on the Johnsburg ledge.[43] Hodges described the perilous ascent: "You switchback among the brush up the face of the mountain, and are kept busy sorting out your legs from among the straggling limbs. Some people use strong language under such circumstances." After climbing about a thousand feet,

> you suddenly emerge on the side of a gulch. . . . Its lower half is filled with snow which by alternate thawing and freezing has become almost transformed into ice. It would make an ideal toboggan slide were it not for a huge cave. . . . You climb through brush again to another gulch, which only needs to be tilted up a little more to attain the perpendicular. Its bed is smooth granite, with only slight occasional projections and is thinly covered with decaying fir needles which have dropped from the overhanging trees on each bank and have matted down into a smooth, hard bed. It is no easy task to make much [of] an impression on this ground as will furnish a foothold and at each step one must stamp one's foot down with some force to make it stay. Mr. Landre, missing the trail, started to climb this gulch like a mountain goat and the writer started to follow, but soon found . . . smooth rock at an angle of 70 degrees. He dug the fingers of one hand into a crack in the rock, hung to a small knob with the other and shouted for the old pioneer to coddle and pull him out. Mr. Landre himself found it impossible to climb further and clambered out on the bank. He reached out his stick and the writer, grasping it with one hand, was hauled up to safety from that informal toboggan slide. If he had relaxed his

hold, he would have rolled down a little matter of 2,000 feet and the only means of gathering up his remains would have been a sponge and a soup handle.[44]

At the end of the 1880 Ruby Creek rush, a few miners remained to keep the dream alive. The payoff came when Alex M. Barron discovered the rich Eureka lode in 1891. Hearing there was free-milling gold ore at the surface (coarse gold that can be recovered without flotation or chemicals), prospectors rushed to the district from both the Methow and Skagit river approaches. The focus of mining moved east from the mouth of Ruby Creek to what became the Slate Creek mining district.[45] This time the argonauts came for lode prospects that contained gold-bearing quartz ore, so this portion of the northern Cascades was explored more thoroughly than it had been earlier. Some did continue placer mining, however, and sometimes used hydraulics; but lode mining, which required capital and the formation of large companies, prevailed. Companies often purchased claims with funds from the sale of stock, the shareholders attracted by the promise of a high return on investment. While some reports were undoubtedly inflated, but it seems likely that at least three hundred lode or placer claims had been staked in the Slate Creek district by 1900.

By 1894, the town of Barron had been built near the Eureka location, and it soon boasted a population of over a thousand people. A stamp mill was erected near Bonita Creek in 1896, and the ore was conveyed from the mine down to the mill by a surface tramway.[46] In two years, the Eureka claim yielded $120,000 in gold. In 1895, John Siegfried founded the North American Mining Company and built a mill close to Mill Creek. To transport ore, the company built a narrow-gauge road from the mill to Barron. A horse trail was constructed from the Methow River across Harts Pass to service those mines and the town, and a three-foot wagon road was built to Barron in 1902–1903.

In the mid-1890s, the Skagit Trail was finally improved with short suspension bridges placed over lateral gorges, but the cost of packing supplies was still high. Getting supplies to the Azurite Mine, for example, cost a hundred dollars per ton, which made most operations unprofitable.[47] In time, a profitable packing service to Ruby Creek developed, and more improvements were made to the trail.

Venturesome prospectors continued to face one danger or another. In late August 1897, for example, Peter Miller of La Conner started up Jack Mountain with Tommy Rowland and another companion. On August 22, they "started to cross the big glacier & got stuck on the middle of it we had a hard time to get off of it it was full of cracks." Miller caught Rowland when he slipped and fell; otherwise, he would have "been no more." The prospectors then crossed Devils Mountain to another glacier, where they became trapped and had to bivouac in an ice hole through a cold night.[48]

In 1898, J.B. Allen staked Allen Basin, an alpine amphitheater west of Bonita Creek, where fifteen claims were patented.[49] Also that year, the Ruby Creek

Mining Company brought in a Pelton wheel—a doughnut-shaped waterwheel turned by jets of water—and built a three-mile flume along the canyon slope to bring water for hydraulic power. The company spent $300,000 for the flume, shops, a sawmill, camp buildings, and a hydraulic mining plant with a return of only $3,000.[50] Remnants of the flume can still be seen at the site.

One of the more successful mining operations was the New Light near the Bonita Creek headwaters, which took an estimated $350,000 in gold between 1896 and 1905 and eventually became part of the Eureka district. The Anacortes, to the northwest, reportedly yielded $76.40 in gold for every ten pounds of ore in 1895. The famous Bonita Mine, on the north fork of Slate Creek, produced $350,000 in gold during the 1890s. The Mammoth vein discovered in 1895 by G.C. Mathews about a mile from the Eureka lode was also rich in gold. A stamp mill was built on the property, and a tram brought ore to Barron. From 1898 to 1901, about $397,000 worth of gold was produced there.[51]

By 1900, the gold rush had subsided, and many miners had left for the Klondike. Barron was abandoned in 1907, with miners hastily discarding tools, wagons, bedding, and cooking utensils.[52] It had become apparent that the free-milling gold ore gave way to base metals at depth. Still, considerable optimism remained at some major properties, and stamp mills were constructed at the North American, Minnesota, Anacortes, and Goat mines.

One of the last companies to operate in the area was the Minnesota Mining Company, organized in 1905. Its developments included a mill to crush ore, an air compressor, and a tramway, which was built in 1912. The ore proved to be of a lower grade than expected, however, and the company and stockholders lost the claims in 1916.[53] Miners at the Azurite Mine, which operated from 1915 on the steep eastern slope of Majestic Mountain, at first thought they had found copper, but the ore was in fact pyrite that contained gold. Silver and gold minerals were found to an altitude of 7,400 feet by the Ballard brothers and C.R. McLean, which led to tunneling in 1918. The mine produced $972,000 in gold from November 1936 to February 1939.[54]

In all, 2,812 claims were staked in the Slate Creek mining district from 1894 to 1937. Of those, fifty-two were patented.[55] The demand for metal during World War I renewed interest in mining in the northern Cascades, and in the 1940s and 1950s some development continued.

Stehekin to Horseshoe Basin

As miners carried supplies up the Columbia River and Lake Chelan, the town of Chelan developed as a small mining community. An 1891 newspaper report explained that

> by taking the steamer at the foot of Lake Chelan any one of the camps on the east side of the mountains may be reached in two days. . . . Those camps on the Stehekin

river and its tributaries lie in a fan-like shape, converging from the mouth of Bridge Creek, and are Bridge Creek, North Bridge Creek, Park Creek, Horseshoe Basin, and Doubtful Lake.[56]

The resources of the Stehekin district were excellent for mining. "Cascades pour into the valley on each side in several places supplying hundreds of thousands of horse power. Pine, fir, and cedar timber of sufficient size for all mining purposes cover the hillsides to the timberline."[57] On April 28, 1896, some miners met in Stehekin and organized a district to protect their interests.

The first dramatic strike occurred in September 1885, when George L. Rouse and John C. Rouse found ore in an alpine basin at the head of a tributary to Lake Chelan. The mineral belt "can be traced by the red iron stain eastward through the Sawteeth to Horseshoe Basin and runs westward through the summit into the Cascade District, where it crops out in the Boston, at the side of Boston Glacier."[58] The find turned out to be rich in silver and galena, and the silver-carrying rock from the Rouse's Quien Sabe claim averaged seven to eight hundred dollars per ton.[59]

When the editor of the *Chelan Leader* visited scenic Doubtful Lake basin (near Cascade Pass) in the summer of 1897, he met one of the Rouses in a cabin and then visited the tunnel at the Quien Sabe by crossing the lake on a pole raft. He reported: "Arriving at 'Marmot' island, we climbed over the snow bridge . . . thence up an incline of 45 degrees . . . thence, through a hole in the snow, into the tunnel." The Rouse millsite was located in September 1903 near the falls below Doubtful Lake. A six-inch pipe led from the falls to a forty-eight-inch Pelton wheel, which powered the sawmill.[60] There was another important discovery in 1889, when

the Rouse boys went in by the way of Lake Chelan. The account of their departure from Seattle was published in one of the papers, a copy of which fell into the hands of Messrs. M.M. Kingman and A.M. Pershall of Davenport, who at once fitted up an outfit and after many vicissitudes found themselves in the camp of the Rouse boys . . . where they were cutting a trail through the heavy undergrowth. Kingman and Pershall went up to the lake and made an examination of the properties located, [and they] concluded that the veins must cut through to the next basin, so went down and passing around the angle of the spur which divides Horseshoe from Doubtful, by tortuous ascents succeeded in getting into what is known as the lower basin, where they beheld the rugged and red peaks at the back of the basin, which appeared well mineralized. . . . The hardy prospectors saw the great "red mountain" and attempted to reach it, but on arriving at the wall which divided the lower basin from the upper one they suddenly stumbled onto a ledge which on closer and later inspection proved to average 16 feet wide and was well mineralized. They lost no time in locating two claims, which occurred on the 20th day of June, 1889, naming the claims the Blue Devil and the Black Warrior; claims which were destined to place these men beyond want.[61]

After bonding the two properties, Kingman and Pershall scaled the wall to the upper basin in 1890 and discovered and located the Davenport group.[62] It was an impressive feat, and they may have been the first people to reach the glacierized upper basin, high above timberline.

The patented Black Warrior Mine yielded copper, zinc, lead, gold, and silver. Donald Ferguson's camp in the lower basin had a log cabin, cookhouse, and blacksmith shop.[63] Some of the other cabins high on Horseshoe Basin were remarkable. One of them, under the towers of Ripsaw Ridge, was wired to the rock and had to be entered by a ladder leading through the floor.

Ore samples from the Davenport Mine near the glacier proved to be nearly solid galena. In 1891, Kingman and Pershall sold their holdings, which eventually became the Horseshoe Basin Mining and Development Company. In 1892, a visitor to Horseshoe Basin observed that ledges "cleave the granite country rock so strongly that they can be traced with the eye . . . on the jagged summits for miles." There was a need for better transportation, however: "We can not progress much more without a railroad, and are in hopes the Northern Pacific will be in there before long."[64] Among the tenuous developments in Horseshoe Basin was a "rawhide tramway" built by Pershall and Kingman. The *Chelan Leader* reported:

> Instead of a steel cable and buckets they will use ropes and a sort of basket fashioned out of rawhides. The rope will run through pulleys at either end and the ore, laced up tightly in the rawhides, will slide down over the glaciers, instead of being suspended in the air. . . . The descending load of ore will be used to carry up timbers in the ascending baskets.[65]

In 1908, the Cascade Mining and Smelting Company built a sawmill at Doubtful Lake, powered by a fifty-four-inch Pelton wheel; water was piped to serve air compressors.[66] J.M. Schenyeaulle staked claims across the Stehekin's headwaters at Trapper Lake, at the time called Shyall Lake. He may have been the first to visit this secluded alpine lake beneath the ramparts of Trapper Peak. Other prospectors traced the galena ledges of Horseshoe Basin twelve miles east to the head of Bridge Creek. The Tiger group, located by E.S. Ingraham and his partners in the north fork, was situated under the face of Goode Mountain.

How much of this rugged landscape in the northern Cascades heartland was examined by prospectors will never be fully known, but a reporter provided this information: "The granite formation carrying this galena belt has been traced northeast across Doubtful and Horse Shoe basin . . . between the north forks of Thunder and Bridge Creeks . . . [to] the southwest through the whole watershed of the Cascade's several forks to Mineral Park."[67] In the 1920s, mining in upper Horseshoe Basin nearly ceased for two decades. In the 1940s, when the Black Warrior began to operate again, a 7,000-foot tramway was built between the lower and upper basins, a remarkable achievement considering the difficult terrain.

In its prime, Horseshoe Basin had three millsites and thirty-two claims. There were relatively few stamp mills in the Stehekin area (as well as elsewhere in the northern Cascades) because it was generally cheaper to haul ore to outside mills. While activity in the Stehekin district continued as late as the 1950s, the ores were not high enough in quality to justify costly transportation. When their operations were finished, the miners left behind a good deal of unsightly trash, including pipe, sheet metal, and drums.

Thunder Creek

In the fall of 1891, John Russner and two partners ascended the snow and glacier in Horseshoe Basin, climbed through the "Sawtooths," and crossed the "Silver Basin" (Boston) glacier, which forms one head of Thunder Creek. The trip involved some serious rock scrambling and was quite dangerous, but the men were rewarded by the discovery of a ledge of green ore rich in silver near 7,500 feet.[68] The ledge, the Willis E. Everette, had the richest values in Thunder Creek, with some assays running as high as 3,400 ounces of gold per ton.[69] The vein headed in the "Saw Tooth Range" and struck northeast, its highest adit being at 7,600 feet on the north ridge of Forbidden Peak. Russner's find precipitated a rush to Thunder Creek in 1892, and soon six more claims were located on the ledge. It was a difficult area to reach because of the condition of the Skagit Trail and its unreliable bridges, and some prospectors preferred to take the more circuitous Stehekin route over Park Creek Pass.

One pioneer who undertook the challenge was Merritt E. Field, who would later build the Field Hotel at Stehekin. Once he packed a mill across to Thunder Creek at the rate of two cents per pound; one piece weighed 450 pounds, and the horses had to take turns carrying it. One summer, Field earned $2,500 from packing, but the work was dangerous. On one wintry trip in November 1908, for example, nine of his twenty-seven horses fell and were killed.

When the Skagit Queen Mining Company was formed in the fall of 1892, it obtained control of the basin's claims. The holdings were near upper Skagit Queen Creek, where avalanches could often be heard, and encompassed a series of twenty-nine separate lodes. Real development was begun in 1905 with a hydroelectric powerhouse and a thirty-inch Pelton wheel that powered an electric generator for lights and machine drills. The camp contained bunk and dining facilities, a powder house, a blacksmith shop, a barn for pack trains, and laboratories. The company also built forty miles of trail. Silver prices were low, however, and the hardness of the granite and the difficulty of transporting the rock increased the cost of mining. The ore veins proved to be shallow and narrow as they were elsewhere in the northern Cascades, and together with the rough topography and transportation difficulties the Skagit Queen folded.[70] The remains of the properties can still be seen today.

During 1912, the mining press reported that there were four groups of claims in the district: the Skagit Queen group of forty claims; the Silver Tip, with twenty claims in Silver Basin; the Thunder Creek group of six claims in the basin to the east (below Park Creek Pass); and George Logan's group of ten claims two miles below the pass.[71] Logan had arrived in the valley in 1896 and spent twenty-one summers driving tunnels on his claims. He also built a log cabin there that became a welcome stopover for hungry packers.

The beginning of the twentieth century saw many changes in ownership in the Thunder Creek district. As in other mining districts, new companies purchased claims from miners who did not have the capital to undertake full-scale development. There were big expectations for the Thunder Creek Mining Company, which incorporated in 1904 and purchased William McAllister's five claims on upper Thunder Creek, but the enterprise was unsuccessful. The *Concrete Herald* reported on another case of a company that failed to live up to its promise:

> . . . the North Coast Mining Company . . . was incorporated in Tacoma on January 21, 1908, with a stock issue of $1,600,000. . . . The company expected to produce five hundred tons of silver ore per year with each ton then valued roughly at ten dollars.
>
> . . . When Henry, Bert and Sheldon Fluheart left their diggings on Thunder Creek for the Klondike in 1897, [vice-president William] McAllister moved in and, as the company prospectus pointed out, "he successfully pioneered this rich mining district destined to rival the Coeur d'Alenes if not surpass it". . . . [The company] advertised the land as being "unbelievably wealthy" and stated that, "It assays at $40 per ton—will last 50 years—will return $2.00 per day to stockholders." But such was not the case, as the silver veins quickly pinched off in the hard granite, and $4 per ton rather than $40 became common.[72]

By 1919, the company had disappeared.

Mt. Baker

The search for gold in the Nooksack region began as early as 1858, when prospectors flocked to Bellingham Bay to reach the Fraser River mines in British Columbia. While waiting for the Whatcom Trail to be completed, a few impatient men found gold nuggets on the nearby Nooksack River. John Tennant and his party, venturing out from Whatcom, spent a night with Chief Hump Clalum of the Nooksack tribe before traveling up the river's middle fork in canoes—possibly traversing some terrain new to non-Indians. In 1877, early Whatcom citizens Judge Edward Eldridge and Capt. Henry Roeder searched for gold up the valley of the south fork (the site of the old Indian trail from the Skagit River near present-day Lyman).

Later, packers from Sumas and Deming were lured by predictions of prosperity made by Charles Bagley and Hamilton Wells, who ventured far up the Nooksack's north fork in 1891. Less than two years later, the State Trail was constructed to Ruth Creek, and packers could find profitable work. When Wells discovered the Silver Tip vein (named for an old grizzly living near Hannegan Pass) near milepost 18 on the trail in 1896, the news quickly brought others to the Mt. Baker district. The *Bellingham Reveille* reported that "on the mountain sides grazing was excellent and these pastures were dotted with the horses of prospectors who had left them and were working the neighboring hills. . . . Ruth Mountain is very rugged and precipitous, and has but little been prospected." During the excitement that, according to Hodges, "caused hundreds of farmers, mechanics and professional men to drop their tools and books and undertake a journey," attention focused on the Swamp Creek trail, a hard day's trek for a man with a pack. Jack Post of Sumas, for example, explored beyond the lakes and found a rich quartz outcrop crossing Bear Mountain on August 23, 1897, at about 5,600 feet. He later returned to the discovery, which became the Lone Jack, with his partners R.S. Lambert and L.G. Van Valkenberg. The three men spent two busy days setting claim stakes and gathering ore samples. The assay report overwhelmed them with excitement—gold in the ore was worth over $10,000 per ton.[73] As the news spread, the rush to the Mt. Baker district began.

Hodges detailed the route to the Lone Jack in the September 29 *Seattle Post-Intelligencer*. It

> involves a climb of 1000 feet or so; a descent still greater, down a very precipitous grass-covered slope; the crossing of two small glaciers [snowfields]; a scramble up and around an enormous mass of debris, and a final climb up in the air, which will be remembered for some time by the few who have taken it.

He warned, however, that not much could be accomplished by rushing to the area at that time, with winter approaching: "Any persons who attempt to go in to the new district now will take chances on being caught there by the snow, and will only get out by a desperate struggle."[74]

Nevertheless, there was a scramble to find other ledges. One, located a mile north of the Lone Jack, was of white quartz. The gold carried in the quartz—"wire gold"—could easily be seen by the naked eye and could be picked out with the fingernails. Finds on nearby "Root Mountain" (Granite Mountain) resulted in more tantalizing stories. Headlines proclaimed: "Enough to Keep Prospectors Busy for Ten Years" and "New Eldorado near Mount Baker." Tent cities sprang up overnight, with names such as Gold Hill, Trail City, and Wilson's Townsite (in the valley at the mouth of Ruth Creek). Union City, with perhaps five hundred tent residents at the forks of Swamp Creek, was soon the doorway to the biggest gold strikes.[75] A Whatcom newspaper reported on the crazy scene. Men started out in "wagons, on horseback, on bicycles and on foot with picks, guns, blankets and provisions." Hodges met a reporter "going in on his bicycle and carrying twenty-five pounds. His nose was broken and two teeth were gone. He said his name was Scarce, and I told him he would be a mighty sight scarcer before he reached the end of his journey."[76]

Post and those who followed him needed to apply feature names to the complicated topography so they could accurately locate claims on mining maps. Post named both Twin Lakes and Winchester Mountain, the latter after placing his rifle to mark a claim. Skagway Pass was the name given to the defile at Twin Lakes. Miners also named Gold Run Pass, the crossing later used by Clyde and LeRoy Gargett of Sumas for bringing pack trains to their mine site. Nearby Goat Mountain received its name because of its good hunting and Red Mountain for the colorful tone of its rocky slopes. Lambert thought that Shuksan must mean "Roaring Mountain" because great avalanches could be seen and heard from the high ridges that he and his partners explored.

Despite warnings about the weather, more than seventeen hundred men (according to the *Seattle Times*) entered the district after they learned about Post's discoveries, and the ledge was traced and staked for three and a half miles. Klondike gold experts considered the Lone Jack a rich find. Because only about eight square miles out of a hundred in the district had been prospected, big plans were made, and there was even talk of a railroad.

When Post and his partners sold out to a syndicate, heavy development followed. In 1899, the Mt. Baker Mining Company sold the Post-Lambert operation to English and Son, which built a 4,000-foot aerial tramway and a fifteen-stamp mill at its base. The mill was hauled uphill from beyond Glacier by a steam donkey and horses and then installed near Silesia Creek in 1900. Forty horses and mules in tandem carried the aerial cable, probably the most difficult such transport operation in the northern Cascades.

The Lone Jack mill and mine could operate only about five months of the year, and snowslides were a constant threat. Still, large amounts of gold were produced. The mill burned in 1900 but was rebuilt and continued operating until 1920, when an avalanche destroyed it. Gold production at the Lone Jack continued until 1924, however, and ore production was estimated at $550,000 in the twenty-two years after the mill was rebuilt.[77]

The other great strike in the Mt. Baker district came in 1898 when an Englishman was hunting on Red Mountain (now Mt. Larrabee). Tom Braithwaite shot a goat, which rolled down to a ledge of quartz gold in schist and diorite on the Silesia Creek flank of the mountain. The discovery would become known as the Boundary Red ledge. A mining report stated:

Across Slesse creek from the Jumbo, and on the western slope of Tamihy [Slesse] mountain, is the Tin Cup mineral claim, the workings on which are 1,000 feet above the creek, and are reached by a steep zig-zag trail. A mountain torrent has here denuded the hillside, laying bare a few stringers of quartz, frozen tight in a granitic formation. . . . Red mountain is a semi-circle of rock towering high above timber line, its sides being covered with blue glaciers, and its summit crowned with perpetual snow. The oxidation of the iron, with which the rock is mineralised, has stained the mountain side, giving the appearance from which its name is derived. On a spur of this mountain, between Glacier and Slesse creeks, a trail leads to the claims of the Red Mountain Company, half a mile south of the International Boundary. Near a cabin built on a shelf of rock on the mountain side, a tunnel and upraise are being driven, to tap a quartz vein which is exposed higher up the mountain.[78]

After a wagon road was built along the Chilliwack River between 1898 and 1905, supplies could be taken to the mine by pack train.

This mine eventually proved to be the richest in the Mt. Baker district after the Lone Jack, yielding a total of $1.5 million in gold out of quartz veins. A sawmill was built for a stamp mill, and a long aerial tram was installed to bring ore from the tunnels. Although the mine yielded great ore values, it was plagued by transportation, labor, and other problems. Located just beneath a glacier, the Lone Jack offered notoriously poor working conditions. Water ran through the main tunnel, and during the summer months as many as five hundred gallons of glacial meltwater drained through the main adit each minute.[79] An avalanche destroyed the mill in 1942.

In general, the best prospecting in this locale was along contacts of Slesse Diorite and the Chilliwack Series of argillites, and the area north of Ruth Creek to the International Boundary and from Silesia (Slesse) Creek westward is the most highly metallized area in the district.[80] The logical approach to prospects and mines in the Silesia Creek Valley was from British Columbia. The 1904 annual report of B.C.'s minister of mines explained:

Slesse creek rises some six miles south of the International Boundary and flows into the Chilliwhack river about twelve miles above the municipality [of Chilliwack], and the majority of the claims in the Mount Baker district are reached by a trail following up this creek from its junction with the Chilliwhack, which river is crossed by a pack bridge. . . . Within half a mile of the International Boundary, a wild mountain stream called Glacier creek, and having its source among the glaciers of Red mountain, falls into Silicia creek from the south-west. About a mile and a half from the Boundary, and east of Slesse creek, is Tamihy mountain, a jagged, irregular peak which is a landmark in the district.

During the mining excitement of a few years ago, some misunderstanding was caused by an observation post placed on Slesse creek when the forty-ninth parallel was first surveyed. . . . The post was taken for a boundary mark.[81]

Another successful mine was the gold- and silver-producing Great Excelsior, discovered in 1899 near Wells Creek above the Nooksack River. It had a long including the construction of a concentrating mill in 1914.

In 1910, the Gargett brothers located four claims at 5,800 feet, well above timberline, on the south flank of Red Mountain. They recruited local men to form the Gold Run Mining and Milling Company. For over thirty years, the Gargetts spent every summer tunneling into the alpine slope, hoping to intersect a gold-bearing quartz vein that cropped out on the cliffs above. To operate a sawmill, they hauled in an old automobile engine on horses. Although they spent some $120,000 on this venture and dug out a 2,000-foot tunnel, the vein was never found.

No portrayal of the Mt. Baker mining district is complete without a tribute to "Mighty" Joe Morovits, a Bohemian who became famous not for success in mining but for his feats of strength.[82] As with many miners of his time, no one seemed to know how he came to the Pacific Northwest nor where he went when he left. In 1908, after Morovits had located the Fourth of July group of claims near the head of Swift Creek on the eastern slope of Mt. Baker, he drove over a thousand feet of tunnel by himself. He built and maintained a forty-mile trail and regularly carried a one-hundred-pound pack for a distance of about thirty-two miles (he was once seen packing a large iron cookstove stuffed with flour, whiskey, and dynamite). Among his legendary feats was the windlassing of a 2,300-pound mortar for his stamp mill, a task that required a full two years and the stringing of a mile of tram cable through trees. Morovits climbed Mt. Baker seven times—once by a new route, along which he used his rifle to cut notches in the steep ice.[83]

Before 1900, the Mt. Baker and the Monte Cristo districts together yielded heavy-ore returns that exceeded a million dollars in value. Between 1900 and 1965, some $2.5 million in metallic minerals was produced in Whatcom County, including the Slate Creek district, with gold accounting for 98 percent of the value.[84] Although over five thousand claims were filed in the Mt. Baker district, only the Lone Jack and Boundary Red were profitable. While the remote district had its improbable discoveries and the usual hardships and hazards of mining, the greatest romance of finding great wealth in the northern Cascades was to bloom in a place whose name would be derived not from geography but from fiction: Monte Cristo.

Monte Cristo: A Prospector's Mecca

As early as 1859, Edward Cady and a companion named Parsons traveled up the north fork of the Skykomish River to blaze what would become known as the Cady Pass trail. Placer gold was soon found on the Skykomish and Sultan rivers and their tributaries, and a few placers were located on the Sultan by 1869. It was not until Hans Hansen found silver in 1874 at his Norwegian Mine at Silver Creek, however, that there was a minor stampede to the area. Local prospectors created a mining district at Silver Creek that year and established its laws and claim parameters.

With a foot trail open, prospectors arrived to stake claims in the drainage. In 1873, Theron Ferguson established Mineral City (a conglomeration of cabins) at the Silver Creek forks. By 1880, there was an arrastra but no horse trail—men served as the packers—and two years later Elisha H. Hubbart improved the trail and located claims. Still, there was little knowledge of the flanking mountains and no correct maps. As far as we know, it was not until 1889 that anyone ventured beyond the headwaters of Silver Creek. The prospectors worked mainly in a forest of gigantic trees so dense that the rays of the sun could not break through. Observers were struck by the silent forest and the bare precipitous rocks that showed the destructive action of avalanches and glaciers on the highly folded metamorphic and volcanic rock.

All the early miners at Silver Creek district were impressed by the sight of Mt. Baring (then called Mt. Index). One traveler, reporting for the *Seattle Press-Times* in 1891, described

> the odd figure which attracts the eye at Sultan. . . . From one side it looks like a Prussian fatigue cap, from another, like an old fashioned hat. . . . It is named Index mountain, and marks the entrance to the valley of the north fork of the Skykomish, which is to be the highway to the grand mining belt.

That highway, he wrote, was "perilous at times and painful throughout."[85] The *Press-Times* writer spent ten days in two districts, and he took the arduous trek up Silver Creek: "The trail grew muddier and muddier as we advanced, save for stretches of it that we ran helter-skelter, up the waterworn bed of the creek. . . ." Beyond the Hubbart cabin at Mineral City, "the pull up the mountain . . . is a wearying one."[86]

The most notable property in the Silver Creek district was that of Bonanza Mining and Smelting, located one mile above Mineral City.[87] Near Mineral City and Galena—the district headquarters, at the mouth of Silver Creek—miners gave their finds hopeful or fanciful names such as the Nest Egg, King Bee, Morning Star, Lucky Day, Orphan Boy, and Great Scott. Some eight hundred locations were reported in 1891, with a hundred in nearby Troublesome Creek Valley. On rugged Sheep Gap Mountain west of Silver Creek, E.R. Krueger, the head of a German syndicate, found an ore ledge in 1889.

William F. Phelps, on a prospecting expedition to the Little Chief lode near Copper Lake, described the almost impenetrable forests men had to make their way through for a chance at wealth.

> The fallen trees of a remote period form a network in places almost covering the surface, making travel among and over them exceedingly difficult and quite exhausting to all pedestrians but miners and mountaineers accustomed to the severest hardships. The excursion through these labyrinths into the hitherto almost unknown regions near the sources of the Sultan and Stillaguamish rivers was undertaken for the purpose of examining certain mineral lodes discovered by adventurous prospectors during the year 1891. Until that time it is claimed that the country had never been penetrated by either white or red men. It may well be believed that the latter had never set foot in it, for there could have been no sufficient induce-

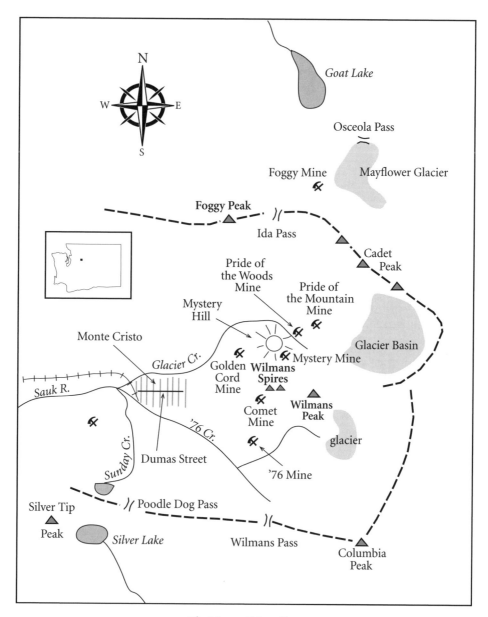

The Monte Cristo Area

ment for them to undergo the labor and hardship, since game is quite rare in those forest fastnesses, while only the unquenchable thirst for the precious metals could have tempted the pale-faces to penetrate them.[88]

Following the Pilchuck River using ponies, the party at one point required six and a half hours to travel two and a half miles. "The severe experience of the day had whetted our appetites, and the coarse, homely fare of the proprietor [of a homestead cabin] was relished better than the most elaborate meal at a first-class hotel," Phelps wrote. Two women visiting from another homestead had already arrived. "One of them, whose avoirdupois could not have been less than 225 pounds, had brought over the mountains on her back a pack of goods weighing sixty pounds."

Among the many fortune seekers in the Silver Creek district, the one who was to make the most important discovery was a restless prospector named Joseph Pearsall. In late spring 1889, Pearsall was tracing an outcrop high on Hubbart's Peak when he spotted a glistening streak on a distant mountain.[89] Red bands covered an entire ledge, from the valley to above timberline. Having explored mountains in Idaho and Colorado for precious metals, Pearsall immediately recognized it as galena stained to reddish gold by surface gossan (the reddish color was caused by the oxidation of rich sulfide ores in contact with the atmosphere). Beneath a cap of gossan there could be a fortune.

Pearsall descended into the precipitous Sauk River drainage to investigate. After reaching the canyon later called '76 Gulch, he scrambled to the bright band to prove out his discovery. Pearsall was probably gone several days before he returned to Mineral City, where he confided the discovery to Frank Peabody, a dreamer and prospector friend who agreed to take some ore samples to Seattle for assay. John MacDonald "Mac" Wilmans, a mining speculator with some influence, saw the samples and immediately decided to return to the discovery site with Peabody. They met Pearsall, and the three of them "climbed Silver Tip Mountain" (probably the divide at Wilmans Pass) and with the aid of glasses saw the ore vein on the mountain (later called Wilmans Peak). Wilmans got far enough to see where the vein cut through the mountain, and Pearsall went farther and brought back more samples.[90]

Wilmans gave the two prospectors direction and hope. After the assay proved good in both silver and gold, he advanced them the small sum of $150 and told them to locate claims and bring more samples. Pearsall and Peabody each were to receive one-eighth of what the property earned, with their shares bonded for $7,500 apiece. The three men agreed to keep the find confidential.

The two adventurers returned to the mountains and staked two claims along the outcrop. Because apparently one was located on July 4, the property was named Independence of 1776 (soon shortened to '76). The second claim, staked on a parallel outcrop (probably on July 5), was named Glacier.[91] The prospectors returned to Snohomish to record the claims and sent a report to Wilmans, who had gone to Utah because of poor health. Wilman's older brother, Fred, was to accompany Pearsall and Peabody to '76 Gulch.

The three men took horses to Scott's camp (a waystation at Galena that would soon have a hotel). They staked another claim, the Ranger, far above the canyon bottom on August 29, and then crossed Wilmans Glacier and the rugged Wilmans Peak divide to a previously unknown alpine basin. Hardly able to believe their eyes, the men saw red streaks of galena below them, an indication that these veins were extensions of those in '76 Gulch.[92] After descending a glacier and steep slopes into the basin—a mountaineering feat—the awestruck men realized that the galena veins did indeed extend through Wilmans Peak. They excitedly staked three claims on the major vein crossing that was to become known as Glacier Basin, naming them Pride of the Mountains, Pride of the Woods, and '89. On the following day, they located the Mystery claim (which would become the first operating mine in the Monte Cristo area) along the vein extension at the edge of the basin, then descended the rushing Glacier Creek to a point where they could see more gossan. The location was later recorded as being in an "unnamed region." The name Monte Cristo did not appear in recordings until 1890.

In the spring of 1890, Mac Wilmans joined his brother Fred in packing loads from Scott's camp to '76 Gulch. Others were also enlisted as packers, some of whom no doubt saw the glitter and staked claims for themselves. Men had to tote loads over the sharp alpine divide at Wilmans Pass, some 3,400 feet higher than Scott's. While a work crew built a cabin in '76 Gulch, gunpowder blasts opened tunnels, and horses packed loads from Scott's on an improved trail along Silver Creek. At the end of 1890, nearby "Silver Lake Pass" was found to be a superior route (the name Poodle Dog Pass came into use about 1900). That summer, Peabody—financed by Mac Wilmans—decided to stake his own claims, and Pearsall divested himself of all his interests for $40,000.

As tunnels were being opened, it was apparent that the exploitation of the rich claims would depend on reliable and efficient transportation to get the ores to a smelter. To attract the necessary capital, the prospectors needed an imaginative name that suggested the wealth of the area. While various sources differ on how and when the name *Monte Cristo* originated, the most reliable story seems to be that Fred Wilmans, who had a copy of Alexandre Dumas's *Count of Monte Cristo*, suggested it to others around the campfire one evening.[93]

Lack of transportation also meant that the heavy machinery necessary for large-scale mining could not be brought to this isolated mountain valley. Tunnels had to be driven through with sledgehammers, and small drills were used to make holes for blasting powder. Until the horse trail from Mineral City was finished in the summer of 1890, everything had to be carried in by men, some of them struggling with loads of up to seventy-five pounds. Roots growing out of the trail's bedrock steps aided the packers. Where there were no roots, an overhead branch of Alaska cedar would hold a tug. The going rate for packing was six cents a pound, and prices for provisions were high: a pound of flour that sold for three cents in Seattle, for example, cost eight cents at Galena. The *Press-Times* reporter who visited the Silver Creek district in 1891 observed the logistics of one packing trip:

> At the summit of the Silver Lake pass we met a packer who was loading up with
> about 65 pounds of fresh beef for the supply camp. An equal amount, for which he

had to return, was cached in a tree, and a sack of flour, which would necessitate another trip still, was placed on the dry side of a cedar to protect it from the rain.[94]

Meanwhile, tales of a "rich mineral girdle" that could be "followed with the naked eye a mile distant" spurred a rush to Monte Cristo. L.W. Getchell, a respected miner, judged that the Monte Cristo discoveries surpassed districts he had seen in Nevada, New Mexico, and California.[95] Mac Wilmans brought in some of his Seattle investment partners, and the Wilmans brothers returned to the Pacific Northwest early in 1891 to renew the mining work at Monte Cristo—Mac Wilmans joining Hiram Bond, a New York judge and property investor. One of the first acts of their Monte Cristo Mining Company was to build the Sauk River "Pioneer Trail." The wagon road, constructed in the spring of 1891, had puncheons (sectioned and split cedar logs) at swamps and soft spots used to form a solid corduroy surface for the heavy, clumsy wagon loads. The technique was efficient and economical—though rough on the heavy gear—and mill machinery, including an entire sawmill, was hauled in as the wagon road progressed. Ahead of four- and six-horse teams, timber fallers and swampers cut the forested right-of-way and built bridges across streams.

By the time the sawmill reached the low ridge between Glacier and '76 creeks, a log-cabin store had been built. Mac Wilmans and his associates decided that the Monte Cristo townsite would be placed just beneath Wilmans Peak, which mining reporter Lawrence Hodges described as "a bold, precipitous headland . . . which ice has carved out right and left of it." The Wilmans brothers were reportedly well liked by miners and had an easy rapport with their employees. The name *Wilmans Peak* was given to the spectacular mountain "by some of Mr. Wilmans friends near the turn of the century."[96]

The Boom Begins

In early summer 1891, as engineer M.Q. Barlow was surveying above the Sauk for a railroad along the wagon-road route, he noted a spring whose water flowed in the opposite direction. Ascending the mountainside, he soon discovered a pass into another drainage that would allow for a more direct approach from the west. In the words of miner Sam Strom: "It so happened this little Spring of Water Changed the Whole Plan."[97] Wilmans and Bond would soon abandon the Sauk project, despite the considerable effort already expended, to focus on the 2,345-foot-high Barlow Pass as an entry route.

Barlow and others quickly realized that Camp Independence, where copper and silver were being discovered, was only about ten miles west and in the same river drainage to Puget Sound. The notion of a railroad route to serve both districts generated much enthusiasm, and Barlow soon put a fifty-man survey crew to work on the Stillaguamish right-of-way. Familiar with the heavy rains and sudden channel changes in the Cascades, he ran his line high above the river's normal water level, even though it would require long, expensive trestles and deep slope cuts. Other engineers disagreed and designated a railroad route far down in the Stillaguamish canyon, planning cribbing at sharp curves and blasting tunnels where the river made a sharp angle.

Northern Pacific Railroad directors Charles L. Colby and Colgate Hoyt visited Puget Sound in the summer of 1890. They envisioned a new seaport and lumber center at Port Gardner on the Sound, an industrial city that would serve Monte Cristo. A syndicate was formed and the decision was made to promote Everett as the headquarters of a new mining district. Early in 1891, wealthy lumberman Henry Hewitt went to New York to meet with Colby and Hoyt to plan the industrial city, railroad transportation, and Monte Cristo enterprises.

The capitalists asked mining engineer Alton L. Dickerman to study the area and its potential. Only three hundred feet of tunneling had been completed, but glaciers had "cut the mountain with deep furrows, leaving exposed upon their broken sides her deep buried mineral treasures."[98] After Dickerman made his report in fall 1891, Colby and Hoyt paid the Wilmans-Bond group $50,000 to hold an option on four important claims in Glacier Basin.[99] That year had seen a boom at Monte Cristo. Thirteen mines and forty claims were reported, with many miners laboring on Mystery Hill. The *Everett Herald* reported that there was more gold and silver in a ten-mile radius than anywhere in the world. Rockefeller's syndicate bought Wilmans's Monte Cristo Mining Company for $47,000 (Wilmans kept his Comet Mine).[100]

After Colby made his first visit to Monte Cristo in the summer of 1892, he was convinced that the mineral deposits "promise the largest development and the easiest working that I have yet heard of." He also believed money could be made in tourist excursions, "if guides are furnished for mountain climbing as in Switzerland. The mines are at the foot of the glaciers, and Thursday I walked on the ice."[101] Unbridled optimism, fueled by the press, prevailed, with one report predicting that the planned $2 million railroad to Monte Cristo would employ three to four thousand men.[102] Returning from the Pride of the Mountains Mine, a mining expert reportedly concluded: "There is enough ore in sight in this one lead to employ the largest smelter in the world for 100 years."[103] Two streams at Monte Cristo provided power for drilling, and there was abundant timber for buildings. The "streets," many named for Dumas characters, were being planked. Men were arriving from Montana and Arizona Territory, Canada and Mexico, Europe and Australia, as well as from Michigan iron mines.

Despite the optimism, life at the mining town was risky. There were explosions, accidental shootings, collapsing mine timbers, falls from cliffs or into ore chutes, and avalanches. Pundits even noted that the plat for Monte Cristo—

filed in Ohio in February 1893—was shaped like a pistol, with Dumas Street pointing like a gun barrel downvalley. In 1892, eighty-foot-wide Dumas Street already boasted a market, post office, tailor shop, blacksmith shop, horse barn, cobbler, machine shop, stores, rooming houses, newspaper office, saloons, and dance halls. One enterprising resident built a two-story outhouse, the height necessary because of the winter snow depth.

Typical of an unruly frontier mining town, Monte Cristo had its share of social problems. Some called it a "Hell Roaring Mining Camp." As a tent city sprang up, whiskey was sold from the Blazing Stump, a combination saloon, gambling hall, and brothel.[104] Most miners had a strong sense of fair play, but there were those "that carried guns and had notches in them." When one miner shot and robbed a jewelry peddler in July 1896, purportedly to gain the favor of a dance-hall girl, a posse hunted him relentlessly. Sam Strom, a Norwegian immigrant, remembered "a few shooting scrapes and knifings, of which three proved fatal."[105] The area was the hangout of a gang of crooks, some of whom concealed themselves below Mt. Forgotten.

There were also numerous accidents on the way to Silverton, which had a population of about five hundred by the spring of 1892. Many a poor fellow "lost his all by a miss step and a plunge into deep pools." One story is particularly unfortunate. Charles McKensey, in an attempt to rectify an error in his claim location, traveled all night from Granite Falls. A bridegroom of only four months, "he was rushing in to 'secure a fortune' for his newly-wed." Some ranchers along the way invited him to spend the night, but he pushed on. The next day, only a few miles from Silverton, the locals "found his lifeless body leaning against a tree half-covered with newly fallen snow."[106]

Railroads to the Mines

The Pride of the Mountains Mine, at 4,500 feet on the slope of rocky Cadet Peak, had the highest ore value in the Monte Cristo area. As the mine was being stoped (terraced) and the ore removed, Dickerman optimistically reported that the veins increased in value with tunnel depth. Tunnels of twenty-five to fifty feet driven at various altitudes showed lead-silver ore of commercial grade. Ore was slowly blocked out of tunnels along the main vein in the basin. This continuous surface outcrop could be traced about one mile from below Mystery Hill to high on Cadet Peak. The ownership of this most promising vein, known as the Monte Cristo, was divided between the Monte Cristo and Pride of the Mountains mining companies.[107]

The Wilmans brothers formed two companies—the Wilmans Mining Company, which consolidated the '76 Creek properties, and the Golden Cord Mining Company, which operated the Glacier Creek mines. Mac Wilmans purchased a 10,000-foot-long tramway from San Francisco to bring ore down from the 5,400-foot Comet Mine, perched at a dizzying location on the Wilmans Spires.

There were rumors that the syndicate might build a smelter at Galena and that a wagon road would be built from Monte Cristo across the Cascade Range crest to the Okanogan region. The wagon road from the Sauk had been completed on August 11, 1891, and four-horse teams could now haul out loads of ore weighing up to four tons. All who worked at the mines, however, were waiting for trams to be installed and the railroad to arrive. Meanwhile, workers at the Monte Cristo sawmill cut timbers for a five-level ore concentrator.

On March 14, 1892, the Everett and Monte Cristo Railroad was incorporated by the New York syndicate, which now controlled the major mines, and $1.8 million was put up for railroad construction. The syndicate ordered the rail line run to Monte Cristo by the most direct route, forty-two miles from the western terminus of Hartford. They ignored Barlow's studies and his recommendation to avoid the Stillaguamish River canyon. Local men also warned them of the folly of their route, which was vulnerable to high water from rain and snowmelt. Nevertheless, three locomotives were shipped from the East, assembled in Seattle, and run to Hartford. Five thousand tons of track and 860 kegs of nails were brought from Philadelphia around Cape Horn in two sailing vessels. Supplies poured into the Stillaguamish River area, where an estimated eighteen hundred men were working to build six tunnels in the five-mile canyon during the summer. No one wanted to work at one particularly dangerous area seven miles below Silverton after a "sand tunnel" caved in. The problem was resolved with a twenty-five-degree shoofly curve around the obstacle. To deal with another type of problem, the sheriff posted notices that anyone selling liquor along the railroad would be prosecuted.

A fatal landslide occurred in June, and in November a storm presaged problems as the river rose alarmingly and caused devastation. The winter of 1892–1893 brought an especially heavy snowfall: a gauge at a road camp seven miles from Monte Cristo measured thirty-six and a half feet. Meanwhile, the syndicate had begun construction of a tram system that would cross Glacier Basin in a 1,200-foot span to the Mystery Mine and bring ore to the townsite. When completed, this 6,600-foot cable-bucket system would be able to carry 230 tons of ore per ten-hour day. Some forty men worked on the installation that winter, but avalanches destroyed many towers. The railroad contractors, Henry and Balch, built a final, 2,000-foot switchback below Monte Cristo because of the Sauk River grade, enabling the line to reach the townsite on August 5, 1893. Six weeks later, the first excursion train brought 156 sightseers. Still, floods played havoc with the railway that year, destroying bridges and killing some workers.[108]

Dickerman spent ten days that year inspecting the syndicate's mines. He announced publicly that he was pleased with the progress and predicted that three thousand men would be employed when the mines were fully equipped and the concentrator completed. Enough silver would arrive at Everett "to pave the streets," he predicted.[109] Despite the 1893 economic depression and plunging silver prices, the future looked bright for Monte Cristo.

In late 1893, the Wilmans's tramway was finished, and about a hundred tons of ore were shipped from the Comet Mine to the concentrator. An aerial tramway lowered the ore from the bunker, on the brink of a rock protrusion, to a rock pinnacle known as "The Count" in a single span, and then on to the concentrator at the townsite. A visitor, A.M. Reynolds, described a precarious route to the mine site, some 1,700 feet above the valley, in 1894: "This is a risky place on account of the rockslides that are continually thundering down the narrow way at a rate that makes it highly interesting for an ascending party." From the notch above the mine, the scene was frightening:

> Rising at the extremities of the dividing ridge—scarcely fifty feet long and so narrow that it can be straddled—two perpendicular obelisk-like shafts of weather beaten rock [the South and East Wilmans Spires] majestically face each other across the narrow gulf of the descending chasm and form gigantic portals to the Eastern view. Looking down between these, 1,300 feet below, can be seen the green, park-like expanse of Glacier basin.[110]

Better Access

The arrival of a steam-driven rotary snowplow early in 1894 meant that trains could run to the townsite during the winter, although with thirty feet of snow, avalanche hazards were great. The tramways began to screech by late winter, when the snow had consolidated, and a production run at the Everett smelter had reduced thirty tons of ore to bullion by March.

By June 7, 1894, the Comet Mine had sent about nine hundred tons of ore down its cables, and in July the main cable of the Golden Cord tramway to the properties on the north slope of Wilmans Peak was stretched and ready for operation. The transportation system from Glacier Basin was finally achieving success, and the tramway began carrying ore down from the Pride of the Mountains Mine on August 1. The concentrator plant, with its three-hundred-ton daily capacity, started up on August 20. There was noise day and night, and burning coal filled the valley with smoke. By year's end, Monte Cristo was a busy production town, and the saloons and dance halls never closed.[111]

It was the boom year of 1894 that saw the first serious pollution at Monte Cristo. The *Everett Herald* reported that "Glacier Creek and Sauk river now look like mining streams. Concentrator tailings have changed the dark green waters to murky white." Still, many residents appreciated the area's natural beauty. A Swiss miner reported that edelweiss grew at the upper end of the moraine of the Monte Cristo Glacier, and flowers on a nearby alp included white trillium, fairy spirea, and bleeding heart.[112] Visitors who had time to climb above Glacier Basin could see Mt. Rainier and even the waters of Puget Sound. Many thought that the Monte Cristo region rivaled Switzerland in its beauty.

What probably most impressed newcomers to Monte Cristo was its rugged landscape. There were no foothills, and peaks, glaciers, canyons, and rockslides rose in the "wildest confusion" from the very outskirts of the town.[113] One visitor arrived with a highly romantic vision of the mining town: "I started for Monte Cristo, half expecting to meet the radiant Count, or to find myself the possessor of some vast treasure, or, perhaps, to gather at least a few gems from the wealth so abundant there." On the railway trip, he reported:

> We come upon the Stillaguamish, serene and peaceful, flowing tranquilly down to meet its destiny in the bosom of blue Puget Sound. The character of the foliage here is varied, and besides the usual growth of giant cedars, with their strong limbs shrouded in glossy robes . . . [are] lithe willows and graceful alders, with their dappled trunks leaning out over the water's edge, their roots reaching down into the cool, moist soil they love so well.
>
> . . . Away above our heads, more than half a mile as the bird flies, we discerned, perched on a craggy point, a tiny building. "That," said Mr. Mercer, the superintendent, "is the entrance to the mine of the Wilman Mining company, and their tunnel runs far back into the mountain."
>
> At another spot, so far that we but just could behold it, we were shown the point where the "Pride" mine tramway passes over the hill, a tram six thousand six hundred feet long, of which fourteen hundred feet spans a gully of over four hundred feet in depth, and the immense buckets come traveling down this endless cable, bringing in the heavy galena ores to the discharge terminal, where they are crushed and sent on their downward course to the immense concentrator.[114]

Another traveler described Glacier Basin—"covered in summer with the greenest of grass and brightest of flowers and shut in on all sides by great, jagged mountains"—and the difficult route from the basin to the Comet Mine, which involved crossing the gap between the Wilmans Spires from the top of the Mystery rockslide. The same gap could be reached from the '76 flank "by a severe, though not necessarily dangerous, climb up the steep, boulder-strewn canyon known as Glacier gulch." Above a mining cabin, the route steepened, and there was a 200-foot-long safety rope.[115]

Winter and spring snowfalls often isolated Monte Cristo, particularly when the trains could not get through. Heavy, fearful slides occurred regularly, and rock and mud slides took a heavy toll. One springtime avalanche wrecked a Comet tram tower, "moving with a terrible and awe inspiring roar carrying great trees and boulders before it." In the fall of 1894, a "tremendous rock slide on the side of Mt. Wilmans . . . shook up the town." On November 23, a snowslide hit a cabin at the Pride mine, killing one man. Unstable soils in the

Stillaguamish canyon caused fatal slides in both 1894 and 1895. On February 20, 1896, a great avalanche struck the Mystery Mine, and men fled for their lives as the snow swept down from high on Wilmans Peak. The wheel at the mine headhouse was broken, and the mine remained closed until another wheel could arrive from San Francisco.[116] In the narrow valley leading to Monte Cristo, a rotary plow could barely make a dent in some of the avalanches that slid across the tracks—particularly when the heavy, wet snow froze. One slide alone piled up forty feet.

During 1895–1897, the fortunes of Monte Cristo rose and fell with the price of gold and silver—and with the Stillaguamish floods, which took out parts of the railroad track at the end of 1896. The contractors' shoofly curve eroded away in the canyon, and Monte Cristo was virtually abandoned for lack of food and transportation. The entire district had to revert to using wagon roads and horses until the line could be repaired. In mid-November 1896, snow turned to rain in the Cascades, and a deluge flowed through two tunnels in the Stillaguamish canyon. A torrential Glacier Creek poured through horse stables and washed away trestles on the Sauk, leaving a train trapped for the winter. The snow melted as temperatures rose to springtime levels, and most of the tracks and bridges in the canyon washed away. On December 11, it was announced that the railroad would not be rebuilt, which angered miners, who had a great stake in the future of Monte Cristo. The following year, Rockefeller initiated mortgage foreclosure on the Mystery and Pride of the Mountains mining companies and gained control of these major properties. There was some evidence that his refusal to rebuild the railroad was a ploy to gain control of all the mines.[117]

Activity in Monte Cristo subsided, giving prospectors more time to investigate adjacent headwater valleys. At Goat Lake, for example, across the rugged divide from Glacier Basin,

> . . . snow fields and glaciers in which the Cascade Range abounds, making it a worthy rival of the Alps in all except the rich store of legends wherewith the Swiss have endowed their beloved land. On the left the shore breaks down to a gentle slope from a line of huge granite cliffs, above which Sloan's Peak soars as a watchtower on an ancient city wall.[118]

This alpine crossing, via Ida Pass, may have been first made on August 9, 1891, when Del Bishop and Henry Cochrane located the Ida claim.[119] Jerome Coffin and James Bedal located eleven claims that fall, and Bedal and William H. Mackintosh returned to the lake in the spring to build a log cabin at its outlet. In the spring of 1893, they traveled the easier Elliott Creek route to the lake on snowshoes. Within three years, they were operating three millsites below the outlet, with the falls providing the water power.

In 1893, Mackintosh and others who had bought pioneer locations sold a partial interest to Pennsylvania investors, and the Penn Mining Company was organized in 1896. The company headquarters—a three-story log house—was built below Goat Lake at a location safe from avalanches; and a seven-mile puncheon wagon road was constructed from Barlow Pass, at a cost of nearly $6,000, to serve as the principal transportation route to the smelter.[120]

The mineral vein of the Foggy ledge, about 5 feet wide and 1,100 feet above the lake, was well exposed. It was traced some 3,500 feet, and red oxidized iron, blue azurite, and green malachite prevailed.[121] A survey was made for a two-mile tramway from Goat Lake, and an air compressor was installed as well as a cable for a sled (pulled by a donkey engine) to haul supplies from the lake to the mine. Hand drills were used to cut a tunnel from the Goat Lake flank of the mountain in 1896. By July 1899, the Penn mining tunnel under Osceola Pass was 2,700 feet long, with men working in it all winter.

When the Foggy ledge was developed, the mine buildings were constructed to conform to the slope, with steep metal roofs to shed snowslides. The blacksmith shop stood "perched like an eagle's nest" on a ledge hewed out of the cliff. The buildings, perfectly secure from snowslides, had water "piped into them from a cascade which leaps from the glacier under Cadet Peak."[122] To reach the boardinghouse above the cliff face, people had to ascend "by swinging up a rope hand over hand with toes resting on notches cut in rock."

There was not only a threatening glacier overhead on Cadet Peak, but the spectacle of another not far to the west. Visiting the Foggy Mine in September 1900, geologist Josiah E. Spurr wrote: "Below tunnel for probably 700–800 feet is a great snow-slide, broken from front of New York Glacier, which itself is half a glacier and does much of the work of one."[123] Hodges climbed to Osceola Pass on the ridge above the Foggy ledge and saw the Mayflower Glacier, its even surface gashed by crevasses, threatening "death to him who seeks to cross the fathomless rivers of ice." The view was breathtaking:

> The marvelously pure air permits you to see in sharp outline every ridge and peak till the farthest cuts off the blue horizon. Myriads of jagged points rise heavenward, like the tips of the waves in a choppy sea, while the white expanse of glaciers and snow fields might be likened to the waters of the ocean lashing themselves into a foam on hidden rocks. . . . A lordly eagle flies far overhead, gazing jealously down at the intruders into his wild wide domain.[124]

Copper Lake

The Silverton and Sultan Basin areas also developed mines in the 1890s. There were almost no trails, and men had to make their way along dangerous river pools and follow overgrown pathways. Prospectors found Copper Lake on June 28, 1891. Named for its "beautiful copper green," it was "on all sides except at the outlet surrounded by almost perpendicular rocky precipices."[125] The first work at the lake was done by the Little Chief group, which had two millsites in the valley below. The 123-foot-thick vein, uncovered by glacial action, carried gold, silver, and copper, and claims ran up the sides of Little Chief Mountain almost to the lake. There were grandiose plans to bring power from the lake's stream falls and a railroad from Sultan.

George Hall, locating claims in the Silverton area, found the "45" vein in August 1891 (named for Alec Jones's forty-five pack animals). The next year, a company spent $2,000 for a pack trail across Marble Pass to the mine site. From the divide at the pass, a "magnificent panorama of mountain peaks" could be seen, "and in the far north snow white Mount Baker."[126] The railroad came to Silverton in 1893, but the boom did not develop for another three years. Discoveries were made high on nearby Helena Peak (north of Silverton) in 1894, and a wagon road was built up Deer Creek. The Consolidated Mining Company, incorporating twenty-five claims that included the 45 Mine, built a 13,750-foot steel cable extending across the Stillaguamish River and Marble Pass. Each of its 265 buckets could hold up to 125 pounds of ore. In 1896, the 45 became the first producer in Sultan Basin, packing its shipments by horse from the sawmill area across Marble Pass to Silverton. During the 1897 boom, there were five saloons, six hotels, and even a band in Silverton, prompting one newspaper to call the town "the coming Denver of the Northwest."[127]

When the 45 Mine's tram was completed on December 3, 1897, there were already 5,000 tons of ore at the mine ready to ship. When the railroad flooded out that winter, the Consolidated Mining Company planned to build its own wagon road and concentrator along the Sultan River, but the company went into debt when it built a long puncheon road to connect with the Great Northern Railway at Sultan. In early 1900, when the owners of the 45 Mine agreed to guarantee a minimum of 3,000 tons of ore a month, the syndicate announced it would rebuild the railroad. By August 1901, the tram was bringing forty tons a day to Silverton, and the future looked promising. Geologists later estimated that the 45, Iowa, Florence Rae, and Sultan King mines—all in Sultan Basin—together produced about 4,016 tons of ore (80 percent of it from the 45 Mine) worth $134,831.[128]

The reopening of the railroad led to a rebirth of mining at Monte Cristo. Mac Wilmans reopened his Comet Mine, and in 1905 he spent a large sum on the concentrator, hoping to repurchase the major mines. Within two years, however, rains and slides had again collapsed his dreams. The Rockefeller syndicate sold the railroad to the Northern Pacific in September 1902, and a train soon bore the new logo of the Monte Cristo Railroad Company, with the letters "M" and "C" in gold against the black backdrop of the tender. Superintendent J.O. Whitmarsh encouraged tourism, and the Sunday trains had four open-top observation cars and a brass band.

Most of the mining properties, which had come under new ownership, produced well in 1906, sending carloads of ore to the smelter, but the owners were forced into receivership in the 1907 depression. Gold extraction dropped sharply in the following years, and in 1918 the silver market collapsed. In 1915, the Northern Pacific gave the Rucker brothers a lease to run the railroad. They renamed it the Hartford Eastern Railway Company and introduced gasoline-operated cars for passenger and light-freight runs. The Rucker brothers prospered, encouraging tourism and spending $150,000 to build the elegant Big Four Inn in 1920 (it was destroyed by fire in 1949).

The investments in Monte Cristo began in an affluent era, when capital could easily be found for projects that promised wealth. The total amount of investment in the area is difficult to calculate, but it likely ran over $4 million. Purchasers had paid nearly $400,000 for the first four principal mining claims. The townsite, tramways, concentrator, mine buildings, and smelter cost far more—not to mention the expenses for railroad construction (about $2 million) and repair—but eastern interests extracted over $7 million in precious metals from the richest gold and silver strike in the Cascades.[129] Still, by 1930, Monte Cristo had become a ghost town, and today only four buildings remain on Dumas Street. Nevertheless, the achievements of the miners were formidable. Many of the prospectors added a great deal to the knowledge about the landscape as the news of their discoveries was spread by local and regional newspapers. The creation of a mining empire in the heart of the Cascade wilderness was evidence not only of a desire for wealth but also of a genuine pioneer spirit.

An aerial view of Mt. Spickard—called Station Glacier by boundary surveyors—taken from the west in late summer, M. Woodbridge Williams, photographer (U.S. Department of the Interior, National Park Service)

15

TOPOGRAPHERS AND GEOLOGISTS

[The forest's] grandeur in an artistic sense is beyond description, and can be fully appreciated only by one who abides for weeks or months in its perpetual twilight.

—Israel C. Russell

The foundation for much of the modern science of geology was laid by James Hutton in the late eighteenth century. His doctrine that "the present is the key to the past"—that the earth's history can be explained by observing the geological forces now at work—was articulated in the early nineteenth century by Sir Charles Lyell, whose description of a continuous development requiring millions of years was a strong influence on Charles Darwin. By the time North American geologists began to study the Cascade Range, Darwin's theory of evolution had been accepted by the scientific world, and paleontology—the study of fossil remains—was a branch of geology. The formidable task of subdividing, classifying, and naming the strata of the earth's crust had been largely completed by the mid-nineteenth century.

Geologist Bailey Willis once pointed out that geology and geography in the 1870s were still sciences of exploration, and the refinements of surveying had not yet been developed. Although famed surveys such as that of the fortieth parallel were the standard of the time, they are now regarded as only high-grade reconnaissance. During the early years of Cascade Range fieldwork, the labors of the Northwest Boundary Survey and the U.S. Geological Survey (USGS) were conducted in largely unmapped country, and a vast amount of topographic work was required just to make base maps on which to plot the geology. Almost from its beginning in 1879, the USGS had a Topographic Branch, whose surveyors and topographers produced contour maps for the geologists who followed them into the field. The first such maps covered a full degree of latitude and longitude at a scale of four miles to the inch, but geologists found it difficult to plot anything but the broadest reconnaissance geology on this small scale. Early in the 1890s, the standard became a more usable half degree (thirty minutes), which is two miles to the inch.

The technique used by USGS field surveyors for quadrangle field maps was to select and survey key summits that they could sight from each station to use as a triangulation network. One network that was developed in the Cascades just before the turn of the century, for example, used the following peaks: Dirtyface, Stormy, Pyramid, Sahale ("Boston"), Gardner, Reynolds, Star,

North and South Navarre, Tiffany, Loop Loop, and Chopaka.[1] It required calculated planning to choose the correct summits, because blocked sight lines and cloudy weather regularly frustrated and delayed the topographers' efforts.

Surveyors determined altitudes by vertical angulation from summits (or other locations of known elevation) and from distant baselines. Altitude figures on ridges or summits were marked on bolts set into bedrock, and such locations were used as plane-table stations (a plane table is a tripod-mounted drawing board for compiling survey and mapping details). Topography was the critical concern, and it was subject to close scrutiny with reports devoted to sighted angles and calculations.

Between 1895 and 1902, the USGS undertook the monumental project of mapping the topography of the Cascade Range from Snoqualmie Pass to near Cascade Pass. Surveyors produced fifteen magnificent thirty-minute topographic quadrangles, each covering about nine hundred square miles of rugged terrain. Those detailed maps became the standard for over sixty years.

The first trip by a survey unit was made in the fall of 1895, from the Skykomish River to Monte Cristo. The summers from 1897 to 1899 were the heyday of the pioneering surveyors, when the extremely rugged and mountainous Sultan, Skykomish, Stillaguamish, Snoqualmie, Glacier Peak, Methow, and Chelan topographic quadrangles were surveyed and mapped.[2] Mapping for the Skykomish quadrangle was carried out under George E. Hyde, who also mapped the Mt. Stuart (with Richard Urquhart Goode) and Cle Elum River areas. Louis C. Fletcher directed the survey of the Stillaguamish quadrangle, and he surveyed a broad area between the Sauk and Stillaguamish rivers between 1897 and 1899.[3]

The Glacier Peak quadrangle and the adjacent Suiattle River area were surveyed under Thomas Golding Gerdine and Edward Chester Barnard during the same years. Much of the fieldwork was done in 1897 and 1898 under Robert A. Farmer and William T. Griswold, who mapped from Lake Chelan to Cascade Pass. The map of the Glacier Peak quadrangle, published in 1899, was the first accurate representation of the complex drainages of the southern Skagit River tributaries. The state surveyor general's maps of this region were almost always out of date (the 1906 map labels all mountainous areas adjacent to the Cascade River as "unsurveyed"), and the Forest Service maps were not published until 1913.

Gerdine's parties explored Illabot, Buck, Downey, and Sulphur creeks and marked Bath, Granite, Jordan, Bench, and Found lakes, as well as Big (Kindy) Creek, Crater Lake, Green Mountain, Totem Pass, Fire Mountain, and the middle fork of the Cascade River. In the summer of 1897, they made the first ascent of Glacier Peak, using it as an observation point and placing a summit marker. "Struggling upward through wisps of fog," Gerdine and his men

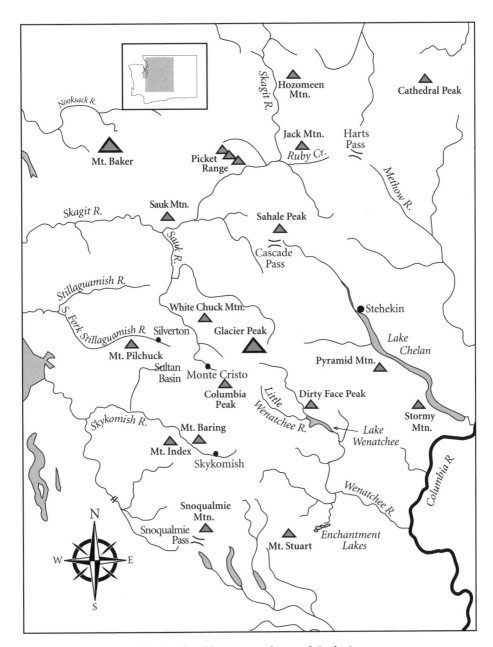

Sites Explored by Topographers and Geologists

reached a high point, started to put up the flag, and were amazed to see through a sudden hole in the drifting fog that the actual peak was still far above and beyond them. They named the false summit Disappointment Peak. They placed a post marked "5423 feet" at Cascade Pass and set a copper bolt atop Sahale Peak, which the surveyors called "Boston."[4]

The Chelan quadrangle was surveyed under Griswold and Farmer. In surveying for the Methow quadrangle, this team appears to have climbed Star, North and South Navarre, and Gardner peaks. The summit of Twisp Pass was marked "6066 feet."[5] During mapping west of Lake Chelan for the Stehekin quadrangle, the name *Bonanza Peak* was incorrectly transferred to what earlier maps called North Star Mountain. Because Bonanza is the highest nonvolcanic peak in the Cascade Range, this error by the USGS is of some importance. Not only was this high, dominant peak named incorrectly on the topographic map, but a triangulation mark was placed on the map to denote the summit—a lofty perch that the surveyors never climbed.[6]

USGS men attached to the Northwest Boundary Survey—Walter B. Reaburn and a companion named Ledgerwood—climbed Davis Peak near the upper Skagit River gorge in 1897. Another party returned in 1905. The J.E. Blackburn party explored the remote Baker River and Bacon Creek drainages in July and August 1909.[7] Photographs taken by the men show that they were east of upper Bacon Creek on July 15. They also conducted triangulation on Mt. Baker and Mt. Shuksan at the Sulphide Glacier on September 8, though it is not known whether they climbed to either summit.

In 1895, Samuel S. Gannett of the USGS climbed Mt. Stuart, the second highest nonvolcanic peak in the Cascades, and left a six-foot-high cairn on the summit. It was noted that "the peak can only be ascended by following a main ridge on the south east side; when about half the way up crossing westward into a gulch leading towards the main summit."[8] Mt. Stuart was climbed again the following year by a party under Goode, and George Otis Smith and probably Israel C. Russell made the ascent in 1898.

Sylvester and Charlton

Albert Hale "Hal" Sylvester and John Charlton left Ellensburg for the Teanaway River in early summer 1897. Neither man was a professional surveyor. The twenty-six-year-old Sylvester, with a degree in engineering, earned $900 a year as a USGS assistant topographer. Charlton, a local schoolteacher who had horse-handling experience, was paid $50 per month to assist him. For their expedition, they purchased six horses for $75 (each was branded "NP" because they had been used in a railroad survey).

Because the melting snows kept streams at high flood, the two men crossed the Yakima River where it broke from Keechelus Lake on a crude ferry operated by a squatter named Chris Hanson. They then followed the cattle road the Smith brothers had opened for driving stock from the Kittitas Valley to Puget Sound. Sylvester and Charlton traveled easily into the Teanaway drainage on horseback. Their precise route is not known, but the first peak they climbed was the magnificent and dominating 9,470-foot-high Mt. Stuart, located a "few years before" by Samuel Gannett.[9] Sylvester described what they did on Mt. Stuart's summit:

> On its highest point, a narrow sloping boulder, we drilled a hole and set a copper plug, set the theodolite, sighted, read and recorded the angles to many peaks, built a rock cairn higher than our heads for a future mark to sight from other stations, while at our backs on the north side of the mountain a precipice fell away a thousand feet to the glaciers below.

From Mt. Stuart, the two men sighted prominent Chimney Rock and decided to seek that rugged summit next. From Snoqualmie Pass, they took a miner's trail up the valley of Gold Creek, where "snow water was pouring in a hundred glittering falls and cascades." They camped on an alp at the head of the canyon "by a crystal clear pond bordered on its upper side by a huge snowbank." The trail ended there; Chimney Rock was still beyond, on another drainage.

> We tied up the tent, hobbled and belled the horses, and with the theodolite, a blanket a-piece, and a scanty grub supply for one night, not forgetting the copper plug, drill and hammer . . . started early up the rocky ridge that separates Gold Creek from Burnt Boot Creek, a tributary of the Middle Fork Snoqualmie River, crossed it, skirted along the west slope of the summit range over snow fields, rock slides and glaciers, above an ice-covered lake, and into a gap under the peak we were after.

Sylvester and Charlton never attempted to ascend the technically difficult Chimney Rock. Instead, they settled on a subsidiary peak they later named Overcoat, because Sylvester left his too-small duck coat buttoned around the summit cairn.

Their next objective was "Index Peak" (Mt. Baring), northward in the Skykomish River drainage. They reached it by following a trail along the railroad line to Doolittle's cabin, "thence up south slope of mountain." The men had to make their way through heavy forest, with "great logs to climb over, pitfalls to stumble into, and stiff underbrush." A grassy chute led to the summit, which they reached in the evening and where they spent the night. They set a copper bolt in rock at the summit and built a six-foot cairn.[10] This was undoubtedly the first ascent of Mt. Baring.

Sylvester then moved up the Skykomish River's north fork and on to Monte Cristo, where he found Louis Fletcher's survey camp (Thomas Gerdine, who had just returned from the ascent of Glacier Peak was also at the camp). Sylvester, Charlton, Fletcher, and Goode climbed Columbia Peak—an excellent strategic viewpoint—for a triangulation survey. The peak was climbed again in 1898, with Sylvester apparently again part of the party. The ascent was made "up the backbone of the ridge" from the divide at the end of the horse trail. Azimuths were taken to Snoqualmie, Baring, Pilchuck, White Chuck, Stuart, Pyramid, Stormy, Dirtyface, and Sauk mountains.[11]

On their 1897 expedition, Sylvester and Charlton followed the wagon road along the Sauk River to the Skagit and established Sauk Mountain as a triangulation station.[12] Using the cable ferry at Marblemount to recross the Skagit River, the two surveyors took their horses up the Cascade River. One stream across the wagon road brought them to a halt:

> It was running at mill race speed, was muddy and appeared deep. The chance of losing horses or at least getting our packs soaked was apparent. A tree fallen across it offered a solution. We unpacked the horses, carried the packs over by way of the log. Tied a rock to the end of a pack rope—one threw while the other retrieved it on the other side. Then with one end of the rope tied to each horse's neck in turn we pulled them in and through the flood, repacked and trailed on.

The route up "Boston" (Sahale) Peak led over rocks, then finally a glacier, "the rocky spine at the top standing but about 100 feet above the ice of the glacier of the south, but falling in sheer descent hundreds of feet on the northeast. This was the sharpest peak I was ever on. No necessity for a cairn here. All that was necessary was to wrap four yards of white cotton around the top of the peak." Sylvester added that north of Glacier Peak "extends a rugged glorious range with evidently hundreds of unscalable peaks, shining waterfalls and ice fields, with deep blue lakes nestled in ancient glacial cirques." Enchanted by his first view of the northern Cascades heartland, Sylvester wrote:

> Glorious Mt. Baker and its understudy Shuksan, not so large but fully as beautiful, seemed but a stone's throw to the northwest across the great canyon of the Skagit, while off to the south Glacier Peak with its glittering snowfields held the eye for long—and still farther away the hoary head of mighty Rainier showed dimly.

Taking the steamer at the head of Lake Chelan, the men met William Griswold's survey party at Railroad Creek at the end of August.

In 1898, Sylvester took part in a surveying ascent of Dirtyface Peak (near Lake Wenatchee), which involved a "foot climb of 5000 ft., very steep and rocky." Horses were taken to within a quarter mile of the summit of Pyramid, a "high bare round-topped mountain on west side of Lake Chelan" and a superb viewpoint.[13] Sylvester was also in a USGS party that made the ascent of Snoqualmie Mountain that year. They followed a horse trail to a miner's cabin at the foot of the mountain and "from here it is a 3000 foot climb to the summit over rocks and through brush." The survey party left a seven-foot cairn with a target marked on a center pole.[14] Sylvester also traveled with another party that reached Mt. Pilchuck by way of the Monte Cristo Railroad.[15] White Chuck Mountain was a more serious ascent. From the mouth of the White Chuck River, "a blind trail runs up either side of river for about ½ mile then turns north. A guide is necessary. The climb is nearly a whole days work and a second camp will probably be required on a bench below and north of ridge ascended."[16]

After his work with the USGS, Sylvester took a position with the U.S. Forest Service. For decades he explored, mapped, and named many of the features in the Wenatchee National Forest, roughly from Mt. Stuart to Glacier Peak and from the Cascade divide to the Columbia River (see chapter 17). He was active in U.S. Forest Service administration until his death in 1944.

The First Geologists in the Cascades

The work of making early geological field maps was certainly no easier than making topographic maps. Geologic mapping required crossing an area several times and carefully tracing rock types, much of the time without instruments. The geologists usually measured distances by pacing from one observation point to another, and the accuracy and detail of their work depended greatly on the time available and the number of observations they could make. The weather and the amount of seasonally snow-free terrain were additional factors.

These early surveyor-explorers—the field geologists and topographers—carried enormous, heavy packs into the wilderness, and they had to work with heavy camping equipment, stubborn mules and packhorses, and unknown and often dangerous routes. They regularly waded icy, hazardous streams, slept in wet blankets, endured leaky tents, and made campfires from wet wood after stripping bark from a fallen cedar or hemlock. "Surveyors of the U.S. Geological Survey go almost everywhere," one observer noted, "without making much ado about it."[17]

The formation of the survey in 1879 is considered by some to mark the end of the era of exploration in the American West, "an era that began with Lewis and Clark's epic march to the Pacific at the opening of the nineteenth century and concluded with Powell and King's institutional victory over the forces of frontier individualism." The purpose of USGS expeditions in the West was seldom to discover the unknown, however, but rather to assess resources.[18] Still, in the Cascades, there were still important discoveries to be made.

Samuel Franklin Emmons, who had a long and distinguished career as a geologist and mining specialist, was the first professional to study the geology and glaciers of the northern Cascades. He was a tall man who gave an impression of dedication, endurance, and steadfastness, and he was known for his painstaking adherence to the scientific method. Representative of a new professionalism in American geology, Emmons had graduated from Harvard College in 1861 and then attended the Royal School of Mines in Germany. There he met Arnold Hague, who recommended him to Clarence King, who hired him to work on the survey of the fortieth parallel.[19] Emmons was twenty-nine years old in 1870, when he made the second ascent of Mt. Rainier (see chapter 13) and carried out a study of its glaciers. He traveled extensively throughout the West and was influential in the establishment of Mt. Rainier National Park. In 1883, he was the USGS geologist in charge of the Rocky Mountain mining district, where he was respected as the man who applied geological knowledge to mining principles. In the summer of 1898, many years after his Mt. Rainier explorations, Emmons briefly studied the rocks and mines of the Blewett Pass area southeast of Leavenworth.[20]

George Mercer Dawson, studying the geology and resources of western Canada for the Geological Survey of Canada, made reconnaissances of the Okanogan and Similkameen country and of the Cascade Range north of Hope from 1875 to 1877. He determined the ages of rocks in sections of British Columbia and concluded that none (except for some gneisses) were older than Carboniferous. Dawson, who was educated in Canada and England, was one of the first to suggest that some granite was of metamorphic origin, referring to the granitic peaks of the Anderson River area and the quite different rocks of the Hope peaks.[21] In 1881, Dawson photographed an immense erratic, assigned its age, and conjectured that ice sheets had transported it from the Precambrian shield in northern Canada.

One of the great men of North American geology was Canadian Reginald Aldsworth Daly. Born in Ontario in 1871, Daly received degrees from Victoria College and obtained his doctorate at Harvard, where he became a professor. He worked and tested his theories in Europe, the Pacific Islands, and South Africa as well as Canada and belonged to scientific societies throughout the world.[22] While employed with the Canadian International Boundary Commission from 1900 to 1907, Daly made exhaustive explorations in the Cascades near the forty-ninth parallel. In 1912, he reported the results of his detailed geological transect from the prairie interior to the Strait of Georgia and outlined the tectonic divisions along the boundary. His report was the first attempt to analyze the rock structures of the boundary belt, a region with an extremely complicated geologic history. His work provided the foundations for broad concepts of Cordilleran tectonics.[23] Daly originated the term *tandem cirques*, a topographic feature often found in the northern Cascades. A particularly fine example was the one containing Hanging Lake, near the south end of Chilliwack Lake. He named the Chilliwack batholith, an extensive pluton that makes up mountains on both sides of the boundary, and studied many rock bodies, including the Castle Peak stock.

A Renaissance Man: Bailey Willis

Bailey Willis—mining engineer, field geologist, author, and professor—was a remarkable interpretive geologist who took part in the USGS investigations in the Cascade Range beginning in 1897. He was born in New York state in 1857 and educated in Germany and at Columbia University. During his many years with the USGS, he was renown for his studies of structural geology, especially for tracing the folds and faults of the Appalachian Mountains and developing a new concept of their deformation.[24] Late in his career—which included explorations in China, Africa, and Patagonia—Willis became interested in seismology, and he became famous as the "Earthquake Professor" at Stanford University.

Willis brought the broad scope of a Renaissance man to his geographical and geological explorations. He was an explorer not only in the sense of traveling widely in little-known landscapes but also in that he reasoned broadly on little-known subjects. His observations show a continuing sense of wonder, and a keen eye for the landscape led him to describe the magnitude of the Cascade Range and speculate on its peculiarities.

After Emmons, Willis was the first geologist to study the Mt. Rainier area. In 1881, he built a horse trail from Wilkeson along the Carbon River. He continued to the Carbon Glacier and was certainly the first to see its snout. In 1883, while employed by the Northern Pacific Railroad, he traced coal beds northwest of Mt. Rainier (which he called Mt. Tacoma). He built a trail to the mountain's meadow slopes and guided German paleontologist Karl von Zittel (see chapter 17).[25]

In a memorial to Willis, Aaron C. Waters wrote: "This frontier wilderness of spectacular river gorges, dense gloomy forests, and huge glacier-clad volcanic cones fascinated the young engineer-geologist." Willis himself penned this tribute to Mt. Ranier in 1883:

> Southward, 9,000 feet above you, so near you must throw your head back to see its summit, is grand Mount Tacoma; its graceful northern peak piercing the sky, it soars single and alone. . . . it is always majestic and inspiring, always attractive and lovely. It is the symbol of an awful power clad in beauty.

His published accounts helped create a demand for preserving Mt. Rainier and its surroundings as a national park. The geologist prepared a document in support of a proposal (which von Zittel endorsed) and in 1894 gained the backing of five scientific and mountaineering societies for a congressional bill to establish a park.[26]

Willis joined the USGS after his work with the Northern Pacific. "Not only was this rigorous field work a delight to Willis," Waters wrote, "but it enabled him to acquire geologic experience and to gain insight into those problems of structural geology and physiography which occupied much of his attention in later years."[27] In the summer of 1895, Willis carried out the first extensive geological reconnaissances in the Cascade Range. The next summer, in July 1896, he ascended Mt. Rainier from its north flank. The party—which included Willis, Smith, Russell, and camp hands Fred Ainsworth and William B. Williams—first ascended the snowfields to Spray Park and passed the prominent peaks that Russell called the Guardian Rocks (Echo and Observation rocks). The route led around the head of the Cataract Creek canyon and followed a "sawtooth crest and had some interesting rock climbing." From a vantage near the Carbon Glacier, Russell commented on the forbidding aspect of this flank of Mt. Rainier: "It rises boldly into the sky as a magnificent snow-clad dome, and appears sufficiently rugged and precipitous to bid defiance to the boldest mountaineer. In fact its northern side is so precipitous that no ascents have been attempted from that direction."[28] He then described the ascent:

> Taking our blankets, a small supply of rations, an alcohol lamp, alpenstocks, a rope 100 feet long to serve as a life line, and a few other articles necessary for traveling above the timber line, we began the ascent of Winthrop Glacier. . . . In several places the névé rises in domes as if forced up from beneath, but caused in reality by bosses of rock over which the glacier flows. These domes are broken by radiating crevasses which intersect in their central portions, leaving pillars and castle-like masses of snow with vertical sides.

The party found its way around the crevassed area and reached

> the sharp ridge of rock which divides the névé snow flowing from the central dome of the mountain, and marks the separation between Winthrop and Emmons glaciers. This prow-like promontory, rising some 500 feet above the glaciers on either hand, we named The Wedge, . . . left in bold relief by the erosion of the valleys on either side. . . .
>
> We found it an utterly desolate rocky cape in a sea of snow. . . . Water was obtained by spreading snow on smooth rocks or on rubber sheets, and allowing it to melt by the heat of the afternoon sun. Coffee was prepared over the alcohol lamp, sheltered from the wind by a bed sheet supported by alpenstocks. After a frugal lunch, we made shelf-like ledges in a steep slope of earth and stones and laid down our blankets for the night. From sheltered nooks amid the rocks, exposed to the full warmth of the declining sun, we had the icy slopes of the main central dome of the mountain in full view and chose what seemed the most favorable route for the morrow's climb.
>
> Surrounded as we were by the desolation and solitude of barren rocks, on which not even a lichen had taken root, and pure white snow fields, we were much surprised to receive passing visits from several hummingbirds, which shot past us like winged jewels.

On July 24, in the early morning, the party began its ascent:

> Roped together as we had been on the previous day, we slowly worked our way upward, in a tortuous course, in order to avoid the many yawning crevasses. . . .
>
> Once while crossing a steep snow slope diagonally, and having a wide crevasse below us, Ainsworth, who was next to the rear of the line, lost his footing and slid down the slope on his back. Unfortunately, at that instant Williams, who was at the rear of the line, removed his alpenstock from the snow, was overturned by the pull on the line, and shot head first down the slope and disappeared over the brink of the

crevasse. A strong pull came on the members of the party who were in advance, but our alpenstocks held fast, and before assistance could be extended to the man dangling in midair, he climbed the taut rope and stood unhurt among us once more. The only serious result of the accident was the loss of an alpenstock. . . .

We crossed many frail snow bridges and climbed precipitous slopes, in some of which steps had to be cut. As we neared the summit we met a strong westerly gale that chilled us and benumbed our fingers. At length, weary and faint on account of the rarity of the air, we gained the lower portion of the rim of stones marking the position of the crater. . . .

Descending into the crater, I discovered crevices from which steam was escaping, and on placing my hands on the rocks rejoiced to find them hot. My companions soon joined me, and we began the exploration of the crater, our aim being to find the least uncomfortable place in which to take refuge from the freezing blast rather than to make scientific discoveries.[29]

On the descent—by Gibraltar on the opposite flank of Mt. Rainier—the men observed that the prow of Little Tahoma was being cut away by the strong ice current: "The descending snow meets the wedge of rock and is parted by it as the current is divided by the prow of a ship at anchor."[30] Willis is remembered on Mt. Rainier in the name Willis Wall, the great north face of the mountain (the Willis Glacier was renamed the North Mowich).

In 1898, Willis studied the geology of the Mt. Stuart area. On September 12, he ascended to 7,300 feet on the divide east of Snow Lakes. He noted the "long narrow glacier" and, lower, how the "rock masses are rounded in form"; the depths of glaciers that formerly occupied the canyon were "traceable on the slopes about Twin [Snow] Lakes." He also observed that "the whole region in sight is of bare granite [the Mt. Stuart batholith] in roches moutonnées." Making only the second description of the now-popular locale (the first was by Israel C. Russell), he mentioned "aiguilles of the most serrate outlines possible" (the Mt. Temple ridge).[31]

In August 1899, while Willis was mapping the Snoqualmie quadrangle (in coordination with Smith and Walter C. Mendenhall), he ascended Gold Creek and also climbed Denny Mountain and Silver Peak. On September 8, while mapping and studying the rock formations near the Teanaway River, he climbed Hawkins Mountain. From the summit, he photographed Mt. Rainier, Mt. Adams, Glacier Peak, Mt. Stuart, and "Wapatus Needle" (Bears Breast Mountain).[32] His notes indicate that on October 1, near the Northern Pacific line, he studied the Keechelus (now Naches) Formation and the Swauk unit.

Willis visited the Lake Chelan area in 1900 and on August 27 ascended to the summit of Stormy Mountain. On September 6, from the Navarre Peaks to the east of the lake, he described the magnificent scenery : "The Cascade Range . . . is stretched in a grand panorama. Including Navarre peaks and the Methow range . . . I counted 60 distinct mountain masses from 7800' to 8000'+ elevation. Glacier Peak 10-400+ towers above all others. Showing that none of them probably rise above 9000'."[33] After taking the steamer to the head of the lake, Willis visited Cascade Pass and climbed Sahale Peak, sighting both Mt. Rainier and Mt. Baker. He also observed the glacier crevasses west of Sahale and mentioned the hornblende gneiss (the Eldorado Orthogneiss) of the area.

The Last Classical Geologists

The scientific efforts of Israel Cook Russell, one of the last classical geologic explorers, contributed much to the knowledge of the northern Cascades. Russell was a self-reliant, restless type who delighted in the challenge of the unknown.[34] In his early years with the USGS, which he joined in 1880, he investigated the desert basins of the West, the Sierra Nevada, and the Cascades. He spent three exploring seasons in Alaska, during which he made two serious attempts on Mt. St. Elias and discovered Canada's highest mountain, later named Mt. Logan.

In 1896, Russell made extensive glacier studies on Mt. Rainier, traversing the mountain during his ascent with Smith and Willis. The Russell Glacier is named for him. In 1897 and 1898, he examined the Mt. Stuart area and became the first to describe the basin of the Enchantment Lakes. In 1897, he studied the Teanaway River drainage and plateau terrain east of the main divide.[35] Conducting a continuing geologic study, he traveled up the Little Wenatchee in the summer of 1898, followed the highland to Glacier Peak, which he apparently climbed alone. Russell also visited Cascade Pass, Ruby Creek, Harts Pass, the Methow River, and Monte Cristo.

No early geologist spent more time in the northern Cascades than the indefatigable George Otis Smith, who visited the range nearly every summer from 1895 to 1906. His first journey, when he was twenty-four years old, was to the Monte Cristo area. Smith traversed below the slopes of Columbia Peak to the '76 Glacier and analyzed the volcanic-flow breccia above nearby Twin Lakes.[36] He also visited Snoqualmie pass on a short mapping reconnaissance with Willis. In his early professional years, Smith, a native of Maine, worked with other Cascade Range geologists, including Bailey Willis, Frank Cathcart Calkins, Walter Mendenhall, George C. Curtis, and Israel Russell. He was with the USGS from 1896 to 1930, and President Theodore Roosevelt made him its fourth director in 1907. Among his many other honors, Smith was president of the Mining and Metallurgic Engineers and chairman of the Federal Power Commission.

Smith was a self-reliant explorer who was ready to venture for weeks into the untracked wilderness equipped with only the bare essentials: tools for measuring and mapmaking, fieldbooks, a geologist's hammer, and a good supply of bacon, beans, and coffee. His pack was always heavier upon his return, the food having been replaced by carefully labeled rock samples. Smith paid close attention to the landscape, its lithology, rock texture, and correlation of units, which allowed him to make detailed descriptions and to speculate on a variety of geologic agents and constructional and erosional processes. He commented on the peculiar shape of Lake Chelan, for example, and on linear glacier-carved valleys such as the Pasayten and the enigma of stranded boulder erratics.

During Smith's geologic investigations on the flanks of Mt. Rainier in 1895 and 1896, he observed what is now known as the Fifes Peak formation on the Mother Mountains and commented on the dip of the bedding of Mt. Rainier's Steamboat Prow. He ascended to 9,000 feet on Ptarmigan Ridge, noting that the lava was highly basaltic—perhaps partly ejected bombs. In the summer of 1898, when he explored the Teanaway River, Mt. Stuart, and Ingalls Creek areas, Smith studied the "Peshastin" and Swauk formations as well as the serpentine of the Ingalls complex. On August 15, he and Curtis made one of the earliest ascents of rugged Mt. Stuart, during which he "attempted in vain to find pass into basin on N side."[37]

Smith commented on the Mt. Stuart batholith at the summit: "The most noticeable feature of granite is its jointing. To this is due the excessive ruggedness of this peak. Perched blocks, seemingly ready to fall at any time are to be found on the highest points." He was impressed with the north face of Mt. Stuart, where "there is an abrupt fall of a thousand feet. Below & lying up against this sheer wall there is a series of small glaciers." He added: "These glaciers tho small are true glaciers & deserve to be so mapped." In 1899 and 1900, Smith, Mendenhall, and Calkins carried out the first thorough geologic and topographic mapping of the Mt. Stuart and Snoqualmie quadrangles. In the summer of 1899, while near Snoqualmie Pass, Smith and Mendenhall climbed Denny Mountain and explored the Gold Creek Valley. Later, Smith studied the Cle Elum River area and climbed Hawkins Mountain.[38]

Together with Calkins—a pioneer petrologist and master field geologist who began his USGS career in 1900—Smith made a geologic reconnaissance of the International Boundary transect in the summer of 1901, working from east to west (see chapter 16). In the summer of 1902, Smith and Calkins surveyed the Ellensburg quadrangle, using packhorses to carry supplies and visiting many locations such as Stampede Pass, Manastash Ridge, Naches Pass, and Arch Rock. In late August, Smith made another geologic study of the Snoqualmie quadrangle. Visiting the rim of Gold Creek, he climbed to above the glacier at the head of Burnt Boot Creek. He also explored Spectacle and Glacier lakes, noting the lava and breccia of the Naches Formation (which he mapped as Keechelus and Teanaway).[39] After conducting triangulation from the summit of Snoqualmie Mountain, Smith again studied the Cle Elum River drainage. In 1906, he ascended Wright Peak and Denny Mountain and traversed from Denny to The Tooth.

Smith's surveying of several quadrangles enabled the USGS to publish accurate topographic maps, and five *Geologic Atlas* folios were based on his work. In addition, his contributions to the study of rock units in the Cascades were of great importance. Together, Smith, Russell, and Calkins established a bedrock stratigraphy that has withstood later geologic scrutiny remarkably well. Their foundational work has been built upon, rather than replaced by, recent studies.[40]

Another important figure in Cascade geology and mapping history is George Carroll Curtis, a Harvard graduate who became the foremost maker of geographic and geologic models. In 1898, at the age of twenty-six, he worked with Smith to map the Mt. Stuart quadrangle. During exploration of the drainages of the Cle Elum and Teanaway rivers and Ingalls Creek, he visited Ingalls Lake, where he noted the glacier striations and assumed that the lake basin was a glacial excavation. His notebook entry reads: "On the eastern side of the Three Sisters Peaks [Ingalls Peak] at 6500 ft. Alt. head of Ingalls Creek, is a small triangular shaped lake about 1/5 of a mile on a side. This—on July 26— was covered with ice, snow, and floating bergs." Observing craggy Ingalls Peak, Curtis wrote that the "dike cuts the mass composing the peaks . . . which is composed of pyroxenite." He found that granite sent dikes into the serpentine, which forms a considerable portion of the peaks: "The weathered surface of the pyroxenite is a light red, which gives a prevailing tint to the mass."[41]

Field geologist Walter Curran Mendenhall spent a brief time working in the Cascades. Born in Ohio, he studied at Harvard and in Heidelberg and was named acting director of the USGS in 1931. In the summer of 1899, working under Smith, Mendenhall thoroughly explored and mapped the Snoqualmie quadrangle. Sometimes alone, sometimes with others, he climbed Snoqualmie Mountain and other summits in the area. The high ridges he traversed included the divide between Burnt Boot Creek and the middle fork of the Snoqualmie and others in the extensive Cle Elum River drainage.[42]

Field Geologists, Unheralded Pioneers

The topographers and geologists who studied the northern Cascades were wilderness pioneers as well as scientists, and they played a pivotal role in deciphering the diverse complexity of the mountain range. It is not easy to imagine the adversities these men endured, and their annual field reports often understated the difficult conditions under which they worked. They often packed their instruments to high, alpine stations in fine weather and ran into unpredictable clouds and foul weather on their descent. It was often necessary to work in the wind and cold, and sometimes the surveyors had to retreat and return later in the season or in a following year. Rains made travel difficult for packhorses, forcing crossings of treacherous side-streams in high water. Successfully packing a fragile eleven-by-fourteen-inch plate camera or surveying instrument on horseback along flimsy, rocky trails required constant vigilance.

Although many of the details of their exploits may never come to light, we know that they discovered, named, and climbed many significant peaks, among them Glacier, Columbia, Sahale, White Chuck, Pilchuck, Vesper (probably), Baring, and Stuart. Before the USGS arrived in the northern Cascades, only isolated geologic studies had been done and topographical explorations had been conducted chiefly by the Northwest Boundary Survey and army expeditions. These studies were well documented, but their reports had appeared only in government publications, where they remained virtually unknown. The maps of the USGS explorers were of great benefit to the continuing explorations of prospectors and to the organized surveys and studies by the U.S. Forest Service, which inherited the administration of most of the land in the northern Cascades near the turn of the century. They stand as a remarkable series of documents in the history of the West.

Pack train crossing a cedar log over the upper Skagit river, 1905, Edward C. Barnard, photographer (International Boundary Commission)

16

THE SECOND NORTHWEST BOUNDARY

SURVEY, 1901–1908

By a curious accident the international boundary line, roughly speaking, divides the coast range into two parts of contrasted scenic quality. In Washington the summits are the higher and more peaked, the ridges the more serrate, while all are dominated by the majestic cone of Mount Baker. On the Canadian side the massifs are somewhat lower, are more rounded, and less abundantly supplied with a perennial snow cover.

—Reginald A. Daly, 1910

The first Northwest Boundary Survey in 1857–1862 produced two sets of official maps—one British and one American. During their final meetings, the two commissions agreed to draw a mean line between conflicting British and American lines, a result of discrepancies in astronomic calculations. That proved to be an inadequate remedy, however, because two or three lines and sets of markers sometimes were left on the ground. In addition, there were some fifteen gaps of information on the 220-mile sector east of Point Roberts. For many years, the condition of the boundary line at the forty-ninth parallel posed no problem. As the country adjacent to the boundary was settled late in the nineteenth century, however, mining claims needed to be located and forest reserves established. A precise demarcation had become necessary.

In 1899, the U.S. Geological Survey suggested to the State Department that the Northwest Boundary line be properly determined and marked by permanent monuments. Of the 409 miles from the Strait of Georgia to the Rocky Mountains, 364 had not been effectively surveyed and marked in 1857–1862.[1] In 1900, a senator from Washington state requested that the boundary line be re-established in the Mt. Baker mining district because valuable mining properties had been discovered there (one disputed American mine was later shown to be several hundred yards inside Canada). Although the original survey's report had been lost for many years, the summary publication of its history, records, and maps in 1900 (through the diligent efforts of Marcus Baker of the USGS) led the U.S. and Canadian governments to undertake a new survey to eliminate misunderstandings about boundary locations.[2]

The commissioners planned to mark the line at shorter intervals, replacing the cairns with stone and iron monuments numbered from west to east (in the

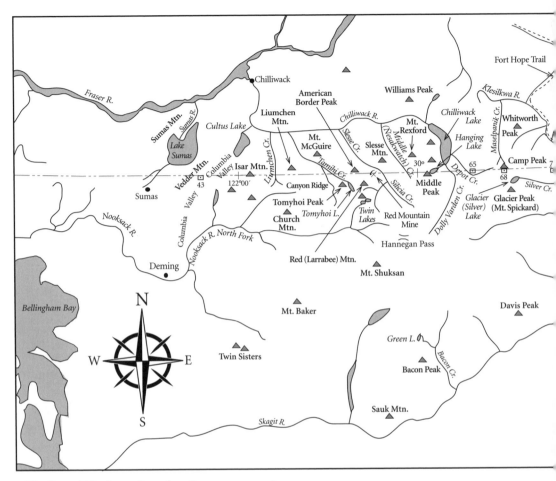

The Second Northwest Boundary Survey, 1901–1908

original survey, the Americans had numbered east to west and the British west to east). The 1857–1862 survey had marked the area from Columbia Valley (Monument 43) through the Cascade Range (including Monuments 44 to 67), with twenty-one stone cairns and one benchmark cut in bedrock. All but two of the original monuments were eventually found and replaced.

Retracing the Northwest Boundary involved three types of field parties: astronomic, topographic, and geologic. The topographic and geologic branches of the USGS joined forces in the summer of 1901 to survey westward from the summit of the Rocky Mountains. USGS Director Charles D. Walcott issued a letter of instruction to George Otis Smith on May 27, 1901, to conduct a geological reconnaissance along the forty-ninth parallel from Osoyoos Lake westward across the Cascade Range. His charge was to investigate mines and prospects and to determine the condition of boundary monuments. Smith and his young assistant, Carl Williams Smith (a cousin), were in the field from July to October.[3]

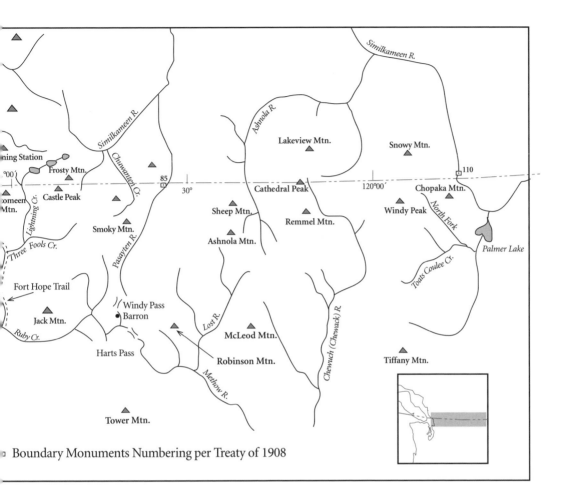

Edward Chester Barnard of the Topographic Branch of the USGS, working in cooperation with Cephas Hempstone Sinclair of the Coast and Geodetic Survey, headed the American field party. Barnard, who became the chief American topographer of the survey from 1903 to 1905, had joined the USGS in 1884 after graduating from Columbia University. In 1898, he had surveyed the Alaska-Yukon boundary and later had charge of Alaskan field parties. The Canadian party was led by James Joseph McArthur, who had performed much of the topographic surveying and marking of the forty-ninth parallel through the Rocky Mountains. He had climbed more than one hundred mountains and was well prepared for the hardships and technical problems of surveying in the Cascade Range. As dominion surveyor, McArthur had made the first ascent of Mt. Stephen in the Canadian Rockies in 1887, and he had climbed four peaks over 10,000 feet in the range by 1892.

The general instructions to the field parties were to determine what parts of the boundary line were still recognizable and whether they corresponded to the treaty boundary (the astronomic forty-ninth parallel of north latitude). They were also charged with recovering the old astronomic stations and determining what parts of the line needed to be surveyed and marked. The U.S. boundary commissioner, Thomas Riggs, later explained the difficulties in determining the boundary:

> At the time the original survey of the Boundary was made, sufficient geodetic work had not been done to permit the determination of the geodetic parallel and it was therefore agreed to determine and adopt the astronomic parallel as the Boundary. The effect of gravity of mountain masses and varying density of the earth's crust was known to the early surveyors, but at the time they had no way of measuring the resulting deflections of the plumb line from the true vertical. All they could do was to note the differences occurring between their own latitude stations where they could be connected by accurate surveys one with another. . . . They took this into account on the western end of the Line and on the intermountain section by establishing a mean astronomic parallel.[4]

The topographic work of the Second Boundary Survey would extend the parallel from a point determined on it, run lines connecting monuments, and map the features adjacent to the boundary.

In the 1901 season, the American party first examined "Silicia" (Silesia or Slesse) Creek, where a boundary misunderstanding had arisen. On May 16, Barnard and Sinclair and their party took a steamer from Seattle to New Whatcom to confer with prospectors who had claims in the stream valley. They then proceeded to Chilliwack and continued from there with twenty-four pack and four saddle animals. Parts of the thirty-two-mile trail were along steep and dangerous cliffs that skirted Chilliwack River and Slesse Creek. Several animals rolled downslope, although without serious consequences.[5]

Cutting trails in the dense forest and locating camps with available horse feed were continual concerns. The party made camp on May 23 near what they thought was an observation post from 1859 in a vista that had been cut through the timber. The field narrative describes the search for the boundary marker and the topographers' subsequent work:

> When the distance to the Boundary had been measured, a thorough search was made for the stone pile placed as a boundary mark in 1859. The Boundary crossed the ravine of Silicia Creek in a place cleared of large timber by snow slides, and its position was also indicated by a waterfall that comes into Silicia Creek from the southwest. Brush and weeds formed a tangled mass that concealed small objects, but after clearing away much of this, a circular stone pile, 6 feet in diameter and about a foot high, was recognized as artificial, amid the debris carried down by torrents. . . .
>
> Owing to unfavorable weather, it was many days before the sun or the stars could be observed for azimuth, but in the meantime, a "Y" cut in a large boulder on the west side of Silicia Creek, to which measurements had been made in 1859, was

found, and by means of this the stone pile was verified as an old boundary mark. When the weather cleared, the azimuth was determined and the true direction was given for opening the line. The first astronomic work, though begun on May 24, was not completed till June 18, on account of rain, snow, and fog. . . .

In order to avoid the expense of cutting the vista from the azimuth station to the nearest summit on an approximate direction, a point was located on the summit by means of building fires, which were moved north or south by signals with a rifle till the correct position was reached. The final cutting was afterwards completed when the true azimuth of the Boundary had been determined.

In this region of immense mountain masses there is a probability of considerable station deflection, and it will be necessary to connect adjacent astronomic stations before the extent of deflection can be determined, and the adjusted line located. It was therefore highly desirable to extend the surveyed line so as to connect with the old boundary monuments . . . but the deep snow still lying on the mountains prevented.[6]

Meanwhile, the topographic party measured a baseline across a ravine and connected it with the astronomic station. A scheme of plane-table triangulation was executed from the ends of the base to the nearby mountaintops, and a closely estimated elevation was assumed. With this control, a topographic map was made of a strip of territory two miles wide on each side of the boundary, from summit to summit across the Silesia Creek Valley.[7] The Boundary Red Mine (see chapter 14) was located in Glacier Basin, and the present-day American Border Peak was called Glacier Peak. The name *Red Mountain* (now Larrabee) was established at that time and probably originated with miners.[8] Monument posts were placed on spur ridges near Silesia Creek, and the line was cut and marked two miles along the forty-ninth parallel.

The American Geologic Field Team

The American geological field party, under George Otis Smith, commenced work on the boundary on July 10, 1901, at the confluence of the Okanogan and Similkameen rivers. The approach took them past the outlet river to Lake Chelan, where Smith described the intense color: "Below where it is full of foam, the river is more beautiful than any water that I've ever seen. I presume this color is due to the same cause as the color of the Swiss lakes, the glacial silt." On July 17, the party visited Chopaka Mountain, the most northeastern peak in the Cascade Range in Washington state.[9]

The exploration team proceeded westward, easily locating the monuments in the high, sparsely timbered country. At Horseshoe Basin, the men probably ascended Arnold Peak and Apex Mountain, which Smith described as a "flat-topped Pk. higher than Chopaca, but lower than pk to NW." On July 22, Calkins climbed to about 8,900 feet (possibly on Cathedral Peak) to study the geology. Between July 23 and 26, the party made a frustrating search for monuments. Smith even offered a five-dollar prize for locating one. The men found a camp and log cabin built forty-two years earlier, and the blocks on which the surveyors had rested their astronomical instruments were still where they had left them.[10]

Smith and his cousin Carl made the first ascent of Cathedral Peak, the jewel of today's Pasayten Wilderness, on August 3. They "climbed to the very tip of the sharpest peak," which looked "something like a big church."[11] Studying the rugged topography, Smith made this astute observation: "The peaks forming the divide & near the divide between the Methow & Ashnola waters are characterized by the cirques on the N faces. Every peak has at least one such ampith. with the flat debris covered bottom, often containing small ponds." He noted that the peaks were remnants of originally dome-shaped masses and that the cutting of cirques rarely produced a matterhorn (a triangular peak sculptured by three or more glaciers).[12]

Before the men worked their way westward in early August, they found a ten-foot ladder on a rock crag between Cathedral Fork and Ewart Creek at the old Monument 99 (the resurvey changed the monument number to 101).[13] Continuing, they visited Bald Mountain and noted the Parson Smith tree (with an 1866 carving by settler Alfred L. Smith in 1866). While in the Chuwanten Valley, they decided that thick smoke from forest fires made it unwise to search for more monuments.

Ascending the Pasayten River southward on August 28, the party reached the head of Canyon Creek, where Smith noted the "remarkable level tops of these EW ridges." They could see the extent of the ancient Pasayten glacier, where granite blocks were "evidence of an ice sheet, possibly with a south movement."[14] From a camp at Windy Pass, there was a splendid view of Jack Mountain, at 9,066 feet, a "bold peak with several glaciers." The men took the well-used miner's trail to the Skagit River, then turned north on the old Fort Hope trail—which was overgrown and choked with windfalls—to the boundary line. Smith lamented "that for hundreds of yards the trail can be followed only by the feet feeling out the worn rut."[15]

While traveling up the Skagit on September 8, Smith noted the old metamorphic-rock series along the river as far as Jackass Point. Discussing the unexplored terrain to the west, he wrote that granite "is believed to make up the very rugged peaks [the Picket Range] at the head of Beaver & Little Beaver creeks." He must have seen these sharp, ice-clad peaks from the head of the Pasayten River and had glimpses of them from the Skagit. Looking west up the valley of the Little Beaver (a branch of the Skagit), he saw glaciers "about N 65 W" and "light colored" rock that "appears to be granite."[16]

In his report, Smith described the primeval mountain wilderness that they saw west of the Skagit River before moving the camp down the Skagit and north to the Nooksack River:

The upper valley of the Skagit extends southward from the 49th parallel as a broad valley with gravel-covered bottom and low grade. The river in this portion of its course has many meanders, and swamps occupy large areas in the valley. Large timber is found here, and the dense undergrowth of the western slope of the Cascades makes its appearance. Below where Beaver and Ruby creeks enter the Skagit, the river turns west and in a wild canyon cuts through the mountains. The spur of the Cascades, which is crossed by the Skagit at this point, extends northwestward, and is the range to which the name of Skagit Mountains is here given. These mountains include some of the most picturesque peaks, of which the sharp pyramidal peak of Mount Shuksan is an example.[17]

Smith observed that granitic rocks (actually largely gneissic) occur west of the Skagit and make up the high and rugged peaks. He added: "In the western portion of the Skagit Mountains, or Mount Baker district, closely folded limestones, slates, schists, and other metamorphic rocks are most important both in their areal distribution and from the gold-quartz veins of which they form the country rock."[18]

From the north fork of the Nooksack River, Smith ascended Swamp Creek to Twin Lakes, a route already well tramped by prospectors. From a camp there, he descended Tomyhoi Creek to the boundary line, along the route pioneered by Henry Custer in 1859. While on the south face of "Red" Mountain (Larrabee) on September 20, he observed that volcanic rocks occurred with dikes and sediments.[19] The party climbed Goat Mountain, visited the famous Lone Jack Mine (see chapter 14), went to Austin and Mamie passes, and studied the volcanic rocks at Hannegan Pass. In early October, when Smith met with McArthur, they ascertained that all of the monuments along the line had been found except two, in the valley of Tamihi Creek.

The Canadian Team

The main Canadian party—which included McArthur, J.M. Bates, E.T. de Coeli, J.W. McArthur, J.M. Macoun (a naturalist), William Spreadborough (the assistant naturalist), and Reginald A. Daly (a geologist)—followed Slesse Creek to the boundary, where they met the American parties. The Canadians then returned to the Chilliwack River and headed east to reopen the trail to Chilliwack Lake. At the lake, the party built a large raft and cedar dugout canoe to ferry supplies to Dolly Varden ("Klahaihu") Creek near the boundary. They located old cairns, cut a vista tangent to the parallel, and opened a foot trail into Depot Creek. Old boundary cairn 52 on Depot Creek (now Monument 65) was found in good condition.

They explored Nesakwatch Creek, a particularly difficult valley, and cut a trail. Later, a horse and foot trail was opened up at Tamihi Creek.[20] They felled a large tree across the Chilliwack River and leveled it so the horses could cross.

Farther east, the boundary cairns and markings from the Similkameen River to the Skagit were examined by another Canadian party.

The Canadian topographic party was the first in the Pacific Northwest to use a camera and to calculate the terrain by photogrammetric and photo-topographical methods. Sometimes "the clouds would lift like magic," McArthur said, "and the landscape be revealed for a short time, during which we would hasten to take the views and make our observations." The Canadian chief noted that the Americans, who were equipped with the plane table, were unable to accomplish any work except on very fine days.[21]

The studies of Canadian geologist Reginald A. Daly for the International Boundary Commission from 1901 to 1907 involved a colossal field task—investigating the geology of the boundary belt from the Strait of Georgia to the Rockies. Daly applied a systematic orography to describe the rocks and suggested many additions to the nomenclature. His three-volume study of the belt is a supreme achievement.[22] Assisted in the field by Fred Nelmes of Chilliwack, Daly began the 1901 season on July 9. Traversing from Chilliwack to the lake, he found that the smoke from forest fires was so thick he could barely map outcrops. During that summer, he covered eighty miles of the boundary belt to ten miles north and was most impressed (and often frustrated) with the area's "windfalls, devil's club, [and] vine-maple" vegetation. He also noticed an interesting coincidence:

> By a curious accident the international boundary line, roughly speaking, divides the coast range into two parts of contrasted scenic quality. In Washington the summits are the higher and more peaked, the ridges the more serrate, while all are dominated by the majestic cone of Mount Baker. On the Canadian side the massifs are somewhat lower, are more rounded, and less abundantly supplied with a perennial snow cover.[23]

The panoramas along the Chilliwack River Valley were imposing: "The inaccessible horn of Slesse mountain, 7,700 feet in height, is the loftiest peak in the belt, and the average height of some fifty other summits, determined barometrically, is over 5,500 feet."[24] At Chilliwack Lake, Daly noted that glacial erosion had given the lake its fjordlike character. He also mentioned the excellent farmland on the broad, timbered benches—formed by the terracing of glacial gravels, sands, and clays deposited by the torrential river—extending from Chilliwack Lake to the Fraser's alluvial flats. Daly certainly made some first ascents of peaks, although which ones may never be known.[25]

The Resurvey Continues

The boundary resurvey continued in the summer of 1904. A Canadian party of some forty men and forty horses took the Chopaka trail to the boundary near the eastern fringe of the Cascades. They did topographic work and cut vistas as far as the Skagit River until August 1, when forest fires seriously interfered with triangulation. By summer's end, the men had built a continuous trail along the line from Chopaka Mountain to the Skagit River and had cut trails along Toats Coulee, up the Similkameen River from Princeton, and along the Pasayten River to the boundary.[26]

The American topographic party, under Barnard, surveyed the same span that summer. The party consisted of DeWitt L. Reaburn (a triangulation assistant), Sledge Tatum (a topographic assistant), J.G. Hefty (a transitman), Thomas Riggs, Jr., J.P. Breckenridge, Walter B. Reaburn, G.H. Wheeler, and forty to sixty-five hands. The Americans used mules because they could pick their way through the forest easier than horses could.[27] A considerable amount of supplies and provisions was needed for such a large expedition. The survey party made local purchases that included two fourteen-by-fourteen-foot tents, three hundred brass keeps (fasteners) for tent ropes, twelve camp chairs, and signal cloth. The line party had one cook tent, three nine-by-nine-foot tents, two ten-by-twelve-foot tents, and five "A" tents. The food rations purchased in August totaled 2,150 pounds.[28]

Members of the American survey party made some remarkable alpine ascents in 1904 and 1905. Working as a triangulation team, Sledge Tatum (as observer) and George E. Loudon, Jr. (as recorder), climbed numerous peaks east of the Skagit River during four months in 1904. The highlights of their achievements were the ascent of Cathedral Peak and first ascents of Hozomeen and Jack mountains.[29] The two men ascended the impressive granite pyramid of Cathedral Peak on July 25 and placed a pole into a four-foot cairn on the summit. Cathedral was climbed again in 1905 by Thomas Riggs and probably Walter Reaburn (on June 30). The fieldbook entry reads: "Riggs set up instrument on leaning rock about 4 x 10 leaning to the north, from there he sighted Mon #10. Had rope around his waist to keep from going over cliff. A very dangerous place."

In the summer of 1905, an American party consisting of Barnard, George Neuner, W.W. Wineland, and fifteen hands began placing monuments from Horseshoe Basin (a total of thirty-eight were placed between the Similkameen and Skagit rivers). Monument 95, on the north shoulder of Cathedral Peak, was the only one that was difficult to set. The knifelike rock ridge was so narrow that a place for the monument had to be blasted out, and the monument and material had to be lifted up by ropes from shelf to shelf on the cliffs. It was dangerous work. "In making the ascent one man lost his footing and fell 30 feet to a rock shelf below, but miraculously sustained only severe body bruises."[30] Horses were generally used to pack loads to the monument sites, but the men had to backpack the loads at craggy and difficult locations such as Monument 95.

On September 9, 1904, Tatum and Loudon became the first to climb Hozomeen's north peak (the higher). From the old "Commissioner's Trail" south of the boundary, which the original survey had built in 1859, they crossed a small glacier and took the northeast ridge to the summit, where they built a cairn. They sighted "Glacier" (Mt. Spickard), Grassy, Frosty, Castle, Smoky, Skagit, and Jack for triangulation.[31] Hozomeen was climbed again on August 25, 1905, by Riggs and Neuner, who took both vertical and horizontal angles from the summit. Their fieldbook entry glumly states: "Cross lower end of glacier and go up first ridge facing East. Or go up North ridge. Both routes equally bum."[32] Tatum and Loudon also made the first ascent of Jack Mountain, probably from Ruby Creek, on September 17, 1904. From its remote summit, they sighted the summits of Robinson, Gardner, Tower, "Boston" (Sahale), Sauk, "Mrs. Davis" (Davis Peak), Shuksan, "Glacier" (Spickard), Hozomeen, Frosty, and Smoky.[33]

On both September 6 and 11, 1905, Walter Reaburn and a companion (probably Riggs) ascended Jack Mountain. On the sixth, they made the climb in four hours from the west fork of Crater Creek. The ascent was difficult and dangerous, and Reaburn recorded that a "very cold and windy snow storm drove us off."[34] The freezing temperatures made it hard to work, and the men often were frustrated when summit points were obscured by clouds.

Tatum and Loudon climbed numerous other peaks in the boundary region in 1904, most of them recording first ascents. On July 3, they climbed Chopaka Mountain, placing a cairn and flag on this popular survey station. Three days later they climbed Windy Peak (near Horseshoe Basin), then crossed the boundary on July 9 to climb Snowy Mountain, "a bald, high summit," to build a six-foot stone cairn. On July 18 and 22, the two surveyors hiked up Tiffany Mountain, and on July 26 they climbed Remmel Mountain, a high, bold, rocky peak about three miles south of Cathedral.[35] They returned to Remmel on October 2 for more triangulation. On July 30, the pair climbed Lakeview Mountain, to the east of the Ashnola River in Canada. Starting from east of Cathedral Peak, this long trek involved passing three divides to the north. They climbed such lesser summits as Ashnola Mountain, Roche, Smoky, Frosty, and Grassy between August 12 and September 11 and the high and conspicuous Robinson Mountain on September 20—another significant first ascent. The surveyors' fieldbook describes Robinson as "a high rock peak in the divide between the Skagit & Methow Rivers about 5 mi. southeast of Barron." They erected a signal tower there.[36]

In 1904, American surveyors climbed another prominent summit, Castle Peak ("Turret"), on the main divide just south of the boundary. Not to be outdone, other American parties under Barnard made first ascents in the bewildering alpine landscape west of the Skagit River. During the summer of 1904, Walter Reaburn climbed "Station Glacier" (Mt. Spickard) on a daring and solitary venture. The survey report stated that this "highest peak of Custer Ridge" was "surrounded by glaciers, and is difficult and dangerous to climb."

Riggs later recalled that "Reaburn climbed the peak and erected a signal, but then he went light, carrying merely a hatchet and a drill. I had not thought to ask him the route he took and his only comment on the trip had been that he had slept out on the mountain for two nights and didn't want any more of it."[37]

"Glacier Peak," as it came to be known on maps for some five decades, was next climbed by Riggs and J. Beall on August 20, 1905. The ascent and return made a three-day adventure from their camp. The approach began from the Skagit River in Canada, along a blazed trail via International Creek and across the intervening ridge to the valley of Silver Creek. Riggs was particularly impressed with nearby Silver Lake—"a lake of indigo," with mini-icebergs and an outflow confined by a narrow rock rim—which he discovered while searching for a route to the summit. "Follow ridge south of creek to station," the fieldbook advises. "Glaciers look easy to cross but are impossible on account of deep crevasses." Another entry warns: "Keep to the rocks as the glaciers are impassable. This route is most hazardous at best." At a distance, the mountain had looked like "a pyramid with glacier on north side."[38] The glacier repulsed Riggs, and eventually he led his party to the southwest slope. The frustrating climb was completed the next day, and from the summit the party sighted Whitworth, Lightning, Hozomeen, Jack, Davis, and Shuksan.

During the 1904 season, surveyors climbed the rugged formation of Davis Peak, a bastion of gneissic rock—"the highest rocky mountain top 3 miles west of the Davis ranch on the Skagit River. . . . It has heretofore been reached by a hard climb on foot from the Davis ranch."[39] A seven-foot cairn was built over an aluminum marker disk by the ascent party (whose members are not known). The peak was climbed again by Riggs and Walter Reaburn on September 23, 1905. They called it a difficult ascent, with only one possible route. Their brief field notation states: "Straight up in the air from Davis roadhouse for a day. Then camp out all night." They made the final ascent by the south ridge. The team spent three hours attempting to sight Sahale Peak and Jack Mountain in the clouds.[40] Davis Peak was visited again in 1926 and used as a first-order triangulation station.

During the summer of 1905, a Canadian trail-building party improved the route from Hope to the Skagit River, then west to Chilliwack Lake. The crew completed the trail from the Skagit River to Depot Creek. A line-surveying party traversed near the head of Depot Creek, crossing five high alpine ridges and three glaciers on the north shoulder of Mt. Spickard and working to an altitude of 7,700 feet. "One of the high ridges crossed is so sharp and the rock so disintegrated that it was impossible to set up a transit without extensive preparation of the station," the survey report noted.[41]

American surveyors R.B. Robertson and Eugene Logan had a difficult wilderness adventure when they climbed to the summit of Bacon Peak—a first ascent—in the summer of 1905. The trek involved ten miles of strenuous climbing through brush and rocks on a route that followed Bacon Creek and its west forks to Green Lake. From the Baker River divide, they crossed an easy glacier at the head of Noisy Creek for about one mile. Then, from a rocky ridge north of the peak, they crossed another glacier to the north summit and possibly went on to the highest summit. The men built a seven-foot stone cairn with a flagpole and took azimuths to "Glacier," Hozomeen, Davis, Jack, and "Boston."[42]

During the 1905 season, Riggs, Walter Reaburn, Beall, and Neuner worked as a team. Reaburn and Riggs ascended "Brush" and Riggs and Neuner ascended "Lightning" in August; Riggs and Beall climbed Frosty West, Roche (Chuwanten), and Smoky during September. The "Lightning" station (Nepopekum Mountain) was a round, bald knob, the most northerly point on the Hozameen ridge about four miles north of the boundary.[43] They also made ascents of Twin Sisters (the South Sister) and Church Mountain, both reached from Deming. Both provided excellent vantage stations because they stand as topographic outliers to higher summits in the western portion of the range.

Of more significance was the August 8 ascent of Whitworth Peak by Riggs and Neuner. The approach to this peak, west of the Skagit River and some five miles north of the boundary, must have been arduous. The triangulation was done on a "sharp point of rotten rock" not quite as high as the most northern one but "better located."[44] This ascent was certainly the first climb of the peak, although it is not certain whether the party reached the very summit. At the beginning of October, snow fell to depths of three to four feet, threatening to maroon men and equipment, and the pack parties headed out of the mountains for the season.

Completing the Resurvey

Field operations in 1906 were carried out in the boundary belt from Sumas Prairie through the mountains to the Skagit River. Robertson and Logan of the American party repeated the ascents of Davis Peak on September 19 and 20, Twin Sisters on August 17, Church Mountain on July 27, and later Jack and Sauk mountains. To reach the South Sister, they left their mules at the head of Skookum Creek and wrote in the fieldbook: "choose your way up peak which is hard to climb." Robertson wrote that "Baker Sawtooth" (West Black Butte) was "solid rock and I doubt if it can be climbed." They also found that it was "not advisable to take animals" up Sauk Mountain.[45]

The same year, the Canadian party—eight surveyors, forty-two hands, and forty-two horses—set out in May from the Columbia Valley, following the existing trail to Isar Mountain.[46] About ten miles from the valley, the line-measurement party crossed the rocky ridge of Liumchen Mountain and diverted to Canyon Ridge (on the Canyon–Tamihi Creek divide, barely south of the boundary). They found a beautiful alpine park that was ideal for camping and forage, but the route soon became difficult as they continued downward and east to the canyon of Tamihi Creek, where the forest was so thick that travel was impossible without trails.

> The windfalls, often 6 to 9 feet in diameter and from 150 to 200 feet long, could be used as footpaths when fortunately lying in the direction of travel, but when lying crosswise, as they perversely seemed to do most of the time, presented an obstacle only to be overcome by improvising a ladder or by crawling around either end through the dense brush and devilsclub.[47]

The party completed the trail along this difficult traverse to Tamihi Creek and also reopened various 1901 trails.

This Canadian party also projected the chord (boundary and vista) east from Tamihi Creek to Slesse/Silesia Creek, crossing an almost unscalable shoulder of "Red" Mountain (Larrabee) at an elevation of 7,300 feet. They ascended the difficult ridge near American Border Peak nine times and cut a vista to timberline on its flanks. (McArthur's party may have climbed "Red" Mountain this season; if so, this was the first ascent). Thick smoke from forest fires prevented observations for days at a time. A party under McArthur climbed Mt. McGuire in 1906, probably for the first time.[48] Attempts to bridge the Chilliwack River near Tamihi Creek failed when large trees "snapped like pipestems" in the swift water; the men eventually secured a steel cable and completed a one-span bridge.[49]

Another Canadian party surveyed the rough, alpine terrain from Slesse to Nesakwatch Creek, during which a southeast peak of Mt. Rexford was apparently ascended. Meanwhile, axemen cut a vista across the difficult valley of Nesakwatch/Ensawkwatch Creek. On July 15, by prearrangement, the topographic party met another group that began a line from the boundary at "Dolly Varden Creek" (upper Chilliwack River) on the high divide between it and Ensawkwatch Creek.[50] Axemen cut a vista across the valley of Middle Creek. At Chilliwack Lake, a large raft was constructed to transport the entire party (including two mules) with supplies, and they moved to a camp about one mile up the river near the boundary.

Parties coming south from Hope also worked at the boundary in the Skagit River area. The men rebuilt trails to monument sites between the Skagit River and Chilliwack Lake, set monuments, and completed triangulation at Whitworth and Glacier stations. A party including Noel J. Ogilvie climbed both "Glacier" and Whitworth in August, taking a route on "Glacier that was different from the one Riggs had used in 1905 (unfortunately, details are not known).

In 1907, the Canadian party was assigned to connect its triangulation with that of USGS parties. Among the seven surveyors in the Canadian party under McArthur were F.H. Mackie, S.S. McDiarmid, and E.T. de Coeli, who were assisted by forty hands. The weather was so wet early in the season that a full day's work of vista cutting (from the Columbia Valley) was seldom possible. The boundary line crossed canyons 500 to 2,000 feet deep, and climbing up and down through wet brush was so trying and dangerous that axemen would not stay long on the job.[51] Problems with bridges across the lower Chilliwack made it necessary to open a new trail, and the wagon road along the raging river was washed out. Monumenting parties were at work that season on the Nesakwatch/Ensawkwatch and Silesia Creek sections of the boundary. Middle Peak, a high summit southwest of Chilliwack Lake, was ascended for triangulation.

By season's end, the boundary resurvey was nearly complete from Point Roberts to the Skagit River. In the summer of 1908, a joint party with Sinclair from the United States and Ogilvie from Canada completed an inspection begun in 1907.[52] This lengthy task, which lasted from June to October, marked the end of surveying, monumenting, and inspection from the Strait of Georgia to the Rocky Mountains.

In 1908, Canadian parties probably made the first ascent of "Red" Mountain (Larrabee) on September 11. The survey report states that Station Red could be reached from the Red Mountain Mine by crossing the snowfield and climbing the glacier to the ridge, then proceeding around to the southwest flank for the final portion.[53] Mt. McGuire was climbed on July 27. Also in July, J.J. McArthur and E.T. de Coeli climbed Williams Peak (Station Silver), probably as a first ascent, and Station Silicia.[54] There were some difficult alpine traverses in the 1908 season. On one occasion, for example, a man fell into a crevasse on the Maselpanik Glacier (east of Monument 68) and had to be pulled out with an alpenstock. The party was probably crossing the glacier from Camp Peak eastward to upper McNaught Creek. The Sinclair-Ogilvie party visited Hanging Lake and climbed westward to the alpine divide.[55]

In 1908, a treaty provided for a complete reestablishment and mapping of the boundary from the Atlantic to the Pacific Ocean. Special boundary commissioners were named: William F. King for Britain and Otto H. Tittmann for the United States. The final map, published in 1913 by the USGS, was divided into nineteen sheets and shows the placement of the monuments. In the Cascade Range, Cathedral Peak is represented with a triangulation mark; Glacier Peak, Glacier Lake, Mt. Redoubt, Red Mountain, and Tomyhoi Peak are also shown, while Henry Custer's "Putlushgohap Lake" of 1859 remains.

Further surveying from high peaks of the northern Cascades continued in 1925, 1926, and 1935. Sheep Mountain in the Pasayten region was climbed in 1925 and Jackita Peak (near Jack Mountain) in 1926. The 1935 ascents include Liumchen Mountain, Station Slesse (third point from the north), Red Mountain, Williams Peak, Middle Peak, Castle Peak, Mt. McGuire, Lone Mountain;

and a peak southeast of Mt. Rexford (Station G) climbed by J. H. Kihl.[56] The 1935 survey parties of had improved camp equipment, including tents with tarps, cookstoves, heating stoves, lanterns, washbasins, and canvas tables.[57]

The 1901–1908 boundary survey had run new lines, cleared old vistas, and replaced missing markers, and it was remarkable that corrections from the original survey were minimal. The early surveyors had fulfilled their difficult task carefully. In a 1937 letter on the second survey, U.S. Boundary Commissioner Thomas Riggs explained that no changes were made in the line as originally laid down and that the subsequent surveys consisted of running straight lines between the original monuments, replacing old monuments with new ones on straight-line courses, and executing triangulation and traverses to determine the geodetic latitude and longitude of the monuments. There would be no changes in the location of the boundary, he reported, because of the discrepancies between the astronomic and geodetic parallels.[58]

The second Northwest Boundary Survey was important for its commendable fieldwork, monumenting, and triangulation, which led to an acceptable confirmation of the boundary line at the forty-ninth parallel. Furthermore, the field travel, topographic studies, and mapping by both the American and Canadian teams significantly advanced the knowledge of the convoluted and mountainous boundary belt, whose true expanse had only been determined by the earlier survey.

Mountaineering with a scientific orientation reached its zenith in the northern Cascades during the boundary resurvey. While a few of the men involved—notably Walter Reaburn and James McArthur—had had previous alpine experience, they generally lacked the technical background of some of the mountaineers and guides who had made early ascents in the Canadian Rockies and on Mt. Rainier. Yet, they performed notable and sometimes amazing feats.

Not much can be learned from the personal accounts of these surveyors—just the dutiful abstracts of the official record—but their extraordinary efforts in the Cascade Range were only an interlude in their topographic careers. The dangers and struggles they faced were also their delights, and they could look back on their achievements with pride.

Crossing the snowfields at Goat Rocks with sheep (Mt. Baker–Snoqualmie National Forest Service Collection)

17

MANAGING THE MOUNTAIN LANDS:
THE FOREST SERVICE AND PARK SERVICE ERA,
1895–1950

> Most striking is the wealth of timber. The roads are little more than vast aisles through the forests. . . . After traveling for days through these dense forests one is very ready to believe what the sawmill men assert—that there is timber enough in the Puget Sound country to supply the whole world for a century to come.
>
> —Alfred Holman, 1891

There is a marvellous fascination about these immense quiet and shady fastnesses of the western valleys," British mountaineer Norman Collie wrote about the forests of western Canada, " . . . the tangled wreck of a lifetime, the luxuriant growth of centuries." The same could be said about the wilderness forests of the northern Cascade Range. Geographer Henry Gannett, writing at the turn of the twentieth century, observed that "with the exception of the redwoods of California, the forests of Washington are the densest, heaviest, and most continuous in the United States."[1] Noted geologist Israel C. Russell was awed by the huge firs and cedars rising to heights of 250 feet or more:

> The trees are frequently 10 to 12 feet or more in diameter at the height of one's head and rise in massive columns without a blemish to the first branches, which are in many instances 150 feet from the ground. The soil beneath the mighty trees is deeply covered with mosses of many harmonious tints, and decked with rank ferns.[2]

The forests of the Canadian and Washington Cascades, as Gannett noted, are essentially continuous in their span. In a 1924 report, the inventory for the Skagit Range (west of the main divide) lists the principal conifers as Douglas fir, western white pine, alpine fir, and Engelmann spruce. An earlier study by naturalist Frederick G. Plummer notes the dominance of western red cedar in the lower west-flank forest and of the yellow (ponderosa) pine east of the divide.[3]

Martin W. Gorman was the first specialist to research the Cascade Range forests. Between August and October 1897, he accompanied a USGS party at Lake Chelan and studied the eastern half of the Washington Forest Reserve, which included Lake Chelan, Railroad Creek, the Stehekin River, Early Winters Creek, the Chewuch (Chewack) River, and other Methow drainages. Another forest scientist who was active at about the same time was Horace B. Ayres, a USGS field assistant. Such early foresters as Gorman and Ayres prepared topographic maps for geologic surveys and the detailed representation of forests. The maps showed types and sizes of trees and included the density of the forests.[4]

At the end of the nineteenth century—when there was a national enthusiasm for "taming" the land—Congress took action to protect the nation's forests. President Grover Cleveland's executive order of February 22, 1897, withdrew vast areas of public domain for forest reserves. In the northern Cascades, 1.5 million acres were set aside as part of the Rainier Forest Reserve. Over 3.5 million acres were withdrawn that year as the Washington Forest Reserve, which closed the land to private exploitation.[5] At first, this acreage was in the custody of the Department of the Interior's General Land Office, which inherited this largely unknown and unsurveyed terrain. Until the USGS completed maps early in the twentieth century, many prospectors may have known the mountain lands better than administrators and surveyors did. Not until 1912 did Congress order that all forest lands be surveyed.

The administration of forest reserves was transferred in 1905 to the Department of Agriculture's Bureau of Forestry, and their official name was changed to national forests. With the creation of the U.S. Forest Service, forest rangers were named as resident managers to enforce government policy, protect resources, settle disputes, and ensure the proper and fair use of the land. The Forest Service became a public-land steward, with policies designed to preserve timber, water, forage, recreational opportunities, and other public resources for future generations.

In 1908, part of the Rainier Forest Reserve became the Columbia National Forest, which in 1949 was renamed the Gifford Pinchot National Forest. Also in 1908, the Washington Forest Reserve was divided into the Chelan, Wenatchee, Snoqualmie, and Washington national forests. To alleviate public confusion, the Washington National Forest was changed to the Mt. Baker National Forest in 1924. Two years later, the Mt. Baker Recreation Area was created—a large region managed for recreation, logging, mining, and hydroelectric development.

In 1931, the Whatcom Primitive Area was established, encompassing over 172,000 acres of largely unexplored country between Mt. Baker and the Skagit River. No roads were to be built in the primitive area and only such trails as were necessary to protect the forest. In 1934, this primitive area was increased in size and renamed the North Cascades Primitive Area, a temporary status before the establishment of the North Cascades National Park in 1968. It was to be a region without the accommodations of modern life, a place that pro-

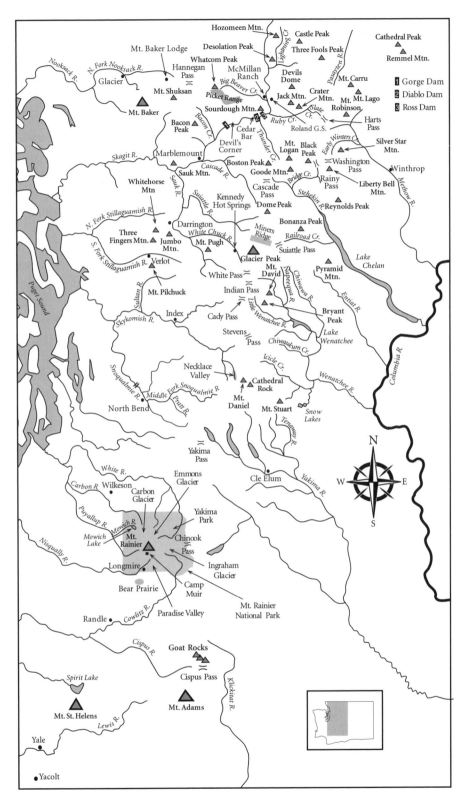

The Northern Cascades in the Forest Service and Park Service Era

vided physical and spiritual rewards for visitors. Also in 1931, a plan was made to keep Glacier Peak in a natural condition, and five chalet sites were proposed near the peak that could be reached by horses and packers.[6] Eventually, the Glacier Peak Wilderness was established.

The Forest Service in the Cascades

Under Forest Service management, Cascade Range forests were surveyed and mapped, and an extensive trail network was built and maintained. Roads were constructed for fire protection and timber harvesting, and most of them were also used for recreation. The Forest Service also built bridges and fire lookouts and constructed campgrounds and trail shelters for the public. The ranger stations varied in size, from the guard stations at the former Rowland and McMillan homesteads to a number of larger establishments. Some of the better-known early stations were the Backus (at Marblemount), Boundary (on the upper Skagit), Winthrop, Glacier, Cle Elum, Randle, Spirit Lake, North Bend, Darrington, and Verlot. Guard stations were maintained during the summer at more remote locations such as Kennedy Hot Springs.

The duties of the district rangers became more complex as the public increased its use of the forests. In addition to their involvement in public recreation, rangers also assisted in mountain rescues—notably in 1939, when an avalanche swept six college students to their deaths on Mt. Baker. Other aspects of ranger duty included clearing miles of foot and horse trails in each district and manning fire lookouts.[7] Most rangers and Forest Service employees wore heavy, calked boots for fieldwork. Some even made their own snowshoes, especially if they trapped animals in the forests. Almost all fieldwork was supported by packhorse supply, and the larger camps used pyramidal sleeping tents and tin cookstoves. The rangers made mess tables and seats from trees and often made cots by laying two logs on the ground with green boughs filling the space between for their bedrolls.

Victor H. Flach reported in a Forest Service bulletin a rewarding part of a day in the field:

> Many years ago Charles Gowan and I arrived at one of these timber survey camps at dinner time. The cook was an exceptionally good one—also thrifty and versatile. Occasionally he had an unusual dessert, which he asked the newcomers to identify. I guessed squash pie; another said pumpkin. Actually, it was made from left-over sweet potatoes, carrots, and mashed potatoes. It was delicious. The next morning, breakfast included hot cakes which were also very good. I complimented the cook and asked how he made them. He told me if I wanted to get up at 5 o'clock the next morning he would show me.

Clifton C. McGuire entered the Forest Service as a guard at Finney Creek (near Darrington) in 1909 and eventually became a district ranger. He later remembered a time in his first year when sixteen potential rangers assembled at the supervisor's headquarters for a required three-day, multi-skill test of their fitness. "As memory serves me," he wrote, "the following tests were given":

(1) From the foliage, identify ten species of trees grown on the Mt. Baker—give common and technical names—if you can spell the latter, more power to you. (2) Fall a tree ten or more inches in diameter with an axe. In giving this test a stake was driven in the ground about 20 feet from the tree. The victim was allowed to select the point where the stake was driven. All he had to do then was to fall the tree so that it would drive the stake further into the ground. His skill was determined by the nearness of the tree bole to the stake. Only three candidates out of the sixteen survived that test, one man actually driving the stake. Most trees went wide of the mark with some trees falling in the opposite direction. (3) Figure magnetic declinations on the four quadrants of the compass. In those days it seems no one thought of the idea of setting off the compass dial. (4) Run and pace a triangle, prepare the field notes and compute the acreage. (5) Demonstrate your ability to use a seven foot cross-cut saw. (6) Tell the boss man what ingredients and how much of each you would use in preparing a batch of bisquits. (7) How to build and put out a campfire (no accent on getting the last spark). (8) Pack a horse. This was a toughy—the pack consisted of two loosely tied sacks of oats, an axe, a mattock, a shovel and a cross-cut saw. Also, five days supply of grub for one man—all unpacked and a conglomeration of cooking equipment. Not only was your skill tested but you worked against time. Many would-be rangers fell by the wayside on this test. One bewildered candidate got the pack saddle on backwards with the britchen over the horses head and used the breast strap for a double cinch. Next he picked up his lash rope and cinch and after he walked around the horse a couple of times he gave up in despair, remarking "there is no ring on this saddle that will fit the big hook on the end of this rope."

. . . only the following four men survived the three day test namely, Ralph Hilligoss, Carl Bell, Grover Burch and C. C. McGuire.[8]

Thomas (Tommy) Thompson began his twenty-eight-year Forest Service career as a fire guard on the upper Skagit River in 1904. He later recalled that at first he had a salary of $60 per month and that he had to furnish his own two horses, a pack and saddle, and all necessary supplies and equipment.[9] Once, Thompson remembered, a fire began near a miner's cabin on Slate Creek and nearly destroyed the town of Barron. Long, strenuous hikes were part of a ranger's job because of the isolation, and Thompson once walked thirty-two miles to Marblemount just to get the mail.

In August 1913, Thompson was in charge of a large crew of men and horses carrying heavy wire rope through the Skagit Canyon for a bridge at Thunder Creek. The cable was in one piece over a thousand feet long and together with the hardware weighed two tons. Herman Rohde's mules and horses worked in tandem to drag the cable, but the men had to carry the stiff wire themselves when they reached the switchbacks of the infamous Goat Trail. Thompson recalled that it was the hardest labor of his career. After securing the swaying, two-hundred-foot cable suspension bridge across the Skagit gorge, they built a bridge across Thunder Creek.[10]

There was a disastrous fire to fight at Gorge Creek in the hot summer of 1922. Some one hundred men were on the fire line, but parts of the blaze were impossible to reach because of the steep, rocky terrain. One man died in the effort. Thompson was also involved with a large fire in Big Beaver Creek Valley that was sighted on July 4, 1926, after it had been burning for some time. Nearly four hundred men fought the blaze, which eventually covered about fifty thousand acres. In mid-July,

> a hot northeast wind started the fire up and set it roaring over our heads. It's a wonder that someone wasn't killed. We had to go back into the burn in order to be safe. That wasn't the only blow-up. Three or four days later there was another hot wind and the fire went three or four miles. That first blowup occurred in the night time. There were several such runs at intervals.

There had been little rain since January—"it was one of the driest years we had ever had and the river was very low"—and the fire burned until rain came in late August. Thompson added:

> I think that it was the big fires in 1926 that started everyone thinking about discovering the fires more quickly and agitating for the establishment of lookouts. . . . That same year the Bacon Creek fire occurred. We had around 300 men on it at one time. . . . The fire started on a trail and must have been from a fisherman because a fisherman had gone up the trail. The city light crew, City of Seattle, thought that they had the fire out but a strong wind came up in the afternoon and blew the fire over their heads.[11]

Thompson's administrative duties included attending meetings about a proposed mining road over Cascade Pass and coordinating dam-building plans with James D. Ross of Seattle City Light. Although the supervision of water power in the national forests had been transferred to the Federal Power Commission, the construction and other activities of the dam-building process were monitored at the local level by the Forest Service.

Lage Wernstedt

The most outstanding forest specialist in the Cascades in the early part of the twentieth century was the prolific and talented Swedish-born Lage Wernstedt. After graduating from Yale University in 1905, he pioneered the use of photogrammetry—surveying and mapping by using photographs—and created forest maps that were the standard for forty years. In 1917, using panoramic photographs taken from summits in the Columbia (now Gifford Pinchot) National Forest, Wernstedt almost single-handedly mapped an area of about seven hundred square miles. Typically, he would take panoramas with a large

Cirkut camera on a tripod and then make supplementary transit triangulations to orient the pictures for later mapping.[12]

In 1923, Victor H. Flach and Roland C. Burgess went to the Willamette National Forest in Oregon to assist Wernstedt, who by then had acquired a reputation for being independent and brilliant. Wernstedt had the quirk of not hobbling his horses, who would stray at night looking for forage, and Burgess and Flach sometimes had to chase after them the entire day. Flach recalled another assignment to find a horse:

Near Oakridge [Oregon] one day, Lage startled me by saying, "Vic, I need another horse, here's fifty dollars to buy one." Why me? Bud was the horse expert. . . . I was a city boy.

Lage insisted, however, and told me to go up the road toward Lowell and talk to the farmers about a horse. He added, "Be sure you get one that's gentle and is both a good saddle and pack horse."

That turned out to be a difficult assignment. There were horses for sale, all right, but at prices of $85 and $100 with nothing said about their abilities as saddle or pack horses. About noon, having walked eight or nine miles, I came across a man plowing his field with a heavy-maned, sway-backed horse weighing perhaps 1,200 pounds. We struck up a conversation. The horse was gentle enough, but had never been ridden with saddle, only bareback around the place by the farmer's children. And he had never been used for packing. Even worse, the farmer felt he couldn't part with him for less than $75.

I was about to give up when I was invited in for lunch. Maybe it was the mellowing effect of the food. Or, being an amateur magician, maybe it was the magic tricks I showed to his children. But after lunch, the farmer said he'd sell me "Old Barney" for the fifty.

I'd never ridden bareback and Barney proved too much for me. He was so sway-backed and so wide in the back that my legs straddled him at about a 100-degree angle. I couldn't take it, so I got off and led him back to the Ranger Station.

Lage was standing on the porch. . . . For a few seconds he said nothing, just looked at the sway-backed plow horse. Then he exploded, "What in the Hell you got there?"

"Lage, you gave me fifty bucks to get a real gentle horse, one that could be saddled or packed, and this is the best I could do. I'll guarantee he's gentle or I never could have gotten back. And with a high enough saddle he ought to ride all right at the speed we'll be going."

Old Barney turned out to be one of Lage's best all-around horses, one of the few he held over to the next season. The following year, working on the Okanogan (Chelan) Forest, Barney got tangled up in some fallen telephone lines and fell over a cliff. In his memory, Lage named that point, "Mount Barney."[13]

Between 1925 and 1929, Wernstedt's work—which was virtually unknown to the public—included some outstanding explorative and mountaineering achievements, the development of highly effective surveying techniques, and the building of photographic equipment for what was likely the first aerial mountain photography for mapping. The detail and accuracy of the 1931 edition of the Mt. Baker Forest map, as well as the number of names of mountain features on it, seem directly attributable to Wernstedt's projects. He saw a strong need for permanent nomenclature in the triangulation networks, and many of the names that first appeared at this stage of cartographic history may have been his. The designation "Picket Range" and several of the dramatic peak names such as Mt. Terror and Mt. Fury made their debut on this map.[14]

Wernstedt spent several summers in the 1920s collecting field data for a new compilation of the Okanogan Forest base map, making his headquarters at Winthrop. Between 1926 and 1931, he took thousands of panoramic photos from high vantage points in the Mt. Baker, Chelan, and Okanogan national forests. He ascended over fifty peaks (mostly in 1925 and 1926), with some important first ascents, such as Silver Star, Mt. Logan, and Black Peak (all in 1926). He also took heavy equipment to many Pasayten-area summits and up Jack Mountain. Wernstedt probably never carried less than forty pounds of surveying and photographic equipment on field ventures. On most of his survey trips, he took two saddle horses, seven packhorses, and his dog. A trip into what is now the Pasayten Wilderness would typically last four to six weeks.

Burgess spent the summer of 1924 with Wernstedt in the Pasayten area and other parts of the Chelan Forest, having been "loaned" to him because of his ability to drive a Model T Ford and ride a horse. Burgess recalled that on June 26 the two men hiked up Tiffany Mountain. In mid-July, while on the summit of nearby Windy Peak during a lightning storm, they drew sparks from static electricity. Farther north, they rebuilt some of the International Boundary markers. During the more dangerous climbs, Wernstedt was quite bold. Usually he would go first, then throw down a rope and pull up the heavy pack.[15] Sometimes the men took along an eight-foot pole, tacked a white cloth triangle on it to serve as a survey target, and wired it down to the rocks. During their climbing and surveying together, which lasted for two years, Wernstedt and Burgess named Mt. Lago and Mt. Rollo after themselves.

In one summer—1923 or 1924—Wernstedt took Frank Burge with him, climbing Remmel, Pistol, Lago, Carru, Castle, Jack, and Robinson. On the ascent of Robinson, "chasms of rock" proved difficult and dangerous, and Wernstedt had to descend some distance to help his partner. When the men were on different peaks, they sometimes sent messages to each other by heliograph. In the summers of 1925 and 1926, Wernstedt and his assistant, Alfred Shull, spent many weeks along the divide between the Chelan and Mt. Baker national forests. Much of their travel was across rough alpine terrain, including snowfields and glaciers. The men ascended Black Peak and possibly Mt. Logan.[16]

Unfortunately, few Forest Service explorers in the Cascade Range left field records as Wernstedt did. An employee named Fred J. Berry, however, kept a trail-crew journal that provides valuable information.[17] Berry began working for the Forest Service in 1925 and was involved in trail work at Silver, Perry, and Little and Big Beaver creeks, west of the upper Skagit River. While working near Whatcom Pass in 1936, he made the first ascent of Whatcom Peak, an anchor of the Picket Range. He also ventured into the high Chilliwack wilderness to the north and explored such unknown valleys as those of McAllister, Marble, and Newhalem creeks.

Names in the Cascades

Forest Service supervisors and district rangers applied innumerable new feature names on their maps of the Cascades. Albert H. Sylvester alone, who was supervisor of the Wenatchee National Forest from 1908 to 1931, is said to have applied over one thousand names. Some colorful examples are Image Lake, named for its reflections of Glacier Peak; Jug Lake; Triad Creek, with its three branches; Itswoot Lake, meaning "bear" in Chinook Jargon (a bear was seen bathing there); Skull Cap and Portal peaks; Helmet Butte and Liberty Cap; Big Snow Mountain, whose snowcap is clearly visible; Rat Trap Pass, whose name came from a backwoods ditty; Dishpan Gap, a divide saddle that reminded someone of a dishpan; and Spark Plug Lake, commemorating a mule. One name that puzzled Sylvester was "Pomas Creek." He later learned that it was a ranger's misspelling of *pumice*, the creek having been named for deposits from Glacier Peak's last eruption.

Sylvester used Chinook Jargon words in some of his naming:

> In counting, three is "klone." Up near the Cascade Summit in the Icicle watershed lie three lakes with a common outlet. I called them "Klonaqua Lakes." You may say I was mixing Indian and Latin, a gross error, but in the Wenatchee tongue "qua" is water, so I feel all right about it with just a mixture of Chinook and Wenatchee.
>
> Klone Peak does not mean Three Peaks, for I named it from a dog of mine for which I paid three dollars and called him Klone. . . .[18]

In 1909, Sylvester named the lakes on Icicle Ridge and near Chiwaukum Creek after female relatives and friends—Mary, Margaret, Flora, Edna, Augusta, and so forth, and one for the British Queen Victoria: "The numbers of ladies' lakes grew until practically all ranger's and other employees wives, sisters, sweethearts, mothers and daughters had lakes named for them."[19] Sylvester also named the peaks of the American Poet Group, where Irving, Poe, Longfellow, Bryant, and Whittier stand guard north of the Little Wenatchee River. The forester explained how some names came about:

> Names of my own choosing followed no definite plan but were often the result of some incident of the trail, fancied resemblances, happy or unhappy whimsies, and what you will. An assistant lost a new camera on a mountain. I called it Kodak Peak. The top of another mountain had a fancied resemblance to an Indian head-dress,

and became Indian Head. Two peaks stand close together on the south side of one of our Indian Creek canyons. I named them David and Jonathan. David now has a trail to its top and a fire lookout on its head. A gloomy peak stands across the canyon from them, glowering I fancied, and that became Mount Saul.

Another name that I felt was a happy one came on a trip I made on foot, the only way, into the head of Snow Creek in the Mount Stuart Range. There are two fine lakes, large for high mountain lakes, near the head of Snow Creek, called Snow Lakes. I camped between them overnight and the next morning went on up the creek to see what I could see. There I found five or six most beautiful small lakes grouped in a wonderful little glacial valley all ringed with alpine larch. From the highest up over an entrancing fall tumbled the water it received from a small glacier. It was an enchanting scene. I named the group Enchantment Lakes. I must presume they had been seen before by some goathunter or seeker of water for irrigation, but the topographer had overlooked them in mapping the Mount Stuart Quadrangle.[20]

Miners also named a great many features, including Sprite Lake, Paddy-Go-Easy Pass, Cathedral Rock, Van Epps Creek, Lynch Glacier, and Foggy Peak. The origins of the names of some of the spectacular granitic formations near Washington Pass are uncertain, but Silver Star Mountain, Snagtooth and Kangaroo ridges, Tower Mountain, Golden Horn, and Liberty Bell obviously acquired their names because of their shapes. (The name Liberty Bell first appeared in a 1916 Forest Service album; the legend "The Towers" appears at this location on an 1895 blueprint map of the state road commissioner, a name apparently bestowed by wagon-road suveryors.[21])

It is still unknown exactly when some of the names in the Cascade Range were applied and who named them, but a review of the maps issued periodically by the Forest Service can give us some guidance. On the 1913 Mt. Baker National Forest map, the entire area between Dome Peak and Cascade Pass is unnamed; present-day Bonanza Peak is still called North Star. There are two Red Mountains and two Glacier Peaks, one of each near the International Boundary. The glaciers on the volcano Glacier Peak are still unnamed. Some of the features identified are Dome Peak, Agnes Mountain, Logan Peak (now Mt. Logan), Reynolds Peak, Washington Pass, Rainy Pass, Mt. Booker, Mt. Higgins, Chiwawa Mountain, Three Fingers, White Horse Mountain, Hozomeen Mountain, Jack Peak (now Jack Mountain), Castle Peak, Monument Peak, Mt. Robinson, Mt. Shuksan, Bacon Peak, Middle Peak, Tomyhoi Peak, Ruth Mountain (at the location of Sefrit), and Green Mountain. Buck Creek and Suiattle passes, Milk Creek, Bridge Creek (and its north fork), the Suiattle River, Hannegan Pass, Whatcom Pass, and the upper Skagit are indicated as having trails. By 1919, most of the peaks of the Dutch Miller Gap–Mt. Daniels area (in the Snoqualmie National Forest) had been located.

Maps from 1922 include Liberty Bell, Bonanza Peak, Clark Mountain, and Goode Mountain. The area between Mt. Shuksan and the Skagit River—including the Pickett Range—is nearly featureless on the maps, as is the span between Boston Peak and Diablo Canyon (although the Beaver Pass trail is shown). Green Lake, Berdeen Lake, and Bald Mountain (Mt. Blum) appear. The 1926 Forest Service map has notable additions: the Mazama and Coleman glaciers on Mt. Baker; Spider, Magic, and Glory mountains; and Le Conte and Sentinel peaks. Trails are shown along Squire and Bedal creeks and between the Crested Buttes. By 1931, four glaciers are named on Glacier Peak's slopes. The Chocolate and Goodell Creek valleys have trails, Lewis Peak is shown at the location of Del Campo Peak, and King George Peak is substituted for Slesse Mountain. The Picket Range finally appears.

Sheep

As a steward of public lands, the Forest Service oversaw not only timber and mining activities but also grazing, which the federal government had authorized in part of the forest reserve. Ever since the reserve was created in 1897, there had been differences of opinion about sheep grazing on public lands. Some believed that it was essential for the livelihood of sheepmen, while others thought it was detrimental to forests and recreational resources.[22] Grazing, however, did reduce the amount of inflammables in the forests and was accepted as helpful in keeping down fire danger.

Among the first areas used by sheep bands were the Lake Chelan and Entiat river drainages, regions with generally thin soils and a short growing season. By the 1890s, sheep were being driven into the upper Entiat to take advantage of the unrestricted use of forage. As many as thirteen thousand head reportedly grazed on Pyramid Mountain, whose slopes soon became terraced and gullied. In the spring, when the lambing season ended, sheep left the low hills along the Columbia River and were driven to the high country, where they remained until fall. Fred Plummer reported in 1900 that on the upper Mad and Entiat rivers, the "trampling and cutting of thousands of hoofs has in many places denuded the ground of every trace of vegetation." Farther south, an estimated fifteen thousand sheep were grazing on the grasses of the Teanaway drainages. In the early 1900s, sheepherder Paul Lozier built the Napeequa River trail to avoid the difficult and steep Little Giant Pass. Herders generally lost a horse per year and always lost sheep on their way to the high country. The animals either wandered off or were killed by bears or coyotes, and most herders killed every bear they saw, including grizzlies.[23]

In the Ashnola River country, near the International Boundary, there were many bands of twelve to fourteen hundred sheep early in the century—all without permit—and some bands went into Canada. As elsewhere, sheep drives devastated the land. At that time, there were still many bighorn sheep in the heights of the Pasayten-Chewuch (Chewack) River country, but they were decimated by the diseases introduced by domestic sheep that were driven to graze in these high regions between 1910 and 1940. In the first two decades of the twentieth century, there were also many sheep bands along the crestline south of Glacier Peak. The alpine grasslands of White, Indian, and Cady passes and the adjoining area were a favorite region for herders; and in 1912 over twenty-five hundred sheep grazed on Miners Ridge and near Buck Creek Pass.[24]

Wenatchee National Forest records indicate that in 1923 there were fifty-three sheep-allotment areas, among them Old Baldy, Cady Pass, Cooper River, Miners Ridge, Teanaway, and Fortune Creek. Each was permitted between twelve hundred and five thousand sheep, depending on the area's capacity and ground cover. The Chumstick-Chiwaukum area was allowed over twenty thousand sheep. Grazing was equally prevalent farther south. The Goat Rocks-Snowgrass Flat area was long used for grazing, and sheep even crossed snow-fields on their way to pastures.[25] In 1885, New Zealand sheepmen Charles and Alexander McAllister had five thousand sheep east and south of Mt. Adams.

On a Mazama club outing to Mt. Adams in 1902, William Lyman wrote: "This paradise, like the ancient Eden, has the trail of the serpent. The serpent in this case is the sheep business." About two hundred thousand sheep were pastured on the flanks of the mountain, and the permit system appeared to have been grossly violated. Lyman added: "The sharp hoofs of the sheep have cut out the turf, defiled the flowery margins of the pools, and polluted the clearness of the fountains. As a result of this Bird Creek Park has in some places become almost a desert." Early in the century, there were perhaps sixty-five to seventy-five thousand sheep in the forest reserve, and by 1930 the number had fallen to about twenty-five thousand.[26]

Grazing declined considerably in the 1930s as the Forest Service studied the carrying capacity of the land and realized that high-meadow grazing caused severe soil damage. The agency consequently reduced sheep allotments. The last record of a band in the Entiat drainage is from 1961. Evidence of some old sheep camps can still be seen on some of the high ridges of this area.

Fire

While grazing affected the ecology of the meadowland belt, particularly in the eastern portions of the range, grass and timber fires sometimes devastated the Cascade Range. Some fires were caused by lightning, but many were started by sheepmen to promote grass growth, by Indians to enhance berry growth, or by careless prospectors, settlers, or campers. Fires and smoke often interfered with the work of surveyors, as evidenced by the frequent complaints of the International Boundary surveyors.

One fire that escaped from an early sheep camp burned out the Whitepine and Wildhorse creek drainages in the Wenatchee River basin. Careless gold diggers supposedly started a large fire in the upper Chiwawa River Valley in about 1862 or 1863. Much of the terrain there is still bare, with ashes and burned and fallen logs on the ground. There was a large burn on Granite Mountain near Snoqualmie Pass in 1865, and dead snags are still plainly visible from Interstate 90. In an attempt to burn out a yellow-jacket nest along the Paradise River near Mt. Rainier in 1894, a fire went out of control and created today's "silver forest." The Great Northern Railway set blazes in the 1890s to clear the right-of-way at Nason Creek east of Stevens Pass. During construction, fires spread into the adjacent hills and valleys.[27] In 1913, the Three Fools Pass fire on the upper Skagit—probably caused by lightning—burned all summer, destroying some 14,000 acres of spruce and lodgepole pine.

The years 1924–1929 were unusually dry in the Pacific Northwest. The two great fires of the Mt. Baker National Forest—the Big Beaver and the Bacon Creek—burned through most of the summer of 1926 and destroyed 43,000 acres. The fire jumped the Skagit, swept across Jack Mountain and Desolation Peak, and spread to Three Fools Creek.[28]

While the Entiat and related fires of the summer of 1970 burned some 99,000 acres and the destructive Entiat and Icicle Creek conflagrations of July 1994 filled the eastern slopes with thick smoke and threatened Leavenworth, the most terrifying and devastating fire in the Cascade Range was the 1902 Yacolt fire in the Rainier Forest Reserve. The fire exploded during extremely hot weather on September 11 as a result of careless burning to clear land, and strong winds spread the fire twenty-five miles in thirty-six hours. The fire quickly made the Lewis River drainage a "valley of death," devastating three counties as it swept to the Columbia River and burning an estimated 240,000 acres of forest.

Some forty woodsmen survived the blast-furnace conditions by taking refuge for three days on Spilyeh Prairie (on Captain McClellan's route of 1853). The inferno destroyed a dozen settlements and left at least thirty-eight persons dead. A picnic party at Yale was struck by an uncontrollable sheet of flame "exploding into balls of fire that went off like torpedoes," Stewart Holbrook wrote in *Burning of an Empire*. There were no survivors. An inch of ash fell on Portland city streets, and the smoke was so dense that the captain of a river steamer had to turn on his running lights in the daytime. In Olympia, a woman warned that Mt. Rainier was in eruption; elsewhere, people were convinced that the last days on earth had arrived.

Fire Lookouts

To protect public resources from uncontrolled fires early in the twentieth century, the Forest Service embarked on a comprehensive protection program that was based on the construction of lookouts. One of the earliest cabins was built in 1912 on the summit of Mt. Pilchuck, an unusual vantage point with a commanding perspective of the western range front and across the Puget Sound Basin. The summit's granite rock was blasted to lower and level it in order to build the lookout cabin, which was used until 1956.[29]

As many as forty-three lookouts were built on summits and ridges in the Mt. Baker National Forest. Church Mountain had the first lookout in the forest in 1928; most of the others were built in the 1930s. They were usually of a standard size and easily constructed, with materials transported to the site by packhorse. The Osborne fire-finder (a sighting device) stood in the center of the building, surrounded by a bunk, stove, table, chairs, lantern, and cooking utensils. The earliest lookouts used army heliographs to transmit and receive messages in Morse code. This device consisted of a mirror and shutter mounted on a tripod. When telephone lines became practical, 3,000-pound test wires were strung to the lookouts; eventually, there were an estimated two hundred miles of telephone lines.

Sourdough Mountain, which commanded a dramatic panorama of the Skagit River and its tributaries, first had a tent lookout. Glee Davis built a horse trail to the location in one week, and in 1917 built a ten-by-ten-foot custom split-cedar cabin with a bunk and Yukon stove. There were no shower facilities, but fresh alpine air was just outside the door. A telephone line of flimsy wire was strung to the site in 1919. The old lookout remained until the 1930s, when the Civilian Conservation Corps (CCC) constructed a new one of Forest Service design. Will Jenkins, a fire and trail worker on Sourdough Mountain in 1919, later remembered that he received $105 per month and had to furnish his own food.[30]

Two buildings were constructed east of the Skagit River, on Crater Mountain (the highest lookout site in the region). The rocky summit had a tent in about 1929, and a cabin was constructed in 1931. The lookout on Jumbo Mountain, near Darrington, provided a vantage to discover the 1916 Fire Creek fire. A message was dispatched to forester Harry Grey, who blazed a route to the locality. Only eight of the sixty men hired finished the difficult march up the untracked White Chuck Valley to the fire.

The most interesting summit lookout project in the northern Cascades was the one on the spectacular South Peak of Three Fingers, which Harry Bedal and Harold Engles reconnoitered in 1929 on a snowy October day. The two men hiked from a trail-crew camp in Canyon Creek close enough to the summit to make a favorable decision about the location.[31] During a snowstorm, they made a perilous crossing of a six-foot rock gap about twenty feet from the summit. They then continued to the Three Fingers-Big Bear saddle and descended Squire Creek in the rain and dark to Darrington to end a remarkable one-day marathon.

The next summer, the men returned to begin blasting and to build a ladder across the gap. During site work in 1931, it was necessary to blast some fifteen feet off the summit to make a level platform for a cabin. Meanwhile, a crew built a trail across the rocky terrain above timberline from Goat Flat to "saddle camp" (Camp Pass), which was used as a construction base. The trail cost $300 per mile, more than was usually spent on such jobs. Beyond Tin Can Gap, gravel was laid on the snow sections so that mules could reach the final camp. During construction of the cabin, a 650-foot tram (with a windlass) was used to haul material for the fourteen-by-fourteen-foot building. It was finally completed in 1932.[32]

Another Darrington-region summit with difficult trail-building and siting problems was 7,201-foot Mt. Pugh, where a lookout cabin was built in 1919. Two cable trams with rock-weight counterbalance systems were built to winch construction materials up the steep, rocky summit slope. Nels Bruseth had previously established a tent lookout there, and one of his most memorable experiences on the mountain was when a lightning strike cracked his tinned food. Both Pugh Mountain and Mt. Higgins, where a cabin was built in 1922, were maintained regularly. Mt. David was another peak on which the summit rock had to be blasted in the 1930s, though the terrain was not as precipitous as that of Three Fingers. Lightning storms on the east side of the range frightened the lookout men, who preferred to sleep in the meadow below.[33]

In Mt. Rainier National Park, a lookout building was constructed at 9,584 feet on Anvil Rock in 1916.[34] By 1934, there were seven more lookouts, all near the 6,000-foot level. Between 1913 and 1935, more than twenty-five lookouts were built in the Columbia (later Gifford Pinchot) National Forest, south of Mt. Rainier. They included Cispus, Sunrise, Burley, Tatoosh Peak, Badger Peak, French Butte, and McCoy Peak. A lookout was even built on top of Mt. St. Helens in about 1913, although the structure did not remain there long.

The lookout system began to decline as aerial surveillance was developed, which was less expensive and more reliable. Eventually, fire-lookout structures were obsolete. Realizing the potential for hiker injuries and litigation, the Forest Service removed most of the lookouts that were no longer in use after 1965. In North Cascades National Park, the only ones remaining on the west side of the crest are at Desolation Peak, Sourdough Mountain, Copper Ridge, and Hidden Lake Peak.[35]

Trails

The initial reason for developing an extensive trail system in the Cascade forests was fire access. The goal was to enable firefighters to get within two miles of any fire by trail. The same was true for Mt. Rainier National Park, although the trails there were planned largely for vacation hikers. Early in the twentieth century, trails were built in the Gifford Pinchot National Forest into the principal valleys and branches beyond the road system. Mountaineering clubs used some of those trails along the Cowlitz, Cispus, Lewis, Tieton, and Klickitat rivers to approach Mt. St. Helens, Mt. Adams, and Goat Rocks.

Before the turn of the century, there were 240 miles of horse trails in the forest reserve north of the Skykomish River. Trails also ran along the Pilchuck, the Sultan, Williamson Creek, Silver Creek, Perry Creek, the north fork of the Stillaguamish, the north fork of the Sauk, the Cascade, the Skagit, Ruby Creek, Canyon Creek, Slate Creek, the Baker, and the north fork of the Nooksack. By 1917, the Stehekin ranger district had built more than twelve shelters for public use along the Stehekin River and Bridge Creek.[36]

During the 1930s, the CCC undertook various jobs in the national forests under Forest Service supervision, including the construction of campsites, telephone lines, lookouts, and trails; fire fighting; and the rejuvenation of environmentally damaged areas. The fifty CCC camps in Washington state were administered by the U.S. Army.

Rivers were a major hindrance in early road and trail building. One notable span in the early part of the twentieth century was the Settler's Bridge across the Skykomish River just west of Index—the only way to reach the district's mining claims. The strategic White Chuck and north-fork Sauk bridges in the Darrington district of the Mt. Baker National Forest were built by the Forest Service in 1912 and used by pack trains.

One of the earliest trails in the Snoqualmie National Forest ran along the Pratt River. In 1910, a twenty-man crew worked on the trail, which was to connect the middle and south forks of the Snoqualmie River. The now-popular Lake Dorothy trail was built from the middle fork in 1913. A Forest Service exploration to find a Cascade Crest trail was made in the summer of 1928. A trail-locating party passed through Necklace Valley, La Bohn Gap, and parts of the Alpine Lakes area, climbing Mt. Hinman on the way.[37]

The first forestry trail in the Mt. Baker area, built in 1904, was along Swift Creek. The Mazama–Wells Creek trail of 1906 was made for summer-outing packers. Similarly, a Mountaineer group in 1908 built a trail to the foot of Boulder Glacier. The Skyline Divide trail was first constructed for riding and for pack animals. In 1925, the Forest Service built a trail around Table Mountain (between Mt. Baker and Mt. Shuksan), which became a popular tourist hike. In the Darrington district, the numerous ambitious trail projects included rebuilding the White Chuck River trail from an old trap-line route. The pleasant, tangy soda from Kennedy Hot Springs, located on this trail, apparently attracted mountain goats, for they visited the springs in large numbers and established a good game trail to Lake Byrne. A trail was also built branching from the Sauk wagon road into the north fork; it was completed to Indian Pass (following an old Indian trail) in 1921. Some of the trail planners hiked through wilderness terrain that very few non-Indians had yet crossed. Fred Cleator walked from Darrington to Lake Chelan in 1927 to probe for new trail routes. In 1929, he was in a party that studied the terrain south of Glacier Peak and climbed to the summit.[38]

During the summer of 1935, a lengthy reconnaissance was made to locate a route for the Cascade Crest trail near the main divide. While on this mission—which included studying a route from Monument 78 on the International Boundary to Harts Pass—Nels Bruseth, Dale Allen, and Hugh Courtney crossed Last Chance Pass (near Corteo Peak) and explored the unknown Seven Sisters and Rimrock Ridge areas. They made their way through the tangle of windfall and undergrowth along Flat Creek to Le Conte Glacier, a location that is now in the heart of the Glacier Peak Wilderness Area. While exploring the rugged alpine terrain at the head of Agnes, Spruce, and Sulphur creeks, they noted the splendor of Bannock Lakes. The party also crossed and named Totem Pass.

The planners decided against a trail route that passed Bannock Lakes because of the delicate vegetation and thin soils. In many places, a trail near the true crest was not practical because of the pristine nature of the terrain and lingering snow on the north and east slopes. Snowslide hazards were a concern for a proposed trail following Spruce Creek to Ross Pass and then Image Lake—a route still without footpaths.

As logging expanded, so did the Forest Service's road network. The Stehekin River Road was built to Bridge Creek before 1928, following the old miners' route. Another forest road that was built far into a mountain valley during this period was along the Suiattle River. The Little Wenatchee and Chiwawa River roads were among the east-slope routes the Forest Service built for fire protection and logging in the 1930s. A road along the middle fork of the Snoqualmie River was to be routed through the Alpine Lakes high country to the Skykomish River, but it was never completed. Other intervalley roads, such as the Mountain Loop Highway (from Granite Falls to Barlow Pass, then Darrington) and the Lewis River–White Salmon road, were built.

In 1913, the state legislature authorized a McClellan Pass Highway to cross the range near Mt. Rainier. (The pass was called both Rainier and McClellan before the name Chinook was adopted.) The road across the pass—of questionable necessity and in fragile terrain—was not opened until July 2, 1932, and is closed in winter.[39]

Resource Issues

In its role as a public-land steward, the U.S. Forest Service has often been embroiled in controversy involving the issuance of special-use permits for harvesting timber, building roads, constructing dams, building recreation homes, and other development. Timber-cutting policy has been a hotly debated issue for the forests of the northern Cascades, which have long supplied lumber for both the United States and other nations. Logging in the region originated near Puget Sound and spread to the forested west-flank valleys in the 1860s. At first, loggers felled trees with axes and later with lengthy crosscut saws. Ox teams hauled the logs to rivers on skid roads greased with fish oil. The steam donkey, which was invented in 1882 and eventually replaced oxen for moving logs, pulled in the logs along the ground by means of a cable wound on a large drum. At about the same time, animal-powered logging railroads began taking timber to the mills; the first tracks along the Skagit River were built in 1882. In time, towns such as Sedro Woolley and Darrington became important timber-harvesting centers.

With the rapid expansion of the timber industry, there were many technological changes. By 1898, wood-burning locomotives were in use. In about 1915, timbermen began to bring logs in on high leads, fastening a lead cable to a high stump so that a log could be lifted off the ground. When gasoline engines replaced steam donkeys in the 1920s, roads were built throughout many principal valleys on both flanks of the range.

Some of the first timber sales in the Washington Forest Reserve were made from 1902 to 1906 in the Slate Creek mining district, which provided logs for flumes and cabins. While there was private land in this area, most timber was taken from the public forests. Farther south along the range, where railroad land grants had led to a mix of public and private ownership, there was more road development and disturbance of the land. Because of heavy timber harvests on intermingled federal and private lands, the ranger districts of the Mt. Baker-Snoqualmie and Gifford Pinchot national forests have faced an unusual management challenge. There has been much controversy over cutting allocations and the methods of timber removal and about how to preserve the land as an everlasting resource. The settlement of such conflicts and the protection of watersheds have been a constant challenge for the Forest Service.

Another contentious resource issue involved the Skagit Canyon, an eleven-mile-long gorge of gneissic rock. In 1907, engineers arrived with transit and level to map the gorge for a new resource—water power. In 1908, the company had established construction camps with plans to build a dam and hydroelectric plant in Diablo Canyon, but it was unable to begin operations before time limits set by the federal government expired. In 1912, the company sold out to Stone and Webster of Boston, but the new developer twice allowed its permit to expire. In 1917, Seattle City Light, headed by James D. Ross, contested the Stone and Webster claim to the Skagit. By late December, Ross's company was in a position to begin its own multi-dam project with enough generating stations to make it the world's largest power project. Harnessing the river, however, was more difficult and costly than anticipated. As historian Paul Pitzer points out, ". . . the struggle to acquire rights to the Skagit and begin construction of a hydro project lasted twelve years and involved elaborate plans and discussions but little actual work toward development. . . ."[40]

At the time, there was no public input and little debate about the desirability of utilizing the Skagit's water power. The river frequently flooded, causing widespread damage in its lower region. Controlling the river flow, however, would benefit agricultural interests at the expense of the upper-valley environment. Furthermore, the wishes of early homesteaders to own and develop land adjacent to the Skagit conflicted with Forest Service policies, which were inclined to support hydroelectric developments.[41]

When Seattle City Light began construction of the dam in 1919, it began a vast transformation of the Skagit River wilderness. The number of men, tents, and buildings in the region increased until, by April 1920, an estimated five hundred workers lived in Newhalem, the new company town. In 1918, Seattle City Light established a base at Rockport with horses to carry construction workers to the damsite. The following year, the Lynch Brothers Diamond Drilling Company undertook boring for a bedrock analysis. The utility quickly realized that it would be most efficient to build its own railroad to transport supplies. By 1920, a twenty-five-mile line was in operation, following the course of the Skagit.[42] President Calvin Coolidge started the generators of the Gorge Dam on September 27, 1924, using a remote-control circuit from Washington.

Exploratory drilling for the massive 389-foot-high Diablo Dam was begun in 1925. The waterworn canyon had bedrock walls of gneiss only some one hundred feet apart and rising 160 feet from the riverbed. The location, about seven miles beyond the Gorge plant, was an ideal damsite. Diablo (formerly Cedar Bar) became another company town. The dam, completed in 1930, was at that time the world's highest. It backed up the new, milky-green, five-mile-long Diablo Lake and entirely changed the appearance of the landscape.[43]

The third dam was to be located at the Rip-raps, just below Ruby Creek. Before construction began in 1937, Seattle City Light bought Ruby Creek Inn and all of the mining claims that might affect the project.[44] Gravel and cement for the Ruby (later Ross) Dam were barged across Diablo Lake in an industrial caravan beneath some glacier-clad alpine peaks that had never been scaled. The first step in the project—a 300-foot-high dam consisting of arch structures that created a nine-mile-long lake—was completed in 1939. The second step was a 545-foot-high dam that created a twenty-four-mile-long lake extending into British Columbia; it was finished in 1949. When spillway gates were added to Ross Dam in 1953, the water rose to 1,600 feet above sea level.

In the 1970s, there was a public dispute over City Light's proposal to again raise the dam and the water level. The Washington Department of Ecology opposed the higher reservoir because of the visual impact on the Ross Lake region.[45] The opposition to licensing the High Ross Dam on environmental grounds provided the impetus for an agreement between Washington state and British Columbia to find an alternative. Political and economic realities had changed, as David Fluharty pointed out in 1989:

If Seattle Light were to be proposing to construct the three dams today . . . the environmental furor they would set off would make the Exxon Valdez disaster seem a mere skirmish. However, when the dam projects on the Skagit were licensed by the Federal Power Commission more than sixty years ago only a few voices mourned the loss of this area and many praised the developers for their foresight. Through the years, those served by Seattle City Light have benefitted from low cost, reliable power supplied by these projects. Floods on the Skagit have been considerably reduced for farms and communities downstream. But these benefits have come at considerable cost to the environment of the Skagit River. Fortunately, the 50-year license of the projects has expired and Seattle City Light, in applying for a new license, must comply with a new set of laws and a new set of political, economic and social conditions.[46]

State, federal, and provincial agencies all became more aware of the new protectionist voice. Complex agreements were made between City Light and the government of British Columbia, and the waters of Ross Lake were not raised.

The Mt. Baker Area

Better access to scenic Mt. Baker was much on the minds of Whatcom County residents early in the twentieth century. In May 1911, some prominent Bellingham citizens became involved in mountaineering when they agreed to promote fund-raising marathon races sponsored by the Mt. Baker Club "to open up this wonderland with road and trail and demonstrate the accessibility of the northernmost fire peak of the Cascade Mountains, Mount Baker."[47] Because the mountain could be approached from different flanks, opinion was sharply divided over where a road should be built. In 1906, the Mazamas had made an ascent via Wells Creek and established a camp on Ptarmigan Ridge northeast of Mt. Baker, christening it Camp Kiser. The club's crowning promotional effort—which helped support such projects as access trails to Heliotrope and Kulshan ridges—was an annual marathon race from Bellingham to the summit of Mt. Baker and back, held from 1911 to 1913. Each sponsoring faction sent its contestants over the route it deemed best. Money to advertise and to award small cash prizes to the racers was raised by public subscription and by the sale of lapel buttons bearing the slogan "Goa-to-it" and a picture of a goat dressed in hiker's clothing and carrying an alpenstock. The marathons verged on the barbaric and were certainly dangerous. A journalist later called the races "without a shadow of doubt the yeastiest chapter in northwest sporting history."[48] One racer fell into a crevasse and nearly died, a grim warning to the race committee. By 1913, many sponsors thought the risks (including running underclad on glaciers during darkness) too great.

At the time, a railroad operated via Sumas to Glacier on the northern valley flank of the mountain and a wagon road ran from Bellingham to Heisler's ranch on the south flank. These were the most popular race routes, and the contestants were about equally divided between them. During the 1912 marathon, some of the fifteen racers took the railroad to Glacier and then were on their own. Harvey Haggard, traveling this route, made the round trip from Bellingham in about fourteen hours—though it probably would have been less if the train had not hit a large bull on the return. Haggard had to complete the trip in a car. Even with this delay, he came in second. Joe Galbraith, the winner, traveled by way of Heisler's ranch.

Opinion remained divided as to where a road should be built near Mt. Baker and if and when funds could be obtained. One group wanted a road to Skyline Ridge, a spur north of the mountain. Others wanted one to Mazama Meadows on the south. A third and stronger vote favored Austin Pass, on the ridge connecting with Mt. Shuksan. Both the Mt. Baker Club and the Bellingham Chamber of Commerce—with public-spirited notions and future profits in mind—agitated to establish a Mt. Baker-centered national park in the exceptionally beautiful rugged alpine region. A 1917 bill was reported on favorably by the Public Lands Committee, but mining interests protested loudly. After many public hearings, Congress failed to pass the bill. Subsequently, the more limited Mt. Baker Recreation Area was set aside, effectively ending the efforts to create a national park. No timber was to be cut there for commercial purposes, and mining was to be carefully supervised to preserve scenery. Recreation was to be the priority. Congress appropriated funds, and the Bureau of Public Roads built twenty-seven miles of road from Glacier to Heather Meadows and Austin Pass.

The Mt. Baker Development Company, formed in 1923, built Heather Inn at the lake-dotted meadows. In July 1927, the lavish Mt. Baker resort, with a hundred rooms, was opened to tourists. That year, an estimated 11,700 guests visited the $225,000 alpine lodge. Among the recreational offerings were miniature golf and pony rides around Table Mountain. The lodge area served as the winter setting for the film *The Call of the Wild*, a location chosen to simulate the Klondike. An improved highway, completed in 1931, allowed thousands to visit the high country, but the intrusion of road slash on the fragile Austin Pass slope was lamented by some members of a 1929 Mazamas outing. The lodge burned in August 1931, and through the Depression years the company never really recovered.

Mt. Rainier National Park

Mt. Rainier National Park, established in 1899, developed out of the Rainier Forest Reserve. The movement for a park had begun in 1880 and had enjoyed strong public support. Concern about protecting the land around Mt. Rainier was expressed by members of Congress, staff of the Department of the Interior, and even some prominent Europeans. Lord James Bryce, a member of the British Parliament, and Karl von Zittel, a German paleontologist, both of whom had visited Rainier in 1883, sent a joint letter endorsing the national park to congressional leaders.

Several seemingly incompatible interests contributed to the park's founding. The Northern Pacific Railroad was supportive, convinced that "the area did indeed have great potential for tourism."[49] Professional and preservation groups such as the National Geographic Society, the Geological Society of America, the American Association for the Advancement of Science, the Appalachian Mountain Club, and the Sierra Club sought congressional support to safeguard the mountain's delicate environment. Scientific groups that endorsed the park for resource preservation eventually agreed to keeping Naches and Cowlitz passes out of the boundary as potential railroad crossings.

It was Mt. Rainier's dominance on the landscape that prompted the surge of public interest. As Israel C. Russell wrote in 1898:

> This grand mountain is not, like Mont Blanc, merely the dominant peak of a chain of snow mountains; it is the only snow peak in view, Mount St. Helens and Mount Adams being, like it, isolated and many miles distant. Rainier is majestic in its isolation, reaching 6,000 to 8,000 feet above its neighbors. It is superb in its boldness, rising from one canyon 11,000 feet in 7 miles. Not only is it the grandest mountain in this country, it is one of the grand mountains of the world, to be named with St. Elias, Fusiyama [sic], and Ararat, and the most superb summits of the Alps.[50]

After his 1896 studies on Mt. Rainier, Russell described the forest that would be such an important part of the future park:

> The mighty forest through which we traveled from Carbonado to the crossing of Carbon River extends over the country all about Mount Rainier and clothes the sides of the mountain to a height of about 6000 feet. From distant points of view it appears as an unbroken emerald setting for the gleaming, jewel-like summit of the snow-covered peak.[51]

Few people had seen the mountain's timberline zone:

> The knolls rising through the snow are gorgeous with flowers. . . . Acres of meadow land, still soft with snow water and musical with rills and brooks flowing in uncertain courses over the deep, rich turf, are beautiful with lilies, which seemed woven in a cloth of gold about the borders of the lingering snow banks. We are near the upper limit of timber growth, where parklike openings, with thickets of evergreens, give a special charm to the mountain side.[52]

While it was the spectacle of the glacier-clad volcano itself that was the impetus for a national park, most visitors would encounter the forests, not the glaciers, and it was the primeval forest that was the most vulnerable.

There had been much careless camping in the park region, and human-caused fires had changed the landscape over the years. Even though the creation of the forest reserve had halted new settlement for a time, loggers anticipated stripping the forests to the mountain's base. In 1891, an Interior Department agent, Cyrus Mosier, expressed astonishment at the indiscriminate logging and timber wreckage in the region. Mosier warned of the potential for floods and erosion as a result of corporate greed. Like an act of vandalism, he wrote, stripping the timber and allowing fires to run over the surface "will tear the frame from this grand painting against the sky."[53] National parks in the United States were intended to preserve a heritage—invaluable assets for the people–and such a heritage must be safeguarded by policies that reflected strong preservation principles. The protection of Mt. Rainier and its forests by setting it aside as the fifth national park, for many, was an appropriate step.

The Northern Pacific and Mt. Rainier

The arrival of the Northern Pacific Railroad at Puget Sound in 1883 marked the beginning of rapid growth and change in communications and the economy of the region. In 1873, railroad surveyors had studied a route to Wilkeson in the Carbon River coalfields. After the railroad was built three years later, the town enjoyed a measure of prosperity from mining. Until 1881, however, when geologist Bailey Willis began his explorations, little was known of the northern and western flanks of the mountain. Over two years, Willis surveyed and explored the region for the Northern Transcontinental Survey. He opened a horse trail from Wilkeson to the Carbon River and in the fall of 1882 extended it south to the Mowich River. The trail, though built to aid in a mineral survey, also attracted visitors and became known as the Willis or Grindstone trail. It led to the north fork of the Puyallup River, where Willis built a cabin.[54]

The enthusiasm of Willis and the curiosity of the railroad's vice-president, Thomas F. Oakes, led to a June 1883 visit by Oakes, Vermont Senator George F. Edmunds, and J.M. Buckley, who was in charge of the railroad's western division. The men were impressed by the glaciers and the scenery. The railroad prepared travel guides, and Olin Wheeler wrote floridly enthusiastic promotional pieces about Mt. Rainier, creating an effusive narrative about a 1894 ascent of the mountain. George O. Shields, who visited the Pacific Northwest and traveled on the Northern Pacific, prophesied in his 1889 book that "Mt. Tacoma will be the future resort of the continent."[55]

Mt. Rainier was brought to the attention of leading Europeans after the 1883 visit by Bryce and von Zittel. Willis guided the September expedition of four Germans and three Englishmen to the Carbon, Mowich, and Puyallup glaciers. Until then, European scientists had been unaware of the glaciers on Mt. Rainier.[56] Willis and his party rode to Palace Camp on the Puyallup River and up the wooded ridge north of the Mowich River and then followed the route of today's road to Mowich Lake. The Willis trail subsequently crossed the steep escarpment to reach Spray Park. The pioneering party hiked almost to lower Ptarmigan Ridge and made a traversing descent onto the "Willis" (North

Mowich) Glacier. After returning to Mowich Lake, they continued to Ipsut Pass, noting the columnar andesite exposures nearby. Reaching Eunice Lake, they climbed Tolmie Peak (which Willis believed Tolmie had climbed in 1833).

In his account of the trip, von Zittel observed that the almost impenetrable forest on the approach to the Cascades presented the greatest difficulty to an ascent. He described his experiences:

> Mr. Villard took care to see that a small number of his guests might find it possible to visit [Mt.] Tacoma. So, on the night of 10. September, in Portland, four Germans (v. Bunsen, Dielitz, v. Schauss, Zittel) and three Englishmen (Prof. Bryce, Benson, McLeod) made preparations, under the leadership of Mr. Willis, to first go to Kalama on the Willamette [Columbia] River with a steamship, to then reach Puget Sound by railroad, and from there to the foot of Tacoma. . . . We arrived in Wilkeson late in the evening, found hospitable lodging there and the next morning a number of small but unbelievably tough Indian horses, which were to carry us through the primeval forest to the half-height of Tacoma.
>
> . . . The bridle-path from Wilkeson to Palace Camp is rather well-kept, so that the Indian horses hasten on at a gallop and with wondrous certainty go forward over thick roots, tree trunks and deep holes. A wide ravine is bridged with a fallen giant fir on which two riders can comfortably pass alongside each other. In the afternoon we took a newly opened side path, which struggles steeply upwards, and reached a wooded rocky ridge, which separates the Carbon River valley from that of the Puyallup River. . . . We rode on the ridge for seven English miles, then the path turned toward the side, crossed a large swampy woods-meadow and then climbs steeply once more until it ends on a rocky terrace at a crystal-clear crater lake, bordered on one side by steep andesite rocks and shaded everywhere by dark evergreens. . . .

The next morning, clouds and thick fog veiled the mountain. At about eight o'clock, however, a "fresh wind" cleared the sky, and the party continued.

> After two hours the woods ceased, steeply rising alpine meadows spread themselves before us and behind them rose the mighty snow peak of Tacoma. The horses were now sent back, we quickly climbed over the meadow. . . . Soon the vegetation became more sparse, we clambered up on rough andesite rocks and finally at 12:30 o'clock stood at the end of a side-arm of the Willis glacier.
>
> Tied to a line, we stepped on the steeply tilted, but only a little fissured, ice surface, climbed upward for about two hours, whereby we could now view the steep side walls of the glacier tongue, which consisted of regularly layered inclined strata of andesite lava, which by their variegated colors already at a distance allowed their construction to be recognized.
>
> Now and then an isolated reef also protruded from the ice, whose black or rust-colored lava chunks appeared so fresh and undecayed, as if they had first congealed yesterday.

At about four o'clock in the afternoon, the explorers reached

> a stone ridge radiating from the peak or Tacoma at an altitude of about 10,000 Engl. feet, alongside and below which the Willis glacier spread out in its fullest glory.

In the depths, a thick sea of fog surged over the primeval forest, but up above the air was of the most transparent clarity and above us a deep blue sky arched. The western horizon was bordered by the many jagged snow-covered, still unexplored, Coast Range between Puget Sound and the Pacific Ocean; in the south Mount Helens rose out of the fog, high above the crags of the Cascade Range, and in the north, from a great distance, the glaciated peak of Mount Baker shone toward us in its lonely bigness. But far more than on this glorious distant view was our attention held by our immediate surroundings. Right before our eyes, the central cone of Tacoma, completely covered with eternal snows, rose up steeply, culminating above in a jagged peak, which drew our sights away from both of the peaks lying behind it. We believed we saw thin steam clouds rising out of the crater, but it could not be decided whether warm steam of condensed moisture caused the phenomenon. Sunk in a deep, wide canyon, right at our feet, lay the mighty Willis glacier. . . . Countless transverse and longitudinal fissures cross in all directions, split up the glacier in light-blue fragments. . . .

No glacier of the Alps surpasses this Tacoma glacier in beauty and grandeur. . . .

Resisting, we separated ourselves from the magnificent presentation, but the sun already was sinking toward the horizon and before us still lay a long, difficult return. In the dark of night we again mounted our horses at the border of the woods, and left it to their sure footing to bring us back to the camp ground at the crater lake [Mowich Lake].[57]

Bryce and von Zittel published a report expressing the hope that the mountain would be treated as a national park. They concluded: "We have nothing more beautiful in Switzerland or Tyrol, in Norway or in the Pyrenees, than the Carbon River glaciers and the great Puyallup glaciers."[58]

The opening of the Carbon River area was significant because it drew public attention to the future parkland. The Bailey Willis trail was popular with tourists in the 1880s and 1890s, and visitors could take the railroad from Tacoma to Wilkeson, where they could procure packhorses.[59] There were other explorations and wanderings onto the mountain's northern flank during this time. Maj. Edward S. Ingraham and Ernest C. Smith hiked to Spray Park late in 1888 and crossed the Carbon Glacier before continuing to the White River. J. Warner Fobes and his party of mountaineers used the Carbon River approach to ascend the Winthrop–Emmons Glacier route to the summit in 1884. In July 1896, Willis, Israel C. Russell, and George Otis Smith, sponsored by the U.S. Geological Survey, made a historic exploration of the north flank to study glaciers and the mountain's volcanic origin.

Still, no great tourist mecca developed there, as the Northern Pacific optimists had hoped. Instead, public attention turned in the 1890s to Longmire Springs and Paradise Valley. What eventually became the more popular route to the south flank of Mt. Rainier had had its beginning in 1861 when settler James Longmire built his trail from Yelm Prairie to Bear Prairie. Longmire's discovery of hot springs in 1883—where he soon developed a claim, then built a trail and road—was another influence. A variety of visitors, including hikers, mountaineers, foresters, and scientists, began to appear on this flank of the mountain even before the national park was formed. Nevertheless, park supporters realized that the Carbon River area would be valuable for its primitive qualities and need not be a resort hub.

Naming Mt. Rainier

When Capt. George Vancouver named the Pacific Northwest's highest mountain on May 8, 1792, he initiated a controversy that lasted for more than a century.[60] In the decades following the creation of Mt. Rainier National Park, the often-bitter dispute created adverse publicity for the park, and at times presented a serious barrier to development plans.

Lewis and Clark used the name *Regnier*, which perpetuated the name bestowed by Vancouver and its application on maps of the time. The 1853 traveler Theodore Winthrop pointed out that the Indians' *Tacoma* was a broad term and refuted those who claimed it was simply a specific name for Mt. Rainier. Throughout his book, *The Canoe and the Saddle*, Winthrop used both *Rainier* and *Tacoma*. Historian Edmond S. Meany believed that "Mr. Winthrop probably heard the Indians use the chinook jargon word 'T'kope', meaning 'white.' Mr. Buchanan thinks it quite likely as the explosive pronunciation of T'kopt [*sic*] by the Indian would somewhat resemble the white man's pronunciation of Tacoma."[61]

It appears that *Tahoma* or *Tacoma* was long used to refer to almost any Pacific Northwest snow mountain. Winthrop wrote: "Tacoma the second, which Yankees call Mt. Adams, is a clumsier repetition of its greater brother." Other witnesses included George Gibbs and later Hazard Stevens, who discussed the name after his ascent of the mountain in 1870.[62]

> Takhoma or Takoma among the Yakimas, Klickitats, Puyallups, Nisquallys, and allied tribes of Indians, is the generic term for mountains, used precisely as we use the word mountain, a Ta-ka-ma Wynatchic or Mount Wynatchic. But they also designate Mount Rainier simply as Tak-ho-ma or the mountain just as the mountain men used to call it "Old He."[63]

Maps varied on the assigning the mountain a name. The 1887 General Land Office map of Washington was ambivalent: "Mt. Rainier or Mt. Tacoma."

In 1883, the Northern Pacific Railroad, in an attempt to advertise its destination city of Tacoma and attract industry, insisted on referring to the mountain as "Mount Tacoma." In the March issue of *The Northwest*, the railway issued this statement:

> The Indian name Tacoma will hereafter be used in the guide books and other publications of the Northern Pacific Railroad and the Oregon Railway and Navigation Company, instead of Rainier, which the English Captain Vancouver gave to this magnificent peak when he explored the waters of Puget Sound in the last century.[64]

Thus began a long controversy over the name, as both the railroad and the city of Tacoma politicked for *Tacoma* in opposition to Seattle's *Rainier*. The *Tacoma Daily Ledger* was especially active in 1883 in supporting the Indian name. The battle was also fought in the House Committee on Public Lands, and its chairman successfully amended the park bill at the last minute to read "Mount Rainier National Park," a change bitterly received in the city of Tacoma.[65] The controversy was finally referred to the U.S. Board on Geographic Names, which in 1890 confirmed *Rainier* as the official name of the mountain

The reaction in Tacoma prompted the *Seattle Daily Times* later to comment:

> It will never cause grand old Mount Rainier the faintest blush of shame, even when her sun-kissed summit beams brightly down on Tacoma—the city of considerable destiny—to reflect that the name of a Briton is associated with its beautiful surroundings, while all the world but Tacoma is pleased to designate the mountain itself with the name which the Congress of the United States has given to the grandest park on the coast. . . . Here is anglomania run riot. The name of Washington National Park has been changed to Rainier, after a British naval officer. It might be in order to likewise change the name of the state, and complete the job.[66]

Tacoma sent protests to the nation's capital, and its business clubs continued to promote the city's preference.[67] The Mt. Tacoma Club kept alive sentiment for a name change even after the turn of the century. In 1917, the Board on Geographic Names again heard evidence for and against a change. On May 28, it announced another decision in favor of *Rainier*.

Tourism and Mt. Rainier

Despite the argument over the name of Mt. Rainier, roads, mining, and tourism continued to grow in the park area. In 1896, Tacoma business interests—who saw themselves as best fitted to develop the mountain's southern approach—endorsed a destination road, one that would serve the city's commercial interests by promoting tourist travel. A wagon road had been completed to Longmire in 1891. Four years later, there was a trail to Paradise Valley, and soon a four-horse stage was taking passengers to that subalpine destination. Meanwhile, the Tacoma and Eastern Railroad was pushing toward Ashford. After its completion in 1904, the line carried thousands of tourists to the mountain's lower forest.

With road construction a high priority for the park, the Army Corps of Engineers, under the direction of civil engineer Eugene Ricksecker, conducted a survey to Paradise Valley in 1904. The road, begun in 1906, was a major policy decision in the park's development. While no road can leave nature untouched, Ricksecker recognized the importance of preserving scenic beauty. Autos, which had reached Longmire in 1908, could be driven along the winding ascent to Paradise in 1911.[68]

When the park was launched in 1899, there were no appropriations for administration and development, and it was fortuitous that the park area held only marginal interest for mining and grazing enterprises. Still, prospectors were delighted with the legislation that established the park, because it allowed for mining and the cutting of timber for cabins. Not until 1908 were new mining claims within the park prohibited. The most aggressive mining operation near the Carbon River was the Washington Mining and Milling Company. Beginning in 1908, the firm located thirty-eight lode claims.

Arguably the most interesting operation within the park was the Mt. Rainier Mining Company. Not only were its silver and copper workings in Glacier Basin (near the Emmons Glacier) the most extensive, but at one time its officers were jailed for mail fraud. Peter Storbo and his associates began extracting ore as early as 1897, before the park was established. In less than a decade, Storbo improved the trail into the White River and its Inter Fork to his mining camp. By 1909, his company had erected a water-powered sawmill; constructed cabins, a barn, and a blacksmith shop; and tunneled some seven hundred feet. It soon built a road over eleven miles long within the park (at a cost of $38,500), with a "wagon trail" following the glacier moraine to a sawmill at an elevation of 5,700 feet. An aerial tramway led from a tunnel to the wagon road, and ore shipments were occasionally taken by wagon and packhorse to Enumclaw. There was also a 2,400-volt electric-power plant and machinery for a one-hundred-ton concentrator. In 1924, the company received patents on eight claims, but in a few years stockholder complaints began to mount. Storbo and a partner were found guilty of fraud in 1930, sending the company into a disarray from which it never recovered. Eventually, new owners rebuilt much of the road and worked the claims, but renewed operations proved unsuccessful.

In the early years of the park, there was little uniformity and no standard policies with respect to concessions, despite their often unreliable nature. Tent camps had been set up at Theosophy Ridge (Paradise) in 1897 and at Indian Henry's Hunting Ground in 1908. Guiding services were offered by pioneer Leonard Longmire after he made his first climb in 1890. Early accidents on Mt. Rainier helped draw attention to the need for regulation of guiding. The first known fatality on the mountain took place during a Mazama outing in August 1897 when Edward McClure slipped and fell while taking a shortcut in his descent of Gibraltar. The large outing, with some two hundred members and friends, received national publicity, and the accident may have helped those in Congress who were attempting to establish the park by pointing up the need for some official supervision. When two climbers died in a storm on Rainier in 1909, it was recommended that the government license guides and build a shelter at Camp Muir. Not long afterwards, in 1911, a system was introduced to regulate guiding. The Stamfler brothers had a guide service from 1906 to 1919. When the Rainier National Park Company was formed in 1916, the guide service was linked with company operations. The Fuhrer brothers (from Switzerland) operated the service with a respectable record from 1919 to 1925. The formation of the park company, which unified nearly all concessions, led to further development.[69] The public was clamoring for better lodging, access roads, camps, and trails; and with a capital of $200,000, it made immediate plans to build Paradise Inn. By 1940, the National Park Service and other agencies had made improvements worth $7.5 million.

Various promotional schemes were aimed at expanding the park's road system. Some hoped to encircle the mountain with a main roadway and then add branches to the meadow regions. In 1921, this envisioned "Wonder Road" was favored by park superintendents and other officials (the Wonderland Trail had fulfilled a similar vision for hikers when it circled the mountain in 1915). After the Mt. Rainier Mining Company built its wagon road along the White River in 1914, the increase in travel to the north flank led to the idea of developing Yakima Park to include tourist facilities, and a terrain-scarring new road opened to the public in 1932.[70] The West Side Highway was begun in the 1920s and completed in 1935 to the north fork of the Puyallup, but the dream of an "around-the-mountain" road connecting the Longmire and Carbon River areas was never fulfilled. The public was clamoring for better lodging, access roads, camps, and trails. The road to subalpine Mowich Lake was completed in 1932 and the disputed Stevens Canyon Road in 1957. Stephen Mather, the first director of the National Park Service, suggested a parkway for the eastern perimeter of the park in 1928—a road that later took his name.

At Mt. Rainier National Park—as at Yellowstone and Yosemite—the road system became a corridor through the wilderness. As in most national parks, 99 percent of visitor travel is accommodated on one to five percent of the total land area. In the 1950s, automobile clubs and chambers of commerce endorsed additional roads and a permanent tramway on the mountain.[71]

When all visitation records were broken at Mount Rainier in 1958, the Park Service recognized the need for serious resource planning. A 1959 ecology study indicated environmental problems. Foot trampling and gully erosion were widespread, and many of the subalpine trails were poorly located (snowdrifts sometimes encouraged hikers to skirt them on wet meadows). Horses had caused trail erosion, and parallel troughs were widespread in meadowlands.[72] There was also a need for additional development at Paradise, the focal point of tourism.

In 1955, a ten-year plan known as Mission 66 was made for the development of all the national parks to rescue them from neglect and to create facilities for visitors. The plan for Mt. Rainier, designed to allow for one million visitors annually, called for new campground units, more development at Paradise and Yakima Park, and new low-level trails.[73] Some opponents of the national plan contended that it catered to recreation seekers, not nature lovers, and that construction of facilities was making resorts out of the national parks. Nevertheless, Congress had clearly spelled out the dual purposes of enjoyment and preservation in the National Park Act of 1916: "To conserve the scenery . . . and to provide for the enjoyment of the same . . . by such means as will leave them unimpaired for enjoyment of future generations."

Stewardship

The forests of the Cascade Range have seen three regimes of land use and management from the time of early Euro-American settlement to the present. In the extractive era, which lasted from the second half of the nineteenth and into the twentieth century, logging removed much of the forest cover. The landscape of the foothills and lower mountain slopes changed considerably, particularly because of clearcuts and the intrusion of roads and railways. Dams were built in the river valleys, and impounded lakes replaced the flowing waterways. Prominent transmission lines marred trunk valleys and transect the foothills. During the custodial era, which lasted for much of the twentieth century, the Forest Service managed timberlands according to the sustained-yield doctrine, emphasizing protection from fire and overcutting. The agency constructed lookouts and hundreds of miles of trails, and extended roads in order to access valley headwaters and flanking ridges.

Recently, forest management has aimed to preserve watershed and recreational opportunities. As the vitality of the Cascades has come into question with the increasing impact of humans on the ecology of the range, management principles have, under the influence of wilderness advocates and scientists, changed to accommodate the concept of protecting the ecosystem. Still, many agree that forests must continue to provide renewable timber, reliable supplies of water, and outdoor opportunities for people.

Such stewardship to preserve the wilderness is critical, according to western author Wallace Stegner. In 1960, he wrote: "Something will have gone out of us as a people if we ever let the remaining wilderness be destroyed. . . . We need wilderness preserved—as much of it as is still left, and as many kinds—because it was the challenge against which our character as a people was formed."[74] That challenge has been taken up by generations of people in the northern Cascades: the Indians who first traveled up the valleys and over the passes; the maritime and overland explorers seeking to establish political and commercial claims; the solitary fur hunters and the hopeful settlers; the surveyors whose task was to find a route for the iron horse or to delineate a boundary between nations; and, finally, those who came to the mountain wilderness to conquer high peaks, find mineral wealth, or study the topography and rocks.

The range of glaciers that make up the northern Cascades has now been thoroughly investigated and its resources widely tapped. For decades after the early land explorers breached the unknown passes, there was but little change in the alpine vista and even the low valleys on the mountain flanks. Those early visitors probably never expected that the apparently boundless prospects of the rich wilderness would so soon be replaced by a need for conservation and its associated limits on economic and human activity.

Illustrations ~

Tramway and cables on Pugh Mountain during lookout construction in 1919. Courtesy of author, Nels Bruseth Collection.

Devil's Corner and the Goat Trail above the Skagit River in the 1890s. Darius Kinsey, photographer; Glee Davis Collection, courtesy Mrs. Jeanita Davis Callahan, OHS neg., OrHi 85675.

261 Skagit River Hotel, in Barron, Washington

(Above left) Dumas Street in Monte Cristo, from behind the main row of buildings, c. 1895. Note the two-storied outhouses, used to cope with deep winter snow. Woodhouse Collection, MSCUA, University of Washington Libraries, UW14024.

(Below left) The Skagit River Hotel at Barron, c. 1895. Darius Kinsey, photographer; Glee Davis Collection, courtesy Mrs. Jeanita Davis Callahan, OHS neg., OrHi 85640.

(Above) The McMillan roadhouse in the upper Skagit River valley, about 1898. The area is now flooded by Ross Lake. Courtesy Vera Thompson Murphy.

(Right) The geologist Samuel F. Emmons, who ascended Mt. Rainier in 1870 with Allen Drew Wilson. Emmons was the first professional to study the geology and glaciers of the northern Cascades. Library of Congress.

Hazard Stevens and Philemon B. Van Trump, about 1915. The flag is one they carried to the summit of Mr. Rainier during their ascent in August 1870. Washington State Historical Society, Tacoma.

American boundary surveyor at Monument 69, at the head of McNaught Creek, west of the Skagit River, in the summer of 1908. The peaks are Devils Tongue (left) and Mt. Rahm, closely south of the forty-ninth parallel. C. H. Sinclair, photographer, RG 76, National Archives.

(Above) Mazama party near large crevasse on Mt. Baker, August 1906. Fred Kiser, photographer, Mazamas—Kiser Collection, album 2B, VM1993.026.P130.

(Left) Lage Wernstedt, Forest Service surveyor. R.C. Burgess, photographer, U.S. Forest Service.

U.S. Geological Survey camp at Snoqualmie Pass, August 1895. Bailey Willis, photographer, U.S. Geological Survey Photographic Library, Denver.

American Boundary Survey party packing equipment to Monument 95 on the north shoulder of Cathedral Peak, 1905. Surveying apparatus had to be pulled with ropes to reach this high, exposed station. RG 76, CB-34-128, National Archives.

ABBREVIATIONS

Alexander C. Anderson Papers	Alexander C. Anderson Papers, Add. MSS 559, BCARS
BCARS	British Columbia Archives and Records Service (B.C. Provincial Archives), Victoria
Gardner, manuscript	George C. Gardner, manuscript, MSS S-1131, George Clinton Gardner Papers, Beinecke Library, Yale University, New Haven, Conn.
Gibbs, journal	George Gibbs, journals, E. 198, RG 76, NA
GNR Records	Great Northern Railway Company Records, Minnesota Historical Society, St. Paul
GSC	Geological Survey of Canada
Harris Papers	Joseph Smith Harris Papers, Beinecke Library, Yale University, New Haven, Conn.
Hill Papers	James J. Hill Papers, Great Northern Railway Company Records, Minnesota Historical Society, St. Paul
IBC	International Boundary Commission
Kennerly, journal	Dr. Caleb B.R. Kennerly, journal, E. 199, RG 76, NA
Macy Papers	Preston Macy Papers, University of Washington Libraries, Seattle
McClellan Papers	George B. McClellan Papers, Manuscripts Division, Library of Congress, Washington, D.C.
NA	National Archives, Washington, D.C.
NWD	*Northwest Discovery*
NPRR Records	Northern Pacific Railroad Company Records, Minnesota Historical Society, St. Paul
OHQ	*Oregon Historical Quarterly*
PNQ	*Pacific Northwest Quarterly*
Rogers, diary	Albert B. Rogers, diary, Albert B. Rogers Papers, Washington State Historical Society, Tacoma
Samuel Anderson Papers	Samuel Anderson Papers, Yale Collection of Western Americana, Beinecke Library, Yale University, New Haven, Conn.
Strom Papers	Sam Strom Papers, University of Washington Libraries, Seattle
USGS	U.S. Geological Service
Van Trump Papers	Philemon B. Van Trump Papers, University of Washington Libraries, Seattle
WHQ	*Western Historical Quarterly*
WSA	Washington State Archives and Records Center, Olympia

NOTES

Introduction

1. Vancouver, *Voyage,* 2:694.

2. Vancouver, *Voyage.*

3. Goetzmann, *Exploration and Empire,* xi.

4. Wagner, *Spanish Explorations,* 17, 82 (map).

5. Ibid., 17.

6. Cline, *Exploring the Great Basin,* 62.

7. Vancouver, *Voyage,* 1:79.

8. Vancouver, *Voyage,* 2:510, 515, 519. (Charles F. Easton noted that Vancouver named the mountain "without any respect to the aboriginal title—Koma Kulshan.") See also Newcombe, ed., *Menzies' Journal,* 17. Vancouver confirmed Menzies's description of the range, stating that the mountains had "grotesque shapes." See *Voyage,* 2:544.

9. Vancouver, *Voyage,* 2:522.Vancouver had served with Peter Rainier of the British Navy two years previously. The publication of Vancouver's work placed the name Mt. Rainier on British maps, from which it was copied onto American maps. In both 1890 and 1917, the U.S. Board on Geographic Names decided to retain the name despite other proposals.

10. Vancouver, *Voyage,* 2:759–61. Samuel Hood was a British admiral who served during the Seven Years' War and the American and French revolutionary wars.

11. The Cascade Range continues to the plateau at the junction of the Fraser and Thompson rivers. See Daly, *Geology of the North American Cordillera,* pt. 1, 22–4, 41; Daly, "Okanogan Composite Batholith," 332.

12. Coues, *New Light,* 2:795. Henry's view was from south of the Kalama River.

13. Winthrop, *Canoe and the Saddle,* 39.

14. Ibid., 36.

15. "Report of George Gibbs upon the Geology of the Central Portion of Washington Territory," May 1, 1854, in *Reports of Explorations and Surveys,* 1:481.

16. Tabor et al., *Accreted Terranes.*

17. Kirk and Daugherty, *Exploring Washington Archaeology,* 13; Crandell, Mullineaux, and Rubin, "Mount St. Helens Volcano," 438–41.

18. See Holmes, *Mount St. Helens,* 13–15. The Reverend Samuel Parker also noted the 1835 eruption but did not publish anything about the event.

19. Thornton, *Oregon and California,* 1:256.

20. Burnett, "Letters," 424.

21. Warre, *Overland to Oregon,* 88. He drew the eruption from the lower Cowlitz River. An earlier sketch of the mountain was included in a coastal profile made in 1792 during the voyage of Dionisio Alcalá Galiano and Cayetano Valdés. See Higueras Rodríguez, ed., *Catálogo Crítico* 2:256, illustration 2573, 334; Kane, *Paul Kane's Frontier,* 99. The watercolor was done March 26, 1847; in his March 30 sketch, the smoke is depicted as originating from either Goat Rock or the

crater behind it. Kane's later oil painting, a dramatic vision of a fiery night eruption and bright lava flow, is a fiction. See Majors, "Paul Kane's Drawing"; *Oregonian*, September 3, 1853.

22. Gibbs, "George Gibbs' Account," pt. 1, 321–2. See also Majors, "First Reference to Glacier Peak." There is disagreement on the date of the last eruption of Glacier Peak (probably the "smaller peak" Gibbs mentioned); estimates range from twelve thousand years ago to A.D. 1750. Gibbs observed lava discharges near Mt. Adams in 1853, some of which had killed fir trees and cooled, but noted elsewhere that no modern reports of eruption were known.

23. Crandell, "Geologic Story"; Willis, "Canyons and Glaciers"; Mullineaux, Sigafoos, and Hendricks, "Historic Eruption," B15–18.

24. Winthrop, *Canoe and the Saddle*, 38; Gibbs, "Report of George Gibbs on a Reconnaissance," 1:469. There are also several newspaper reports of eruptions. See the *Olympia Pioneer and Democrat*, December 28, 1860; the *Victoria Daily British Colonist*, July 27, 1863; and the *Olympia Washington Standard*, August 1, 1863.

25. Davidson, "Recent Volcanic Activity," 262. Davidson stated that between 1852 and 1877, when he was often in sight of Mt. Baker's features, no catastrophe such as the summit's falling in had taken place. There had been press reports that the summit had formerly been a sharp point and was now much flattened.

26. Davidson, "Recent Volcanic Activity," 262; "Mount Baker an Active Volcano," *West Shore* 16 (March 22, 1890), 376.

27. Post et al., "Inventory of Glaciers," A1. This figure includes the Olympic Mountains. Of the Cascade Range glaciers, 756 occur north of Snoqualmie Pass (A4). See also Pelto, "Current Behavior."

28. Denton and Hughes, *Last Great Ice Sheets*, 132–3.

29. Waitt and Thorson, "Cordilleran Ice Sheet," 53. The maximum extent of the Puget lobe, which reached to just south of the forty-seventh parallel, was about fifteen thousand years ago. When the vast continental icecap in Canada reached its maximum, a great peninsula of ice— probably thousands of feet high—protruded southward to near the present location of Coeur d'Alene Lake in western Idaho, effectively blocking the voluminous glacial meltwaters. The icecap flow pooled into a frigid reservoir existing from about twenty-two thousand to eighteen thousand years ago. Geologists refer to the impounded waters as Lake Missoula and compare it in size to Lake Michigan. In time, the deepening waters broke under or around the ice blockade to release a flood surge perhaps many times the combined flow of all the world's rivers. It tore through the basalt plateau of central Washington, scoured the bedrock, and excavated great canyons as it overwhelmed the Columbia River valley and flowed against the eastern flank of the Cascade Range. Geologists surmise that a version of the phenomenal lake re-formed at least six times, the last one forming about seventeen thousand years ago—which Native Americans may have witnessed.

30. Denton and Hughes, *Last Great Ice Sheets*, 132–3.

31. The glacier that occupied the Chelan Valley was the longest on the east slope of the range, cutting to some four hundred feet below sea level. At the last glacial maximum, valley glaciers in the northern Cascades terminated as much as fifty kilometers east of the drainage divide. Porter, Pierce, and Hamilton, "Late Wisconsin Mountain Glaciation." In the northern part of the range (roughly north of Darrington), Cascade glaciers in drainage headwaters probably merged with the Puget lobe, creating a nearly continuous ice cover across this portion of the range. (Tabor et al., *Preliminary Geologic Map*, 9). Deposits derived from the Puget lobe of the ice sheet fill many lower valleys; these date from glaciation culminating about fifteen thousand years ago.

32. Porter, Pierce, and Hamilton, "Late Wisconsin Mountain Glaciation," 86, fig. 4-12.

33. Diary of Dr. William F. Tolmie, Add. MSS 557, p. 24, BCARS. It has been suggested that the geologist Clarence King deserves the credit for the first true discovery of glaciers in the continental

United States when he spent six weeks studying Mt. Shasta's glaciers. See Bartlett, *Great Surveys*, 181. See also King, "On the Discovery." King climbed Mt. Shasta on September 12, 1870, in the company of other scientists—including Samuel F. Emmons, who conducted a survey of Mt. Rainier's glaciers in 1870 (see chap. 15).

34. Kautz, "Ascent of Mount Rainier."

35. Hazard Stevens, typescript, folder 25b, Stevens Papers, Washington State Historical Society, Tacoma.

36. Gibbs, "Physical Geography," pt. 2, 351.

37. Bayley, "Ascent of Mount Tacoma," 273.

38. Russell, "Glaciers of Mount Rainier," 341.

39. Russell, "Existing Glaciers," 341.

40. See Borden, "Peopling," 963–5; Kirk and Daugherty, *Exploring Washington Archaeology*, 9, 26–9. Early archaeological sites west of the Cascade foothills give radiocarbon dates of nine thousand to six thousand years ago (Kirk and Daugherty, *Exploring Washington Archaeology*, 82–3). There are material traces of humans along the Columbia River in central Washington from the early Holocene Epoch, ten thousand to three thousand years ago. See also Jermann and Mason, *Cultural Resource Overview*; Collins, *Valley of the Spirit*, 21.

41. Mierendorf, *People of the North Cascades*, 55.

42. Anastasio, "The Southern Plateau." See also Mierendorf, *People of the North Cascades*, 63.

43. Robert Mierendorf, personal communication, March 6, 1989. Mierendorf has found through radiocarbon dating that the prehistory of the northern Cascades extends back 4,500 years.

44. Lyman, "Switzerland of the Northwest," 304.

45. Clark, *Indian Legends*, 7–8; Bruseth, *Indian Stories and Legends*. The Lummi name *Kulshan* means "bleeding wound," probably referring to prehistoric eruptions, and first appeared in Winthrop's *Canoe and the Saddle*. See also Miles, *Koma Kulshan*.

46. R.N. McIntyre, "Mather Memorial Highway: A Brief History," unpublished manuscript, 1952, Mount Rainier National Park Library, Tahoma Woods, Washington; Brown, "Ascent of Mount Rainier," 49–50.

47. The figures are given in Stevens, *Life of Isaac Ingalls Stevens,* 504. Gibbs estimated the Skagit population at three hundred in 1854 ("Report of Mr. George Gibbs to Captain McClellan," 1:433). Gibbs's 1855 journal figures are generally lower than Stevens's. According to Gibbs, the Snoqualmie and "Stoluchwhch" tribes had 556 persons and 100 canoes; the Snohomish, 141 persons; the Nisqually, 250 persons; the Puyallup, 390 persons; the Skagit, 1,675 persons and 130 canoes (the discrepancy with Gibbs's 1854 figures for the Skagit has not been explained); and the Lummi and Nooksack, 680 persons (Gibbs, journal 3, [1855]). In 1877, Gibbs believed the Indian population west of the Cascades in Oregon and Washington was 26,800 at its peak (*Tribes of Western Washington and Northwestern Oregon*). The numbers of Indians in Oregon Territory were provided in HBC trading lists (Schafer, ed., "Warre and Vavasour's Reconnoissance," 61–2).

48. Gibbs, "Indian Tribes of the Territory of Washington," 434.

49. Mooney, *Aboriginal Population*, 29. See also Teit, *Thompson Indians*, 175.

50. Coleman, "Puget Sound."

51. Gunther, *Indian Life on the Northwest Coast*.

52. David R. Buerge, "The Sacred Snoqualmie," *Seattle Weekly*, August 5, 1987, 24–31.

53. A. Smith, *Ethnography*, 16–30. See also Collins, *Valley of the Spirit*, 21–2.

54. A. Smith, *Ethnography*, 18, 31; Collins, *Valley of the Spirit*, 18–19. See also Sampson, *Indians of Skagit County*, frontispiece, 159; Collins, *Valley of the Spirit*, 11, 13.

55. Smith, "The Nooksack," 331–2, 340; Amoss, *Spirit Dancing*, 5–6. Nooksack hunting territories were bounded on the south by the Skagit River, on the west by Lummi territory, and on the

north by the territory of the Halkomelem peoples. See Amoss, *Spirit Dancing,* 4.

56. Alexander C. Anderson Papers, vol. 2, file 8, P. 84 (1867 notes). See also Duff, *Upper Stalo Indians,* 11, 43, 46.

57. Smith, *Ethnography,* 82; Duff, *Upper Stalo Indians,* 37–9, 87, 43. The Chilliwack villages are described and mapped in M. Smith, "The Nooksack," 340–1. Duff identifies twenty-two village sites, most near the Fraser, all being occupied after about 1830, when the lower Chilliwack River changed its westerly course away from Lake Sumas. Smith identifies ten villages in the narrow canyon above Vedder Crossing. See Smith, *Ethnography,* 85, 94.

58. Duff, *Upper Stalo Indians,* 44; Smith, *Ethnography,* 94; Wells, *The Chilliwacks,* 16–17.

59. Hill-Tout, "Notes on the Ntlakapamuq," 1:52–3; Smith, *Ethnography,* 146, 199.

60. Teit, *Thompson Indians,* 166–71, passim; Collins, *Valley of the Spirit,* 14–15.

61. Ray, "Native Villages," 107. See also Gibbs, "Indian Tribes of the Territory of Washington."

62. Spier and Sapir, *Wishram Ethnography*; Teit, *Middle Columbia Salish,* 99. See also Spier, *Tribal Distribution,* 25. By 1800, the Klickitat population had split into two groups; one moved west of the range between the Lewis and Columbia rivers. See Curtis, *North American Indian,* 7:37; Norton, Boyd, and Hunn, "Klickitat Trail," 132; see also Bennett, *Cultural Resource Overview.*

63. Ray, "Native Villages," 148–9; Norton, Boyd, and Hunn, "Klickitat Trail."

64. Gibbs, "Indian Tribes of the Territory of Washington," 403.

65. Ross, *First Settlers*; Ray, "Native Villages," 146.

66. Martinson, "Mountain in the Sky," 9. See also Smith, *Ethnographic Guide,* 256–65; Turek and Keller, "Sluskin," 2.

67. Ray, "Native Villages," 144.

68. Ibid., 142. For more on the Wenatchee, see Curtis, *North American Indian,* 69; Spier, *Tribal Distribution,* 14; Thompson, "Journal of David Thompson" (this is a copy of the original Thompson journal from the Archives of Ontario, "Voyage to the Mouth of the Columbia, by the Grace of God, by D. Thompson and Seven Men on the Part of the N.W. Company"); and Hollenbeck and Carter, *Cultural Resource Overview,* 142.

69. Ray, "Native Villages," 122; Merk, *Fur Trade,* 168.

70. Ray, "Native Villages," 122, 141; Bruseth, *Indian Stories and Legends,* 13. Ethnographers Verne Ray and Leslie Spier regarded the Chelan as distinct from the Wenatchee, but James Teit did not. (See Ray, "Native Villages"; Spier, *Tribal Distribution*; Teit, *Middle Columbia Salish*). For more on the Chelan Indians, see Hodgson, "Hunting Mazamas," 316; Lyman, "Lake Chelan," 198; Gorman, "Washington Forest Reserve," 318; Miller, "Native People."

71. Gibbs, "Indian Tribes of the Territory of Washington"; Bennett, *Cultural Resource Overview,* 30; Barry, "Indians in Washington." The tribe dwindled from about 2,200 members in 1780 to 500 in 1906 (Teit, *Middle Columbia Salish*).

72. Indians living along the Similkameen River have sometimes been considered a separate group from the Okanogan nation—which included twelve tribes, each with a petty chief. See Teit, "Salishan Tribes," 204. Their origin can only be surmised. See Cameron, "History and Natural Resources," 6.

73. Borden, "Peopling," 970.

74. Collins, *Valley of the Spirit,* 46. The Skagit had dip nets and three-pronged spears to take salmon; spears had a deer-antler or goat-horn tip (p. 50–1).

75. These racks were similar to those of Missouri Indians; tons of salmon hung under long sheds. To begin a fire, the Indians used a vine-maple fire drill that sparked on dry moss.

76. Duff, *Upper Stalo Indians,* 60, 67; Coleman, "Mountaineering on the Pacific," 799.

77. Duff, *Upper Stalo Indians,* 67; Teit, *Thompson Indians,* 247. See also Smith, *Ethnography,* 153–4.

78. Journal of Samuel Anderson, Samuel Anderson Papers; Rice, "Indian Utilization," 14. See also Neils, *Klickitat Indians,* 142.

79. Hollenbeck and Carter, *Cultural Resource Overview,* 134; Journal of Daniel C. Linsley, file 156, NPRR Records; Scheuerman, *Wenatchi Indians,* 25. See Spier and Sapir, *Wishram Ethnography,* 191.

80. Stewart, *Cedar,* 45, 97–8, 113–28, 144, 171–7; Underhill, *Indians of the Pacific Northwest,* 116–19; Coleman, "Puget Sound," 251; Rice, "Indian Utilization," 14.

81. Jermann and Mason, *Cultural Resource Overview,* 54; Curtis, *North American Indian,* 5.

82. See Ray, "Native Villages," 148–50; Ray, *Cowlitz Indians,* a-12; Norton, Boyd, and Hunn, "Klickitat Trail."

83. Ray, "Native Villages," 148–9; Duff, *Impact of the White Man,* 73; Hollenbeck and Carter, *Cultural Resource Overview.* See also Martinson, "Mountain in the Sky"; Norton, "Association between Anthropogenic Prairies," 189; and Plummer, "Forest Conditions," 29.

84. Spier and Sapir, *Wishram Ethnography,* 181.

85. Spier, *Tribal Distribution,* 39. Bows and arrows were usually made of serviceberry, yew, rosewood, or hemlock. Some arrow shafts were of ironwood, having a stone point.

86. See the snowshoe illustrations in Teit, "Salishan Tribes," 256–7. To trap animals, a concealed hole and snare with a bent-sapling spring pole were set up at an open gate. Another way was to tie a deerhide noose to a tree so that the animal's legs caught in the noose (p. 241)

87. Tinkham, "Railroad Report," 1:186; Duff, *Upper Stalo Indians,* 53. See also Teit, "Salishan Tribes," 249.

88. Norton, Boyd, and Hunn, "Klickitat Trail," 121, 126.

89. Haeberlin and Gunther, *Indians of Puget Sound,* 11.

90. Gibbs, "Indian Tribes of the Territory of Washington." The Snoqualmie Pass trail was described by Maj. J.H. van Bokkelen in 1856.

91. Splawn, *Ka-mi-akin,* 255; Hollenbeck and Carter, *Cultural Resource Overview,* D-8.

92. Dow, *Passes to the North,* 34–35. The route across Colockum Pass, established as a wagon road by 1881, may not have followed a trail. See Hollenbeck and Carter, *Cultural Resource Overview,* D-9.

93. Gibbs, "Shoalwater Bay and Puget Sound," 472. On October 7, 1867, Northern Pacific Railroad surveyor Albert J. Treadway confirmed this portage (at present-day Darrington), which he estimated at three miles. See also Braun, "History of Sauk-Suiattle Tribe." Indians were portaging canoes here as late as 1887. See Albert B. Rogers, diary.

94. The trail is shown on the Northwest Boundary Survey's 1866 *Map of Western Section* (Cartographic Archives, NA).

95. Willis stated that the trail presented little difficulty to horse passage, "the ridges followed being of gentle rise" ("Physiography and Deformation," 65).

96. Gibbs noted the disuse of trading routes in an 1856 paper that was not published until 1877. See *Tribes of Western Washington,* 169–70.

97. Ross, *First Settlers,* 313. The direct route was said to cross the mountains almost due west, to where they fall on the seacoast. In 1853, the factor at Fort Okanogan, Mr. La Fleur, informed McClellan of an Indian trail believed to exist between Cascade Pass and the Fraser route. This route originated along the Methow River. See McClellan, "General Report," 197.

98. The name "S'cho-kehn," used on Gibbs's 1860 manuscript map (*Tribes of Western Washington*), was later modified and appeared as "Stehekin" on the General Land Office map of Washington Territory for 1883. On Bridge Creek, see Rogers, diary; Pierce, *Expedition from Fort Colville to Puget Sound.*

99. Mayne, *Four Years,* 106–7.

100. Smith, *Ethnography,* 95.

Chapter 1: Mapping the Unknown and Early Exploration

1. See L. Brown, *Story of Maps,* chap. 3; Boorstin, *The Discoverers.*

2. Wheat, *Mapping the Transmississippi West,* 1:139.

3. At President Thomas Jefferson's request, King had prepared a manuscript map of western North America in 1803, summarizing what was known. It depicts a conjectural river trending eastward from the Columbia, reflecting the belief in a water route to the Pacific.

4. The 1814 map was the progenitor of, for example, the 1826 Anthony Finley map of North America. In it, the Columbia continues to be termed "Clark's R," above "Lewis' R" (the Snake); the Yakima is called "Tapetette."

5. Farley, "Historical Cartography of British Columbia," 159.

6. Wheat, *Mapping the Transmississippi West,* 2:102. The manuscript map is in the British Museum, London.

7. "Journal of John Work," 308.

8. Meany, *Geographic Names,* 173.

9. Goetzmann, *Army Exploration,* 57. On another 1844 map, drawn by Robert Greenhow, the range running through Oregon and Washington was called the Far West Mountains. The 1859 John Arrowsmith map, *The Provinces of British Columbia and Vancouver Island* (located at the Bancroft Library, Univeristy of California), still showed exaggerated elevations for certain peaks of the Canadian Rockies.

10. Two contemporary maps rivaled Frémont's in scope, if not in fame. Capt. Benjamin Bonneville's map (1837) distributes some mountains over the West where none exist; the Cascades are depicted as a single long chain. The similar Albert Gallatin map (1836) presents an idea of the West based largely on explorers' reports. The map does, however, portray the route of the American fur trader and explorer Jedediah Smith, and it shows the Fraser and Columbia as separate rivers.

11. Wheat, *Mapping the Transmississippi West,* 4:144; *Preliminary Sketch of the Northern Pacific Rail Road Exploration and Survey from the Rocky Mountains to Puget Sound,* map 3 in *Reports of Explorations and Surveys,* vol. 11.

12. "Topographical Report of Lieutenant J.K. Duncan," in *Reports of Explorations and Surveys,* 1:218.

13. See Wheat, *Mapping the Transmississippi West,* 4:12. Yakima Pass was explored by Lt. Abiel Tinkham in 1854, and it is shown on his map.

14. Possible errors in geographic positioning due to the traditional use of compass courses and odometer distances are found on the Stevens map. See *Reports of Explorations and Surveys,* 11:108.

15. See Gibbs, "Physical Geography," pt. 1, 152.

16. Ibid.

17. Gibbs, "Shoalwater Bay and Puget Sound," 471. Lake Chelan appeared on a map as early as 1827, called "clear lake" by HBC trader Archibald McDonald. The 1859 John Arrowsmith map *The Provinces of British Columbia and Vancouver Island* has the legends "Clear Water or Chelan R and L." Yet, on the mostly accurate General Land Office map of the United States and its territories (1855), the lake is omitted; not until 1860 did the territorial survey map include Lake Chelan. The modern name of Lake Wenatchee first appeared on the Northwest Boundary Survey map of 1866 ("Tah-kwt or Wenatchee L"). The John Arrowsmith *British North America* maps of 1824 and 1840 depict the lake in outline with the legend "Piscous R" to the southeast; this indicates that HBC trappers knew of the lake.

18. See Wheat, *Mapping the Transmississippi West,* 4:45.

19. The map (at a scale of 1:300,000) was published in *Reports of Explorations and Surveys,* vol. 11; Gannett, "The Mother Maps," 105.

20. In the period before the Civil War, there were still some surprising omissions; for example, the otherwise quite accurate *Map of the West* (1857) by Maj. William H. Emory, who drew on Pacific Railroad maps and those of the General Land Office, shows Lake Chelan and Mt. Stuart yet omits Mt. Rainier and Mt. St. Helens.

21. Russell, *North America*, 168. R.T. Williams's 1884 *New Map of British Columbia* has the label "Cascade Range" inland from Vancouver Island.

22. Palmer, "Report on Country between Fort Hope on the Fraser and Fort Colville on the Columbia River," November 23, 1859, B.C. Papers, pt. 3, 82, BCARS.

23. This manuscript map is at the Bancroft Library, University of California, and at BCARS.

24. See Gilbert, *Exploration of Western America*, 21–4; and Wheat, *Mapping the Transmississippi West*, 4:1.

25. Watson, "Role of Illusion," 15.

26. Moulton, ed., *Journals*, 5:298, 6:13.

27. Moulton, ed., *Journals*, 5:304, 6:16, 6:18, 6:87, 6:112, 11:385. See also Farquhar, "Naming America's Mountains," 62.

28. Moulton, ed., *Journals*, 7:59, 7:33. The explorers were near present-day Vancouver.

29. See Cline, *Exploring the Great Basin*, 65–8, 69. Clark's map is called *A Map of the Continent of North America . . . Showing Lewis and Clark's Route over the Rocky Mountains in 1805 on Their Route to the Pacific from the United States*.

30. See Coues, *History of the Expedition*, vol. 3.

31. Thompson, "Journal of David Thompson."

32. For information on John Dollond and his invention, see Pannekoek, *History of Astronomy*, 295.

33. Thompson, *Narrative*, 480.

34. Thompson, *Narrative*, 480–1, 493. The only location on the middle river where both volcanos are visible is just opposite present Hood River.

35. Alexander Ross, biography, typescript, HBC Archives, Winnipeg.

36. A. 34/1, 107, HBC Archives.

37. Except where otherwise noted, the account of Ross's journey given here is from *Fur Hunters of the Far West*, 29–39. A 1956 edition edited by Kenneth A. Spaulding contains the original Ross manuscript, located at Yale University. Ross's crossing—or partial crossing, as the case may be—of the Cascade Range is found on 36–43 of the 1956 edition; Spaulding proposes that he crossed at Cascade Pass.

38. Ross, *First Settlers*, 313. The "Pacific" meant Puget Sound or the Strait of Georgia.

39. Smith, *Ethnography*, 94.

40. In *First Settlers*, Ross calls the river the Buttlemuleemauch, meaning "Salmon-fall River." On Archibald McDonald's 1827 map, the river is the "Meat who."

41. Ross's map of 1821 erroneously shows him traveling along the east flank of the river. To his west were the high crests of the Chelan Mountains (Sawtooth Ridge).

42. Where Ross left the Methow is the first problem in deciphering the route. See Majors, ed., "First Crossing of the North Cascades," 156. The problems of plotting Ross's route become greater because he admits not consistently using his compass—it "made us lose too much time."

43. Twisp Pass would have been a more logical route than Copper Pass, for it is lower and less steep, but at that time of summer snow would probably not have been nearby. William C. Brown believes Ross crossed Twisp Pass and eventually reached the Skagit, although he feels it is impossible to learn from his writings where he was at a given time (*Early Okanogan History*).

44. His map ignores the southerly direction; he does not indicate a stream-valley descent.

45. The description suggests Cascade Pass.

46. Majors believes Ross had by this time reached the lower Cascade River ("First Crossing of the North Cascades," 161).

47. Majors believes this was along the Skagit, although the description also fits the Sauk Valley.

48. Majors believes the campsite of the fifth was near Sedro Woolley, where trees were five to six feet in diameter ("First Crossing of the North Cascades," 162). It is unlikely, however, that Ross could have come so far or made the wide Skagit River fords.

49. Although Lake Chelan would seem to offer the natural route between the west and the interior, Indians seem to have avoided the dangerous, windy lake waters.

50. The original manuscript map, located in the British Museum, is depicted (poorly) in Wheat, *Mapping the Transmississippi West*, facing 2:106.

51. Ross was fairly close in stating that the mouth of the Okanogan is six hundred miles up the Columbia.

52. Ross could not possibly have forded the Skagit below present Marblemount; the water depth, even in late summer, would have been above his neck (author's discussions with staff of Skagit County Department of Public Works, April 20, 1988, and with local residents).

53. It is unlikely that Ross crossed Harts Pass. In examining the upper Methow Valley in 1883, 2d Lt. Samuel Rodman reported that "no signs could be found of any previous visitation by man." Rodman's Indian guide said he knew of no pass in the locality (Rodman, "Explorations in the Upper Columbia Country," 262). It is also unlikely that Ross descended the virtually impassable Skagit Canyon. In August 1858, George Gibbs found Indians who stated that even they had never traversed the "Great Rapids" in the canyon.

54. Ross Pass appeared on Forest Service maps during the 1940s.

55. Multiple fords would have been arduous but possible, in contrast to crossings of the Skagit. The Suiattle, a feeder to the Skagit, is but a fraction of its size.

56. See A. Smith, *Ethnography*, 258; and Ross, *Fur Hunters*, 41 n. 25, regarding Cascade Pass and River. Most written interpretations of the route agree that Ross crossed from the Methow River to the Bridge Creek drainage.

57. Tolmie, *Journals*, 181.

58. Diary of Dr. William F. Tolmie, Add. MSS 557, BCARS; Tolmie, *Journals*, 230. Except where otherwise noted, the account of Tolmie's expedition given here is from his *Journals*.

59. See Fauré, "The Real Tolmie's Peak," 69–70.

60. See also Diary of Dr. William F. Tolmie, Add. MSS 557, p. 233, BCARS.

61. Douglas, *Douglas of the Forests*, 13, 39. See also Douglas, *Journal*.

62. Douglas, *Douglas of the Forests*, 98. See also Harvey, *Douglas of the Fir*, 58. After the name *Cascade Range* was used in Douglas's journal and on the 1844 map by Charles Wilkes, it appeared in Alexander C. Anderson's 1858 supplement to one of his maps (E/B/An 3.3, Add. MSS 559, BCARS).

63. Douglas, *Douglas of the Forests*, 123. See also Wheeler, "Mts. Brown and Hooker," 163, 166–7; and Holway, "Mounts Brown and Hooker," 45–6.

64. See Wilkes, *Narrative*; and Barker, *The Wilkes Expedition*. American trading ships had entered Puget Sound in 1830, but Wilkes's expedition was the first official one.

65. Wilkes, *Narrative*, 413.

66. Ibid., 414, 413, 319, 309, 303.

67. Ibid., 305, 310.

68. Ibid., 419.

69. Barry, "Pickering's Journey," 55.

70. Morgan, *Puget's Sound*, 55. Except where otherwise noted, the following account of Johnson's expedition is taken from Brackenridge, "Our First Official Horticulturist."

71. Wilkes, *Narrative*, 419, 528.

72. Barry, "Pickering's Journey," 55.

73. Wilkes, *Narrative*, 422.

74. Ibid., 423.

75. Goetzmann, *Army Exploration*, 5.

76. Ibid., 18–19, 86.

77. Ibid., 4.

78. Ibid., 103–4. See also Wheat, *Mapping the Transmississippi West*, 2:181.

79. Goetzmann, *Army Exploration*, 92–3.

80. Frémont, *Report of the Exploring Expedition*, 184, 193–4.

81. Ibid., 194; Goetzmann, *Army Exploration*, 102.

82. Kane, *Paul Kane*, 5. See also Kane, *Paul Kane's Frontier*.

83. Winthrop, *Canoe and the Saddle*, 283.

84. Ibid., 30.

85. Ibid, 40–1.

86. John Williams, introduction to Winthrop, *Canoe and the Saddle*, xxi.

87. See Chittenden and Richardson, *De Smet*; Goetzmann, *Army Exploration*, 26.

88. Chittenden and Richardson, *De Smet*, 555.

89. Ibid., 742.

Chapter 2: "Absolute Lordes and Proprietors"

1. Rich, *Hudson's Bay Company*, vol. 1; Ross, "Retreat of the Hudson's Bay Company."

2. International Boundary Commission, *Joint Report*, app. 1, 166. Such chartering of an immense land monopoly had become standard practice for Great Britain as early as the sixteenth century; the East India Company is another example.

3. Hudson's Bay Company, *Copy-book of Letters Outward*, xi.

4. Kenneth A. Spaulding, introduction to Ross, *Fur Hunters*, xvii.

5. Cline, *Exploring the Great Basin*, 79. The detailed reports of Lewis and Clark also spurred American traders; pioneer merchants such as John Jacob Astor were eager to exploit the fur trade.

6. Ibid., 63. The 1793 Aaron Arrowsmith map of America indicates that Mackenzie believed the Fraser and Columbia were the same, and the 1802 revision continued the error. Albert Gallatin's map of 1836 shows the rivers correctly as separate streams.

7. See Mackenzie, *Voyage to the Pacific Ocean*, 148; Mackenzie, *Journals*, 321. Mackenzie had evidently seen a copy of the *Voyages* of Capt. John Meares (1790), who visited the coast of what is now British Columbia in 1786 and 1788 (Mackenzie, *Journals*, 320, n. 3).

8. Ross, *First Settlers*, 151.

9. Davidson, *North West Company*.

10. Report of Colvile District, 1827, HBC Archives.

11. Cline, *Exploring the Great Basin*, 28.

12. Ibid., 87.

13. Rich, *Hudson's Bay Company*, 2:749; Merk, *Fur Trade*, 243.

14. Johansen and Gates, *Empire of the Columbia*, 146.

15. For more on Fort Okanogan, see Brown, "Old Fort Okanogan," 31.

16. Swan, *Northwest Coast*, 307. George Gibbs's *A Dictionary of the Chinook Jargon, or Trade Language of Oregon* defines more than 450 words. See also Howard R. Lamar, ed., *The Reader's Encyclopedia of the American West* (New York: Thomas Y. Crowell, 1977), s.v. "Chinook Jargon."

17. Merk, *Fur Trade*, 52. The Wenatchee River is also referred to as the "Pisquowsh." See also

Simpson to H.U. Addington, January 5, 1826, cited in Merk, *Fur Trade*, 265.

18. Fort Langley journal (written by George Barnston), b. 113/a/1, HBC Archives. See also Murphy, "History of Fort Langley."

19. The Puget Sound Agricultural Company—which included the Cowlitz Farm (the PSAC's actual first site was at Cowlitz Portage), as well as a farm on the prairie west of the Chilliwack River in 1858—was involved with domestic animals, lumber mills, and agriculture. See Galbraith, *Hudson's Bay Company*, 217.

20. Bagley, "Journal of Occurrences," 179–97.

21. Edward Huggins Papers, University of Washington Libraries, Seattle.

22. Sir James Douglas to George Davidson, May 12, 1868, cited in Davidson, *Alaska Boundary*, 117.

23. Magnusson, "Naches Pass," 172–3.

24. Historical study of Naches Pass, U.S. Forest Service, Naches Ranger Station, Natches, Washington.

25. See Hull, *History of Central Washington*, 17. See also Rogers, diary, 68; Schafer, "Warre and Vavasour," 43.

26. Work's journals are at BCARS; there is a copy in the John Work Papers, University of Washington Libraries, Seattle.

27. Meinig, *Great Columbia Plain*, 496.

28. See Henry Peers's journal, EA P34A, BCARS.

29. Simpson to Addington, January 5, 1826, cited in Merk, *Fur Trade*, 265.

30. Merk, *Fur Trade*.

31. Although the 1846 treaty guaranteed free navigation to the HBC on the Columbia, it became obvious that American officials had no intention of honoring this proviso (Hatfield, *36th Annual Report*, 44).

32. Anderson's 1867 map showing exploring and trading routes in southern British Columbia is included in Farley's *Historical Cartography of British Columbia*. His 1846 and 1858 maps, showing communication routes, are at BCARS; the account of his journeys in this chapter draws on the Alexander C. Anderson Papers.

33. Anderson's 1846 map (cma 18941, BCARS) depicts his route from the Coquihalla River to Blackeye's Trail. The map shows that understanding of the northern Cascades drainage patterns was still incomplete.

34. Hatfield, "Old Trails," 104.

35. Now called Snass Creek; the present-day Skaist River is to the east. The Punch Bowl that Anderson saw, about thirty-two miles north of the International Boundary, is at the head of the Tulameen River. See Merk, *Fur Trade*, 34.

36. This map was sent to Lord Stanley, the British statesman and former colonial secretary, in 1858. See Alexander C. Anderson Papers; B.C. Papers, pt. 1, 17, BCARS; and Reid, "Whatcom Trails," 273–4.

37. Akrigg and Akrigg, *British Columbia Chronicle*, 7–8.

38. Akrigg and Akrigg, *British Columbia Chronicle*, 12–13; Ormsby, *British Columbia*, 91; Hatfield, *36th Annual Report*, 45. See also Henry Peers's journal, EA P34A, BCARS.

39. Akrigg and Akrigg, *British Columbia Chronicle*, 13. Peers probably received his instructions from Manson, who was in charge of the New Caledonia brigade (Hatfield, *36th Annual Report*, 45). The confirmation to recheck the 1846 Anderson route was probably given by J.M. Yale, the officer in charge of Fort Langley.

40. Hatfield, "Old Trails," 93. The Brigade Trail has also been called the "Dalles" or "Colvile" Trail; it was shown on an 1827 map by Archibald McDonald.

41. "Old Pack Trails," 11; Hatfield, *36th Annual Report*, 18.

42. See Elliott, "Fur Trade."

43. Gardner, 1858 report, Northwest Boundary Survey, RG 76, NA.

44. McDonald, "Few Items," 227.

Chapter 3: McClellan's Railroad-Pass Survey

1. Smalley, *Northern Pacific,* 58.

2. Ibid., 66; Modelski, *Railroad Maps,* xiii.

3. Johnson, *Railroad to the Pacific,* 43.

4. Northern Pacific Railroad, *Life of Canfield.*

5. Smalley, *Northern Pacific,* 77; Overmeyer, "McClellan," 5.

6. Goetzmann, *Army Exploration,* 274–5. See also Goetzmann, *Exploration and Empire,* 281.

7. Goetzmann, *Army Exploration,* 275.

8. Stevens, "Narrative and Final Report," 31. The Stevens report is also published in House Exec. Doc. 129, vol. 1, 33d Cong., 1st sess., serial 736, 1855.

9. Goetzmann, *Army Exploration,* 278.

10. I.I. Stevens, "Narrative and Final Report," 331; George Suckley to John Suckley, June 30, 1853, George Suckley Papers, Yale Collection of Western Americana, Beinecke Library, Yale University, New Haven, Conn.

11. See Stevens, *Life of Isaac Ingalls Stevens.*

12. Stevens, "Narrative and Final Report," 32.

13. Overmeyer, "McClellan," 7.

14. Powell and Shippen, *Officers of the Army and Navy,* 256.

15. Morgan, *Puget's Sound,* 84–5; Overmeyer, "McClellan," 8.

16. McClellan Papers; and Overmeyer, "McClellan," 9–10; Stevens to McClellan, May 9, 1853, in *Reports of Explorations and Surveys* 1:203; Stevens to McClellan, April 18, 1853, McClellan Papers. On the military road, see chapter 4.

17. McClellan to Duncan, May 12, 1853, letter book, McClellan Papers.

18. Ogden to McClellan, undated, McClellan Papers.

19. McClellan to Duncan, May 12, 1853, McClellan Papers.

20. McClellan to Gibbs, July 9, 1853, McClellan Papers.

21. Gibbs, "Pacific Northwest Letters," 191. See Beckham, "George Gibbs." See also the correspondence and reports of George Gibbs IV, MSS 1117, Gibbs Papers, State Historical Society of Wisconsin, Madison.

22. McClellan, "General Report," 202.

23. Gibbs, "Pacific Northwest Letters," 194.

24. Cooper's notebook is in the Smithsonian Institution Archives. See also Cooper and Suckley, *Natural History.*

25. McClellan, "General Report," 188; Stevens to McClellan, May 9, 1853, in *Reports of Explorations and Surveys* 1:203; Overmeyer, "McClellan," 20.

26. McClellan to Office of Chief of Engineers, July 15, 1853, Letter M 2532, RG 77, NA.

27. Overmeyer, "McClellan," 20. In a letter to Secretary of War Jefferson Davis of September 18, 1853, McClellan gave the number of men as sixty-eight (in *Reports of Explorations and Surveys* 1:25). In his report to Stevens, McClellan gave the number of animals as 173, "73 for the saddle; 100 for packing." Of the total number, forty-six were mules ("General Report," 188). See also McClellan, journal, McClellan Papers, 5. McClellan's daily record of the expedition was this 185-page journal (which he did not publish). His "General Report" of February 25, 1854, is a fifteen-page outline taken from it.

28. There is no evidence of Euro-American penetration prior to 1853 of the mountainous region traversed by the Klickitat Trail. Descriptions of the trail and campsites are given in Norton, Boyd, and Hunn, "Klickitat Trail," 124–9, 144–7.

29. McClellan, journal, 8, McClellan Papers.

30. Cooper, notebook; McClellan, journal, 24, McClellan Papers. At this time the expedition was only two weeks in advance of the party of Portland newspaper publisher Thomas Dryer, which was to climb Mt. St. Helens.

31. Plamondan, "McClellan's Trail," pt. 4, 3.

32. "Report of George Gibbs upon the Geology," 474.

33. McClellan to Davis, September 18, 1853, in *Reports of Explorations and Surveys* 1:25; Plamondan, "McClellan's Trail," pt. 4, 4. This portion of the Lewis River is now inundated by the Swift Reservoir.

34. Plamondan, "McClellan's Trail," pt. 4, 4–5.

35. Cooper, notebook; Plamondan, "McClellan's Trail," pt. 4, 5.

36. "Report of George Gibbs upon the Geology," 475; Duncan, "Topographical Report," 208. Duncan probably saw the Tatoosh Range from present-day Red Mountain. See Plamondan, "McClellan's Trail," pt. 2, 4.

37. McClellan, "General Report," 189. In his journal, McClellan had added Mt. Baker (36); he probably realized later that Mt. Baker was out of sight. The survey charted both Mt. St. Helens and Mt. Adams, decisively ending their confusion.

38. On the map, the 121° meridian crosses Mt. Adams and passes west of The Dalles (see *Reports of Explorations and Surveys* vol. 11, map 3). Lt. Henry L. Abbot, on his *Pacific Railroad Map of Oregon*, places Mt. Adams at 46°12' latitude and 120°19' longitude, which is 2' south and 15' west of its position on the Duncan-McClellan map. Abbot also places Mt. St. Helens 10' south and 4' west of where Duncan did. Another of Duncan's errors was running the Klickitat River into the "Nikepun" (White Salmon) River; in fact, the rivers begin on opposite flanks of Mt. Adams.

39. Duncan, "Topographical Report," 207.

40. McClellan, journal, 35, McClellan Papers.

41. Ibid., 72; Gibbs, "Indian Tribes of the Territory of Washington," 403.

42. McClellan, journal, 37, 38–9, McClellan Papers.

43. Ibid., 38–9. See Guie, *Bugles in the Valley*. During the Indian wars, the military used a trail from Fort Dalles to Fort Simcoe; McClellan traveled along part of this route.

44. McClellan, journal, 48, McClellan Papers. Gibbs described these in "Indian Tribes of the Territory of Washington," 409.

45. McClellan, journal, 48, McClellan Papers.

46. Gibbs, "Indian Tribes of the Territory of Washington," 410, 407; McClellan, journal, 95, McClellan Papers. Charles William Wilson, with the British party surveying the International Boundary in 1860, gave another description of the chief: "Kamiakan, the great war chief, was here too the other day; he was the heart & soul of the last war against the Americans & a finer looking fellow & more graceful rider I hardly ever saw, in his war costume & fully armed he looks very formidable" (Wilson, *Mapping the Frontier*, 113).

47. Overmeyer, "McClellan," 28.

48. McClellan, journal, 51, McClellan Papers; McClellan, "General Report," 202, 190.

49. McClellan, "General Report," 202, 190, 191–2.

50. McClellan, journal, 58, 61, McClellan Papers; McClellan to Davis, September 18, 1853, in *Reports of Explorations and Surveys* 1:25.

51. McClellan, "General Report," 192; McClellan, journal, 60, McClellan Papers. See also Meany, "Mount Stuart," 33–5.

52. McClellan, "General Report," 192; McClellan, journal, 66–7, McClellan Papers.

53. McClellan, journal, 69–70, McClellan Papers. *Iktas* is Chinook Jargon for "things" (Overmeyer, "McClellan," 34).

54. McClellan, journal, 71, 73, McClellan Papers.

55. McClellan, "General Report," 194.

56. McClellan, journal, 73, McClellan Papers.

57. "Report of George Gibbs upon the Geology," 479.

58. McClellan, journal, 74, McClellan Papers; McClellan, "General Report," 194; "Report of George Gibbs upon the Geology."

59. McClellan, journal, 76, McClellan Papers; McClellan, "General Report," 193, 194.

60. McClellan, "Railroad Practicability," in *Reports of Explorations and Surveys* 1:182. McClellan also reported on the possibility of a tunnel at the level of Keechelus Lake.

61. McClellan, letter book, n.d., McClellan Papers; McClellan, journal, 78, McClellan Papers.

62. McClellan, journal, 82, 83, McClellan Papers. The contract apparently displeased Stevens, for, immediately upon his arrival in Washington, he ordered McClellan to lay it before the secretary of war for his decision (Stevens to McClellan, March 6, 1854, McClellan Papers). See also Overmeyer, "McClellan," 37.

63. McClellan, "General Report," 196; Duncan, "Topographical Report," 211. McClellan had already seen and named the mountain from near Naches Pass.

64. "Report of George Gibbs upon the Geology," 481.

65. McClellan, "General Report," 196; "Report of George Gibbs upon the Geology," 481.

66. McClellan, "General Report," 196; "Report of George Gibbs upon the Geology," 483.

67. McClellan, journal, 107, McClellan Papers.

68. McClellan, "General Report," 197.

69. Morgan, *Puget's Sound*, 85.

70. Stevens, "Narrative and Final Report," 154.

71. McClellan, journal, 161, McClellan Papers; McClellan to Lander, November 8, 1853. Overmeyer points out McClellan's shrewdness: he declined responsibility and left Lander still facing the questionable venture ("McClellan," 49).

72. McClellan, journal, 161, McClellan Papers.

73. Ibid., 165.

74. Stevens to Tinkham, December 12, 1853, in *Reports of Explorations and Surveys* 1:617–19; Stevens, "Narrative and Final Report," 164.

75. Tinkham to Stevens, February 1, 1854, in *Reports of Explorations and Surveys* 1:630.

76. Ibid., 1:631.

77. Stevens to Jefferson Davis, January 31, 1854, in *Reports of Explorations and Surveys* 1:622; McClellan, "General Report," 200.

78. McClellan to Stevens, January 31, 1854, in *Reports of Explorations and Surveys* 1:623.

79. Ibid.

80. Gibbs, journal 3, 1854.

81. Gibbs, "Pacific Northwest Letters," 195.

82. Overmeyer, "McClellan," 57.

83. McClellan, "Railroad Practicability," in *Reports of Explorations and Surveys* 1:183.

84. Davis, "Report of the Secretary of War on the Several Railroad Explorations," in *Reports of Explorations and Surveys* 1:12.

85. Overmeyer, "McClellan," 3.

86. Goetzmann, *Army Exploration*, 336, 295.

87. See Isaac Stevens Letters, Secretary of the Interior, Office of Explorations and Surveys, RG

48, NA; Davis, "Report of the Secretary of War on the Several Railroad Explorations," 9, 11. Washington Territory settlers were acutely concerned about the objections to the northern route, so a territorial assembly had authorized Lander to conduct a special exploration from South Pass to Puget Sound.

88. George Suckley to Rutsen Suckley, December 9, 1853, and George Suckley to John Suckley, January 25, 1854, George Suckley Papers, Yale Collection of Western Americana, Beinecke Library, Yale University, New Haven, Conn.

Chapter 4: The First Wagon Roads

1. Gates, *Messages of the Governors,* 5.

2. The most common spelling of the time was *Nachess Pass*. Surveyor General James Tilton used "Nacheess" on an 1859 map of Washington Territory. Lt. Robert Johnson's party, of the Wilkes expedition in 1841, called the Naches River the "River Spipen."

3. Meeker, *Pioneer Reminiscences,* 157, 481. After the 1841 harvest, HBC's Alexander C. Anderson and his men followed an Indian trail over the "Sinahomish" pass; they may have crossed Naches Pass, but, according to Edward Huggins, "Sinahomish" referred to Snoqualmie Pass.

4. Mahlberg, "Edward J. Allen," 157. See also Winther, "Inland Transportation," 376–7; Prosch, "Military Roads," 121.

5. Robert E. More, "Reminiscences," *Puyallup Valley Tribune,* June 14, 1904; see also Edward Huggins Papers, University of Washington Libraries, Seattle.

6. John Williams, introduction to Winthrop, *Canoe and the Saddle,* xx.

7. Prosch, "Military Roads," 122.

8. See Longmire, "Narrative," 59; and Magnusson, "Naches Pass," 177–79; Walter Evans, "By Covered Wagon through the Naches Pass," *Seattle Post-Intelligencer,* November 16, 1975, 10.

9. Magnusson, "Naches Pass," 177. As late as 1899, it was reported that many bleached horse skeletons lined the road (George E. Hyde, notebook SB 52, p. 189, Oregon Historical Society Research Library, Portland).

10. Evans, "By Covered Wagon."

11. Hyde, notebook, SB 52, Oregon Historical Society Research Library, Portland; McClellan to Arnold, May 19, 1854, McClellan Papers.

12. Arnold, "Report on the Military Road," 532. The following account of his expedition is from this report.

13. Gibbs, journal 3, 1854. The following account of the reconnaissance is from this journal.

14. Meeker, *Pioneer Reminiscences,* 98.

15. Magnusson, "Naches Pass," 173; Denny, *Pioneer Days,* 64.

16. Denny, *Pioneer Days,* 65. Although Bagley states that the Lander party crossed Snoqualmie Pass (*History of Seattle* 1:210), they actually went to Yakima Pass. Probably it was Lt. Richard Arnold's report that drew attention to the "Snoqualmie" Pass.

17. See Coleman, "Puget Sound," 246; and Field, *Washington National Guard* 1:38. The date of the crossing was supposedly June 20.

18. Letter of van Bokkelen to Adj. Gen. James Tilton, June 24, 1856, in manuscripts prepared by Mary W. Ferrell for Snoqualmie Valley Historical Society, North Bend, Wash.

19. Denny, *Pioneer Days,* 73. Bagley, in contrast to Denny, stated that the exploration party consisted of Denny, Perkins, L. V. Wyckoff, and John Ross (*History of Seattle* 1:212).

20. Bagley, *History of Seattle* 1:212.

21. Coleman, "Puget Sound," 249–50, 246, 253. The date of Coleman's journey is not evident, but it had to be no later than 1875.

22. See Gossett, "Stock Grazing," 120; Oliphant, "Cattle Trade," 203, 205. See also Splawn, *Ka-mi-akin*, 290; Bagley, *History of Seattle* 1:214; Oliphant, "Cattle Trade," 198.

23. Oliphant, "Cattle Trade," 193–4, 212; Morgan, *Puget's Sound*, 185. The Snoqualmie wagon road intersected with the Northern Pacific's tracks at 2,310 feet in the Yakima Valley.

24. Bagley, *History of Seattle* 1:219–20; Morris, "Blasting the Cascade Barrier," 68–70.

25. *Everett Herald*, January 16, 1971. See also Whitfield, *History of Snohomish County*.

26. *Index News*, October 13, 1910.

Chapter 5: Indian Wars in the Cascades

1. Splawn, *Ka-mi-akin*, 18, 21–2, 24–5. Owhi's territory ran to the heads of the Cle Elum and Teanaway rivers. Northward, extending to Lake Chelan, were the Wenatchee, with To-qual-e-can as their chief. See also Bischoff, *Yakima Campaign*, 165.

2. Kautz to McClellan, June 13, 1853, McClellan Papers.

3. Berland, "Strategy Strife," 7.

4. Ibid., 4.

5. Dryden, *History*, 129. See Tucker, "The Governor and the General." Edward Huggins's scrapbook, Huggins Papers, University of Washington Libraries, Seattle.

6. Berland, "Strategy Strife," 5.

7. See Stevens, *Life of Isaac Ingalls Stevens* 2:226; Stevens Papers, folder 9a; and Tucker, "The Governor and the General."

8. Stevens, "The Pioneers," 176–7.

9. Stevens, "The Pioneers," 177; Kautz, "Ascent of Mount Rainier," 395; Glassley, *Indian Wars*, 128.

10. Emmons, *Leschi of the Nisquallies*, 227–8. See Cram, "Topographical Memoir and Report," 92.

11. Haines, *Mountain Fever*, 20.

12. See Field, *Washington National Guard* 2:66, 86; Wallace, "Kautz," 22; Glassley, *Indian Wars*, 129.

13. *Message of the Governor;* "Report of Isaac W. Smith to Gen. J. W. Sprague, Cascade Mountain Surveys to Close of Year 1880," 8–9, Secretary Series, NPRR Records.

14. See Hicks, *Yakima and Clickitat Indian Wars*, 7; Hicks, *Reminiscences*.

15. Hicks, *Yakima and Clickitat Indian Wars*, 45.

16. *Sunday Ledger* (Port Townsend), July 10, 1892, cited in Reese, *The Northwest Was Their Goal* 3:516; Reese, *The Northwest Was Their Goal* 3:519.

17. See Bischoff, *Yakima Campaign*, 171.

18. Dryden, *History of Washington*, 126; Splawn, *Ka-mi-akin*, 38–41; Glassley, *Indian Wars*, 112.

19. Splawn, *Ka-mi-akin*, 41–43; Bischoff, *Yakima Campaign*, 178.

20. Cram, "Topographical Memoir and Report," 90.

21. See Splawn, *Ka-mi-akin*, 50; Bischoff, *Yakima Campaign*, 168; Splawn, *Ka-mi-akin*, 51.

22. Splawn, *Ka-mi-akin*, 62.

23. De Lacy kept a diary from June 12 to August 29, 1856; the following account of the expedition is in Field, *Washington National Guard* 2:104–7.

24. Cram, "Topographical Memoir and Report," 69.

25. Cited in Bischoff, *Yakima Campaign*, 195.

26. Bischoff, *Yakima Campaign*, 195–6; see also Wright to Capt. D. R. Jones (Assistant Adjutant General, Headquarters, Department of the Pacific), July 7, 1856, Senate Exec. Doc. 5, 34th Cong., 3d sess., serial 876, 1857, 174–5.

27. Schmitt, ed., *Crook*, 58. Yakama tribes had long camped in the area and had a fort here as early as 1849 for protection against the Cayuse. The post was also used as an Indian agency (Guie, *Bugles in the Valley*).

28. Gen. N. S. Clarke to Col. Samuel Cooper, June 1, 1858, House Exec. Doc. 2, 35th Cong., 2d sess., serial 998, 1858, 343–4.

29. Hull, *History of Central Washington*, 15–16. See also Maj. R. S. Garnett to Maj. W. W. Mackall, August 30, 1858, in *Report of the Secretary of War, 1858*, Senate Exec. Doc. 1, 35th Cong., 2d sess., serial 975, 1858, 379–80; and Dow, *Passes to the North*, 31.

30. Mackall to Garnett, July 18, 1858, in *Report of the Secretary of War, 1858*, Senate Exec. Doc. 1, 35th Cong., 2d sess., serial 976, 1858, 364–5. Garnett to Mackall, July 17, 1858, Records of the U.S. Army Continental Command, pt. 1, E. 3584, Letters Received, Headquarters, Department of Pacific, no. 77-g-1858, RG 393, NA.

31. See Garnett to Mackall, August 30, 1858.

32. Garnett to Mackall, August 15, 1858, in *Report of the Secretary of War, 1858,* 371–2; Guie, *Bugles in the Valley,* 113; Splawn, *Ka-mi-akin,* 102. See Brown, *Indian Side,* 218–19.

33. Splawn, *Ka-mi-akin,* 104. See Scheuerman, *The Wenatchi Indians.* Splawn states that Crook, McCall, and Turner rode via Swauk Creek to "Pish-pish-ash-tan Creek" and the Wenatchee River, then moved up to the falls—a fishing locale—where Indians were encamped (*Ka-mi-akin,* 104). If this version is correct, the force visited present-day Leavenworth before proceeding to meet Garnett. Whether this detour was made is not clear from the official and autobiographical reports. Dow states that the soldiers crossed Blewett Pass (*Passes to the North*, 32).

34. See Schmitt, *Crook*; Scheuerman, *The Wenatchi Indians*; and Ruby and Brown, *Half-Sun on the Columbia,* 38–9.

35. Garnett to Mackall, August 30, 1858.

36. Autobiography of General George Crook, holograph manuscript, Crook-Kennon Papers, U.S. Army Military History Institute, Carlisle Barracks, Pennsylvania. This manuscript occasionally differs from the presumably later typescript (held in the Army War College, also at Carlisle Barracks) used by Schmitt. This is the first published use of material from this valuable document.

37. Schmitt, *Crook,* 60. Crook's command probably followed the north bank of the Wenatchee River to near present-day Leavenworth, but it is difficult to be certain because there are only minimal route details in his autobiography. It is improbable that he ascended Tumwater Canyon, since there was a trail and easier route along Chumstick Creek, crossing the ridge to the Wenatchee River above the canyon. The narrative does not appear to describe the canyon's topography, except when Crook neared the Indians' camp.

38. Autobiography of General George Crook, holograph manuscript, Crook-Kennon Papers, U.S. Army Military History Institute, Carlisle Barracks, Pennsylvania. The fallen timber and boggy ground may have been near the Wenatchee-Chiwawa juncture.

39. Ibid.

40. Ibid. See also Schmitt, *Crook,* 62. This description fits the lower Chiwawa River area.

41. This may have been near present-day Plain, or it may have been farther upstream, near Lake Wenatchee. Scheuerman evades the problem of Crook's route, but states that the soldiers spent a cold night along the swollen river in the vicinity of the lake (*The Wenatchi Indians,* 92).

42. Schmitt, *Crook,* 62–3. Although the crags described resemble those of Tumwater Canyon, the narrative of the trek—the described sequence of heavy timber, bogs, etc.—does not fit with the terrain below the canyon.

43. Schmitt, *Crook,* 63. See also *Report of the Secretary of War, 1858,* 379.

44. See Scheuerman, *The Wenatchi Indians,* 94; Splawn, *Ka-mi-akin,* 104–5; and Sylvester Papers, University of Washington Libraries, Seattle.. Sylvester believed that one band fled up the Chiwawa River, while another took the trail to huckleberry grounds at the head of Raging Creek. Indians fleeing from troops probably camped on the flats of Chikamin Creek and used their ruse of riding in a circle to obliterate the trail, then branching off in various directions. See also Dow,

Passes to the North, 32–3; and Scheuerman, *The Wenatchi Indians,* 94.

45. Garnett to Mackall, August 30, 1858.

46. Ibid. On Qual-chan's involvement in various attacks on whites, see Col. George Wright to Maj. W.W. Mackall, September 30, 1858, in *Report of the Secretary of War, 1858,* Senate Exec. Doc. 1, 35th Cong., 2d sess., serial 975, 1859, 403–4.

47. "Report of Lt. Thomas W. Symons, Corps of Engineers, for the fiscal year ending June 30, 1881," in *Report of the Secretary of War, 1881,* vol. 2, pt. 3, House Exec. Doc. 1, 47th Cong., 1st sess., serial 2013, 1882, Appendix CCC, 2868–70.

Chapter 6 : A Mountainous Crown Colony

1. Fraser, *Letters and Journals.* See also Holman, "Discovery and Exploration," 1–15.

2. Farley, "Historical Cartography of British Columbia," 156.

3. Fraser, *Letters and Journals,* 27.

4. Fraser, *Letters and Journals,* 102, 109; Farley, "Historical Cartography of British Columbia," 157–8.

5. "Captain John Palliser's Exploring Expedition to British North America in the Years 1857, 58, and 59," p. 3, E. 230, RG 76, NA.

6. Ibid. See also Great Britain, Parliament, *Papers Relative to the Exploration by Captain Palliser;* and Spry, *The Palliser Expedition.* See Palliser, *Papers,* 530–31; *Papers Relative to the Exploration by Captain Palliser,* 39.

7. Cope, "Colonel Moody," 3.

8. Howay, *Royal Engineers,* 1; James Douglas to William G. Smith, June 20, 1858, Record Office Transcripts, HBC, vol. 727, BCARS.

9. Wilson, *Mapping the Frontier,* 25.

10. Rich, *Hudson's Bay Company* 2:782.

11. Letter by C.C. Gardiner, November 1858, cited in *British Columbia Historical Quarterly,* October 1937.

12. Gibbs, journal, 1858.

13. John Ledell, letter in *Northern Light* (Whatcom), June 13, 1858.

14. Horatio Webb, "Chilliwack Valley and Its Pioneers," manuscript, BCARS. The lush prairie seasonally became Lake Sumas.

15. *Weekly Ledger,* May 18, 1893, cited in Hicks, *Reminiscences.*

16. Hicks, *Reminiscences.*

17. Jeffcott, *Nooksack Tales,* 58–123.

18. For more on de Lacy, see "Walter Washington De Lacy," 184–7.

19. See Winther, "Pack Animal Transportation," 135.

20. *Northern Light,* September 4, 1858, cited in Jeffcott, *Nooksack Tales,* 110.

21. Reid, "Whatcom Trails," pt. 1, 203.

22. Reid, "Whatcom Trails." Indians with Townsend had not been past the north end of the lake.

23. J.M. Hurd, letter in *Northern Light,* July 3, 1858, cited in Jeffcott, *Nooksack Tales,* 69–72; M.G.W. Case, letter in *Northern Light,* July 17, 1858, cited in Jeffcott, *Nooksack Tales,* 83–4.

24. Reid, "Whatcom Trails," pt. 1, 206.

25. Reid, "Whatcom Trails," pt. 2, 271; "Walter Washington De Lacy," 186–87; *Northern Light,* September 4, 1858, cited in Jeffcott, *Nooksack Tales,* 110–19.

26. *Victoria Gazette,* July 17, 1858. The lowest pass to the Maselpanik is about 4,500 feet. De Lacy's trail route unnecessarily took a higher line that climbed to altitudes of 5,664 feet and 5,718 feet, crossing the ridge north of Depot Creek about two-thirds of a mile northwest of the lowest pass.

27. *Northern Light*, cited in Jeffcott, *Nooksack Tales*, 111, 112.

28. *Northern Light*, September 4, 1858, cited in Jeffcott, *Nooksack Tales*.

29. Jeffcott, *Nooksack Tales; Victoria Gazette*, August 3, 1858.

30. Reid, "Whatcom Trails," pt. 2, 272–3.

31. Reid, *Mountains, Men, and Rivers.*

32. Gibbs, Report of September 22, 1858, Appendix E, Envelope 4, E. 196, RG 76, NA.

33. *Victoria Gazette*, September 3, 1858, cited in Reid, "Whatcom Trails," pt. 2, 273.

34. Scholefield, *British Columbia* 1:30.

35. *Victoria Gazette*, September 9, 1858, cited in Reid, "Whatcom Trails," pt. 2, 275; Cited in Reid, "Whatcom Trails," pt. 2, 275.

36. Reid, "Whatcom Trails," pt. 1, 199.

37. Gibbs, journal 3, February 4, 1855.

38. Rich, *Hudson's Bay Company* 2:783. See *Gold Discovery Papers*, 17, cited in Cope, "Colonel Moody," 6.

39. Rich, *Hudson's Bay Company* 2:783. See Begg, *History of British Columbia*, 221; Akrigg and Akrigg, *British Columbia Chronicle*, 137.

40. See Ormsby, *British Columbia;* and Howay, *Fraser River Mines.*

41. Hazlitt, *Gold Fields*, 162.

42. Rich, *Hudson's Bay Company* 2:782.

43. Lytton to Douglas, July 30, 1858, B.C. Papers, pt. 1, 44, BCARS. Some sappers were already on the mainland as part of the boundary commission under the Royal Engineer Maj. John S. Hawkins.

44. Wilson, *Mapping the Frontier*, 32.

45. Sage, *Sir James Douglas*, 227–8.

46. Howay, *Fraser River Mines*, viii.

47. Mayne, *Four Years*, 52–3.

48. See Basque, "Ned McGowan's War," 52–7. See Mayne, *Four Years*, 59.

49. B.C. Papers, pt. 2, 55–6. See also Murphy, "History of Fort Langley," 106.

50. Mayne, *Four Years*, 67.

51. Mayne, *Four Years*, 70; Hall, "Royal Engineers,"50–1. See Howay, *British Columbia* 2:61–5.

52. Rich, *Hudson's Bay Company* 2:784.

53. Douglas to Lytton, November 4, 1858, B.C. Papers, pt. 2, 21.

54. B.C. Papers, pt. 1, 55.

55. Akrigg and Akrigg, *British Columbia Chronicle*, 118.

56. Moody to Douglas, July 2, 1859, letter book 3, 59, Royal Engineers, BCARS.

57. Palmer, "Report on Country," B.C. Papers, 79–80. Okanagan Historical Society, *51st Annual Report*. See also Colvile, *London Correspondence.*

58. Palmer, "Report on Country," B.C. Papers, 80, 88.

59. Okanagan Historical Society, *36th Annual Report*, 26.

60. Palmer, "Report on Country," B.C. Papers, 82.

61. Ibid., 83.

62. Ibid., 84, 85. This is now the site of Princeton. Palmer afterwards found that the peak was situated near the southern portion of the Similkameen Valley, "near the junction of that river and the Okanagan," with the parallel cutting across its northern slope.

63. *Daily British Colonist*, October 2, 1860.

64. See Harris, *British Columbia Historical News* 12, no. 3 (1979).

65. Geologist George M. Dawson gave a report on this trail and the nearby mountains; see *Report of Progress*, 38b–41b.

66. Hatfield, *51st Annual Report*, 96; Harris, *British Columbia Historical News* 14, no. 3 (1981); B.C. Papers, pt. 3, 67.

67. See Moberly, *Rocks and Rivers*, 33–4. The Dewdney Trail route followed Nicolum Creek, the Sumallo and Skagit rivers, and Canyon (Snass) Creek, then went northward to present-day Princeton. It eliminated the old Brigade Trail over Manson Ridge.

68. See Hatfield, "Proposed Cascade Wilderness"; R. C. Harris, *British Columbia Historical News* 17, no. 4 (1984); and Dawson, *Report of Progress*, 45b–48b.

69. Interesting map references found in BCARS include *British Columbia—Hope to Similkameen and Rock Creek, Lillooet to Kamloops and Okanagan Lake*, by Col. John S. Hawkins (1861); *Gold Regions of Fraser River, B.C.*, by John Begbie (1861); and the Joseph Trutch map drawn by J. B. Launders (1871), showing the trail up to Hope Pass east of Skaist Mountain. The Cairnes report of 1920 mentioned that the "old Dewdney trail" was well preserved—in contradiction to the report of the Gen. William T. Sherman expedition, which in 1883 stated that the trail was overgrown and impassible. See also Okanagan Historical Society, *51st Annual Report*, 97.

70. Ormsby, *British Columbia*, 181.

71. John F. Damon, Jr., journal (1859), Huntington Library, San Marino.

72. Ormsby, *British Columbia*, 185; Akrigg and Akrigg, *British Columbia Chronicle*, 249–50; Howay, *Royal Engineers*, 8.

73. See Rattray, *Vancouver Island*, 93.

74. Berton, *The Last Spike*, 233–5, 251.

75. Ibid.

76. At the time the line was being constructed through the Fraser Canyon and along the Thompson River, the Canadian Pacific directors had not yet been able to settle on the best passes through the Rocky Mountains and Selkirk Range. Albert Rogers spent the summers of 1881 and 1882 proving out the route over Rogers Pass; eventually it was decided to follow this route through the Selkirks and Kicking Horse Pass in the Rockies. Rogers, diary.

77. Okanagan Historical Society, *36th Annual Report*, 131–4.

78. See Dolmage, *Geology*.

79. Cairnes, *Coquihalla Area*.

80. *Annual Report*, Minister of Mines, British Columbia (1915), BCARS.

81. Ibid.; *Annual Report*, Minister of Mines, British Columbia (1924), BCARS. See Daly, "The Geology of the Region Adjoining the Western Part of the International Boundary," in *Summary Report* 14, pt. a, GSC [1901].

82. *Annual Report*, Minister of Mines, British Columbia (1919), BCARS.

83. Bauerman, "Geology of the Country" (written in 1862 during the boundary survey). See also Daly, *Geology of the North American Cordillera*; and Cairnes, "Reconnaissance."

84. Sargent, "South-Western District," F3–23.

Chapter 7: The Northwest Boundary Survey, 1857–1858

1. International Boundary Commission, *Joint Report*, appendix 1, 165.

2. Greenhow, *Oregon and California*; International Boundary Commission, *Joint Report*, appendix 1, 167.

3. See George F. G. Stanley, introduction to Wilson, *Mapping the Frontier*, 4.

4. Bancroft, *History of the Northwest Coast* 1:332–4; International Boundary Commission, *Joint Report*, appendix 1, 181. HBC partners were the first to suggest the forty-ninth parallel as a line of demarcation between the British in the north and the French in Louisiana. Certain British geographers at the time of the convention adopted the contention that this parallel should be the

southern boundary of HBC territory, and their maps reflected this.

5. Schafer, "Warre and Vavasour," 3.

6. See Warre Papers, vol. 16, reel h-1700, mg 24, National Archives of Canada; Schafer, "Warre and Vavasour," 10; Morgan, *Puget's Sound,* 64–7; and Vavasour typescript (Colonial Office copy), Special Collections, University of Washington Libraries.

7. See Winther, *The Old Oregon Country,* 7.

8. See Cline, *Exploring the Great Basin,* 92; Merk, *Oregon Question;* and Carey, "British Side," 263–94.

9. See McCabe, *Water Boundary Question,* 59.

10. George F. G. Stanley, preface to Wilson, *Mapping the Frontier.*

11. Deutsch, "Contemporary Report," 17. See also Boggs, *International Boundaries;* and Jones, *Boundary Making.*

12. Klotz's 1902 *Foreign Office Correspondence* is the American edition of his *Certain Correspondence of the Foreign Office and of the Hudson's Bay Company,* which was copied from original documents in London in 1898 and printed in Ottawa in 1899. See part 3, "Foreign Office Correspondence: International Boundary, 49th Parallel. British Columbia, 1858–1864," 3-5. The British at first seemed the more eager to begin a survey. See Deutsch, "Contemporary Report," 18 n. 7.

13. Baker, *Survey of the Northwestern Boundary,* 13–15.

14. An 1851 map by Parke and Richard H. Kerr was a dependable depiction of the Southwest territory. Parke mapped from Sonora to Pikes Peak—a large region, but he could draw on the work of Frémont, Lt. J. W. Abert, and others. See Records of the Adjutant General, RG 94, NA; *Reports of Explorations and Surveys* 5, 11; and Cullum, *Biographical Register* 2:370.

15. Col. J. Mansfield to Maj. Irvin McDowell, January 25, 1859, "Report of the Inspection of the Port of Semi-ah-moo in December 1858," 5, Records of the Adjutant-General's Office, RG 94, NA [hereafter Mansfield to Mcdowell].

16. Joseph S. Harris to his brother, April 25, 1857, WA MSS S-1293, box 1, folder 21, Harris Papers.

17. Gardner, manuscript, 2:325.

18. Baker, *Survey of the Northwestern Boundary,* 14.

19. See *Historische-Biografisches Lexicon der Schweiz* (Nuremberg, 1924), 657.

20. Letter to the author from Dr. Ernesto Menolfi, Basel, Switzerland, April 24, 1989; letter to the author from Henry L. Custer, St. Gall, Switzerland, May 17, 1989.

21. See Zollinger, *Sutter.*

22. See "Report of Explorations for That Portion of a Railroad Route Near the Thirty-second Parallel of North Latitude Lying between Dona Ana, on the Rio Grande and Pimas Villages, on the Gila," in *Reports of Explorations and Surveys,* 2:3–19. See also *Reports of Explorations and Surveys* vol. 7; "Report of Lieutenant John G. Parke, Topographical Engineers, upon That Portion of the Route Near the 32nd Parallel from Preston to the Rio Grande," in *Report of the Secretary of War,* House Exec. Doc. 1, 33d Cong., 1st sess., serial 736, 1855, 3:5, 24 (vol. 3 is unpublished); and Wheeler, *100th Meridian* 1:582–3.

23. See Wheeler, *100th Meridian* 1:654–5; King to Brig. Gen. Andrew A. Humphreys, April 6, 1867, letter book, 1867–79, microcopy 622, 6, Records of the Geological Exploration of the Fortieth Parallel, roll 3, RG 57, NA. See also Bartlett, *Great Surveys,* 147; Goetzmann, *Exploration and Empire,* 440–1; Leviton, *Frontiers,* 28.

24. "Northwest Boundary Commission," 2.

25. Harris to brother, April 25, 1857, Harris Papers.

26. Harris to sister, April 25, 1857, Harris Papers.

27. Harris to brother, April 25, 1857, Harris Papers.

28. Ibid.

29. See Baker, *Survey of the Northwestern Boundary,* 14–15.

30. Gardner, manuscript.

31. Campbell to William H. Seward, February 3, 1869, House Exec. Doc. 86, 40th Cong., 3d sess., 93–6.

32. Parke to Campbell, December 9, 1857, envelope 1, E. 196, RG 76, NA.

33. Harris to mother, November 28, 1857, Harris Papers. He enclosed a sketch map showing two chains in the range, a legacy of the Pacific Railroad survey maps.

34. For information about the zenith telescope, see Baker, *Survey of the Northwestern Boundary,* 40.

35. Gardner, manuscript; Harris to brother, February 15, 1858, Harris Papers; Mansfield to McDowell, 5.

36. See "Northwest Boundary Commission."

37. Series 223, RG 76, NA; Report of Henry Custer to Archibald Campbell, "Reconnaissances Made in 1859 over the Routes in the Cascade Mountains in the Vicinity of the 49th Parallel," May 1866, envelope 4, E. 196, RG 76, NA (hereafter Custer to Campbell, May 1866). Between 1864 and May 1866, Custer prepared this forty-seven-page report for Campbell from field journals; someone in the survey office subsequently edited the enthusiastic document. Custer also wrote a sequel to Campbell, dated July 1866.

38. See "Northwest Boundary Commission," 2–22; Report of Parke to Campbell, September 26, 1857, E. 196, RG 76, NA.

39. See E. 229, RG 76, NA.

40. Gardner to Parke, September 3, 1857, and report of Parke to Campbell regarding the 1858 season, E. 196, RG 76, NA. The Nikomekl River (today crossed by the freeway just north of the boundary) provided a useful canoe route toward the fort.

41. Custer had already surveyed the lengthy shoreline from the camp to the Fraser River. During the fall, he also made a reconnaissance to Fort Langley, then Sumas, E. 199, RG 76, NA.

42. Gardner to Parke, November 20, 1857, E. 196, RG 76, NA. Gardner's manuscript gives the date as September 28.

43. The Indians had trails here to hunt beaver in swamps and to tend potato patches. In 1858 the British made a new station between Sumas and Tamihi Creek. The bed of the former Lake Sumas is now crossed by the Trans-Canada Highway.

44. Gardner, manuscript, 1:16.

45. Gardner to Parke, November 20, 1857, E. 196, RG 76, NA.

46. Ibid. See also International Boundary Commission, *Joint Report.*

47. A portion of the route along the river had already been explored. By 1855 (or earlier), a Mr. Reid had followed the river to near Mt. Baker. Gibbs learned of this venture, the account of which described Nooksack villages and potato cultivation, when he canoed from Victoria to Bellingham in June 1855 (see Gibbs, journal 3). An American prospecting party ascended the river to about Canyon Creek in August 1858.

48. Gardner to Parke, November 20, 1857, E. 196, RG 76, NA.

49. Prevost to Campbell, December 1, 1857, reel b-1129, p. 198, RG 17, National Archives of Canada; Campbell to Prevost, December 2, 1857.

50. Letter book, "Correspondence to the Hydrographer of the Navy—1859–62," 39, 36, cited in Akrigg and Akrigg, *British Columbia Chronicle,* 101.

51. Harris to brother, January 15, 1858; Harris to sister, October 24, 1857, Harris Papers.

52. Harris to brother, December 12, 1857; to sister, December 12, 1857; to mother, November 2, 1857, Harris Papers.

53. Harris to mother, November 28, 1857; Harris to sister, December 25, 1857, Harris Papers.

54. See Campbell file, E. 226, RG 76, NA.

55. See Hayman, "The Wanderer," 38–47; George F.G. Stanley, introduction to Wilson, *Mapping the Frontier*, 10. Bauerman's report was not published until 1884, when at George M. Dawson's suggestion it appeared in *Report of Progress of the Geological and Natural History Survey of Canada for 1882–3–4*, pt. 3 (Ottawa, 1884).

56. For more, see George F.G. Stanley, introduction to Wilson, *Mapping the Frontier*, 2.

57. Expense estimate of Capt. Hawkins, March 20, 1858, microfilm B-1143, National Archives of Canada.

58. Watson, *Life of Wilson*, 19.

59. Ibid., 20.

60. Hawkins to Secretary of State for Foreign Affairs, July 26, 1858, cited in Klotz, *Foreign Office Correspondence*, pt. 3, 7.

61. Harris to Parke, June 21, 1858, envelope 4, E. 196, RG 76, NA.

62. See Smith, "Boundary." The effect of gravity due to the mountain masses and varying density of the earth's crust resulted in deflections of the plumb line from true vertical that could not be measured at the time. Gravity anomalies affected the precise level tubes on instruments for making astronomical observations of latitude.

63. Goetzmann, *Army Exploration*, 428.

64. Custer, report to Parke, April 7, 1858, E. 196, RG 76, NA.

65. Harris to brother, January 31, 1859, Harris Papers.

66. Report of Gardner to Parke, April 17, 1858, E. 196, RG 76, NA.

67. Gardner, manuscript, 1:38, 18.

68. Gardner to Parke, April 17, 1858, E. 196, RG 76, NA..

69. Ibid.

70. Ibid.

71. Gardner, manuscript, 1:30.

72. Kennerly, journal, 7–8, 12–13.

73. Ibid., 111.

74. Gardner, manuscript, 1:40.

75. Gibbs, "Physical Geography," pt. 2, 345.

76. See Kennerly, journal, 41.

77. Harris to Gardner, December 10, 1858, E. 196, RG 76, NA.

78. Report of Gardner to Campbell, Gardner, manuscript, 1:44.

79. See E. 201, RG 76, NA.

80. Report of Gardner to Parke, December 15, 1858, E. 196, RG 76, NA.

81. Gibbs to Gardner, September 3, 1858.

82. Wilson, *Mapping the Frontier*, 28.

83. Ibid.

84. Ibid., 30.

85. Baker, *Survey of the Northwestern Boundary*, 19, 32.

86. Wilson, *Mapping the Frontier*, 30.

87. Baker, *Survey of the Northwestern Boundary*, 15–16. See also Klotz, *Foreign Office Correspondence*, pt. 3, 16–17, 20–7, 41; George F.G. Stanley, introduction to Wilson, *Mapping the Frontier*, 11.

88. See Deutsch, "Contemporary Report," 32; and Klotz, *Foreign Office Correspondence*, pt. 3, 45, 51, 66–8, 106–7.

89. Watson, *Life of Wilson*, 20. See Hawkins to Secretary of State for Foreign Affairs, March 28, 1859; and Klotz Papers, vol. 7, B-13, MG 30, National Archives of Canada; .

90. Klotz, *Foreign Office Correspondence*, pt. 3, 11.

91. Hawkins to Secretary of State for Foreign Affairs, March 28, 1859, in Klotz, *Foreign Office Correspondence,* pt. 3, 10.

92. Ibid.

93. Watson, *Life of Wilson,* 22.

94. Ibid., 23.

95. Ibid., 23–4.

96. Ibid., 24.

97. Ibid., 25.

98. See Hawkins to Secretary of State for Foreign Affairs, March 28, 1859, dispatch no. 3, in Klotz, *Foreign Office Correspondence,* pt. 3, 11.

99. Lord, *Naturalist* 1:99, 2:64.

100. Watson, *Life of Wilson,* 25.

101. Hawkins to Secretary of State for Foreign Affairs, March 28, 1859, in Klotz, *Foreign Office Correspondence,* pt. 3, 12, 15.

102. Gardner, manuscript, 45. Gardner wondered about the geographic accuracy of Alexander C. Anderson's earlier sketch map, which implied that the main drainage to the east discharged near Bellingham Bay.

103. Report of Gardner to Parke, E. 196, RG 76, NA.

104. Gardner, manuscript, 46.

105. Ibid., 47, 48.

106. Kennerly, journal, 101.

107. Gardner, manuscript, 52.

108. Ibid., 49.

109. Harris to Gardner, December 10, 1858, Harris to Gardner, October 12, 1858, Harris Papers.

110. See E. 201, RG 76, NA.

111. Gardner, manuscript, 53–4.

112. Gibbs, "Physical Geography," pt. 2, 343. He also observed that the highest peaks of the Chilliwack-Nooksack region are situated not on the main divide, but on spur and secondary ridges.

113. Ibid.

114. Harris to brother, January 8, 1859, Harris Papers; Gardner to father, October 15, 1860, George Clinton Gardner Papers, Beinecke Library, Yale University, New Haven, Conn.

115. Gardner, manuscript, 1:288–89; Gardner to father, October 15, 1860, Gardner Papers.

116. Gardner to Campbell, Gardner, manuscript, vol. 1.

117. Wilson, *Mapping the Frontier,* 45.

118. Ibid.

119. Hawkins to Secretary of State for Foreign Affairs, March 28, 1859, in Klotz, *Foreign Office Correspondence,* pt. 3, 14.

Chapter 8: The Northwest Boundary Survey, 1859–1862

1. Hawkins to Secretary of State for the Colonies, November 22, 1859, in Klotz, *Foreign Office Correspondence,* pt. 3. One reason Hawkins wanted a continuous forest vista cut may have been that it would serve as a safeguard against Americans' later disputing the boundary. See Samuel Anderson, letter, January 20, 1860, WA MSS S-1291, Samuel Anderson Papers.

2. See Parke to Campbell, November 12, 1859, Senate Exec. Doc. 16, 37th Cong., 1st sess., serial 1031, 1860, 3.

3. Hawkins to Secretary of State for Foreign Affairs, March 28, 1859, in Klotz, *Foreign Office Correspondence,* pt. 3, 13.

4. Anderson to Janet (sister), January 6, 1860, Samuel Anderson Papers.

5. George F.G. Stanley, introduction to Wilson, *Mapping the Frontier,* 12.

6. Anderson to Janet, January 6, 1860, Samuel Anderson Papers.

7. Wilson, diary, cited in Porter, *History of the Corps,* 3:262.

8. Ibid., 3:261.

9. Watson, *Life of Wilson,* 29.

10. Gardner, manuscript, 38.

11. Samuel Anderson, letter, January 6, 1860, Samuel Anderson Papers.

12. Wilson, *Mapping the Frontier,* 64.

13. Ibid., 47. The location may have been Tamihi Creek; Wilson obtained the description secondhand from other party members.

14. Ibid., 48.

15. Ibid., 49.

16. Ibid., 49–50. This is Tomyhoi Peak, just south of the parallel; it is very conspicuous when viewed up the Tamihi Creek valley.

17. Ibid., 50.

18. Ibid., 53.

19. Ibid., 58.

20. Ibid., 60.

21. Gardner, manuscript, 63.

22. Ibid., 67.

23. Report by Parke, November 12, 1859, cited in Baker, *Survey of the Northwestern Boundary,* 67; Gardner, manuscript, 68. Boundary-survey trails are depicted on various manuscript maps located in the Cartographic Archives, RG 76, NA. In particular, see map 12, series 69; field sheets 101 and 111, series 69; progress sketch, 1:120,000 (1857); map 51, showing Vedder Crossing, HBC 1855 trail, and Whatcom Trail; map 66, series 69, 1:720,000 (1866); and map 2, series 68.

24. Gardner, manuscript, 70. Baker published the magnetic observations of Harris and Haig (see *Survey of the Northwestern Boundary,* 41–2). Those of Harris are shown as magnetic bearings and given as declinations between 21° and 23° at various points.

25. Custer's reconnaissances were based on a system of triangulation points "for which numerous sharply defined peaks gave an excellent opportunity" (Custer to Campbell, May 1866). On this exploration, see Custer's report to Parke, "Report of Henry Custer of Reconnaissances along the 49th Parallel and Vicinity, between Schweltcha Lake and Senehsay River, Chiloweyuck Depot," July 2, 1859, E. 196, RG 76, NA (hereafter Custer to Parke, July 2, 1859). The report covers the period from June 5 to June 27. A course notebook covering June 6–August 15 is titled "Reconaissances. Sketches and Bearings Tacken during the Summer of 1859" (holograph manuscript, 112 pp.), E. 202, box 7, bk. 1, RG 76, NA (hereafter Custer, "Reconnaisances").. The Custer manuscript narrative, including some notebook data, maps, and sketches, is printed in Majors, "Discovery of Mt. Shuksan," and "First Crossing of the Picket Range." Although these are valuable renditions of the handwritten account, they are marred by some erroneous captions and interpretive errors. Custer's discoveries are included on the *U.S. North West Boundary Survey, Map of Western Section* (1866), series 66, RG 76, NA. This important printed map has the first complete depiction of the alpine region and the location of numerous peaks near the International Boundary. It should be noted that the map contains some nomenclature errors.

26. In June 1859, Thiusoloc made Custer a map (drawn in Custer's hand) that helped plan the first reconnaissance in this region (map 43, series 69, RG 76, NA). Thiusoloc also provided data for maps based on Custer's topographic efforts (*Map of Reconnaissance of June 1859 by Mr. H. Custer,* maps 19-1 and 19-2, series 69). Another map that was important to the American surveyors was

drawn by an Indian (probably Thiusoloc), with names from the Indian provided by George Gibbs (maps 26 and 27, series 69).

27. Baker, *Survey of the Northwestern Boundary,* 45–6.

28. See maps 19-1 and 19-2, series 69, RG 76, NA. These maps, modified from Custer's work, depict the route taken and the camps, but there are some errors in camp locations.

29. Custer to Parke, July 2, 1859.

30. Most of Custer's barometric elevations closely approximate today's. Some readings are given in his report; some are cited in Baker's published listings (*Survey of the Northwestern Boundary,* 45–47). Custer's barometric notebook, for the recording of aneroid readings at various sites, has not been located, but it was periodically copied into a Gibbs notebook (E. 200, RG 76, NA). Custer's narrative for sighting peaks and providing stream directions indicates that his bearings were based on magnetic north. See E. 200, box 5, RG 76, NA; and Baker, *Survey of the Northwestern Boundary,* 46.

31. Custer to Parke, July 2, 1859; Custer to Campbell, May 1866.

32. Custer, "Reconaissances"; Custer to Parke, July 2, 1859. Custer, Gardner, and Gibbs must be given credit as the first men to recognize the existence of glaciers in the range north of Mt. Rainier.

33. Custer to Parke, July 2, 1859. The steep slope is near the top of Point 5281, almost due northeast from Church Mountain.

34. Camp 4 was made on Bald Mountain's northwest shoulder, probably at the minor notch at 4,880 feet (plus) (see Custer, "Reconaissances," 86–87). The rock that Custer described as "trapp or granite" is today called the Chilliwack Group; it consists of arc volcanic rocks and associated ancient, thick, marine sedimentary rocks (see Tabor, et al., *Accreted Terranes,* 9).

35. Custer, "Reconaissances." Black Mountain is 2.8 miles northwest of Bald Mountain.

36. Custer to Parke, July 2, 1859.

37. Ibid.

38. See map 43, series 69, RG 76, NA.

39. Custer, "Reconaissances."

40. Custer to Parke, July 2, 1859.

41. Ibid. The canyon includes Nooksack Falls, just below the entrance of Wells Creek.

42. Ibid.

43. Custer, "Reconaissances" (July 27).

44. Ibid.

45. Ibid. This, along with Custer's report of grizzlies near their camp the following day, is a valuable early eyewitness recording of the presence of grizzly bears in the region. See also Alexander C. Anderson Papers, vol. 2, file 8, P. 65 (1867 notes).

46. Custer to Parke, July 2, 1859. His estimated altitude of 7,000 feet means that he was probably on the glacier. His notebook states that he was "near summit of Putlushgohap Mtn" between "11 am & 12 noon" ("Reconaissances," 19). The true summit (7,435 feet) was still some distance away.

47. Custer, "Reconaissances," 19.

48. From Winchester (now a popular trail hike), Custer drew a profile sketch that afternoon that included Slesse and Goat mountains. It has been proposed that Custer climbed Mt. Larrabee on June 23 (Majors, "First Crossing of the Picket Range," 114–15). But there is no evidence of such an ascent in Custer's narrative, field notebook, or barometric notations. An altitude (6,633 feet) given in Baker, *Survey of the Northwestern Boundary,* and on the 1866 map suggests that a surveyor climbed Mt. McGuire (which in Custer's notebook is termed "West Tumehay peak"), yet there is no evidence of such an ascent. The altitude may have been triangulated by Harris or another surveyor.

49. Custer, "Reconaissances."

50. Custer to Parke, July 2, 1859. This location was not far north of the forty-ninth parallel and was near the later Red Mountain Mine.

51. Ibid.

52. Ibid.

53. Ibid.

54. Gardner to Campbell, Gardner, manuscript, vol. 1.

55. *Annual Report of Regents of the Smithsonian Institution.*

56. Kennerly, journal.

57. See Custer to Campbell, May 1866. See also Majors, "First Crossing of the Picket Range," 120–41, for a rendition of Custer's field report for this expedition.

58. Custer, E. 196, RG 76, NA.

59. Custer's evaluation was correct. Not until the 1960s was a successful ascent done here.

60. It should be noted that Custer's latitude estimates were subject to considerable error unless he was at or near an astronomical station. His latitude and longitude figures for field stations are given in Baker, *Survey of the Northwestern Boundary*, but are not reliable to position on today's maps. En-saw-kwatch station would later be established very closely north of the parallel, to be occupied by both American and British astronomers.

61. The map by an Indian giving native names (written by Gibbs) shows "Kla hái h" for the stream and "S' háh-cha-ka" for the lake (maps 26 and 27, series 69, RG 76, NA).

62. Custer's remaining journeys are reported in his May 1866 narrative report to Campbell. Only this July reconnaissance and the one in June are described in contemporary field reports.

63. Wilson, *Mapping the Frontier*, 60.

64. Ibid., 64, 65.

65. Ibid.

66. Ibid., 65.

67. Ibid.

68. Ibid., 66.

69. Ibid., 69.

70. Ibid., 67–8.

71. Ibid., 69–70. The stream draining the glaciers beneath the American Border Peak and Mt. Larrabee is the one Custer called "Chuch-chech."

72. Ibid., 70.

73. Hawkins treated the creek as the west fork of the upper Similkameen, while Baker (*Survey of the Northwestern Boundary*) regarded it as a branch of the Pasayten.

74. Gardner, manuscript, 1:72.

75. Baker, *Survey of the Northwestern Boundary*, 67.

76. Gardner, manuscript, 1:77–8.

77. Unfortunately, no journal notes show his bearings or route, although it was probably along the northwest ridge. Evidence of the vast fire on the subrange can still be seen.

78. The map drawn by Thiusoloc for Gibbs calls the Skagit the "Smallá-o."

79. In Baker, *Survey of the Northwestern Boundary*, the stream name was misprinted as "Klabneh." On map 26 (series 69, RG 76, NA), the upper Chilliwack is "Kla hái-hu." That summer Gibbs sketched Bear Mountain from the forest edge at the lake ("Mountain on Klahaihu creek").

80. Bear Creek is labeled "S'Kaan-1' p" on map 26, series 69, RG 76, NA.

81. Baker refers to Easy Ridge as "Goat Mountain," giving its elevation as 5,862 feet (its highest point is actually 6,613 feet) and mentioning that it is on the "Klab-neh–Zakeno" divide (*Survey of the Northwestern Boundary*, 48).

82. Baker, *Survey of the Northwestern Boundary*, 48.

83. The 1866 map has the spelling "Wil-a-kin-a-haist" for Mt. Challenger. For an earlier account of Custer's discovery, see Beckey, *Challenge*. Gibbs reviewed Custer's description of the region, the mountain, and the glacier in "Physical Geography," pt. 2, 351. In his notebook for August 11, Custer called the massif "glaciers Mt"; and he made the first drawing of Mt. Challenger.

84. Custer to Parke, July 2, 1859, 35. While Custer was leading this important reconnaissance, Charles Gardner continued a survey eastward from Camp Chuchchehum, finishing at Camp Skagit on August 13. He apparently followed the rugged 1858 route of Gardner and Peabody, crossing the second divide north of the Maselpanik Glacier, then descending St. Alice Creek.

85. Gardner, manuscript, 1:98.

86. See map 2, series 68, RG 76, NA.

87. Gardner, manuscript, 1:79.

88. Baker, *Survey of the Northwestern Boundary*, 48; Gardner, manuscript, 1:80. This crest separates Lightning from Nepopekum Creek.

89. Gardner, manuscript, 1:81. Gardner had a copy of the Pacific Railroad survey map.

90. Ibid. See also Gardner's *Sketch of Reconnaissances in August 1859*, map 17, series 69, RG 76, NA.

91. Baker, *Survey of the Northwestern Boundary*, 68; Gardner, manuscript, 1:83.

92. Gardner, manuscript, 1:87, 89.

93. Summit Cache was at 5,819 feet (see map 2, series 68, RG 76, NA).

94. Gardner, manuscript, 1:89.

95. Ibid., 1:90.

96. Baker, *Survey of the Northwestern Boundary*, 71.

97. The route is shown on map 2, series 68, RG 76, NA. Numerous regional topographic features have changed both their name and location on maps since 1859. The name used by the survey, now spelled *Skaist*, was first recorded for this location by Alexander C. Anderson in 1846. Now the river and mountains (today the Snass Mountains) are placed on the next valley east.

98. Gardner to Campbell, Gardner, manuscript, 1:96.

99. Parke to Campbell, November 12, 1859. See Baker, *Survey of the Northwestern Boundary*, 16, 69, 70.

100. Hawkins to Secretary of State for War, October 19, 1859, in Klotz, *Foreign Office Correspondence*, pt. 3.

101. Wilson, *Mapping the Frontier*, 78.

102. Hawkins to Secretary of State for War, November 9, 1859; Hawkins to Secretary of State for the Colonies, December 20, 1859, in Klotz, *Foreign Office Correspondence*, pt. 3.

103. Watson, *Life of Wilson*, 28.

104. Anderson to Jack, March 28, 1860, Samuel Anderson Papers.

105. Anderson to Janet, January 6, 1860, Samuel Anderson Papers.

106. Ibid.

107. Ibid.

108. Box 1, folder 19, letters, p. 133, Samuel Anderson Papers.

109. Anderson to Janet, January 6, 1860, Samuel Anderson Papers.

110. Anderson, letter of February 1861 concerning the New Year's celebration, and Anderson to Jack, March 28, 1860, Samuel Anderson Papers

111. Anderson to Jack, March 28, 1860, Samuel Anderson Papers.

112. Anderson to Janet, January 6, 1860, Samuel Anderson Papers.

113. Ibid.

114. Anderson to Aunt Harriet, February 7, 1860, Samuel Anderson Papers.

115. Anderson to Jack, March 28, 1860, and Anderson to Aunt Harriet, February 7, 1860, Samuel Anderson Papers.

116. Wilson, *Mapping the Frontier,* 83.

117. Anderson to Jack, May 27, 1860, Samuel Anderson Papers.

118. Anderson to Janet, March 6, 1860, Samuel Anderson Papers.

119. Anderson to Jack, May 27, 1860, Samuel Anderson Papers.

120. Anderson to Jack, March 28, 1860, Samuel Anderson Papers.

121. Anderson to Janet, April 23, 1860, Samuel Anderson Papers.

122. Anderson to Janet and Aunt Harriet, March 28, 1860, Samuel Anderson Papers. Some of the photographs are preserved in the Museum of Royal Engineers in Kent, England, and in the Harris Papers at Yale University.

123. Hawkins to Secretary of State, May 29, 1860, in Klotz, *Foreign Office Correspondence,* pt. 3, 39–41; Hawkins to Secretary of State for the Colonies, February 18, 1860, in Klotz, *Foreign Office Correspondence,* pt. 3.

124. Hawkins to Secretary of State, May 29, 1860, in Klotz, *Foreign Office Correspondence,* pt. 3, 39–40.

125. Watson, *Life of Wilson,* 32.

126. Wilson, *Mapping the Frontier,* 95.

127. Hawkins to Secretary of State for Foreign Affairs, March 28, 1861, cited in Deutsch, "Contemporary Report," 22–3.

128. Watson, *Life of Wilson,* 33.

129. Hawkins to Secretary of State for Foreign Affairs, March 28, 1861, in Klotz, *Foreign Office Correspondence,* pt. 3, 43.

130. Wilson, *Mapping the Frontier,* 119.

131. Ibid., 121. This was likely the spruce grouse, known colloquially as the fool hen. It has now almost vanished because of its overconfident nature.

132. Ibid.

133. Ibid., 122.

134. Ibid., 123.

135. Anderson to Janet, September 26, 1860, Samuel Anderson Papers.

136. Hawkins to Lord Lyons, December 3, 1860, Museum of Royal Engineers, Kent, England.

137. Baker, *Survey of the Northwestern Boundary,* 17.

138. Wilson, *Mapping the Frontier,* 134.

139. Lord, *Naturalist.*

140. Anderson to Jack, February 2, 1862, Samuel Anderson Papers.

141. Ibid.

142. Anderson to Janet, May 2, 1862, Samuel Anderson Papers.

143. Ibid.

144. Ibid.

145. See Gardner, manuscript, 2:214.

146. Baker, *Survey of the Northwestern Boundary,* 18.

147. Deutsch, "Contemporary Report," 29.

148. See Klotz, *Foreign Office Correspondence,* pt. 3, 36, 38–9, 66, 69–71; and Hawkins to Secretary of State, August 26, 1861, in Klotz, *Foreign Office Correspondence,* pt. 3.

149. George F.G. Stanley, introduction to Wilson, *Mapping the Frontier,* 17.

150. "Northwest Boundary Commission." This valuable document (House Exec. Doc. 86, 40th Cong., 3d sess., serial 1381) summarizes the entire history of the survey operation and includes a tabular exhibit of the survey's expenditures, as well as a list of personnel and helpers. See also Baker, *Survey of the Northwestern Boundary,* 75.

151. The British maps are in Cartographic Series 67, RG 76, NA.

152. For a review of the meeting, see Klotz, *Foreign Office Correspondence,* pt. 4, 6–7.

153. Baker, *Survey of the Northwestern Boundary,* 18.

154. The manuscript was reportedly last seen at the office of the Northern Boundary Commission (Wheeler, *100th Meridian,* 1:617).

155. Klotz, "Forty-ninth Parallel." Klotz's papers are in the Public Archives of Canada.

Chapter 9: Legacy of the Land Grants

1. Goetzmann, *Exploration and Empire,* 265.

2. Hidy, Hidy, and Scott, *Great Northern Railway,* 19.

3. The line as first surveyed was largely theoretical. (*Report of Johnson, 1867*).

4. Tilton to Canfield, September 24, 1867. Unless otherwise stated, all reports by Tilton or Walker are in the Secretary Series, Lake Superior and Puget Sound Company, Northern Pacific Railroad Company (NPRR) Records. The Indian name for the river was "Tanum"; Lt. Richard Arnold called it the Bumping River in his 1854 military-road report. Bumping Lake is shown on Tilton's 1855 map of Washington Territory.

5. Ibid.; Walker to Canfield, September 16, 1867.

6. Report of R. M. Walker to Henry S. Welles, September 7, 1867, "Survey of Passes through Cascade Mountains," Chief Engineer, Old Vault Files, file 156, folder 1, p. 5, NPRR Records.

7. Ibid., 2. These conclusions were also stated in Walker's reports to Johnson, Canfield, and Smith (all in the NPRR Records).

8. Tilton to Canfield, September 12, 1867.

9. Report of Walker to Welles, September 7, 1867, 7–8; Walker to Canfield, September 16, 1867.

10. Tilton to Johnson, August 7, 1867; Tilton to Canfield, September 24, 1867; *Report of Johnson, 1869,* 68.

11. Tilton to Canfield, September 24, 1867.

12. See also *Report of Johnson, 1869.*

13. Ibid., 73.

14. Tilton to Johnson, August 7, 1867. Tilton's conclusion relied in part on the explorations of the Northwest Boundary Survey. See also Tilton to Canfield, September 12, 1867; and Tilton, "Report of Surveys Made in 1867, to Edwin F. Johnson," October 2, 1867, 73.

15. *Report of Johnson, 1869,* sketch no. 4.

16. Tilton to Canfield, October 19, 1867.

17. Ibid.; *Report of Johnson, 1867,* 31.

18. *Report of Johnson, 1869,* 76, 17. The details of the survey are not known. See file 66, 3E79B, NPRR Records.

19. Smalley, *Northern Pacific,* 185. See also Frank Billallby to Edwin F. Johnson, October 9, 1870, Letters Received, 3f67b, Lake Superior and Puget Sound Company, NPRR Records.

20. *Report of Johnson, 1869,* 15.

21. W. Milnor Roberts, "Cascade Range" (draft), 1875, NPRR Records.

22. Thomas B. Morris to W. Milnor Roberts, December 1, 1872, NPRR Records.

23. Smalley, *Northern Pacific,* 153–4. See also Renz, *Northern Pacific Railroad.*

24. Northern Pacific Railroad, *Life of Canfield,* 35.

25. Roberts, *Reconnaissance,* 17; *Wilkeson's Notes,* 18, 10, 24–5. For more on Wilkeson, see Smalley, *Northern Pacific,* 283.

26. *Wilkeson's Notes,* 18, 7–8.

27. Johnson, *Trans-Continental Railways.*

28. Smalley, *Northern Pacific,* 187. See Linsley's twenty-six-page report to Johnson, September

26, 1870, Chief Engineer, Old Vault Files, file 157, appendix D, NPRR Records. Linsley's 165-page manuscript journal is in file 156. See also his "Pioneering in the Cascade Country," 339–44; "Sauk and Wenatchee Rivers," 201–66; and "Lake Chelan and Agnes Creek," 382–401. Unless otherwise stated, the account of Linsley's exploration and the accompanying quotations are from his journal.

29. Linsley to Johnson, September 26, 1870, 25–6, NPRR Records.

30. For more on Linsley, see *Biographical Directory of the Railway Officials;* see also Smith, *Addison County,* 770–2.

31. Johnson to Linsley, April 28, 1870, Chief Engineer, Old Vault Files, file 156, NPRR Records.

32. See Linsley to Johnson, September 26, 1870, 3, NPRR Records.

33. This would logically be Glacier Peak, despite Linsley's mistaken bearing of S 58 W (his directions often erred, inconsistent with magnetic declination). The perennial snows were glaciers near the head of Dome Creek, to the north of "Kaiwhat Pass."

34. Linsley to Johnson, September 26, 1870, 5, NPRR Records.

35. Ibid., 11. The defile became informally known as Linsley's Pass and is now known to hikers as Little White Pass.

36. Ibid., 12.

37. The Great Northern Railway later followed this precise route, digging a tunnel through the soft sandstone to avoid Tumwater Canyon.

38. Linsley to Johnson, September 26, 1870, 19–20, NPRR Records. During a later year (possibly 1886), James R. Maxwell is said to have made two surveys of Lake Chelan and the Stehekin and abandoned them; apparently, he was guided by William L. Sanders, who assisted Albert B. Rogers of the Great Northern Railway in 1887 (see Rogers to J.J. Hill, July 2 and 5, 1887, Albert B. Rogers Papers, Washington State Historical Society, Tacoma).

39. See J.T. Sheets's report, accompanying appendix D to Virgil G. Bogue's report of April 25, 1882, in Chief Engineer, Old Vault Files, file 157-D, NPRR Records.

40. Report of Thomas B. Morris, July 26, 1872, Chief Engineer, Old Vault Files, file 156, folder 2, p. 3, 4, 5, NPRR Records. See also Morris to W. Milnor Roberts, July 26, 1872, Chief Engineer, Old Vault Files, file 157, appendix D, NPRR Records.

41. Hubert C. Ward to Thomas B. Morris, October 31, 1872, Chief Engineer, Old Vault Files, file 156, folder 2, p.9, NPRR Records.

42. Report of Morris on his return from the surveys of Ward Sheets, Skagit River, July 26–August 19, 1872, Chief Engineer, Old Vault Files, file 156, folder 2, NPRR Records.

43. See Morris to Roberts, December 1, 1872, Chief Engineer, Old Vault Files, NPRR Records; and Report of Morris, July 26, 1872, 13, NPRR Records.

44. Smalley, *Northern Pacific,* 193–4.

45. Ibid., 194.

46. Ibid., 205, 212.

47. Ibid., 206, 208, 217, 219.

48. For more on Clarke, see D.D. Clarke, manuscript, Oregon Historical Society Research Library, Portland (hereaftered cited as Clarke, manuscript).

49. See "Preliminary Report (with map) of W. Milnor Roberts, Chief Engineer of the Northern Pacific Railroad Company on the Surveys for the Branch from Tacoma across the Cascade Range, in 1878," 1879, file 66, 3E79B, NPRR Records. Because almost all surveying was done on sloping ground, the transit measurements became slope distances (a stretched tape would include the horizontal distance and the altitude gained). Computations later determined the correct horizontal distance for mapping purposes.

50. Clarke, manuscript.

51. Report of Isaac W. Smith to Gen. J. W. Sprague, December 27, 1880, "Cascade Mountain Surveys to Close of Year 1880," 9, Secretary Series, Lake Superior and Puget Sound Company, NPRR Records. See Virgil G. Bogue to Gen. Adna Anderson, Engineer-in-Chief, August 5, 1887, NPRR Records.

52. Report of Smith to Sprague, December 27, 1880, 3.

53. Ibid.

54. Ibid., 5–6.

55. Bogue's report, originally published in *Bulletin of the American Geographical Society*, was reprinted in the *Seattle Post-Intelligencer*, October 27, 1895. Bogue's story is also told in a typescript (Special Paper no. 65, President and Vice President Correspondence, NPRR Records). See also the account in Morgan, *Puget's Sound*, 195–9.

56. *Oregonian*, November 1, 1895, 10.

57. Bonney, "Stampede Pass," 278. See also Morgan, *Puget's Sound*, 199–200.

58. See *Memoirs of Henry Villard*, vol. 2.

59. Morgan, *Puget's Sound*, 186–7.

60. Ibid., 191; Hedges, *Henry Villard*, 127–8.

61. Chief Engineer, Old Vault Files, file 36-11, box 4, NPRR Records.

62. Anderson to Oakes, July 11, 1884, file 66, 3E79B, NPRR Records.

63. Bogue to Oakes, December 1, 1883, file 66, A3E79B, 5, NPRR Records.

64. See Morgan, *Puget's Sound*, 203–11.

65. *Engineering News*, October 3, 1891, October 10, 1891, Chief Engineer, Old Vault Files, file 36, miscellaneous, NPRR Records.

66. Chief Engineer, Old Vault Files, file 36-18, NPRR Records. Morgan states that the switchback crossing was a symbol of the Northern Pacific's intent to complete the route, not a practical system (*Puget's Sound*, 210).

67. Smalley, *Northern Pacific*.

68. Knappen, "Every Odd Section."

69. Ibid.

70. Griffith, "Pacific Northwest," 77. See also *Northern Pacific Land Grants*, report of the Joint Committees on Investigation of the Northern Pacific Railroad Land Grants.

Chapter 10: Army Explorations North of Lake Chelan

1. Symons, "Explorations and Surveys," 2552. See also Ruby, "Moses Reservation," 17–23.

2. See Symons, "Report for the Fiscal Year Ending June 30, 1881," 40–1.

3. Symons, "Explorations and Surveys," 2552–3.

4. Russell, *North America*, 157–8; Lyman, "Lake Chelan," 199.

5. Ross, *First Settlers*, 151.

6. Rodman, "Explorations in the Upper Columbia Country," 265.

7. Lyman, "Lake Chelan," 198.

8. Statements that prospectors ascended the lake in 1858 are erroneous. See Majors, "Backus Explores the Twisp and Methow Valleys," 48.

9. Symons, *Report of an Examination of the Upper Columbia River*, 6:40.

10. This river exploration is described in Symons's *Report of an Examination of the Upper Columbia River*.

11. Downing, *Upper Columbia*, 26. See also Majors, ed., "Alfred Downing's Misadventures." Downing also wrote his little-known *Brief Narrative of a Misadventure on the Columbia River, Washington Territory* (Portland, 1880) while he was stationed at Columbia Barracks.

12. Except where otherwise noted, the account of the expedition given here, including all quotations, is from Pierce's *Report of an Expedition from Fort Colville to Puget Sound*. See also Majors, "Army Expedition," 4–84. Pierce's expedition is summarized in Symons's "Report of the Chief of Engineers, U.S. Army," 2412. His original manuscript is in the National Archives (5658 AGO, 1882, RG 94).

13. The prospector may have been a man named McKee (or McGee), who apparently ventured nearly to Harts Pass in January 1877. See Majors, "Backus," 35–7; and *Chelan Falls Leader*, October 1, 1891, cited in Majors, "Army Expedition," 33, 80. McKee was in the area by 1875 (*Illustrated History of Stevens, Ferry, Okanogan, and Chelan Counties*).

14. Majors points out Swa-u-lum's error in "Army Expedition," 33, 35. "Captain Jim" lived on the Twisp River and knew the local route.

15. Majors, "Army Expedition," 35.

16. As early as September 1882, Symons disputed this claim. Lt. Samuel Robertson and Lt. Samuel Rodman would both disprove Pierce's belief in summer 1883.

17. See Symons, "Report for the Fiscal Year Ending June 30, 1881."

18. Majors, "Army Expedition," 79, 81.

19. It has been conjectured that the elder prospector had already ascended to the pass from the west (see Majors, "Backus," 38).

20. This is one of the most devastating avalanche tracks in the northern Cascades.

21. Majors, "Army Expedition."

22. Symons, "Report of the Chief of Engineers," 2412.

23. See Goethals, "Report for the Fiscal Year Ending June 30, 1883," 2412. One of Pierce's soldiers was with Robertson, whose report has never been located.

24. Except where otherwise noted, the account of Rodman's expedition given here, including all quotations, is from his "Explorations in the Upper Columbia Country."

25. Griffin, "George W. Goethals," 137. See also "Report of Reconnaissance Made While with Scouting Party under Command of 1st Lt. George B. Backus, 1st U.S. Cavalry," July 14, 1884, file 3781 AGO 1884 (filed with 5658 AGO 1882), Letters Received (Main Series), 1881–89, microcopy 689, roll 143 (1882), Records of the Adjutant General's Office, RG 94, NA. Alfred Downing drew the *Map of Reconnaissance Showing Route Followed by Scouting Party under 1st Lieut. G. B. Backus* (W-402-1, RG 77, NA). Goethals also made another report, "Explorations and Surveys in the Department of the Columbia," in *Annual Report of the Chief of Engineers,* pt. 3, app. BBB, 2407–9; Symons, "Report of the Chief of Engineers," 2410–12.

26. John C. Tidball, "Report of Journey Made by General W. T. Sherman," 231. There was a usable Indian trail along the Similkameen as early as 1812; the HBC trader Samuel Black depicted it on his map of the Thompson's River District, c. 1833.

Chapter 11: The Great Northern's Search for a Pass

1. Berton, *The Last Spike,* 23. For more on the Great Northern Railway, see Hidy and Hidy, "John Frank Stevens," 343–4.

2. Martin, *James J. Hill,* 390.

3. Berton, *The Last Spike,* 19, 178, 179. See also Cruise and Griffiths, *Lords of the Line,* 102–3.

4. Berton, *The Last Spike,* 181.

5. Secretan, *Canada's Great Highway,* 182, 186.

6. Rogers, diary.

7. Ibid.

8. Ibid.

9. This and other estimates on the expedition are quite accurate.

10. Rogers to Hill, August 19, 1887, Hill Papers.

11. Rogers to Hill, August 27, 1887, Hill Papers.

12. Rogers to Hill, October 7, 1887, Hill Papers.

13. Martin, *James J. Hill,* 389–91.

14. Beckler to Hill, June 8, 1890, Hill Papers. See also Hidy and Hidy, "John Frank Stevens," 348.

15. Leyden to J. Beckler, March 22, 1890, President's Office, 22.E.5.6 F, Hill Papers.

16. Stevens, "Great Northern Railway," 111–12; Beckler to Hill, June 22, 1890, President's Office, 22.E.5.6 F, Hill Papers.

17. *Seattle Post-Intelligencer,* August 16, 1894, 3; Beckler to Hill, June 22, 1890, Hill Papers. Beckler was aware of Daniel C. Linsley's 1870 exploration for the Northern Pacific from the Suiattle River to Lake Chelan. See July 2, 1890, President's Office, 22.E.5.6 F, Hill Papers.

18. Stevens to Beckler, June 11, 1890, President's Office, 22.E.5.6 F, Hill Papers.

19. Haskell to mother, January 18, 1890, in Haskell, *On Reconnaissance,* 63.

20. Ibid.

21. Beckler to Hill, June 22, 1890, Hill Papers.

22. Martin, *James J. Hill,* 379.

23. Stevens to Beckler, May 30, 1890, President's Office, 22.E.5.6 F, Hill Papers.

24. Stevens, "Cascade Crossing," 20.

25. Stevens, "Great Northern Railway," 112.

26. Stevens, "Cascade Crossing," 19.

27. Ibid., 20.

28. Stevens, memorandum, September 25, 1928, GNR Records.

29. Stevens, "Cascade Crossing," 20.

30. Stevens, memorandum. The discovery of Stevens Pass must have been on about July 1.

31. Stevens, "Cascade Crossing," 21.

32. Haskell to mother, June 5, 1891, in Haskell, *On Reconnaissance,* 136.

33. Hidy, Hidy, and Scott, *Great Northern Railway,* 82–4.

34. "Great Northern Railway Tunnel through the Cascade Mountains," 456; Kerr, "Preliminary Studies," 186. for a map of the switchback routes, see Hidy, Hidy, and Scott, *Great Northern Railway,* 114.

35. Kerr, "Preliminary Studies," 188.

36. Johansen and Gates, *Empire of the Columbia;* Kerr, "Preliminary Studies," 189 (table).

37. See Hult, *Northwest Disaster.*

38. See Wood, *Lines West; Seattle Times,* July 4, 1965.

39. Hult, *Northwest Disaster,* 50–1.

40. Wood, *Lines West,* 32.

41. Kerr, "Preliminary Studies," 193; Baxter, "Construction Plans and Methods," 230–3; P.N. Peterson, "Great Northern Opens World's Fifth Largest Railroad Bore: 8-Mile Cascade Tunnel," *Pacific Builder and Engineer,* February 2, 1929, Special Collections, University of Washington Libraries, Seattle.

42. Hidy and Hidy, "John Frank Stevens," 357.

43. Stevens, "The Cascade Tunnel," 23–6.

44. GNR Records, HE 2791.G7.

45. Rinehart, *Tenting To-Night,* 118.

46. Ibid., 121.

47. GNR Records.

Chapter 12: From Wagon Roads to Highways

1. *Report of the Secretary of War, 1859,* Senate Exec. Doc. 2, 36th Cong., 1st sess, 1859–60, 877.

2. *Index News,* October 9, 1913.

3. See H.A. Annen Papers, University of Washington Libraries, Seattle.

4. Murray, "Wagon Road," 51. Accounts disagree on the year, but a *Seattle Post-Intelligencer* story (August 16, 1894, 3) stated that it was 1891.

5. Murray, "Wagon Road," 51. See also Roth, *History of Whatcom County,* 570–1; RG 53, Department of Highways, Washington State Archives and Records Center, Olympia (hereafter WSA).

6. Minutes of the State Road Commission, New Whatcom, October 13, 1893, 61, WSA.

7. Ibid., 65.

8. Ibid., 65–6.

9. Jeffcott, *Chechaco and Sourdough,* 48–56; *Seattle Post-Intelligencer,* August 16, 1894, 3.

10. *Seattle Post-Intelligencer,* August 16, 1894, 3.

11. Murray, "Wagon Road," 53; Engineer's Report, September 23, 1895, Washington State Road Commission Report, MSS. 157, State Library, Olympia, 4.

12. Engineer's Report, September 23, 1895, Washington State Road Commission Report, MSS. 157, State Library, Olympia, 7–8, 11, 12. The final report of the Board of State Road Commissioners was made by Wilson, Welts, and Watson on December 17, 1896 (see *Washington Highways,* September 1972, 1–9). The altitudes given, determined by aneroid barometer, all concur with today's measurements.

13. Murray, "Wagon Road," 54.

14. North Cascades Study Team, *North Cascades,* 50. A copy of this report is located in the Washington State Archives at Bellingham.

15. Ibid., 50–1.

16. Murray, "Wagon Road," 54–5.

17. Washington State Highway Commission, *1st Biennial Report* (1906).

18. Report of Charles I. Signer to James Allen, Superintendent of Highways, RG 53, WSA, 7.

19. File B 53, RG 53, WSA.

20. Ibid.

21. The state Mine to Market Roads law of 1939 was enacted to provide access to mineralized areas of the state for development. See RG 9/6-10, Department of Natural Resources, box 8, WSA.

22. The Forest Service had first built a trail through Rainy Pass in 1906.

23. Haines, *Mountain Fever,* 29–30.

24. Martinson, "Mountain in the Sky," 28.

25. Robert N. McIntyre, "History of Mount Rainier National Park" (1952), box 3, Macy Papers; Martinson, "Mountain in the Sky," 33. Longmire was later the site of the park headquarters.

26. Clevinger, "Migration of Southern Appalachian Mountain Highlanders," 6, 21.

27. Sylvester Papers, University of Washington Libraries, Seattle.

28. Nels Bruseth Papers, University of Washington Libraries, Seattle.

29. Ibid.

30. Strom Papers, 145.

31. Ibid.

32. Ayres, "Washington Forest Reserve," 285.

33. Pitzer, "Upper Skagit Valley," 54.

34. Ibid.

35. Jenkins, *Last Frontier,* 113.

36. Dayo tape recording, North Cascades National Park library, Sedro Woolley, Washington.

37. North Cascades Study Team, *North Cascades,* 74, 92.

38. *Northern Star* (Snohomish, Wash.), June 12, 1878.

39. North Cascades Study Team, *North Cascades,* 94. When the Forest Homestead Act was passed in 1906, the Forest Service questioned the Dohne claim. See the article by Paul C. Pitzer in the *Concrete Herald,* June 21, 1951.

40. Glee Davis, "Pioneering in Upper Skagit Recalled by Early Settler," *Bellingham Herald,* June 26, 1953, 8.

41. North Cascades Study Team, *North Cascades,* 105. See also *Seattle City Light News,* June 1967, 105; and Pitzer, "Upper Skagit Valley," 36–53.

42. Petta, taped interview, University of Washington Libraries, Seattle.

43. Ernest Kobelt Papers, University of Washington Libraries, Seattle.

44. *Chelan Falls Leader,* August 6, 17, 1891.

45. *Chelan Falls Leader,* April 19, May 10, June 19, 1900. A general reference for the Stehekin area is *Wenatchee Daily World,* special supplement, May 25, 1965.

46. North Cascades Study Team, *North Cascades,* 179–80.

47. "Lake Chelan," 198–9.

48. *Chelan Falls Leader,* September 6, 1895.

Chapter 13: Early Mountaineering on the Volcanos

1. Wilkes, *Narrative,* 303; Tolmie, *Journals,* 201; Custer, "Reconaissances."

2. Coleman, "Mountains and Mountaineering," 387–90; *Whatcom Reveille,* August 3, 1883.

3. Coleman, "Mountaineering on the Pacific," 793. See Edmond S. Meany Papers, box 41, file 7, University of Washington Libraries, Seattle; and Mumm, *Alpine Club Register.*

4. See Miles, *Koma Kulshan,* 21; and Majors, *Mount Baker.*

5. John A. Tennant, journal, Lummi Reservation Archives.

6. Coleman, "Mountaineering on the Pacific."

7. Ibid., 798.

8. Thomas Stratton, "Ascent of Mount Baker," *Weekly Message* (Port Townsend), September 3, 10, 1868, cited in Majors, *Mount Baker,* 175.

9. Ibid.

10. Coleman, "Mountaineering on the Pacific," 806.

11. Stratton, "Ascent of Mount Baker," 179.

12. Ibid., 180.

13. Ibid., 181.

14. Ibid.

15. Coleman, "Mountaineering on the Pacific," 809.

16. Coleman's ice axe was the first to be used in the Pacific Northwest, probably in all of North America.

17. Coleman, "Mountaineering on the Pacific," 812.

18. Stratton, "Ascent of Mount Baker," 183.

19. Although naming the peak was superfluous, "Grant Peak" has gained official recognition on maps.

20. Coleman, "Mountaineering on the Pacific," 813.

21. Ibid.

22. Stratton, "Ascent of Mount Baker," 184.

23. Winthrop, *Canoe and the Saddle,* 36; Coleman, "Mountains and Mountaineering," 389–90.

24. Kautz, "Diary of Gen. A. W. Kautz," 116; Kautz, "Ascent of Mount Rainier," 393.

25. Wallace, "Kautz," 10; Powell and Shippen, *Officers of the Army and Navy,* 224.

26. Kautz, "Ascent of Mount Rainier," 393.

27. Kautz, *Northwest Journals.*

28. Kautz, "Ascent of Mount Rainier," 393–4.

29. Ibid., 395–6.

30. Ibid., 396.

31. Haines, *Mountain Fever,* 23.

32. Kautz, *Northwest Journals.*

33. Kautz, "Ascent of Mount Rainier," 398.

34. Kautz, *Northwest Journals.*

35. Kautz, "Ascent of Mount Rainier," 401; Kautz, *Northwest Journals.*

36. See Haines, *Mountain Fever,* 219 n. 67; Meany and Farrar, *Mount Rainier,* 71–93.

37. Kautz, "Ascent of Mount Rainier," 400.

38. Haines, *Mountain Fever,* 26.

39. Kautz, "Ascent of Mount Rainier," 403.

40. *Tacoma Ledger,* January 29, 1893, cited in Haines, *Mountain Fever,* 151; see also 149–50.

41. Kautz, "Ascent of Mount Rainier," 394, 403.

42. "Visit to Mt. Ranier [*sic*]," *Columbian* (Olympia), September 18, 1852, cited in Scott, "News and Comment," 338. See also Haines, *Mountain Fever,* 10–12.

43. Himes, "Very Early Ascents," 199. See also Scott, "News and Comment," 337.

44. See McWhorter, "Sluskin's True Narrative." See also Lucullus McWhorter transcript, folder 25b, Stevens Papers, Washington State Historical Society, Tacoma; and Splawn, *Ka-mi-akin,* 340. Splawn, who met Sluskin in 1861, indicates that the event took place shortly after the 1855 Indian war.

45. Van Trump, "Mount Tacoma: The Story of Its First Sucessful [*sic*] Ascent," manuscript, 1909, P. 5, Van Trump Papers.

46. Heitman, *Historical Register and Dictionary of the United States Army.*

47. Majors, "The Stevens and Van Trump Ascent," pt. 1, 20.

48. Ibid.

49. Except where otherwise stated, my exposition is based on the first published narrative of the expedition, Stevens, "Ascent of Takhoma," 513–30 (Stevens preferred to call Mt. Rainier "Takhoma"). This was for many decades the only reliable account, save for newspaper stories, until the appearance of Meany and Farrar, *Mount Rainier.* Other primary materials were published by Coleman ("Ascent of Mount Rainier," in *Illustrated Travels* [1873]) and Van Trump ("Mount Rainier" [1900]). The first secondary source to add new insight into the expedition was Aubrey Haines's *Mountain Fever* (1962). Another account is provided in Dee Molenaar, *The Challenge of Rainier.* Harry M. Majors's 1985 four-part series, "The Stevens and Van Trump Ascent," is based on little-known newspaper accounts.

50. Stevens, "Ascent of Takhoma."

51. Coleman, "Ascent of Mount Rainier," 161. There was a wagon road as far as Lackamas Prairie.

52. Haines, *Mountain Fever,* 35–6.

53. Coleman, "Ascent of Mount Rainier."

54. Van Trump, "Mount Rainier," 9.

55. Ibid., 8–10.

56. See Majors, "The Stevens and Van Trump Ascent," pt. 1, 42–72.

57. Haines, *Mountain Fever,* 39–40.

58. Van Trump, "Mount Rainier," 11–12.

59. Ibid., 12.

60. Stevens, "Ascent of Takhoma," 520.

61. Van Trump, "Mount Rainier," 13.

62. Stevens, typescript, folder 25b, 8, Stevens Papers.

63. Stevens, "Ascent of Takhoma," 522.

64. Ibid., 523; Van Trump, "Mount Tacoma," 17, Van Trump Papers.

65. Van Trump, "Mount Tacoma," 18, Van Trump Papers; Stevens, "Ascent of Takhoma," 523.

66. Stevens, "Ascent of Takhoma," 524.

67. Ibid.

68. Van Trump, "Mount Rainier," 15; Van Trump, "Mount Tacoma," Van Trump Papers.

69. Stevens, "Ascent of Takhoma," 526. It appears that their plate and canteen were deposited on rocks of the Columbia Crest slope or on the north rim of the west crater (Majors, "The Stevens and Van Trump Ascent," pt. 1, 76). Samuel Emmons did not find these items two months later (Emmons, "Ascent of Mt. Rainier," 312).

70. Majors, "The Stevens and Van Trump Ascent," pt. 3, 252; see also pt. 1, 73–96; Haines, *Mountain Fever*, 47; and Molenaar, *The Challenge of Rainier*, 38. Majors has made a case that Stevens and Van Trump did not reach the true summit. The main body of mountaineering opinion, however, does give Stevens and Van Trump their summit credentials. See Russell, "Glaciers of Mount Rainier"

71. Stevens, "Ascent of Takhoma," 527.

72. Van Trump, "Mount Tacoma," Van Trump Papers.

73. Foster, *Summits to Reach*, 119–26.

74. Emmons, "Volcanoes."

75. Ibid.

76. Emmons, diary, container 2, Emmons Papers, Manuscripts Division, Library of Congress, Washington, D.C.

77. Emmons, "Volcanoes," 59.

78. Ibid.; Emmons, diary, container 2, Emmons Papers, Manuscripts Division, Library of Congress, Washington, D.C..

79. Emmons, "Volcanoes," 63.

80. The space between the ice and the rock was described by Israel C. Russell after his descent of the mountain in 1896. See "Glaciers of Mount Rainier," 374.

81. Majors, "The Stevens and Van Trump Ascent," pt. 3, 226.

82. Haines, *Mountain Fever*, 56; Emmons, "Volcanoes," 64.

83. King, "Actual Glaciers," 161–5; Stevens, "Ascent of Takhoma," 530.

84. Emmons, "Volcanoes."

85. Except where otherwise stated, all quotations from Bayley in this chapter, as well as the account of his expedition, are from his 1886 article in *Overland Monthly*, "Ascent of Mount Tacoma."

86. Wheeler, "Mount Rainier,"

87. Haines, *Mountain Fever*, 68.

88. On their ascent, see Haines, *Mountain Fever*, 70–9; and Schullery, *Island in the Sky*, 101–12.

89. Fobes, "Summit of Mount Rainier," 265. The account of the expedition given here, including all quotations, is from this article.

90. Muir, "Ascent of Mount Rainier," 197. Quotations from Muir in the following account are from this article.

91. Arthur C. Warner Papers, University of Washington Libraries, Seattle. See also Schullery, *Island in the Sky*.

92. Warner Papers, University of Washington Libraries, Seattle.

93. Haines, *Mountain Fever,* 94.

94. *Seattle Telegraph,* January 6, 1895. See also Haines, *Mountain Fever,* 183–5.

95. *Seattle Post-Intelligencer,* January 6, 1895.

96. *Seattle Telegraph,* January 6, 1895.

97. Lyman, "Switzerland of the Northwest," 304.

98. See Majors, "First Ascent of Mount St. Helens," 166, 176. Dryer's narrative appeared in the *Oregonian,* September 3, 1853, and was reprinted in *Mazama* 50, no. 13 (1968), 45–9. The account of the expedition given here, including all quotations, is from Dryer's narrative.

99. Loo-wit-lat-kla, *Gold Hunting.*

100. S. A. Clark, scrapbook, vol. 6, Oregon Historical Society (see article of Ruth E. Sheldon); *Oregonian,* August 2, 1920.

101. Himes, "Very Early Ascents."

102. *Portland Evening Telegram,* November 11, 1909.

103. *Oregonian,* July 28, 1895, 8.

104. See Rusk, *Tales of a Western Mountaineer.*

Chapter 14: Prospectors and the Mining Boom

1. Huntting, "Gold in Washington."

2. The story of the expedition appeared in the *Tacoma Sunday Ledger* on May 1, 1892 (see Reese, *The Northwest Was Their Goal* 3:574–608; the account given below, including all quotations, is from this source).

3. Pringle, *Roadside Geology of Mount St. Helens,* 15.

4. Weaver, "Geology and Ore Deposits of the Blewett Mining District." The arrastra, devised by the Spanish, was a circular stone trough for ore grinding. A mule supplied power, dragging a large, smooth stone around the trough.

5. *Seattle Post-Intelligencer,* September 6, 1896.

6. Ibid.

7. L. D. Lindsley Papers, University of Washington Libraries, Seattle; *Seattle Post-Intelligencer,* June 1, 1888.

8. See Ellis, "Geology of Dutch Miller Gap."

9. Patty, "Metal Mines of Washington," 145.

10. Weaver, "Geology and Ore Deposits of the Index Mining District."

11. Patty, "Metal Mines of Washington," 265, 283.

12. *Seattle Post-Intelligencer,* August 16, 1896, 20.

13. Ibid.

14. Ibid.

15. Adams, *Holden Mine,* 73.

16. Ibid., 7.

17. *Chelan Leader,* November 22, 1900.

18. See Granby Mining Company Papers, University of Washington Libraries, Seattle. The Forest Service informed Granby that it was illegal to allow tailings to slide into Railroad Creek—the first instance of environmental intervention in this large district.

19. See P. T. Harris, Okanogan Forest supervisor, to district forester, Portland, January 6, 1921, Okanogan National Forest Papers, 95-59a 242, box 9715, Federal Records Center, Seattle.

20. Waring, *My Pioneer Days,* 197–8; Hodges, *Mining in the Pacific Northwest,* 97; and Louis, "History of Ruby City," 68.

21. The geologist Reginald A. Daly named this biotite granite the Cathedral Batholith.

22. Pitzer, *Concrete Herald,* June 21, 1951; Mount Baker National Forest Papers, Federal Records Center, Seattle.

23. Otto Klement, "Early Skagit Recollections," *Mount Vernon Daily Herald,* October 19, 1926; and Ethel Van Fleet Harris, "Early Historical Incidents of Skagit County," *Mount Vernon Daily Herald,* October 19, 1926. The Harris typescript is in Special Collections, University of Washington Libraries, Seattle. The account of the journey that follows is from the *Mount Vernon Daily Herald* article.

24. Pitzer, "Upper Skagit Valley"; see also *Concrete Herald,* June 21, 1951.

25. Pitzer, "Upper Skagit Valley," 4–5; *Concrete Herald,* June 21, 1951.

26. *Bellingham Bay Mail,* April 24, 1880; *Annual Report,* Minister of Mines, British Columbia (1910), 131, BCARS.

27. See *North Pacific Coast,* December 1879, 29, cited in Pitzer, "Upper Skagit Valley," 37.

28. This rock corner is below Gorge Dam, where the present-day highway's first tunnel cuts the cliff.

29. *Concrete Herald,* June 21, 1951.

30. *North Pacific Coast,* December 1879, 29, cited in Pitzer, "Upper Skagit Valley," 9, 11, 13.

31. *Bellingham Bay Mail,* April 10, 1880, cited in *Concrete Herald,* November 2, 1966.

32. *Concrete Herald,* December 14, 1966.

33. Ibid.; Glee Davis, interview with the author.

34. *Bellingham Bay Mail,* April 24, 1880, 3.

35. "Memoirs of C. C. McGuire," Special Collections, University of Washington Libraries, Seattle.

36. Pitzer estimates that the number never exceeded one thousand to fifteen hundred ("Upper Skagit Valley").

37. *North Pacific Coast,* May 1, 1880, 133.

38. *Puget Sound Mail,* October 30, 1880, cited in Pitzer, "Upper Skagit Valley," 13. See also Huntting, "Gold in Washington."

39. The Soldier Boy, Boston, Midas, and Johnsburg claims were later patented. The tunnels followed quartz veins in schist bedrock. The size of the Midas mine camp and mill indicates that the owners expected the veins to increase in size at greater depth. *Seattle Post-Intelligencer,* October 25, 1896; Paul W. Law, report, December 9, 1892, University of Washington Libraries, Seattle.

40. *Seattle Post-Intelligencer,* October 25, 1896.

41. Ibid.

42. Ibid.

43. Paul W. Law, report, December 9, 1892, University of Washington Libraries, Seattle.

44. *Seattle Post-Intelligencer,* October 25, 1896.

45. Pitzer, "Upper Skagit Valley," 16–17. County auditor reports stated that 740 claims were located in the Ruby Creek drainage during 1890–91.

46. Ibid. Gold-bearing quartz veins are most numerous in the Bonita Creek drainage (Moen, "Mines and Mineral Deposits," 96.

47. Moen, "Mines and Mineral Deposits," 102.

48. Peter H. Miller, diary, Skagit County Historical Museum, La Conner.

49. Moen, "Mines and Mineral Deposits," 100.

50. Pitzer, "Upper Skagit Valley."

51. Moen, "Mines and Mineral Deposits," 96. At the time a second mill was built in 1905, miners' wages were $2.50 per day.

52. Mount Baker National Forest Papers.

53. *Northwest Mining Journal,* August 1906.

54. Milnor Oakes Roberts Papers, University of Washington Libraries, Seattle; Moen, "Mines and Mineral Deposits." At that time, gold brought thirty-two dollars per ounce.

55. Moen, "Mines and Mineral Deposits," 97.

56. *Chelan Falls Leader,* October 1, 1891.

57. "Lake Chelan Mining Region," *Chelan Leader,* December 20, 1892.

58. Hodges, *Mining in the Pacific Northwest,* 83.

59. *Chelan Falls Leader,* October 1, 1891, 1.

60. *Chelan Leader,* August 31, 1897; Okanogan National Forest Papers.

61. *Chelan Leader,* December 29, 1892.

62. Ibid.

63. See *Chelan Falls Leader,* October 1, 1891; and Anderson, "Lake Chelan and the American Alps," 300–308.

64. *Chelan Leader,* October 1, 1891, December 29, 1892.

65. *Chelan Leader,* August 29, 1901

66. Ibid.; *Concrete Herald,* June 21, 1951.

67. Hodges, *Mining in the Pacific Northwest,* 54–6. See also *Seattle Post-Intelligencer,* October 25, 1896, 18.

68. Hodges, *Mining in the Pacific Northwest,* 58.

69. *Washington Miner,* October 15, 1908; Milnor Oakes Roberts Papers, University of Washington Libraries, Seattle. See also Hodges, *Mining in the Pacific Northwest,* 58–9.

70. *Concrete Herald,* November 23, 1966.

71. "Thunder Creek Mining District."

72. *Concrete Herald,* November 16, 1966.

73. *Seattle Post-Intelligencer,* September 29, 1897; Jeffcott, *Chechaco and Sourdough,* 76; Moen, "Mines and Mineral Deposits," 11, 88.

74. *Seattle Post-Intelligencer,* September 29, 1897.

75. Ibid., Jeffcott, *Chechaco and Sourdough,* 83.

76. *Seattle Post-Intelligencer*, September 25, 1897.

77. Moen, "Mines and Mineral Deposits," 88.

78. *Annual Report,* Minister of Mines, British Columbia (1904), G267, BCARS.

79. Moen, "Mines and Mineral Deposits," 82, 63.

80. Moen, "Mines and Mineral Deposits," 80, 82; *Annual Report,* Minister of Mines, British Columbia (1915), BCARS.

81. *Annual Report,* Minister of Mines, British Columbia (1904), g266, BCARS.

82. Dolly Connelly, personal communication, November 25, 1968.

83. Connelly, "Mighty Joe Morovits," 52–7.

84. Moen, "Mines and Mineral Deposits," 1.

85. *Seattle Press-Times,* June 18, 1891, 5; June 22, 1891, 2.

86. *Seattle Press-Times,* June 19, 1891, 6; June 20, 1891, 5.

87. Hodges, *Mining in the Pacific Northwest,* 26–33. See also *20th Annual Report,* USGS, pt. 1 (1899), 495.

88. The following account of the journey is from Phelps's "In the Cascade Mountains," 3–5.

89. Although some accounts credit both Pearsall and his friend Frank Peabody with the discovery, the most reliable sources state that Pearsall was alone. See Hodges, *Mining in the Pacific Northwest,* 267; and Woodhouse, *Monte Cristo,* 13.

90. John MacDonald Wilmans Papers, folder VF 802B, University of Washington Libraries, Seattle.

91. Snohomish County mining records.

92. Woodhouse, *Monte Cristo*, 19.

93. Woodhouse, *Monte Cristo*, 27.

94. *Seattle Press-Times*, June 20, 1891, 5.

95. Woodhouse, *Monte Cristo*, 29.

96. Josiah E. Spurr's *Geological Sketch Map of the Vicinity of Monte Cristo, Washington* (in *22nd Annual Report*, USGS, pt. 2 [1901], plate 80) calls the higher peak "Wilman Peak" and the spires "Needle Peaks" (see also plate 81). In a forestry report by Horace B. Ayres, the spires were "The Needles" ("Washington Forest Reserve," plate 95); a photo in *The Coast* calls them "The Sentinels." In 1917, the Mountaineers officially proposed "Wilman Peaks" for "two sharp peaks one mile southeast of the town of Monte Cristo" (*The Mountaineer* 10 [December 1917], p. 92); these would be the North and South Wilmans Spires.

97. Strom Papers, 19.

98. *Everett Herald*, May 5, 1892, cited in Woodhouse, *Monte Cristo*, 43, 44.

99. Woodhouse, *Monte Cristo*, 44.

100. *Everett Herald*, December 17, 1891. By exercising its option to purchase a portion of the Pride of the Mountains Mining Company in December 1891, the Colby-Hoyt syndicate became the major Monte Cristo holder. Wilmans wisely retained a one-third interest in the form of stock options. The Wilmans brothers' share of the transaction was $86,000 cash and a bond for $67,000, to be paid from mine earnings. At this time, miners' wages were two to three dollars a day.

101. *Everett Herald*, August 4, 1892, 47.

102. *Everett Herald*, January 28, 1892, 7

103. *Everett Herald*, September 8, 1892, 61.

104. Strom Papers, 44, 52; *Everett Herald*, August 26, October 26, 1893.

105. Strom Papers.

106. "From Ocean Shore to Mountain Crest," 147.

107. Francis H. Brownell, "Reminiscences of the Monte Cristo Mines in the Cascades," Nordlund Papers, University of Washington Libraries.

108. See Whitfield, *History of Snohomish County*; and Frances Tanner, "Monte Cristo from Boom to Bust," *Snohomish County Review*, January 14, 1965.

109. Woodhouse, *Monte Cristo*, 76, 79.

110. *Seattle Post-Intelligencer*, March 12, 1894. The Comet Mine had a three-hundred-foot tunnel through the mountain that opened toward Glacier Basin.

111. "Ascent of a Mountain," 7.

112. *Everett Herald*, August 30, 1894; Denny, "Monte Cristo," 13.

113. "Monte Cristo Alps," *Seattle Post-Intelligencer*, March 12, 1894, 2.

114. Newell, "Washington's Monte Cristo," 1–2.

115. *Seattle Post-Intelligencer*, March 12, 1894, 2.

116. *Everett Herald*, September 27, November 29, 1894; Woodhouse, *Monte Cristo*, 129–30.

117. *Everett Herald*, November 26, 1897; Woodhouse, *Monte Cristo*, 151, 161–2. See *Seattle Post-Intelligencer*, December 13, 1897.

118. *Seattle Post-Intelligencer*, October 18, 1896. See also Hodges, *Mining in the Pacific Northwest*, 15–17, which includes the Webster Brown map of mining claims; and *19th Annual Report*, USGS, pt. 1 (1898), pt. 5 (1899), plates 76, 77, and 373.

119. There has been confusion regarding the position of Ida Pass. Its location is marked correctly on the Webster Brown map (which, however, reverses the positions of Halls Peak and Big Four

Mountain) and on a Forest Service map of 1914 (55 a [p] 32, Federal Records Center, Seattle). The current USGS topographic map locates the pass incorrectly.

120. *Everett Herald,* September 24, 1896.

121. *Seattle Post-Intelligencer,* October 18, 1896.

122. *Seattle Post-Intelligencer,* October 22, 1896.

123. Josiah E. Spurr, notebook 2, RG 57, NA. Josiah Spurr, one of the foremost American authorities on the geology of ore deposits, arrived at Monte Cristo in July 1900 to make a comprehensive survey of the district (see Spurr, "Ore Deposits of Monte Cristo," 785–865).

124. *Seattle Post-Intelligencer,* October 22, 1896.

125. *Northwest Illustrated Monthly Magazine,* May 10, 1892, 40.

126. *Everett Herald,* October 27, 1892. In one bizarre event at Marble Pass, a goat jumped from a telephone pole, caught its throat and choked to death (*Everett Herald,* July 1, 1898).

127. *Seattle Times,* April 23, 1896; Mount Baker National Forest Papers, Federal Records Center, Seattle, Wash.

128. Mount Baker National Forest Papers.

129. See Woodhouse, *Monte Cristo,* 10.

Chapter 15: Topographers and Geologists

1. USGS, Triangulation Records, RG 57, NA.

2. The Skykomish quadrangle was surveyed in 1897 and 1902; the Snoqualmie in 1897, 1898, 1900, and 1901; the Glacier Peak in 1897 and 1899; the Chelan in 1897 and 1898; the Methow in 1897 and 1899; the Stehekin in 1901 and 1902; the Chiwaukum in 1900 and 1901; the Mt. Stuart in 1896 and 1897; the Mt. Aix in 1900–02; and the Mt. Adams in 1903.

3. See *20th Annual Report,* USGS, pt. 1 (1899); *18th Annual Report,* USGS, pt. 1 (1897); *19th Annual Report,* USGS, pt. 1 (1898).

4. Nels Bruseth, "Tall, Little-Known Glacier Peak," *Seattle Times,* magazine section, May 18, 1947; *19th Annual Report,* USGS, pt. 1 (1898), 364–65.

5. *21st Annual Report,* USGS, pt. 1 (1900), 579–80.

6. Forester Martin Gorman wrote in 1899 (in "Eastern Part of Washington Forest Reserve") that the two mountains at the head of Railroad Creek were known locally as Bonanza and North Star. Bonanza was shown as "North Star" on the 1909 General Land Office map of Washington and on the Forest Service map of 1913, but as "Bonanza Peak" on the 1922 Forest Service map. On an early list of peaks made by the Washington Geological Survey, the altitude of "North Star" was given as 10,000 feet (it is now triangulated at 9,511 feet). The symbol should have been placed on what is now known as North Star, which surveyors climbed about 1904. Similar triangulation-station marks were placed during this period on Pyramid, Stormy, Sahale, and Glacier peaks (whose summits were occupied by surveyors).

7. Glee Davis, interview with the author; *Topography A* (album), USGS Library, Denver.

8. USGS, Triangulation Records, vol. 3, 187, RG 57, NA. Mt. Stuart may also have been climbed by Frank Tweedy, possibly during a railroad reconnaissance prior to 1895.

9. Sylvester Papers, University of Washington Libraries, Seattle. Except where otherwise stated, all quotations in the account of this expedition are from the Sylvester Papers.

10. USGS, Triangulation Records, vol. 4, 225, RG 57, NA.

11. Ibid. An azimuth is a reading of the bearing in degrees, minutes, and seconds to another triangulation station.

12. Sauk was described in 1898 as "a mountain forming the western rim of an extinct volcano. It has eight or nine small tops of nearly equal height" (USGS, Triangulation Records, vol. 4, 228a,

RG 57, NA). A foot trail, which horses could take halfway, led from von Pressentin's store to the summit.

13. USGS, Triangulation Records, vol. 4, 230–31, RG 57, NA.

14. USGS, Triangulation Records, vol. 4, 223, RG 57, NA.

15. USGS, Triangulation Records, vol. 4, 227, RG 57, NA.

16. USGS, Triangulation Records, vol. 4, 228, RG 57, NA.

17. Hart, "Unexplored Mountains," 403.

18. Goetzmann, *Exploration and Empire*, 592.

19. See Bartlett, *Great Surveys*, 148; and Goetzmann, *Exploration and Empire*, 434. For more on King, see Clifford M. Nelson and Mary C. Rabbitt, "The Role of Clarence King in the Advancement of Geology in the Public Service, 1867–1881," in Leviton, *Frontiers*, 19–35.

20. Emmons, notebook 1146, RG 57, NA. A *massif* is described as a large granite batholith (igneous rock mass) eroded to form a mountain. See Southwick, "Geology of the Alpine-Type Ultramafic Complex," 391–7; and Tabor et al., *Geologic Map of the Wenatchee*, 5, 11.

21. Dawson, notebook 2796, RG 45, vol. 134, microfilm C4838, National Archives of Canada.

22. See Billings, "Memorial," 115–21.

23. See Daly, *Geology of the North American Cordillera;* Monger, "Cordilleran Tectonics," 256; Monger, "Cordilleran Tectonics," 256.

24. Waters, "Memorial to Bailey Willis," 60.

25. Willis, "Canyons and Glaciers."

26. Waters, "Memorial to Bailey Willis," 58.

27. Ibid., 59.

28. Russell adapted an 1896 manuscript map by H.M. Sarvant and G.F. Evans that included early glacier names, publishing it with his account of the exploration. The party probably crossed the Mt. Pleasant–Fay Peak ridge. Russell was unaware of the 1884 ascent of the Fobes party. Russell, "Glaciers of Mount Rainier," 358, 362.

29. Ibid., 369–71.

30. Ibid., 378.

31. Willis, notebook 1212, USGS Library, Denver. Roches moutonnées are glacially rounded outcrops. Aiguilles are rock needles in an alpine setting.

32. Willis, notebook 1220, USGS Library, Denver.

33. Willis, notebook 199, USGS Library, Denver.

34. Mary C. Rabbitt, "I. C. Russell: Frontiersman of Science," in Leviton, *Frontiers*, 79.

35. See Russell, "Glaciers of Mount Rainier," 416–23, and Russell, "Geology of the Cascade Mountains," 140–4. His photograph album depicts his ascent of Glacier Peak (USGS Library).

36. Smith, notebook 1202, USGS Library, Denver.

37. Smith, notebook 1209, USGS Library, Denver. See also Curtis, notebook 1214, USGS Library, Denver; Smith, "Rocks of Mount Rainier," 417–23.

38. Smith, notebook 1209, notebook 1222, USGS Library, Denver.

39. Smith, notebook 1223, USGS Library, Denver. See Smith and Calkins, "Description of the Snoqualmie Quadrangle," 4–5.

40. Smith's papers include "Geology and Physiography of Central Washington," *Professional Paper No. 19*, USGS (1903), pp. 9–34; *Description of the Mount Stuart Quadrangle, Washington*, Folio No. 106, USGS Geologic Atlas (1904); and *Description of the Ellensburg Quadrangle, Washington*, Folio No. 86, USGS Geologic Atlas (1903).

41. See *Geographical Review*, April 1926; Curtis, notebook 1216, USGS Library, Denver; see also Smith, notebook 1211, and Curtis, notebook 1216, USGS Library, Denver.

42. Mendenhall, notebook 1231, USGS Library, Denver.

Chapter 16: The Second Northwest Boundary Survey

1. International Boundary Commission (hereafter IBC), "Narrative of Field Reports," 92.

2. See Baker, *Survey of the Northwestern Boundary.*

3. *Northwest Boundary Report*, U.S. Coast and Geodetic Survey, USGS (1901), 32. Bailey Willis and F. Leslie Ransome received the same instructions to examine the terrain eastward to the Rocky Mountains. See also *Bangor (Maine) News*, May 14, 1901.

4. Riggs to S.B. Jones, January 22, 1937, IBC correspondence. The difference between the geodetic and astronomic parallels at the monument at Sumas was +284.26 meters. Eastward, into the mountains, the difference dropped very rapidly, to a low of −236 meters.

5. IBC, "Narrative of Field Reports," 37. See also E. 285, RG 76, NA.

6. IBC, "Narrative of Field Reports," 38–9.

7. IBC, *Joint Report,* 40. See also *23rd Annual Report*, USGS (1902), 148–50. The report of the 1901 season included an atlas containing six maps, three diagrams, and a photo album.

8. See Barnard, photo album (1901), NA.

9. Smith to mother, June 30, 1901, Smith Papers, USGS Library, Denver; Smith, notebook 1232, and Calkins, notebook 1235, USGS Library, Denver. The reconnaissance is summarized in IBC, "Narrative of Field Reports." There is in fact no glacial silt in the outlet stream, for it has all settled out in the lake.

10. Smith to Grace (wife), July 28, 1901, Smith Papers.

11. Smith to Grace, August 4, 1901; Smith to "Little Chum," August 4, 1901, Smith Papers.

12. Smith, notebook 1232, USGS Library, Denver.

13. Ibid.

14. Ibid. Later investigations confirmed Smith's observations on the former glacier.

15. Smith to Grace, August 28, 1901, Smith Papers; Smith, notebook 1232, USGS Library, Denver.

16. Smith, notebook 1232, USGS Library, Denver.

17. IBC, "Narrative of Field Reports," 143–4. Smith's was one of the first descriptions of the Skagit River valley.

18. IBC, "Narrative of Field Reports," 156.

19. See Calkins's sketch maps, USGS Library, Denver.

20. IBC, *Joint Report,* 37–8.

21. Rodger, "Photography and the International Boundary," 7. The British commission had taken photographs during the first boundary survey, but not for surveying. Dr. C.B.R. Kennerly of the American commission also had done some photography, but there is no record of its use for surveying. See Kennerly Papers, 1855–60, box 1, Record Unit 7202; and Spencer F. Baird Collection, 1793–1923, box 26, Record Unit 7002, Smithsonian Institution Archives, Washington, D.C.

22. Daly's *Geology of the North American Cordillera at the Forty-ninth Parallel* was published as an appendix to the report of the chief astronomer (Ottawa, 1910), then republished in 1912 as Memoir No. 38 (in three parts) by the Geological Survey of Canada. Part 3 contains the earliest topographic maps of the boundary area.

23. Daly, "Western Part of the International Boundary," 41-a.

24. Ibid., 43.

25. Ibid., 45-a; Daly, *Geology of the North American Cordillera*, pt. 1, 501.

26. IBC, *Joint Report,* 67, 69. A line of levels was run from the USGS benchmark near Barron down the Pasayten River some thirty miles to provide a check on vertical angle elevations carried out from the Similkameen River.

27. Ibid., 65–66, 70.

28. See survey notes by D. L. Reaburn, August 9, 1904, GB 1904, E. 285, RG 76, NA.

29. See triangulation fieldbooks, GTZ 1904-B, box 5, 43–44, E. 285, RG 76, NA. See also GH 1904-B, 83 NW, box 2, E. 285, RG 76, NA.

30. Triangulation fieldbooks, GTZ 1905-B, box 5, E. 285, RG 76, NA. Presumably, they climbed to the summit of Cathedral; one entry states, "On Rock cliff slope of Cathedral," which might indicate they triangulated below the summit. See IBC, *Joint Report,* 77, 419.

31. Triangulation fieldbooks, GTZ 1904-B, box 5, E. 285, RG 76, NA. September 6, a date mentioned in another entry, may have been when they made their first ascent.

32. Triangulation fieldbooks, GTZ 1905-R, box 5, 22, E. 285, RG 76, NA.

33. Triangulation fieldbooks, GTZ 1904-B, box 5, E. 285, RG 76, NA. No other details of the ascent are given in the fieldbooks.

34. Triangulation fieldbooks, GH 1905-B, NW, E. 285, RG 76, NA. See also GH 1905, 83 N, vol. 4, 6–7, E. 285, RG 76, NA.

35. Triangulation fieldbooks, GTZ 1904-B, box 5, E. 285, RG 76, NA. See also IBC, *Joint Report,* 337.

36. Triangulation fieldbooks, GTZ 1904-B, box 5, E. 285, RG 76, NA. See also GTZ 1905-R, box 5, E. 285, RG 76, NA.

37. IBC, *Joint Report,* 336; Riggs, "Ascent of Glacier Peak," 161.

38. Triangulation fieldbooks, GH 1905, 83 NW, vol. 5, box 3; GTZ 1905-R, box 5, E. 285, RG 76, NA. See also Riggs, "Ascent of Glacier Peak."

39. IBC, *Joint Report,* 336–7. The first ascent of Davis had been made in 1897 by the USGS.

40. See triangulation fieldbooks, 83 N, box 3, 14–19, E. 285, RG 76, NA.

41. IBC, *Joint Report,* 71.

42. Triangulation fieldbooks, GH 1906-R, box 3, E. 285, RG 76, NA. See also IBC, *Joint Report,* 336. The documentation regarding Robertson and Logan is unclear, but they most likely were the party that made this ascent. An ascent of "Boston" (Sahale) Peak for triangulation was also made in 1905.

43. Triangulation fieldbooks, GTZ 1905-R, box 5, E. 285, RG 76, NA.

44. Triangulation fieldbooks, GH-1905, 83 NW, vol. 5, E. 285, RG 76, NA. See also GTZ 1905-R, box 5, E. 285, RG 76, NA; and IBC, *Joint Report,* 417.

45. Triangulation fieldbooks, GH 1906-R, box 3, E. 285, RG 76, NA.

46. IBC, *Joint Report,* 79. The field party was the same as in 1905, except that W.P. Near had replaced J.W. McArthur.

47. Ibid., 80–1.

48. The IBC's *Joint Report* states that the party made the ascent in 1908 (415), but the position of the photo on page 82 suggests that the first ascent may have been in 1906.

49. IBC, *Joint Report,* 81.

50. Ibid., 83, 85 (photo).

51 Ibid., 87.

52. Ibid., 89.

53. E.T. de Coeli is listed as observer for this station; J.J. McArthur likely took part in the ascent (IBC, *Joint Report,* 415).

54. Triangulation fieldbooks, GH 1908, 83 NE, E. 285, RG 76, NA. The fieldbooks contain a triangulation map (triangulation fieldbooks, GH 1908, 83 NW, E. 285, RG 76, NA).

55. See photo, E. 287, RG 76, Cartographic Archives, NA.

56. IBC, *Joint Report,* 337–8, 415–19.

57. See E. 286, RG 76, NA.

58. Riggs to Jones, January 22, 1937, IBC correspondence.

Chapter 17: Manging the Mountain Lands

1. Gannett, "Forest Reserves," 26.

2. Russell, "Glaciers of Mount Rainier," 362.

3. Cairnes, *Coquihalla Area;* Plummer Papers, Washington State University Library, Pullman. See also Plummer's "Forest Conditions in the Cascade Range."

4. Rabbitt, *Minerals, Lands, and Geology* vol. 2; Mount Baker National Forest Papers, Federal Records Center, Seattle. See also Gorman, "Eastern Part of Washington Forest Reserve," 317–18, 349. Near the head of Twenty-five Mile Creek, he studied a tract of lodgepole pine and subalpine fir that fires and sheep had desolated.

5. Mount Baker National Forest Papers, Federal Records Center, Seattle. See also North Cascades Study Team, *North Cascades,* p. 304. The Public Lands Commission, appointed by President Theodore Roosevelt, found that the previous lack of control over public lands had allowed millions of acres of valuable grazing lands to be seriously depleted (*Report of the Public Lands Commission,* Senate Doc. 1103, 58th Cong., 3d sess.); the findings of this commission had a strong bearing on the creation of the forest reserves.

6. U.S. Forest Service Papers, VF 1360, University of Washington Libraries, Seattle.

7. Snoqualmie National Forest Papers, Federal Records Center, Seattle.

8. Mount Baker National Forest Papers.

9. Thomas Thompson Papers, Washington State University Library, Pullman.

10. Pitzer, "Upper Skagit Valley"; Thomas Thompson Papers, Washington State University Library, Pullman. See also Jenkins, *Last Frontier,* 115.

11. Thomas Thompson Papers, Washington State University Library, Pullman..

12. MacArthur and Flach, "Lage Wernstedt," 146–7; Flach, "Mapping Reflections."

13. Flach, "Mapping Reflections."

14. The previous planimetric map (1926) portrays no skeleton for the Picket Range. How incompletely this area was known is suggested by the exaggerated length of McMillan Creek and the absence of Luna Creek.

15. Burgess, personal communications, April 3 and May 14, 1974; Burge, interview with the author, October 7, 1975.

16. Burge, interview with the author, October 7, 1975; Archie C. Walter to Roland C. Burgess, December 15, 1975.

17. See Fred J. Berry Papers, University of Washington Libraries, Seattle.

18. Sylvester Papers, University of Washington Libraries, Seattle.

19. Ibid.

20. Ibid.

22. Rakestraw, *History of Forest Conservation.*

23. Wenatchee National Forest Papers, Wenatchee, Washington. See also William O. Burgess, tape recording, University of Washington Libraries, Seattle (Burgess was a Forest Service grazing ranger); Plummer, report (1900), 36–7, Plummer Papers; Douglas, "Preliminary Biological Survey"; William F. Burge, "Early Experiences in the Forest Service," typescript, U.S. Forest Service records, Portland.

24. Mount Baker–Snoqualmie National Forest Papers; see photo albums, vol. 16, where sheep are pictured on Benchmark Mountain and a herder cabin at White Pass is shown in a 1924 photo.

25. See album 16, Snoqualmie National Forest Papers, Federal Records Center, Seattle.

26. Lyman, "Mount Adams Outing," 168; Burge, "Early Experiences."

27. Plummer, report (1900), 47.

28. *Timber-Lines* 14 (June 1960), 60.

29. H.A. Annen Papers, University of Washington Libraries, Seattle.

30. Jenkins, *Last Frontier,* 32, 34; North Cascades Study Team, *North Cascades,* 327; Jenkins, *Last Frontier.*

31. Harold Engles, interview with the author.

32. Engles, personal communications, 1973, 1975.

33. U.S. Forest Service records. See also Mount Baker National Forest, vf 679, University of Washington Libraries.

34. Park superintendent's annual report for 1917, Mount Rainier National Park Library. In 1920, the Park Service proposed building a fire lookout on Mt. Rainier's summit.

35. Newton Field, "A Book of Historical Facts and Figures," U.S. Forest Service (1950), Mount Baker–Snoqualmie National Forest Papers, Mountlake Terrace, Wash.

36. North Cascades Study Team, *North Cascades,* 330.

37. Mount Baker–Snoqualmie National Forest Papers,

38. Photographs among the Mount Baker–Snoqualmie National Forest Papers testify to the extensive exploration done, although documentation of early Forest Service exploration is meager.

39. McIntyre, "Mather Memorial Highway."

40. Pitzer, "Upper Skagit Valley."

41. Ibid.

42. Ibid. See also North Cascades Study Team, *North Cascades,* 115.

43. The striking color is a result of the suspension of glacially ground "rock flour."

44. See Pitzer, "Upper Skagit Valley," 79–80.

45. John A. Biggs to John A. Nassilkas, chairman of the Federal Power Commission, December 6, 1971; and State of Washington Position Statement, 2, both in the Washington State Archives, Olympia.

46. Fluharty, "Relicensing the Skagit Dams," 2.

47. Charles Easton, "Mt. Baker," Whatcom Museum of History and Art, Bellingham, Washington.

48. Connelly, "Mount Baker Marathon."

49. Martinson, *Wilderness above the Sound,* 12.

50. Russell, "Glaciers of Mount Rainier," 412.

51. Ibid., 363.

52. Ibid., 364.

53. Mount Rainier National Park archives.

54. Martinson, "Mountain in the Sky," 14, 15; *Tacoma Daily Ledger,* May 8, July 8, 1883. See Everett Smith Papers, University of Washington Libraries, Seattle. In 1886, the railroad charged $2.40 for the thirty-mile trip.

55. Martinson, "Mountain in the Sky," 16; Shields, *Cruisings in the Cascades.*

56. The map Willis made after the expedition was drawn in Germany and printed in *Berghaus Physical Atlas,* no. 6 (1887). This first map of the mountain identified the Mowich Glacier as "Von Bailey Willis Glacier."

57. Von Zittel, "Volcanos and Glaciers," See also *Alpine Journal* 15, no. 3 (1891), 383.

58. Robert N. McIntyre, "Short History of Mount Rainier National Park" (1952), Mount Rainier National Park Library, Tahoma Woods, Wash., 73.

59. McIntyre, "Short History," 55; Martinson, "Mountain in the Sky," 16.

60. Farquhar, "Naming America's Mountains," 60–2.

61. Farquhar points out that the spelling "Regnier" was also applied on Albert Gallatin's 1836 *Map of the Indian Tribes of North America* and the 1837 map to accompany William Irving's *Journal*

of Captain Bonneville ("Naming America's Mountains"). Meany, *Geographic Names*.

62. Winthrop, *Canoe and the Saddle*, 39.

63. Stevens, "Ascent of Takhoma," 513, n. 1.

64. Quoted in Conover, *Proposal to Change the Name of Mount Rainier*, 11. This publication's purpose was to disseminate knowledge about the Northwest—its resources, opportunities for acquiring land, and expanding population. It was called *Northwest Illustrated Monthly Magazine* from 1885 to 1898 and *Northwest Magazine* from 1898 to 1903.

65. Martinson, "Mountain in the Sky," 54, citing *Congressional Record*, 55th Cong., 3d sess., 32, pt. 3, 2667.

66. *Seattle Daily Times*, March 4, 1899, 4.

67. See Denman, *Name of Mount Tacoma*; and *Tacoma Daily Ledger*, March 3, 1899.

68. See park superintendent's annual reports for 1904, 1905, and 1906, Mount Rainier National Park Library; "Glaciers and Gasoline." At the time, there were only three national parks in the United States where autos were permitted.

69. Francois Matthes Papers, Mount Rainier National Park Library; Box 3, folder 3-25, Macy Papers. In that year (1916), Congress established the National Park Service, under the Department of the Interior. Asahel Curtis was chief of the Mount Rainier National Park Committee at the time.

70. The Rainier National Park Company spent a large sum on a spacious Yakima Park resort and deluxe cabins (see box 1, Macy Papers).

71. Conrad Wirth to the Secretary of the Interior, March 10, 1961, folder 3-14, Macy Papers; Martinson, "Mountain in the Sky."

72. Box 3, Macy Papers.

73. Box 3, Macy Papers.

74. Wallace Stegner to David E. Pesonen, December 3, 1960, in Brower, *Wilderness*, 97–8.

SOURCES

The primary and secondary literature on the exploration and survey of the American West is vast. A familiarity with at least the broad outlines of Western history is useful to fully understand events in the northern Cascades. Below is a discussion of some of the most important publications, followed by a bibliography of published works and archival sources consulted.

For readers interested in the geography of the northern Cascades, *Landforms of Washington* (1970), by Don J. Easterbrook and David A. Rahm, is an excellent source. For a review of the forest cover, see Stephen Whitney, *Western Forests* (1985). On the subject of Native American culture in this region, we are fortunate to have the writings of James A. Teit, George Gibbs, and Erna Gunther, whose *Indian Life on the Northwest Coast of North America* (1972) is a classic guide. Most useful also is Frederick W. Hodge, *Handbook of American Indians North of Mexico* (1907–10).

The best overall early introduction to the Spanish, British, and American navigators who explored the Pacific Northwest's coastlines is Hubert H. Bancroft's *History of the Northwest Coast* (vol. 1, 1884). Other valuable sources include W. Kaye Lamb's edition of the voyages of Capt. George Vancouver, Murray Morgan's portrayal of events of discovery nearer the Cascade Range, the works of Henry R. Wagner and Herbert K. Beals on the important early Spanish voyages, and Comdr. Charles Wilkes's *Narrative of the United States Exploring Expedition* (1849). Carl I. Wheat's five-volume *Mapping the Transmississippi West* (1957–63) assembles a large number of remarkable maps of western North America.

The pathways of the early overland pioneers are chronicled in such classic works as Gary Moulton's edition of the journals of Lewis and Clark as well as Reuben Gold Thwaites's thirty-two-volume series *Early Western Travels, 1748–1846*. We also have the journals of David Thompson and Alexander Henry the Younger (edited by Elliott Coues) and Milo Milton Quaife's Lakeside Classics, including the travels of Alexander Mackenzie and Alexander Ross. For a rather sentimental view of the Cascade Range by an early visitor, see Theodore Winthrop's *The Canoe and the Saddle*. For a much later descriptive account of vistas, see William Watson Woollen, *The Inside Passage to Alaska, 1792–1920* (vol. 1, 1924).

Introductions to the history of the Hudson's Bay Company can be found in Frederick Merk, *Fur Trade and Empire* (1968) and Hiram M. Chittenden, *The American Fur Trade of the Far West* (1954). For another study of the HBC, see Arthur Morton, *Sir George Simpson: Overseas Governor of the Hudson's Bay Company* (1944). The Hudson's Bay Record Society has accumulated vast materials on this commercial enterprise. Gordon Davidson's *The North West Company* (1918) tells the story of a rival trading firm.

The most readable review of the vast subject of the army on the frontier is William T. Jackson's *Wagon Roads West* (1952). A pioneering work on the Corps of Topographical Engineers is Edward S. Wallace, *The Great Reconnaissance* (1955). There is also William H. Goetzmann's superb *Army Exploration in the American West, 1803–1863* (1959).

Many government publications, particularly the House and Senate document series, contain material on army explorations. The annual reports of the Secretary of War include reports from the various military districts; from 1839 to 1861 they also include the annual report of the Chief of Topographical Engineers. These records illustrate the wide range of projects undertaken by the army—most importantly, the exploration of the West through railroad surveys (see especially the annual reports for 1853–58).

The reports of some of the army exploring expeditions were published as separate documents, the model for the Topographical Corps being John Charles Frémont's *Report of the Exploring Expedition to the Rocky Mountains in the Year 1842, and to Oregon and North California in the Years 1843–1844.* (Frémont's 1887 *Memoirs* contains accounts of his Western explorations, supplementing his official reports.) In the northern Cascades, Lt. Henry Hubbard Pierce's 1882 exploration was described in his *Report of an Expedition from Fort Colville to Puget Sound.* The subsequent explorations by Lts. Backus, Goethals, and Rodman in the same region are far less well known because they are embodied only in obscure government documents. Several engineering reports were made as a result of river surveys; the most important are those of Lt. Thomas W. Symons in the early 1880s.

The outstanding publication of the Topographical Corps is the twelve-volume series of Pacific Railroad reports (originally submitted as congressional documents) entitled *Reports of Explorations and Surveys, to Ascertain the Most Practicable and Economical Route for a Railroad from the Mississippi River to the Pacific Ocean.* This official mid-century set contains the comprehensive field journals and correspondence of the various railroad exploring parties of 1853–55, as well as scientific reviews on botany and zoology. Included in volume 1 are the controversial route evaluations by Secretary of War Jefferson Davis and Gen. Andrew A. Humphreys. Volume 11 has Lt. Gouverneur K. Warren's landmark "Memoir to Accompany the Map of the Territory of the United States from the Mississippi River to the Pacific Ocean." The Isaac I. Stevens report on a northern route through the Cascades includes the details of Capt. George B. McClellan's surveys and the scientific observations of George Gibbs. Also included in the report is Frederick W. Lander's exploration of a line from Fort Vancouver to the emigrant route (sponsored by the territorial legislature of Oregon). A later review of these explorations is provided in George L. Albright, *Official Explorations for the Pacific Railroad* (1921).

The most accessible review of the Northwest Boundary Survey is Marcus Baker's summary report, *Survey of the Northwestern Boundary of the United States, 1857–1861* (1900). Included are the full texts of the reports of Commissioner Archibald Campbell (February 3, 1869) and Lt. John G. Parke (November 12, 1869). Relevant reports are contained in House Exec. Doc. 86, 40th Cong., 3d sess., and Senate Exec. Doc. 29, 40th Cong., 2d sess. There is also the 1937 review *Joint Report upon the Survey and Demarcation of the Boundary between the United States and Canada from the Gulf of Georgia to the Northwesternmost Point of Lake of the Woods.*

The political and diplomatic events of the survey and its progress can be followed in *Foreign Office Correspondence, 1856–71*, edited by Otto Klotz (1902), and in the summary by Herman J. Deutsch ("A Contemporary Report on the 49° Boundary Survey," 1962). George Gibbs described the geography of the boundary belt in "Physical Geography of the North-Western Boundary of the United States" (1873–74).

A valuable work dealing with the post–Civil War frontier is Earl S. Pomeroy, *The Territories and the United States, 1861–1890* (1947). Equally important are the works of Dale L. Morgan, E.W. Gilbert's *The Exploration of Western America, 1800–1850* (1933), and William Goetzmann's excellent *Exploration and Empire* (1966).

Useful books more directly related to the northern Cascades are David Lavender, *Land of Giants: The Drive to the Pacific Northwest, 1750–1950* (1958); Oscar Osburn Winther, *The Old Oregon Country* (1950); Dorothy O. Johansen and Charles M. Gates, *Empire of the Columbia* (1957); Ray Hoard Glassley, *Pacific Northwest Indian Wars* (1953), which provides information on conflicts that affected settlement near the Cascade Range; and Edmond S. Meany, *History of the State of Washington* (1909).

A study of early western Canada would not be complete without reading Frederic W. Howay, *British Columbia* (1928); Walter N. Sage, *Sir James Douglas and British Columbia* (1930); and *British Columbia Chronicle, 1847–1871*, by G.P.V. and Helen B. Akrigg. Lt. Richard Charles Mayne's *Four Years in British Columbia and Vancouver-Island* provides interesting anecdotes. A sense of the region's wilderness is given in John Keast Lord, *The Naturalist in Vancouver Island and British Columbia* (1866).

Books on railroads are many. The standard, Robert E. Riegal's *Story of Western Railroads* (1926), can be complemented by James Blaine Hedges, *Henry Villard and the Railways of the Northwest* (1930). Edwin Ferry Johnson's *Railroad to the Pacific* (1854) is typical of the private surveys for transcontinental railroads.

Annual reports and bulletins published by the U.S. Geological Survey after 1879 include material relevant to the northern Cascades—particularly the writings of Bailey Willis, Israel C. Russell, and George Otis Smith. *Frontiers of Geological Exploration of Western North America* (1979), edited by Alan E. Leviton, includes biographies of leading scientists. See also Wallace Stegner, *Beyond the Hundredth Meridian* (1954), on the U.S. Geological Survey; and George P. Merrill, *The First One Hundred Years of American Geology* (1924).

There are numerous printed guides to materials on various subjects that were useful for this study. The U.S. National Archives' *Records Relating to the International Boundary* (Preliminary Inventory 170) is an essential beginning for this subject. The *Catalog of the Exhibition of Geographical Exploration and Topographical Mapping by the United States Government* (publication 53-2, 1952) describes many important maps housed in the Cartographic Records Division. For materials in Canada, see D. W. Parker, *Guide to the Materials for United States History in Canadian Archives* (1913).

Other useful publications are *Handbook of Manuscripts in the Library of Congress*; D. W. Parker, *Calendar of Papers in Washington Archives Relating to the Territories of the United States* (1911); Charles W. Smith, *A Union List of Manuscripts in Libraries of the Pacific Northwest* (1931); *North Cascades Archival Resources in Washington State Repositories* (University of Washington Libraries, 1974); and Maureen J. Leverty, *Guide to the Records of the Northern Pacific Branch Lines, Subsidiaries, and Related Companies* (1977).

Important periodicals include *The American West*, *The Beaver*, *British Columbia Historical Quarterly*, *Canadian Geographical Journal*, *Canadian Historical Review*, *Century Magazine*, *Harper's Monthly Magazine*, *The Mazama*, *Minnesota History*, *The Mountaineer*, *The Northwest* (after 1885, *Northwest Illustrated Monthly Magazine*), *Oregon Historical Quarterly*, *Overland Monthly*, *Pacific Monthly*, *Pacific Northwest Quarterly*, *Sierra Club Bulletin*, *Sunset*, *Washington Historical Quarterly*, and *West Shore*. Other valuable sources are the many professional scientific articles (especially geological papers), university theses on history and geology, environmental statements and reviews, travel books, emigrant guidebooks, promotional literature, and endless newspaper files.

Published Works

Adams, Nigel B. *The Holden Mine: Discovery to Production, 1896–1938.* Tacoma: Washington State Historical Society, 1981.

Akrigg, G. P. V., and Helen B. Akrigg. *British Columbia Chronicle, 1847–1871.* Vancouver, B.C.: Discovery Press, 1977.

Alley, B. F. *History of Clarke County, Washington Territory.* Portland, Ore: Washington Publishing, 1885.

Amoss, Pamela. *Coast Salish Spirit Dancing: The Survival of an Ancestral Religion.* Seattle: University of Washington Press, 1978.

Anastasio, Angelo. "The Southern Plateau: An Ecological Analysis of Intergroup Relations." *Northwest Anthropological Research Notes* 6, no. 2 (1972): 209–29.

Anderson, Ada Woodruff. "Lake Chelan and the American Alps." *Pacific Monthly* 11, no. 5 (1904): 300–308.

Anderson, Alexander C. *Hand-book and Map to the Gold Region of Frazer's and Thompson's Rivers, with Table of Distances.* San Francisco: J. J. LeCount, 1858.

Anderson, Bern. *Surveyor of the Sea: The Life and Voyages of Captain George Vancouver.* Seattle: University of Washington Press, 1960.

Anderson, Donald L. "Prospecting in Washington." Information Circular No. 31, Washington Division of Mines and Geology. Olympia: State Printing Plant, 1959.

Arnold, Lt. Richard. "Lieutenant Richard Arnold's Report on the Military Road from Wallah-Wallah to Steilacoom," January 26, 1855. In *Report of the Secretary of War*, pp. 532–8. House Exec. Doc. 1, 34th Cong., 1st sess., 1855. Serial 841.

"The Ascent of a Mountain." *Northwest Illustrated Monthly Magazine* 13, no. 8 (1895).

Ayres, H. B. "Washington Forest Reserve." In *19th Annual Report*, USGS, pt. 5 (1899), pp. 283–313.

Bagley, Clarence B. *History of Seattle*. Vol. 1. Chicago: S. J. Clarke, 1916.

————, ed. "Journal of Occurrences at Nisqually House, 1833." *WHQ* 6, no. 3 (1915): 179–97.

Baker, Marcus. *Survey of the Northwestern Boundary of the United States, 1857–1861*. Bulletin No. 174, USGS. 1900.

Bancroft, Hubert H. *History of British Columbia*. San Francisco: The History Co., 1887.

————. *History of the Northwest Coast*. Vol. 1. San Francisco: A. L. Bancroft, 1884.

Barker, Frances B., ed. *The Wilkes Expedition: Puget Sound and the Oregon Country*. Olympia: Washington State Capital Museum, 1987.

Barry, J. Neilson. "The Indians in Washington, Their Distribution by Languages." *OHQ* 28, no. 2 (1927): 147–62.

————. "Oregon Boundaries." *OHQ* 33, no. 3 (1932): 259–67.

————. "Pickering's Journey to Fort Colville in 1841." *WHQ* 20, no. 1 (1929): 54–63.

Bartlett, Richard A. *Great Surveys of the American West*. Norman: University of Oklahoma Press, 1962.

Basque, Garnet. "Ned McGowan's War." *Canadian West* 2, no. 7 (1991): 52–7.

Bates, Malcom S. *Three Fingers: The Mountain, the Men, and a Lookout*. Seattle: Cloudcap Press, 1987.

Bauerman, Hilary. "Report on the Geology of the Country near the Forty-ninth Parallel of North Latitude West of the Rocky Mountains." In *Report of Progress, 1882–3–4*, GSC, pp. 5b–42b.

Baxter, J. C. "Construction Plans and Methods." In *The Eight-Mile Cascade Tunnel, Great Northern Railway: A Symposium*, 218–68. American Society of Civil Engineers Papers, 1931.

Bayley, George. "Ascent of Mount Tacoma." *Overland Monthly*, 2d ser., 8 (September 1886): 266–78.

Beals, Herbert K., trans. and ed. *For Honor and Country: The Diary of Bruno de Hezeta*. Portland: Oregon Historical Society Press, 1985.

————. *Juan Pérez on the Northwest Coast: Six Documents of His Expedition in 1774*. Portland: Oregon Historical Society Press, 1989.

Beckey, Fred. *Cascade Alpine Guide: Climbing and High Routes*. Vol. 1. *Columbia River to Stevens Pass*. 3d ed. Seattle: The Mountaineers, 2000.

————. *Cascade Alpine Guide: Climbing and High Routes*. Vol. 2. *Stevens Pass to Rainy Pass*. 2d ed. Seattle: The Mountaineers, 1996.

————. *Cascade Alpine Guide: Climbing and High Routes*. Vol. 3. *Rainy Pass to Fraser River*. 2d ed. Seattle: The Mountaineers, 1995.

————. *Challenge of the North Cascades*. 2d ed. Seattle: The Mountaineers, 1996.

Beckham, Stephen Dow. "George Gibbs, 1815–1873: Historian and Ethnologist." Ph.D. diss., University of California, Los Angeles, 1969.

Begg, Alexander H. *History of British Columbia: From Its Earliest Discovery to the Present Time*. Toronto: William Briggs, 1894.

Bennett, Lee A. *Cultural Resource Overview*. Okanogan, Wash.: Okanogan National Forest, 1979.

Berland, Sidney. "Strategy Strife on the Indian War Front." *Columbia* 2, no. 1 (1988).

Berton, Pierre. *The Last Spike: The Great Railway, 1881–1885*. Markham, Ont.: Penguin Books Canada, 1989.

Billings, Marland P. "Memorial to Reginald A. Daly." In *Proceedings for 1958*, Geological Society of America, pp. 115–21.

Bischoff, William N. *The Yakima Campaign of 1856*. Reprinted from *Mid-America*, new ser., 20, no. 3 (1949).

—————. "The Yakima Indian War, 1855–56." Ph.D. diss., Loyola University, 1950.

Bonney, William P. *History of Pierce County, Washington*. Chicago: Pioneer Historical Publishing, 1927.

—————. "Naming Stampede Pass." *WHQ* 12, no. 4 (1921): 272–8.

Borden, Charles E. "Peopling and Early Cultures of the Pacific Northwest: A View from British Columbia, Canada." *Science* 203 (March 9, 1979).

Brackenridge, William. "Our First Official Horticulturist—The Brackenridge Journal." Parts 1–3. Ed. O. B. Sperlin. *WHQ* 21, nos. 3–4 (1930): 218–29, 298–305; 22, no. 1 (1931): 42–58.

Braun, Leo. "History of Sauk-Suiattle Tribe." *Concrete Herald* 50 (1951).

Brown, Allison. "Ascent of Mount Rainier by the Ingraham Glacier." *The Mountaineer* 13 (1920): 49–50.

Brown, E. H., and R. C. Ellis. *Geologic Excursions in the Pacific Northwest*. Bellingham: Western Washington University, 1977.

Brown, Lloyd A. *The Story of Maps*. New York: Bonanza Books, 1949.

Brown, William C. *Early Okanogan History*. Okanogan, Wash.: Press of the *Okanogan Independent*, 1911.

—————. *The Indian Side of the Story*. Spokane, Wash.: C. W. Hill, 1961.

—————. "Old Fort Okanogan and the Okanogan Trail." *OHQ* 15, no. 1 (1914): 1–38.

Bruseth, Nels. *Indian Stories and Legends of the Stillaguamish, Sauks, and Allied Tribes*. 2d ed. Arlington, Wash.: Arlington Times Press, 1950.

—————. "Tall, Little-Known Glacier Peak." *Seattle Times*, magazine section, May 18, 1947.

Bryce, George. "Alexander Ross." *The Canadian Magazine* 44 (June 1917): 163–8.

—————. "Alexander Ross, Fur Trader and Philanthropist." *Queen's Quarterly* 11 (July 1903): 26–56.

Buchanan, Charles M. "The Origin of Mounts Baker and Rainier: The Indian Legend." *The Mountaineer* 9 (December 1916): 32–5.

Buerge, David R. "The Sacred Snoqualmie." *Seattle Weekly*, August 5, 1987, 24–31.

Bunte, Alfred. "Burlington Northern and the Legacy of Mount Saint Helens." *PNQ* 74, no. 3 (1983): 116–23.

Burnett, Peter H. "Letters of Peter H. Burnett." *OHQ* 3, no. 4 (1902): 398–426.

Buzzetti, Bea. *The Mount St. Helens Area, Historical and Legendary*. Longview, Wash., 1951.

Cairnes, Clive E. *Coquihalla Area, British Columbia*. Memoir No. 139, GSC. 1924.

—————." Reconnaissance of Silver Creek, Skagit and Similkameen Rivers, Yale District, British Columbia." In *Summary Report*, pt. a, Canada Department of Mines. 1923.

Cameron, John N. "The History and Natural Resources of Manning Park." Thesis, University of British Columbia, 1970.

Campbell, Marjorie Wilkins. *The North West Company*. Vancouver, B.C.: Douglas and McIntyre, 1973.

Canfield, Thomas H. *Northern Pacific Railroad: Partial Report to the Board of Directors, of a Portion of a Reconnoissance Made in the Summer of 1869, between Lake Superior and the Pacific Ocean*. New York, 1870.

Carey, Charles H. "British Side of Oregon Question." *OHQ* 36, no. 3 (1935): 263–94.

Carithers, Ward, and A. K. Guard. "Geology and Ore Deposits of Snohomish County, Washington." Bulletin No. 36, Washington Division of Mines and Geology. Olympia, 1945.

Carpenter, Cecelia S. *Fort Nisqually: A Documented History of Indian and British Interaction*. Tacoma, Wash.: Tahoma Research Service, 1986.

Carver, Jonathan. *Travels through the Interior Parts of North-America in the Years 1766, 1767, and 1768*. London, 1778.

Chase, Evelyn H. *Mountain Climber: George B. Bayley, 1840–1894*. Palo Alto, Calif.: Pacific Books, 1981.

Chittenden, Hiram Martin, and Alfred Talbot Richardson. *Life, Letters, and Travels of Father Pierre-Jean De Smet, S.J., 1801–1873*. Vol. 2. New York: Francis P. Harper, 1905.

Clark, Ella E. *Indian Legends of the Pacific Northwest*. Berkeley: University of California Press, 1953.

Clevinger, Woodrow R. "Migration of Southern Appalachian Mountain Highlanders." *PNQ* 33, no. 1 (1942): 3–25.

——————. "The Western Washington Cascades: A Study of Migration and Mountain Settlement." Ph.D. diss., University of Washington, 1955.

Cline, Gloria Griffin. *Exploring the Great Basin*. Norman: University of Oklahoma Press, 1963.

Coleman, Edmund T. "The Ascent of Mount Rainier." In *Illustrated Travels: A Record of Discovery, Geography, and Adventure*, vol. 5. London, 1873.

——————. "Mountaineering on the Pacific." *Harper's New Monthly Magazine* 39 (November 1869): 793–817.

——————. "Mountains and Mountaineering in the Far West." Part 2. *Alpine Journal* 8, no. 59 (1878): 387–90.

——————. "Puget Sound and the Northern Pacific Railroad." *PNQ* 23, no. 4 (1932): 243–60. Also published as *Puget Sound, and the Northern Pacific Railroad. II*. London: Cassell, Petter and Galpin, 1875[?].

Coleman, Winifred S. "Exploring Expeditions through the North Cascades." *The Mountaineer* (1964): 27–37.

Collins, June McCormick. *Valley of the Spirit: Upper Skagit Indians of Western Washington*. Seattle: University of Washington Press, 1974.

Connelly, Dolly. "Mighty Joe Morovits: Real-Life Bunyan." *Sports Illustrated*, January 7, 1963, 52–7.

Conover, C. T. *Proposal to Change the Name of Mount Rainier: Before the United States Geographic Board, 1917*. Seattle: Lowman and Hanford, n.d.

Cook, James. *The Journals of Captain James Cook on His Voyages of Discovery*. Ed. J. C. Beaglehole. Cambridge, England: Hakluyt-Society, 1967.

Northern Pacific Railroad Company. *The Northern Pacific Railroad's Land Grant, Resources, Traffic, and Tributary Country*. Philadelphia: Jay Cooke & Company, 1873.

Cooper, James G., and George Suckley. *The Natural History of Washington Territory*. New York: Baillière Brothers, 1859.

Cope, Lillian. "Colonel Moody and the Royal Engineers in British Columbia." Thesis, University of British Columbia, 1940.

Coues, Elliott, ed. *History of the Expedition under the Command of Lewis and Clark, to the Sources of the Missouri River, Thence across the Rocky Mountains and down the Columbia River to the Pacific Ocean, Performed during the Years 1804–5–6, by Order of the Government of the United States*. Vol. 3. New York: Francis P. Harper, 1893.

——————. *Journey across the Rocky Mountains to the Pacific, 1799–1816, by Alexander Henry, the Younger*. New York, 1897.

——————. *New Light on the Early History of the Greater Northwest: The Manuscript Journals of Alexander Henry . . . and of David Thompson . . . 1799–1814*. Vol. 2. New York: Francis P. Harper, 1897.

Coutant, Frank R. *Fraser-Cariboo Gold Rush: The Boom That Founded British Columbia*. Monroe, Conn.: Privately printed, 196?.

Cram, Capt. Thomas Jefferson. "Topographical Memoir and Report of Captain T. J. Cram, on Territories of Oregon and Washington," March 3, 1859. House Exec. Doc. 114, 35th Cong., 2d sess., 1859. Serial 1014. Pp. 2–123, 379.

Crandell, Dwight R. "The Geologic Story of Mount Rainier." *Bulletin No. 1292*, USGS. 1969.

——————. "The Glacial History of Western Washington and Oregon." In *The Quaternary of the United States*, ed. H. E. Wright, Jr., and David G. Frey. Princeton, N.J.: Princeton University Press, 1965.

Creech, E. P. "Brigade Trails of British Columbia." *The Beaver*, March 1953.

Crowder, Dwight F., and R. W. Tabor. *Routes and Rocks: Hiker's Guide to the North Cascades from Glacier Peak to Lake Chelan*. Seattle: The Mountaineers, 1965.

Cruise, David, and Alison Griffiths. *Lords of the Line*. Markham, Ont.: Viking/Penguin, 1988.

Cullum, Maj. Gen. George. *Biographical Register of the Officers and Graduates of the U.S. Military Academy at West Point, N.Y.* 2 vols. Boston: Houghton, Mifflin, 1891.

Curtis, Edward S. *The North American Indian*. Vol. 7. Seattle: E. S. Curtis, 1911.

Daly, Reginald A. *Geology of the North American Cordillera at the Forty-ninth Parallel*. Memoir No. 38, GSC. 1912.

—————. "The Geology of the Region Adjoining the Western Part of the International Boundary." In *Summary Report* 14, pt. a, GSC (1901), pp. 39–51.

—————. "The Nomenclature of the North American Cordillera between the 47th and 53rd Parallels of Latitude." *Geographical Journal* 27 (1906).

—————. "The Okanogan Composite Batholith of the Cascade Mountain System." *Bulletin of the Geological Society of America* 17 (1906).

Davidson, George. "Recent Volcanic Activity in the United States: Eruptions of Mount Baker." *Science* 6 (September 25, 1885).

Davidson, Gordon Charles. *The North West Company*. Berkeley: University of California Press, 1918.

Davis, Jefferson. "Report of the Secretary of War on the Several Railroad Explorations." In *Reports of Explorations and Surveys*, 1:3–33.

Davis, John W. "The Unguarded Boundary." *Geographical Review* 12 (1922): 585–601.

Dawson, George M. *The Journals of George M. Dawson: British Columbia, 1875–1878*. Ed. Douglas Cole and Bradley Lockner. Vancouver: University of British Columbia Press, 1989.

—————. "Preliminary Report on the Physical and Geological Features of the Southern Portion of the Interior of British Columbia—1877." GSC. 1879.

—————. *Report of the Canadian Pacific Railway*. Appendix E. Montreal, 1877.

de Lacy, Walter Washington. "Roads in Washington Territory." In *Report of the Secretary of War, 1858*, pp. 1216–30. Senate Exec. Doc. 1, 35th Cong., 2d sess., 1858. Serial 976.

Denman, A. H. *The Name of Mount Tacoma*. Tacoma, Wash.: Rotary Club, Kiwanis Club [etc.], 1924.

Denny, Arthur A. *Pioneer Days on Puget Sound*. Seattle: C. B. Bagley, 1888.

Denny, E. I. "A Monte Cristo in the Cascades." *Northwest Illustrated Monthly Magazine* 15, no. 4 (1893).

Denton, George H., and Terence J. Hughes. *The Last Great Ice Sheets*. New York: John Wiley and Sons, 1981.

De Smet, Father Pierre-Jean. "Missions and Travels over the Rocky Mountains, 1845–1846." In *Early Western Travels, 1748–1846*, vol. 29, ed. Reuben Gold Thwaites. New York: AMS Press, 1966.

Deutsch, Herman J. "A Contemporary Report on the 49° Boundary Survey." *PNQ* 53, no. 1 (1962): 17–33.

Dolmage, V. *Geology and Ore Deposits of Copper Mountain, British Columbia*. Memoir No. 171, GSC. 1934.

Douglas, David. *Douglas of the Forests: The North American Journals of David Douglas*. Ed. John Davies. Seattle: University of Washington Press, 1980.

—————. *Journal Kept by David Douglas during His Travels in North America, 1823–1827*. London: William Wesley and Son, 1914.

—————. *The Oregon Journals of David Douglas*. Ed. David Lavender. Ashland: Oregon Book Society, 1972.

Douglas, George W. "A Preliminary Biological Survey of the North Cascades National Park and the Ross Lake and Lake Chelan National Recreation Areas." Seattle: Prepared for the National Park Service, 1969.

Dow, Edson. *Passes to the North: History of the Wenatchee Mountains*. Wenatchee, Wash.: Outdoor Publishing, 1963.

Downing, Alfred. *The Region of the Upper Columbia and How I Saw It*. Fairfield, Wash.: Ye Galleon Press, 1980.

————. "Report of the Chief of Engineers, U.S. Army." In *Report of the Secretary of War* 2, pt. 3, appendix BBB, pp. 2410–12. House Exec. Doc. 1, pt. 2, 48th Cong., 1st sess., 1883. Serial 2185.

Dryden, Cecil. *Dryden's History of Washington*. Portland: Binfords and Mort, 1968.

Dryer, Thomas J. "The 1853 Ascent of Mt. St. Helens." *Mazama* 50, no. 13 (1968): 45–9. *See also* Majors, Harry M., "First Ascent of Mount St. Helens."

Duff, Wilson. *The Impact of the White Man*. Indian History of British Columbia, vol. 1; Anthropology in British Columbia, Memoir No. 5. Victoria, B.C.: Provincial Museum of Natural History and Anthropology, 1964.

————. *The Upper Stalo Indians of the Fraser Valley, British Columbia*. Anthropology in British Columbia, Memoir No. 1. Victoria: British Columbia Provincial Museum, 1952.

Duncan, Lt. Johnson K. "Topographical Report of Lieutenant J.K. Duncan, U. S. A., Topographer of the Western Division," February 21, 1854. In *Reports of Explorations and Surveys* 1:203–19.

Easterbrook, Don J., and David A. Rahm. *Landforms of Washington*. Bellingham: Western Washington University, 1970.

Easton, Charles F. "Mt. Baker—Its Trails and Legends." *Northwest Journal of Education* 3, no. 5 (1917): 382–7.

————. "The Story of Mt. Baker." *Mazama* 6, no. 1 (1920): 45–53.

Elliott, T. C. "The Fur Trade in the Columbia Basin Prior to 1811." *WHQ* 6, no. 1 (1915): 3–10.

————. "Journal of John Work, November and December, 1824." *WHQ* 3, no. 3 (1912): 198–228.

————. "The Northwest Boundaries." *OHQ* 20, no. 4 (1919): 331–44.

Emmons, Della F.G. *Leschi of the Nisquallies*. Minneapolis, Minn.: T. S. Denison, 1965.

Emmons, Samuel F. "Ascent of Mt. Rainier, with Sketch of Summit" and letter to editor. *The Nation* 23 (November 23, 1876): 312–13.

————. "The Volcanoes of the Pacific Coast of the United States." *Journal of the American Geographical Society of New York* 9, no. 4 (1879): 45–65.

Evans, Brock. *The Alpine Lakes*. Seattle: The Mountaineers, 1971.

Farley, Albert Leonardo. *Historical Cartography of British Columbia*. Vancouver, B.C.: n.p., 1960.

Farquhar, Francis P. "Naming America's Mountains—The Cascades." *American Alpine Journal* 12, no. 1 (1960): 49–65.

Fauré, Gene. "The Real Tolmie's Peak." *The Mountaineer* 60, no. 5 (1967): 61–71.

Field, Col. Virgil. *The Official History of the Washington National Guard: Washington Territorial Militia in the Indian Wars of 1855–56*. 2 vols. Camp Murray, Wash.: Washington State Adjutant-General's Office, 1961–62.

Fisher, Robin. "Lamb's Vancouver Voyage." *PNQ* 76, no. 4 (1985): 132–6.

Fluharty, David. "Relicensing the Skagit Dams." *The Wild Cascades*, Fall 1989.

Fobes, J. Warner. "To the Summit of Mount Rainier." *West Shore* 11, no. 9 (1885): 265–9.

Foster, Mike, ed. *Summits to Reach: Report on the Topography of the San Juan Country*. Boulder, Colo.: Pruett, 1984.

Foxworthy, Bruce L., and Mary Hill. "Volcanic Eruptions of 1980 at Mount St. Helens: The First 100 Days." *Professional Paper No. 1249*, USGS. 1982.

Fraser, Simon. *The Letters and Journals of Simon Fraser, 1806–1808*. Ed. W. Kaye Lamb. Toronto: Macmillan, 1960.

Frémont, Capt. John C. *Report of the Exploring Expedition to the Rocky Mountains in the Year 1842, and to Oregon and North California in the Years 1843–1844*. Senate Exec. Doc. 174, 28th Cong., 2d sess. 1845. Serial 461.

"From Ocean Shore to Mountain Crest and Back Again in a Day." *The Coast* 4 (June 1902).

Fuller, George W. *A History of the Pacific Northwest*. New York: Alfred A. Knopf, 1931.

Galbraith, John. *The Hudson's Bay Company as an Imperial Factor, 1821–1869*. New York: Octagon Books, 1977.

Gannett, Henry. "Forest Reserves." In *19th Annual Report*, USGS, pt. 5 (1899).

————. "Lake Chelan." *National Geographic* 9, no. 10 (1898): 417–28.

——————. "The Mother Maps of the United States." *National Geographic* 4 (1892).

Gates, Charles M., ed. *Messages of the Governors of the Territory of Washington to the Legislative Assembly, 1854–1889*. Seattle: University of Washington Press, 1940.

Gibbon, John Murray. *The Romantic History of the Canadian Pacific: The Northwest Passage of Today*. New York: Tudor Publishing, 1937.

Gibbs, George. *A Dictionary of the Chinook Jargon, or Trade Language of Oregon*. Smithsonian Miscellaneous Collections 7, no. 10. Washington, D.C.: Smithsonian Institution, 1863.

——————. "George Gibbs' Account of Indian Mythology in Oregon and Washington Territories." Parts 1 and 2. Ed. Ella E. Clark. OHQ 56, no. 4 (1955): 293–325; 57, no. 2 (1956): 125–67.

——————. "Pacific Northwest Letters of George Gibbs." *OHQ* 54, no. 1 (1953): 190–239.

——————. "Physical Geography of the North-Western Boundary of the United States." Parts 1 & 2. *Journal of the American Geographical Society of New York* 3 (1873): 134–57; 4 (1874): 298–415.

——————. "Report of George Gibbs upon the Geology of the Central Portion of Washington Territory," May 1, 1854. In *Reports of Explorations and Surveys* 1:473–86.

——————. "Report of George Gibbs on a Reconnaissance of the Country Lying upon Shoalwater Bay and Puget Sound," March 1, 1854. In *Reports of Explorations and Surveys* 1:465–73.

——————. "Report of Mr. George Gibbs to Captain McClellan, on the Indian Tribes of the Territory of Washington," March 4, 1854. In *Reports of Explorations and Surveys* 1:402–34. Reprinted as *Indian Tribes of Washington Territory*. Fairfield, Wash.: Ye Galleon Press, 1967.

——————. *Tribes of Western Washington and Northwestern Oregon*. Contributions to North American Ethnology, U.S. Geographical and Geological Survey. Washington, D.C., 1877.

Gilbert, E. W. *The Exploration of Western America, 1800–1850*. New York: Cooper Square Publishers, 1966.

Glascock, Raglan. "How We Climbed Rainier." *Sunset* 16, no. 1 (1905): 49–55.

Glassley, Ray Hoard. *Pacific Northwest Indian Wars*. Portland: Binfords and Mort, 1953.

Glover, Sheldon L. "One Hundred Years of Mining." In *Biennial Report No. 5*, Washington Division of Mines and Geology. Olympia, 1954.

Goethals, Lt. George W. "Report of Lieutenant George W. Goethals, Corps of Engineers, for the Fiscal Year Ending June 30, 1883," October 1, 1883. In *Report of the Secretary of War* 2, pt. 3, p. 2412. House Exec. Doc. 1, pt. 2, 48th Cong., 1st sess., 1883. Serial 2185.

Goetzmann, William H. *Army Exploration in the American West, 1803–1863*. New Haven, Conn.: Yale University Press, 1959.

——————. *Exploration and Empire: The Explorer and the Scientist in the Winning of the American West*. New York: Alfred A. Knopf, 1966.

Gorman, Martin W. "Eastern Part of Washington Forest Reserve." In *19th Annual Report*, USGS, pt. 5 (1899), pp. 315–50.

Gossett, Gretta. "Stock Grazing in Washington's Nile Valley." *PNQ* 54, no. 3 (1964): 119–27.

Great Northern Railway Company. *Dedication and Opening of the New Cascade Tunnel, a Monument to James J. Hill*. St. Paul, 1929.

——————. "The Great Northern Railway Tunnel through the Cascade Mountains." *Engineering News* 29 (May 18, 1893).

Greenhow, Robert. *The History of Oregon and California*. Boston: Little and Brown, 1845.

Griffin, Walter R. "George W. Goethals, Explorer of the Pacific Northwest, 1882–84." *PNQ* 62, no. 4 (1971): 129–41.

Griffith, Thomas. "The Pacific Northwest." *Atlantic Monthly*, April 1976.

Guie, H. Dean. *Bugles in the Valley: Garnett's Fort Simcoe*. Yakima, Wash., 1956.

——————. *Tribal Days of the Yakimas*. Yakima, Wash.: Republic Publishing, 1937.

Gunther, Erna. *Indian Life on the Northwest Coast of North America, as Seen by the Early Explorers and Fur Traders during the Last Decades of the Eighteenth Century*. Chicago: University of Chicago Press, 1972.

Haeberlin, Hermann, and Erna Gunther. *The Indians of Puget Sound*. University of Washington Publications in Anthropology, vol. 4, no. 1. Seattle: University of Washington Press, 1930.

Haines, Aubrey L. *Mountain Fever: Historic Conquests of Rainier*. Portland: Oregon Historical Society, 1962.

Hall, Winnifred M. "The Royal Engineers in British Columbia, 1858–1863." Thesis, University of British Columbia, 1925.

Harris, Bob, Harley Hatfield, and Peter Tassie. *The Okanagan Brigade Trail in the South Okanagan, 1811 to 1849*. 1989.

Hart, Allen E. "The Unexplored Mountains of North America." *Geographical Review* 7 (June 1919).

Harvey, Athelstan G. *Douglas of the Fir: A Biography of David Douglas, Botanist*. Cambridge: Harvard University Press, 1947.

Haskell, Daniel C., ed. *On Reconnaissance for the Great Northern: Letters of C.F.B. Haskell, 1889–1891*. New York: New York Public Library, 1948.

Hatfield, Harley R. "Brigade Trail Fort Hope to Campment des Femmes." In *36th Annual Report*, Okanagan Historical Society. 1972.

——————. "Old Trails of the Cascade Wilderness from the Days of Blackeye the Similkameen to Those of the Royal Engineers." In *51st Annual Report*, Okanagan Historical Society. 1987.

——————. "The Proposed Cascade Wilderness." In *44th Annual Report*, Okanagan Historical Society. 1980.

Hayman, John. "The Wanderer, John Keast Lord in Colonial British Columbia, 1858–62." *The Beaver* 70, no. 6 (1990): 38–47.

Hazlitt, William C. *The Great Gold Fields of Cariboo*. London: Routledge, Warme, and Routledge, 1862.

Hedges, James Blaine. *Henry Villard and the Railways of the Northwest*. New Haven, Conn.: Yale University Press, 1930.

Heitman, Francis B. *Historical Register and Dictionary of the United States Army*. Washington, D.C.: GPO, 1903.

Hicks, Urban E. *Yakima and Clickitat Indian Wars, 1855 and 1856: Personal Recollections of Capt. U. E. Hicks*. Portland, Ore.: Himes the Printer, 1885.

——————. *Pioneer Reminiscences of Urban E. Hicks*. Compiled by Gary F. Reese. Tacoma, Wash.: Tacoma Public Library, 1984.

Hidy, Ralph W., and Muriel E. Hidy. "John Frank Stevens: Great Northern Engineer." *Minnesota History* 41, no. 8 (1969): 343–61.

Hidy, Ralph W., Muriel E. Hidy, and Roy V. Scott. *The Great Northern Railway: A History*. Boston: Harvard Business School Press, 1988.

Highsmith, Richard M., Jr., and A. Jon Kimmerling. *Atlas of the Pacific Northwest*. 7th ed. Corvallis: Oregon State University Press, 1983.

Higueras Rodríguez, Ma. Dolores, ed. *Catálogo Crítico de los Documentos de la Expedición Malaspina (1789–1794)*. Vol. 2. Madrid: Museo Naval, 1985.

Hill-Tout, Charles. "Ethnological Studies of the Mainland Halkomelem, a Division of the Salish of British Columbia." In *The Salish People*, ed. Ralph Maud, vol. 3. Vancouver, B.C.: Talonbooks, 1978.

——————. "Notes on the Ntlakapamuq (Thompson) of British Columbia, a Branch of the Great Salish Stock of North America." In *The Salish People*, ed. Ralph Maud, vol. 1. Vancouver, B.C.: Talonbooks, 1978.

Himes, George H. "Very Early Ascents." *Steel Points* 1 (July 1907): 199.

Hodges, L. K. *Mining in the Pacific Northwest*. Seattle, Wash.: *Post-Intelligencer*, 1897.

Hodgson, Caspar W. "Hunting Mazamas in the Cascades." *Sunset* 9, no. 5 (1902): 313–18.

Hollenbeck, Jan L. *A Cultural Resource Overview: Prehistory, Ethnography, and History: Mt. Baker–Snoqualmie National Forest*. Portland, Ore.: U.S. Forest Service, 1987.

Hollenbeck, Jan L., and Susan L. Carter. *A Cultural Resource Overview: Prehistory and Ethnography*. Wenatchee, Wash.: Wenatchee National Forest, 1986.

Holman, Frederick V. "The Discovery and Exploration of the Fraser River." *OHQ* 10, no. 2 (1909): 1–15.

Holmes, Kenneth L. *Mount St. Helens: Lady with a Past*. Salem, Ore.: Salem Press, 1980.

Howay, Frederic W. *British Columbia from the Earliest Times to the Present*, vol. 2. Vancouver, B.C.: S.J. Clarke, 1914.

——————. *The Early History of the Fraser River Mines*. Memoir No. 6, Archives of British Columbia. Victoria, B.C.: Printed by C.F. Banfield, 1926.

——————. *The Work of the Royal Engineers in British Columbia, 1858–1863*. Victoria, B.C.: R. Wolfenden, 1910.

Hudson's Bay Company. *Copy-book of Letters Outward &c, Begins 29th May, 1680, Ends 5 July, 1687*, ed. E.E. Rich (Toronto: Champlain Society, 1948).

Huggins, Edward. *Reminiscences of Puget Sound*. Ed. Gary F. Reese. Tacoma, Wash.: Tacoma Public Library, 1984.

Hull, Lindley M. *A History of Central Washington*. Spokane, Wash.: Shaw and Borden, 1929.

Hult, Ruby El. *Northwest Disaster: Avalanche and Fire*. Portland: Binfords and Mort, 1960.

Hunt, Herbert, and Floyd C. Kaylor. *Washington, West of the Cascades*. 2 vols. Chicago: S.J. Clarke, 1917.

Huntting, Marshall T. "Gold in Washington." *Bulletin No. 42*, Washington Division of Mines and Geology. Olympia, 1955.

Hutchison, Bruce. *Rivers of America: The Fraser*. Toronto: Clarke, Irwin, 1950.

An Illustrated History of Skagit and Snohomish Counties. Spokane, Wash.: Interstate Publishing Co., 1906.

An Illustrated History of Stevens, Ferry, Okanogan, and Chelan Counties. Spokane, Wash.: Interstate Publishing Co., 1904.

Ingersoll, Ernest. "From the Fraser to the Columbia." Parts 1 and 2. *Harper's New Monthly Magazine* 68 (April 1884): 706–21; (May 1884): 869–82.

International Boundary Commission. *Joint Report upon the Survey and Demarcation of the Boundary between the United States and Canada from the Gulf of Georgia to the Northwesternmost Point of Lake of the Woods*. Washington, D.C., 1937.

Jeffcott, Percival R. *Chechaco and Sourdough*. Bellingham, Wash.: Pioneer Printing Co., 1963.

——————. *Nooksack Tales and Trails*. Ferndale, Wash.: Sedro Woolley *Courier-Times*, 1949.

Jenkins, Will D. *Last Frontier in the North Cascades: Tales of the Wild Upper Skagit*. Mt. Vernon, Wash.: Skagit County Historical Society, 1984.

Jermann, Jerry V., and Roger D. Mason. *A Cultural Resource Overview of the Gifford Pinchot National Forest, South-Central Washington*. Reconnaissance Reports No. 7, University of Washington, Office of Public Archaeology. 1976.

Jervey, James P. "George W. Goethals—The Man." *Military Engineer* 20 (1928): 161–2.

Johansen, Dorothy O., and Charles M. Gates. *Empire of the Columbia: A History of the Pacific Northwest*. New York: Harper and Brothers, 1957.

Johnson, Dorothy H., and Percival R. Jeffcott. *John A. Tennant: Early Pioneer and Preacher*. Bellingham, Wash.: Fourth Corner Registry, 1978.

Johnson, Edwin Ferry. *Railroad to the Pacific: Northern Route*. New York: Railroad Journal, 1854.

——————. *Report of Edwin F. Johnson, Engineer-in-Chief, to the Board of Directors, Northern Pacific Railroad Company, November, 1867*. Hartford, Conn.: Northern Pacific Railroad Company, 1867.

——————. *Report of Edwin F. Johnson, Engineer-in-Chief, to the Board of Directors, Northern Pacific Railroad Company, April 1869, and Report of Surveys Executed in 1867, by General Ira Spaulding and General James Tilton*. Hartford, Conn.: Northern Pacific Railroad Company, 1869.

Kane, Paul. *Paul Kane, the Columbia Wanderer, 1846–47*. Ed. Thomas Vaughan. Portland: Oregon Historical Society, 1971.

——————. *Paul Kane's Frontier*. Ed. J. Russell Harper. Austin: University of Texas Press, 1971.

Kautz, August V. "Ascent of Mount Rainier." *Overland Monthly* 14, no. 5 (1875): 393–403.

——————. *The Northwest Journals of August V. Kautz*. Ed. Gary F. Reese. Tacoma, Wash.: Tacoma Public Library, 1978.

Kautz, Frances. "Extracts from the Diary of Gen. A.W. Kautz." *Washington Historian* 1 (April 1900).

Kerr, Duncan J. "Preliminary Studies and Results of Improving Cascade Crossing." In *The Eight-Mile Cascade Tunnel, Great Northern Railway: A Symposium*, 185–93. American Society of Civil Engineers Papers. New York, 1931.

King, Clarence. "On the Discovery of Actual Glaciers on the Mountains of the Pacific Slope." *American Journal of Science and Arts*, 3d ser., 1, no. 3 (1871): 158–65.

Kirk, Ruth, and Richard D. Daugherty. *Exploring Washington Archaeology*. Seattle: University of Washington Press, 1978.

Klotz, Otto. *Certain Correspondence of the Foreign Office and of the Hudson's Bay Company*. Part 3, "Foreign Office Correspondence: International Boundary, 49th Parallel. British Columbia, 1858–1864." Ottawa: Government Print. Bureau, 1899.

—————. *Foreign Office Correspondence, Forty-ninth Parallel West of the Summit of the Rocky Mountains, 1856–1871*. Washington, D.C., 1902.

—————. "The History of the Forty-ninth Parallel West of the Rocky Mountains." *Geographical Review* 3, no. 5 (1917): 382–7.

Knappen, Theodore M. "Every Odd Section." *Sunset* 53, no. 6 (1924): 11–13, 54–6.

"Lake Chelan: A Summer Resort." *The Coast* 8, no. 3 (1904): 78–88.

"Lake Chelan, Washington's Wonderland." *The Coast* 16, no. 4.

Lambert, John. "Report of the Topography of the Route from the Mississippi River to the Columbia," June 1, 1854. In *Reports of Explorations and Surveys*, 1:160–77.

Lavender, David. *Land of Giants: The Drive to the Pacific Northwest, 1750–1950*. Garden City, N.Y.: Doubleday, 1958.

LeRoy, Bruce. "Mosquitoes, Mules, and Men." *American Heritage* 16, no. 3 (1965): 102–7.

Leviton, Alan E., ed. *Frontiers of Geological Exploration of Western North America*. American Association for the Advancement of Science symposium, University of Idaho, 1979. San Francisco: Pacific Division, AAAS, 1982.

Linsley, Daniel C. "Lake Chelan and Agnes Creek in 1870." Ed. Harry M. Majors. *NWD* 2, no. 6 (1981): 382–401.

—————. "Pioneering in the Cascade Country." *Civil Engineering* 6 (June 1932): 339–44.

—————. "A Railroad Survey of the Sauk and Wenatchee Rivers in 1870." Ed. Harry M. Majors. *NWD* 2, no. 4 (1981): 201–66.

Lipman, Peter W., and Donal R. Mullineaux. "The 1980 Eruptions of Mount Saint Helens, Washington." *Professional Paper No. 1250*, USGS. 1981.

Little, Elbert, Jr. *Check List of Native and Naturalized Trees of the United States (including Alaska)*. Agricultural Handbook No. 41. U.S. Forest Service, 1953.

Longmire, David. "First Immigrants to Cross the Cascades." *WHQ* 8, no. 1 (1917): 22–8.

Longmire, James. "Narrative of James Longmire, a Pioneer of 1853." Parts 1 and 2. *WHQ* 23, nos. 1, 2 (1932): 47–60, 138–50.

Loo-wit-lat-kla [pseud.]. *Gold Hunting in the Cascade Mountains*. Vancouver, Wash.: L.E.V. Coon, 1861.

Lord, John Keast. *The Naturalist in Vancouver Island and British Columbia*. 2 vols. London: Richard Bentley, 1866.

Louis, Loretta. "History of Ruby City: The Life and Death of a Mining Town." *PNQ* 32, no. 1 (1941): 61–78.

Luxenberg, Gretchen A. *Historic Resource Study, North Cascades National Park Complex, Washington*. Seattle: National Park Service, 1986.

Lyman, William D. *The Columbia River, Its History, Its Myths, Its Scenery, Its Commerce*. New York: G.P. Putnam's Sons, 1917.

—————. "Lake Chelan, the Leman of the West." *Overland Monthly*, 2d ser., 33 (March 1899): 195–201.

—————. "Mount Adams Outing, 1902." *Mazama* 2, no. 3 (1903): 164–75.

—————. "The Switzerland of the Northwest: I. The Mountains." *Overland Monthly*, 2d ser., 2 (September 1883): 300–312.

MacArthur, Lewis A., and Victor H. Flach. "Lage Wernstedt: Pioneer in Photogrammetry." *Journal of Forestry* 43 (1945).

Mackenzie, Alexander. *Alexander Mackenzie's Voyage to the Pacific Ocean in 1793.* Ed. Milo Milton Quaife. Chicago: Lakeside Press, 1931.

—————. *The Journals and Letters of Sir Alexander Mackenzie.* Ed. W. Kaye Lamb. Cambridge, England: Hakluyt Society, 1970.

Magnusson, Elva C. "Naches Pass." *WHQ* 25, no. 3 (1934): 171–81.

Mahlberg, Blanche B. "Edward J. Allen, Pioneer and Road Builder." *PNQ* 44, no. 4 (1953): 157–60.

Majors, Harry M., ed. "Alfred Downing's Misadventures on the Columbia River in 1880." *NWD* 4, no. 1 (1983): 4–33.

—————. "An Army Expedition across the North Cascades in August 1882." *NWD* 3, no. 1 (1982): 4–84.

—————. "Backus Explores the Twisp and Methow Valleys, August–September 1883." *NWD* 4, no. 1 (1983): 33–80.

—————. "Discovery of Mount Shuksan and the Upper Nooksack River, June 1859." *NWD* 5, no. 21 (1984): 4–84.

—————. "First Ascent of Mount St. Helens: The Dryer Party of 1853." *NWD* 1, no. 3 (1980): 164–80.

—————. "The First Crossing of the North Cascades." *NWD* 1, no. 3 (1980).

—————. "First Crossing of the Picket Range, 1859." *NWD* 5, no. 22 (1984): 88–168.

—————. *Mount Baker: A Chronicle of Its Historic Eruptions and First Ascent.* Seattle: Northwest Press, 1978.

—————. "Paul Kane's Drawing of Goat Rock, 1847," *NWD* 1, no. 2 (1980): 107–8.

—————. "The Stevens and Van Trump Ascent of Mount Rainier, August 1870." Parts 1–4. *NWD* 6, nos. 26–29 (1985).

Manning, Harvey. *The Wild Cascades: Forgotten Parkland.* San Francisco: Sierra Club, 1965.

Martin, Albro. *James J. Hill and the Opening of the Northwest.* New York: Oxford University Press, 1976.

Martinson, Arthur D. "Mountain in the Sky: A History of Mount Rainier National Park." Ph.D. diss., Washington State University, 1966.

—————. *Wilderness above the Sound: The Story of Mount Rainier National Park.* Flagstaff, Ariz.: Northland Press, 1986.

Mayne, Richard Charles. *Four Years in British Columbia and Vancouver Island.* London: John Murray, 1862.

McCabe, James O. *The San Juan Water Boundary Question.* Toronto: University of Toronto Press, 1964.

McClellan, Capt. George B. "General Report of Captain George B. McClellan," February 25, 1853. In *Reports of Explorations and Surveys*, 1:188–202.

—————. "Railroad Practicability of the Cascades and of the Line of the Snoqualme Pass," February 8, 1854. In *Reports of Explorations and Surveys*, 1:180–3.

McDonald, Angus. "A Few Items of the West." Ed. F. W. Howay, William S. Lewis, and Jacob A. Meyers. *WHQ* 8, no. 3 (1917): 188–229.

McKee, Bates. *Cascadia: The Geologic Evolution of the Pacific Northwest.* New York: McGraw-Hill, 1972.

McLoughlin, John. *The Letters of John McLoughlin from Fort Vancouver to the Governor and Committee, First Series, 1825–1838.* Ed. E.E. Rich. Hudson's Bay Record Society Publications, no. 4. London, 1941.

—————. *The Letters of John McLoughlin from Fort Vancouver to the Governor and Committee, Second Series, 1839–1844.* Ed. E. E. Rich. Hudson's Bay Record Society Publications, no. 5. London, 1943.

McNeil, Fred H. "In the Glacier Peak Region, 1926." *Mazama* 8, no. 2 (1926): 7–30.

McTaggart, K. C., and R. M. Thompson. "Geology of Part of the Northern Cascades in Southern British Columbia." *Canadian Journal of Earth Science* 4, no. 6 (1967): 1199–1228.

McWhorter, Lucullus V. "Chief Sluskin's True Narrative." *WHQ* 8, no. 2 (1917): 96–101.

Meany, Edmond S. *Diary of Wilkes in the Northwest*. Seattle: University of Washington Press, 1926.

——————. "History of Mount Stuart and Vicinity." *The Mountaineer* 18 (1925): 33–5.

——————. *Origin of Washington Geographic Names*. Seattle: University of Washington Press, 1923.

Meany, Edmond S., and Victor J. Farrar, eds. *Mount Rainier: A Record of Exploration*. New York: Macmillan, 1916.

Meeker, Ezra. *Pioneer Reminiscences of Puget Sound*. Seattle: Lowman and Hanford, 1905.

Meinig, D.W. *The Great Columbia Plain*. Seattle: University of Washington Press, 1968.

Menzies, Archibald. *Menzies' Journal of Vancouver's Voyage*. Ed. Charles F. Newcombe. Victoria, B.C.: W.H. Cullin, 1923.

Merk, Frederick. *The Oregon Question*. Cambridge: Harvard University Press, 1967.

——————, ed. *Fur Trade and Empire: George Simpson's Journal, 1824–1825*. Cambridge: Harvard University Press, 1968.

Mierendorf, Robert R. *People of the North Cascades*. Seattle: National Park Service, 1980.

Miles, John. *Koma Kulshan: The Story of Mount Baker*. Seattle: The Mountaineers, 1984.

Mitchell, Bruce. "By River, Trail, and Rail." Supplement to the *Wenatchee Daily World*, 1968.

Moberly, Walter. *The Rocks and Rivers of British Columbia*. London: H. Blacklock and Co., 1885.

Modelski, Andrew M. *Railroad Maps of North America: The First Hundred Years*. Washington, D.C.: Library of Congress, 1984.

Moen, Wayne S. "Mines and Mineral Deposits of Whatcom County, Washington." *Bulletin No. 57*, Washington Division of Mines and Geology. Olympia, 1969.

Molenaar, Dee. *The Challenge of Rainier*. Seattle: The Mountaineers, 1971.

Monger, James W.H. "Cordilleran Tectonics: A Canadian Perspective." *Bulletin de la Société géologique de France* 7th ser., 26, no. 2 (1984).

Montgomery, J. Peak. "The Mazamas' Outing at Mount Rainier." *Overland Monthly*, 2d ser., 32, no. 188 (1898): 114–23.

Morgan, Murray. *Puget's Sound: A Narrative of Early Tacoma and the Southern Sound*. Seattle: University of Washington Press, 1979.

Morris, Clyde L. "Blasting the Cascade Barrier." *Sunset*, April 1916.

Moulton, Gary E., ed. *Journals of the Lewis and Clark Expedition*. Vols. 5–7, 11. Lincoln: University of Nebraska Press, 1983–2001.

Muir, John. "The Ascent of Mount Rainier." *Pacific Monthly* 8, no. 5 (1902): 197–203.

Mullineaux, D.R., R.S. Sigafoos, and E.L. Hendricks. "A Historic Eruption of Mount Rainier, Washington." *Professional Paper 650–b*, USGS. 1969.

Murphy, Paul. "The History of Fort Langley." Thesis, University of British Columbia, 1929.

Murphy, William. "The North-West Company in British Columbia." Thesis, University of British Columbia, 1926.

Murray, Keith A. "Building a Wagon Road through the Northern Cascade Mountains." *PNQ* 56, no. 2 (1965): 49–56.

Neils, Selma M. *The Klickitat Indians*. Portland, Ore.: Binfords and Mort, 1985.

Newell, Bernice E. "Washington's Monte Cristo." *Northwest Illustrated Monthly Magazine* 8, no. 2 (1895): 1–2.

North Cascades Study Team. *The North Cascades: A Report to the Secretary of Interior and the Secretary of Agriculture*. Washington, D.C.: U.S. Dept. of the Interior, U.S. Dept. of Agriculture, 1965.

Northern Pacific Railroad. *Life of Thomas Hawley Canfield*. Burlington, Vt.: n.p., 1889.

Norton, Helen H. "The Association between Anthropogenic Prairies and Important Food Plants in Western Washington." *Northwest Anthropological Research Notes* 13, no. 2 (1979).

Norton, Helen H., Robert Boyd, and Eugene S. Hunn. "The Klickitat Trail of South-Central Washington: A Reconstruction of Seasonally Used Resource Sites." In *Prehistoric Places on the Southern Northwest Coast*, ed. Robert E. Gringo. Research Report No. 4, Thomas Burke Memorial Washington State Museum. Seattle: University of Washington Press, 1983.

Ogden, Peter Skene. *Peter Skene Ogden's Snake Country Journal, 1826–27*. Ed. K. G. Davies and A. M. Johnson. London: Hudson's Bay Record Society, 1961.

Oliphant, J. Orin. "The Cattle Trade through the Snoqualmie Pass." *PNQ* 38, no. 3 (1947): 193–213.

Ormsby, Margaret A. *British Columbia: A History*. Vancouver, B.C.: Macmillans in Canada, 1958.

Overmeyer, Philip H. "George B. McClellan and the Pacific Northwest." *PNQ* 32, no. 1 (1941): 3–60.

Palliser, John. *The Papers of the Palliser Expedition, 1857–1860*. Toronto: Champlain Society, 1968.

Pannekoek, Anton. *A History of Astronomy*. New York: Interscience Publishers, 1961.

Parrish, Josiah L. "Eruption of Mount St. Helens." *Steel Points* 1 (October 1906): 25–6.

Patterson, H. S. "54° 40' or Fight." *The Beaver* (June 1936): 38–44.

Pattullo, A. S. "Lake Chelan and Mount Sahale." *Mazama* 2, no. 3 (1903): 138–42.

Patty, Ernest N. *The Metal Mines of Washington*. Bulletin No. 23, Washington Geological Survey. Olympia: F.M. Lamborn, Public Printer, 1921.

Pelto, Mauri S. "Current Behavior of Glaciers in the North Cascades and Effect on Regional Water Supplies." *Washington Geology* 21 (July 1993): 3–10.

Perko, Richard C. "A Forgotten Passage to Puget Sound." *Montana* 35, no. 1 (1985): 38–47.

Pethick, Derek. *James Douglas: Servant of Two Empires*. Vancouver, B.C.: Mitchell Press, 1969.

Phelps, William F. "In the Cascade Mountains: A Tramp in Search of Silver Mines." *Northwest Illustrated Monthly Magazine* 10, no. 12 (1892): 3–5.

Pierce, Lt. Henry H. *Report of an Expedition from Fort Colville to Puget Sound, Washington Territory, by Way of Lake Chelan and Skagit River, during the Months of August and September, 1882*. Washington, D.C.: GPO, 1883.

Pitzer, Paul C. "A History of the Upper Skagit Valley, 1880–1924." Master's thesis, University of Washington, 1966.

Plamondan, Martin, II. "A Search for McClellan's Trail across Skamania County, 1853." Parts 1–4. *Skamania County Heritage* 10, no. 4 (1982); 11, nos. 1–3 (1982).

Plummer, Fred G. "Forest Conditions in the Cascade Range, Washington." *Professional Paper No. 6*, USGS. 1902.

———. "Mount Rainier Forest Reserve, Washington." In *21st Annual Report*, USGS, pt. 5 (1900), pp. 81–143.

Porter, Stephen C., Kenneth L. Pierce, and Thomas B. Hamilton. "Late Wisconsin Mountain Glaciation in the Western United States." In *Late-Quaternary Environments of the United States*, vol. 1, *The Late Pleistocene*, ed. Stephen C. Porter, pp. 71–111. Minneapolis: University of Minnesota Press, 1983.

Porter, Whitworth. *History of the Corps of Royal Engineers*. Vol. 3. London: Longmans, Green, 1915.

Post, Austin, et al. "Inventory of Glaciers in the North Cascades, Washington." *Professional Paper 705–a*, USGS. 1971.

Powell, Fred Wilbur, ed. *Hall J. Kelley on Oregon*. Princeton, N.J.: Princeton University Press, 1932.

Powell, Maj. William H., and Edward Shippen, eds. *Officers of the Army and Navy Who Served in the Civil War*. Philadelphia: L. R. Hamersly and Co., 1892.

Prater, Yvonne. *Snoqualmie Pass: From Indian Trail to Interstate*. Seattle: The Mountaineers, 1981.

Pringle, Patrick T. *Roadside Geology of Mount St. Helens National Volcanic Monument and Vicinity*. Information Circular 88, Washington Division of Geology and Earth Resources. Olympia: Washington State Department of Natural Resources, 1993.

Prosch, Thomas W. "The Military Roads of Washington Territory." *WHQ* 2, no. 2 (1908): 118–26.

Rabbitt, Mary C. "I.C. Russell: Frontiersman of Science." In Leviton, *Frontiers*, p. 79.

———. *Minerals, Lands, and Geology for the Common Defense and General Welfare*. Vol. 2, *1879–1904*. [Reston, Va.?]: USGS, 1980.

Rakestraw, Lawrence. *A History of Forest Conservation in the Pacific Northwest, 1891–1913.* New York: Arno Press, 1979.

Ray, Verne F. "Ethnohistorical Notes on the Columbia, Chelan, Entiat, and Wenatchee Tribes." In *American Indian Ethnohistory: Indians of the Northwest,* ed. David A. Horr. New York: Garland, 1974.

——————. *Handbook of the Cowlitz Indians.* Seattle: Northwest Copy Company, 1966.

——————. "Native Villages and Groupings of the Columbia Basin." *PNQ* 27, no. 2 (1936): 99–152.

Reese, Gary F. *The Northwest Was Their Goal.* 3 vols. Tacoma, Wash.: Tacoma Public Library, 1984.

——————, ed. *The Terriblest Route of All.* Tacoma, Wash.: Tacoma Public Library, 1984.

Reid, Harry Fielding. "The Glaciers of Mt. Hood and Mt. Adams." *Mazama* 2, no. 4 (1905): 195–200.

Reid, J.H. Stewart. *Mountains, Men, and Rivers: British Columbia in Legend and Story.* New York: Bouregy and Curl, 1954.

Reid, R. L. "Early Days at Fort Langley." *British Columbia Historical Quarterly* 1, no. 4 (1937).

——————. "The Whatcom Trails to the Fraser River Mines in 1858." Parts 1 and 2. *WHQ* 18, nos. 3, 4 (1927): 199–206, 271–6.

Renz, Louis Tuck. *The History of the Northern Pacific Railroad.* Fairfield, Wash.: Ye Galleon Press, 1980.

Reports of Explorations and Surveys, to Ascertain the Most Practicable and Economical Route for a Railroad from the Mississippi River to the Pacific Ocean. Vols. 1, 11, 12. Senate Exec. Doc. 78, 33d Cong., 2d sess., 1855. Serial 758.

Rice, David. "Indian Utilization of the Cascade Mountain Range in South Central Washington." *Washington Archaeologist* 8, no. 1 (1964): 5–20.

Rich, Edwin E. *The History of the Hudson's Bay Company, 1670–1870.* 2 vols. London: Hudson's Bay Record Society, 1958–59.

——————, ed. *Simpson's 1828 Journey to the Columbia.* London: Hudson's Bay Record Society, 1947.

Riggs, Thomas. "Ascent of Glacier Peak." *American Alpine Journal* 7, no. 2 (1949): 160–4.

Rinehart, Mary Roberts. "A Pack Train in the Cascades." *Cosmopolitan* 63, nos. 3–5 (1917).

——————. *Tenting To-Night.* Boston: Houghton, Mifflin, 1918.

Roberts, W. Milnor. *Special Report of a Reconnaissance of the Route for the Northern Pacific Railroad between Lake Superior and Puget Sound via the Columbia River.* Philadelphia: Jay Cooke and Co., 1869.

Rodger, Andrew. "Photography and the International Boundary." *The Archivist* 4, no. 4 (1976).

Rodman, Samuel, Jr. "Explorations in the Upper Columbia Country." *Overland Monthly,* 2d ser., 7 (March 1886): 255–66.

Roe, Frank Gilbert. *The Indian and the Horse.* Norman: University of Oklahoma Press, 1955.

Roe, Jo Ann. *Stevens Pass: The Story of Railroading and Recreation in the North Cascades.* Seattle: The Mountaineers, 1995.

Ross, Alexander. *Adventures of the First Settlers on the Oregon or Columbia River, 1810–1813.* Ed. Milo Milton Quaife. Chicago: R.R. Donnelly and Sons, 1923.

——————. *The Fur Hunters of the Far West.* Ed. Milo Milton Quaife. Chicago: R.R. Donnelly and Sons, 1924. Reprint, ed. Kenneth A. Spaulding, Norman: University of Oklahoma Press, 1956.

Ross, Frank E. "The Retreat of the Hudson's Bay Company in the Pacific Northwest." *Canadian Historical Review* 8 (September 1937).

Roth, Lottie R., ed. *History of Whatcom County.* Vol. 1. Chicago: Pioneer Historical Pub. Co., 1926.

Ruby, Robert H., and John A. Brown. *Half-Sun on the Columbia: A Biography of Chief Moses.* Norman: University of Oklahoma Press, 1976.

——————. *Indians of the Pacific Northwest.* Norman: University of Oklahoma Press, 1981.

Rusk, Claude E. *Tales of a Western Mountaineer.* Boston: Houghton, Mifflin, 1924.

Russell, Israel C. "Existing Glaciers of the United States." In *5th Annual Report*, USGS (1885), 303–55. 1885.

————. "A Geological Reconnaissance in Central Washington." *Bulletin No. 108*, USGS. 1893.

————. "Glaciers of Mount Rainier." In *18th Annual Report*, USGS, pt. 2 (1898), 349–423.

————. *North America*. New York: D. Appleton and Co., 1904.

————. "A Preliminary Paper on the Geology of the Cascade Mountains in Northern Washington." In *20th Annual Report*, USGS, pt. 2 (1900), 83–210.

Sage, Donald. "Gold Rush Days on the Fraser River." *PNQ* 44, no. 4 (1913): 161–5.

Sage, Walter N. *Sir James Douglas and British Columbia*. Toronto: University of Toronto Press, 1930.

Sampson, Martin J. *Indians of Skagit County*. Mt. Vernon, Wash.: Skagit County Historical Society, 1972.

Schafer, Joseph, ed. "Documents Relative to Warre and Vavasour's Military Reconnoissance in Oregon, 1845–6." *OHQ* 10, no. 1 (1909): 1–99.

————. "Letters of Sir George Simpson, 1841–43." *American Historical Review* 14 (October 1908).

Scheuerman, Richard D., ed. *The Wenatchi Indians: Guardians of the Valley*. Fairfield, Wash.: Ye Galleon Press, 1982.

Schmitt, Martin F., ed. *General George Crook: His Autobiography*. Norman: University of Oklahoma Press, 1960.

Scholefield, E.O.S. *British Columbia from the Earliest Times to the Present*. Vol. 1. Vancouver, B.C.: S.J. Clarke, 1914.

Schullery, Paul. *Island in the Sky: Pioneering Accounts of Mt. Rainier, 1833–1894*. Seattle: The Mountaineers, 1987.

Schwantes, Carlos A. *The Pacific Northwest: An Interpretive History*. Lincoln: University of Nebraska Press, 1989.

Scott, James W., and Roland L. De Lorme. *Historical Atlas of Washington*. Norman: University of Oklahoma Press, 1988.

Secretan, J.H.E. *Canada's Great Highway*. London: John Lane, 1924.

Shields, George O. *Cruisings in the Cascades: A Narrative of Travel, Exploration, Amateur Photography, Hunting, and Fishing*. Chicago: Rand McNally, 1889.

Short, Steve, and Rosemary Neering. *On the Path of the Explorers: Tracing the Expeditions of Vancouver, Cook, Mackenzie, Fraser, and Thompson*. Vancouver, B.C.: Whitecap Books, 1992.

Siemens, Alfred H., ed. *Lower Fraser Valley: Evolution of a Cultural Landscape*. B.C. Geographical Series, no. 9. Vancouver, B.C.: Tantalus Research, 1968.

Smalley, Eugene V. *History of the Northern Pacific Railroad*. New York: G.P. Putnam's Sons, 1883.

Smith, Allan H. *Ethnographic Guide to the Archaeology of Mount Rainier National Park*. [Pullman]: National Park Service and Washington State University, 1964.

————. *Ethnography of the North Cascades*. Pullman: Washington State University, Center for Northwest Anthropology, 1988.

Smith, George Otis. "Description of the Ellensburg Quadrangle, Washington." Folio No. 86, *Geologic Atlas of the United States*. USGS, 1903.

————. "Description of the Mount Stuart Quadrangle, Washington." Folio No. 106, *Geologic Atlas of the United States*. USGS, 1904.

————. "Geology and Physiography of Central Washington." *Professional Paper No. 19*, USGS, pp. 9–34. 1903.

————. "The Rocks of Mount Rainier." In *18th Annual Report*, USGS, pt. 2 (1898).

Smith, George Otis, and Frank C. Calkins. "Description of the Snoqualmie Quadrangle, Washington." Folio No. 139, *Geologic Atlas of the United States*. USGS, 1906.

————. "A Geological Reconnaissance across the Cascade Range near the Forty-ninth Parallel." *Bulletin No. 235*, USGS. 1904.

Smith, H. P., ed. *History of Addison County, Vermont*. Syracuse, N.Y.: D. Mason & Co., 1886.

Smith, Marian W. "The Nooksack, the Chilliwack, and the Middle Fraser." *PNQ* 41, no. 4 (1950): 330–41.

Smith, Winston. "A Boundary between Friends." *Professional Surveyor* 8, no. 6 (1988): 18–24.

Spier, Leslie. *Tribal Distribution in Washington*. General Series in Anthropology, no. 3. Menasha, Wis.: George Banta Publishing Co., 1936.

Spier, Leslie, and Edward Sapir. *Wishram Ethnography*. University of Washington Publications in Anthropology, vol. 3, no. 3. Seattle: University of Washington Press, 1930.

Splawn, Andrew J. *Ka-mi-akin: The Last Hero of the Yakimas*. 1917. Reprint. Portland: Binfords and Mort, 1944.

Spry, Irene M. *The Palliser Expedition: An Account of John Palliser's British North American Expedition, 1857–1860*. Toronto: Macmillan of Canada, 1963.

Spurr, Josiah E. "The Ore Deposits of Monte Cristo, Washington." In *22nd Annual Report*, USGS, pt. 2 (1901), pp. 785–865.

Staatz, Mortimer H., et al. "Geology and Mineral Resources of the Northern Part of the North Cascades National Park, Washington." *Bulletin No. 1359*, USGS. 1972.

Stanton, William. *The Great United States Exploring Expedition of 1838–1842*. Berkeley: University of California Press, 1975.

Steel, William G. "Lake Chelan and the Valley of the Stehekin." *Oregon Native Son* (January 1900).

Steelquist, Robert. "Juan De Fuca's Strait." *Washington* 3, no. 4 (1986): 36–43.

Stenzel, Franz. *James Madison Alden: Yankee Artist of the Pacific Coast, 1854–1860*. Fort Worth, Tex.: Amon Carter Museum, 1975.

Stevens, Hazard. "The Ascent of Mt. Rainier." *The Nation* 23 (November 23, 1876): 312.

──────. "The Ascent of Takhoma." *Atlantic Monthly* 38 (November 1876): 513–30.

──────. *The Life of Isaac Ingalls Stevens*. Vol. 2. Boston: Houghton, Mifflin, 1900.

──────. "The Pioneers and Patriotism." *WHQ* 8, no. 3 (1917): 172–9.

Stevens, Isaac I. "Narrative and Final Report of Explorations for a Route for a Pacific Railroad, near the Forty-seventh and Forty-ninth Parallels of North Latitude, from St. Paul to Puget Sound." 1855. In *Reports of Explorations and Surveys*, 12, bk. 1.

──────. *Preliminary Sketch of the Northern Pacific Rail Road Exploration and Survey from the Rocky Mountains to Puget Sound*. Map 3 in *Reports of Explorations and Surveys*, 11.

──────. "Report of Explorations for a Route for the Pacific Railroad, near the Forty-seventh and Forty-ninth Parallels of North Latitude, from St. Paul to Puget Sound." In *Reports of Explorations and Surveys*, 1.

──────. *A True Copy of the Record of the Official Proceedings at the Council in Walla Walla Valley, 1855*. Ed. Darrell Scott. Fairfield, Wash.: Ye Galleon Press, 1985.

Stevens, John F. "The Cascade Tunnel: Great Northern Ry." *Engineering News* 45 (1901): 23–6.

──────. *An Engineer's Recollections*. New York: McGraw-Hill, 1936.

──────. "Great Northern Railway." *WHQ* 20, no. 2 (1929): 111–13.

Stewart, Hilary. *Cedar: Tree of Life to the Northwest Coast Indians*. Vancouver, B.C.: Douglas and McIntyre, 1984.

Suksdorf, William, and Thomas Howell. "The Flora of Mount Adams." *Mazama* 1 (1896): 68–97.

Swan, James G. *The Northwest Coast; or, Three Years' Residence in Washington Territory*. New York: Harper and Brothers, 1857.

Symons, Lt. Thomas W. "The Army and Exploration of the West." *Journal of the Military Service Institution of the United States* 4 (1883): 205–49.

──────. *Report of an Examination of the Upper Columbia River and the Territory in Its Vicinity in September and October 1881*. Senate Exec. Doc. 86, 47th Cong., 1st sess., 1882. Serial 1991, vol. 6.

──────. "Explorations and Surveys in the Department of the Columbia" (report for the fiscal year ending June 30, 1880). In *Report of the Secretary of War, 1880*, vol. 2, pt. 3. House Exec. Doc. 1, pt. 2, 46th Cong., 3d sess., 1881. Serial 1955, vol. 5.

──────. "Report of Lt. Thomas W. Symons, Corps of Engineers, for the Fiscal Year Ending

June 30, 1881." In *Report of the Secretary of War, 1881*, vol. 2, pt. 3, appendix CCC, pp. 2868–70. House Exec. Doc. 1, 47th Cong., 1st sess., 1882. Serial 2013.

——————. *The Symons Report on the Upper Columbia River and the Great Plain of the Columbia*. Fairfield, Wash.: Ye Galleon Press, 1967.

Tabor, R.W., et al. *Accreted Terranes of the North Cascades Range, Washington*. Field Trip Guidebook T307, 28th International Geologic Congress. Washington, D.C.: American Geophysical Union, 1989.

——————. *Geologic Map of the Wenatchee 1:100,000 Quadrangle, Central Washington*. Misc. Inv. Series 1-1311. USGS (1982).

——————. *Preliminary Geologic Map of the Sauk River 30 by 60 Minute Quadrangle, Washington*. Open-File Map 88-692. USGS [1988].

Teit, James. *The Middle Columbia Salish*. Ed. Franz Boas. University of Washington Publications in Anthropology, vol. 2, no. 4. Seattle: University of Washington Press, 1928.

——————. "The Salishan Tribes of the Western Plateaus." In *45th Annual Report*, U.S. Bureau of American Ethnology, pp. 23–396. Washington, D.C., 1930.

——————. *The Thompson Indians of British Columbia*. Memoirs of the American Museum of Natural History, vol. 2. New York: Knickerbocker Press, 1900.

Thompson, David. *David Thompson's Narrative of His Explorations in Western America, 1784–1812*. Ed. J. B. Tyrrell. Toronto: Champlain Society, 1916.

——————. "Journal of David Thompson." Ed. T. C. Elliott. *OHQ* 15, no. 2 (1914): 39–63.

Thompson, Erwin N. *Mount Rainier National Park Historic Resource Study*. Denver: National Park Service, 1981.

——————. *North Cascades National Park, Ross Lake NRA, and Lake Chelan NRA—History, Basic Data*. Washington, D.C.: Office of Archaeology and Historic Preservation, 1970.

Thornton, Jessy Quinn. *Oregon and California in 1848*. Vol. 1. New York: Harper and Brothers, 1855.

"Thunder Creek Mining District." *Pacific Mining Journal*, August 1912.

Thwaites, Reuben Gold, ed. *Original Journals of the Lewis and Clark Expedition, 1804–1806*. 8 vols. New York: Dodd, Mead, and Co., 1904–5.

Tidball, John C. "Report of Journey Made by General W. T. Sherman in the Northwest and Middle Parts of the United States in 1883," October 27, 1883. In *Report of the Secretary of War, 1883*, 1:203–52. House Exec. Doc. 1, pt. 2, 48th Cong., 1st sess., 1883. Serial 2182.

Tilton, Gen. James. "Report of Gen. James Tilton to Edwin F. Johnson," October 21, 1867. In Johnson, *Report of Edwin F. Johnson*, 1869.

Tinkham, Abiel W. "Railroad Report of the Practicability of the Snoqualme Pass, and the Obstructions to Be Apprehended from Snow," June 19, 1854. In *Reports of Explorations and Surveys*, 1:184–6.

Tolmie, William F. *The Journals of William Fraser Tolmie, Physician and Fur Trader*. Ed. R.G. Large. Vancouver, B.C.: Mitchell Press, 1963.

Tucker, Louis L. "The Governor and the General: The Isaac Stevens–John Ellis Wool Controversy." In *Kansas and the West*, ed. Forrest R. Blackburn et al. Topeka: Kansas State Historical Society, 1976.

Turek, Michael F., and Robert H. Keller, Jr. "Sluskin: Yakima Guide to Mount Rainier." *Columbia* (Spring 1991): 1–7.

Tyler, David B. *The Wilkes Expedition: The First United States Exploring Expedition (1838–1842)*. Philadelphia: American Philosophical Society, 1968.

U.S. Congress. *Report, Joint Committees on Investigation of the Northern Pacific Railroad Land Grants*. Washington, D.C., 1928.

——————. Senate. *Hearings before the Committee on Interior and Insular Affairs* (North Cascades). 89th Cong., 2d sess., February 11–12, 1966.

Vancouver, George. *A Voyage of Discovery to the North Pacific Ocean and Round the World, 1791–1795*. 1798. Reprint. Ed. W. Kaye Lamb. 4 vols. London: Hakluyt Society, 1984.

Van Trump, Philemon B. "Mount Rainier." *Mazama* 2, no. 1 (1900): 1–18.

Villard, Henry. *Memoirs of Henry Villard, Journalist and Financier, 1835–1900*. Boston: Houghton, Mifflin, 1904.

Waddington, Alfred. *Overland Route through British North America*. London: Longmans, Green, Reader, and Dyer, 1868.

Wagner, Henry R. *The Cartography of the Northwest Coast of America to the Year 1800*. Vol. 1. Berkeley: University of California Press, 1937.

——————. *Spanish Explorations in the Strait of Juan de Fuca*. Santa Ana, Calif.: Fine Arts Press, 1933.

Waitt, Richard B., Jr., and Robert Thorson. "The Cordilleran Ice Sheet in Washington, Idaho, and Montana." In *Late-Quaternary Environments of the United States*, vol. 1, *The Late Pleistocene*, ed. Stephen C. Porter, 53–70. Minneapolis: University of Minnesota Press, 1983.

Wallace, Andrew. "General August V. Kautz and the Southwestern Frontier." Ph.D. diss., University of Arizona, 1968.

Wallace, William S., ed. *Documents Relating to the North West Company*. Champlain Society Publications, no. 22. Toronto: The Society, 1934.

"Walter Washington De Lacy, a Pioneer of Pioneers." *Washington Historian* 2, no. 4 (1901): 184–7.

Waring, Guy. *My Pioneer Days*. Boston: Bruce Humphries, 1936.

Warre, Sir Henry James. *Overland to Oregon in 1845: Impressions of a Journey across North America*. Ottawa: National Archives of Canada, 1976.

——————. *Sketches in North America and the Oregon Territory*. Barre, Mass.: Imprint Society, 1970.

Warren, Lt. Gouverneur K. "Memoir to Accompany the Map of the Territory of the United States from the Mississippi River to the Pacific Ocean." In *Reports of Explorations and Surveys*, 11.

Waters, Aaron C. "Memorial to Bailey Willis." *Geological Society of America Bulletin* 73 (1962): 58.

Watson, Sir Charles M. *The Life of Major-General Sir Charles William Wilson*. London: John Murray, 1909.

Watson, J. Wreford. "The Role of Illusion in North American Geography: A Note on the Geography of North American Settlement." *Canadian Geographer* 13, no. 1 (1969).

Weaver, Charles E. *Geology and Ore Deposits of the Blewett Mining District*. Bulletin No. 6, Washington Geological Survey. Olympia: E.L. Boardman, Public Printer, 1911.

——————. *Geology and Ore Deposits of the Index Mining District*. Bulletin No. 7, Washington Geological Survey. Olympia: E.L. Boardman, Public Printer, 1912.

Weeks, Kathleen. "Monuments Mark This Boundary." *Canadian Geographic Journal* 31, no. 3 (1945): 120–33.

Wells, Oliver N. *The Chilliwacks and Their Neighbors*. Vancouver, B.C.: Talonbooks, 1987.

Wheat, Carl I. *Mapping the Transmississippi West, 1540–1861*. 5 vols. San Francisco: Institute of Historical Cartography, 1957–63.

Wheeler, Lt. George M. *Report upon Geographical and Geological Explorations and Surveys West of the 100th Meridian*. Vol. 1. Washington, D.C.: GPO, 1889.

Wheeler, Olin D. "Mount Rainier: Its Ascent by a Northern Pacific Party." *Wonderland* (Northern Pacific Railroad) (1895): 52–103.

Whitfield, William. *History of Snohomish County, Washington*. Vol. 1. Chicago: Pioneer Historical Publishing Co., 1926.

Wilkes, Charles. *Narrative of the United States Exploring Expedition during the Years 1838, 1839, 1840, 1841, and 1842*. Vol. 4. Philadelphia: Lea and Blanchard, 1849.

Wilkeson, Samuel. *Wilkeson's Notes on Puget Sound: Charter and Amendments*. Burlington, Vt.: Northern Pacific Railroad, 1870. Reprint. Fairfield, Wash.: Ye Galleon Press, 1994.

Wilkie, Rosemary. *A Broad, Bold Ledge of Gold: Historical Facts, Monte Cristo, Washington*. Seattle: n.p., 1958.

Williams, John H. *The Guardians of the Columbia: Mount Hood, Mount Adams, and Mount St. Helens*. Tacoma, Wash.: J.H. Williams, 1912.

—————. *The Mountain That Was God.* New York: G. P. Putnam's Sons, 1911.

Willis, Bailey. "Canyons and Glaciers: A Journey to the Ice Fields of Mount Tacoma." *The Northwest* 1 (April 1883).

—————. "Physiography and Deformation of the Wenatchee-Chelan District, Cascade Range." *Professional Paper No. 19,* USGS, pp. 49–79. 1903.

Wilson, Charles William. *Mapping the Frontier: Charles Wilson's Diary of the Survey of the 49th Parallel, 1858–1862, While Secretary of the British Boundary Commission.* Ed. George F. G. Stanley. Seattle: University of Washington Press, 1970.

Winther, Oscar Osburn. "Inland Transportation and Communication in Washington, 1844–1859." *PNQ* 30, no. 4 (1939): 371–86.

—————. *The Old Oregon Country: A History of Frontier Trade, Transportation, and Travel.* Stanford, Calif.: Stanford University Press, 1950.

—————. "Pack Animal Transportation." *PNQ* 34, no. 2 (1943): 135–46.

Winthrop, Theodore. *The Canoe and the Saddle.* Ed. John H. Williams. 1862. Reprint. Tacoma, Wash.: John H. Williams, 1913.

Wood, Charles, R. *Lines West.* Seattle: Superior Publishing Co., 1967.

Woodhouse, Philip R. *Monte Cristo.* Seattle: The Mountaineers, 1979.

Work, John. "Journal of John Work: April 30th to May 31st, 1830." Ed. T. C. Elliott. *OHQ* 10, no. 3 (1909): 296–313.

—————. *The Journal of John Work.* Ed. William S. Lewis and Paul C. Phillips. Cleveland: Arthur H. Clark, 1923.

Zaslow, Morris. *Reading the Rocks: The Story of the Geological Survey of Canada, 1842–1972.* Ottawa: Macmillan, 1975.

von Zittel, Karl. "Volcanos and Glaciers in the North American West." Trans. Rev. Carl A. Nitz. *Journal of the German and Austrian Alpine Verein* (1890): 1–20.

Archival Sources

Bancroft Library, University of California, Berkeley
Alexander C. Anderson. "History of the Northwest Coast."
Arthur A. Denny. Dictations, 1878 and 1890.
Sir James Douglas. Private paper.
Simon Fraser. Manuscript.
George Clinton Gardner Papers.
Alexander Henry. Manuscript.
Northern Pacific Railroad holdings, including "Official Northern Pacific Railroad Guide for Use of Tourists and Travellers," 1897; "Report of Edwin F. Johnson to the Board of Directors, Nov. 1867"; and Albert B. Guptill, "A Ramble in Wonderland."
David Thompson. Manuscript.
William F. Tolmie. Manuscript.
Maps: Arrowsmith, 1859; Royal Engineers (Parsons, Conroy, Moody).
Photographs: Sierra Club outing, 1905 (3 volumes); John Muir.

British Columbia Archives and Records Service (B.C. Provincial Archives), Victoria
Alexander C. Anderson Papers.
Hudson's Bay Company, Record Office Transcripts.
Minister of Mines—Province of British Columbia: Annual reports (printed).
William F. Tolmie. Manuscript.
Charles William Wilson. Manuscript.
Maps: Extensive collection of original and rare maps by the Royal Engineers and of gold regions and early roads.
Photographs: Extensive collection, including Royal Engineers and British Boundary Commission.

British Museum (British Library), London
Alexander Ross. Manuscript map, 1821.
Royal Engineers. Journal.

Bureau of Land Management, Portland, Oregon
Field notes of surveyors, 1880–1940.
Plat and tract books.
Township maps.
Old county maps.

Colby College, Waterville, Maine
George Otis Smith Papers.

Department of Lands and Forests, Toronto, Ontario
David Thompson. Journals and survey records, 1801–40.

Everett Public Library, Everett, Washington
Everett Herald: articles on Monte Cristo and Great Northern Railway disaster.
J.A. Juleen. Photographic panoramas.

Federal Records Center, Seattle, Washington
U.S. Forest Service. Documents and photographs. Includes Chelan, Mount Baker, Okanogan, Snoqualmie, and Wenatchee national forests. Historical maps, albums, and wilderness-hearing papers.
Bureau of Land Management. Surveyor General records.

James Jerome Hill Reference Library, St. Paul, Minnesota
James J. Hill Papers.

Hudson's Bay Company Archives (Provincial Archives of Manitoba), Winnipeg
Alexander Ross Papers.
Journal of Occurrences: Forts Langley, Colvile, Vancouver, and Nisqually.
Letter books: Fort Nisqually, 1850–58; Fort Langley, 1867–68, 1871.
Correspondence books: Fort Langley, 1830–31.
Reports on Districts: Fort Colvile, 1827–30.
Microfilm copies of manuscripts relating to explorers, including David Thompson, John Work, and David Douglas.

Huntington Library, San Marino, California
John F. Damon, Jr. Manuscript, 1859.
James Wickersham. Manuscript, 1853.
Fort Nisqually Collection: Journal of Occurrences (3 journals).
Pamphlet on Skagit gold mines, 1880.

International Boundary Commission, Washington, D.C.
Papers relative to diplomacy, proceedings, and surveys.
Northwest Boundary photograph collection.

International Boundary Commission, Ottawa, Ontario
Papers relative to diplomacy, proceedings, and surveys.
Northwest Boundary: Extensive fieldbook records and photography of Canadian surveyors.

Lake Chelan Historical Society, Chelan, Washington
Historical photographs, including the L. O. Barnes album.
Copies of *Chelan Falls Leader* and *Chelan Leader*.

Library of Congress, Manuscripts Division, Washington, D.C.
George B. McClellan Papers; letter book, 1852–56.
Samuel Emmons Papers.
Edwin F. Johnson. Report (1869) to the board of directors of the Northern Pacific Railroad and
  Reports of 1867 surveys by Gen. Ira Spaulding and Gen. James Tilton.

The Mazamas, Portland, Oregon
Historical photographs, including outings.

Minnesota Historical Society, St. Paul
Eugene V. Smalley. Book of references.
Isaac W. Smith Papers.
Northern Pacific Railroad Company (NPRR) Records: Lake Superior and Puget Sound Company
  Secretary Records (including the Thomas Canfield correspondence, in Letters Sent, General
  Agent); correspondence of W. Milnor Roberts (the letters of 1867 and 1873 deal extensively with
  Cascade Range exploration); Secretary's unregistered correspondence, as well as possible addi-
  tional registered correspondence; Chief Engineer—Old Vault Files. In the Chief Engineer files,
  the most relevant are file 36, file 66 (includes correspondence of Virgil B. Bogue, Adna Ander-
  son, Thomas Oakes, and report of Roberts), file 156 (includes Daniel C. Linsley diary; reports of
  R. M. Walker, Thomas B. Morris, David D. Clarke, and Charles White; and W. Milnor Roberts's
  "Cascade Range" draft), file 157 (includes Cowlitz Pass explorations and Bogue's 1880 explorations), and file 158 (includes Cowlitz Pass explorations).
Great Northern Railway Company (GNR) Records: James J. Hill Papers; other records and printed
  material.

Mount Baker–Snoqualmie National Forest, Mountlake Terrace, Washington
Newton Field. "Mount Baker Almanac."
Typescripts, memoirs, papers, and photographs.

Mount Rainier National Park, Tahoma Woods, Washington
Frank Brockman Papers.
Richard D. Daugherty. Manuscript.
James Longmire material.
Arthur Martinson. Theses.
Paul Sceva. Recollections.
National park records.

National Archives, Washington, D.C.
RG 48, Records of the Office of the Secretary of the Interior: Letter books from the Pacific Railroad
  Surveys (including correspondence of Isaac I. Stevens); Office of Explorations and Surveys,
  letters received; railroad maps and sketches.
RG 49, Records of the Bureau of Land Management: Surveyor General's records; cartographic
  materials.
RG 57, Records of the U.S. Geological Survey: Includes records of the Clarence King survey;
  manuscript maps. Fieldbooks are located in the Geologic Division and triangulation books in
  the Topographic Division.
RG 75, Records of the Bureau of Indian Affairs: Yakama Indian war, microfilm, M-505 and M-506.
RG 76, Records of Boundary and Claims Commissions and Arbitrations: Department of State
  records, including material on the Northwest Boundary Survey. E. 196 and E. 197, reports on
  surveys; E. 198, journals and sketches; E. 199, special survey books; E. 200, surveyors' field notes;
  E. 201, topographic notes; E. 202, reconnaissance books; E. 226–33, correspondence related to
  the Northwest Boundary, including the files of Archibald Campbell and Capt. Palliser and the

correspondence of Campbell, Lewis Cass, and Capt. James Prevost; E. 285, fieldbooks, 1901–33; maps and drawings of the Northwest Boundary; and Northwest Boundary Survey photographs, 1901–. The thirty-eight envelopes of correspondence concerning the Northwest Boundary Survey remain the only original source material, since the official report has never been located. They include the reports of the field parties and subordinate officers to the chief commissioner.

RG 77, Records of the Office of the Chief of Engineers: War Department records, including the bulk of the Topographical Bureau records. E. 311, annual reports; E. 315, register of letters received, 1832–65; letters sent, 1829–67; letters received, 1850–66; letters issued to the Secretary of War, 10 vols., December 6, 1843–January 21, 1867; Office of Explorations and Surveys, records, 1856–61, four boxes related to the Topographical Engineers. Most valuable are the departmental letter files and the long series of public documents printed for the House and Senate. The records of the Wagon Roads Office also cast light on the army's wagon-road program.

RG 94, Records of the Adjutant General's Office: letters, reports, and other documents relating to Indian wars in the Cascade Range, 1855–58. Many reports from field officers are in these files, because they were forwarded up the chain of command. Records of the Secretary of the Interior: railroad surveys; Adjutant General for Washington Territory, records (especially the Goethals report, on microfilm).

RG 95, Records of the Forest Service (Suitland Reference Branch).

The Cartographic and Architectural Records Unit contains the manuscripts of most of the printed maps that accompanied the official reports of exploration, many of which have notations or markings by various cartographers, and the originals of many of the maps, drawings, and paintings made by the boundary-survey parties. Particularly noteworthy are the drawings by George Gibbs and Henry Custer, the joint American-British maps, and the series of beautiful watercolor paintings done by James W. Alden to accompany the unpublished report.

National Archives of Canada, Ottawa

MG 11. Colonial Office 6, British North America. Colonial Office 60, 61, 63, 64, British Columbia, reels B 1127–28 and 1136–38 (British claims in Oregon); reels B 1129–50, B 1940, and B 1150–53 (Northwest Boundary).

MG 16. Foreign Office Correspondence, FO 302, reels 5317–26; FO 5 (Northwest Boundary Survey), reels B 1129–34 and B 1143–44. Northwest Boundary Survey, Colonial Office Correspondence, CO 381, vol. 18, reel B 890; CO 398, reels B 890–92; CO 410, reel 216.

MG 19. Materials on the fur trade and Indians.

MG 24. Sir Henry James Warre Papers.

MG 30. Otto J. Klotz Papers.

RG 21. Records of the Department of Energy, Mines, and Resources.

RG 45. Geological Survey of Canada, vols. 123–77 (field notebooks, 1875–1900, including those of George M. Dawson), and 178–242 (field notebooks, 1900–25).

RG 88. Records of the Survey and Mapping Branch (relating to surveying in British Columbia, lands, Indians and Indian reserves, forest reserves, and railway belts).

Hudson's Bay archives, 1670–1870, microfilm

David Thompson, survey records and journals (copied from the originals in Toronto).

Considerable material (on microfilm) on the Northwest Boundary Survey's explorations and correspondence, including information concerning the Royal Engineers, maps, plans, drawings, and journals relating to activities of the boundary commissioners in Oregon Territory.

New York Public Library, New York

Charles F. B. Haskell Papers, Rare Books and Manuscripts Division.

New York State Library, Albany

G.K. Warren Papers.

John E. Wool Papers.

North Cascades National Park, Sedro Woolley, Washington
Numerous reports on history, archaeology, planning, landforms, hearings, and various study commissions; photograph albums; taped interviews with pioneers.

Okanogan National Forest, Okanogan, Washington
Historical and photographic material (additional material may be found at the Chelan and Winthrop ranger stations).

Oregon Historical Society Research Library, Portland
David D. Clarke Papers.
John S. Hawkins. Letter books.
Extensive historical map and photograph collections.

Public Records Office, London
Sketches of early Washington Territory.
Maps of the Fraser gold region.

Royal Engineers Museum, Chatham, Kent, England
John S. Hawkins. Letter book.
Maps and photographs from the British North American Boundary Commission.

Rutherford B. Hayes Library, Fremont, Ohio
Gen. George Crook. Letter books.

Skagit County Historical Museum, La Conner, Washington
Darius Kinsey. Photographs.
Historical interviews.
Mining files.

Smithsonian Institution, Manuscripts Division, Washington, D.C.
James G. Cooper. Notebook.
Dr. Caleb Burwell Rowan Kennerly Papers, 1855–60, Record Unit 7202.
Spencer F. Baird Collection, 1793–1923, Record Unit 7002.
George Gibbs. Manuscript on Indian vocabularies, in the Smithsonian National Anthropological Archives.

State Historical Society of Wisconsin, Madison
George Gibbs IV Papers, including maps, drawings, and photographs; extensive correspondence on Indian tribes, natural history, and geologic structures; and reports to Capt. George B. McClellan and Governor Isaac I. Stevens.
Gibbs family papers.

Tacoma Public Library, Northwest Room, Tacoma, Washington
Gary F. Reese. Compilations.
Journal of Occurrences, Nisqually House.
Military microfilms.
Conservation and North Cascades National Park files.

Toronto Public Library, Toronto, Ontario
Simon Fraser. Journal, 1808.

Trinity College Library, Hartford, Connecticut
Lieutenant Henry H. Pierce material.

U.S. Army Military History Institute, Carlisle Barracks, Pennsylvania
Texts of Gen. George Crook documenting his Cascade Range campaigns (3 versions, including the
    Crook-Kennon Papers); Arnold R. Pilling comparative study of Crook's autobiographies.

U.S. Forest Service Archives, National Agricultural Library, Beltsville, Maryland
Historical photographs from various national forests and regional offices.

U.S. Forest Service, Pacific Northwest Region, Portland, Oregon
Historical photographs.
Early topographic and Forest Service maps.

U.S. Forest Service, Naches Ranger Station, Natches, Washington
Historical study of Naches Pass.

U.S. Geological Survey Library, Denver
Field notebooks, reconnaissance maps, and photography of early geologists and topographers.

U.S. Geological Survey Library, Reston, Virginia
Topographic maps, historical typescripts, and records of early geologists and topographers, includ-
    ing Bailey Willis, Israel C. Russell, George Otis Smith, George C. Curtis, Walter C. Mendenhall,
    J. E. Blackburn, and Frank C. Calkins.

University of British Columbia, Special Collections, Vancouver
Royal Engineers, records related to British Columbia history.

University of Pittsburgh, Special Collections, Pittsburgh, Pennsylvania
Hervey Allen Collection. Edward J. Allen diaries.

University of Washington Libraries, Seattle
Manuscripts and University Archives Division: Manuscripts and typescripts of Clarence A. Bagley,
    Nels Bruseth, Gen. George Crook, Asahel Curtis, Arthur A. Denny, Pierre-Jean De Smet,
    Granby Mining Company, Ethel Van Fleet Harris, Edward Huggins, Ernest Kobelt, James
    Longmire, Preston Macy, Edmond S. Meany, H. M. Myers, Milnor Oakes Roberts, Hazard
    Stevens, Isaac I. Stevens, Henry Struve, Albert H. Sylvester, Dr. William F. Tolmie, Philemon B.
    Van Trump, Hermann F. Ulrichs, A. C. Warner, John MacDonald Wilmans, and John Work;
    the Nordlund Papers; Yakima River documents; sketches by Alfred Downing; historical tape
    recordings.
Special Collections Division: Extensive photograph collections, including those of The Mountain-
    eers and L. D. Lindsley, the Woodhouse Collection on early Monte Cristo, mining photographs,
    and miscellaneous images of the Cascade Range; extensive collection of rare printed material
    on the Cascade Range.

University of Wyoming, Western History Research Center, Laramie
George Otis Smith Collection, including correspondence.
Josiah Spurr Collection, including reports, notations, and photographs related to the Monte Cristo
    area.

Washington State Archives and Records Center, Olympia
RG 2, North Cascades National Park.
RG 9, public lands, mines, and geology.
RG 53, Department of Highways.
RG 71, conservation.
RG 90, Washington State Planning Council.
Governor Daniel Evans files.

Washington State Department of Natural Resources, Geology Library, Olympia
Early geology bulletins and papers, including the annual reports and bulletins of the Washington
   Geological Survey; all theses on Washington geology; other published papers.

Washington State Historical Society, Tacoma
Asahel Curtis. Photograph album.
Alfred Downing. Sketches.
Albert B. Rogers. Papers.
Paul Sceva Papers.
Isaac I. Stevens Papers.
Stevens family papers.
Great Northern Railway and Northern Pacific Railroad photographs.
Manuscript maps.

Washington State Library, Olympia
Early territorial maps and wagon-road documents.

Washington State University, Pullman
Fred Plummer Papers.
Thomas Thompson Papers.

Wenatchee National Forest, Wenatchee, Washington
Historical material and photographs.

Western Washington University, Center for Pacific Northwest Studies, Bellingham
A.J. Allen Collection.
Percival R. Jeffcott Collection.
Maps collection, including those of the Bellingham Bay and British Columbia Railroad and its
   surveys.
Photographs collection.

Whatcom Museum of History and Art, Bellingham, Washington
Charles F. Easton. Scrapbook.
Darius Kinsey. Photographs.

*Yale Collection of Western Americana, Beinecke Library, Yale University, New Haven,
Connecticut*
Samuel Anderson Papers, including letters and miscellaneous documents.
Henry Eld. Journal dealing with Oregon explorations conducted by Comdr. Charles Wilkes.
George Clinton Gardner Papers (the journals and correspondence relating to the survey total 385
   pages).
George Gibbs Papers, including three original notebooks on Indians, natural history, and regional
   journeys.
Joseph S. Harris Papers.
Isaac I. Stevens Papers.
George Suckley Papers.

INDEX